EQUITY MARKETS AND PORTFOLIO ANALYSIS

Since 1996, Bloomberg Press has published books for financial professionals on investing, economics, and policy affecting investors. Titles are written by leading practitioners and authorities, and have been translated into more than 20 languages.

The Bloomberg Financial Series provides both core reference knowledge and actionable information for financial professionals. The books are written by experts familiar with the work flows, challenges, and demands of investment professionals who trade the markets, manage money, and analyze investments in their capacity of growing and protecting wealth, hedging risk, and generating revenue.

For a list of available titles, please visit our web site at www.wiley.com/go/ bloombergpress.

EQUITY MARKETS AND PORTFOLIO ANALYSIS

R. Stafford Johnson

BLOOMBERG PRESS
An Imprint of
WILEY

For general information on our other products and services or for technical support, please contact our Customer Care Department within the United States at (800) 762-2974, outside the United States at (317) 572-3993 or fax (317) 572-4002.

Wiley also publishes its books in a variety of electronic formats. Some content that appears in print may not be available in electronic books. For more information about Wiley products, visit our web site at www.wiley.com.

Library of Congress Cataloging-in-Publication Data:

Johnson, R. Stafford.
  Equity markets and portfolio analysis / R. Stafford Johnson.
    pages cm. — (Bloomberg financial series)
  Includes index.
  ISBN 978-1-118-20268-5 (cloth)
  1. Stock exchanges.   2. Investment analysis.   3. Portfolio management.   4. Investments.   I. Title.
HG4551.J645 2014
332.63′2—dc23

                                                                    2013049989

ISBN 9781118202685 (Hardcover)
ISBN 9781118228272 (ePDF)
ISBN 9781118240656 (ePub)

Printed in the United States of America

10 9 8 7 6 5 4 3 2 1

This book is dedicated to the memory of my beloved wife, Jan—mother, grandmother, and educator—a beautiful person.

Contents

Preface

Over the past 30 years, the investment industry has seen stock market and real estate bubbles, interest rates approaching zero, the emergence of hedge funds and private equity companies, the globalization of financial markets, the proliferation of derivative securities, and the growth of securitized assets and structured financing. Mirroring these events has been the academic contributions to the investment discipline: the development of capital market theories, the derivation of option pricing models, and the explorations into efficient market theories. The financial events and the academic contributions together point out the challenges in mastering an understanding and developing a knowledge of investments and financial markets.

Today, managing securities in this dynamic and innovative investment environment is a challenge. In this increasingly complex environment, many practitioners manage their securities and portfolios using a Bloomberg terminal. Bloomberg is a computer information and retrieval system providing access to financial and economic data, news, and analytics. Bloomberg terminals are common on most trading floors and are becoming more common in universities where they are used for research, teaching, and managing student investment funds.

The purpose of this text is to provide professionals and finance students with an exposition on equity investments and financial markets that will take them from the basic concepts, strategies, and fundamentals to a more detailed understanding of the markets, advanced strategies, and models. Given the widespread use of the Bloomberg system, this text also includes detailed descriptions of the Bloomberg system, a listing of many of the analytical functions that can be applied to investment analysis, and detailed explanations of how Bloomberg information and analytical functions can be applied to the investment topics covered in the text. It is my hope that the synthesis of fundamental and advanced topics with Bloomberg information and analytics will provide professionals and students of finance with not only a better foundation in understanding the complexities and subtleties of the financial markets, but also with the ability to apply that understanding to real-world investment decisions—to grasp how "it is done on the street."

This book is the second in a three-part series. The first, *Debt Markets and Analysis,* covered fixed-income securities. This book, in turn, focuses on stock and stock portfolios. The third covers derivatives. Like the debt markets book, this book covers subjects presented in many investment texts: equity markets, how stocks are traded, investment funds, return and risk, portfolio theory, capital market theory, fundamental analysis, technical analysis, efficient markets, and equity derivatives. Different from other investment texts is the integration of Bloomberg into the presentation. For those readers who have access to a Bloomberg terminal, it is my hope that they will be able to use the Bloomberg information and the end-of-the-chapter exercises in this book to develop the practical skills needed to apply traditional investment concepts to the real world. It is also my hope that the integration of Bloomberg with investment concepts and theories enhances the readers' intellectual depth and understanding of finance. Finance and economics professors frequently require that students explain a theory, strategy, or idea mathematically, graphically, and intuitively. By so doing, students' depth of understanding, as well as retention, of the theory and idea is often enhanced. It has been my experience in using Bloomberg in my classes that it too enhances a student's depth and knowledge of finance.

Depth of understanding is also accomplished by mastering seminal works. Whether it is Keynesian economic theory, a work of Shakespeare, Einstein's theory of relativity, or the philosophy of Descartes, a student who studies such intellectual works inevitably learns how great minds work, the subtleties inherent in great ideas, the power of logic, and the beauty of thoughts and ideas. The finance and economics disciplines are replete with great thinkers. Like other investment books, this book presents many of the seminal works in financial economics, including the works of Nobel Laureates such as Tobin, Modigliani, Miller, Markowitz, Sharpe, Scholes, Merton, Fama, Hansen, and Shiller.

Furthermore, I strongly believe that intellectual depth is achieved when students are able to relate theory to the real world. In writing about the differences between science and the humanities, the novelist Tom Robbins wrote that "the scientist needs the humanist to keep the scientist human, and the humanist needs the scientist to keep the humanist honest." Over the years, I have found that my finance students need to see more than an abstract concept, a statistic, or a dollar sign; they also need to be able to connect the idea to what is real. The growth in America's gross domestic product from $3 trillion in 1984 to over $16 trillion today, or the Dow Jones Average increase from 700 in 1982 to over 16,000 today, I tell my students, can also be explained as an economy that has evolved into one that can take an office building filled with information and put it on a small computer chip, as one in which planes can take off every minute from any major urban airport and go anywhere in the world, and as one in which data and information can be accessed in seconds via satellites and through the Internet. Again, students of finance who can access information from Bloomberg will be better able to connect the ideas and theories of finance to their practical applications.

The book is written for finance professors interested in incorporating Bloomberg as part of their class instructions, as well as facilitating their own research. The book can also be used as an MBA, MS, and undergraduate finance text. With the emphasis just on equity and equity derivatives, the book is tailored for departments with curricula requiring separate investments-type classes for equity and fixed-income. As an equity market text, the book is designed for a one-semester investment course. The Bloomberg material is presented in boxes in each chapter, and Chapter 2 provides an overview and guide to the Bloomberg system. Finally, the book is written for professionals in the investment industry involved in stock and stock portfolio management. For professionals, the text can be used as an instructional source and as a guide on how to apply Bloomberg to equity markets and analysis, as well as a review of fundamental investment concepts and theories.

Content

The book is comprehensive, covering equity securities and markets, the major theories and models, the practical applications of the models, and cases and empirical studies. Chapter 1 presents an overview of the investment environment, examining the nature of financial assets, the types of securities that exist, the nature and types of markets that securities give rise to, and the general characteristics of assets. Chapter 2 presents an overview and guide to the Bloomberg system. Chapter 3 looks at how equity and debt instruments are valued and how their rates of return are measured. This is followed by two chapters that examine the equity markets, securities, and funds. In Chapter 4, equity securities and their markets are examined in terms of the rules, participants, and forces that govern them; in Chapter 5, investment funds and intermediary securities are examined.

Chapters 6–10 cover expected return and risk, portfolio analysis, and capital market theory: Chapter 6 examines the expected return and risk for stock; Chapter 7 looks at the return and risk of a portfolio of stocks; Chapter 8 examines the Markowitz portfolio selection model; Chapters 9 and 10 present Capital Market Theory—the Capital Asset Pricing Model and the Arbitrage Pricing Theory. Chapters 11–15 examine the fundamental valuation of stocks, technical analysis, and the efficient market hypothesis. Chapter 11 examines the financial anatomy of company and the factors that determine equity value; Chapter 12 looks at empirical approaches to stock valuation and selection; Chapter 13 examines fundamental valuation of the overall market and industry and the top-down approach to stock evaluation. In Chapter 14, technical analysis and behavioral finance are described, and in Chapter 15, the efficient market hypothesis is examined in terms of the theory and its empirical tests. Finally, the last two chapters cover equity derivatives: Chapters 16 provides an overview of the markets, uses, and pricing of stock and stock index options, and Chapter 17 examines the markets, uses, and pricing of futures and futures options.

The text stresses concepts, model construction, numerical examples, and Bloomberg applications and information sources. The text also includes Bloomberg exercises at the end of each of the chapters. These exercises are designed for practitioners who have access to such terminals at their jobs, for professors and students who have access to Bloomberg terminals at their universities, and for students who have access to Bloomberg either at their university or possibly through internships they may have at financial companies. As I noted previously, it is my hope that the Bloomberg exercises will add depth to the understanding of investments, as well as an appreciation of the breadth of financial information and analytics provided by the Bloomberg system. Instructors are invited to visit www.wiley.com for additional materials, such as appendices explaining different Bloomberg applications in more detail, supplemental appendices, and end-of-the-chapter review questions and problems with accompanying solutions that are provided to reinforce concepts. The site also includes Excel spreadsheet programs that can be used to solve a number of the problems, and chapter PowerPoint slides.

The book draws some material from one of my earlier texts published by Wiley: *Bond Evaluation, Selection, and Management* (Wiley, 2010). The Bloomberg material presented here comes from knowledge picked up from using the terminal (or learned from my students who used Bloomberg) when I was the fund professor for the student equity investment fund and bond investment fund at Xavier University.

Acknowledgments

Many people have contributed to this text. First, I wish to thank Mary Beth Shagena, the O'Conor family, my colleagues at Xavier University, and two special colleagues, Rick Zuber, University of North Carolina at Charlotte, and Tom O'Brien, University of Connecticut, who have helped me in many different ways. My appreciation is extended to the editors and staff at John Wiley & Sons, Inc., particularly Bill Falloon, Executive Editor; Judy Howarth, Senior Production Editor; Meg Freeborn, Senior Development Editor; and Angela Urquhart, Thistle Hill Publishing, who oversaw the book's development and were a continued source of encouragement. My appreciation is also extended to Stephen Isaac, Bloomberg Press, for his support, help, and encouragement on this project.

I also wish to thank my children and their spouses, Wendi, Jamey, Matt, Shayna, and Scott, and my grandchildren, Bryce, Kendall, Malin, and Kylee Lynn, for their support, encouragement, and understanding. I also would like to recognize the pioneers in financial economics: James Tobin, Harry Markowitz, William Sharpe, Eugene Fama, Franco Modigliani, Merton Miller, Frank Fabozzi, Fisher Black, Robert Merton, Stephen Ross, Frank Reilly, Jack C. Francis, Mark Rubinstein, and others cited in the pages that follow. Without their contributions, this text could not have been written. Finally, I extend my gratitude to the many people who make up the soul of the Bloomberg system—analysts, programmers, systems experts, reps, and journalists. It is truly a remarkable system.

I encourage you to send your comments and suggestions to me:

johnsons@xavier.edu
R. STAFFORD JOHNSON
Xavier University

CHAPTER 1

Overview of the Financial System

Real and Financial Assets

Most new businesses begin when an individual or a group of individuals come up with an idea: manufacturing a new type of cell phone, developing land for a future housing subdivision, launching a new Internet company, or exploring for crude oil. To make the idea a commercial reality, however, requires funds that the individual or group generally lacks or personally does not want to commit. Consequently, the fledgling business sells *financial claims* or *instruments* to raise the funds necessary to buy the capital goods (equipment, land, etc.), as well as human capital (architects, engineers, lawyers, etc.), needed to launch the project. Technically, such instruments are claims against the income of the business represented by a certificate, receipt, or other legal document. In this process of initiating and implementing the idea, both real and financial assets are therefore created. The *real assets* consist of both the tangible and intangible capital goods, as well as human capital, which are combined with labor to form the business. The business, in turn, transforms the idea into the production and sale of goods or services that will generate a future stream of earnings. The *financial assets*, however, consist of the financial claims on the earnings. Those individuals or institutions that provided the initial funds and resources hold these assets. Furthermore, if the idea is successful, then the new business may find it advantageous to initiate other new projects that it again may finance through the sale of financial claims. Thus, over time, more real and financial assets are created.

The creation of financial claims, of course, is not limited to the business sector. The federal government's expenditures on national defense, entitlements, and infrastructures and state governments' expenditures on the construction of highways, for example, represent the creation of real assets that these units of government often finance through the sale of financial claims on either the revenue generated from a particular public sector project or from future tax revenues. Similarly, the purchase of a house or a car by a household often is financed by a loan from a savings and loan or commercial bank. The loan represents a claim by the financial institution on a portion of the borrower's future income, as well as a claim on the ownership of the real asset (house or car) in the event the household defaults on its promise.

Modern economies expend enormous amounts of money on real assets to maintain their standards of living. Such expenditures usually require funds that are beyond the levels a business, household, or unit of government has or wants to commit at a given point in time. As a result, to raise the requisite amounts, economic entities sell financial claims. Those buying the financial claims therefore supply funds to the economic entity in return for promises that the entity will provide them with a future flow of income. As such, financial claims can be described as financial assets.

All financial assets provide a promise of a future return to the owners. Unlike real assets, however, financial assets do not depreciate (because they are in the form of certificates or information in a computer file), and they are *fungible*, meaning they can be converted into cash or other assets. There are many different types of financial assets. All of them, however, can be divided into two general categories—equity and debt. Common stock is the most popular form of equity claims. It entitles the holder to dividends or shares in the business's residual profit and participation in the management of the firm, usually indirectly through voting rights. The stock market where existing stock shares are traded is the most widely followed market in the world, and it receives considerable focus in many investment and security analysis texts. The other general type of financial asset is debt. Businesses finance more of their real assets and operations with debt than with equity, whereas governments and households finance their entire real assets and operations with debt. This chapter provides an overview of the types of equity and debt securities and their markets. The first book in the Bloomberg investment series, *Debt Markets and Analysis*, focused on debt securities. The focus of this book is on equity. This chapter provides an overview of both types of securities and markets.

Types of Equity Claims

Firms need capital to grow and acquire additional assets. When a corporation decides to finance its capital formation with equity, it will do so either internally by retaining earnings or externally by issuing common stock, preferred stock, or perhaps forming a limited partnership.

Common stock is an equity or ownership claim entitling the holder to dividends and ownership rights. Issued shares include outstanding shares held by investors that are used for per share calculations and treasury shares held by the firm, often through a repurchase of stock by the firm. As discussed in more detail in Chapter 4, the ownership rights of common stock can be classified into four categories: collective rights, specific rights, cumulative voting rights, and preemptive rights. Two important features of common stock are limited liability and double taxation. *Limited liability* means that the most one shareholder of a company can lose if the company goes bankrupt is his or her original investment. Thus, unlike proprietorships and partnerships in which the business ownership is defined in terms of the individuals and not a legal entity, the extent of the liability for an individual shareholder of a corporation is limited to his or her shares, with no risk of personal liability. *Double taxation* means that earnings of a company are taxed twice. First, before the payments to shareholders, the earnings of the company are subject to a corporate tax, and then the dividend payments to shareholders are subject to personal taxes.

Preferred stock can be thought of as a limited ownership share. It provides its owners with only limited income potential in the form of a stipulated dividend (*preferred dividend*), and it gives its holders fewer voting privileges and less control over the business than common stock does. To make preferred stock more attractive, companies frequently sell preferred stock with special rights. Among the most common of these special rights is the priority over common stockholders over earnings and assets upon liquidation and the right to cumulative dividends—if preferred dividends are not paid, then all past dividends must be paid before any common dividends are paid. To the investor, preferred stock is similar to a bond in its priority of claims and its fixed income feature, and it is similar to common stock in that there is no maturity and there is no corporate default if preferred dividends are not paid by the company. Hence, preferred is commonly referred to as a *hybrid security*.

A *limited partnership* is a business structure consisting of a general partner who usually initiates, organizes, and manages a business venture, and limited partners who provide the investment funds by buying limited partnership shares. The limited partnership share, in turn, represents an equity position with limited participation in the management of the company. More importantly, in accordance with current tax and corporate laws, all tax obligations and deductions flow directly to the partners and not to the corporation. Thus, earnings go directly to the partners, with no corporate taxes applied. In addition, the usual corporate deductions for depreciation, interest paid on debt, and the like are also used by the individuals as part of their personal income tax deductions. Thus, a limited partnership share is similar to proprietorship or partnership in the way taxes are applied. However, limited partnerships do not subject their holders to personal liabilities in the case of a bankruptcy or an adverse legal judgment; that is, by law, limited partner shares have a limited liability feature like a common stock. Thus, limited partnership shares have the limited liability benefit of common stock without the disadvantage of double taxation.

Types of Debt Claims

Debt claims are loans whereby the borrower agrees to pay a fixed income per period, defined as a coupon or interest, and to repay the borrowed funds, defined as the principal (also called redemption value, maturity value, par value, and face value). Within this broad description, debt instruments can take on many different forms. For example, debt can take the form of a loan by a financial institution. In this case, the terms of the agreement and the contract instrument generally are prepared by the lender/creditor, and the instrument often is nonnegotiable, meaning it cannot be sold to another party. A debt instrument also can take the form of a bond or note, whereby the borrower obtains her loan by selling (also referred to as issuing) contracts or IOUs to pay interest and principal to investors/lenders. Many of these claims, in turn, are negotiable, often being sold to other investors before they mature.

Debt instruments also can differ in terms of the features of the contract: the number of future interest payments; when and how the principal is to be paid (e.g., at maturity, or the end of the contract) or spread out over the life of the contract (amortized); and the recourse the lender has should the borrower fail to meet her contractual commitments (i.e., collateral or security). For many debt instruments, standard features include the following:

> *Term to maturity*: Number of years over which the issuer promises to meet the obligations. (Maturity refers to the date that the debt will cease to exist.) Generally, bonds with maturities between 1 and 5 years are considered short term; those with maturities between 5 and 12 years are considered intermediate term; and those with maturities greater than 12 years are considered long term.
>
> *Principal* is the amount that the issuer/borrower agrees to repay the bondholder/lender.
>
> *Coupon rate* (or nominal rate) is the rate the issuer/borrower agrees to pay each period. The dollar amount is called the coupon. There are, however, zero-coupon bonds for which the investor earns interest between the price paid and the principal, and floating-rate notes for which the coupon rate is reset periodically based on a formula.
>
> *Amortization*: The principal repayment of a bond can be either repaid at maturity or over the life of the bond. When principal is repaid over the life of the bond, there is a schedule of principal repayments. The schedule is called the amortization schedule. Securities with an amortization schedule are called amortizing securities, whereas securities without an amortized schedule (those paying total principal at maturity) are called nonamortizing securities.
>
> *Embedded options*: Bonds often have embedded option features in their contracts, such as a call feature giving the issuer the right to buy back the bond from the bondholder before maturity at a specific price (*callable bond*).

Finally, the type of borrower or issuer—business, government, household, or financial institution—can differentiate the debt instruments. Businesses sell three general types of debt instruments, *corporate bonds, medium-term notes*, and *commercial paper*, and borrow from financial institutions, usually with a long-term or intermediate-term loan from commercial banks or insurance companies and with short-term *lines of credit* from banks. The corporate bonds they sell usually pay the buyer/lender coupon interest semiannually and a principal at maturity. For example, a manufacturing company building a $100 million processing plant might finance the cost by selling 100,000 bonds at a price of $1,000 per bond, with each bond promising to pay $50 in interest every June 15 and January 15 for the next 10 years and a principal of $1,000 at maturity. In general, corporate bonds are long-term securities when they are issued, and they are sometimes secured by specific real assets that bondholders can claim in case the corporation fails to meet its contractual obligation (defaults). Corporate bonds also have a priority of claims over stockholders on the company's earnings and assets in the case of default. Medium-term notes (MTNs) issued by a corporation are debt instruments sold through agents on a continuing basis to investors who are allowed to choose from a group of bonds from the same corporation, but with different maturities and features. Such instruments allow corporations flexibility in the way in which they can finance different capital projects. Commercial paper is a short-term claim (less than one year) that usually is unsecured. Typically, commercial paper is sold as a zero-discount note for which the buyer receives interest equal to the difference between the principal and the purchase price. For example, a company might sell paper promising to pay $1,000 at the end of 270 days for $970, yielding a dollar return of $30. Term loans to businesses have original maturities that are intermediate or long term, often with the principal amortized. Like all debt instruments, these loans have a priority of claims on income and assets over equity claims, and the financial institution providing the loan often requires collateral. Finally, lines of credit are short-term loans provided by banks and other financial institutions with which the business can borrow up to a maximum amount of funds from a checking account created for it by the institution.

The federal government sells a variety of financial instruments, ranging from short-term *Treasury bills* to intermediate-term and long-term *Treasury notes* and *Treasury bonds*. These instruments are sold by the Treasury to finance the federal deficit and to refinance current debt. In addition to Treasury securities, agencies of the federal government, such as the Tennessee Valley Authority, and government-sponsored corporations, such as the Federal National Mortgage Association and the Federal Farm Credit Banks, also issue securities, classified as *Federal Agency Securities*, to finance a variety of government programs ranging from the construction of dams to the purchase of mortgages to provide liquidity to mortgage lenders. The agency sector includes securities issued by federal agencies and also federally related institutions, referred to as *government-sponsored enterprises*. Similarly, state and local governments, agencies, and authorities also offer a wide variety of debt instruments, broadly classified as either *general obligation bonds* or *revenue bonds*. The former are bonds financed through general tax revenue, whereas the latter are instruments financed from the revenue from specific state and local government projects and programs.

Finally, there are financial intermediaries such as commercial banks, savings and loans, credit unions, savings banks, insurance companies, and investment funds that provide debt and equity claims. These intermediaries sell financial claims to investors and then use the proceeds to purchase debt and equity claims or to provide direct loans. In general, financial institutions, by acting as intermediaries, control a large number of funds and thus have a significant impact on financial markets. For borrowers, intermediaries are an important source of funds; they buy many of the securities issued by corporations and governments and provide many of the direct loans. For investors, intermediaries create a number of securities for them to include in their short-term and long-term portfolios. These include negotiable certificates of deposit (CDs), bankers' acceptances, mortgage-backed instruments, asset-backed securities, collateralized debt obligations, investment fund shares, annuities, and guaranteed investment contracts.

Financial Markets

Markets are conduits through which buyers and sellers exchange goods, services, and resources. In an economy there are three types of markets: a product market where goods and services are traded; a factor market where labor, capital, and land are exchanged; and a financial market where financial claims are traded. The financial market, in turn, channels the savings of households, businesses, and governments to those economic units needing to borrow.

The financial market can be described as a market for loanable funds. The supply of loanable funds comes from the savings of households, the retained earnings of businesses, and the surpluses of governments; the demand for loanable funds emanates from businesses that need to raise funds to finance their capital purchases of equipment, plants, and inventories; households that need to purchase houses, cars, and other consumer durables; and the Treasury, federal agencies, and municipal governments that need to finance the construction of public facilities, projects, and operations. The exchange of loanable funds from savers to borrowers is done either directly through the selling of financial claims (stock, bonds, commercial paper, etc.) or indirectly through financial institutions.

The financial market facilitates the transfer of funds from *surplus economic units* to *deficit economic units*. A surplus economic unit is an entity whose income from its current production exceeds its current expenditures; it is a saver or net lender. A deficit unit is an entity whose current expenditures exceed its income from its current production; it is a net borrower. Although businesses, households, and governments fluctuate from being deficit units in one period to surplus units in another period, on average households tend to be surplus units, whereas businesses and government units tend to be deficit units. A young household usually starts as a deficit unit as it acquires homes and cars financed with mortgages and auto loans. In its midlife, the household's income usually is higher and its mortgage and other loans are often paid; at that time the household tends to become a surplus unit, purchasing financial claims. Finally, near the end of its life, the household lives off the income from its financial claims. In contrast, businesses tend to invest or acquire assets that cost more than the earnings they retain. As a result, businesses are almost always deficit units, borrowing or selling bonds and stocks; furthermore, they tend to remain that way throughout their entire life. Similarly, the federal government's expenditures on defense, education, and welfare have more often exceeded its revenues from taxes. Thus, the federal government, as well as most state and local governments, tend to be deficit units.

Types of Financial Markets

Financial markets can be classified in terms of whether the market is for new or existing claims (primary or secondary market); for short-term or long-term instruments (money or capital market); for direct or indirect trading between deficit and surplus units (direct or intermediary market); for domestic or foreign securities; and for immediate, future, or optional delivery (cash, futures, or options markets).

Primary and Secondary Markets

The *primary market* is the market where financial claims are created. It is the market in which new securities are sold for the first time. Thus, the sale of new government securities by the U.S. Treasury to finance a government deficit, or a $500 million bond issue by Duke Energy to finance the construction of an electrical generating plant, is an example of a security transaction occurring in the primary market. The principal function of the primary market is to raise the funds needed to finance investments in new plants, equipment, inventories, homes, roads, and the like—it is where capital formation begins.

The *secondary market* is the market for the buying and selling of existing assets and financial claims. Its economic function is to provide marketability—ease or speed in trading a security. Given the accumulation of financial claims over time, the volume of trading on the secondary market far exceeds the volume in the primary market. The buying and selling of existing securities is done primarily through a network of brokers and dealers who operate through organized security exchanges, the over-the-counter market, and electronic communication networks. Brokers and dealers serve the function of bringing buyers and sellers together by finding opposite positions or by taking positions in a security. By definition, *brokers* are agents who bring security buyers and sellers together for a commission. *Dealers*, in turn, provide markets for investors to buy and sell securities by taking a temporary position in a security; they buy from investors who want to sell and sell to those who want to buy. Dealers receive compensation in terms of the spread between the *bid price* at which they buy securities and *asked price* at which they sell securities. Whereas brokers and dealers serve the function of bringing buyers and seller together, exchanges serve the function of linking brokers and dealers together to buy and sell existing securities. In the United States, there is the New York Stock Exchange Euronext and several regional organized exchanges. Outside the United States, there are major exchanges in such cities as London, Tokyo, Hong Kong, Singapore, Sydney, and Paris. In addition to organized exchanges, a large number of existing securities and a large proportion of bonds are traded on the over-the-counter (OTC) market. In linking traders, exchanges and the OTC markets operate through humans, electronically, or both. Finally, there are *third markets* in which exchange-listed securities are traded on the OTC market, and a *fourth market* in which there is direct trading between financial institutions and not through the exchange and OTC markets.

New York Stock Exchange Euronext

The New York Stock Exchange (NYSE) was formed in 1792 by a group of merchants who wanted to trade notes and bonds. Since then it has grown to an exchange in which stocks and a limited number of bonds, exchange-traded funds (ETFs), and other securities are traded. The NYSE and a number of other organized exchanges provide a continuous market. A continuous market attempts to have constant trading in a security. This is accomplished by having *specialists* or *designated market makers* (DMMs). Specialists and DMMs are dealers who are part of the exchange and who are required by the exchange to take opposite positions in a security if conditions dictate. Under a specialist system, the exchange board assigns a specific security to a specialist to deal. In this role, a specialist acts by buying the stock from sellers at low bid prices and selling to buyers at higher asked prices. Specialists and DMMs quote a bid price to investors when selling the security and an asked price to investors interested in buying. They hope to profit from the difference between the bid and asked prices, that is, the *bid-ask spread*.

In April 2007, the NYSE became part of *NYSE Euronext*, a holding company created by combining the NYSE Group, Inc. and Euronext N.V. NYSE Euronext can be described as a transatlantic exchange group that brings together six equities exchanges and six derivatives exchanges that provide physical and electronic trading in stocks, bonds, and derivatives. In the UnitedStates, NYSE Euronext includes the NYSE physical exchange and NYSE Arca. NYSE Arca is a fully electronic stock exchange, trading more than 8,000 exchange-listed equity securities. NYSE Arca's trading platform links traders to multiple U.S. market centers and provides customers with fast electronic execution and open, direct, and anonymous market access. NYSE Arca's functions are based on a price-time priority system.

Over-the-Counter Market

The over-the-counter (OTC) market is an informal exchange for the trading of stocks, corporate and municipal bonds, investment fund shares, asset-backed securities, and Treasury and federal agency securities. It can be described as a fragmented, noncentralized market of brokers and dealers linked to each other by a computer, telephone, and telex communications system. To trade, dealers must register with the Securities and Exchange Commission (SEC). As dealers, they can quote their own bid and asked prices on the securities they deal, and as brokers, they can execute a trade with a dealer providing a quote. The securities traded on the OTC market are those in which a dealer decides to take a position. Dealers on the OTC market range from regional brokerage houses making a market in a local corporation's stocks or bonds; to large financial companies, such as Merrill Lynch, making markets in Treasury securities; to investment bankers dealing in the securities they had previously underwritten; to dealers in federal agency securities and municipal bonds. Like the specialist on the organized exchanges, each dealer maintains an inventory in a security and quotes a bid and an asked price at which she is willing to buy and sell. Initially, the *National Association of Securities Dealers* (NASD) regulated OTC trading. In July 2007, the *Financial*

Industry Regulatory Authority (FINRA), the largest independent regulator for all securities firms doing business in the United States, consolidated NASD and the member regulation, enforcement, and arbitration functions of the NYSE. Even though no physical exchange exists, communications among brokers and dealers takes place through a computer system known as the *National Association of Securities Dealers Automated Quotation System (NASDAQ)*. NASDAQ is an information system in which current bid-ask quotes of dealers are offered, and also a system that sends brokers' quotes to dealers, enabling them to close trades.[1]

Electronic Trading Market

There are several other types of secondary market trading for stock. For example, the NYSE features both a physical auction convened by DMMs and a completely automated auction that includes algorithmic quotes from DMMs and other participants. As noted, NYSE Arca is an electronic stock exchange, trading more than 8,000 exchange-listed (NASDAQ included) equity securities. There are also other *electronic communication network* (ECN) systems provided by the OTC markets, regional exchanges, and exchanges in other countries. These crossing network systems allow institutional investors to cross order, matching buy and sell orders directly via computers. The history of these exchanges and their convergence to form today's global electronic exchange system are described in Chapter 4.

Secondary Market for Bonds

The secondary market for bonds in the United States and throughout the world is not centralized, but rather is part of the OTC market. As noted, the OTC consists of a network of noncentralized or fragmented market makers who provide bids and offer quotes for each issue in which they participate. There are some corporate bonds that are listed on physical exchanges. Such bonds are sometimes said to be trading in the bond room. Although they may be listed, they are more likely to be traded through dealers on the OTC market than on the exchange. There is also a transition to electronic trading. For example, the NYSE Euronext recently began offering an all-electronic platform for trading NYSE bonds based on a price-time priority system. Also, there are multi-dealer systems being developed that allow customers to execute bond trades from multiple quotes. The systems display the best bid or offer prices of those posted by all dealers. The participating dealers usually act as the principal in the transaction. There are also single-dealer systems developing that allow investors to execute a transaction directly with the specific dealers desired.

Direct and Intermediate Financial Markets

In addition to dividing the markets for financial instruments into primary and secondary ones, the markets can also be classified in terms of being either part of the direct financial market or the intermediary financial market.

Direct Financial Market

The *direct financial market* is where surplus units purchase claims issued by the ultimate deficit unit. This market includes the trading of stocks, corporate bonds, Treasury securities, federal agency securities, and municipal bonds. The claims traded in the direct financial market are referred to as *primary securities*.[2]

As is the case with many security markets, the direct financial market can be divided into primary and secondary markets. The secondary market for direct financial claims takes place in both the organized exchanges and the OTC market just discussed. In the primary market, new securities are sold either in a negotiated market or an open market. In a *negotiated market*, the securities are issued to one or just a few economic entities under a private contract. Such sales are referred to as a *private placement*. In an open market transaction, the securities are sold to the public at large. The key participant in an *open market trade* is the *investment banker*. The investment banker is a middleperson or matchmaker who, for a fee or share in the trading profit, finds surplus units who want to buy the security being offered by a deficit unit. The major investment bankers include such firms as Bank of America Merrill Lynch and Goldman Sachs. Investment bankers sell a security issue for the issuer for a commission (i.e., for a percentage of the total issue's value) using their *best effort*, *underwrite* the securities (i.e., buy the securities from the issuer and then sell them at, it is hoped, a higher price), or form an *underwriting syndicate* whereby a group of investment bankers buys and sells the issue. Whatever the arrangements, the primary function of the investment banker is to match the needs of the surplus and deficit units. By performing this function, the investment banker reduces the search and information costs to both the investors and the issuer, facilitating the efficient operation of the primary market.

Intermediary Financial Market

The intermediary financial market consists of financial institutions such as commercial banks, savings and loans, credit unions, insurance companies, pension funds, trust funds, and mutual funds. In this market, the financial institution sells financial claims (checking accounts, savings accounts, certificates of deposit[CDs], investment fund shares, payroll deduction plans, insurance plans, etc.) to surplus units and uses the proceeds to purchase claims (stocks, bonds, etc.) issued by ultimate deficit units or to create financial claims in the form of term loans, lines of credit, and mortgages. Through their intermediary function, financial institutions in turn create intermediate securities, referred to as *secondary securities*.

Financial institutions making up the intermediary market can be divided into three categories: *depository institutions, contractual institutions*, and *investment companies*. Depository institutions include commercial banks, credit unions, savings and loans, and savings banks. These institutions obtain large amounts of their funds from deposits, which they use primarily to fund commercial and residential loans and to purchase Treasury, federal agency, and municipal securities. Contractual institutions include life insurance companies, property and casualty insurance companies, and pension funds. They obtain their funds from legal contracts to protect businesses and households from risk (premature death, accident, etc.) and from savings plans. Investment companies include mutual funds, money market funds, and real estate investment trusts. These institutions raise funds by selling equity or debt claims and then use the proceeds to buy debt securities, stocks, real estate, and other assets. The claims they sell entitle the holder/buyer either to a fixed income each period or a pro rata share in the ownership and earnings generated from the asset fund. Also included with the securities of investment companies are *securitized assets.* Banks, insurance companies, and other financial intermediaries, as well as federal agencies, sell these financial assets. In creating a securitized asset, an intermediary will put together a package of loans of a certain type (mortgages, auto, credit cards, etc.). The institution then sells claims on the package to investors, with the claim being secured by the package of assets—a securitized asset. The package of loans, in turn, generates interest and principal that is passed on to the investors who purchased the securitized asset.[3]

Some of the financial claims created in the intermediary financial market do not have a secondary market; that is, secondary markets in which investors sell their bank saving accounts or insurance or pension plans to other investors are rare. However, there are secondary markets for many intermediary securities: negotiable CDs, investment fund shares, and securitized assets.

Money and Capital Markets

Financial markets can also be classified in terms of the maturity of the instrument traded. Specifically, the *money market* is defined as the market where short-term instruments (by convention defined as securities with original maturities of one year or less) are traded, and the *capital market* is defined as the market where long-term securities (original maturities over one year) are traded. The former would include such securities as CDs, commercial paper (CP), Treasury bills, savings accounts, and shares in money market investment funds, whereas the latter would include common and preferred stock, limited partnership shares, corporate bonds, municipal bonds, securitized assets, Treasury bonds, and investment fund shares. Investors with long-term liabilities or investment horizons buy securities in the capital markets. This includes many institutional investors, such as life insurance companies and pensions. The issuers of capital market securities include corporations and governments that use the market to finance their long-term capital formation projects or debt. Investors use the money market to earn interest on excess funds that they expect to have only temporarily. They also hold funds in money market securities as a store of value when they are waiting to take advantage of investment opportunities or when they fear that precarious economic conditions are possible. The sellers of money market securities use the market to raise funds to finance their short-term assets (inventory or accounts receivable); to take care of cash needs resulting from the lack of synchronization between cash inflows and outflows from operations; or, in the case of the U.S. Treasury, to finance the government's deficit or to refinance its maturing debt. It should be noted that the money market functions primarily as a *wholesale market*, in which many of the transactions are done by large banks and investment firms that buy and sell in large denominations. This feature helped to promote the popularity of money market funds. These funds pool the investments of small investors and invest them in money market securities, providing small investors an opportunity to obtain higher returns than they could obtain from individual bank savings accounts.

Foreign Security Markets

Over the past three decades, there has been a substantial growth in the number of equity and fixed-income securities traded globally. This growth in the size of world equity and debt markets is reflected by the significant increase in global security investments among nonresidents. The popularity of global investments is generally attributed to the growing number of corporations, governments, and financial intermediaries issuing securities in foreign countries; to the emergence of currency futures, options, and swaps markets that have made it possible for investors to better manage exchange-rate risk; and to the potential diversification benefits investors can obtain by adding foreign stocks and bonds to their portfolios.

In general, an investor looking to internationally diversify her portfolio has several options. First, she might buy a stock or bond of a foreign government or foreign corporation that is issued in the foreign country or traded on that country's exchange. These securities are referred to as *domestic bonds*.[4] Second, the investor might be able to buy bonds or stocks issued in a number of countries through an international syndicate. Securities sold in this market are known as *Eurobonds* or *Euroequity*. Finally, an investor might be able to buy a bond of a foreign government or the bonds or corporation being issued or traded in his own country. Such bonds are called *foreign bonds*. Similarly, an investor may be able to buy a foreign stock in his own country that is listed on the local stock exchange. Many multinational corporations are listed not only on their national exchanges, but also on security exchanges in other countries, often where they have subsidiaries or conduct considerable business. If the foreign stock of interest is listed on a U.S. stock exchange, then a U.S. investor could easily purchase the stock there. If she did, she would, in turn, avoid the risk of currency conversions and possibly foreign taxes.

If the investor were instead looking for short-term foreign investments, his choices could similarly include buying short-term domestic securities such as CP, CDs, and Treasuries issued in those countries; Eurocurrency CDs issued by Eurobanks; and foreign money market securities issued by foreign corporations and the government in the local country. Similarly, a domestic financial institution or nonfinancial multinational corporation looking to raise funds may choose to do so by selling debt securities or borrowing in the company's own financial markets, the foreign markets, or the Eurobond or Eurocurrency markets. The markets where domestic, foreign, and Euro securities are issued and traded can be grouped into two categories—the *internal bond market* and the *external bond market*. The internal market, also called the *national market*, consists of the trading of both domestic bonds and foreign bonds; the external market, also called the *offshore market*, is where Eurobonds and Eurodeposits are bought and sold.

For foreign investments, one of the most important factors for an investor to consider is that their price, interest payments, and principal are in a different currency. This currency component exposes them to *exchange-rate risk* and affects their returns and overall risk. Most of the currency trading takes place in the *Interbank Foreign Exchange Market*. This market consists primarily of major banks that act as currency dealers, maintaining inventories of foreign currencies to sell to or buy from their customers (corporations, governments, or regional banks). The price of foreign currency or the exchange rate is defined as the number of units of one currency that can be exchanged for one unit of another. It is determined by supply and demand conditions affecting the foreign currency market.

Spot, Futures, Options, and Swap Markets

A *spot market* (also called a *cash market*) is one in which securities are exchanged for cash immediately (in practice, within one or two business days). An investor's buying a stock or a Treasury bill, for example, is a transaction that takes place in the spot market. Not all security transactions, however, call for immediate delivery. A *futures or forward contract* calls for the delivery and purchase of an asset (either real or financial) at a future date, with the terms (price, amount, etc.) agreed upon in the present. For example, a contract calling for the delivery of a Treasury bill in 70 days at a price equal to 97 percent of the bill's principal would represent a futures contract on a Treasury bill. This agreement is distinct from buying a Treasury bill from a Treasury dealer in the spot market, where the transfer of cash for the security takes place almost immediately. Similar to a futures contract, an option is a security that gives the holder the right (but not the obligation) either to buy or to sell an asset at a specific price on or possibly before a specific date. Options include calls, puts, warrants, and rights. Both futures and options are traded on organized exchanges and through dealers on the OTC market. In the United States, the major futures exchange is the Chicago Mercantile Exchange and the major options exchange is the Chicago Board Options Exchange. Options and futures are referred to as *derivative securities* because their values are derived from the values of their underlying securities. In contrast, securities sold in the spot market are sometimes referred to as *primitive securities*. Derivatives have become important to both borrowers and investors in managing the risk associated with issuing and buying securities. Chapters 16 and 17 focus on the markets and the uses of derivative securities.

In addition to derivative securities, bonds often have *embedded option* features in their contracts. As noted earlier, many bonds have a call feature giving the issuer the right to buy back the bond from the bondholder before maturity at a specific price. In addition to these so-called callable bonds, there are putable bonds, giving the bondholder the right to sell the bond back to the issuer at a specified price, sinking fund clauses in which the issuer is required to orderly retire the bond by either buying bonds in the market or by calling them at a specified price, and convertible bonds that give the bondholder the right to convert the bond into a specified number of shares of stock. The inclusion of option features in a bond contract makes the valuation of such bonds more difficult.

Today, there is a large swap market. A swap is an exchange of cash flows. It is a legal arrangement between two parties to exchange specific payments. There are four types of swaps:

1. *Interest rate swaps*: Exchange of fixed-rate payments for floating-rate payments.
2. *Currency swaps*: Exchange of liabilities in different currencies.
3. *Cross-currency swaps*: Combination of interest rate and currency swap.
4. *Credit default swaps*: Exchange of premium payments for default protection.

The swap market primarily consists of financial institutions and corporations that use swap contracts to hedge more efficiently their liabilities and assets. For example, many institutions create synthetic fixed- or floating-rate assets or liabilities with better rates than the rates obtained on direct liabilities and assets or as a tool to change the rate on their existing debt.

Gold and Precious Metals

In addition to domestic and foreign bonds and stocks, investment funds, and derivatives, many investors include gold and other precious metals such as silver as part of their portfolios. Since gold does not generate an income, its attraction as an international asset comes from its tradition of being regarded as an international store of value. Gold is a precious metal that is unaffected by water, weather, and oxygen. Investors have often purchased it during periods of economic or political crisis.

The price of gold is determined by supply and demand. The demand for gold comes from its use in industry, jewelry manufacturing, coin production, and as an investment. South Africa is the largest supplier of gold. It also is mined in the United States, Canada, Latin American, and a number of other places. To acquire gold, an investor can either buy gold bullion or purchase gold-related assets, such as gold coins, equity shares in gold mines, gold bonds, and futures and options contracts on gold bullion. Gold coins trade at prices reflecting the value of their metal content, plus a premium. Actively traded coins include the U.S. Double Eagle, South African Krugerrand, Canadian Maple Leaf, French Napoleon, and Swiss Vreneli. Gold bonds are securities whose coupon and principal are paid in gold or gold coins or whose values are indexed to gold prices. For example, the Pinay, a French government bond, is indexed to the Napoleon. Shares in gold-mining companies are traded on a number of stock exchanges. Over the years, there has been a high (though not perfect) positive correlation between the prices of gold-mining shares and the price of gold bullion. Finally, as a short-run strategy, investors can buy options and futures on gold bullion. These constructs are offered on several options and futures exchanges.

Regulations

Prior to the enactment of federal security laws in 1933 and 1934, the regulations of security trading in the United States came under the auspices of state governments, which had passed a number of laws to prevent fraud and speculative schemes. The state security laws, known as the *blue-sky laws*, were often hard to enforce because many fraudulent promoters could operate outside a state's jurisdiction. With the passage of the *Securities Act of 1933* and the *Securities Exchange Act of 1934*, however, security regulations came more under the providence of the federal government. The 1933 act, known as the *truth-in-securities law*, requires registration of new issues, disclosure of pertinent information by issuers, and prohibits fraud and misrepresentation. The Securities Exchange Act (SEA) of 1934 established the *Securities and Exchange Commission*, extended the disclosure requirements of the 1933 act to include traders and participants in the secondary market, and outlawed fraud and misrepresentation in the trading of existing securities. Today, five commissioners appointed by the president and confirmed by the Senate for five-year terms run the SEC. The SEC is responsible for the administration of both the 1933 and 1934 acts, as well as the administration of a number of other security laws that have been enacted since then. The 1934 act gave the SEC authority over organized exchanges. Historically, the SEC has exercised its authority by setting only general guidelines for the bylaws and rules of an exchange, allowing the exchanges to regulate themselves. The SEC does have the power, however, to intervene and change bylaws, as well as to close exchanges.

The 1933 and 1934 security acts are aimed at ensuring that information is disseminated efficiently to all investors and that fraud and misrepresentation are outlawed. Specifically, the acts outlaw price manipulation schemes such as wash sales, pools, churning, and corners. To comply with the disclosure provisions of the SEA (and its 1964 amendments), companies listed on the exchanges and those traded on the OTC market are required to file with the SEC *10-K reports*, which are audited financial statement forms; *10-Q reports*, which are quarterly unaudited financial statement forms; and *8-K forms*, which report significant developments by the company. Exhibit 1.1 summarizes the provisions in the security acts of 1933 and 1934, and Exhibit 1.2 describes some of the other important security laws in the United States.

There are also laws, regulations, and regulatory agencies that work to ensure that the financial system is sound. Of particular note is the Federal Reserve System. Created in 1913, the Federal Reserve (Fed) is the most important central bank in the world. The Fed is responsible for managing the economy's money supply and the general level of interest rates. The Fed does this by open market operations, changing the reserve requirements that banks maintain, and changing the discount rate they charge commercial banks on loans.

EXHIBIT 1.1 Security Acts of 1933 and 1934: Price Manipulation

Price Manipulation	Description
Wash Sale	A wash sale is a sale and subsequent repurchase of a security or purchase of an identical security. It is done in order to establish a record to show, for example, a capital loss for tax purposes or to deceive investors into thinking there is large activity on the stock. The SEA of 1934 prohibits wash sales.
Pool	A pool is an association of people formed to manipulate the price of a security. For example, a pool might be formed with a group of brokers, specialists, corporate executives, and news reporters. Initially, the group could collude to bring a stock's price down through short sales and the dissemination of negative information; then, after the price has decreased to a certain level, they could buy the securities and use their connections and authority to increase the security's price to a level at which they could profit when they liquidate. The 1934 act forbids such pool activities, requires all pools to be reported, makes it illegal for members to be part of a pool, and requires corporate executives and other insiders to report their transactions in their own securities with the SEC.
Churning	Churning occurs when a broker manipulates his client to make frequent purchases and sales of a security in order to profit from increased commissions. Section 10(b) of SEA of 1934 forbids churning, but it is very difficult to prove in a court of law.
Corner	A corner occurs when someone buys up all or most of the security issues (or commodities) in order to have the monopolistic power to raise its price and to pressure short sellers to sell at higher prices. An investor or group of investors who try to corner the market could do so by forming pools to manipulate the security's price. Such manipulation is outlawed by the SEA of 1934.
Insider Activity	The SEA requires that all officers, directors, and owners of more than 10 percent file an *insider report* each month in which they trade their securities. This information is publicly reported in the financial press. The purpose of this requirement is to eliminate an insider from profiting from inside information.

Identification

There are thousands of bonds, stocks, and investment fund shares outstanding. Publicly traded stocks can be identified by their *ticker* symbol. Most fixed-income securities can be identified by a nine-character *CUSIP* number. CUSIP stands for the Committee on Uniform Securities Identification Procedures. CUSIP is owned by the American Bankers Association and operated by Standard & Poor's (S&P). It is used to identify trades and for clearing. There is also a 12-character foreign security identification system known as the CUSIP International Numbering System (CINS).

Efficient Financial Markets

As defined earlier, an asset is any commodity, tangible or intangible good, organization, or financial claim that generates future benefits. The value of an asset is equal to

EXHIBIT 1.2 U.S. Federal Laws Related to Security Training

Legislation	Description
Glass-Steagall Act (enacted 1933; major provisions repealed 1999)	The Glass-Steagall Act, also known as the Banking Act of 1933, prohibited commercial banks from acting as investment bankers. Enacted after the 1929 stock market crash, the act also prohibited banks from paying interest on demand deposits (a prohibition that was later eliminated under the Monetary Control Act of 1980), and created the Federal Deposit Insurance Corporation. As a result of the Glass-Steagall Act, for years most commercial banks in the United States were not allowed to underwrite securities, act as brokers and dealers, and offer investment company shares. The Glass-Steagall Act also served to differentiate U.S. banking activities from those of many countries in which banks were allowed to provide investment banking and security services (merchant banking). Recognizing these differences, the U.S. Congress repealed many of the provisions of the Glass-Steagall Act.
Financial Services Modernization (Gramm-Leach-Bliley) Act (1999)	The act permitted finance companies and banks to form financial holding companies to offer banking, insurance, securities, and other financial services under one controlling corporation.
Federal Reserve Regulations T and U	Regulations T and U give the Board of Governors of the Federal Reserve the authority to set margin requirements for security loans made by banks, brokers, and dealers. Regulation T sets loan limits made by brokers and dealers, and regulation U sets loan limits made by banks for securities transactions.
Maloney Act (1936)	This act requires associations such as NASD to register with the SEC and allows them to regulate themselves within general guidelines specified by the SEC.
Trust Indenture Act (1939)	This act gave the SEC the authority to ensure that there are no conflicts of interest between bondholders, trustees, and an issuer. The act was in response to abuses in the 1930s that resulted from the issuer having control over the trustee. Among its provisions, the act requires that the bond indenture clearly delineate the rights of the bondholders, that periodic financial reports be given to the trustee, and that the trustee act judiciously in bringing legal actions against the issuer when conditions dictate.
Investment Company Act (ICA) (1940)	This act extends the provisions of the security acts of 1933 and 1934 to investment companies. Like the security acts, it requires a prospectus to be approved and issued to investors with full disclosure of financial statements, and it outlaws fraud and misrepresentations. In addition, the act requires investment companies to state their goals (growth, balance, income, etc.), to have a management firm approved by the investment company's board, and to manage funds for the benefit of the shareholders. The 1940 act was amended in 1970 (Investment Company Amendment Act of 1970) with provisions calling for certain restrictions on management fees and contracts.
Investment Advisers Act (IAA) (1940)	This act requires individuals and firms providing investment advice for a fee to register with the SEC. The act does not, however, require certification of an adviser's qualifications. The act also outlaws fraud and misrepresentation.

(Continued)

EXHIBIT 1.2 (*Continued*)

Legislation	Description
Employee Retirement Income Security Act (ERISA) (1974)	This act requires that managers of pension funds adhere to the prudent man rule (a common-law principle) in managing retirement funds. When applied to investment management, this rule requires average portfolio returns and risk levels to be consistent with that of a prudent man. The probable interpretation (which is subject to legal testing) would be that pension managers be adequately diversified to minimize the risk of large losses.
Securities Investor Protection Corporation (SIPC) (1970)	This act provides investors with insurance coverage against losses resulting from the bankruptcy of brokerage firms. The act stipulates that all registered brokers, dealers, and exchange members be members of the SIPC.
Sarbanes-Oxley Act of 2002	This act mandated a number of reforms to enhance corporate responsibility, enhance financial disclosures, and combat corporate and accounting fraud, and it created the Public Company Accounting Oversight Board (PCAOB) to oversee the activities of the auditing profession.

the current value of all of the asset's future expected cash flows, that is, the present value of the expected cash flow. Thus, if an investor requires a rate of return (R) of 10 percent per year on investments in a corporate bond that matures in one year, he would value (V_0) a bond promising to pay $100 interest and $1,000 principal at the end of one year as worth $1,000 today:

$$V_0 = \frac{\text{Interest} + \text{Principal}}{1 + R} = \frac{\$100 + \$1,000}{1.10} = \$1,000$$

Similarly, an investor who expected ABC stock to pay a dividend of $10 and to sell at a price of $105 one year later would value the stock at $100 if she required a rate of return of 15 percent per year on such investments:

$$V_0 = \frac{\text{Dividend} + \text{Expected Price}}{1 + R} = \frac{\$10 + \$105}{1.15} = \$100$$

Stock and bond valuation is examined in Chapter 3.

In the financial market, if stock investors expecting ABC stock to pay a $10 dividend and be worth $105 one year later required a 15 percent rate of return, then the equilibrium price of the stock in the market would be $100. Similarly, if one-year corporate bond investors required a 10 percent rate of return, then the equilibrium price of the corporate bond would be $1,000. The equilibrium price often is ensured by the activities of *speculators*: those who hope to obtain higher rates of return (greater than 15 percent in the case of the stock or 10 percent in the case of the bond) by gambling that security prices will move in certain directions. For example, if ABC stock sold below the $100 equilibrium value, then speculators would try to buy the underpriced stock.

As they tried to do so, however, they would push the underpriced ABC stock toward its equilibrium price of $100. However, if ABC stock were above $100, investors and speculators would be reluctant to buy the stock, lowering its demand and the price. These actions might also be reinforced with some speculators selling the stock short—a short sale. In a *short sale*, a speculator sells the stock first and buys it later, hoping to profit, as always, by buying at a low price and selling at a high one. For example, if ABC stock is selling at $105, a speculator could borrow a share of ABC stock from one of its owners (i.e., borrow the stock certificate, not money) and then sell the share in the market for $105. The short seller/speculator would now have $105 cash and would owe one share of stock to the share lender. Since the speculator believes the stock is overpriced, she is hoping to profit by the price of the stock decreasing in the near future. If she is right, such that ABC stock decreases to its equilibrium value of $100, then the speculator could go into the market, buy the stock for $100, and return the borrowed share, leaving her with a profit of $5. However, if the stock goes up and the share lender wants his stock back, then the short seller would lose when she buys back the stock at a price higher than $105. In general, speculators help to move the market price of a security to its equilibrium value.

By definition, a market in which the price of the security is equal to its equilibrium value at all times is known as a *perfect market*. For a market to be perfect requires, among other things, that all the information on which investors and speculators base their estimates of expected cash flows be reflected in the security's price. Such a market is known as an *efficient market*. In a perfect market, speculators would not earn abnormal returns (above 15 percent in our stock example). However, if the information the market receives is *asymmetrical* in the sense that some speculators have information that others do not or some receive information earlier than do others, then the market price will not be equal to its equilibrium value at all times. In this inefficient market, there would be opportunities for speculators to earn abnormal returns.

Efficient markets would also preclude arbitrage returns. An *arbitrage* is a risk-free opportunity. Such opportunities come from price discrepancies among different markets. For example, if the same car sells for $10,000 in Boston but $15,000 in New York, an *arbitrageur* (one who exploits such opportunities) could earn a risk-free profit by buying the car in Boston and selling it in New York (assuming, of course, that the transportation cost is less than $5,000). In the financial markets, arbitrageurs tie markets together. For example, suppose there were two identical government bonds, each paying a guaranteed interest and principal of $1,100 at the end of one year, but with one selling for $1,000 and the other selling for $900. With such price discrepancies, an arbitrageur could sell short the higher-priced bond at $1,000 (borrow the bond and sell it for $1,000) and buy the underpriced one for $900. This would generate an initial cash flow for the arbitrageur of $100 with no liabilities. That is, at maturity the arbitrageur would receive $1,100 from the underpriced bond that he could use to pay the lender of the overpriced bond. Arbitrageurs, by exploiting this arbitrage opportunity, however, would push the price of the underpriced bond up and the price of the overpriced one down until they were equally priced and the arbitrage was gone. Thus, arbitrageurs would tie the markets for the two identical bonds together.

Characteristics of Assets

The preceding discussion on the types of financial claims and their markets suggests that there are considerable differences among assets. All assets, however, can be described in terms of a limited number of common characteristics or properties. These common properties make it possible to evaluate, select, and manage assets by defining and comparing them in terms of these properties. In fact, as an academic subject, the study of investments involves the evaluation and selection of assets. The evaluation of assets consists of describing them in terms of their common characteristics, whereas selection involves selecting assets based on the trade-offs between those characteristics (e.g., higher return for higher risk). The characteristics common to all assets are value, rate of return, risk, life, divisibility, marketability, liquidity, and taxability.

Value

As defined earlier, the value of an asset is the present value of all of the asset's expected future benefits. Moreover, if markets are efficient, then in equilibrium the value of the asset would be equal to its market price.

Rate of Return

The rate of return on an asset is equal to the total return received from the asset per period of time expressed as a proportion of the price paid for the asset. The total return on the security includes the income payments the security promises (interest on bonds, dividends on stock, etc.), the interest from reinvesting the coupon or dividend income during the life of the security, and any capital gains or losses realized when the investor sells the asset. Thus, if a corporate bond cost $P_0 = \$1,000$ and was expected to pay a coupon interest of $C = \$100$ and a principal of $F = \$1,000$ at the end of the year, then its annual rate of return would be 10 percent if all the expectations hold true:

$$R = \frac{C + (F - P_0)}{P_0} = \frac{\$100 + (\$1,000 - \$1,000)}{\$1,000} = 0.10$$

It should be noted that value (or price) and rate of return are necessarily related. If an investor knows the price she will pay for a security and the expected future benefits of the security, then she can determine the security's rate of return. Alternatively, if she knows the rate of return she wants or requires and the expected future benefits of the security, then she can determine the security's value or price.

Risk

The third property of an asset is its risk. Investment risk can be defined as the possibility that the rate of return an investor will obtain from holding an asset will be less than expected. For stock, realized returns can deviate from expected returns when there are changes in the underlying factors that determine a firm's earnings, dividends, growth rates, and required return. The total risk of stock is often explained in terms of three general factors that influence a stock's return: factors related to the individual firm, the industry in which the firm competes, and the market in general.

For bonds, risk comes from concerns that a bond issuer might fail to meet contractual obligations (default risk), or it could result from an expectation that conditions in the market will change, resulting in a lower price of the security than expected when the holder plans to sell the bond (bond market risk). Bond investors are exposed to one or more of thefollowing risks:

- *Interest rate risk*: The risk that interest rates change, causing the bond price to change (part of bond market risk).
- *Reinvestment risk*: The risk that the cash flows on the bond are reinvested at lower rates (part of bond market risk).
- *Call risk*: The risk that the issuer will call the bond prior to maturity and the investor will have to reinvest in a market with lower rates.
- *Credit risk* or *default risk*: The risk that the issuer/borrower will fail to meet contractual obligations. Such risk is evaluated in terms of quality ratings by rating agencies (Moody's, S&P, and Fitch). Ratings range from triple A (high quality, low credit risk) to D.
- *Credit spread risk*: The risk that the bond's credit risk will increase, causing the bond's price to decrease relative to other bonds.
- *Liquidity risk*: The risk that the bond will be hard to sell at a price near its value.
- *Risk risk*: The risk of not being able to fully understand the risk of the security because of unexpected future events.

In the case of credit/default risk, investors often rely on bond rating companies to provide information about the default risk associated with a specific company, municipality, or government. The major rating companies in the United States are Moody's Investment Services, S&P, and Fitch Investors Service. Moody's and S&P have been rating bonds for almost 100 years. Today, they rate over 2,000 companies in addition to municipals, sovereigns, asset-backed securities, and other debt obligations. Moody's, S&P, and Fitch evaluate bonds by giving them a quality rating in the form of a letter grade (see Exhibit 1.3). The grades start at "A" with three groups: triple A bonds (Aaa for Moody's and AAA for Standard and Poor's) for the highest-grade bonds, double A (Aa or AA) for bonds that are considered prime, single A for those considered high quality. Grade A bonds are followed by B-rated bonds, classified as either triple B (Baa or BBB), which have a medium grade; double B (Ba or BB) bonds; and single B bonds. Finally, there are C-grade and lower-grade bonds. Moody's also breaks down bonds by using a 1, 2, or 3 designation, whereas S&P does the same with a plus or minus designation. In interpreting these ratings, triple A bonds are considered to have virtually no default risk, whereas low B-rated or C-rated bonds are considered speculative, having some chance of default. In general, bonds with relatively

EXHIBIT 1.3   Bond Ratings

Standard	Very High Quality	High Quality	Speculative	Very Poor
& Poor's	AAA AA	A BBB	BB B	CCC D
Moody's	Aaa Aa	A Baa	Ba B	Caa C

Moody's	S&P	Description
Aaa	AAA	Bonds have the highest rating. Ability to pay interest and principal is very strong.
Aa	AA	Bonds have a very strong capacity to pay interest and repay principal.
A	A	Bonds have a strong capacity to pay interest and repay principal, although they are somewhat susceptible to the adverse effects of changes in economic conditions.
Baa	BBB	Bonds are regarded as having an adequate capacity to pay interest and repay principal. Adverse economic conditions or changing circumstances are more likely to lead to a weakened capacity to pay interest and repay principal for debt in this category than in higher-rated categories. These bonds are medium-grade obligations.
Ba	BB	Bonds are regarded as predominantly speculative with respect to capacity to
B	B	pay interest and repay principal in accordance with the terms of the
Caa	CCC	obligation. BB and Ba indicate the lowest degree of speculations, and CC
Ca	CC	and Ca the highest degree of speculation.
C	C	This rating is reserved for income bonds on which no interest is being paid.
D	D	Bonds rated D are in default, and payment of interest and/or repayment of principal is in arrears.

Note: At times both Moody's and Standard & Poor's have used adjustments to these ratings. S&P uses plus and minus signs: A+ is the strongest A rating and A– the weakest. Moody's uses a 1, 2, or 3 designation, with 1 indicating the strongest.

low chance of default are referred to as *investment-grade bonds*, with quality ratings of Baa (or BBB) or higher; bonds with a relatively greater chance of default are referred to as *non-investment-grade, speculative-grade*, or *junk bonds* and have a quality rating below Baa.

Risk, rate of return, and the value of an asset are necessarily related. In choosing between two securities with the same cash flows but with different risks, most investors will require a higher rate of return from the riskier of the two securities. For example, we would expect investors averse to risk to require a higher rate of return on a corporate bond issued by a fledgling company than on a U.S. government bond. If for some reason both securities traded at prices that yielded the same expected rates, then we would expect that investors would want the government bond but not the corporate. If this were the case, the demand and price of the government bond would increase and its rate of return would decrease, whereas the demand and price of the corporate would fall and its rate of return would increase. Thus, if investors are risk averse, riskier securities must yield higher rates of return in the market or they will languish untraded.

Life

The fourth characteristic of an asset is its life. In the case of stock, the life of the stock is indefinite. For bonds, life is typically defined in term of the bond's maturity. Maturity is the length of time from the present until the last contractual payment is made. Maturity can vary anywhere from one day to indefinitely, as in the case of a consul (a bond issued with no maturity). In defining a bond's life in terms of its maturity, however, one should always be aware of provisions such as a sinking fund or a call feature that modifies the maturity of a bond. For example, a 10-year callable bond issued when interest rates are relatively high may be more like a 5-year bond given that a likely interest rate decrease would lead the issuer to buy the bond back.

Divisibility

The fifth attribute, divisibility, refers to the smallest denomination in which an asset is traded. Thus, a bank savings deposit account, in which an investor can deposit as little as a penny, is a perfectly divisible security; a jumbo certificate of deposit, with a minimum denomination of $10 million, is a highly indivisible security. Moreover, one of the economic benefits that investment funds provide investors is divisibility; that is, an investment company, by offering shares in a diversified portfolio of stocks, makes it possible for small investors to obtain the returns and risk of a portfolio.

Marketability

The sixth characteristic is marketability. It can be defined as the speed at which an asset can be bought and sold. As a rule, for an asset to be highly marketable, its price should be independent of the time spent searching for buyers or sellers. Many tangible assets, such as houses, as well as a number of financial assets, require a certain length of time before they can be bought or sold at their fair market values. This does not mean that they can't be sold in a short period of time; but if they must be sold, then they typically fetch a price substantially lower than what the market would yield if adequate time were allowed. In general, highly marketable securities tend to be very standardized items with a wide distribution of ownership. Thus, the stock of large corporations listed on the NYSE Euronext or Treasury issues are highly marketable securities that can be bought or sold on the exchanges electronically or through dealers in the OTC market in a matter of minutes. One way to measure a security's marketability is in terms of the size of the bid and asked spread that dealers offer. Dealers who make markets in less-marketable securities necessarily set wider spreads than do dealers who have securities that are bought and sold by many investors and that therefore can be traded more quickly.

Liquidity

The seventh property, liquidity, is related to marketability. Liquidity can be defined as how cash-like or money-like a security is. For an instrument to be liquid, it must be highly marketable and have little, if any, short-run risk. Thus, a Treasury security that can be bought and sold easily and whose rate of return in the short-run is known with a high degree of certainty is said to be liquid. However, a security such as an exchange-listed stock is marketable but is not considered liquid given its day-to-day price fluctuations. Technically, the difference between marketability and liquidity is the latter's feature of low or zero risk, which makes the security cash-like. It should be noted that although there is a difference between marketability and liquidity, the term *liquidity* is often used to describe a security's marketability.

Liquidity and marketability are often described in terms of price continuity and depth. *Price continuity* refers to a security's trading at its current level in the absence of any new information. A security with depth, or one with a *deep market*, is one for which there are a large number of buyers and sellers willing to trade at a price without a large change in price.

Taxability

The eighth characteristic of an asset is taxability. Taxability refers to the claims that the federal, state, and local governments have on the cash flows of an asset. Taxability varies in terms of the type of asset. For example, the coupon interests on most municipal bonds are tax exempt, whereas the interest on a corporate bond is not. To the investor, the taxability of a security is important because it affects his after-tax rate of return.

Indexes

Security evaluation and selection are based on comparing the characteristics of different securities. In comparing securities, investors often compare their securities or portfolios to an index. They also constantly monitor trends in the market by following indexes. Indexes are constructed so as to provide an indication of how the market for a particular group of securities is performing. The index could be broad based, measuring the performance of the overall market; sector specific, measuring the performance of an particular industry or sector; or style specific, measuring the performance of certain type of investment (e.g., small-cap companies or investment-grade bonds). The oldest and still most frequently quoted index is the *Dow Jones Industrial Average (DJIA)*. Created in 1896, this broad-based stock index is computed as a price-weighted average of 30 large blue-chip stocks (not all of them being industrials). The other popular broad-base index is the *Standard & Poor's Composite 500 Index (S&P 500)*. In calculating this index, the price of each stock is multiplied by the number of outstanding shares, divided by the aggregate market value of the 500 stocks from a base year. The S&P 500 includes mostly mid- and large-cap stocks.

Financial service and information firms such as Dow Jones, Standard and Poor's, Moody's, Russell, and Wilshire also compute indexes for different caps. For example, the Russell 2000 Index, the Standard & Poor's 600, the Wilshire 1750, and the Dow Jones Small Cap Index are indexes comprised of small-cap companies. There are also indexes constructed for mid-cap and large-cap stocks, as well as indexes composed of stocks that reflect a particular style. For example, there are indexes composed of growth stock and value stocks. Finally, there are indexes that combine style and size: small-cap growth, small-cap value, mid-cap growth, mid-cap value, large-cap growth, and large-cap value.

The most widely known bond indexes are those constructed by Barclay's and Merrill Lynch. These indexes cover different segments and parts of the bond market from investment-grade to lower-quality bonds, from governments to corporate, from short-term to long-term bonds. Ibbotson and Associates also has a set of indexes on T-bills, long-term and intermediate-term Treasuries, and long-term corporate. These indexes do not cover as many segments of the bond market as do the indexes of Barclay's and Merrill Lynch, but they do have a longer historical period, dating back to 1926. Finally, there are indexes for the major foreign stock exchanges and world indexes, such as the Nikkei 225 Index for the Tokyo Stock Exchange. Morgan Stanley, Dow Jones, and other financial service firms also calculate a number of indexes (in the local currency and in dollars), including national indexes, international industry indexes, a European index, an Asian index, and a world index.

Conclusion

In this chapter, we have given an overview of the financial system by examining the nature of financial assets, the types of markets that they give rise to, and their general characteristics. With this background, in the next chapter we will examine how news and information about securities and markets can be accessed and analyzed using the Bloomberg platform.

Web Site Information

- NYSE Euronext: www.nyse.com
- OTC market: www.finra.org/index.htm and www.nasdaq.com
- For financial information on securities, market trends, and analysis:
  - www.Finance.Yahoo.com
  - http://seekingalpha.com
  - http://bigcharts.marketwatch.com
  - http://free.stocksmart.com
  - http://online.wsj.com/public/us
- Data on most financial intermediaries is prepared by the Federal Reserve and is published in the *U.S. Flow of Funds* report. The report can be accessed from www.federalreserve.gov/releases (search for "Flow of Funds Account").

- For information on investment funds, see the Investment Company Institute's Web site: www.ici.org
- For information on derivatives, see:
  - CME Group: www.cmegroup.com
  - Chicago Board Options Exchange: www.cboe.com
- For information on the laws, regulations, and litigations of the SEC, go to www .sec.gov.
- For information on monetary policy, economic data, and research from the Federal Reserve, go to www.federalreserve.gov.
- For more on the efficient market hypothesis, go to www.investorhome.com/ emh.htm.

Notes

1. For a security to qualify for the system, it must have at least two market makers, and its issuer must meet certain financial requirements. For a company to have its stock listed on the NASDAQ system, it must satisfy requirements related to its net worth and shares outstanding.
2. Some scholars refer to direct financial claims as those in which only the ultimate borrowers and lenders trade with each other and a *semidirect market* as one in which brokers and dealers bring borrowers and lenders together. The definition of direct financial market here includes both of these markets.
3. An occasional trend in the financial markets is toward disintermediation. *Disintermediation* refers to the shifting from intermediary financing to direct financing. This occurs when a surplus unit withdraws funds from a financial institution and invests the funds by buying primary claims from an ultimate borrower.
4. Security exchanges in different countries can be grouped into one of three categories: public bourse (exchange), private bourse, and banking bourse. A *public bourse* is a government security exchange in which listed securities (usually both bonds and stocks) are bought and sold through brokers who are appointed by the government. A *private bourse* is a security exchange owned by its member brokers and dealers. In countries where there are private exchanges, a number of the exchanges will usually compete with each other; this is not the case in countries using a public bourse structure. A *banker bourse* is a formal or informal market in which securities are traded through bankers. This type of trading typically occurs in countries where historically commercial and investment banking have not separated.

Selected References

Fabozzi, F. J. 2009. *Bond Markets, Analysis and Strategies*, 5th ed. Upper Saddle River, NJ: Prentice-Hall, 214–321.

Fabozzi, F. J., A. K. Bhattacharya, and W. S. Berliner. 2007. *Mortgage-Backed Securities: Products, Structuring, and Analytical Techniques*. Hoboken, NJ: John Wiley & Sons.

Feldstein, S. G, F. J. Fabozzi, A. M. Grant, and P. M. Kennedy. 2005. *Handbook of Fixed Income Securities*. Edited by F. J. Fabozzi. New York: McGraw-Hill, 251–280.

Jensen, M. C. 1989. Eclipse of the public corporation. *Harvard Business Review* 89: 61–62.

Johnson, R. Stafford. 2013. *Debt Markets and Analysis*. Hoboken, NJ: John Wiley & Sons, 3–29.

Miller, Merton, and Franco Modigliani. 1961. Dividend policy, growth, and valuation of shares. *Journal of Business* 34 (October): 411–433.

Mishkin, F. S., and S. G. Eakins. 2010. *Financial Markets and Institutions*, 6th ed. Boston: Addison-Wesley.

Revell, J. 1997. *The Recent Evolution of the Financial System*. New York: MacMillan.

CHAPTER 2

Overview and Guide to the Bloomberg System

Introduction

Bloomberg is a computer information and retrieval system providing access to financial and economic data, news, and analytics. Bloomberg terminals are common on most trading floors and are becoming more common in universities where they are used for research, teaching, and managing student investment funds. The Bloomberg system provides 24-hour instant access to information on most U.S. and foreign securities: stocks, bonds, asset-backed securities, swaps, and derivatives; economic information by country; current and historical news and information on corporations and countries; and analytical packages for evaluating bonds, stocks, indexes, derivatives, and portfolios. Moreover, many of the models used by financial economists to evaluate, select, and manage securities and portfolios that are described in subsequent chapters are accessible on the Bloomberg system.

In this chapter, we present an overview and introductory guide to the Bloomberg system: how the system works, its functionality, and some of the information that can be accessed from its monitors, screens, and search tools. As we examine the investment environment in future chapters, we will show many of the Bloomberg descriptive and analytical screens and explain how they can be used in the study of investments. This chapter serves as a foundation for understanding how one can access such information and tools with a Bloomberg terminal and provides a "show-and-tell" presentation of the Bloomberg screens.

Bloomberg System—Bloomberg Keyboard

The Bloomberg keyboard allows one to access information within the "Bloomberg system." The keyboard consists of several specialized, color-coded function keys and yellow functional buttons:

- **Green action keys** send a specific request to the system with the system in turn responding:
  - **Enter:** Press <Enter> for entering commands.
  - **NEWS:** Press <News> for accessing 24-hour, online global news service.
  - **HELP:** Press <Help> for terminology, formulas, and defaults. For specific information, type a name and then press <Help>; for help from a Bloomberg representative, press <Help> twice.
  - **MENU:** Press <Menu> to back up to the previous screen or menu.
  - **PRINT:** To send a document to the printer.
  - **PAGE FWD.**
  - **PAGE BACK.**
- **Yellow functional buttons** take the user to information and analytical functions for specific markets:
  - **GOVT:** Domestic and foreign securities.
  - **EQUITY:** Equity news, company information, company financial information, historical prices, mutual fund information, equity derivatives (a company's option, futures, warrants, convertibles, and swaps), and equity analytical functions.
  - **CMDTY:** Commodities by sector, futures, options, and over-the-counter (OTC) pricing contributors.
  - **CORP:** Corporate bonds and bond analytical functions.
  - **INDEX:** Indexes for markets and countries, index composition, index derivatives, and other information and analytics.
  - **CRNCY:** Foreign exchange spot rates, forward rates, and cross rates, currency monitors, and currency indexes.
  - **M-MKT:** Money market rates and indexes (e.g., London Interbank Offered Rate [LIBOR], commercial paper rates, and federal funds rates).
  - **MRTG:** Mortgage securities, agency pool reports, and prepayment statistics.
  - **MUNI:** Municipal bonds and municipal information.
  - **PFD:** Preferred stocks and related information.
  - **ALPHA/CLIENT:** General function for creating, customizing, and updating portfolios.
  - **LAW:** Law menu (BLAW).

    Note: One can also type "Main" and hit <Enter> to bring up the Bloomberg "Main" menu where one can access specific market screens.

The yellow functional buttons are a good way for one to get started on Bloomberg. One can simply enter the yellow key to bring up a menu screen that provides access to information and analytical functions related to the category. For example, to access information on a company and its securities, one presses the "Equity" key, <Equity>, and then presses the "Enter" key, <Enter>. A menu will appear that will identify where a function or information is located. One can then move one's cursor to the subscreen of interest and click it, or one can type the screen's name (e.g., DES) or its number (#2) in the top left corner of the screen and hit <Enter>. For example, to find a company's stock ticker symbol from the Equity menu screen, one would do the following:

- Press <Equity> and hit <Enter>.
- Click "Security Finder" to bring up the "SECF" screen, or just type SECF in the left corner and hit <Enter>.
- On the SECF screen, click the tab for the type of security (e.g., "Eqty" for equity) and then type the name of the company as accurately as possible in the "Search" box to bring up a list of companies.
- Scroll down to find the name of the company.
- Click the name of the company or type the ticker symbol (in the left column of the screen), press <Equity>, and hit <Enter> to access a menu of information and functions for that company: Company Information/Description, Historical Prices, News/Research.

Similar procedures can be followed using the SECF screen to find the menus for securities and to find tickers or identifiers (CUSIPS or ISN numbers) for bonds, corporate securities, countries, commodities, currencies, and indexes: Type SECF in the left corner, click the tab for the type of security (e.g., "FI" for fixed income) and then type the name of the company. Note, if one knows the ticker symbol or identifier, then one can access the stock, bond, index, or currency directly by typing the ticker/identifier and then pressing the relevant key; for example, to access IBM, enter IBM <Equity> <Enter>.

Uploading Information on a Stock, Bond, Currency, or Index

In general, to upload a corporation's security (e.g., stock or bond), index, currency, or commodity in Bloomberg: (1) type in the ticker or identifier, (2) press the yellow key that represents the type of asset (e.g., <Equity> or <Corp>), and (3) hit <Enter>. Here are some examples:

- To pull up IBM's stock screen: IBM <Equity> <Enter>.
- To pull up the screen for the IBM's 6.5 percent coupon bond maturing in 01/15/2028: IBM 6.5 01/15/2028 <Corp> <Enter> or CUSIP <Corp> <Enter>.
- To pull up the S&P 500 index screen: SPX <Index> <Enter>.
- To pull up the British Pound screen: GBP <Crncy> <Enter>.
- To pull up the screen for crude oil futures contracts traded on the New York Mercantile Exchange: Enter CLa <Cmdity> <Enter>.
- To pull up the screen for the U.S. Treasury note paying a 2 percent coupon and maturing 01/31/16: T 2 01/31/16 <Govt> <Enter>.

It should be noted that when one begins typing the name of the security, a dropdown will appear on the screen that lists securities corresponding with the information being typed; clicking the security from the dropdown will bring up its menu. Once a security or index has been loaded, one is taken to a "homepage" menu that categorizes all the functions on the selected security and submenu screens. The functions can be accessed by either clicking the name on the menu option page or by typing the name of the function in the left corner of the screen. Additional menu screens can be found on the homepage menu by clicking a topic heading (e.g., "Company Overview").

There are two main types of screens in Bloomberg: descriptive and analytical. Descriptive screens provide information about the underlying security, such as trade information, expiration, and risk information. Descriptive screens pull data from Bloomberg and present it in an orderly fashion; they usually do not perform calculations. Analytical screens, on the other hand, determine prices, returns, variability, and other statistical and mathematical calculations based on customized inputs. In Bloomberg, many of the functions that are used for evaluating securities are common and as a result have a common command. For instance, the GP function is a price graph that can be used for each security type. Derivatives, indexes, interest rates, currencies, commodities, and bond futures often use many of the same functions. If you know the name of the function (e.g., DES for description) and the security is already loaded, then you can access the function's screen directly by simply typing the name of the function (e.g., DES) in the top left corner. If the security is not loaded, then you can type the ticker, hit the yellow key, and type the function, for example, IBM <Equity> DES <Enter>. Also note that once you have accessed the function screen, you can always press the "Help" key to bring up a screen with information, defaults, and instructions related to that function or hit "Help" twice to access a message box to send questions to the Bloomberg help desk.

Accessing Some of the Information Discussed in Chapter 1

In Chapter 1, we examined the types and markets for equity and debt securities. A myriad of information and analytical function on many of these asset classes can be easily accessed using a Bloomberg terminal. Of note are the menus for stocks, corporate bonds, and government securities.

Bloomberg Menu for a Stock: Ticker <Equity> <Enter>

The Bloomberg menu for a stock (e.g., IBM: IBM <Equity> <Enter>) provides information on the stock and company: company information, historical prices, financials, derivatives, and news (see Exhibit 2.1). Some of the functions and information on a stock's equity menu related to Chapter 1 include the following:

- **DES:** Provides details about the company. The description screen usually has a number of pages summarizing products, management, stock information, board members, financial summaries, and geographical distribution.
- **EVT:** List past and current events, such as earning announcements, stockholders' meeting, security issues, and the like.

EXHIBIT 2.1   Bloomberg Description (DES) and Price Graph (GP)

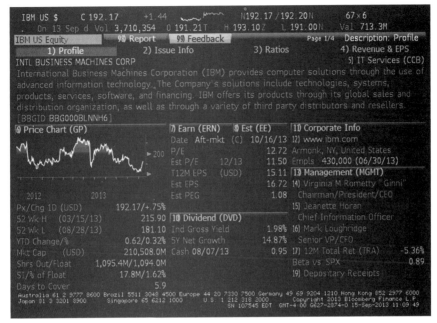

(a)

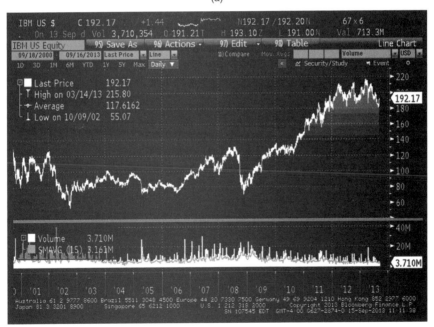

(b)

- **CF:** Corporate filings and SEC filings (EDGAR [Electronic Data Gathering, Analysis, and Retrieval system]), 10-K reports, 10-Q reports, and other filings.
- **GP:** Price and volume graph.
- **SPLC:** Supply chain.

Bloomberg Corporate Bond Information and Functions: Ticker <Corp> <Enter>

To find a corporate bond for a company (IBM), one first accesses the screen for all of the company's bonds (e.g., IBM <Corp> <Enter>. From this screen, one can bring up a menu screen for a specific bond by clicking the bonds of interest (see Exhibit 2.2). Some of the functions and information on that menu that relate to Chapter 1:

- **DES:** Description.
- **HDS:** Shows the holders of the bond.
- **CSHF:** Shows the cash flows promised on the bond: semiannual interest and principal.
- **GP** graphs historical closing prices.

Bloomberg Government Bond Information and Functions: Ticker GOVT <Enter>

To access a specific government bond, one first needs to find a government bond's ticker. As noted, one can find a ticker either by going to the GOVT menu page (<Govt> <Enter>) and then clicking the ticker lookup (TK), using SECF (FI tab and "Govt" tab) or find the ticker directly by entering <GOVT> TK <Enter>. The direct approach will bring up a country screen in which one can click the country (e.g., U.S.A.) and then select the bond group of interest (e.g., T for "U.S. Treasury Notes and Bonds" or CT for "Current U.S. Treasury Notes and Bonds"), as shown in Exhibit 2.3. Finally, one can click the bond of interest to bring up its menu (e.g., 5-year note) and then click DES to bring up the note's description page (Exhibit 2.4).

On the description page one will find the bond's CUSIP number, which, as noted, can also be used to bring up the bond's menu screen: CUSIP <Govt> <Enter> (912810QA9 <Govt> <Enter>). As noted, one other way to bring up the menu page for a specific bond is to start typing the bond's coupon interest and maturity: T 3.5 2/15/39 (for Treasury, coupon, and maturity). This will bring up a dropdown list of bonds; clicking the bond of interest will bring up its screen. Some of the information screens found on a specific government or corporate bond's menu include the following:

- **DES:** Issue and issuer information, access to the TRACE, prospectus, and other screens.
- **HDS:** Bondholders.
- **CSHF:** Shows the cash flows promised on the bond.
- **QR:** Trade recap: Tick-by-tick prices reported from TRACE.
- **GP:** Historical price graph.

Some of these screens will be examined in subsequent chapters.

EXHIBIT 2.2 Bloomberg Menu and Description (DES) for a Bond

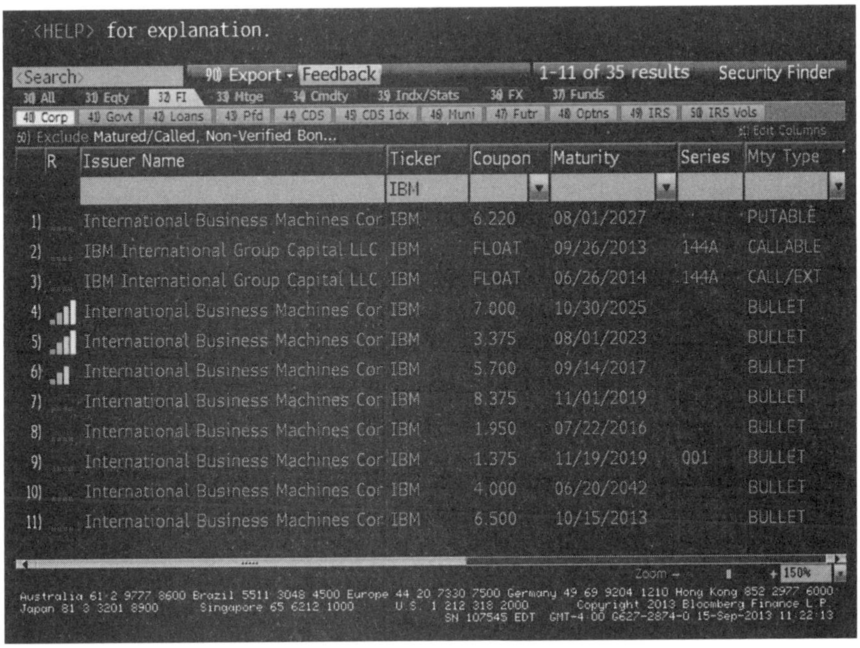

(a)

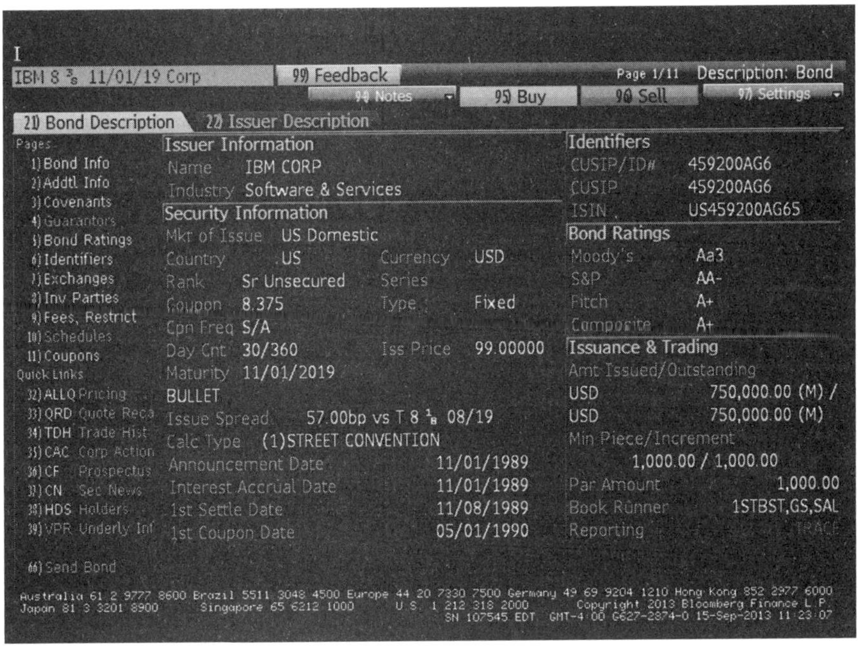

(b)

(a) IBM <Corp> <Enter>: Listing of IBM Bonds. (b) *Note:* The CUSIP is 459200AG6. On the left column of the screen, you can find additional information, such as covenants or current trading prices, by clicking the entry.

EXHIBIT 2.3 Bloomberg Government Bond

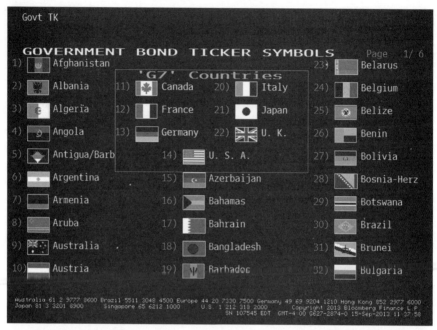

(a)

(b)

(a) Ticker Symbols: <GOVT> TK <Enter>. (b) Clicking U.S.A. on the Government Bond Ticker Symbols screen brings up the SECF screen set for fixed-income government bonds (Ticker = T).

EXHIBIT 2.4   Bloomberg Government Bond Description Slide

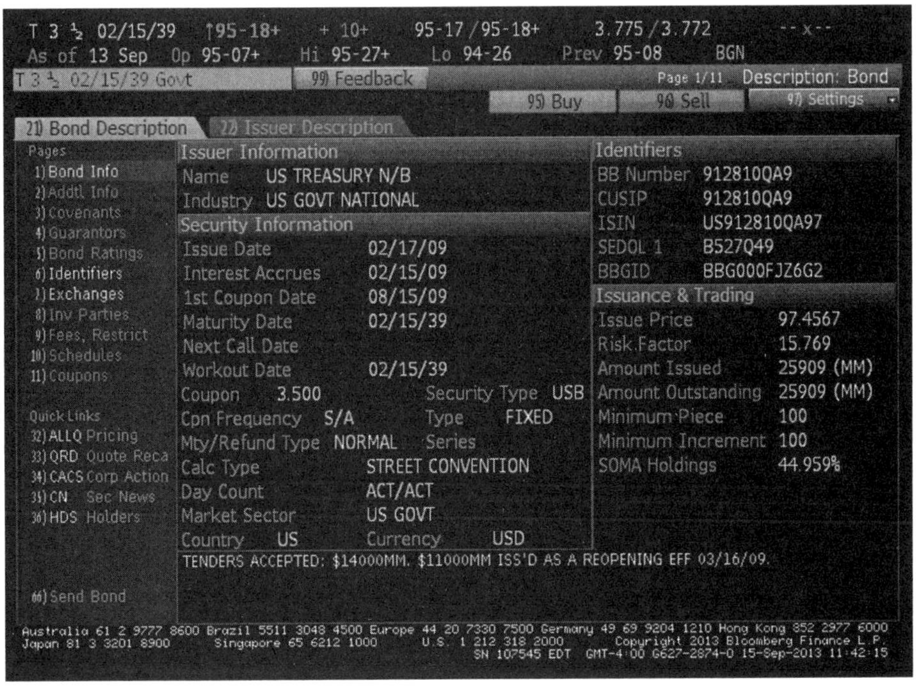

Note: The description screen is for U.S. Treasury, paying 3.5 percent coupon and maturing on 2/15/39. To bring up the bond's menu page, enter: Cusip Number (912810QA9) <Govt> <Enter>.

Finding Other Security Types

As noted, to directly find a government bond's ticker one enters <Govt> TK <Enter>. This will bring up a country screen in which one can click the country (e.g., U.S.A.) and then select the bond group of interest. This approach can be used to quickly search for other securities: foreign government securities (<Govt>), agencies (<Govt>), municipals (<Muni>), money market securities (<M-Mkt>), preferred securities (<Pfd>), and currency (<Curncy>).

Foreign Government Bonds

- <Govt> TK <Enter>.
- Example: Click U.K.
- Select type, such as UKT for all British gilts (bonds).
- Or enter: UKT <Govt> <Enter>.
- Click bond of interest to bring up its menu screen or CUSIP <Govt> <Enter>.

Municipal (Ohio State) Bonds

- <Muni> TK <Enter>.

- Enter State (e.g., Ohio).
- Select type (Ohio State) to bring up menu or CUSIP <Muni> <Enter>.

Preferred Stocks

- <Pfd> TK <Enter>.
- Enter company name or ticker in the yellow box (e.g., D or Dominican Resources or ticker <Pfd>.

Currency

- <Curncy> TK <Enter>.
- Find country's menu (e.g., Swiss Franc [CHF]) or ticker <Curncy> (<Enter> (CHF <Curncy> <Enter>).
- On menu, click function (description [DES], price graph [QP], news [N] or other entries).

The other approach to finding securities is to use the SECF screen and then click the tab and sub-tabs for the type of securities.

Indexes

The menu page for indexes provides information on different indexes by category, such as equity, world indexes, bonds, real estate, and municipals. One way to find the ticker for a specific index is to go to the SECF screen (see Exhibit 2.5) and then select an index from the index tab: SECF <Enter>; click "Index/Stats" tab; type general name of the index (e.g., S&P, Russell, or Dow) or Click "Index/Stats" tab and sub-tab for type (e.g., "Eqty") and then select the index group from the dropdown "Source" (e.g., All, Bloomberg, Dow Jones, etc.). A second way to find indexes is to use the WEI menu screen. On the WEI screen, one can click the "Settings" tab and change the index listing from "names" to "tickers." Also on that screen, one can click the gray area above the geographical area (e.g., Americas) to bring up more indexes.

Two well-known indexes are the S&P 500 and the Dow Jones Industrial Average. Entering their tickers (SPX and INDU), pressing <Index>, and hitting <Enter> brings up their menu screens showing descriptive and analytical functions: description (DES), holdings (in Description), index weighting (MEMB), price graph (GP), and stock movers in the index (MOV) (see Exhibit 2.6).

From the SECF or WEI screen, one can identify the tickers for different indexes constructed for style, industry, sector or area. Entering that index's ticker (ticker <Index> <Enter>) brings up the menu for that index. Another way to identify different indexes is to enter the general index name (e.g., SPX for S&P 500 or RUSS for the Russell index) and hit <Enter>. This will bring up a menu showing different indexes.

EXHIBIT 2.5   Bloomberg Index Search (SECF)

```
RDG          C 621.88   +1.12
On 13 Sep    O 621.74  H 622.20  L 618.87  Prev 621.88
<Search>              90 Export ▾ Feedback              1-19 of 10000+ results   Security Finder
30 All   31 Eqty   32 FI   33 Mtge   34 Cmdty   39 Indx/Stats   36 FX   37 Funds
40 All   41 Eqty   42 FI   43 Cmdty   44 Fund   45 CDS   46 Vols   47 Futr   48 Other   49 Stats   50 ECO   51 Opts
                                                                              61) Edit Columns
```

R	Ticker	Name	Country	Currency	Source	Members	Groups	Options	Futures
					Russell				
1)	RTY	Russell 2000 Index	US	USD	Russell	1966	Yes	Yes	Yes
2)	RIY	Russell 1000 Index	US	USD	Russell	1004	Yes	Yes	Yes
3)	RAY	Russell 3000 Index	US	USD	Russell	2970	Yes	Yes	No
4)	RLG	Russell 1000 Growth Index	US	USD	Russell	610	Yes	No	Yes
5)	RLV	Russell 1000 Value Index AMEX	US	USD	Russell	649	Yes	No	Yes
6)	RUO	Russell 2000 Growth Index	US	USD	Russell	1119	Yes	Yes	No
7)	RUJ	Russell 2000 Value Index	US	USD	Russell	1345	Yes	Yes	No
8)	RUY	Russell 2000 Index for Options	US	USD	Russell	1966	Yes	Yes	No
9)	RMV	Russell Midcap Value Index	US	USD	Russell	521	Yes	No	No
10)	RDG	Russell Midcap Growth Index	US	USD	Russell	488	Yes	No	No
11)	RMC	Russell Midcap Index	US	USD	Russell	809	Yes	Yes	No
12)	R2500	Russell 2500 Index	US	USD	Russell	2476	Yes	No	No
13)	RGUSFL	Russell 1000 Financial Services Index	US	USD	Russell	226	No	No	No
14)	RAG	Russell 3000 Growth Index	US	USD	Russell	1729	Yes	No	No
15)	RAV	Russell 3000 Value Index	US	USD	Russell	1994	Yes	Yes	No
16)	RMICRO	Russell Microcap Index	US	USD	Russell	1507	Yes	No	No
17)	R2500G	Russell 2500 Growth Index	US	USD	Russell	1412	Yes	No	No
18)	RTYFAST	Russell 2000 Fast Cash Index	US	USD	Russell	0	No	No	No
19)	R2500V	Russell 2500 Value Index	US	USD	Russell	1693	Yes	No	No

```
                                                              Zoom  —          100%
Australia 61 2 9777 8600 Brazil 5511 3048 4500 Europe 44 20 7330 7500 Germany 49 69 9204 1210 Hong Kong 852 2977 6000
Japan 81 3 3201 8900      Singapore 65 6212 1000      U.S. 1 212 318 2000      Copyright 2013 Bloomberg Finance L.P.
                                            SN 107545 EDT   GMT-4:00 G627-2874-0 15-Sep-2013 12:33:54
```

SECF <Enter>: Index Search

- SECF <Enter>; click "Index/Stat" tab; type general name of the index (e.g., S&P, Russell, or Dow).
- Or SECF <Enter>; Click "Index/Stat" tab and sub-tab for type (e.g., "Eqty") and then select the index group from the dropdown "Source" (e.g., Russell).

Functionality

Many Bloomberg screens provide functions and links that facilitate one's analysis of a company, security, market, fund, portfolio, or an economy. For example, the relative valuation (RV), financial analysis (FA), and fundamental graphs (GF) functions are provided for companies, indexes, portfolios, governments, and municipals. These functions allow the user to access key financial information for a company, index, or municipality (FA and GF) or for a group of peers (RV). For a company (e.g., Green Mountain Coffee Roasters [GMCR]), its FA, RV, and GF screens can be accessed from its equity menu screen or accessed directly: GMCR <Equity> RV <Enter>; GMCR <Equity> FA <Enter>; GMCR <Equity> GF <Enter>).

Financial Analysis: FA

The FA screen displays financial history for a specific company, equity index, or municipality (Exhibit 2.7). Using the FA screen, one can either select from a list of standard

EXHIBIT 2.6   Bloomberg DES and MEMB Screens for S&P 500

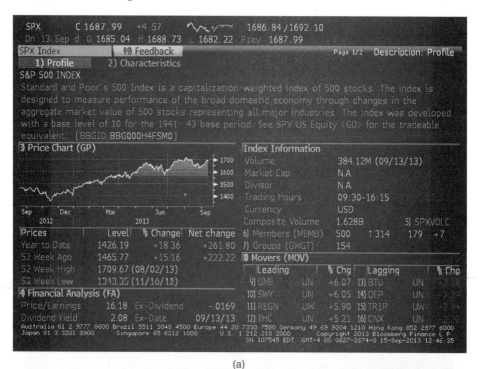

(a)

(b)

(a) DES: S&P 500. SPX <Index> <Enter>. (b) MEMB Screen for S&P 500.

EXHIBIT 2.7   Bloomberg's Financial Analysis (FA) Screen, GMCR

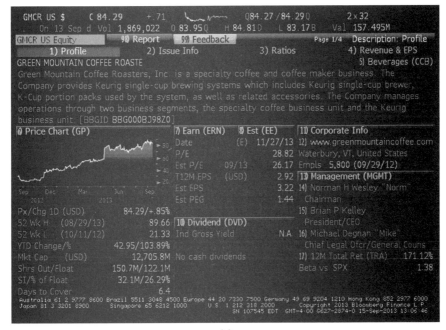

(a)

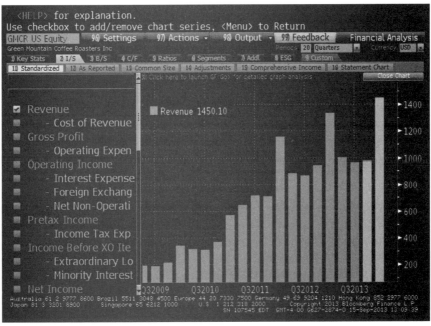

(b)

templates (e.g., income statements, ratio analysis, or detailed financial statements) or customize one's own template. The data can be seen on a quarterly, semiannual, annual, or trailing 12-month basis. On the FA screen, the template information can be viewed on the right panel and can be changed to chart form by clicking the chart icon in the left corner. Using the dropdown "Output" tab, one can create a PDF report of the table, graph, or table and graph, as well as send the data to Excel.

Relative Valuation: RV

The RV screen shows financial and market information of a company relative to its peers (Exhibit 2.8). On the screen, one can change the peer grouping by selecting a different peer group from the dropdown "Comp Source" menu tab. From the peers menu, one can then select a larger sector or subsector. In addition, one can also bring up a portfolio that one has constructed or a group of stocks identified from an equity screen/search that one has conducted and saved (portfolio construction and security searches are discussed later in this chapter). In addition to changing peers, the RV menu also allows one to change the template (gray tabs: Overview, Comp Sheets, Markets, EPS Preview, and Credit).

The gray "Custom" tab on the right of the RV screen allows one to customize the table. The statistics settings box at the bottom of the screen (Select Stats) can be changed by clicking the averages, minimums, maximums, and standard deviations

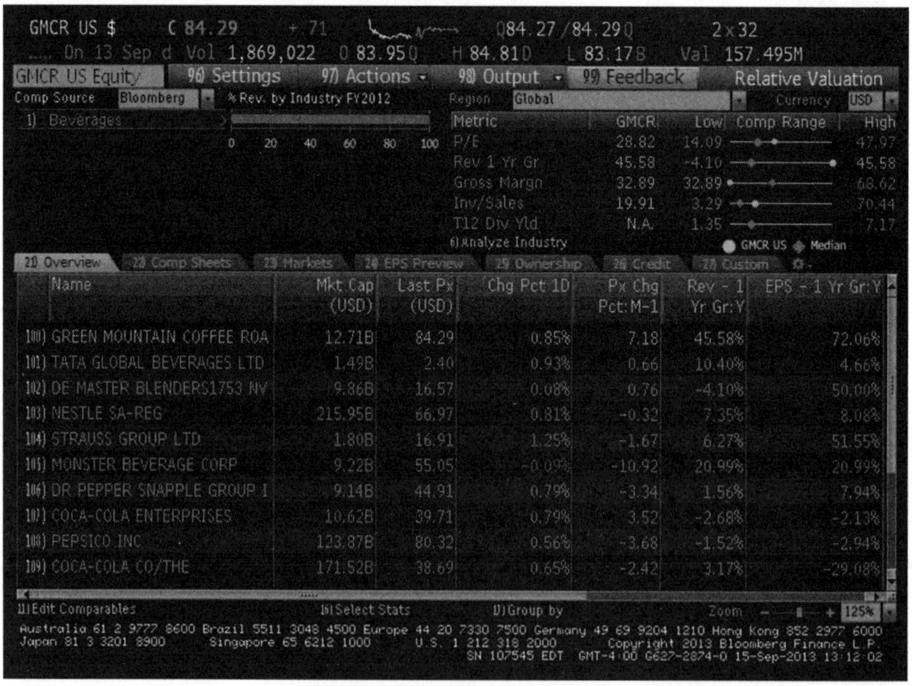

EXHIBIT 2.8   Bloomberg's Relative Valuation (RV) Screen, GMCR

boxes. Alternatively, one can customize the screen by setting one's cursor in the column heading area and holding the right clicker down on the mouse to access a menu. From the dropdown menu, one can bring up a description of the measure and how it is calculated; add a row displaying minimums, maximums, averages, and standard deviations (Show Statistics); delete the column, insert a new entry (Edit Column); and change the order for one of the measures (sort ascending or descending). New columns with new measures can also be added by clicking the gray button on the far right of the screen to bring up a menu and clicking "Add Column" from the menu to bring up an "Add Column" ribbon box area in the middle of the screen (this can also be done in the custom mode). In the box, one can type the name of the measure (e.g., market cap) and then hit <Enter> to activate. Doing this, the new entry will appear in the right column. Information on each of the companies can also be accessed by right clicking the company's name. This will bring up a menu that will allow one to access the company's description page (DES), its financials (FA), and other information. Finally, from the "Output" tab, one can send the screen data and information to Excel.

Fundamental Graphs: GF

The GF function (graphical financial analysis) allows one to graphically compare company fundamentals and ratios against other companies and indexes (see Exhibit 2.9).

EXHIBIT 2.9 Bloomberg's Graphical Financial Analysis (GF) Screen, GMCR

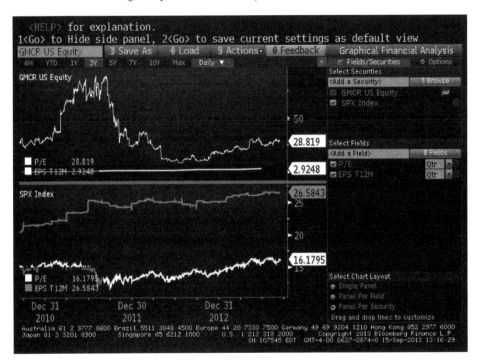

On the screen, one selects a fundamental measure or measures from a field (e.g., the price-to-earnings ratio [P/E] and earnings-per-share for Green Mountain, GMCR), and panels to display the measure over time, as well as other companies and indexes (e.g., S&P 500) for comparisons. Using the functions found in the tabs at the top of the GF screen, one can create a report (Actions) and save the settings (Save As) for future access. Similarly, the data or the graph images can be imported to a clipboard by right clicking in the graph area to bring up a menu of functions and then clicking the Copy/Export Options.

Note that there are GF, RV, and FA screens for indexes. The RV screen for an index consists of the stocks making up the index. Like the stock RV screen, these screens also have considerable functionality. The screens can be accessed from the index's menu screen: Index ticker <Index> <Enter>.

Economic, Industry, Law, and Municipal Information Screens

Many screens in Bloomberg can be accessed directly by typing in the name of the screen and hitting <Enter>. As noted, if a stock or security is loaded, typing in the name of the screen function, such as DES or GP, brings up that security's screen. There are also a number of screens that can be accessed by typing in the appropriate screen name. For example, typing EPR bring up a page showing the listing of exchanges with information on each exchange and its Web site; PRTU takes one to a screen for constructing portfolios; CIXB brings up a screen for inputting securities, indexes, or a portfolio in which historical prices and returns are calculated. This data can be later used in other functions to analyze the portfolio. Some useful screens for investments include those for economic, industry, municipal, and legal analysis.

Economic Information Screens: ECOF, ECO, and ECST

ECOF

Country and regional economic data on employment, business conditions, housing, balance of payments, prices, and other macroeconomic data can be accessed from the ECOF screen (Exhibit 2.10). Clicking an entry (e.g., nominal gross domestic product [GDP]) on the ECOF menu screen brings up a screen showing a graph of an economic measure (top left corner) and a listing of related measures whose graphs can be accessed by clicking the measure's entry. Using the dropdown "Chart" tab above the graph on the ECOF screen, one can copy the data or image to a clipboard by right clicking in the graph area to bring up a menu and then clicking the Copy/Export Options. One can also find regional data by typing the name of a metropolitan city or state in the ribbon area above the graph. Finally, using the ticker for the economic series, one can upload a menu of screens for the series on the index screen: Ticker <Index> <Enter>.

EXHIBIT 2.10   Bloomberg's ECOF Screen

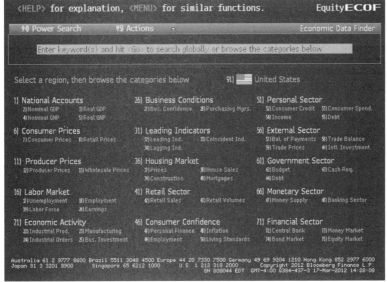

(a)

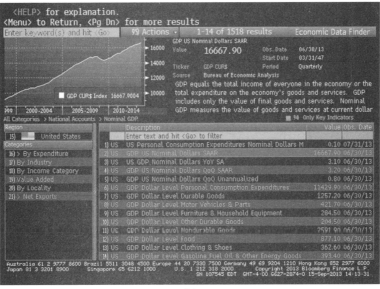

(b)

(a) ECOF <Enter>: Clicking an entry (e.g., nominal GDP) on the ECOF menu screen brings up a screen showing a graph of an economic measure (top left corner) and a listing of related measures whose graphs can be accessed by clicking the measure's entry.
(b)

- Using the dropdown "Chart" tab above the graph on the ECOF screen, you can copy the data or image to a clipboard, allowing you to move the data to Excel or Word.
- You can find regional data by typing the name of a metropolitan city or state in the ribbon area above the graph.
- Using the ticker for the economic series (GDP CUR$), you can upload a menu screen for the series on the index screen: GDP CUR$ <Index> <Enter>.

ECO

The ECO screen displays current, historical, and upcoming economic releases and events by region, country, and event type. Clicking an entry (e.g., Industrial Production) brings up a screen showing a graph of the economic measure or indicator and a listing of news stories and commentaries related to the release or event. Using the dropdown tabs on the ECO screen, one can bring up ECO screens for different releases and events by countries. Also, by moving one's cursor to an entry and right clicking, one can access a menu of additional functions (e.g., description or graphs). On the ECO graphs, one can copy the data or image to a clipboard, allowing one to move the data to Excel or Word, or one can bring up the menu screen: Ticker <Index> <Enter> (see Exhibit 2.11).

ECST, ECOW, and ECMX

The ECST, ECOW, and ECMX screens display current and historical economic statistics by country (Exhibit 2.12). The screens provide functions for changing the country and economic measure, converting the data to graphs, changing the time period, and exporting the information to Excel.

Sector and Industry Information: BI

The BI platform (BI <Enter>) is Bloomberg's proprietary industry research portal (Exhibit 2.13). Information on the BI screen includes data, research, and analysts' insights about industries and the companies in an industry. On the BI screen, one can click an industry (e.g., large pharmaceutical) to bring up its screen. On a selected industry's screen, one can then click entries under the gray "Monitor" tab for events, markets, comp sheets, and credit ratings. Historical financial data and information for the industry and the companies composing it can be found by accessing the "Data Library" tab, and industry insights and analysis by sector analysis experts is found by accessing the "Analysis" tab.

Municipal Screens

The municipal MIFA screen can be used to access financial information on state governments (MIFA <Enter>). The screen allows one to select a state and then access information on the state from a dropdown. On the dropdown, the state's identification number is also shown (e.g., California: stocal US). Using the identification number, one can access the state's menu directly: Stocal <Index> <Enter> or Stocal <Equity> <Enter>. Information that can be accessed on the dropdown or state screen includes description (DES), financials (FA), relative evaluations (RV), demographics, (DEMS), employment (BLS), and a municipal search (SMUN). The municipal FA and RV screen displays income statements, balance sheets, and other information useful for evaluating the government's financial strength. On the FA and RV screens, one

EXHIBIT 2.11   Bloomberg's ECO Screen

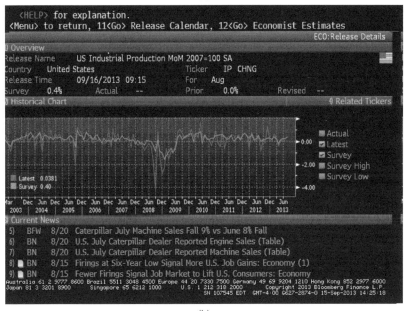

(a)

(b)

(a) ECO <Enter>: Clicking an entry (e.g., Industrial Production MoM) on the ECO menu screen to bring up a screen showing the measure and related news.

- Use the country box to find the economic releases of other countries.
- Use the Economic Releases box to find other economic information.

(b)

- Current news related to the economic release can be accessed by clicking the story in "Current News."
- Using the ticker for the economic series (IP CHNG), you can upload a menu screen for the series on the index screen: IP CHNG <Index> <Enter>.

EXHIBIT 2.12   Bloomberg's ECST

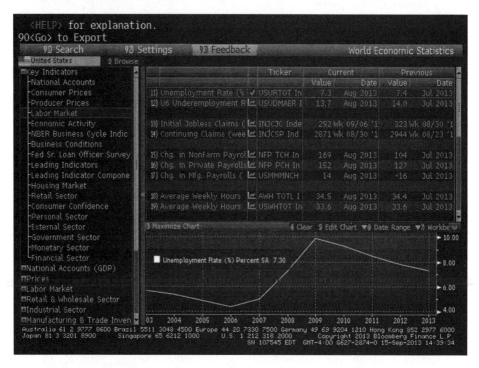

- Use the graph icon to bring up a chart.
- Use the country box to find the ECST screen for other countries.
- To copy the data or image to a clipboard, right click in the graph area to bring up a menu and then click the Copy/Export Options.

can also change the fund category from general to pension to view the municipal pension position. Information on municipals securities of the state or municipalities in the state can be accessed by clicking the municipal screener (SMUN) from the drop-down MIFA menu screen for a state. Municipalities can also be accessed directly by entering SMUN <Enter>. Finally, municipals can be found using the SECF screen: SECF <Enter>, click FI tab and "Muni" tab, and type the name of the municipality (e.g., California) in the "Issuer Name" box.

Legal Information: BLAW

The BLAW menu provides legal, regulatory, and compliance information and functions. The menu is useful not only for accessing laws as they relate to certain industries and regions, but also for identifying judgments, rulings, and pending cases. The BLAW menu is extensive. A good starting point is to use the search functions (BBLS) to look for laws, codes, filings, decisions, and other information. Such information can be found by country and region.

EXHIBIT 2.13   Bloomberg's Sector and Industry Information (BI) Screen

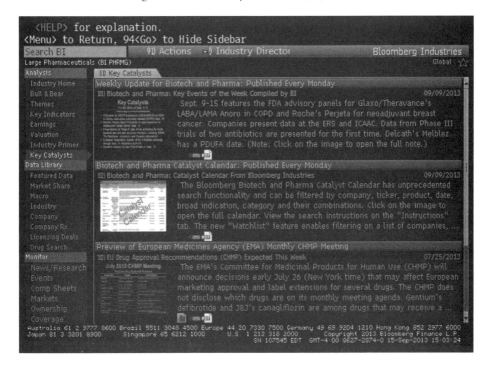

Monitor and Portal Screens

There are a number of screens that monitor current prices and events occurring in the various markets, as well as economic and financial events in different countries. Many of these screens appear in other chapters.

Bond Monitors: FIT, WB, RATT, RATC, CSDR, IM, and BTMM

Using the FIT screen, one can access U.S. Treasuries and other sovereign securities directly. For the United States FIT screen, one can select the types of Treasuries based on their maturities (bills, notes, bonds, TIPs, and strips) or those most recently issued and more actively traded (Actives). To access the menu screen for a particular bond, one places the cursor on the bond of interest, right clicks to access the description (DES) screen to obtain a CUSIP or ISN number, and then enters CUSIP <Govt> <Enter>.

Like the FIT screen, the WB monitor (WB <Enter>) displays and compares bonds by different global areas. From the monitor, one can compare bonds of different countries in terms of yields. From the screens (icons), one can also bring up historical yields and current yield curves.

Three other bond monitors to note are RATC, RATT, and CSDR. RATC displays and searches for credit rating changes, RATT shows trends in quality ratings, and CSDR shows sovereign debt ratings.

The IM screen displays a directory of bond monitors for each country. Clicking the country brings up a BTMM screen for that country. Alternatively, one can bring up the BTMM screen (BTMM <Enter>), which shows the U.S. bond monitor, and then use the dropdown to "Change Country" tab to select a country.

Stock Monitors: WEI, IMAP, MMAP, and MOST

The IMAP screen displays intraday price movements and news across industries, regions, and the companies (Exhibit 2.14). It includes a heat map showing the performances of stocks and sectors. Using the "Source" dropdown menu, one can select all securities, different indexes, constructed portfolios, and saved searches. On the table menu listing stocks or areas, one can select sectors or regions, and on the table menu for stocks and areas, one can access both price information and news information.

WEI

The World Equity indexes (WEI) screen (WEI <Enter>) monitors world equity indexes. As noted previously, this index is a good way to find an index's ticker

EXHIBIT 2.14   Bloomberg IMAP Screen

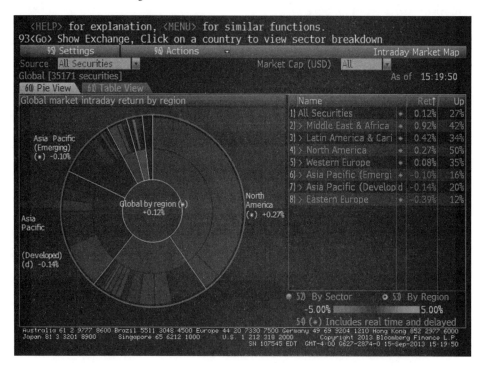

symbols. On the WEI screen, one can also select different information about the indexes, such as futures prices, movers (advances and declines), ratios (e.g., P/E ratio), and currency. On the screen, one can click the country area to bring up more indexes for that geographical area.

MMAP

MMAP displays global market segments, and the companies that operate within those segments. The user can select investment parameters (e.g., growth in earnings) for different global areas and sectors to do a comparative evaluation of stocks in a sector or a region.

MOST

MOST displays the day's most active stocks by volume, the leading advancers and decliners by percentage or net gain/loss, stocks with the most value traded on an exchange, and stocks with the largest volume increase for the day. On the screen, one can change to different indexes, sectors, and time periods, as well as access portfolios and searches created by the user.

New Bond and Equity Offerings: NIM and IPO

The NIM screen monitors news headlines and security data for new issues. Clicking a category on the NIM screen (e.g., U.S. Bond Market) brings up a screen showing new or pending bond issues; clicking an issue brings up a description screen with details about the issue. Equity issues can be accessed from the IPO screen: IPO <Enter>. On the IPO screen, one can search for issues in different stages of the issuance process.

COUN and BTMM: Country Information Indicators

Selecting a country on the COUN screen takes one to that country's screen where there is summary information on the country's security markets, debt ratings, events, and most active stocks (Exhibit 2.15). On the country screen, one can click several tabs to bring up screens with more detail information and other links. The BTMM screen (BTMM <Enter>) provides interest rate and security price information by country.

Calendar Screens

Bloomberg has several event calendar screens that allow users to monitor events, securities, and corporate actions. Two screens of note are EVTS and CACT.

EXHIBIT 2.15   Bloomberg Country Information and Indicators, COUN

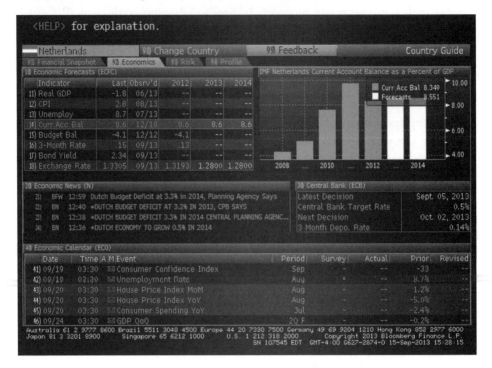

EVTS

The EVTS calendar screen displays a calendar of corporate events and corresponding details, including transcripts and audio recordings (Exhibit 2.16). One can opt to display historical or upcoming events on a daily, weekly, or monthly basis. One can also select from the dropdown "Source" tab all securities, securities from an index, securities from a search, or securities from a portfolio created in Bloomberg. The user can also save the screen (Calendars tab) and set up alerts (click bell icon in the "A" column) in which Bloomberg will notify the user through Bloomberg's message system.

CACT—Class Action and Corporate Action Filings

The CACT monitor screen displays a calendar of class actions and corporate action filings of corporations and municipalities, such as stock buybacks, capital changes, and mergers and acquisitions. At the top of the CACT screen, one can select time period, geographical area, and types of actions (e.g., merger and acquisition or stock splits). One can also customize the actions.

EXHIBIT 2.16 Bloomberg's EVTS Screen

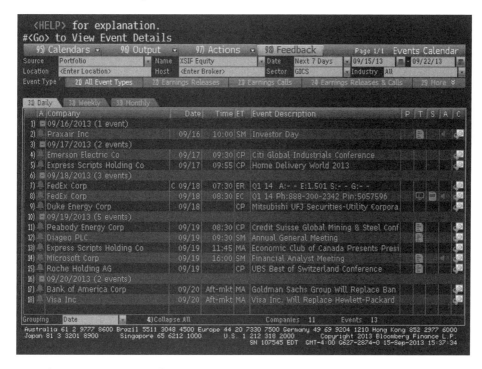

- Use the "Source" tab to select from a menu of all securities, securities from an index, securities from a search, or securities from a portfolio created in Bloomberg.
- You can save the screen (Calendars tab) and set up alerts in which Bloomberg will notify the user through Bloomberg's message system.

Other Monitors and Portals

MNSA	Today's announced merger and acquisition deals.
PREL	Pipeline of announced bonds.
DIS	Distressed bonds.
PE	Private equity.
TACT	Trade activity.
BRIEF	Daily economic newsletter.
EIU	Economist intelligence unit.
IECO	Global comparison of economic statistics.
FXIP	Foreign exchange information portal.
CENB	Central bank menu: Use to access platforms of central banks.
FED	Federal Reserve Bank portal.
ECB	European Central Bank portal.
LTOP	Top underwriters.
FICM	Fixed-income monitor.
PGM	Money market lookup by program type.

EXHIBIT 2.17   Portfolio Screens, PMEN: PORT, Characteristics Tab

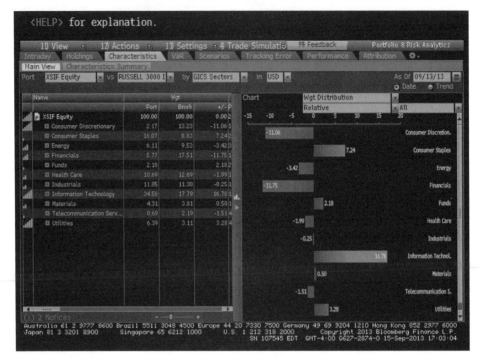

PORT: Characteristics tab, Main View. Portfolio sector allocations relative to Russell 3000 sector allocations.

Portfolios and Baskets

Portfolio Construction and Analysis: PRTU and PMEN

A user can set up a stock or fixed-income portfolio on Bloomberg using PRTU and, once loaded, analyze and monitor the portfolio using screens on the Portfolio menu, PMEN. See Bloomberg exhibit box: "Creating Portfolios in Bloomberg."

Many of the screens found on the PMEN menu can be used for in depth portfolio analysis (see Exhibit 2.17). The "Portfolio Risk & Analytics Screen (PORT), for example, allows one to evaluate a portfolio's features and performance. By accessing the screen tabs (e.g., "Holdings," "Characteristics," "Performance," and "Attributions"), one can evaluate the features, drivers, and historical performances of the portfolio, securities in the portfolio, and the portfolio's index. (Note: Many of these same functions can be accessed directly: PORT HD to access holdings, PORT CH to access characteristics, and PORT PA to access performance attributes.) Other screens of note on the PMEN menu screen include Portfolio News (NPH), Events Calendar (EVTS), and Expected Cash Flow (PCF). Many of these screens have tabs for accessing different information, sending information to Excel, and downloading information to PDF and Excel reports. A number of PMEN screens are presented in Chapter 7 and Chapter 8 when we examine portfolio evaluation and selection.

Once a portfolio is created, it can be exported to other screens or imported from other screens. For example, if one wanted to analyze a portfolio created in PRTU using relative valuation, one could select a stock in the portfolio (e.g., Apple [AAPL]), access the stock's menu (AAPL <Equity> <Enter>), and then bring up the stock's RV menu. On the stock's RV menu, one can then import the portfolio by selecting "Portfolio" from the dropdown "Comp Source" tab and the name of the portfolio from the dropdown "Name" menu. Similarly, one can also import the portfolio from other screens, such as the CACT, MOST, IMAP, EVTS, and MMAP screens, and also from Excel using the Bloomberg Excel Add-In.

CREATING PORTFOLIOS IN BLOOMBERG

Steps for Creating Portfolios

Step 1: PRTU: PRTU displays a list of portfolios. To create a portfolio using PRTU:

1. PRTU <Enter>
2. On the PRTU screen, click the "Create" tab. This will bring up a two-page screen for inputting information:
   a. Settings Page: Name of your portfolio, asset class (equity, fixed income, balanced), and benchmark (e.g., S&P 500).
   b. Portfolio Display Page: Screen for inputting securities by their identifiers.
3. Securities can be inputted by:
   a. Entering tickers or identifiers (e.g., CUSIP for bonds) in the security boxes.
   b. Importing securities from searches, indexes, or other portfolios that have been saved in Bloomberg. To import, you click the "Actions" tab on the PRTU screen, click "Import," and then identify the specific portfolio, search, or index from a dropdown.
   c. Drag and drop securities from another screen (e.g., RV or a member-holding screen of a fund (MHD). The entire portfolio can be dropped by using the dragging green arrow icon appearing in the right corner.
4. Once the portfolio is loaded, hit "Save." The name given to the portfolio will then be displayed on the PRTU screen.
5. Note: Different indexes for comparing portfolios can be added by accessing the Benchmark Screen (Click Benchmark tab found on the left of the PRTU screen).

(Continued)

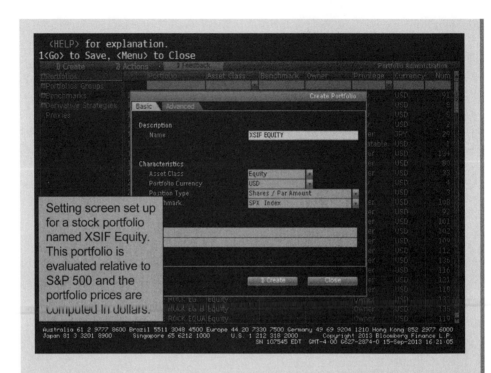

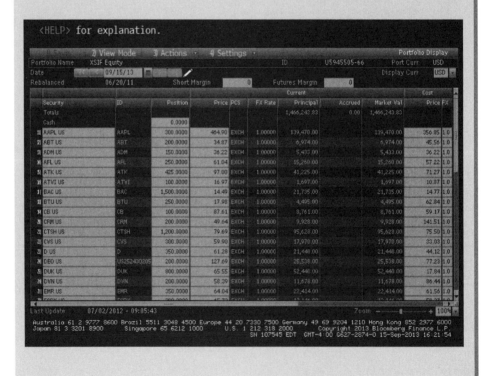

Step 2: PMEN: With the portfolio loaded, type PMEN to access a menu of functions to apply to the portfolio.

Historical Portfolio Returns

To analyze the past return performances of a portfolio, a history of portfolio rates of return needs to be created in PRTU. With history, the historical performance of the portfolio can then be analyzed from the performance tab on the PORT screen.

Steps for Creating Historical Data for Portfolios in PRTU
Bring up the PRTU screen for your portfolio. On the screen, change the date in the amber "Date" box (e.g., Month/Day/2006). Click the "Edit" tab and then the "Actions" tab. From the "Actions" dropdown, select "Import" to bring up the import box. On the import box, select "Portfolio" from the "Source" dropdown, the name of your portfolio from the "Name" dropdown, change the date (e.g., back to the current period), hit the "Import" tab, and then click "Save." You should now have a portfolio with historical data.

Creating Baskets: CIXB

Portfolios created in PRTU and securities found from searches (discussed in the next section) can be imported into CIXB. In CIXB, the portfolio's historical return data,

EXHIBIT 2.18   GP Screen for CIXB-Created Portfolio

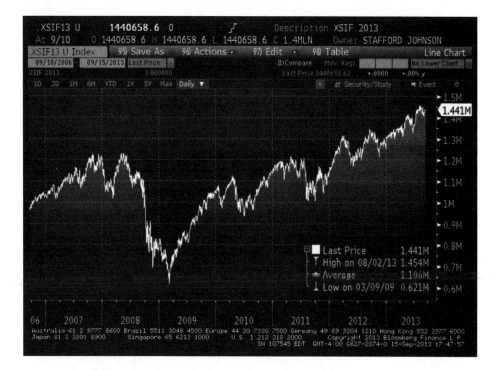

- .XSIF13 is a CIXB Basket of XSIF Equity Portfolio with historical data.
- A CIXB basket can be evaluated as an index: Ticker <Index> <Enter>.
- .XSIF13 <Index> <Equity>; GP Screen.

in turn, can be created and stored in a CIXB basket, where it can be evaluated as an index using the screens on the basket's index menu.

From the index menu, the portfolio can be analyzed by accessing Description (DES), Price Graph (GP), Market Heat Map (MMAP), Intraday Market Map (IMAP), Comparative Total Return (COMP), Historical Regression (HRA), and other functions applicable to indexes (Exhibit 2.18).

STEPS FOR CREATING AND ANALYZING A CIXB INDEX BASKET

CIXB:

The returns of a portfolio in PRTU (or from a search or index) can be evaluated by putting the portfolio into a CIXB basket, creating historical data, and then treating the portfolio as an index so that it can be evaluated using the screens on the index menus.

Steps:
1. CIXB <Enter>.
2. On the CIXB screen, name the ticker and the portfolio in the "Ticker." and "Name" yellow box and hit <Enter> to update (XSIF13 for ticker and XSIF 2013 for Name).

3. Click "Import" from the Actions dropdown tab.
4. On the "Import from Excel" box, click "Import from List" tab at bottom to bring up "Import from List" tab.
5. On "Import from List" tab: Select Portfolio (or EQS search or index) from the "Source" dropdown and the name of the portfolio (search or index) from the "Name" dropdown, and then click the "Import" tab. These steps will import the portfolio's stocks, shares, and price to the CIXB screen.
6. On CIXB screen, click the "Create" tab to bring up a time period box for selecting the time period for price and return data. After selecting the time period, hit "Save." This will activate a Bloomberg program for calculating the portfolio's daily historical returns.
7. The data will be sent to a report, RPT. To access this report, type "RPT" and hit<Enter>.

Index Menu Screen:

To analyze a CIXB-generated portfolio as an index enter Ticker Name (remember the period) <Index> <Enter> (e.g., .XSIF13 <Index> <Enter>) and then pull up screens from the index menu.

Screening and Search Functions

Given the hundreds of thousands of securities and funds that exist globally, investment analysis requires being able to search and screen for securities. Bloomberg provides screening and search functions for most security types and funds.

Equity Screener Analysis: EQS

Equity Screener Analysis, EQS, searches for equity securities. Using this screen, one can screen by general categories, such as countries, exchanges, indexes, security types, and security attributes; by security lists; and by data categories, such as fundamentals, estimates, financial and price ratios, and technical fields. One can also save the screening criteria so that the identified securities can be analyzed using other functions or imported to form a portfolio in PRTU. See Bloomberg exhibit box: "EQS Search Example Steps."

EQS SEARCH EXAMPLE STEPS

- Bring up EQS screen: EQS <Enter>.
- Select a category such as "Indexes."

(Continued)

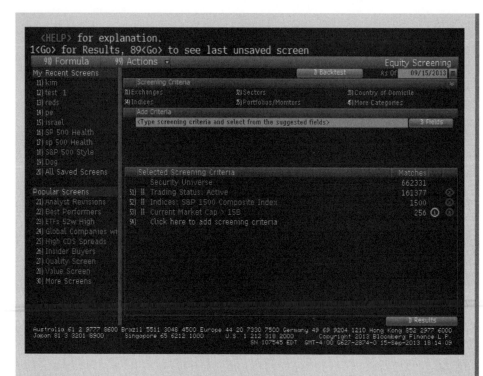

- Scroll down the list of indexes and identify a specific index (e.g., S&P 1500 Composite index)
- In the amber ribbon box, type in screening features, such as market cap greater than $15 billion, price-to-earnings ratio greater than 10, debt-to-total capital greater than 20 percent and less than 50 percent.
- Save the search by clicking "Save As" from the "Actions" tab dropdown and then name the search (e.g., Equity SP 1500 Style). Note: Saved screens are found on the left panel. Also, you can import the stocks from your search to other Bloomberg screens such as relative valuation analysis (RV).
- Click the "Results" tab at the bottom right corner to see the stocks found from the search.
- On the "Results" screen, one can click a stock on the output screen to access information on the stock (e.g., DES) or its menu.

Other Search Screens: Fund Searches (FSRC), Bond Searches (SRCH), Municipal Bond Searches (MSRC), and News Searches (NI)

Fund Searches: FSRC

From the FSRC screen, one can search and screen investment funds by general investment criteria, such as asset class (stock, bonds, balance, type (open, closed, unit investment trust, or exchange-traded product), by country, by asset holding criteria (industry, market cap, maturity, or ratings), and by adding fields. The user can save the search. The screen menus of any of the funds listed from the search can be accessed by clicking the name of the fund. On the fund menu, the fund can be evaluated. Some of the uses of the FSRC screen are presented in our examination of investment funds in Chapter 5.

Bond Searches: SRCH and MSRC

From the SRCH screen, one can search for bonds that fit specified criteria based on coupon, maturity, country, currency, and structure type for government, corporate, structured notes, and private securities. Using the MSRC screen, one can search and screen the universe of municipal bonds. Information on municipal securities and other information of a state or municipality in the state can also be accessed from the municipal screener (SMUN): SMUN <Enter>.

News Searches: NI and TNI

The menu screens for each stock, bond, government security, and commodity provide a news function in which news and information on a selected company, country, or commodity can be accessed. The Bloomberg system also has news platforms that one can use to select areas for news or to conduct new searches. Two areas of note are "News, by Category" (NI) and "News Search" (TNI). NI can be used to search and screen the universe of news by category. TNI can be used to conduct advanced news searches. Using TNI, the selected news search criteria can be saved and a corresponding custom news alert can be set so that one can receive messages from Bloomberg.

Other Bloomberg Searches and Screeners

MA	Merger and acquisition searches.
RATC	Search for credit rating changes.
PSCH	Preferred stock search.
MSCH	Money market search.
CTM	Search commodities exchanges.
AV	Bloomberg's media links.
LIVE	Bloomberg's live links.
BBLS	Search for legal documents.
ETF	Exchange-traded products.
BMAP	World Energy and Commodity Map and Platform.

STEPS FOR USING BLOOMBERG SEARCH SCREENS

SRCH Search Example Steps
- Bring up SRCH screen: SRCH <Enter>.
- Enter search information into amber "Ask a Question:" box.

MRSC Search Example Steps
- Bring up MSRC screen: MSRC <Enter>.
- Select features.
- Save the search by clicking the "Actions" tab, clicking "Save As," and then naming the search. By clicking the "My Searches" tab at the bottom of the MSRC screen, one can find the identified search. Also, other Bloomberg functions can import bonds from one's search for analysis.
- Click the gray "Results" tab at the bottom right corner to see output.
- Place cursor on a bond on the Results screen and left click to see a menu of information (e.g., description, DES).
- Use the CUSIP number (found on the Results Screen) to access the bond's menu: Cusip # <Muni> <Enter>.

NI Search Example Steps
- NI <Enter>.
- Select type of news from menu (e.g., Economic News).
- Select type of selected news, such as Country Economies and China Economy.
- Click a specific news story to bring up a PDF of that story.
- On the dropdown tabs above the news stories, screen the news by sources, language, type, and time period.

TNI Search Example Steps
- TNI <Enter>.
- Type key words, (e.g., Greece).
- Click the "Save and Set Alerts" tab to save the search.
- Click a specific news story to bring up a PDF of that story.
- On the dropdown tabs above the news stories, screen the news by sources, language, type, and time period.

The Bloomberg Excel Add-In: Importing Bloomberg into Excel

In Bloomberg, the data shown on many screens can be exported to Excel by clicking Excel from the "Actions" dropdown tab. The data behind many graphs also can be sent to a clipboard where it can be moved to Excel. Instead of exporting Bloomberg data, one can alternatively import Bloomberg information from Excel using the Bloomberg Excel Add-In. Using Excel to import Bloomberg data and information enables one to develop customized programs for analyzing securities and portfolios. On the Bloomberg Add-In, there are a number of templates, data wizards, screeners, and other functions. The DAPI screen in Bloomberg also provides a list of Bloomberg Add-In functions and how to use them. From the list, the "Import Data Wizard," "Fundamental Analysis Wizard," and "Template Library" are good ways to get started using the Bloomberg Add-In functions.

Import Data Wizard

Using the Import Data Wizard, Bloomberg data can be imported into an Excel spreadsheet where the data can be customized using a variety of functions and formulas. The Import Data Wizard generates tables for times series and cross-sectional data for companies, stocks, bonds, and indexes. The wizard moves sequentially, starting from a window where securities, portfolios, searches, and indexes are selected; to a field window where data can be selected from an extensive list of financial, economics, and market information, then to a time period window for selecting the number of periods (for historical wizard), and finally to a window for selecting the Excel table layout.

Fundamental Analysis Wizard

Using the Fundamental Analysis Wizard (accessed from the Financial/Estimates tab in the Import Data Wizard), one can import customized data such as income statements, balance sheets, and cash flow statements on a company, index, or portfolio of stocks. The information can be viewed for selected single or multiple periods.

Template Library

The Template Library enables one to locate and download a preconstructed Bloomberg spreadsheet from an extensive list of available spreadsheets. One can then save the spreadsheet to use as a template for future analysis. The sheets are grouped by categories: Equity, Fixed-Income, Industry, Currency, In-the-News, Markets, and New Templates. The templates can be accessed directly from the Bloomberg Add-In in Excel or by clicking "Excel Template Library" from the DAPI screen in Bloomberg, selecting the template, and then clicking "Open" to open the customized workshop in Excel.

Some of the templates and uses of Bloomberg Excel Add-in functions are presented in a number of the chapters in this text.

STEPS TO LOAD "BLOOMBERG ADD-IN" IN EXCEL

- On computer, click Start.
- Click "All Programs."
- Click Bloomberg.
- Click Excel Add-In.
- Press Install.

EXHIBIT 2.19   Launchpad, Xavier Student Equity Fund

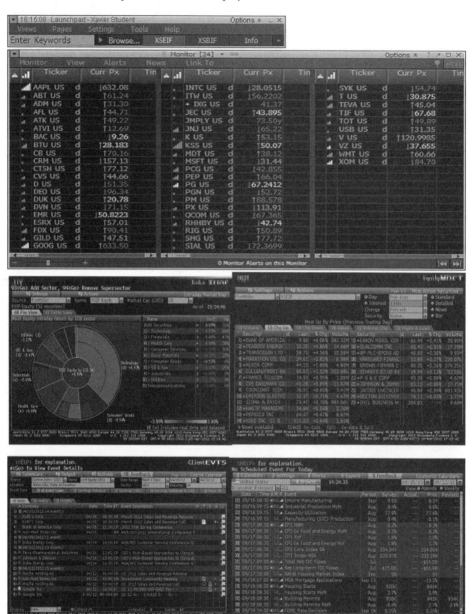

Launchpad

The types of analysis that financial analysts do can vary: managing a portfolio, analyzing stocks in a particular industry, identifying new security offerings, monitoring markets, or identifying relevant economic news and events. Each of these different types of analysis requires accessing specific types of information. Given the myriad Bloomberg screens, Bloomberg's Launchpad function enables one to customize a Window-esque interface, allowing easy access to information needed to conduct a specific type of analysis. Exhibit 2.19 shows an example of a Bloomberg Launchpad created for a student investment fund portfolio. The steps for generating a Launchpad are described in the Bloomberg exhibit box: "Steps for Creating a Launchpad Window."

STEPS FOR CREATING A LAUNCHPAD WINDOW

Step 1: BLP <Enter>: Brings up the Bloomberg toolbar.
Step 2: Toolbar: Click "Options" to bring up the toolbar showing the tabs with Views, Pages, Setting, and Tools.
Step 3: Load Screens: On the Launchpad toolbar, load Bloomberg screens.

To find a screen, type in a key word (e.g., FX to find and load the Foreign Exchange Information platform, WB for the World Bond Monitor, MOST for the most active stocks monitor, or IMAP for the stock index heat map).

In the Views dropdown tab on the toolbar, save the screen being created by clicking "SaveView" and then name the screen (e.g., Monitors). To create new screens or access previously created screens, use the "New" and "Open" tabs in the Views tab.

On the Launchpad toolbar, the Views, Pages, Settings, and Tools tabs can be used to manage and customize screens:

- In the Pages dropdown, you can create, delete, share, and send pages in the view.
- In the "Setting" tab, you can set the default option for one's Launchpad View, such as "XSIF Equity."
- The Tools tab allows you to create groups of functions.

Step 4: Load Screens from Browse:

One quick and efficient way to load screens is to click the "Browse" tab. The Browse option tab lists common categories to load, or you can type in a name in the amber search field box (e.g., MOST) to find and load a screen.

(Continued)

Example: To load securities, currencies, or portfolios, a frequently used panel is the "Monitor" panel. Clicking "Monitor" and the "Launch Component" brings up a stock monitor screen similar to PRTU. From that screen, you can load securities by entering their tickers in the "Ticker" boxes. If you want to import a portfolio that has been created in PRTU or from a search, or if you want to load an index, you can click the "Monitor" tab and then "Import Securities." This will bring up a box where you can select from a source type: portfolios (PRTU), equity searches (EQS), equity indexes, fund screens (FSRC), Bloomberg peers, and other sources. After selecting the type, you then select the portfolio, index, or search, and then click "Import." For example, to download one of Xavier's Student funds, the author selected Portfolio and then "XSIF Equity." See Exhibit 2.19 for an example.

The loaded monitor screen can be further customized using tab functions on the screen: Monitor, Views, Alerts, News, and Link to:

- Using the "Views" tab, you can change the view to show securities grouped by industries or sectors (Group by), different panels (Panel), size (Zoom), and add or delete columns (Manage Columns).
- Using the "Alerts" tab, you can set alerts, such as security prices changing by a specified percentage or by volume changes.
- Using the "News Alerts," you can enable the "News Alert" to create a column to click on news for each security.
- Using the "link to" tab, you can bring up the portfolio or index's heat map.

> **Step 5: Loading Other Screens:** Going back to the Launchpad toolbar, you can use the Browse option to find other screens to load, or use the amber keyword box to search for other items. For example, type in ECO to find the ECO screen to load or "Live" to bring up the menu showing live news events to monitor.
>
> **Step 6: Saving Screen:** Once the screens are loaded on the Views screen (or as they are being loaded), the view can be saved by clicking "Save View" in the "Views" tab of the toolbar.
>
> **Step 7: Creating Additional Pages:** Additional pages in the saved view can be created by clicking the + icon next to the "Pages" tab, for example, pages for each sector in the portfolio and stocks in each sector, other funds, and stock index and economic calendars. Pages in a view can be deleted by going to the page tab.
>
> **Step 8: Creating New Views:** New views focusing on a different topics can also be created by clicking the "Views" tab and then "New."
>
> **Step 9: Exiting Bloomberg:** One can exit Launchpad and return to a general Bloomberg screen by clicking x on the Launchpad toolbar (or by clicking "Exit Launchpad" from the Views tab). To access Launchpad again, one can type in BLP and hit <Enter>.

Other Bloomberg Functions

In subsequent chapters, we will identify many of the screens discussed in this chapter and how to access them. A directory listing of many of the screens by functions can be found in Appendix A. A cursory look at these functions shows the breadth and depth of the Bloomberg system and its value in the study of financial markets and investments. For detailed applications of the system, one should view the Bloomberg video tutorials and training documents. The tutorials training documents (with topical cheat sheets) can be accessed directly from the Bloomberg system by typing BU to bring up the Bloomberg information menu. Bloomberg is also constantly adding and improving its platforms. Bloomberg's NEXT screen (NEXT <Enter>) provides brochures, fact sheets, and videos about new Bloomberg enhancements.

Conclusion

In this chapter, we have given an overview of the Bloomberg system and a starting guide on to how to access financial and economic news, information, and analytics from the system. In subsequent chapters, we will use this powerful system as a guide to the study of investments. Given the overview of the financial system explained in Chapter 1 and the Bloomberg news, data, and analytical retrieval system in this chapter, we now take up the study of equity markets and investment.

Bloomberg Exercises

1. Select a stock of interest and study it by going to its equity menu and accessing the following screens:
   a. DES   Description.
   b. CF   Corporate filings (view or download the company's 10-K).
   c. SPLC Supply chain.
   d. RELS Related securities (e.g., debt, preferred stocks).
   e. HDS   Major holders of the stocks.
   f. CN   Company news.
   g. GP   Stock price graph (vary time period and activate events and volume).
   h. GIP   Intraday price graph.
2. Study some of the market trends by using MOST: MOST <Enter>. Using the MOST screen, examine the S&P 500 stocks by selecting "Equity Indexes" and "SPX" from the dropdowns.
3. Using the WEI screen, identify a broad-based index such as the S&P 500 and a sector index. Find the index's ticker by going to the WEI "Settings" window and clicking "Ticker." Access the following information about the indexes from their menus (Index ticker <Index> <Enter>):

      a. DES   Description of index.

      b. IMOV Index movers.

      c. MRR   Member returns.

      d. IMAP   Industry market heat map.

      e. GP   Price graph (vary time period and activate events and volume).

4. Using the index's RV screen, compare the features of the stocks that comprise the index.

5. Using the index's FA screen, examine the index's summary statement and then select a stock that is a member of the index to compare its financials with the index: type the stock's ticker and hit <Equity> in "Compare" box.

6. Select a corporation of interest and examine one of its bonds: Ticker <Corp> <Enter> and then select a bond. Possible screens to examine the selected bond include the following:

      a. DES   Description of the bond (see prospectus).

      b. HDS   Bondholders.

      c. AGGD Largest creditors.

      d. DDIS   Debt distribution.

      e. GP   Price graph.

      f. GRBI   Guarantors of the bond.

      g. CRPR   Credit rating.

      h. CSHF   Bond payment schedule.

      i. QR   Trade recap.

7. Select and examine a U.S. Treasury note that was recently issued: <Govt> TK <Enter> and then select U.S.A. and CT (or use the SECF screen to find the issue). Possible screens to examine include the following:

      a. DES   Description of the bond.

      b. HDS   Bondholders.

      c. DDIS   Debt distribution.

      d. GP   Price graph.

      e. GIP   Intraday.

      f. CSHF   Bond payment schedule.

      g. QR   Trade recap.

8. Explore different sources of economic information using some of the following screens:

      a. Examine the economic statistics of the U.S. and other countries by going to ECST:

            a. GDP.

            b. Population.

            c. Housing.

            d. International Trade.

      b. Examine the economic statistics of the U.S. and other countries by going to ECOF:

            a. National Accounts.

            b. Business Conditions.

     c. Prices.

     d. Labor Conditions.

     e. Housing Conditions.

     f. Leading Economic Indicators.

     g. Government Sector.

     h. Balance of Payments.

     i. Monetary Sector.

     j. Financial Sector.

  c. Get an economic snapshot of several countries by going to ECOW (ECOW <Enter>).

  d. Review some recent economic releases for the United States by going to ECO: ECO <Enter>.

  e. Review some recent economic releases for a country or area by going to WECO: WECO <Enter>.

  f. Study economic trends and analysis by going to BRIEF and downloading the "Economics" PDF.

  g. Study the economy or a market by going to AV. On the AV screen, select a topic from AV Categories dropdown. To connect to a live broadcast, click "Live" tab; to connect to Bloomberg's radio and TV broadcast, click the "TV and Radio" tabs.

  h. Go to EIU to access news information and analysis from the *Economist* by topical areas (suggestion: economic information on countries can be found in "Economic Structure" and "Economic Indicators").

  i. Go to NI to access news on a country: (1) NI <Enter>; (2) click "Topics," "Business News," "Economic News," "Country Economies"; (3) select country; and (4) download story.

9. Using the BI screen, select an industry sector (e.g., Health Care, Biotechnology) and evaluate the sector using the following screens:

  a. Key Catalysts.

  b. Comp sheets.

  c. News/research.

  d. Events.

  e. Data library.

  f. Analysis.

10. Analyze an industry by examining the sector's index on the Index menu. The index ticker can be found from the BI screen (e.g., BIMATUSB for Biotechnology) or from SECF. Possible screens to examine include the following:

  a. DES   Description.

  b. IMAP Heat map.

  c. GP   Price graph (vary time period and activate events and volume).

  d. FA   Financials.

  e. GF   Fundamental graphs.

11. Select research, news stories, and videos on a sector using the following screens:

    a. TNI   Advanced News Search (click "Industries").

    b. NI   News Search.

    c. AV   Videos.

12. Conduct a simple screen and stocks search using EQS. Suggestion: Limit search to S&P 500 stocks (search for the S&P 500 stocks using the "Indexes" dropdown) and a market cap greater than $20 billion (in the ribbon box, type in "Market Cap" to bring down dropdown and follow input instructions). Be sure to save your search (go to "Actions" tab to find "Save As").

13. Select one of the stocks from the search you did in Exercise 12 and bring up its RV screen, then import your search to the RV screen: Company ticker <Equity> <Enter>; click RV; in "Comp Source" dropdown tab, click "Equity Screen" (EQS), and in "Name" tab, click the name of your search and hit <Enter> to activate. On the RV screen, evaluate your stocks by selecting different templates (gray tabs).

14. Create a basket consisting of the stocks from your search in Exercise 13 using the CIXB screen. See Bloomberg exhibit box: "Steps for Creating and Analyzing a CIXB Index Basket." After creating the basket, evaluate your portfolio of stocks from the search using the index menu (Basket ticker name [e.g., .Name] <Index> <Enter>). Possible screens to consider on the index screen are as follows:

    a. DES   Description.

    b. GP   Price graph.

    c. IMAP   Intraday market map.

15. Create a portfolio of the stocks of interest or a portfolio from stocks created in your EQS search done in Exercise 12. See Bloomberg exhibit box "Creating Portfolios in Bloomberg." Create historical data for your portfolio.

16. Using the PMEN screen, analyze the portfolio you created in Exercise 15. Possible screens to consider on the PMEN screen include the following:

    a. PORT Portfolio Risk and Analytics (select some of the gray tabs).

    b. PDSP Portfolio Display.

    c. NPH   Portfolio News.

17. Select one of the stocks from the portfolio you created in Exercise 15 and bring up its RV screen, then import your portfolio to the RV screen: Company ticker <Equity> <Enter>; click RV; in the "Comp Source" dropdown tab, click "Portfolio," and in the "Name" tab, click the name of your portfolio, and hit <Enter> to activate. On the RV screen, evaluate your portfolio by selecting different tabs.

18. Using the EVTS screen, load the portfolio you created in Exercise 15 on that screen: EVTS <Enter>, on the "Source" dropdown tab click "Portfolio," and on the "Name" dropdown tab click the name of your portfolio. Once your portfolio is loaded, click the news announcement you want to monitor (e.g., All Event Types, Earnings Releases, etc.). Next, set alerts by clicking the bell icon in the "A" column and then setting the type and timing of the alert (this will send Bloomberg messages to you). This is the type of screen that you might want to send to a Launchpad page that you have created.

19. Two important security laws are the Securities Act of 1933 and the Securities Exchange Act of 1934. Learn more about these acts and others (e.g., Sarbanes-Oxley Act of 2002) by going to the BLAW screen: BLAW <Enter> and clicking PRAC (Practice Areas), "Securities Law," and "Securities Act of 1933," "Securities Exchange Act of 1934," and "Sarbanes-Oxley Act of 2002."

20. Explore the following Wizards in Bloomberg's Excel Add-Ins:
    • Click "Import Data," "Real Time/Historical," and "Historical End of the Day."
    • Click "Import Data," "Real Time/Historical" and "Real Time/Current."
    • Click "Import Data," "Financial/Estimates," and "Fundamental Data."

21. Explore the Template Library found in the Bloomberg Excel Add-In from Excel or by going to the DAPI screen: DAPI <Enter> and click "Excel Template Library."

22. Learn about the NYSE Euronext and other exchanges in the United States and throughout the world by going to their Web sites. To find general information about exchanges and their Web sites, go to Bloomberg's EPR screen.

23. Conduct a research and advanced news search to find stories related to a financial crisis (e.g., sovereign debt crisis): TNI <Enter>.

24. Create a Launchpad view with pages for one or more categories described in the chapter. Some possible views include the following:
    a. Stock portfolio monitor of the portfolio or search you created.
    b. Economic monitor that includes screens such as ECO.

CHAPTER 3

Stock and Bond Valuation and Return

Introduction

In Chapter 1, we discussed how securities can be evaluated in terms of eight common characteristics: value, rate of return, risk, life, divisibility, marketability, liquidity, and taxability. For most investors, the most important of these characteristics are value and return. In this chapter, we examine the valuation of bonds and stocks and how to measure the rates of return from investing in such securities. In Chapter 11, we will examine more closely the value, return, and risk relations for stocks when we begin our analysis of equity securities. Understanding how securities are valued and their rates determined, however, is fundamental to being able to evaluate and select these securities.

Rate of Return

Holding Period Yield

The rate of return an investor earns from holding a security is equal to the total dollar return received from the security per period of time (e.g., year) expressed as a proportion of the price paid for the security. The total dollar return includes income payments (coupon interests or dividends), interest earned from reinvesting the income during the period, and capital gains or losses realized when the security is sold or matures. For example, an investor who purchased XYZ stock for $S_0 = \$100$, then received $10 in dividends ($D$) two years later when he sold the stock for $S_T = \$110$, would realize a rate of return for this two-year period of 20 percent:

$$\text{Rate of Return} = \frac{D + S_T - S_0}{S_0} = \frac{\$10 + \$110 - \$100}{\$100} = 0.20$$

Similarly, a bond investor who bought a Treasury bond on April 20 for $P_0^B =$ $95,000 and then sold it for $P_T^B = \$96,000$ on October 20 just after receiving a coupon of $C = \$4,000$, would earn a rate of return for this six-month period of 5.263 percent:

$$\text{Rate of Return} = \frac{C + P_T^B - P_0^B}{P_0^B} = \frac{\$4,000 + \$96,000 - \$95,000}{\$95,000} = 0.05263$$

Both the bond and stock rates of return are measured as *holding period yields, HPY.* The *HPY* is the rate earned from holding the security for one period (e.g., one year or six months). The *HPY* can alternatively be expressed in terms of the security's *holding period return, HPR,* minus one, where the *HPR* is the ratio of the ending-period value (e.g., $D + S_T$) to the beginning period value (S_0). That is:

$$HPY = \frac{\text{Ending Value}}{\text{Beginning Value}} - 1$$

$$HPY = HPR - 1$$

$$HPY = \frac{D + S_T}{S_0} - 1; \quad HPY = \frac{C + P_T^B}{P_0^B} - 1$$

Annualized HPY

To evaluate alternative investments with different holding periods, investment analysts often annualize the rate of return. The simplest way to annualize a return is to multiply the periodic rate of return by the number of periods of that length in a year. Thus, to annualize the *HPY* on the bond investment, we would multiply the six-month *HPY* of 0.05263 by 2 to obtain 0.10526; to annualize the stock's rate of return, we would multiple the two-year *HPY* of 0.20 by 1/2 to get 0.10. This method for annualizing rates of return, however, does not take into account the interest that could be earned from reinvesting the cash flows. That is, a $1 investment in the bond would yield $1.0526 after six months, which could be reinvested. If it is reinvested for six months at the same six-month rate of 5.26 percent, then the dollar investment would be worth $1.108 after one year. Thus, the *effective annual rate* (i.e., the rate that takes into account the reinvestment of interest or the compounding of interest) is 10.8 percent. The *effective annualized HPY* (HPY^A) can be calculated using the following formula:

$$HPY^A = HPR^{1/M} - 1$$

where: $M =$ number of years the investment is held.

Thus, the effective annualized *HPY* for the bond investment would be 10.8 percent, and the effective *HPY^A* for the stock investment would be 9.544 percent:

$$HPY^A = HPR^{1/M} - 1$$

$$HPY^A = \left[\frac{\$4,000 + \$96,000}{\$95,000}\right]^{1/0.5} - 1 = 0.108$$

$$HPY^A = \left[\frac{\$10 + \$110}{\$100}\right]^{1/2} - 1 = 0.0954$$

The two-year *HPY* on the stock of 20 percent reflects annual compounding. That is, $1 after one year would be worth $1.0954, which reinvested for the next year would equal $1.20:

$$\$1.00(1.0954)(1.0954) = (1.0954)2 = \$1.20$$

Required Rates of Return and Value for a Single-Period Cash Flow

The price of a security and its rate of return are related. When an investor knows the price of the security and its cash flow, she can determine the rate of return. Alternatively, when the investor knows her *required rate of return* and the security's cash flow, she can determine the value of the security or the price she is willing to pay. For example, an investor who requires an annual 10 percent rate of return in order to invest in a one-year AAA bond paying a single cash flow (coupon interest) of $10 and a principal of $100 at maturity would value the bond at $100. This price can be found by expressing the equation for the *HPY* in terms of its price:

$$\text{Rate of Return} = R = \frac{C + P_T^B}{P_0^B} - 1$$

$$P_0^B(1 + R) = C + P_T^B$$

$$P_0^B = \frac{C + P_0^B}{(1 + R)}$$

$$P_0^B = \frac{\$10 + \$100}{1.10} = \$100$$

If the bond were priced in the market below $100, the investor would consider it underpriced, yielding a rate of return that exceeds her required rate of 10 percent; if the bond were priced above $100, she would consider the bond to be overpriced, yielding a rate of return less than 10 percent.

Future and Present Values

Future Value

The above value and return relations can be described in terms of the present values and future values of investments and future receipts. More formally, the future value of any amount invested today is

$$P_N = P_0(1 + R)^N$$

where:

N = number of periods of the investment

P_N = future value of investment N periods from present (future value, FV)

P_0 = initial investment value (present value, PV)

R = rate per period (periodic rate)

$(1 + R)^N$ = future value of $1 invested today for N periods at a compound rate of R

In terms of the preceding bond example, the future value (FV) of the bond investment of $100 at 10 percent is $110 (coupon and principal):

$$P_1 = P_0(1 + R)^1$$
$$P_1 = \$100(1.10) = \$110$$

An investment fund that invested $1,000,000 in a security that paid 10 percent per year for three years would in turn have $1,331,000 at the end of three years:

$$P_N = P_0(1 + R)^N$$
$$P_3 = \$1,000,000\,(1.10)^3 = \$1,331,000$$

If the interest is paid more than once a year, then the rate of return and the number of periods must be adjusted. Specifically, let

n = the number of times interest is paid per year

M = number of years of the investment

$$\text{Period Rate} = R = \frac{\text{Annual Rate}}{n}$$

N = number of periods of the investment = $(n)(M)$

If an investment fund invested $1,000,000 in a three-year security that paid annual interest at 10 percent for three years with the interest paid semiannually, then the investment would be worth $1,340,095.64 after three years:

$$n = 2$$

$$M = 3 \text{ years}$$

$$\text{Period Rate} = R = \frac{\text{Annual Rate}}{n} = \frac{0.10}{2} = 0.05$$

$$N = \text{number of periods of the investment} = (n)(M) = (2)(3) = 6$$

$$P_N = P_0(1 + R)^N$$

$$P_6 = \$1,000,000 \, (1.05)^6 = \$1,340,095.64$$

Note that with semiannual interest payments, there are more opportunities for reinvesting the interest received. As a result, the future value of the investment is greater with interest paid semiannually than annually.

Future Value of an Annuity

An annuity is a periodic investment or receipt. For example, an investment of $1 million each year for three years would be an example of an investment annuity, and a security paying $50 every six months for 10 years would be an example of a receipt annuity. The future value of an annuity (A) is equal to the sum of the future values of each investment at the investment horizon:

$$P_N = A(1 + R)^{N-1} + A(1 + R)^{N-2} + A(1 + R)^{N-3} + \cdots + A(1 + R)^{N-N}$$

$$P_N = \sum_{t=1}^{N} A(1 + R)^{N-t}$$

As an example, suppose an investment fund owned $50,000,000 of bonds maturing in three years that promised to pay 10 percent per year and $50,000,000 at the end of three years. If the fund reinvested the annual interest of $5,000,000 at a rate of 10 percent, then at the end of three years the sum of the annual interest payments would be worth $16,550,000:

Year	0	1	2	3	3	Values
A		$5,000,000			$5,000,000(1.10)^2$	$6,050,000
A			$5,000,000		$5,000,000(1.10)^1$	$5,500,000
A				$5,000,000	$5,000,000(1.10)^0$	$5,000,000
					Horizon Value = P_N	$16,550,000

$$P_N = \sum_{t=1}^{N} A(1 + R)^{N-t}$$

$$P_3 = \sum_{t=1}^{3} \$5,000,000 \, (1 + R)^{3-t}$$

$$P_N = \$5,000,000(1.10)^{3-1} + \$5,000,000(1.10)^{3-2} + \$5,000,000(1.10)^{3-3}$$
$$P_N = \$16,550,000$$

At the end of three years, the fund would have $500 million in principal, $15 million in interest, and $1,550,000 (= $16,550,000 − $15,000,000) in interest earned from reinvesting the interest.

The equation for the future value of an annuity is equal to the annuity times the future value of $1 invested each period for N periods:

$$P_N = \sum_{t=1}^{N} A(1+R)^{N-t}$$

$$P_N = A \sum_{t=1}^{N} (1+R)^{N-t}$$

The future value of $1 invested each period for N periods is defined as the future value interest factor of an annuity, $FVIF_a$. The formula for determining $FVIF_a$ is:

$$FVIF_a = \sum_{t=1}^{N} (1+R)^{N-t} = \left[\frac{(1+R)^N - 1}{R} \right]$$

Substituting the formula for the $FVIF_a$ into the equation for P_N, the future value of annuity can alternatively be expressed as:

$$P_N = A \sum_{t=1}^{N} (1+R)^{N-t}$$

$$P_N = A \left[\frac{(1+R)^N - 1}{R} \right]$$

In terms of our example:

$$P_3 = \$5,000,000 \sum_{t=1}^{3} (1.10)^{3-t}$$

$$P_3 = \$5,000,000 \left[\frac{(1.10)^3 - 1}{0.10} \right]$$

$$P_3 = \$16,550,000$$

Note: If the bond investment fund received interest semiannually, then the fund would receive $2,500,000 every six months. If the semiannual reinvestment rate were

5 percent, then the sum of the future values of the interest payments would be $17,004,782:

Year	0.0	0.5	1.0	1.5	2.0	2.5	3.0	3		Values
N		1	2	3	4	5	6	6		
A		$2,500,000							$2,500,000(1.05)^5$	$3,190,704
A			$2,500,000						$2,500,000(1.05)^4$	$3,038,766
A				$2,500,000					$2,500,000(1.05)^3$	$2,894,063
A					$2,500,000				$2,500,000(1.05)^2$	$2,756,250
A						$2,500,000			$2,500,000(1.05)^1$	$2,625,000
A							$2,500,000		$2,500,000(1.05)^0$	$2,500,000
									Horizon Value $= P_N$	$17,004,782

$$P_N = A \sum_{t=1}^{N} (1 + R)^{N-t}$$

$$P_6 = \$2,500,000 \sum_{t=1}^{6} (1.05)^{6-t}$$

$$P_6 = \$2,500,000 \left[\frac{(1.05)^6 - 1}{0.05} \right]$$

$$P_6 = \$17,004,782$$

Present Value

The present value is the amount that must be invested today to realize a specific future value. The present value of one future receipt is:

$$P_0 = \frac{P_N}{(1 + R)^N}$$

Thus, $1,331,000 received three years from now would be worth $1 million given a rate of return of 10 percent and annual compounding:

$$P_0 = \frac{P_N}{(1 + R)^N}$$

$$P_0 = \frac{\$1,331,000}{(1.10)^3} = \$1,000,000$$

The amount of $1,340,095.64 received three years from now ($M = 3$), would be worth $1 million given a 5 percent semiannual rate and two compoundings per year ($n = 2$

and $N = nM = (2)(3) = 6$:

$$P_0 = \frac{P_N}{(1 + R)^N}$$

$$P_0 = \frac{\$1,340,095.64}{(1.05)^6} = \$1,000,000$$

The method of computing the present value is referred to as *discounting,* and the interest rate used to discount is referred to as the *discount rate.*

Present Value of an Annuity

When a fixed dollar annuity is received each period, the series is also called an annuity. If the first payment is received one period from the present, the annuity is referred to as an *ordinary annuity;* if the first payment is immediate, then the annuity is called an *annuity due.* The present value of an ordinary annuity is the sum of the present values of each annuity received:

$$P_0 = \frac{A}{(1 + R)^1} + \frac{A}{(1 + R)^2} + \frac{A}{(1 + R)^3} + \cdots + \frac{A}{(1 + R)^N}$$

$$P_0 = \sum_{t=1}^{N} \frac{A}{(1 + R)^t}$$

$$P_0 = A \sum_{t=1}^{N} \frac{1}{(1 + R)^t}$$

$\sum_{t=1}^{N} \frac{1}{(1+R)^t}$ is the present value of $1 received each period for N periods. It is referred to as the present value interest factor of an annuity, $PVIF_a$. $PVIF_a$ is equal to:

$$PVIF_a = \sum_{t=1}^{N} \frac{1}{(1 + R)^t} = \left[\frac{1 - (1/(1 + R)^N)}{R} \right]$$

Thus, an investor who received $100 at the end of each year for three years would have an investment currently worth $248.69 given a discount rate of 10 percent:

Year	0	0	1	2	3
A	$90.91	$100/(1.10)^1	$100.00		
A	$82.64	$100/(1.10)^2		$100.00	
A	$75.13	$100/(1.10)^3			$100.00
	$248.69	Present Value = P_0			

$$P_0 = \sum_{t=1}^{3} \frac{\$100}{(1.10)^t} = \frac{\$100}{(1.10)^1} + \frac{\$100}{(1.10)^2} + \frac{\$100}{(1.10)^3}$$

$$P_0 = \$100 \sum_{t=1}^{3} \frac{1}{(1.10)^t}$$

$$P_0 = \$100 \left[\frac{1 - (1/(1.10)^3}{.10} \right]$$

$$P_0 = \$248.69$$

If the investment paid $50 every six months and the appropriate six-month rate were 5 percent, then the present value of the $50 annuity would be $253.78:

Year		0	0		0.5	1.0	1.5	2.0	2.5	3.0
Number of Semiannual Periods from Present		0	0		1	2	3	4	5	6
A		$47.62	$50/(1.05)^1		$50					
A		$45.35	$50/(1.05)^2			$50				
A		$43.19	$50/(1.05)^3				$50			
A		$41.14	$50/(1.05)^4					$50		
A		$39.18	$50/(1.05)^5						$50	
A		$37.31	$50/(1.05)^6							$50
		$253.78	Present Value = P_0							

$$P_0 = \$50 \sum_{t=1}^{6} \frac{1}{(1.05)^t}$$

$$P_0 = \$50 \left[\frac{1 - (1/(1.05)^6}{0.10} \right]$$

$$P_0 = \$253.78$$

Bond Valuation

Like the value of any asset, the value of a bond is equal to the sum of the present values of its future cash flow:

$$V_0^B = \sum_{t=1}^{N} \frac{CF_t}{(1+R)^t} = \frac{CF_1}{(1+R)^1} + \frac{CF_2}{(1+R)^2} + \cdots + \frac{CF_N}{(1+R)^N} \qquad (3.1)$$

where

V_0^B = the value or price of the bond

CF_t = the bond's expected cash flow in period t, including both coupon income and repayment of principal

R = the discount rate

N = the term to maturity on the bond

The discount rate is the required rate, that is, the rate investors require to buy the bond. This rate is typically estimated by determining the rate on a security with comparable features: same risk, liquidity, taxability, and maturity.

Many bonds pay a fixed coupon interest each period, with the principal repaid at maturity. The coupon payment, C, is typically quoted in terms of the bond's coupon rate, C^R. The coupon rate is the contractual rate the issuer agrees to pay on the bond. This rate is often expressed as a proportion of the bond's face value (or par) and is usually stated on an annual basis. Thus, a bond with a face value (F) of $1,000 and a 10 percent coupon rate would pay an annual coupon of $100 each year for the life of the bond: $C = C^R F = (0.10)(\$1,000) = \$100$. The value of a bond paying a fixed coupon interest each year (annual coupon payment) and the principal at maturity (M), in turn, would be

$$V_0^B = \frac{C}{(1+R)^1} + \frac{C}{(1+R)^2} + \cdots + \frac{C}{(1+R)^M} + \frac{F}{(1+R)^M} \qquad (3.2)$$

$$V_0^B = \sum_{t=1}^{M} \frac{C}{(1+R)^t} + \frac{F}{(1+R)^M}$$

The fixed coupon payments are an annuity, and their value can be found by computing the present value of an annuity. The value of the principal payment, in turn, can be found by simply computing the present value of the principal:

$$V_0^B = \sum_{t=1}^{N} \frac{C}{(1+R)^t} + \frac{F}{(1+R)^N}$$

$$V_0^B = C \sum_{t=1}^{N} \frac{1}{(1+R)^t} + \frac{F}{(1+R)^N}$$

$$V_0^B = C \left[\frac{1 - 1/(1+R)^N}{R} \right] + \frac{F}{(1+R)^N}$$

Thus, if investors require a 10 percent annual rate of return on a 10-year, corporate bond paying a coupon equal to 9 percent of par each year and a principal of $1,000 at maturity ($N = M = 10$ years), then they would price the bond at \$938.55:

$$V_0^B = \sum_{t=1}^{M} \frac{C}{(1+R)^t} + \frac{F}{(1+R)^M}$$

$$V_0^B = \sum_{t=1}^{10} \frac{\$90}{(1.10)^t} + \frac{\$1,000}{(1.10)^{10}}$$

$$V_0^B = \$90 \sum_{t=1}^{M} \frac{1}{(1.10)^t} + \frac{\$1,000}{(1.10)^{10}}$$

$$V_0^B = \$90[PVIF(10\%, 10 \text{ yrs}] + \frac{\$1,000}{(1.10)^{10}}$$

$$V_0^B = \$90 \left[\frac{1 - [1/1.10]^{10}}{0.10} \right] + \frac{\$1,000}{(1.10)^{10}}$$

$$V_0^B = \$938.55$$

Bond Price Relations

In the above example, the value of the bond is not equal to its par value. This can be explained by the fact that the discount rate and coupon rate are different. Specifically, for investors in the above case to obtain the 10 percent rate per year from a bond promising to pay an annual rate of $C^R = 9$ percent of par, they would have to buy the bond at a value, or price, below par: The bond would have to be purchased at a discount from its par, $V_0^B < F$. In contrast, if the coupon rate is equal to the discount rate (i.e., $R = 9$ percent), then the bond's value would be equal to its par value, $V_0^B = F$. In this case, investors would be willing to pay \$1,000 for this bond, with each investor receiving \$90 each year in coupons. Finally, if the required rate is lower than the coupon rate, then investors would be willing to pay a premium over par for the bond, $V_0^B > F$. This might occur if bonds with comparable features were trading at rates below 9 percent. In this case, investors would be willing to pay a price above \$1,000 for a bond with a coupon rate of 9 percent.

In addition to the above relations, the relation between the coupon rate and required rate also explains how the bond's value changes over time. If the required rate is constant over time, and if the coupon rate is equal to it (i.e., the bond is priced at par), then the value of the bond will always be equal to its face value throughout the life of the bond. This is illustrated in Exhibit 3.1 by the horizontal line that shows that the value of the 9 percent coupon bond is always equal to the par value. Here investors would pay \$1,000 regardless of the terms to maturity. On the other hand, if the required rate is constant over time and the coupon rate is less (i.e., the bond is priced at a discount), then the value of the bond will increase as it approaches maturity; if the required rate is constant and the coupon rate is greater (i.e., the bond is priced at

EXHIBIT 3.1   The Value Over Time of an Original 10-Year, 9 Percent Annual Coupon Bond Selling at Par, Discount, and Premium

Year	Discount Bond Price of Bond Selling to Yield 11%	Par Bond Price of Bond Selling to Yield 9%	Premium Bond Price of Bond Selling to Yield 7%
10	$882.22	$1,000.00	$1,140.47
9	$889.26	$1,000.00	$1,130.30
8	$897.08	$1,000.00	$1,119.43
7	$905.76	$1,000.00	$1,107.49
6	$915.39	$1,000.00	$1,095.33
5	$926.08	$1,000.00	$1,082.00
4	$937.95	$1,000.00	$1,067.74
3	$951.13	$1,000.00	$1,052.49
2	$965.75	$1,000.00	$1,036.16
1	$981.98	$1,000.00	$1,018.69
0	$1,000.00	$1,000.00	$1,000.00

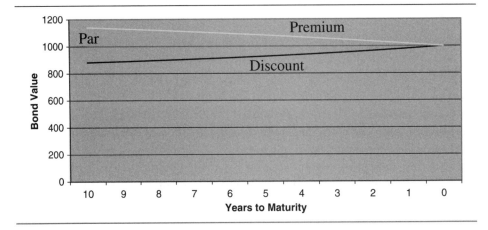

a premium), then the value of the bond will decrease as it approaches maturity. These relationships are also illustrated in Exhibit 3.1.

Another bond relationship to note is the inverse relation between the price of the bond and its rate of return. That is, given known coupon and principal payments, the only way an investor can obtain a higher rate of return on a bond is for its price (value) to be lower. In contrast, the only way for a bond to yield a lower rate is for its price to be higher. Thus, an inverse relationship exists between the price of a bond and its rate of return.

Finally, it should be noted that a bond's price sensitivity to interest rate changes and will be greater the longer its maturity and the lower its coupon rate. Specifically, the greater the bond's term to maturity, the greater its price sensitivity to a given change in interest rates. This relationship can be seen by comparing the price sensitivity to interest rate changes of the 10-year, 9 percent coupon bond in our above example with a 1-year, 9 percent coupon bond. If the required rate is 10 percent for both bonds, then the 10-year bond would trade at $938.55, whereas the 1-year bond would trade at $990.91 ($1,090/1.10). If the interest rate decreases to 9 percent for each bond (a 10 percent change in rates), both bonds would increase in price to $1,000. For the 10-year bond, the percentage increase in price would be 6.55 percent [($1,000 − $938.55)/$938.55], whereas the percentage increase for the 1-year bond would be only 0.9 percent. Thus, the 10-year bond's price is more sensitive to the interest rate change than the 1-year bond. Similarly, a lower coupon bond's price is more responsive to a given interest rate change than the price of the higher coupon bond.

Valuing Bonds with Different Cash Flows and Compounding Frequencies

Equation (3.2) defines the value of a bond that pays coupons on an annual basis and a principal at maturity. Bonds, of course, differ in the frequency in which they pay coupons each year, and many bonds have maturities less than one year. Also, when investors buy bonds, they often do so at noncoupon dates. Equation (3.2), therefore, needs to be adjusted to take these practical factors into account.

Semiannual Coupon Payments

Many bonds pay coupon interest semiannually. When bonds make semiannual payments, three adjustments to Equation (3.2) are necessary: (1) The number of periods is doubled; (2) the annual coupon rate is halved; (3) the annual discount rate is halved. Thus, if our illustrative 10-year, 9 percent coupon bond trading at a quoted annual rate of 10 percent paid interest semiannually instead of annually, it would be worth $937.69:

$$V_0^B = \sum_{t=1}^{20} \frac{\$45}{(1.05)^t} + \frac{\$1,000}{(1.05)^{20}} = \$937.69$$

$$V_0^B = \$45 \left[\frac{1 - [1/(1.05)]^{20}}{0.05} \right] + \frac{\$1,000}{(1.05)^{20}} = \$937.69$$

Note that the rule for valuing semiannual bonds is easily extended to valuing bonds paying interest even more frequently. For example, to determine the value of a bond paying interest four times a year, we would quadruple the periods and quarter the annual coupon payment and discount rate. In general, if we let n be equal to the number of payments per year (i.e., the compoundings per year), M be equal to the maturity in years, R^A be the discount rate quoted on an annual basis (simple annual rate), and R be equal to the periodic rate, then we can express the general formula for valuing a bond as follows:

$$V_0^B = \sum_{t=1}^{N} \frac{C^A/n}{(1 + (R^A/n))^t} + \frac{F}{(1 + (R^A/n))^{Mn}}$$ (3.3)

where:

$$
\begin{aligned}
C^A &= \text{annual coupon} = (C^R)(F) \\
n &= \text{number of payments per year} \\
\text{Periodic coupon} &= \text{annual coupon}/n \\
M &= \text{term to maturity in years} \\
N &= \text{number of periods to maturity} = (n)(M) \\
\text{Required periodic rate} &= R = \text{annual rate}/n = R^A/n
\end{aligned}
$$

Valuing Zero-Coupon Bonds with Maturities Less than One Year

Some bonds do not make any periodic coupon payments. Instead, the investor realizes interest as the difference between the maturity value and the purchase price. These bonds are called *zero-coupon bonds* (also called *zeros* and *pure discount bonds*, PDB). The value of a zero-coupon bond is

$$V_0^B = \frac{F}{(1 + R)^N}$$

For example, a zero-coupon bond maturing in 10 years and paying a maturing value of $1,000 would be valued at $385.54 if the required rate is 10 percent and annual compound is assumed:

$$V_0^B = \frac{\$1,000}{(1.10)^{10}} = \$385.54$$

If the convention is to double the number of years and half the annual discount rate, then the bond would be valued at $376.89 to yield a semiannual rate of 5 percent, simple annual rate of 10 percent, and effective annual rate of 10.25 percent ($= 1.05)^2 - 1$):

$$V_0^B = \frac{\$1,000}{(1.05)^{20}} = \$376.89$$

Many *zero-coupon bonds* have maturities less than a year. In valuing such bonds, the convention is to discount by using an annual rate and to express the bond's maturity as a proportion of a year. Thus, on March 1 a zero-coupon bond promising to pay $100 on September 1 (184 days) and trading at an annual discount rate of 8 percent would be worth $96.19:

$$V_0^B = \frac{\$100}{(1.08)^{184/365}} = \$96.19$$

Valuing Bonds at Noncoupon Dates

The above equations for pricing a bond are for valuing at dates in which the coupons are to be paid in exactly one period. However, most bonds purchased are not bought on coupon dates, but rather at dates between coupon dates. An investor who purchases a bond between coupon payments must compensate the seller for the coupon interest earned from the time of the last coupon payment to the settlement date of the bond. This amount is known as *accrued interest* (*AI*). (An exception to this rule would occur when a bond is in default. Such a bond is said to be quoted flat, that is, without accrued interest.) The formula for determining accrued interest is:

$$AI = \text{Coupon} \left[\frac{\text{Number of Days from Last Coupon to Settlement Date}}{\text{Number of Days in the Coupon Period}} \right]$$

For U.S. Treasury coupon securities, the convention is to use the actual number of days since the last coupon date and the actual number of days between coupon payments: an actual/actual ratio. For example, consider a T-note whose last coupon payment was on March 1 and whose next coupon is six months later on September 1. Suppose the note is purchased with a settlement date of July 20. The actual number of days in the coupon period (sometime referred to as the basis) is 184 days, and the actual number of days between coupons is 43:

- July 20 to July 31 = 11 days.
- August = 31 days.
- September 1 = 1 day.
- Total = 43 days.

For corporate, agency, and municipal bonds, the practice is to use 30-day months and a 360-day year: 30/360 ratio for which each month is assumed to have 30 days and each year is assumed to have 360 days. If the preceding T-note were a corporate credit with a 30/360 day count convention, then the number of days in the coupon period would be 180 and the days between coupons would be 41:

- Remainder of July = 10 days.
- August = 30 days.

- September 1 = 1 day.
- Total = 41 days.

In trading bonds on a noncoupon date, the amount the buyer pays to the seller is the agreed-upon price plus the accrued interest. This amount is often called the *full-price* or *dirty price*. The price of a bond without accrued interest is called the *clean price*:

$$\text{Full Price} = \text{Clean Price} + \text{Accrued Interest}$$

The full price of the bond can be found by doing the following:

1. Move to the next coupon date and determine the value of the bond at that date based on the future coupons.
2. Add the coupon at the next coupon date to the value of the bond.
3. Discount the bond value plus coupon back to the current date.

Thus, the 8 percent corporate bond maturing in 2019, purchased with a settlement date of July 20, 2013, at a required yield of 10 percent would have value of 91.693586 per $100 face at the next coupon date. Discounting the sum of that value and the $4 coupon back to the settlement date (0.227778 years) yields the full-bond price of $94.636:

- Value of the bond at next coupon date in 41 days or 41/180 = 0.227778 year.
- Value of the bond at the next coupon date plus coupon paid at that date.

$$V^B = \sum_{t=1}^{11} \frac{\$4}{(1.05)^t} + \frac{\$100}{(1.05)^{11}} = \$91.693586$$

$$\$91.693586 + \$4 = \$95.693586$$

- Current value of the bond—full price:

$$V^B = \frac{\$95.693586}{(1.05)^{0.227778}} = \$94.636$$

The full or dirty price of $94.636 includes the portion of the coupon interest the buyer will receive but the seller has earned. Even though the price the buyer pays the seller is the full price, in the United States the convention is to quote a bond's clean price. In this example, given that there are 41 days to the next coupon and 180 days in the coupon period, the number of days from the last coupon is 139 (= 180 − 41). The accrued interest (*AI*) per $100 par is $3.0222, and the clean price or flat price is

$91.547 (full price minus the *AI*):

$$AI = \$4(139/180) = \$3.089$$
$$\text{Clean Price} = 94.636 - \$3.089 = \$91.547$$

Exhibit 3.2 shows Bloomberg Description and Yield Analysis (YAS) screens for a Procter & Gamble bond that pays an annual coupon of 2.3 percent, principal of $1,000, and matures on 2/6/2022. On 7/5/2013, the bond was trading at 96.335 per $100 face value (clean price). As shown on the bond's YAS screen, the bond has a settlement date of 7/10/2013, 154 days of accrued interest on that date of $9.84 (for $1,000 face), and an invoice price of $973.19. Finally, the bond yields a rate of return of 2.7834 percent; that is, 2.7834 percent is the discount rate that equates the price of the bond to the present value of its semiannual coupon payments and principal payment at 2/6/2022.

Price Quotes, Fractions, and Basis Points

Whereas many corporate bonds pay principals of $1,000, this is not the case for many non-corporate bonds and other fixed income securities. As a result, many traders quote bond prices as a percentage of their par value. For example, if a bond is selling at par, it would be quoted at 100 (100 percent of par); thus, a bond with a face value of $10,000 and quoted at 80 1/8 would be selling at (0.80125)($10,000) = $8,012.50. When a bond's price is quoted as a percentage of its par, the quote is usually expressed in points and fractions of a point, with each point equal to $1. Thus, a quote of 97 points means that the bond is selling for $97 for each $100 of par. The fractions of points differ among bonds. Fractions are either in thirds, eighths, quarters, halves, or 64ths. On a $100 basis, a 1/2 point is $0.50 and a 1/32 point is $0.03125. A price quote of 97 4/32 (97 − 4) is 97.125 for a bond with a 100 face value. It should also be noted that when the yield on a bond or other security changes over a short period, such as a day, the yield and subsequent price changes are usually quite small. As a result, fractions on yields are often quoted in terms of basis points (bp). A bp is equal to 1/100 of a percentage point, or 100 bps = 1 percent. Thus, 6.5 percent may be quoted as 6 percent plus 50 bps or 650 bps, and an increase in yield from 6.5 percent to 6.55 percent would represent an increase of 5 bps.

Exhibit 3.3 shows the Bloomberg FIT screen showing the prices and yields of U.S. Treasury bonds, Treasury notes, and Treasury bills that were recently issued and actively traded as of 2/15/2013. As shown on the screen, there is an approximate 10-year T-note paying a coupon of 2 percent. The Bloomberg description screen (DES) for the Treasury provides more details; specifically, the bond was issued on 2/15/13, matures on 2/15/23, pays a 2 percent coupon semiannually, its average quoted bid and ask prices from dealers (ALLQ screen) are 94-11 and 94-12. The Bloomberg yield analysis (YAS) screen shows that for an investment period from the settlement date of 7/8/13 to the 2/15/23 maturity, the yield or total return on the bond

EXHIBIT 3.2   P&G Bond, Bloomberg Screens: DES and YAS

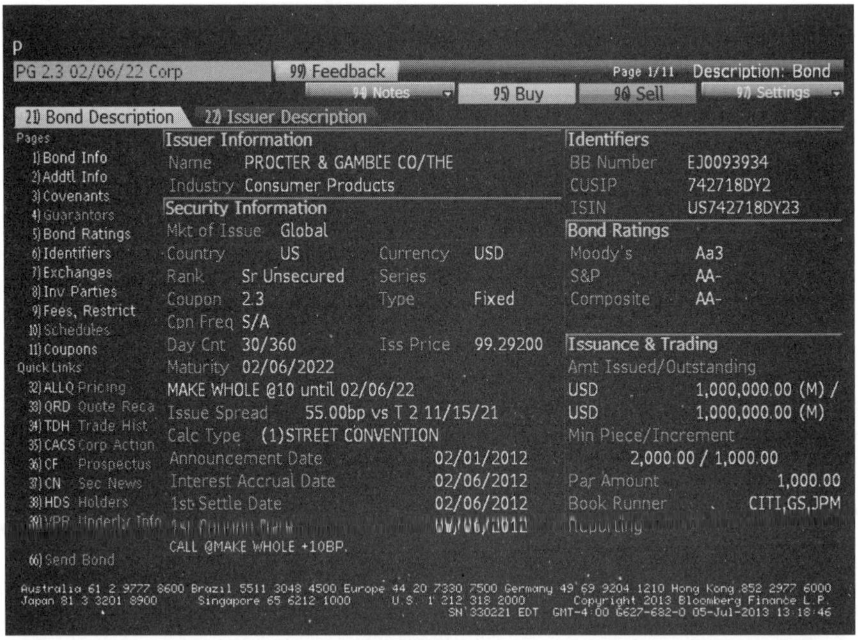

(a)

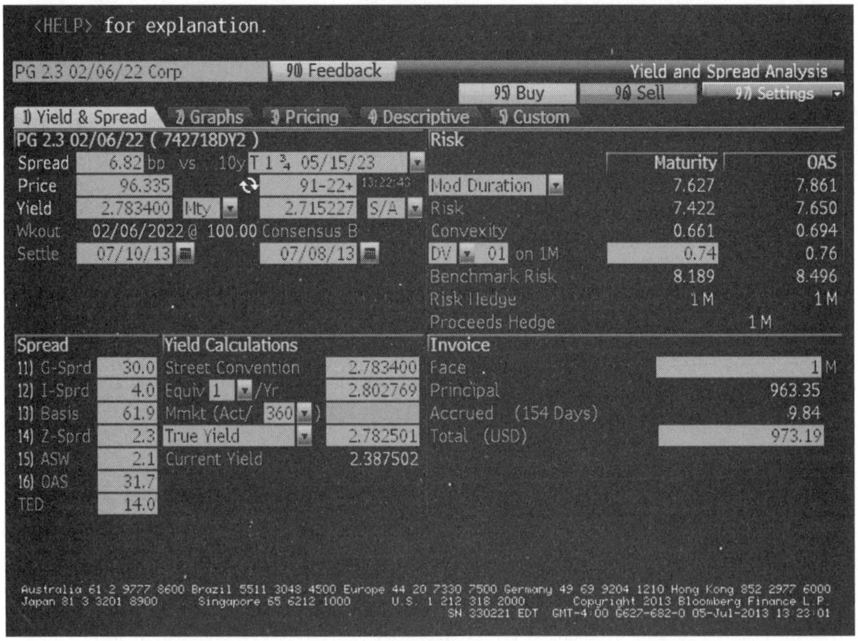

(b)

EXHIBIT 3.3   Bloomberg Price Quotes and Descriptions of U.S. Treasury Securities: Bloomberg FIT, YAS, Cash Flows (CSHF), Composite Quotes (ALLQ)

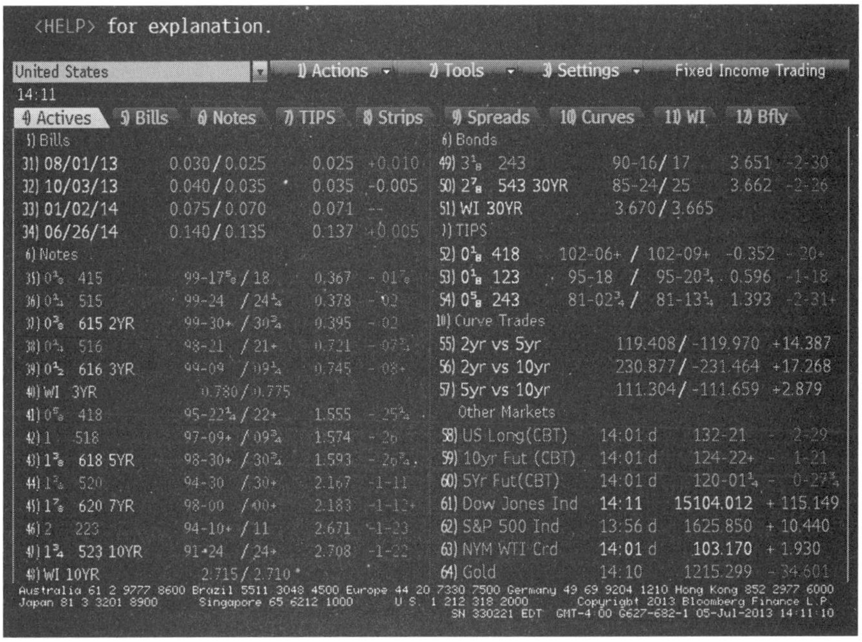

(a)

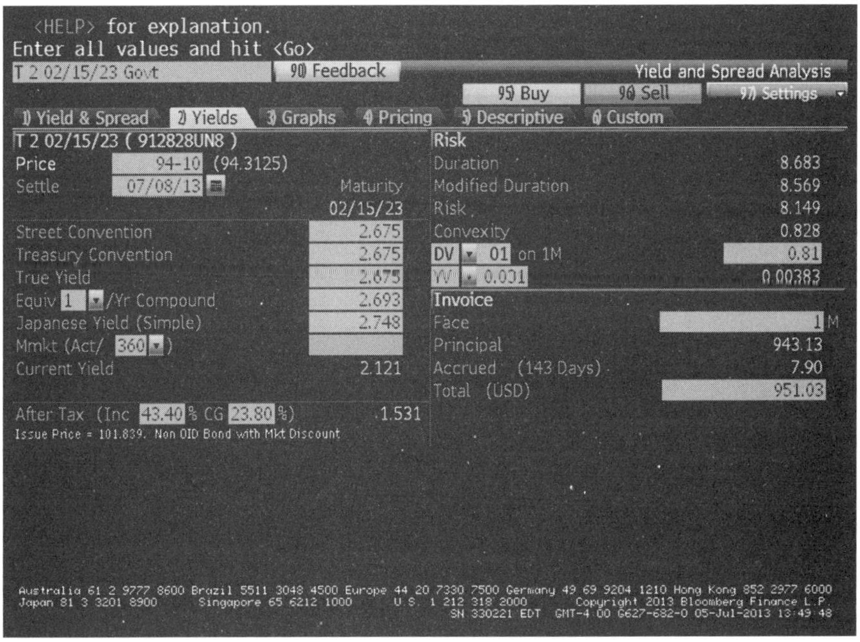

(b)

(*Continued*)

EXHIBIT 3.3   (*Continued*)

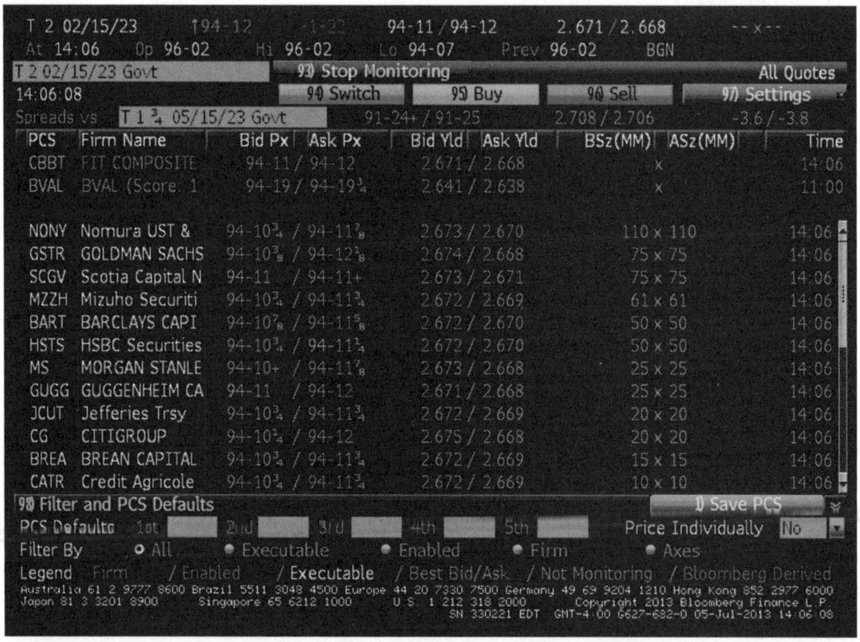

(c)

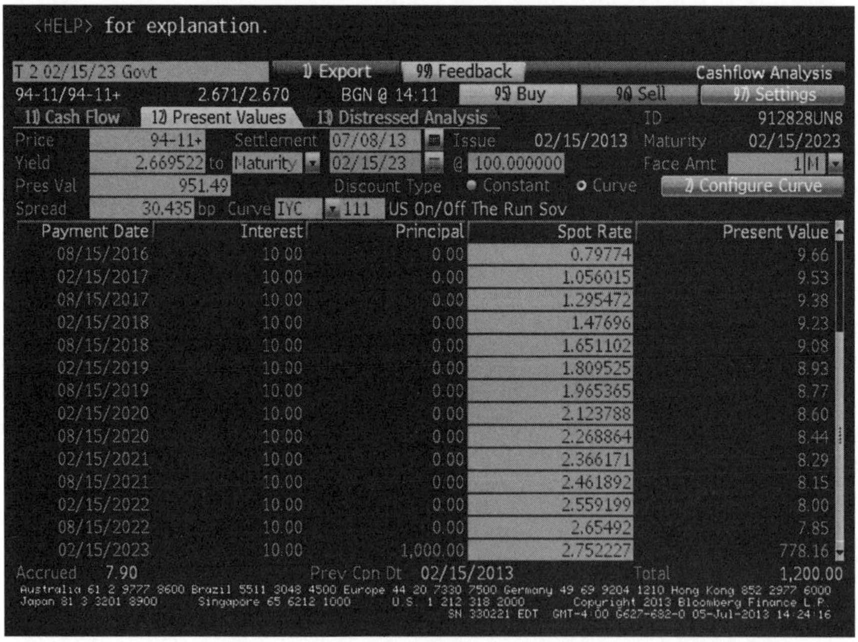

(d)

(with semiannual compounding) is 2.675 percent given a clean price of 94-10 (94.3125 per $100 face); the full price is $951.03, and the accrued interest is 7.90 per $1,000 face.

The Yield to Maturity and Other Rates of Return Measures for Bonds

The financial markets serve as conduits through which funds are distributed from borrowers to lenders. The allocation of funds is determined by the relative rates paid on bonds, loans, and other financial securities, with the differences in rates among claims being determined by risk, maturity, and other factors that serve to differentiate the claims. There are a number of different measures of the rates of return on bonds and loans. Some measures, for example, determine annual rates based on cash flows received over 365 days, whereas others use 360 days; some measures determine rates that include the compounding of cash flows, whereas some do not; and some measures include capital gains and losses, whereas others exclude price changes. In this section, we examine some of the measures of rates of return, including the most common measure—the yield to maturity—and in subsequent sections we look at three other important rate measures for bonds—the spot rate, the total return, and the geometric mean.

Common Measures of Rates of Return

When the term "rate of return" is used, it can mean a number of different rates, including the interest rate, coupon rate, current yield, or discount yield. The term *interest rate* is sometimes referred to the price a borrower pays a lender for a loan. Unlike other prices, this price of credit is expressed as the ratio of the cost or fee for borrowing and the amount borrowed. This price is typically expressed as an annual percentage of the loan (even if the loan is for less than one year). Today, financial economists often refer to the yield to maturity on a bond as the interest rate. In this book, the term interest rate will mean yield to maturity.

Another measure of rate of return is a bond's *coupon rate*. As noted in the last section, the coupon rate, C^R, is the contractual rate the issuer agrees to pay each period. It is usually expressed as a proportion of the annual coupon payment to the bond's face value:

$$C^R = \frac{\text{Annual Coupon}}{F}$$

Unless the bond is purchased at par, the coupon rate is not a good measure of the bond's rate of return because it fails to take into account the price paid for the bond.

In examining corporate bond quotes, the *current yield* on a bond is often provided. This rate is computed as the ratio of the bond's annual coupon to its current price. This measure provides a quick estimate of a bond's rate of return, but in many cases not an accurate one because it does not capture price changes. The current yield is a good approximation to the bond's yield, if the bond's price is selling at or near its face value or if it has a long maturity. That is, we noted earlier that if a bond is selling at par, its coupon rate is equal to the discount rate. In this case, the current yield is equal to the bond's yield to maturity. Thus, the closer the bond's price is to its face value, the closer the current yield is to the bond's yield to maturity. As for maturity, note that a coupon bond with no maturity or repayment of principal, known as a *perpetuity* or *consul,* pays a fixed amount of coupons forever. As shown in Exhibit 3.4, the value of such a bond is:

$$V_0^B = \sum_{t=1}^{\infty} \frac{C}{(1+R)^t} \rightarrow \frac{C}{R}$$

If the bond is priced in the market to equal V_0^B, then the rate on the bond would be equal to the current yield: $R = C/V_0^B$. Thus, when a coupon bond has a long-term

EXHIBIT 3.4   Value of Perpetuity

$$V_0^B = \sum_{t=1}^{\infty} \frac{C}{(1+R)^t} = \frac{C}{(1+R)^1} + \frac{C}{(1+R)^2} + \frac{C}{(1+R)^3} + \cdots$$

Factor out C·

$$V_0^B = C\left[\frac{1}{(1+R)^1} + \frac{1}{(1+R)^2} + \frac{1}{(1+R)^3} + \cdots\right]$$

Multiply through by $(1+R)$

$$V_0^B(1+R) = C\left[1 + \frac{1}{(1+R)^1} + \frac{1}{(1+R)^2} + \frac{1}{(1+R)^3} + \cdots\right]$$

Subtract V_0^B from both sides

$$V_0^B(1+R) - V_0^B = C\left[1 + \frac{1}{(1+R)^1} + \frac{1}{(1+R)^2} + \frac{1}{(1+R)^3} + \cdots\right] - V_0^B$$

Note: $V_0^B = C\left[\frac{1}{(1+R)^1} + \frac{1}{(1+R)^2} + \frac{1}{(1+R)^3} + \cdots\right]$. Thus

$$V_0^B(1+R) - V_0^B = C\left[1 + \frac{1}{(1+R)^1} + \frac{1}{(1+R)^2} + \frac{1}{(1+R)^3} + \cdots\right]$$
$$-C\left[\frac{1}{(1+R)^1} + \frac{1}{(1+R)^2} + \frac{1}{(1+R)^3} + \cdots\right]$$

$$V_0^B(1+R) - V_0^B = C$$

$$V_0^B[(1+R) - 1] = C$$

$$V_0^B R = C$$

$$V_0^B = \frac{C}{R}$$

EXHIBIT 3.4 *(Continued)*

$$V_0^S = \sum_{t=1}^{\infty} \frac{d_0(1+g)^t}{(1+k_e)^t} = \frac{d_0(1+g)^1}{(1+k_e)^1} + \frac{d_0(1+g)^2}{(1+k_e)^2} + \frac{d_0(1+g)^3}{(1+k_e)^3} + \cdots$$

Factor out d_0.

$$V_0^S = d_0 \left[\frac{(1+g)^1}{(1+k_e)^1} + \frac{(1+g)^2}{(1+k_e)^2} + \frac{(1+g)^3}{(1+k_e)^3} + \cdots \right]$$

Multiply through by $(1+k_e)/(1+g)$

$$V_0^S \left[\frac{1+k_e}{1+g} \right] = d_0 \left[1 + \frac{(1+g)^1}{(1+k_e)^1} + \frac{(1+g)^2}{(1+k_e)^2} + \frac{(1+g)^3}{(1+k_e)^3} + \cdots \right]$$

Subtract V_0^S from both sides

$$V_0^S \left[\frac{1+k_e}{1+g} \right] - V_0^S = d_0 \left[1 + \frac{(1+g)^1}{(1+k_e)^1} + \frac{(1+g)^2}{(1+k_e)^2} + \frac{(1+g)^3}{(1+k_e)^3} + \cdots \right] - V_0^S$$

Note: $V_0^S = d_0 \left[\dfrac{(1+g)^1}{(1+k_e)^1} + \dfrac{(1+g)^2}{(1+k_e)^2} + \dfrac{(1+g)^3}{(1+k_e)^3} + \cdots \right]$. Thus

$$V_0^S \left[\frac{1+k_e}{1+g} \right] - V_0^S = d_0 \left[1 + \frac{(1+g)^1}{(1+k_e)^1} + \frac{(1+g)^2}{(1+k_e)^2} + \frac{(1+g)^3}{(1+k_e)^3} + \cdots \right]$$

$$- d_0 \left[\frac{(1+g)^1}{(1+k_e)^1} + \frac{(1+g)^2}{(1+k_e)^2} + \frac{(1+g)^3}{(1+k_e)^3} + \cdots \right]$$

$$V_0^S \left[\frac{1+k_e}{1+g} \right] - V_0^S = d_0$$

$$V_0^S \left[\left[\frac{1+k_e}{1+g} \right] - 1 \right] = d_0$$

$$V_0^S \left[\left[\frac{1+k_e}{1+g} \right] - \left[\frac{1+g}{1+g} \right] \right] = d_0$$

$$V_0^S \left[\frac{k_e - g}{1+g} \right] = d_0$$

$$V_0^S = \frac{d_0(1+g)}{k_e - g} = \frac{d_1}{k_e - g}$$

maturity (e.g., 20 years), then it is similar to a perpetuity, making its current yield a good approximation of its rate of return.

Finally, the *discount yield* is the bond's return expressed as a proportion of its face value. For example, a one-year zero-coupon bond costing $900 and paying a par value of $1,000 yields $100 in interest and a discount yield of 10 percent:

$$\text{Discount Yield} = \frac{F - P_0}{F} = \frac{\$100}{\$1,000} = 0.10$$

The discount yield used to be the rate frequently quoted by financial institutions on their loans (because the discount rate is lower than a rate quoted on the borrowed amount). The difficulty with this rate measure is that it does not capture the conceptual notion of the rate of return being the rate at which the investment grows. In this example, the $900 bond investment grew at a rate of over 11 percent, not 10 percent:

$$\frac{F - P_0}{P_0} = \frac{\$100}{\$900} = 0.111$$

Because of tradition, the rates on Treasury bills are quoted by dealers in terms of the bills' discount yield (R_D). Whereas Treasury bills have maturities less than one year, the discount yields are quoted on an annualized basis. Dealers quoting the annualized rates use a day count convention of actual days to maturity but with a 360-day year:

$$\text{Annual Discount Yield} = R_D = \frac{F - P_0}{F} \frac{360}{\text{Days to Maturity}}$$

Given the dealer's discount yield, the bid or ask price can be obtained by solving the yield equation for the bond's price, P_0. Doing this yields.

$$P_0 = F\left[(1 - R_D(\text{Days to Maturity}/360)\right]$$

Yield to Maturity

The most widely used measure of a bond's rate of return is the *yield to maturity* (YTM). As noted previously, the YTM, or simply the yield, is the rate that equates the purchase price of the bond, P_0^B, with the present value of its future cash flows. Mathematically, the YTM (y) is found by solving the following equation for y (YTM):

$$P_0^B = \sum_{t=1}^{M} \frac{CF_t}{(1 + y)^t} \tag{3.4}$$

The YTM is analogous to the internal rate of return used in capital budgeting. It is a measure of the rate at which the investment grows. From our first example, if the 10-year, 9 percent annual coupon bond were actually trading in the market for $938.55, then the YTM on the bond would be 10 percent. The 2.3 percent P&G bond with a maturity of 2/16/2022 shown in Exhibit 3.2, in turn, is priced at 96.335 (per $100 face value). At the 7/10/13 settlement date, the cost of the bond (per $1,000 face value) is $973.19 (equal to the clean price of $963.35 plus 9.84 of 154 days of accrued interest). Based on this cost and using semiannual compounding the annualized yield of the P&G bond is 2.7824 percent. Unlike the current yield, the YTM incorporates all of the bonds cash flows (CFs). It also assumes the bond is held to maturity and that of all CFs from the bond are reinvested to maturity at the calculated YTM.

Estimating YTM: Average Rate to Maturity

If the cash flows on the bond (coupons and principal) are not equal, then Equation (3.4) cannot be solved directly for the YTM. Alternatively, one must use an iterative (trial and error) procedure: substituting different y values into Equation (3.4), until that y is found that equates the present value of the bond's cash flows to the market price. An estimate of the YTM, however, can be found using the bond's *average rate to maturity* (ARTM; also referred to as the *yield approximation formula*). This measure determines the rate as the average return per year as a proportion of the average price of the bond per year. For a coupon bond with a principal paid at maturity, the average return per year on the bond is its annual coupon plus its average annual capital gain. For a bond with an M-year maturity, its average gain is calculated as the total capital gain realized at maturity divided by the number of years to maturity: $(F - P_0^B)/M$. The average price of the bond is computed as the average of two known prices, the current price and the price at maturity (F): $(F + P_0^B)/2$. Thus, the ARTM is:

$$\text{ARTM} = \frac{C + [(F - P_0^B)/M]}{(F + P_0^B)/2} \tag{3.5}$$

The ARTM for the 10-year, 9 percent annual coupon bond trading at \$938.55 is 0.0992:

$$\text{ARTM} = \frac{\$90 + [(\$1,000 - \$938.55)/10]}{(\$1,000 + \$938.55)/2} = 0.0992$$

Bond Equivalent Yields

The YTM calculated above represents the yield for the period (in the above example this was an annual rate, given annual coupons). If a bond's *CF*s were semiannual, then solving Equation (3.4) for y would yield a six-month rate; if the *CF*s were monthly, then solving (3.4) for y would yield a monthly rate. To obtain a *simple annualized rate* (with no compounding), y^A, one needs to multiply the periodic rate, y, by the number of periods in the year. Thus, if a 10-year bond paying \$45 every six months and \$1,000 at maturity were selling for \$937.69, its six-month yield would be 0.05 and its simple annualized rate, y^A, would be 10 percent:

$$\$937.69 = \sum_{t=1}^{20} \frac{\$45}{(1+y)^t} + \frac{\$1,000}{(1+y)^{20}} \Rightarrow y = 0.05$$

$$y^A = \text{Simple Annualized Rate} = (n)(y) = (2)(0.05) = 0.10$$

In this example, the simple annualized rate is obtained by determining the periodic rate on a bond paying coupons semiannually and then multiplying by two. Because Treasury bonds and many corporate bonds pay coupons semiannually, the rate obtained by multiplying the semiannual periodic rate by two is called the *bond-equivalent yield*. Bonds with different payment frequencies often have their rates expressed in terms of their bond-equivalent yields so that their rates can be compared to each other on a common basis. This bond-equivalent yield, though, does not take into account the reinvestment of the bond's cash flows during the year. Therefore, it underestimates the actual rate of return earned. Thus, an investor earning 5 percent semiannually would have $1.05 after six months from a $1 investment that she can reinvest for the next six months. If she reinvests at 5 percent, then her annual rate would be 10.25 percent $(= (1.05)(1.05) - 1 = (1.05)^2 - 1)$, not 10 percent. As noted earlier, the 10.25 percent annual rate, which takes into account compounding, is known as the effective rate.

Yield to Call, Yield to Put, and Yield to Worst

Yield to Call

Many bonds have a call feature that allows the issuer to buy back the bond at a specific price known as the call price (CP). Given a bond with a call option, the *yield to call* (YTC) is the rate obtained by assuming the bond is called on the call date. Like the YTM, the YTC is found by solving for the rate that equates the present value of the *CF*s to the market price:

$$P_0^B = \sum_{t=1}^{N_{CD}} \frac{CF_t}{(1+y)^t} + \frac{CP}{(1+y)^{N_{CD}}}$$

where:
$\quad CP$ = call price
$\quad N_{CD}$ = number of periods to the call date

Thus, a 10-year, 9 percent coupon bond callable in 5 years at a call price of $1,100, paying interest semiannually and trading at $937.69, would have a YTM of 10 percent and an annualized YTC of 12.2115 percent:

$$\$937.69 = \sum_{t=1}^{10} \frac{\$45}{(1+y)^t} + \frac{\$1,100}{(1+y)^{10}} \quad \Rightarrow \quad YTC = 0.0610575$$

Simple Annualized YTC = (2)(0.0610575) = 0.122115

Yield to Put

An issue can be putable, allowing the bondholder the right to sell the bond back to the issuer at a specified price, known as the put price (PP). As with callable bonds, putable bonds can have a constant put price or a put schedule. When a bond is putable, the convention is to calculate the yield to put (YTP). Like the YTM and YTC, the YTP is found by solving for the rate that equates the present value of the *CF*s to the market price:

$$P_0^B = \sum_{t=1}^{N_{PD}} \frac{CF_t}{(1 + YTP)^t} + \frac{PP}{(1 + YTP)^{N_{PD}}}$$

where:

PP = put price
N_{PD} = number of periods to the put date

A 10-year, 9 percent coupon bond, first putable in five years at a put price of $950, paying interest semiannually and trading at $937.69, would have an annualized YTP of 9.807741 percent:

$$\$937.69 = \sum_{t=1}^{10} \frac{\$45}{(1 + YTP)^t} + \frac{\$950}{(1 + YTP)^{10}} \Rightarrow YTP = 0.04903870$$

Simple Annualized YTP = (2)(.04903870) = 0.09807741

Yield to Worst

Many investors calculate the YTC for all possible call dates and the YTP for all possible put dates, as well as the YTM. They then select the lowest of the yields as their yield return measure. The lowest yield is sometimes referred to as the *yield to worst.* Exhibit 3.5 shows the Bloomberg call schedule from the Bloomberg's YAS screen (Call tab) for a 3.5 percent Dow Chemical bond with a maturity of 12/15/16. The Dow bond has a YTM of 3.766 percent, yield to the first call of 6.5866 percent, and a yield to worst of 3.766 percent.

Bond Portfolio Yields

The yield for a portfolio of bonds is found by solving the rate that will make the present value of the portfolio's cash flow equal to the market value of the portfolio. For example, a portfolio consisting of a two-year, 5 percent annual coupon bond priced at par (100) and a three-year, 10 percent annual coupon bond priced at 107.87 to yield 7 percent (YTM) would generate a three-year cash flow of $15, $115, and $110 and would have a portfolio market value of $207.87. The rate that equates this portfolio's cash flow to its portfolio value is 6.2 percent:

$$\$207.87 = \frac{\$15}{(1 + y)^1} + \frac{\$115}{(1 + y)^2} \frac{\$110}{(1 + y)^3} \Rightarrow y = 0.062$$

EXHIBIT 3.5 Call Schedule and Yield-to-Call Calculations, Bloomberg YAS Screen (Call Tab)

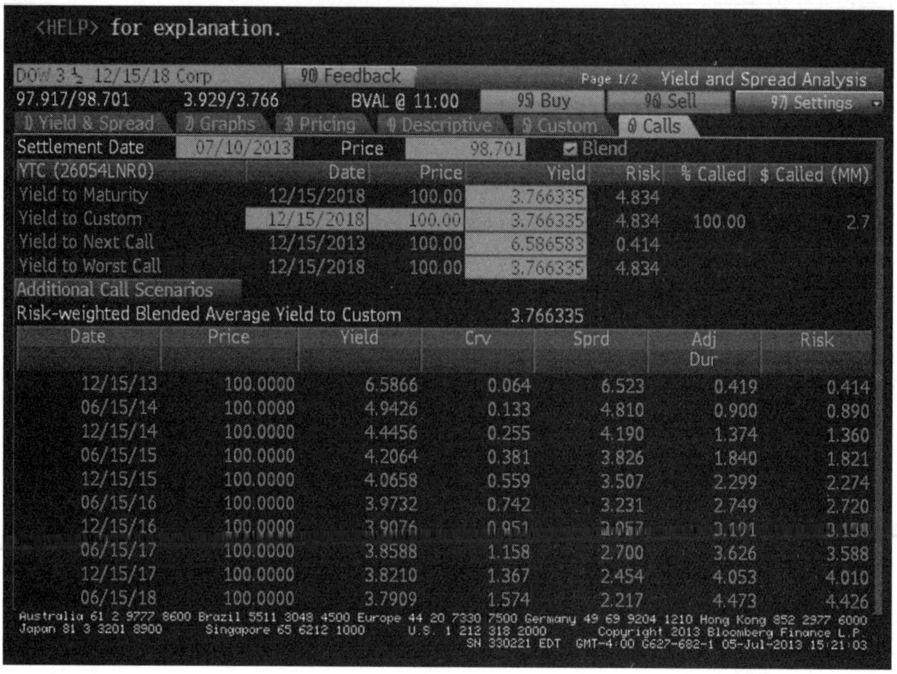
<HELP> for explanation.

DOW 3 ½ 12/15/18 Corp | 90 Feedback | Page 1/2 Yield and Spread Analysis

97.917/98.701 3.929/3.766 BVAL @ 11:00 | 95 Buy | 96 Sell | 97 Settings

1) Yield & Spread | 2) Graphs | 3) Pricing | 4) Descriptive | 5) Custom | 6) Calls

Settlement Date 07/10/2013 Price 98.701 Blend

YTC (26054LNR0)	Date	Price	Yield	Risk	% Called	$ Called (MM)
Yield to Maturity	12/15/2018	100.00	3.766335	4.834		
Yield to Custom	12/15/2018	100.00	3.766335	4.834	100.00	2.7
Yield to Next Call	12/15/2013	100.00	6.586583	0.414		
Yield to Worst Call	12/15/2018	100.00	3.766335	4.834		

Additional Call Scenarios

Risk-weighted Blended Average Yield to Custom 3.766335

Date	Price	Yield	Crv	Sprd	Adj Dur	Risk
12/15/13	100.0000	6.5866	0.064	6.523	0.419	0.414
06/15/14	100.0000	4.9426	0.133	4.810	0.900	0.890
12/15/14	100.0000	4.4456	0.255	4.190	1.374	1.360
06/15/15	100.0000	4.2064	0.381	3.826	1.840	1.821
12/15/15	100.0000	4.0658	0.559	3.507	2.299	2.274
06/15/16	100.0000	3.9732	0.742	3.231	2.749	2.720
12/15/16	100.0000	3.9076	0.951	2.957	3.191	3.158
06/15/17	100.0000	3.8588	1.158	2.700	3.626	3.588
12/15/17	100.0000	3.8210	1.367	2.454	4.053	4.010
06/15/18	100.0000	3.7909	1.574	2.217	4.473	4.426

Australia 61 2 9777 8600 Brazil 5511 3048 4500 Europe 44 20 7330 7500 Germany 49 69 9204 1210 Hong Kong 852 2977 6000
Japan 81 3 3201 8900 Singapore 65 6212 1000 U.S. 1 212 318 2000 Copyright 2013 Bloomberg Finance L.P.
SN 330221 EDT GMT-4:00 G627-682-1 05-Jul-2013 15:21:03

Note that this yield is not the weighted average of the YTMs of the bonds comprising the portfolio. In this example, the weighted average (R_p) is 6.04 percent:

$$R_p = w_1(YTM_1) + w_2(YTM_2)$$

$$R_p = \left[\frac{\$100}{\$207.87}\right](0.05) + \left[\frac{\$107.87}{\$207.87}\right](0.07) = 0.0604$$

Rate on Zero-Coupon Bond

Whereas no algebraic solution for the YTM exists when a bond pays coupons and principal that are not equal, a solution does exist in the case of a zero-coupon bond or pure discount bonds (PDBs; we will use both expressions) in which there is only one cash flow (F). That is

$$P_0^B = \frac{F}{(1 + YTM_M)^M}$$

$$(1 + YTM_M)^M = \frac{F}{P_0^B} \tag{3.6}$$

$$YTM_M = \left[\frac{F}{P_0^B}\right]^{1/M} - 1$$

where M = maturity in years. Thus, a zero-coupon bond with a par value of $1,000, a maturity of three years, and trading for $800 would have an annualized YTM of 7.72 percent:

$$YTM_3 = \left[\frac{\$1{,}000}{\$800}\right]^{1/3} - 1 = 0.0772$$

If the convention is to assume semiannual compounding, then the semiannual YTM would be 3.798 percent and the simple annual rate or bond-equivalent yield would be 7.55782 percent:

$$M = 3\,\text{years}$$
$$n = \text{compound frequency} = 2$$
$$N = nM = (2)(3) = 6$$
$$\text{Semiannual YTM} = \left[\frac{\$1{,}000}{\$800}\right]^{1/6} - 1 = 0.03789$$
$$\text{Bond-Equivalent Yield} = (2)(0.03789) = 0.075782$$

Similarly, a pure discount bond paying $100 at the end of 182 days and trading at $96 would yield an annual rate of 8.53 percent (using a 365-day year):

$$YTM = \left[\frac{\$100}{\$96}\right]^{365/182} - 1 = 0.0853$$

Total Return

Equation (3.6) provides the formula for finding the YTM for a zero-discount bond. A useful extension of Equation (3.6) is the *total return* (*TR*), also called the *realized return* and *average realized return* (ARR). The total return is the yield obtained by assuming the cash flows are reinvested to the investor's horizon at an assumed reinvestment rate and at the horizon the bond is sold at an assumed rate given the horizon is not maturity or pays its principal if the horizon is maturity. The *TR* is computed by first determining the investor's horizon, HD; next, finding the HD value, defined as the total funds the investor would have at HD; and third, solving for the *TR* using a formula for the zero-coupon bond [Equation (3.6)].

To illustrate, suppose an investor buys a four-year, 10 percent coupon bond, paying coupons annually, and selling at its par value of $1,000. Assume the investor needs cash at the end of year three (HD = 3), is certain he can reinvest the coupons during the period in securities yielding 10 percent, and expects to sell the bond at his HD at a rate of 10 percent. To determine the investor's *TR*, we first need to find the HD value. This value is equal to the price the investor obtains from selling the bond at HD and the value of the coupons at the HD. In this case, the investor, at his HD, will be able to sell a one-year bond paying a $100 coupon and a $1,000 par at maturity for $1,000, given an assumed discount rate of 10 percent:

$$P_0^B = \frac{\$100 + \$1,000}{(1.10)^1} = \$1,000$$

Also at the HD, the $100 coupon paid at the end of the first year will be worth $121, given the assumption it can be reinvested at 10 percent for two years and there is annual compounding, $100(1.10)^2 = \$121$, and the $100 received at the end of year two will, in turn, be worth $110 in cash at the HD, $100(1.10) = \$110$. Finally, at the HD the investor would receive his third coupon of $100. Combined, the investor would have $1,331 in cash at the HD: HD value = $1,331. The horizon value of $1,330 consists of a bond valued at $1,000, coupons of $300, and interest earned from reinvesting coupons of $31 (HD coupon value – total coupon received = $331 – $300 – $31; see Exhibit 3.6). Note that if the rates at which coupons can be reinvested

EXHIBIT 3.6   Total Realized Return

• Example: You buy 4-year, 10% annual coupon bond
  at par (F = 1,000). *Assuming* you can reinvest CFs at
  10%, your *TR* would be 10%:

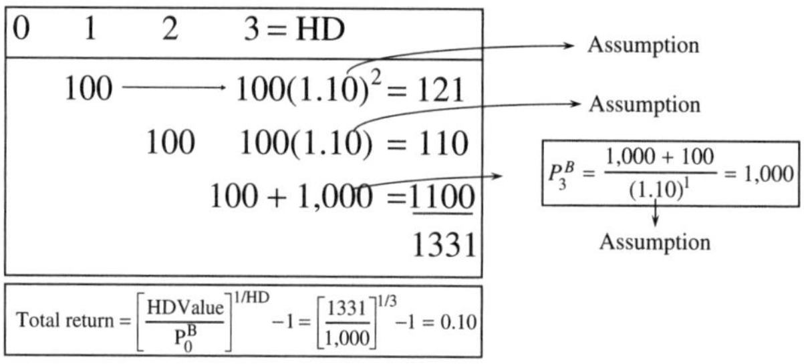

$$\text{Coupon Value} = \sum_{t=0}^{HD-1} C(1+R)^t = \$100 \left[\frac{(1.10)^3 - 1}{.10}\right] = \$331$$

Interest on Interest = $331 − $300 = $30

$$P_{HD}^B = \frac{\$1,000 + \$100}{1.10} = \$1,000$$

Horizon Value = Coupon Value + P_{HD}^B = $331 + $1,000 = $1,331

$$\$1,000 = \frac{\$1,331}{(1 + \text{Total return})^3}$$

$$\text{Total return} = \left[\frac{\$1,331}{\$1,000}\right]^{1/3} - 1 = 0.10$$

(reinvestment rates) are the same (as assumed in this example), then the coupon value at the horizon would be equal to the periodic coupon times the future value of an annuity of ($FVIF_a$):

$$\text{Coupon Value at HD} = \sum_{t=0}^{HD-1} C(1+R)^t$$

$$\text{Coupon Value at HD} = C \sum_{t=0}^{HD-1} (1+R)^t$$

$$\text{Coupon Value at HD} = C\, FVIF_a$$

$$\text{Coupon Value at HD} = C \left[\frac{(1+R)^{HD} - 1}{R} \right]$$

$$\text{Coupon Value at HD} = \$100 \left[\frac{(1.10)^3 - 1}{0.10} \right] = \$331$$

The reinvestment income or interest earned from reinvesting coupons (interest on interest), in turn, is equal to the coupon value at HD minus the total coupons received, $(N)(C)$:

$$\text{Reinvestment Income} = \text{Coupon Value at HD} - \text{Total Coupons}$$

$$\text{Reinvestment Income} = \sum_{t=0}^{HD-1} C(1+R)^t - (N)(C)$$

$$\text{Reinvestment Income} = \$100 \left[\frac{(1.10)^3 - 1}{0.10} \right] - (3)(\$100)$$

$$\text{Reinvestment Income} = \$331 - \$300 = \$31$$

Given the HD value of \$1,331, the *TR* is found in the same way as the YTM for a zero-coupon bond. In this case, a \$1,000 investment in a bond returning \$1,331 at the end of three years yields a total return of 10 percent:

$$P_0^B = \frac{\text{HD Value}}{(1+\ TR)^{HD}}$$

$$(1+TR)^{HD} = \frac{\text{HD Value}}{P_0^B}$$

$$TR = \left[\frac{\text{HD Value}}{P_0^B} \right]^{1/HD} - 1 \tag{3.7}$$

$$TR = \left[\frac{\$1,331}{\$1,000} \right]^{1/3} - 1 = 0.10$$

Note that the total return is the rate that makes the initial investment grow to equal the horizon value. That is, $1,000 grows at an annual rate of 10 percent to equal the horizon value of $1,331 at the end of year three:

$$\$1,000(1.10)^3 = \$1,331$$

The total return can be applied to any period length. For example, if the four-year bond purchased by the investor made semiannual payments and the six-month yield were at 5 percent (a simple annual yield of 10 percent and an effective annual yield of 10.25 percent $[=(1.05)^2 -1)]$, then the investor's coupon value, reinvestment income, price at HD, and HD value at his HD would respectively be $340.10, $40.10, $1,000, and $1,340.10 (see Exhibit 3.7):

$$\text{Coupon Value} = \sum_{t=0}^{6-1} \$50\,(1.05)^t = \$50 \left[\frac{(1.05)^6 - 1}{0.05} \right] = \$340.10$$

$$\text{Reinvestment Income} = \$340.10 - (6)(\$50) = \$40.10$$

$$\text{HD Price} = \sum_{t=1}^{6} \frac{\$50}{(1.05)^t} + \frac{\$1,000}{(1.05)^6} = \$50 \left[\frac{1 - (1/(1.05)^6)}{0.05} \right]$$

$$+ \frac{\$1,000}{(1.05)^6} = \$1,000$$

$$\text{HD Value} = \$340.10 + \$1,000 = \$1,340.10$$

The investor's semiannual total return would be 5 percent, the simple annual rate would be 10 percent, and the effective annual rate would be 10.25 percent:

$$\text{Semiannual Total Return} = \left[\frac{\$1,340.10}{\$1,000} \right]^{1/6} - 1 = 0.05$$

$$\text{Simple Annual Rate} = 2 \left[\left[\frac{\$1,340.10}{\$1,000} \right]^{1/6} - 1 \right] = 0.10$$

$$\text{Effective Annual Rate} = (1.05)^2 - 1 = 0.1025$$

In this example, the semiannual TR of 5 percent is the same rate at which the bond was purchased; that is, a 10 percent coupon bond, paying interest twice a year, and selling at par, yields a semiannual YTM of 5 percent and bond-equivalent yield of 10 percent. In this case, obtaining a total return equal to the initial YTM should not be surprising because the coupons are assumed to be reinvested at the same semiannual rate as the initial YTM (5 percent) and the bond is also assumed to be sold at that rate as well (recall, the YTM measure assumes that all coupons are reinvested at the calculated YTM).

EXHIBIT 3.7 Total Realized Return with Semiannual Cash Flows

Maturity = 4-years, annual coupon rate = 10%, interest paid semiannually, par = $1,000, reinvestment rate = 5% semiannually, purchase price = $1,000, horizon = 3 years, bond expected to sell at the HD at a 5% semiannual rate.

Horizon Value = $1,340, Semiannual Total Return = 5%, Simple Total Return = 10%, and Effective Total Rate = 10.25%:

Year 0.0	0.5	1.0	1.5	2.0	2.5	3.0		Values
	$50.00						$50(1.05)^5$	$63.81
		$50.00					$50(1.05)^4$	$60.78
			$50.00				$50(1.05)^3$	$57.88
				$50.00			$50(1.05)^2$	$55.13
					$50.00		$50(1.05)^1$	$52.50
						$50.00	$50	$50.00
						$1,000.00	$50/1.05+($1,050/(1.05)^2$	$1,000.00
							Horizon Value	$1,340.10

$$\text{Coupon Value} = \sum_{t=0}^{6-1} \$50(1.05)^t = \$50 \left[\frac{(1.05)^6 - 1}{0.05} \right] = \$340.10$$

Interest on Interest = $340.10 − $300 = $40.10

$$\text{Horizon Price} = P_{HD}^B = \frac{\$50}{1.05} + \frac{\$50 + \$1,000}{(1.05)^2} = \$1,000$$

HD Value = $340.10 + $1,000 = $1,340.10

$$\text{Initial Price} = \sum_{t=1}^{6} \frac{\$50}{(1.05)^t} + \frac{\$1,000}{(1.05)^6} = \$50 \left[\frac{1 - (1/(1.05)^6)}{0.05} \right] + \frac{\$1,000}{(1.05)^6} = \$1,000$$

$$\text{Semiannual Total Return} = \left[\frac{\$1,340.10}{\$1,000} \right]^{1/6} - 1 = 0.05$$

$$\text{Simple Annualized Rate} = 2 \left[\left[\frac{\$1,340.10}{\$1,000} \right]^{1/6} - 1 \right] = 0.10$$

Effective Annual Rate = $(1.05)^2 - 1 = 0.1025$

It should be noted that the yield on the Procter & Gamble bond shown on the YAS screen in Exhibit 3.2 is obtained by using a total return calculation and assuming the coupons are reinvested at the YTM.

Market Risk and Horizon Analysis

If the coupons in our above total return examples were expected to be reinvested at different rates or the bonds sold at a different YTM, then a total return equal to the initial

YTM would not have been realized. For example, if the rates on all maturities were to increase from 10 percent to 12 percent (simple annual rate), just after the four-year, 10 percent bond was purchased at par, then the total semiannual total return would decrease to 4.8735 percent and the simple annual rate would be 9.7471 percent:

$$\text{Coupon Value at HD} = \sum_{t=0}^{HD-1} \$50(1+R)^t = \$50 \left[\frac{(1.06)^6 - 1}{0.06} \right] = \$348.77$$

$$\text{Reinvestment Income} = \$348.77 - (6)(\$50) = \$48.77$$

$$\text{HD Price}: P_{HD}^B = \frac{\$50}{(1.06)} + \frac{\$1,000 + \$50}{(1.06)^2} = \$981.67$$

$$\text{Horizon Value} = \text{Total Dollar Return} + P_{HD}^B = \$348.77 + \$981.67$$
$$= \$1,330.44$$

$$\text{Total Return} = \left[\frac{\$1,330.44}{\$1,000} \right]^{1/6} - 1 = 0.048735$$

$$\text{Simple Annualized Total Return} = (?)(0.048735) - 0.097471$$

In this case, the rate increase has augmented the reinvestment income by $0.67 from to $48.10 to $48.77, but it has also lowered the horizon price by $18.33 from $1,000 to $981.67. As a result, the price decrease has reduced the total return more than the interest-on-interest increase has increased the realized return. Thus, the increase in rates from 10 percent to 12 percent lowers the total return from 10 percent to 9.7471 percent.

Exhibit 3.8 shows the Bloomberg Total Return Analysis (TRA) screen for the P&G bond paying a coupon of 2.3 percent and maturing on 2/6/22 with a settlement date of 7/10/13 and a selected one-year horizon. The screen shows the calculated price of the bond at the horizon at the yield reflecting the different yield shifts ranging from plus 75 basis points to minus 75 basis points and the total return based on the price, coupon, and interest on interest at the horizon.

The possibility of the actual return on a bond deviating from the expected return because of a change in interest rates is known as *market risk*. As illustrated in the above total return example, a change in interest rates has two effects on a bond's return. First, interest rate changes affect the price of a bond; this is referred to as *price risk*. If the investor's horizon is different from the bond's maturity date, then the investor will be uncertain about the price he will receive from selling the bond (if HD < M), or the price he will have to pay for a new bond (if HD > M). Also, as we noted earlier in discussing the properties of bonds, the price of a bond is inversely related to interest rates and is more price responsive to a change in interest rates if it has a longer term to maturity and its coupon rates are less. Thus, if interest rates change, the price effect on the total return will be negative (i.e., lower rates increase the horizon price and therefore the total return), with the effect being greater for bonds with greater terms to maturity and lower coupon rates. Secondly, interest rate changes affect the return the investor expects from reinvesting the coupon—*reinvestment risk*. If an investor

EXHIBIT 3.8 Total Return, P&G Bond

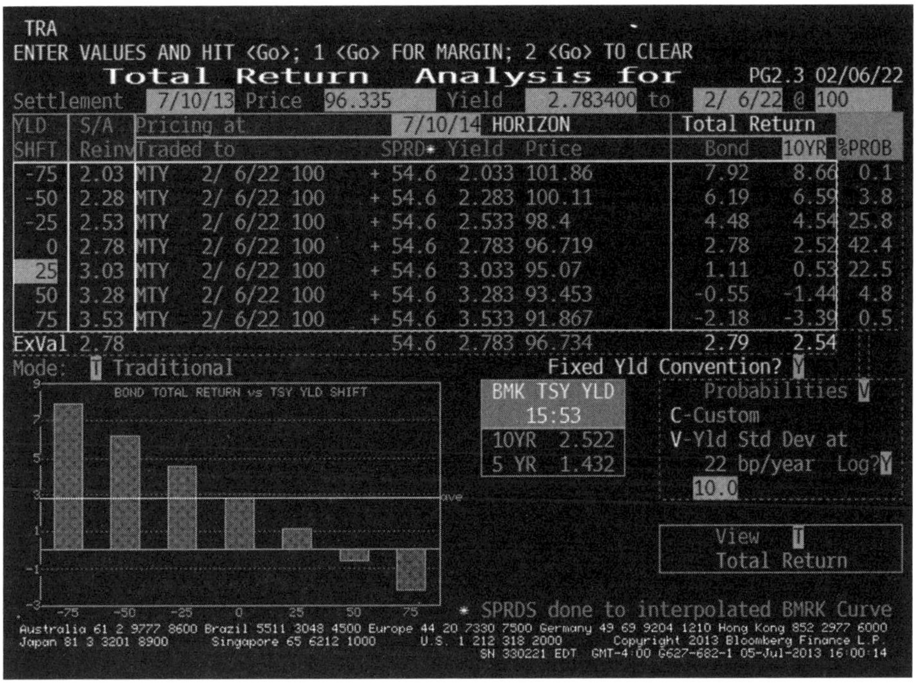

buys a coupon bond, he automatically is subject to market risk. Thus, if interest rates change, the interest-on-interest effect on the total return will be direct (i.e., greater rates increase the reinvestment return and therefore the total return), with the effect being greater for bonds with greater coupon rates.

One way to evaluate market risk for a bond is to estimate the bond's total returns given different interest rate scenarios. Such analysis is known at *horizon analysis.* Moreover, by conducting horizon analysis on one or more bonds or bond portfolios, an investor or portfolio manager can project the performance of the bonds or portfolios and can compare different bonds or bond portfolios based on a planned investment horizon and expectations concerning the market. Exhibit 3.9 shows the total returns for a three-year horizon for four bonds with different coupons and maturities under three interest rate scenarios: yields stay at 7.5 percent, yields decrease to 5 percent, and yields increase to 10 percent. For each scenario, it is assumed the reinvestment rate and the rate for determining the horizon price of the bond are equal to the scenario yield. In terms of market risk, Bond A has the smallest deviations in total returns, with the lowest rate being 7.23 percent and the highest being 7.77 percent. Bond A's total return also decreases when rates decrease and increases when rates increase, suggesting Bond A's interest-on-interest effect dominates its price effect. In contrast, longer-term Bond D has the greatest market risk, with the range in total returns being 2.01 percent to 13.8 percent, and with its total return increasing when rates decrease and decreasing when rates increase, implying its price effect dominates its interest-on-interest effect.

EXHIBIT 3.9   Horizon Analysis

Total returns for a 3-year horizon for four bonds under three interest rate scenarios: yields stay at 7.5%, yields decrease to 5%, and yields increase to 10%. For each scenario it is assumed the reinvestment rate and the rate for determining the horizon price of the bond are equal to the scenario yield.

Bond	Annual Coupon Rate	Maturity	Price at 7.5%	Total Return 5.00%	Total Return 7.50%	Total Return 10.00%
A	10.00%	3 yrs	106.61	7.23%	7.50%	7.77%
B	7.50%	5 yrs	100.00	8.59%	7.50%	6.48%
C	10.00%	10 yrs	117.37	10.85%	7.50%	4.47%
D	5.00%	15 yrs	77.71	13.80%	7.50%	2.01%

Horizon = 3 years
Semi-annual payments
Yield same on all matuirites

Ultimately, which bond an investor should select depends on her expectations about futures interest rates and the degree of market risk she wants to assume. Horizon analysis, though, is a useful tool for analyzing market risk and facilitating bond investment decisions.

BLOOMBERG BOND YIELD AND RETURN ANALYSIS SCREENS

Bloomberg Bond Yield Analysis Screen: YAS calculates the yield on the bond given the bond's prices using different market conventions: Current yield = coupon / price; street convention = yield based on the convention the bond is calculated on in the market; corporate bond equivalent, and after-tax yield (see Exhibits 3.2 and 3.3).

   Bond Payment Schedule: The **CSHF** screen shows the bond's cash-flow schedule. On the CSHF screen, you can select either the cash flow or its present value.

   FIHZ Screen: The BLOOMBERG FIHZ Screen calculates the total return on a selected bond. You can select the horizon period, the discount yield at the HD, and the reinvestment rate.

   COMP Screen: Historical Comparative Return Screen compares a bond's historical total returns with a comparable bond index and other selected bonds.

   Bloomberg Total Return Screen: The **TRA** screen calculates total returns given different interest rate cases. You can select different horizons, reinvestment rates (semiannual rate, S/A Reinv), and yield shifts (YLD SHFT). See Exhibit 3.8.

   FISA: FISA compares and analyzes the profit/loss and percentage return of a selected bond under different scenarios based on changes in specific yields, dates, reinvestment rates, or specified yield curve shifts.

   See Bloomberg Web Exhibit 3.1.

Spot Rates and Equilibrium Prices

The rate on a zero-coupon bond is called the *spot rate*. We previously examined how bonds are valued by discounting their cash flows at a common discount rate. Given different spot rates on similar bonds with different maturities, the correct approach to valuing a bond, however, is to price it by discounting each of the bond's *CF*s by the appropriate spot rates for that period (S_t). Theoretically, if the market does not price a bond with spot rates, arbitrageurs would be able to realize a free lunch by buying the bond and stripping it into a number of zero-coupon bonds or by buying strip bonds and bundling them into a coupon bond to sell. Thus, in the absence of arbitrage, the *equilibrium price* of a bond is determined by discounting each of its *CF*s by its appropriate spot rates.

To illustrate this relationship, suppose there are three risk-free zero-coupon bonds, each with principals of $100 and trading at annualized spot rates of $S_1 = 7$ percent, $S_2 = 8$ percent, and $S_3 = 9$ percent, respectively. If we discount the *CF* of a three-year, 8 percent coupon bond, paying an $8 coupon annually and a principal of $100 at maturity at these spot rates, its equilibrium price, P_0^*, would be $97.73:

$$P_0^* = \frac{C_1}{(1+S_1)^1} + \frac{C_2}{(1+S_2)^2} + \frac{C_3+F}{(1+S_3)^3}$$

$$P_0^* = \frac{\$8}{(1.07)^1} + \frac{\$8}{(1.08)^2} + \frac{\$108}{(1.09)^3} = \$97.73$$

Suppose this coupon bond is trading in the market at a price (P_0^B) of $95.03 to yield 10 percent:

$$P_0^B = \sum_{t=1}^{3} \frac{\$8}{(1.10)^t} + \frac{\$100}{(1.10)^3} = \$95.03$$

At the price of $95.03, an arbitrageur could buy the bond, then strip it into three risk-free zero-coupon bonds: a one-year zero paying $8 at maturity, a two-year zero paying $8 at maturity, and a three-year zero bond paying $108 at maturity. If the arbitrageur could sell the bonds at their appropriate spot rates, she would be able to realize an initial cash flow (CF_0) from the sale of 97.73 and a risk-free profit of $2.70 (see Exhibit 3.10). Given this risk-free opportunity, this arbitrageur, as well as others, would exploit this strategy of buying and stripping the bond until the price of the coupon bond was bid up to equal its equilibrium price of $97.73.

However, if the 8 percent coupon bond were trading above its equilibrium price of $97.73, then arbitrageurs could profit by reversing the above strategy. For example, if the coupon bond were trading at $100, then arbitrageurs would be able to go into the market and buy proportions (assuming perfect divisibility) of the three pure discount bonds (8 percent of Bond 1, 8 percent of Bond 2, and 108 percent of Bond 3) at a cost of $97.73, and bundle them into one three-year, 8 percent coupon bond to be

EXHIBIT 3.10   Equilibrium Bond Price: Arbitrage for Underpriced Bond

---

Market price of 3-year, 8% coupon bond $= 95.03$
Arbitrage:
  Buy the bond for 95.03
  Sell three stripped zeros:

  1-year zero with $F = 8 : P_0 = \dfrac{8}{1.07} = 7.4766$

  2-year zero with $F = 8 : P_0 = \dfrac{8}{(1.08)^2} = 6.8587$

  3-year zero with $F = 108 : P_0 = \dfrac{108}{(1.09)^3} = 83.3958$

  Sale of stripped bonds $= \$97.73$
$CF_0 = 97.73 - 95.03 = 2.70$

EXHIBIT 3.11   Equilibrium Bond Price Arbitrage for Overpriced Bond

---

Market price of 3-year, 8% coupon bond $= 100$.
Arbitrage:
  Buy 3 zeros:

  8% of 1-year zero with $F = 100 :$ Cost $= (0.08)\dfrac{100}{1.07} = 7.4766$

  8% of 2-year zero with $F = 100 :$ Cost $= (0.08)\dfrac{100}{(1.08)^2} = 6.8587$

  108% of 3-year zero with $F = 100 :$ Cost $= (1.08)\dfrac{100}{(1.09)^3} = 83.3958$

  Cost $= 7.4766 + 6.8587 + 83.3958 = 97.73$
  Bundle the bonds and sell them as 3-year, 8% coupon bond for 100
$CF_0 = 100 - 97.73 = 2.27$

---

sold at \$100. As shown in Exhibit 3.11, this strategy would result in a risk-free cash flow of \$2.27.

BLOOMBERG SCREENS FOR STRIPS AND STRIP ANALYSIS

CSHF Screen: On the CSHF screen for a selected bond, one determines the present value of each payment using spot rates selected from a yield curve. See the CSHF screen for the Treasury security in Exhibit 3.3.

Strip Analysis Screen, SP: On the SP screen, one can analyze stripping a selected bond of its interest and principal payments.

Treasury Strips: U.S. Treasury Strip securities can be found from FIT, Strips Tab, and using the SECF screen.

See Bloomberg Web Exhibit 3.2.

Geometric Mean

Another useful measure of the return on a bond is its *geometric mean*. Conceptually, the geometric mean can be viewed as an average of current and future rates. To see this, consider one of our previous examples in which we computed a YTM of 7.72 percent for a zero-discount bond selling for $800 and paying $1,000 at the end of year three. The rate of 7.72 percent represents the annual rate at which $800 must grow to be worth $1,000 at the end of three years assuming annual compounding. If we do not restrict ourselves to the same rate in each year, then there are other ways $800 could grow to equal $1,000 at the end of three years. For example, suppose one-year bonds are currently trading at a 10 percent rate, a one-year bond purchased one year from the present is expected to yield 8 percent ($R_{Mt} = R_{11} = 8$ percent), and a one-year bond to be purchased two years from the present is expected to be 5.219 percent ($R_{Mt} = R_{12} = 5.219$ percent). With these rates, $800 would grow to $1,000 at the end of year 3. Specifically, $800 after the first year would be $880 = $800(1.10)$, after the second, $950.40 = $800(1.10)(1.08)$, and after the third, $1,000 = $800(1.10)(1.08)(1.05219)$. Thus, an investment of $800 that yielded $1,000 at the end of three years could be thought of as an investment that yielded 10 percent the first year, 8 percent the second, and 5.219 percent the third. Moreover, 7.72 percent can be viewed not only as the annual rate at which $800 grows to equal $1,000, but also as the average of three rates: one-year rates today ($R_{Mt} = R_{10}$), one-year rates available one year from the present ($R_{Mt} = R_{11}$), and one-year rates available two years from the present ($R_{Mt} = R_{12}$):

$$P_0^B(1 + \text{YTM}_M)^M = F = P_0^B[(1 + R_{11})(1 + R_{11})(1 + R_{12})(1 + R_{13}) \cdots (1 + R_{1,M-1})]$$

$$(1 + \text{YTM}_M)^M = \frac{F}{P_0^B} = [(1 + R_{11})(1 + R_{11})(1 + R_{12})(1 + R_{13}) \cdots (1 + R_{1,M-1})]$$

$$(1.0772)^3 = \frac{\$1,000}{\$800} = [(1.10)(1.08)(1.05219)] \tag{3.8}$$

Mathematically, the expression for the average rate on an *M*-year bond in terms of today's and future one-year rates (and assuming annual compounding) can be found by solving Equation (3.8) for YTM_M:

$$\text{YTM}_M = [(1 + R_{11})(1 + R_{11})(1 + R_{12})(1 + R_{13}) \cdots (1 + R_{1,M-1})]^{1/M} - 1$$
$$\text{YTM}_3 = [(1.10)(1.08)(1.05219)]^{1/3} - 1 = 0.0772 \tag{3.9}$$

Equation (3.9) defines the rate of return on an *M*-year bond in terms of expected future rates. A more practical rate than an expected rate, however, is the implied forward rate.

Implied Forward Rate

An implied forward rate, f_{Mt}, is a future rate of return implied by the present interest rate structure. This rate can be attained by going long and short in current bonds. To see this, suppose the rate on a one-year, zero-coupon bond is 10 percent (i.e., spot rate is $S_1 = 10$ percent) and the rate on a similar two-year zero is $S_2 = 9$ percent. Knowing these current rates, we could solve for f_{11} in the equation below to determine the implied forward rate. That is:

$$S_2 = [(1 + S_1)(1 + f_{11})]^{1/2} - 1$$
$$f_{11} = \frac{(1 + S_2)^2}{(1 + S_1)} - 1$$
$$f_{11} = \frac{(1.09)^2}{(1.10)} - 1 = 0.08$$

With one-year and two-year zeros presently trading at 10 percent and 9 percent, respectively, the rate implied on 1-year bonds to be bought one year from the present is 8 percent. This 8 percent rate, however, is simply an algebraic result. This rate actually can be attained by implementing the following locking-in strategy:

1. Execute a short sale by borrowing the one-year bond and selling it at its market price of $909.09 = $1,000/1.10 (or borrow $909.09 at 10 percent).
2. With two-year bonds trading at $841.68 = $1,000/(1.09)^2, buy $909.09/ $841.68 = 1.08 issues of the two-year bond.
3. At the end of the first year, cover the short sale by paying the holder of the one-year bond his principal of $1,000 (or repay loan).
4. At the end of the second year, receive the principal on the maturing two-year bond issue of (1.08)($1,000) = $1,080.

With this locking-in strategy the investor does not make an investment until the end of the first year when he covers the short sale; in the present, the investor simply initiates the strategy. Thus, the investment of $1,000 is made at the end of the first year. In turn, the return on the investment is the principal payment of $1,080 on the 1.08 holdings of the two-year bonds that comes one year after the investment is made. Moreover, the rate of return on this 1-year investment is 8 percent [($1,080 – $1,000)/ $1,000]. Hence, by using a locking-in strategy, an 8 percent rate of return on a one-year investment to be made one year in the future is attained, with the rate being the same rate obtained by solving algebraically for f_{11}.

Given the concept of implied forward rates, the geometric mean now can be formally defined as the geometric average of the current one-year spot rate and the implied forward rates:

$$YTM_M = [(1 + YTM_1)(1 + f_{11})(1 + f_{12})(1 + f_{13}) \cdots (1 + f_{1,M-1})]^{1/M} - 1 \quad (3.10)$$

Two points regarding the geometric mean should be noted. First, the geometric mean is not limited to one-year rates. That is, just as 7.72 percent can be thought of as an average of three one-year rates of 10 percent, 8 percent, and 5.219 percent, the implied rate on a two-year bond purchased at the end of one year, $f_{Mt} = f_{21}$, can be thought of as the average of one-year implied rates purchased one and two years, respectively, from now. Second, note that for bonds with maturities of less than one year, the same general formula for the geometric mean applies. For example, the annualized YTM on a zero-coupon maturing in 182 days (YTM_{182}) is equal to the geometric average of a current 91-day bond's annualized rate (YTM_{91}) and the annualized implied forward rate on a 91-day investment made 91 days from the present, $f_{91,91}$:[1]

BLOOMBERG FORWARD RATE CURVE MATRIX: FWCM

The FWCM screen can be used to find projected forward rates based on current interest rate.

Stock Valuation and Return

Stock Returns

An investor who has purchased common stock can expect to earn a possible return from the stock's periodic dividends, capital gains (or losses) when the stock is sold, and interest earned from reinvesting dividends. As noted, the stock's rate of return or yield is that rate that equates the present value of the stock's cash flow to its market price. For example, an investor planning to buy a stock currently priced in the market at $100 ($P_0$) and expected to pay dividends (d_t) of $10 in each of the next three years, and to sell for $100 at end of the third year (P_3), would expect to earn a rate of return of 10 percent; that is, the rate that equates the present value of the stock's expected cash flows to the market price of $100 is 10 percent:

$$P_0^S = \frac{d_1}{(1+R)^1} + \frac{d_2}{(1+R)^2} + \frac{d_3 + P_3^S}{(1+R)^3}$$

$$\$100 = \frac{\$10}{(1+R)^1} + \frac{\$10}{(1+R)^2} + \frac{\$10 + \$100}{(1+R)^3} \Rightarrow R = 0.10$$

Like the total return on a bond, the *total return on a stock* is obtained by assuming the expected cash flows (dividends) are reinvested to the investor's horizon at an assumed reinvestment rate and at the horizon the stock is valued at a forecasted expected price. In this case, the investor's total return would be 10 percent if she could reinvest the dividends at the discount rate of 10 percent and the stock was worth $100 at the investor's three-year horizon.

Year	1	2	3	CF	Values
	$10			$10(1.10)^2	$12.10
		$10		$10(1.10)	$11.00
			$10	$10	$10.00
			$P_3^S = \$100$	$100	$100
$P_0^S = \$100$				Horizon Value	$133.10

$$\text{Dividend Value} = \$10(1.10)^2 + \$10(1.10)^1 + 10 = \$33.10$$

$$\text{Dividend Value} = \sum_{t=0}^{3-1} \$10\,(1.10)^t = \$10\left[\frac{(1.10)^3 - 1}{0.10}\right] = \$33.10$$

$$\text{HD Value} = \text{Dividend Value} + P_3^S = \$33.10 + \$100 = \$133.10$$

Total return:

$$P_0^S = \frac{\text{HD Value}}{(1 + TR)^{HD}}$$

$$TR = \left[\frac{\text{HD Value}}{P_0^S}\right]^{1/HD} - 1$$

$$\$100 = \frac{\$133.10}{(1 + TR)^3}$$

$$TR = \left[\frac{\$133.10}{\$100}\right]^{1/3} - 1 = 0.10$$

BLOOMBERG TOTAL RETURN ANALYSIS FOR STOCK: TRA

The TRA screen for a selected stock can be used to analyze the historical cumulative total returns for a selected stock.

Stock Valuation

Alternatively, if an investor knows the rate she requires on a stock, then she can determine the value of the stock (V_0^S) by discounting the stock's expected cash flows by her required return. Thus, if our above investor required a rate of return of 10 percent on the stock based on her assessment of the stock's risk, then she would value the stock at

$100 and would consider the stock to be correctly priced if it were trading for $100 in the market:

$$V_0^S = \frac{\$10}{(1.10)^1} + \frac{\$10}{(1.10)^2} + \frac{\$10 + \$100}{(1.10)^3} = \$100$$

If she required a rate of return of 15 percent, however, then she would value the stock at $88.58 and would consider it to be overpriced at $100 and not a good investment:

$$V_0^S = \frac{\$10}{(1.15)^1} + \frac{\$10}{(1.15)^2} + \frac{\$10 + \$100}{(1.15)^3} = \$88.58$$

On the other hand, if the investor required a return of only 7.5 percent, then she would value the stock at $106.50 and consider it to be underpriced at $100 and therefore a good investment:

$$V_0^S = \frac{\$10}{(1.075)^1} + \frac{\$10}{(1.075)^2} + \frac{\$10 + \$100}{(1.075)^3} = \$106.50$$

Note, that like bonds, there is an inverse relationship between the value of stock and the required return.

In addition to determining the required return, the valuation of stocks also requires estimating dividends that can be expected to change over time given changes in the company's earnings and investment prospects. In valuing stocks, many analysts try to determine the stock's *growth rate* in dividends over time, g_t. Given the estimated growth rate, expected dividends can then be related to previous dividends to determine the stock's value. For example, suppose instead of a constant annual dividend of $10 over the next three years, the investor in the above example estimates that the projected future revenue of the company will result in an annual growth rate of 3 percent in dividends for the next three years. Given this growth rate, in year 1 the investor would expect a dividend of $10.30 [= $10(1+.03)]; in year two, $10.61 [= $10.30(1.03) = $10(1.03)^2]; and in year 3, $10.93 [= $10.61(1.03) = $10(1.03)^3]. Suppose the investor also projects that the company would be worth $109.30 at the end of year three and estimates her required rate of return to be 10 percent. Given these estimates, the investor would value the stock at $108.46:

$$V_0^S = \frac{\$10(1.03)}{(1.10)^1} + \frac{\$10(1.03)^2}{(1.10)^2} + \frac{\$10(1.03)^3 + \$109.30}{(1.10)^3} = \$108.46$$

Based on her cash flow analysis, the investor would consider the stock to be underpriced if it were trading below $108.46 in the market and overpriced if it were trading above $108.46.

Note, if the investor can reinvest her expected dividends at the discount rate of 10 percent to her three-year horizon, then her total return would be equal to the required return of 10 percent:

Year	0	1	2	3	CF	Values
		$10(1.03)$			$10(1.03)(1.10)^2$	$12.46
			$10(1.03)^2$		$10(1.03)^2 (1.10)$	$11.67
				$10(1.03)^3$	$10(1.03)^3$	$10.93
				$P_3^S = \$109.30$	$109.30	$109.30
	$P_0^S = \$108.46$				Horizon Value	$144.36

Total return:

$$P_0^S = \frac{\text{HD Value}}{(1 + TR)^{HD}}$$

$$TR = \left[\frac{\text{HD Value}}{P_0^S}\right]^{1/HD} - 1$$

$$\$108.46 = \frac{\$144.36}{(1 + TR)^3}$$

$$TR = \left[\frac{\$144.36}{\$108.46}\right]^{1/3} - 1 = 0.10$$

Fundamental Stock Valuation

The above example suggests that determining the value of a stock requires estimating the stock's growth rate in dividends, g, required return, k_e, and future price, V_t^S. Since the future price of a stock depends on the remaining future dividends, this valuation approach can be simplified by valuing the stock solely in terms of its future dividends. Thus, the stock value of a company expected to last N periods can be expressed as:

$$V_0^S = \sum_{t=1}^{N} \frac{d_t}{(1 + k_e)^t} = \frac{d_1}{(1 + k_e)^1} + \frac{d_2}{(1 + k_e)^2} + \cdots + \frac{d_N}{(1 + k_e)^N} \quad (3.11)$$

where: k_e = required rate ($k_e = R$).

This stock valuation expression can be simplified further by relating dividends in different periods to the growth rate in dividends: $d_t = d_{t-1} (1 + g_t)$, and by assuming the growth rate is constant over a certain number of periods. These assumptions allow one to relate dividends in one period all the way back to the current period. For example, if the growth rate in dividends is constant over the first T periods, as in our previous example ($T = 3$ years), then the dividend in period T can be related to the dividend in the current period, d_0:

$$d_T = d_0 (1 + g_t)^T$$

If we assume dividends will grow at a constant rate, g, over the entire life of the stock of N years, then the value of the stock would be:

$$V_0^S = \sum_{t=1}^{N} \frac{d_0(1 + g)^t}{(1 + k_e)^t} = \frac{d_0(1 + g)^1}{(1 + k_e)^1} + \frac{d_0(1 + g)^2}{(1 + k_e)^2} + \cdots + \frac{d_0(1 + g)^N}{(1 + k_e)^N} \quad (3.12)$$

Valuing a stock solely in term of its dividends and growth rate in dividends (and not in terms of its expected future prices), requires that one estimate the life of the firm—N. Most companies have an indefinite life, with many expected to last many years. It is interesting that, as N gets large, Equation (3.12) for the value of the stock approaches a maximum value equal to $d_1/(k_e - g)$ at a discrete N value, such as 30 to 50 years (see Exhibit 3.4 for a proof). The N value where a variable approaches its optimum (maximum or minimum) is known as the asymptote or critical number and the relationship is described as an asymptotic relation. Thus, for a company expected to have a constant growth rate in dividends for the next 40 to 50 years—a profile that describes many large, blue-chip companies—the value of its stock would be:

$$V_0^S = \sum_{t=1}^{N} \frac{d_0(1 + g)^t}{(1 + k_e)^t} = \frac{d_0(1 + g)^1}{k_e - g} = \frac{d_1}{k_e - g} \quad \text{for large N}$$

Thus, if the investor in our above example expected the stock to grow at an annual rate of 3 percent for a long time and required a return of $k_e = 0.10$, she would value the stock at \$147.14:

$$V_0^S = \frac{d_0(1 + g)^1}{k_e - g} = \frac{d_1}{k_e - g} = \frac{\$10(1.03)}{0.10 - 0.03} = \$147.14$$

Exhibit 3.12 shows the relation between value of the stock and its life, N. The graph highlights the asymptotic relation in which the stock value increases at a decreasing rate, with the asymptote occurring at N^* equal to 60, where the maximum stock price is approaching \$147: $d_1/(k_e - g) = \$10(1.03)/(0.10 - 0.03) = \$147$. Note that the value of the stock would still be \$147.14 even if the investor planned to sell the stock at a future horizon date, provided that the expected selling price at the investor's horizon is equal to the present value of the stock's future dividends. For example, in term of our previous example, if the investor's horizon were three years, then dividends in year four would be \$11.25 [= $\$10(1.03)^4$] and the value of the stock at year three

EXHIBIT 3.12   Stock Values for Different N

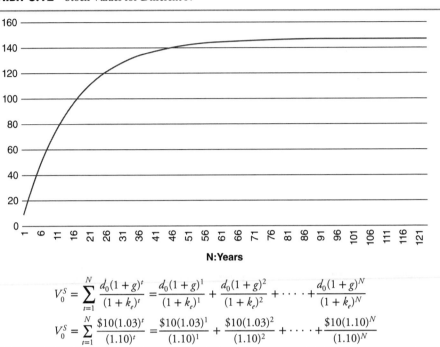

$$V_0^S = \sum_{t=1}^{N} \frac{d_0(1+g)^t}{(1+k_e)^t} = \frac{d_0(1+g)^1}{(1+k_e)^1} + \frac{d_0(1+g)^2}{(1+k_e)^2} + \cdots + \frac{d_0(1+g)^N}{(1+k_e)^N}$$

$$V_0^S = \sum_{t=1}^{N} \frac{\$10(1.03)^t}{(1.10)^t} = \frac{\$10(1.03)^1}{(1.10)^1} + \frac{\$10(1.03)^2}{(1.10)^2} + \cdots + \frac{\$10(1.10)^N}{(1.10)^N}$$

would be \$160.79. Discounting this value and the dividends back to the present yields a current value of the stock of \$147.14:

$$V_3^S = \frac{d_4}{k_e - g} = \frac{d_0(1+g)^4}{k_e - g} = \frac{\$10(1.03)^4}{0.10 - 0.03} = \frac{\$11.25}{0.10 - 0.03} = \$160.79$$

$$V_0^S = \frac{d_0(1+g)^1}{(1+k_e)^1} + \frac{d_0(1+g)^2}{(1+k_e)^2} + \frac{d_0(1+g)^3 + V_3^e}{(1+k_e)^3}$$

$$V_0^S = \frac{\$10(1.03)}{1.10} + \frac{\$10(1.03)^2}{(1.10)^2} + \frac{\$10(1.03)^3 + \$160.79}{(1.10)^3} = \$147.14$$

In practice, estimating a stock's future dividend growth is very challenging, requiring knowledge of the company's operations, the external factors that affect the company, and the company's investment opportunities. The two most important factors influencing the equity value of a company, however, are its potential earnings from current operations and its potential investments. Exhibit 3.13 shows Bloomberg dividend per share (DVD) and earnings per share (ERN) screens for P&G stock. In Chapter 11, we examine how a company's operations and investment decisions determine its earnings, dividends, and dividend growth rates.

EXHIBIT 3.13   Bloomberg Dividends and Earnings for P&G: Bloomberg DVD and ERN Screens, 7/5/13

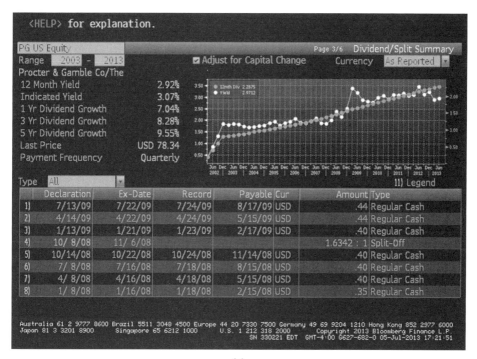

(a)

(b)

Two-Stage and Three-Stage Growth Models

The assumption that a company can maintain a constant growth rate for a long time fits the profile of many well-established companies. However, companies in relatively new industries that may be in their early stages of development or companies in industries going through fundamental changes may experience different stages of growth. Valuing the stocks of these firms requires assuming different growth rates. The two most common models are the two-stage growth model and the three-stage growth model.

The two-stage growth model assumes that dividends will grow at an extraordinary growth rate of g_1 for N years and then grow at a steady-state rate of g_2 thereafter. The value of the stock given these assumptions is

$$V_0^S = \frac{d_0(1+g_1)^1}{(1+k_e)^1} + \frac{d_0(1+g_1)^2}{(1+k_e)^2} + \cdots + \frac{d_0(1+g_1)^N}{(1+k_e)^N} + \frac{V_N^S}{(1+k_e)^N}$$

where:

$$V_N^S = \frac{d_N(1+g_2)}{k_e - g} = \frac{d_0(1+g_1)^N(1+g_2)}{k_e - g}$$

Thus, if a company's current dividends per share were $d_0 = \$10$, and as a result of its current and potential investment opportunities investors expected dividends to grow at a rate $g_1 = 5$ percent for three years and thereafter at $g_2 = 3$ percent, then they would value the stock to be $155.34:

$$V_0^S = \frac{d_0(1+g_1)^1}{(1+k_e)^1} + \frac{d_0(1+g_1)^2}{(1+k_e)^2} + \frac{d_0(1+g_1)^3}{(1+k_e)^N} + \frac{V_3^S}{(1+k_e)^N}$$

$$V_0^S = \frac{\$10(1.05)^1}{(1.10)^1} + \frac{\$10(1.05)^2}{(1.10)^2} + \frac{\$10(1.05)^3}{(1.10)^3} + \frac{\$170.34}{(1.10)^3} = \$155.34$$

where:

$$V_3^S = \frac{d_3(1+g_2)}{k_e - g} = \frac{d_0(1+g_1)^3(1+g_2)}{k_e - g} = \frac{\$10(1.05)^3(1.03)}{0.10 - 0.03} = \$170.34$$

The three-stage growth model assumes a period with an extraordinary growth rate of g_1, a transitional period in which the growth rate moves from the extraordinary rate to the steady-state rate, and then a steady-state period in which the stock dividend grows at the steady-state rate. During the transitional period, it is generally assumed that the growth rate in dividends will change at a constant rate. In terms of the above example, suppose investors expect the dividends to initially grow at an annual rate of 6 percent for three years, then steadily decline with growth rates of 5 percent,

EXHIBIT 3.14 Three-Stage Growth

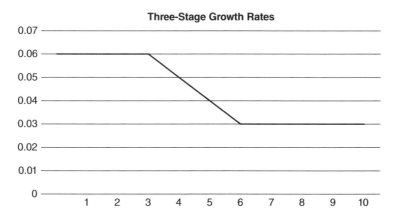

4 percent, and 3 percent in years 4, 5, and 6, respectively, and then starting in year 6 to grow at a constant steady-state rate of 3 percent (see Exhibit 3.14). Given these assumptions, the investor would value the stock at $163.31:

$$
V_0^S = \frac{d_0(1+g_1)^1}{(1+k_e)^1} + \frac{d_0(1+g_1)^2}{(1+k_e)^2} + \frac{d_0(1+g_1)^3}{(1+k_e)^3} + \frac{d_0(1+g_1)^3(1+g_2)}{(1+k_e)^4}
$$

$$
+ \frac{d_0(1+g_1)^3(1+g_2)(1+g_3)}{(1+k_e)^5} + \frac{d_0(1+g_1)^3(1+g_2)(1+g_3)(1+g_4)}{(1+k_e)^6}
$$

$$
+ \frac{\dfrac{d_0(1+g_1)^3(1+g_2)(1+g_3)(1+g_4)(1+g_4)}{k_e - g_4}}{(1+k_e)^6}
$$

$$
V_0^S = \frac{\$10(1.06)^1}{(1.10)^1} + \frac{\$10(1.06)^2}{(1.10)^2} + \frac{\$10(1.06)^3}{(1.10)^3} + \frac{\$10(1.06)^3(1.05)}{(1.10)^4}
$$

$$
+ \frac{\$10(1.06)^3(1.05)(1.04)}{(1.10)^5} + \frac{\$10(1.06)^3(1.05)(1.04)(1.03)}{(1.10)^6}
$$

$$
+ \frac{\dfrac{\$10(1.06)^3(1.05)(1.04)(1.03)(1.03)}{0.10 - 0.03}}{(1.10)^6}
$$

$$
V_0^S = \frac{\$10.60}{(1.10)^1} + \frac{\$11.24}{(1.10)^2} + \frac{\$11.91}{(1.10)^3} + \frac{\$12.51}{(1.10)^4}
$$

$$
+ \frac{\$13.01}{(1.10)^5} + \frac{\$13.40}{(1.10)^6} + \frac{\$197.11}{(1.10)^6}
$$

$$
V_0^S = \$163.31
$$

Determining which growth-rate model an analyst should use to estimate the value of a stock depends on the type of the company being evaluated. As noted, companies in emerging industries such as new technology, for example, are typically characterized by multistage growth periods. For such companies, there is often an initial period of extraordinary growth in which the companies in the new industry are expanding their manufacturing and marketing base to meet the immense domestic and possibly world demand for their products. The length of this initial period can vary depending on capital requirements, the ease of entry of new firms into the industry, the emergence of subsequent technology, and the potential demand. The initial growth stage for General Motors, Ford, and Chrysler arguably lasted as long as 50 years (from 1920 to 1970), whereas the initial growth stage for companies in the consumer product industry may have been only 10 years. In contrast, companies in more mature industries, such as metals, manufacturing, food processing, or mining, may be better characterized by a constant growth rate model in which their dividends and earnings are expected to grow at a steady-state rate. However, it is important to remember that such companies can be influenced by external factors, both good and bad, which can transform them into an emerging industry again. For example, many analysts considered the banking industry to be mature and stable in the 1960s, and then to become again a growth industry as a result of the liberalization of banking laws and the emergence of new technology. Similarly, the fall of Communism in the 1980s or the rise of emerging economies like China and India in 2000 led to new markets for the products of many companies in mature industries.

The Bloomberg Three-Stage Growth Model—DDM

Growth rate stages can also be classified based on cross-sectional trends. The Bloomberg DDM screen, for example, determines the values of a loaded stock using a three-stage growth model. Based on the stock's growth rate, the program defaults to one of four growth stage scenarios: explosive growth, high growth, average growth, and slow/mature growth. This classification is based on the normalized distribution of the forecasted growth rate for all equities.

Explosive growth firms are at the high end of the distribution, with growth rates significantly above the normalized mean or median, whereas low/mature growth firms are those at the low end of the distribution. The Bloomberg DDM model initially sets the length of the growth stage to three years for explosive growth, five years for high growth, seven years for average growth, and nine years for slow growth. The growth rate defaults to the mean secular growth rate.

In the third stage—steady state or mature stage—the DDM model assumes the growth rate is equal to the retention rate (100 percent minus the dividend-payout rate) times the stock's required rate. The growth rates in the transition period are based on assuming that the growth rate decreases annually from the rate in the growth stage period to the rate in the mature stage. In the Bloomberg DDM model, EPS for FY1, FY2, and FY3 are based on consensus earnings projections. The EPS for the remaining years in the initial growth period reflect the long-term growth rate assumption: $EPS_{FY4} = EPS_{FY3}(1 + \text{growth rate})$, $EPS_{FY5} = EPS_{FY4}(1 + \text{growth rate})$ and so on.

Given EPS growth, dividends per share (DPS) for FY2 and FY3 and the growth years' periods are based on the current dividend-payout ratio (DPS/EPS). This ratio is multiplied by EPS in FY2 times the payout ratio to obtain the DPS in FY2. Similarly, DPS in FY3 is obtained by multiplying EPS in FY3 by the dividend-payout ratio [= (DPS/EPS)(EPS$_{FY3}$)], and so on. The DDM model defaults to a dividend-payout ratio of 45 percent starting in the first year of the mature stage. For the transition period, the model assumes that the payout ratio moves to 45 percent (e.g., if payout ratio in the initial growth period is 20 percent, and the transition period is five years, then the payout ratio would increase by annual increments of 5 percent to reach 45 percent).

Finally, the DDM model defaults to a discount rate equal to the risk-free rate of the 10-year Treasury bond plus a risk premium (also known as the market's required rate of return) as the discount rate. Required returns on stock are examined in Chapter 9. The boxes on the DDM screen allow one to change the default assumptions (see Bloomberg exhibit box: "Bloomberg DDM Screen").

DDM Example

Exhibit 3.15 shows the DDM screen for Disney on 8/29/2013. The intrinsic value of the stock of approximately $44 is determined by discounting the flow of estimated DPS by a required rate based on the following estimates and assumptions:

1. As shown in the Bloomberg slide in Exhibit 3.15, the default model EPS is $3.37 for FY1, $3.91 for FY2, and $4.56 for FY3. These estimates are based on Bloomberg's consensus estimates drawn from the ANR screen.
2. For Disney, the length of the initial growth stage is seven years, with the annual growth rate estimated to be 9.94 percent for that period (see Bloomberg slide box). The length of the transitional stage is 10 years.
3. The mature growth period starts in year 20 with an assumed dividend payout ratio of 45 percent and with a growth rate of 5.636 percent. The mature growth rate is equal to the discount rate of 10.26 percent times the retention ratio: $(1 - 0.45)$.
4. The transition period starts in year 11, with the growth rate decreasing by increments of 0.43 percent per year (= 9.94 percent − 5.636 percent/10) from the 9.94 percent to 5.636 percent. Column 3 in the table in Exhibit 3.15 shows the growth rates for each year (starting in year 4) and its corresponding EPS (EPS$_t$ = EPS$_{t-1}(1 + g_t)$].
5. The dividend-payout ratio for the first 10 years (FY1 to FY3 plus the seven year growth year) is 0.217 (Column 5) and is equal to the current dividend-payout ratio (= DPS$_{FY1}$/EPS$_{FY1}$ = $0.733/$3.374).
6. Starting in year 11 (the first year of the transition period), the payout ratios start to increase by annual increments of 2.33 percent [= (45 percent − 21.7 percent)/10] to reach the model's assume payout rate 45 percent at year 20, the last year of the transition period.
7. From year 20 on, the dividend payout stays at 45 percent.

EXHIBIT 3.15 Valuation of Disney Using Bloomberg's DDM Model DDM Screen for Disney, 8/29/2013

<HELP> for explanation.

DIS US Equity — Dividend Discount Model — Walt Disney Co/The

Dividend Discount Model

		Risk Premium Country	United States
Earnings Per Share FY1	3.374	Bond Rate	2.754%
Earnings Per Share FY2	3.913	Country Premium	6.549%
Earnings Per Share FY3	4.555	Beta	1.144
Dividends Per Share FY1	0.733	1) Risk Premium	7.493%
Growth Years	7	Payout during Growth yrs	21.725%
Transitional Years	10	Payout at Maturity	45.000%
Long Term Growth Rate	9.944%	Growth Rate at Maturity	5.636%
Closing Price	61.405	Currency	USD

Computed values based on above assumptions

Theoretical Price	44.035
Percentage Change from Close	-28.287%
Internal Rate of Return	9.183%
Expected Return	-7.994%
Implied Growth Rate	13.794%

Australia 61 2 9777 8600 Brazil 5511 3048 4500 Europe 44 20 7330 7500 Germany 49 69 9204 1210 Hong Kong 852 2977 6000
Japan 81 3 3201 8900   Singapore 65 6212 1000   U.S. 1 212 318 2000   Copyright 2013 Bloomberg Finance L.P.
SN 330221 EDT GMT-4:00 H706-284-1 29-Aug-2013 17:11:57

(a)

1	2	3	4	5	6	7
Stage	Year	Growth Rate	EPS	Dividend Payout Ratio	DPS	PV at $k = 0.1026$
Analysts' EPS Estimates	1		3.3740	0.217	$0.733	$0.66
	2		3.9130	0.217	$0.850	$0.70
	3		4.5550	0.217	$0.990	$0.74
	4	0.0994	5.0078	0.217	$1.088	$0.74
	5	0.0994	5.5055	0.217	$1.196	$0.73
Growth Years	6	0.0994	6.0528	0.217	$1.315	$0.73
Growth Rate = 0.0994	7	0.0994	6.6544	0.217	$1.446	$0.73
Current Dividend Payout Rate = 0.733/3.374 = 0.217	8	0.0994	7.3159	0.217	$1.589	$0.73
	9	0.0994	8.0431	0.217	$1.747	$0.73
	10	0.0994	8.8426	0.217	$1.921	$0.72
	11	0.0951	9.6835	0.241	$2.329	$0.80
Transitional	12	0.0908	10.5626	0.264	$2.786	$0.86
Annual Growth Rate Decrease:	13	0.0865	11.4762	0.287	$3.295	$0.93
0.004304	14	0.0822	12.4193	0.310	$3.854	$0.98
Annual Payout Rate Increase:	15	0.0779	13.3866	0.334	$4.466	$1.03
0.023275044	16	0.0736	14.3715	0.357	$5.129	$1.07
	17	0.0693	15.3670	0.380	$5.842	$1.11
	18	0.0650	16.3654	0.403	$6.603	$1.14
	19	0.0607	17.3582	0.427	$7.407	$1.16
	20	0.0564	18.3365	0.450	$8.251	$1.17
Maturity	20	0.05636	19.36994441	0.45	$188.51	$26.73
Dividend Payout Rate = 0.45					V_{20}	Intrinsic Value
Growth Rate = (1 − Payout Rate)(Discount Rate)						$44.19

Growth Rate = (0.55)(0.1026) = 0.0563
$EPS_{21} = EPS_{20}(1 + g) = 8.25(1.0563) = 19.37$
$DPS_{21} = (Payout\ Rate)EPS_{21} = (0.45)(19.37) = 8.72$
$V_{20} = DPS_{21}/(k - g) = 8.72/(0.1026 - 0.0563) = 188.51$

IRR: Rate that equates the PV of projected CF to market price of $61.405: $k = 0.09183$

EXHIBIT 3.15 *(Continued)*

$$P_0 = \$61.405 = \frac{\$0.73}{(1+k)^1} + \frac{\$0.85}{(1+k)^2} + \frac{\$1.99}{(1+k)^3} + \frac{\$1.09}{(1+k)^4} + \frac{\$1.20}{(1+k)^5}$$

$$+ \frac{\$1.31}{(1+k)^6} + \frac{\$1.45}{(1+k)^7} + \frac{\$1.59}{(1+k)^8} + \frac{\$1.75}{(1+k)^9} + \frac{\$1.92}{(1+k)^{10}}$$

$$+ \frac{\$2.33}{(1+k)^{11}} + \frac{\$2.79}{(1+k)^{12}} + \frac{\$3.29}{(1+k)^{13}} + \frac{\$3.85}{(1+k)^{14}} + \frac{\$4.47}{(1+k)^{15}}$$

$$+ \frac{\$5.13}{(1+k)^{16}} + \frac{\$5.84}{(1+k)^{17}} + \frac{\$6.60}{(1+k)^{18}} + \frac{\$7.41}{(1+k)^{19}} + \frac{\$8.25}{(1+k)^8}$$

$$+ \frac{\frac{\$8.72}{k-0.05636}}{(1+k)^9} \Rightarrow k = 0.09183$$

(b)

8. The dividends per share each year are equal to the EPS times the payout ratio. They are shown for each year in Column 6 of the exhibit table.
9. The value of Disney's equity in year 20 is determined in the DDM by using the constant growth model $(V = d/(k_e - g)$. As shown in the table, dividends in year 21 are estimated to be 8.7164. With the discount rate at 10.26 percent and the steady-state growth rate at 5.636, the value of the stock at that year is $188.51 [= 8.7164/(0.1026 − 0.05636)].
10. Finally, the intrinsic value of approximately $44 is calculated by discounting each DPS and the terminal value by the discount rate of 10.26 percent (Column 7). The difference in the Bloomberg screen value shown at $44.035 and the Table value of $44.19 is due to rounding differences.

In addition to determining the intrinsic value of the stock, the DDM also calculates the rate of return—internal rate of return (IRR)—by solving for the discount rate that equates the present value of the projected dividends to the current market price. The market price of Disney at the time of the analysis was $61.40. The IRR based on that price is 9.183 percent (see bottom of Exhibit 3.15).

BLOOMBERG DDM SCREEN

Bloomberg's DDM model estimates the intrinsic value of a selected equity using a three-stage growth model. The screen also can be used to calculate the IRR, expected return, and implied growth rate based on a series of assumptions. Estimates for EPS for FY1–FY3, dividend payout ratio, growth rates, length of years for stage 1 growth and transition years, and discount rates appear in the amber boxes. You can change any of the assumptions.

(Continued)

Bloomberg defaults:
1. Discount Rate: The model uses the risk-free rate of the 10-year Treasury bond plus a risk premium (also known as the market's required rate of return) as the discount rate. Required returns on stock are examined in Chapter 9. You can select you own risk-free rate and risk premium.
2. EPS for FY1, FY2, and FY3 are pulled from Bloomberg analysts' estimates. You can change these values based on your own estimates.
3. Growth Stages: DDM defaults to a three-stage dividend discount model consisting of a growth, transition, and mature or steady-state stage.
4. The long-term growth rate is Bloomberg's consensus estimate.
5. The dividend payout ratio for the first three years and growth years defaults to the current payout ratio.
6. The dividend payout rate for the mature stage defaults to 45 percent.
7. Growth rate in the mature stage is equal to the required rate times retention ratio [= (Discount Rate) (1 – dividend payout ratio)].
8. Growth rate in the transitional period decreases annually from the rate in the growth stage period to the rate in the mature stage.
9. The payout ratios in the transitional period change by annual increments to reach the payout rate at the mature stage (set at 45 percent).

Note: You can modify both the payout rate and the growth rate in the mature stage, but the growth rate cannot exceed the market's required rate of return.

See Bloomberg Web Exhibit 3.3.

Valuation of Preferred Stock

As noted in Chapter 1, preferred stock can be thought of as a limited ownership share. It provides its owners with only limited income potential in the form of a stipulated dividend (preferred dividend) that is usually expressed as a percentage of a stipulated par value. Preferred stock also gives its holders fewer voting privileges and less control over the business than common stock does. To make preferred stock more attractive, companies frequently sell preferred stock with special rights. Among the most common of these special rights is the priority over common stockholders over earnings and assets upon dissolution of the company and the right to cumulative dividends: If preferred dividends are not paid, then all past dividends must be paid before any common dividends are paid. Many preferred stocks are sold by financial institutions as a trust preferred and by utilities.

With a dividend payment that is fixed and with an indefinite life or long-term maturity, preferred stock takes the form of a bond perpetuity. As noted, the value of a perpetuity is equal to the coupon divided by the discount rate (= C/R). Similarly, the value of a preferred stock with a fixed dividend and long-term maturity or indefinite life is equal to the dividend divided by the required rate, k_e^{PS}, (the rate preferred investor's require for investing in the preferred stock). The rate of return on a preferred stock, in turn, is equal to its dividend divided by its market prices, P^{PS}:

$$V_0^S = \frac{\text{preferred dividend}}{k_e^{PS}}$$

$$\text{Rate of return on preferred} = \frac{\text{preferred dividend}}{P_0^{PS}}$$

Conclusion

For most investors the most important characteristics of an asset are its value and its rate of return. In this chapter, we have examined how the value and rate of return for bonds and stocks are measured. The measurement of security value and return, however, is based on future cash flows—coupons, dividends, and future prices—that are uncertain. Uncertainty, in turn, means that investors have to deal with risk—the possibility that their realized return will deviate from their expected return. In Chapters 6 and 7, we will examine in more detail the value, return, and other stock characteristics such as risk that are needed to evaluate and select stocks and construct stock portfolio.

Web Site Information

Bond Information

Investinginbonds.com

Go to http://investinginbonds.com.

FINRA

Go to http://www.finra.org/index.htm, Sitemap, Market Data, and Bonds.

Wall Street Journal

Go to http://online.wsj.com/public/us, Market Data, Rates.

Yahoo.com

Go to http://finance.yahoo.com/bonds, click "Advanced Bond Screener."

Finance Calculator—FICALC

The online FICALC calculator computes a bond's price given its yield or its yield given its price, as well as other information, such as cash flows and total returns. The FICALC calculator is designed so it can either be used as a stand-alone fixed income calculator, or integrated into a Web site that has information on fixed income securities: http://www.ficalc.com/calc.tips

Note

1. One of the practical uses of the geometric mean is in comparing investments in bonds with different maturities. For example, if the present interest rate structure for zero-coupon bonds were such that two-year bonds were providing an average annual rate of 9 percent and

one-year bonds were at 10 percent, then the implied forward rate on a one-year bond, one year from now, would be 8 percent. With these rates, an investor could equate an investment in the two-year bond at 9 percent as being equivalent to an investment in a one-year bond today at 10 percent and a one-year investment to be made one year later yielding 8 percent (possibly through a locking-in strategy). Accordingly, if the investor knew with certainty that one-year bonds at the end of one year would be trading at 9 percent (6 percent)—a rate higher (lower) than the implied forward rate—then he would prefer an investment in the series of one-year bonds (two-year bond) over the two-year bond (series of one-year bonds). That is, by investing in a one-year bond today and a one-year bond one year from now, the investor would obtain 10 percent and 9 percent, respectively, for an average annual rate on the two-year investment of 9.5 percent.

Selected References

Bierwag, G. 1977. Immunization, duration and the term structure of interest rates. *Journal of Financial and Quantitative Analysis* 12: 725–743.

Bierwag, G. O., G. G. Kaufman, and A. Toevs. 1983. Duration: Its development and use in bond portfolio management. *Financial Analysts Journal* (July–August): 15–35.

Cox, J. C., J. Ingersoll, and S. Ross. 1981. A re-examination of traditional hypotheses about the term structure of interest rates. *Journal of Finance* 36: 769–799.

Fama, E. 1984. The information in the term structure. *Journal of Financial Economics* 13 (December): 509–528.

Fama, E. F. 1976. Forward rates as predictors of future spot-rates. *Journal of Financial Economics* 3: 361–377.

Fama, E. F. 1990. Term structure forecasts of interest rates, inflation and real returns. *Journal of Monetary Economics*, 25: 59–76.

Fisher, I. 1930. *The Theory of Interest*. New York: Macmillan.

Hicks, John R. 1946. *Value and Capital*. 2nd ed. London: Oxford University Press, 141–145.

Johnson, R. S. 2013. *Debt Markets and Analysis*. Hoboken, NJ: John Wiley & Sons, 85–135.

Johnson, R. S., R. Zuber, and J. Gandar. 2010. A re-examination of the Market Segmentation Theory as a pedagogical model. *Journal of Financial Education* 36 (Spring/Summer): 1–37.

Macaulay, F. R. 1938. *The Movement of Interest Rates, Bond Yields, and Stock Prices in the United States Since 1856*. New York: National Bureau of Economic Research.

Malkiel, B. G. 1962. Expectations, bond prices and the term structure of interest rates. *Quarterly Journal of Economics* 76(2): 197–218.

Mishkin, F. 1990. What does the term structure tell us about future inflation? *Journal of Monetary Economics* 25: 77–95.

Rose, P. S., 2003. *Money and Capital Markets*. New York: McGraw-Hill/Irwin.

Sargent, T. J. 1972. Rational expectations and the term structure of interest rates. *Journal of Money, Credit and Banking* 4(1): 74–97.

Stambaugh, R. 1988. The information in forward rates: Implications for models of the term structure. *Journal of Financial Economics* 21: 41–70.

Weil, R. L. 1973. Macaulay's duration: An appreciation. *Journal of Business* 46(4): 589–592.

Bloomberg Exercises

1. Select an option-free (bullet) corporate bond of interest. Evaluate the bond in terms of its price, yield, yield spread, and price-yield curve. In your

evaluations, you may want to consider the following screens on the bond's menu screen:

   a. CSHF screen to find the bond's cash flow.

   b. YAS screen to determine price and yield.

   c. TDH and ALLQ to determine the liquidity on the bond based on its trading activity and bid-ask spreads.

2. Select a U.S. Treasury bond with a long-term maturity (15 to 20 years). You may want to use the FIT screen to find your bond. Conduct a total return analysis of the bond using the TRA screen. Select different horizon periods (current date, one-year horizon, etc.), yield shifts, and reinvestment rates. Comment on the bond's sensitivity to interest rate changes.

3. Select a U.S. Treasury bond or note with an intermediate-term or long-term maturity (5 to 10 years). You may want to use the FIT screen to find your bond. Conduct a total return analysis of the bond using the TRA screen. Select different horizon periods (current date, one-year horizon, etc.), yield shifts, and reinvestment rates. Comment on the bond's sensitivity to interest rate changes.

4. Select an intermediate-term to long-term investment grade corporate bond (quality ratings of BBB or higher). Using the bond's GP screen, examine its price, yield to maturity, yield to next call (if applicable) and spread over its benchmark over the past year (price dropdown). Click the "Event" checkbox and set the event settings to see if the spikes in spreads can be explained by certain events.

5. Select an intermediate-term to long-term speculative-grade corporate bond (quality ratings less than BBB). Using the bond's GP screen, examine its price, yield to maturity, and yield to next call (if applicable), and spread over its benchmark over the past year (price dropdown). Click the "Event" checkbox and set the event settings to see if the spikes in spreads can be explained by certain events.

6. Select a U.S. Treasury bond or note with an intermediate-term or long-term maturity (10 to 20 years). You may want to use the FIT screen to find your bond. Use the SP screen on the selected bond's menu screen (CUSIP <Govt> <Enter>) to evaluate the profitability of stripping the bond.

7. Select a stripped U.S. Treasury bond with at least a 10-year maturity. You may want to use the FIT screen to find your bond.

   a. Use the bond's YAS, GP, and CSHF screens to find the strip bond's price, yield to maturity, and cash flows.

   b. Using the TRA screen, conduct a one-year total return analysis of the bond. Comment on the interest-rate risk of the bond given a one-year horizon.

8. Select several stocks of interest and analyze their historical prices, returns, dividends, and EPS over different time periods using GP, TRA, DVD, and ERN screens.

9. Examine several stocks of interest using the DDM model: Ticker <Equity> <Enter>; DDM.

   a. For several of your stocks, examine the impact on the stock's value when you change the discount rate, the growth rate for the growth years, and the growth rate for the mature stage.

b. Given the current prices of your stocks, compare their IRRs to their required returns. Comment on what stocks you believe would be good investments and which would be bad.

10. Excel Exercise: Create an Excel spreadsheet for determining the intrinsic value of one of the stocks you analyzed in Exercise 9, using the DDM model (see Exhibit 3.15 for a guide).

CHAPTER 4

Equity Securities, Markets, and Trading

Introduction

Major corporations can be viewed as perpetual investment machines: constantly developing new products and technologies, regularly expanding their markets, and from time to time acquiring other companies. To finance these investments, corporations obtain funds both internally and externally. With *internal financing*, companies retain part of their earnings that otherwise would go to existing shareholders in the form of dividends, whereas with *external financing*, companies generate funds from outside by selling new shares of stock, selling debt instruments, or borrowing from financial institutions. From the corporation's perspective, decisions on internal versus external financing depend on the dividend policy it wants to maintain and the cost of raising funds from the outside.[1]

When firms need capital to grow and acquire additional assets, they usually finance their capital formation with the following equity and debt sources or instruments:

- Retained earnings
- Common stock
- Preferred stock
- Straight debt
- Medium-term notes
- Commercial paper
- Leases
- Direct financing
- Limited partnerships
- Debt and stock with options

At a given point in time, a company's core operations and its past investments are reflected in its current balance sheet. Exhibit 4.1 provides a financial snapshot of

EXHIBIT 4.1   Kraft: Bloomberg Screens: DES, CF, and SPLC

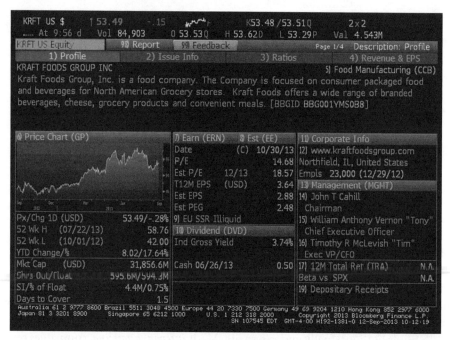

(a)

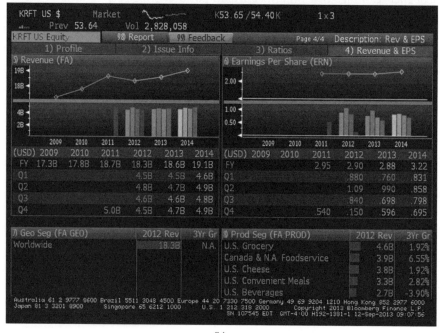

(b)

EXHIBIT 4.1 *(Continued)*

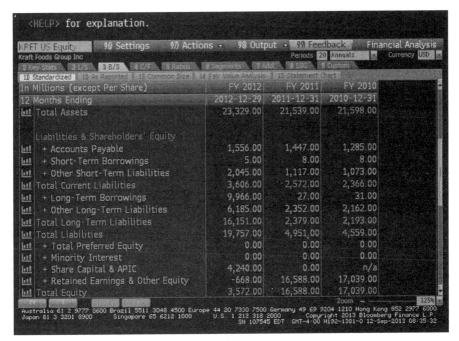

(c)

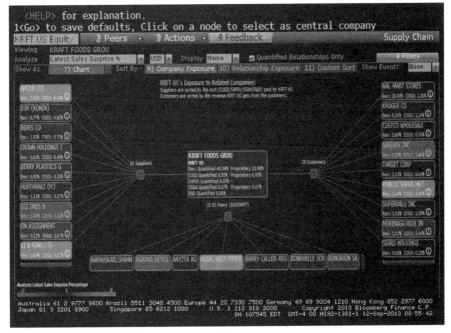

(d)

Kraft Foods Group from several Bloomberg screens accessed on September 12, 2013: description (DES) screen, key financials (FA), and supply chain (SPLC). Some other screens that were used to gather information on Kraft but that are not shown here include Kraft's 10-K corporate filing report found on the CF screen, debt and equity breakdowns on the ISSD screen, outstanding equity holders on HDS, bondholders on AGGD, and corporate actions (CACS). From these compiled screens, we find that in 2012 Kraft Foods Group was one of the largest packaged food and beverage companies in North America with net revenues of over $18.3 billion and operating earnings of $2.8 billion (10-K from CF screen and FA screen). Of its $18.3 billion in revenue, 24.8 percent came from grocery sales and 21.3 percent from Canadian and North American Food service (FA, Segment tab, By Measure tab), with Wal-Mart and Kroger being its biggest customers (SPLC). In 2012, the company had 23,000 employees, sold products in 14 countries, operated 37 manufacturing and processing plants (10-K), and owned 29 major subsidiaries (RELS). As of December 29, 2012, Kraft's gross assets were $23.3 billion and its total liabilities were $19.75 billion, of which $16.1 billion were long-term liabilities (FA, B/S tab), with 76 percent in bonds and 23 percent in loans (ISSD, Debt Summary page). On September 12, 2013, Kraft had 595.6 million shares outstanding and a market cap of $31.856 billion (DES), with its principal equity holders being Blackrock (6.28 percent), Capital Group (5.26 percent), State Street (5.15 percent), Vanguard (4.85 percent), and Wellington Management (4.67 percent) (HDS) and its principal bondholders being Vanguard (2.11 percent), Prudential (2.04 percent), and Capital Research and Management (2.03 percent) (AGGD).

Like many large companies, Kraft is an investment machine. Set up as Kraft Foods Global, Inc. (Delaware Company) in 1980, Kraft grew over the years into a global conglomerate, becoming a wholly owned subsidiary of Mondelez International Inc. In 2011, the company had total assets of $93.8 billion, employed 126,000 workers, operated in 75 countries, and had 220 manufacturing and processing plants (10-K, 2011; CF). On March 8, 2010, the conglomerate acquired Cadbury PLD for 13.5 billion British pounds (CACS). To finance part of that acquisition and to meet antitrust compliance they were active in divesting some of their other holdings, including the sale of North American frozen pizza business to Nestle USA (information on the Cadbury and other deal can be found on Kraft's "Company Research" screen [BRC]). On October 11, 2011, however, Mondelez International spun off Kraft Food Groups with a series of transactions that separated the assets and entities: Mondelez owning the snack food business and Kraft Food Group owning the North American grocery business. To complete the spin-off, on September 29, 2011, Mondelez distributed all of its shares of Kraft Foods Group to its holders (holders of Mondelez International received one share of Kraft for three shares of Mondelez International). As a result, Kraft Foods Group became an independent publicly traded company.

When corporations such as Kraft decide to finance their investments, they may do so internally by retaining earnings, using their cash position, or selling a division, or externally by issuing common stock or preferred stock, forming a limited partnership, borrowing directly from a financial institution, or issuing bonds. In this chapter, we examine the types of equity securities issued by businesses such as Kraft and the primary and secondary markets in which investors buy and sell such securities.

Types of Equity Securities

Common Stock

Common stock is the most popular form of equity. As defined in Chapter 1, common stock is an equity or ownership claim entitling the holder to dividends and ownership rights (*registered claim*) in which the holder's name is recorded on the company's books to determine dividend payments and voting privileges. Issued shares include outstanding shares held by investors and used for per share calculations and treasury shares held by the firm often via a repurchase of stock by the firm. The ownership rights of common stock can be classified into four categories: collective rights, specific rights, cumulative voting rights, and preemptive rights.

Collective rights often include the right to vote on the adoption of amendments to the company's bylaws, elect directors, authorize asset sales, approve mergers, change the amount of outstanding stock, and approve new security offerings. Although all stockholders are entitled to vote on such matters, most relinquish such rights to a proxy. A *proxy* is a legal instrument giving an agent the right to vote in the name of the shareholder. Usually the management of a company obtains the proxies of shareholders who cannot attend the annual or special meetings. There are special circumstances, such as the poor performance of the company, when some shareholders come together and try to take control of management or stop a management action by engaging in a *proxy fight* in which they try to obtain the proxies of other shareholders.

Specific rights give each holder the right to sell stock, inspect the books, share in earnings, and establish claims upon dissolution. *Cumulative voting rights*, in turn, provide for multiple voting for a single director. For example, with cumulative voting rights, the owner of 100 shares could cast either 100 votes for each of, say, six directors or 600 votes for one, or some other combination.

The *preemptive right* gives the common stockholders the first option to purchase additional shares. This right is usually required of corporations in accordance with state laws. However, many state laws allow the shareholders of a corporation to waive their right by voting to amend the preemptive right in their bylaws. The objective of the preemptive provision is to ensure a stockholder's right to maintain her share of ownership. The preemptive right means that when a company issues new shares, the existing shareholders must be given the first right of refusal. Companies whose shareholders have not waived their preemptive right often comply with this law by issuing each stockholder a certificate, known as a *right* (or *subscription warrant*). This right gives the existing shareholders the right to buy new issues of the company's stock at a specified price, known as the *subscription price*, for a specified period of time before the stock is sold to the general public. Rights are usually issued just before a company sells new stock and often can be sold in the secondary market.

In addition to collective, specific, and preemptive rights, the laws governing corporations provide two other features important to common stock—limited liability and double taxation. As noted in Chapter 1, *limited liability* means that the most one shareholder of a company can lose if the company goes bankrupt is his original investment. Thus, unlike proprietorships and partnerships in which the business ownership is defined in terms of the individuals and not a legal entity, the extent of the liability for an individual shareholder of a corporation is limited to his shares, with no risk of personal liability. *Double taxation* means that earnings of a company are taxed twice. First, before the payments to shareholders, the earnings of the company are subject to a corporate tax, and then the dividend payments to shareholders are subject to personal taxes.

Two other features of common stock should also be noted. First, some companies issue two classes of common stock—A and B. *Class A* common stock has voting rights, whereas *Class B* does not. Several firms have also issued one or more classes of common stock with dividend tied to the performance of a particular subsidiary, known as *targeted common stock*. General Motors was one of the first to do this when it issued GM Class E in 1984 when it acquired EDS. Targeted common stocks enable investors to invest in a specific business of the corporation. Second, some companies attach a par value on their common stock. The par value is an arbitrary value assigned by the company. However, some companies do define provisions in their charter in terms of the par value of their stock. For example, there may be a provision prohibiting a company from issuing new stock that would cause the company's value to go below its par value. Similarly, in some states, there may be laws that prohibit companies from issuing new shares at prices below their par value. As a result, companies required to specify par values often make the values very small. If not required, companies often will issue stock without a par value.

Stock Dividends, Stock Splits, and Reinvestment Plans

Although most dividends that are paid to shareholders are paid in cash, some companies from time to time pay their shareholders a *stock dividend* in addition to, or instead of, a cash dividend. A stock dividend pays the shareholder in shares of stock instead of cash. For example, a company declaring a 3 percent stock dividend would give each shareholder a dividend equal to 3 percent of each share they have. Thus, an investor with 100 shares would now have 103 shares. A company could declare a stock dividend instead of a cash dividend to conserve on cash. This would represent a way of financing.

Companies will occasionally declare a *stock split* or *reverse split* when they find their stock at a price that is too high or low. If a stock is trading for $100, a 2-for-1 split would mean that for each share a shareholder would now have two shares, each worth $50. If a stock is trading at $10, a 1-for-2 reverse split would mean that for every two shares, the shareholder would now have one share worth $20. Note: Stock dividends and stock split are equivalent. For example, take a company with one million shares outstanding priced at $30/share. If it has a 100 percent stock dividend, it would create one million new shares. This would lead to a new stock price of $15, which would be the same impact as a 2:1 split. Also note that a company can have a split and then keep its dividends the same. This would be the equivalent of an increase in dividends per share. Similar to a stock dividend is a *dividend reinvestment plan* (DRP). This plan allows shareholders to use their dividends to purchase shares of the firm's stock. In a newly issued DRP, the firm often sells newly issued shares to shareholders as part of a DRP at prices below market.

BLOOMBERG CORPORATE ACTION CALENDARS, CACS AND CACT

CACS: Stock dividends, stock splits, divestures, merger and acquisitions, and other information on corporate actions are found for each company by accessing CACS on the company's equity menu (or Ticker <Equity> CACS).

CACT: To search for corporate actions, you can use CACT. You can set your searches for dividends, splits, M&A, and IPO/ADDL (divestures), for different time periods, and for different groups of securities.

See Bloomberg Web Exhibit 4.1.

Dividend Mechanics: Dividend Payments and the Ex-Dividend Date

Dividends, as well as stock splits and stock dividends, must be declared by the firm's board of directors. When a firm's board declares a dividend it specifies a *record date* and a *payment date*. The record date is established to determine who will get the dividends, and the payment date is the date when payments are made to the shareholders of record (owners determined on the record date).

By exchange rules, stock transactions must be settled by the third business day after the transaction. As a result, the major exchanges and the over-the-counter (OTC) market establish ex-dividend dates at least two business days prior to the record date. On that date, shares begin to trade ex-dividend (without a dividend). Investors who purchase shares of stock before the ex-dividend date are entitled to receive the dividend—*cum-dividend*—while those who buy on or after the ex-dividend date are not. For example, suppose Kraft established the following dates on it first quarter dividend payment:

Declaration Date	Ex-Dividend Date	Record Date	Payment Date
2/25/Y1	3/29/Y1	3/31/Y1	4/14/Y1

On the ex-dividend date, the stock will open at the previous day's closing price minus the dividend (or the present value of the dividend); that is, the price of the stock will decrease by an amount approximately equal to the dividend, since those who buy the stock at such time do not receive the dividend. For example, suppose investors expected ABC stock to sell for $E(S) = \$54$ at the end of the period and to pay a $1 dividend. If investors required a 10 percent expected rate of return for the period from buying the stock, then just prior to the ex-dividend date they would pay $S_0 =$ $50 for ABC stock and at the ex-dividend date they would pay $49.09. Thus, on the ex-dividend date the price of the stock would have to fall by an amount approximately equal to the dividend to yield investors the same rate:

$$\text{Cum-Dividend: } E(r) = \frac{Div + E(S) - S_0}{S_0} = \frac{\$1 + \$54 - \$50}{\$50} = 0.10$$

$$\text{Ex-Dividend: } E(r) = \frac{E(S) - S_0}{S_0} = \frac{\$54 - \$49.09}{\$49.09} = 0.10$$

BLOOMBERG DIVIDEND CALENDAR, DVD

DVD: Bloomberg dividend information such as past and expected dividends, dividend splits, and dividend record, ex div, and payment dates can be found on the stock DVD screen.
   See Bloomberg Web Exhibit 4.2.

Preferred Stock

As noted in Chapter 1, preferred stock can be thought of as a limited ownership share. It provides its owners with only limited income potential in the form of a stipulated dividend (*preferred dividend*), which is usually expressed as a percentage of a stipulated par value. Preferred stock also gives its holders fewer voting privileges and less control over the business than common stock does. To make preferred stock more attractive, companies frequently sell preferred with special rights. Among the most common of these special rights is the priority over common stockholders over earnings and assets upon dissolution and the right to cumulative dividends—if preferred dividends are not paid, then all past dividends must be paid before any common dividends are paid. A variation of a preferred stock is a *preference stock*. Preference stock is a preferred stock that is subordinate in claims to preferred. Other possible rights and features of preferred are as follows:

1. The right to vote on new stock issues.
2. The right to vote on the levels of retained earnings the company can maintain before dividends are declared.
3. The election of directors under certain circumstances.
4. The conversion of the preferred stock to common stock or another security of the company.
5. The payment of a variable dividend rate in which the dividend is tied to the rate on another security.
6. A call feature or optional redemption provision giving the company the right to buy the preferred stock from the holder.
7. A sinking fund clause used by the issuer to buy back the issue.

To the investor, preferred stock is similar to a bond in its priority of claims and its fixed income feature, and it is similar to common stock in that there is no maturity and no corporate default if preferred dividends are not paid by the company. Hence, preferred is commonly referred to as a *hybrid security*. Exhibit 4.2 shows a Bloomberg description and price graph screens of a preferred stock issue of Pacific Gas & Electric. The preferred is a perpetual, pays a fixed dividend of $6.00 per quarter, is noncallable, and from 9/12/2008 to 9/12/2013 traded between $23.30 and $31.98. Like common stock, one of the disadvantages of preferred is that it has the double taxation feature. For corporate investors, this feature is minimized to some extent by the *70 percent dividend exclusion rule*. Based on federal tax laws, other corporations who buy the equity of domestic companies can exclude 70 percent of the dividends they receive from corporate taxes. From a corporate perspective, if a firm does not have taxable income to take advantage of debt financing, it may consider preferred as an alternative to debt financing. Preferred stock tends to be offered by financial institutions and utilities.

Limited Partnership Shares

The third type of equity instrument is a *limited partnership share*. As defined in Chapter 1, a limited partnership is a business structure consisting of a general partner who usually initiates, organizes, and manages a business venture, and limited partners who provide the investment funds by buying limited partnership shares. The limited partnership share, in turn, represents an equity position with limited participation in the management of the company. An important feature of limited partnership is that in accordance with current tax and corporate laws all tax obligations and deductions flow directly to the partners and not to the corporation. Thus, $100 in business earnings goes directly to the partners, with no corporate taxes applied; the partners do, in turn, pay personal taxes on the income received. In addition, the usual corporate deductions for depreciation, interest paid on debt, and the like are also used by the individuals as part of their personal income tax deductions. Thus, a limited partnership share is similar to proprietorship or partnership in the way taxes are applied. However, limited partnerships do not subject their holders to personal liabilities in the case of a bankruptcy or an adverse legal judgment; that is, by law, limited partner shares have a limited liability feature like a common stock. Thus, limited partnership shares have the limited liability benefit of common stock without the disadvantage of double taxation. In addition, limited partnerships are exempt from many of the burdensome Securities and Exchange Commission (SEC) disclosure regulations. One of the disadvantages of limited partnerships is that they usually do not have a wide distribution of ownership and therefore lack marketability. Companies that do not have wide ownership distribution are often referred to as a *closely held firm*.

Limited partnerships are used extensively in real estate development projects (malls, office buildings, etc.), sports franchises, film making, research and development (R&D) projects, and gas- and oil-drilling ventures. Limited partnerships are also used as the organization structure by private equity firms for venture capital and capital buyouts (discussed in the next section). Unlike leasing and project financing

EXHIBIT 4.2   Pacific Gas & Electric Preferred Description

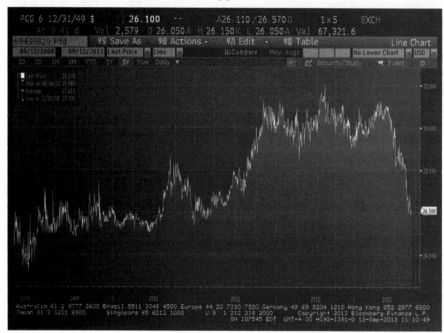

(a)

(b)

with debt, limited partnership represents a form of equity financing for a corporation. A limited partnership is a particularly good form of equity investment for a firm that plans a tax-intensive investment where there are depreciation deductions, depletion allowances, and interest deductions and where the project is expected to have sufficient taxable income to use the deductions. Limited partnerships can take different forms in their structure. For example, a structure could take the following form:

1. The general partners contributed 10 percent of the partnership's capital and the limited partners contribute 90 percent.
2. The limited partners are promised 98 percent of the profits, losses, tax credits, and cash distributions until they recover their investment. Thereafter they are promised 80 percent until they receive cash representing in the aggregate 200 percent of the investment.
3. General partners receive a management fee equal to 4 percent of the limited partnership's net worth and 100 percent of the profits, tax credits, and cash distributions after the limited partnership agreement has been met.

Private Equity Investments

Limited partnerships are often used as the organization structure for *private equity investment*. In contrast to public equity financing where companies sell stocks and bonds in the open market with SEC oversight, private equity investment raises funds from a limited number of investors, often by forming a limited partnership firm. Two investment areas that private equity firms tend to focus are in venture capital and capital buyout. Some large private equity firms, such as KKR (Kohlberg, Kravis, and Roberts & Co.), Blackstone Group, and Bain Capital, are active in both (see Exhibit 4.3 for description and corporate action KKR).

Venture Capital

Venture capital firms provide funds for start-up companies. In the 1970s, many of these firms were organized as closed-end mutual funds. Since the 1980s, more venture capital firms have been set up as limited partnerships, partly to avoid disclosure requirements of the Investment Securities Act of 1940. As limited partnership, funds are raised from limited partners and invested by the general partner in fledgling businesses. Venture capital firms have provided the start-up funding for such companies as Apple, Microsoft, Cisco, Starbucks, Staples, and Genentech. The source of funding (i.e., those with limited partnership shares) often comes from other corporations or institutional investors, notably pension funds.[2] For corporations, investing in a venture capital firm as a limited partner or managing one as a general partner represents an alternative financing option for its research and development.

Funds raised by venture capital firms are often made in the form of commitments by investors/limited partners to provide funds over a period of time for seed money, early-stage funding, and later-stage funding. With such commitments, the venture

EXHIBIT 4.3   Private Equity Firm KKR

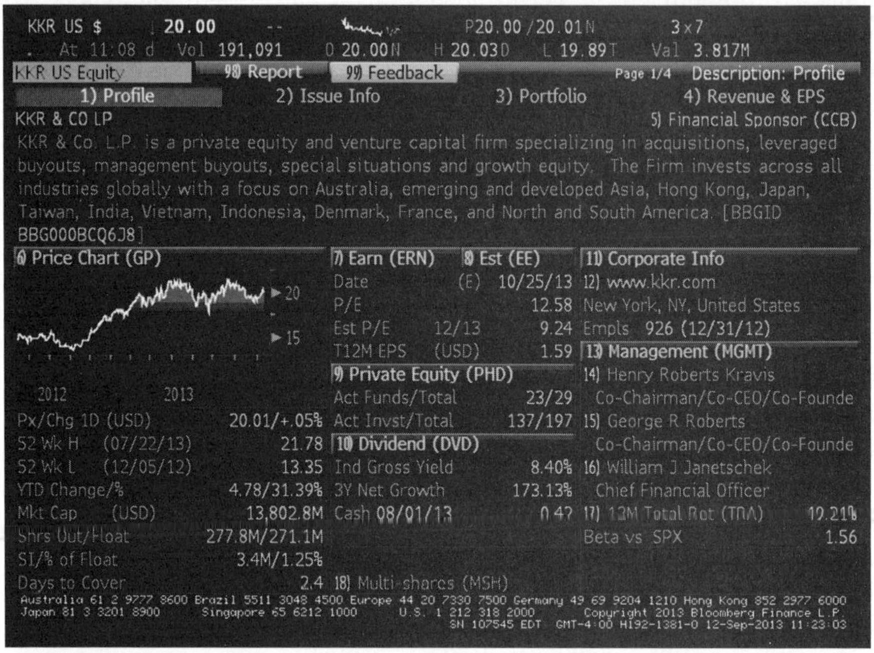

(a)

(b)

capital firm/general partners will call for funds as needed. Such calls are referred to as *takedowns* or *paid-in-capital*. Most venture capital firms are set up to take a business idea and nurture it from its early stage of development to a mature stage where the business is an attractive acquisition for another corporation or where the business is in a position to go public. When that stage is reached, the venture capital firm will take the company public through an *initial public offering, IPO* (a stock sold to the public for the first time) or it will arrange for a merger with another company, profiting, in turn, from the sale. At that point, the venture capital firm is dissolved.

Private-Equity Buyouts

In contrast to venture capital firms who often take a fledging private company public, capital buyout firms often take public companies private. In a private equity capital buyout, a limited partnership is often formed to raise funds to buy the shares of a publicly traded company. Once the shares are acquired, they are retired, and the private equity company takes control. Once the formerly public company goes private, it is often able to pursue changes that require less scrutiny than when it was public.[3] Often private equity buyout companies purchase poorly performing public companies that they try to turn around. As part of their strategy, they may bring in a CEO to revise the company. If successful, the private equity buyout firm may then take the company public again through an IPO or sell it to another company.

BLOOMBERG: BLOOMBERG CORPORATE ACTION CALENDARS: CACS, CACT, EVTS, AND FLNG; ACQUISITIONS, PRIVATE EQUITY, AND IPOS

Bloomberg information on corporate actions such as acquisitions and limited partnership deals by company can be accessed on the CACS screen found on the company's equity menu (or Ticker <Equity> CACS). To search for corporate actions related to acquisitions and IPOs, use CACT and set your search for M&A or IPO. For pending corporate deals, use EVTS and set search for M&A (found in "More" tab). Another information screen to note is FLNG. This screen reports 13F filings and it can be used to search for investment activities of venture capital and private equity holdings.

Bloomberg IPO Screen: IPO <Enter>

Information on an IPO can be found on the IPO screen: IPO <Enter>. On the screen, one can access pending IPOs by clicking "IPO" and the deal.

Bloomberg Private Equity Menu: PE <Enter>

Bloomberg's Private Equity screen displays a menu of links that provide access to specific Bloomberg private equity analysis functions.

(Continued)

Bloomberg PHDC: PHDC <Enter>

PHDC searches for institutional and insider holders whose trading activity may influence the price of a selected security: PHDC <Enter>.

How Stocks and other Securities are Traded—Primary Market

Markets are conduits through which buyers and sellers exchange goods, services, and resources. The financial market, in turn, channels the savings of households, businesses, and governments to those economic units needing to borrow. As noted in Chapter 1, financial markets can be classified in terms of whether the market is for new or existing claims—primary or secondary market. In this section and the next, we examine the primary and secondary market for securities in the United States, with emphasis on stock, and describe the types of transactions that investors make and their costs. In Chapter 5, we look at the global markets for stocks.

Billions of dollars of corporate bonds and stock are sold each year in the primary market. New corporate bonds are either sold in the open market or are privately placed to a limited number of investors, whereas stocks issued in the primary market are either initial public offerings or seasoned issues. As noted, an IPO is a stock sold to the public for the first time by a previously privately owned company. In contrast, a new seasoned issue is an issue of a company that has sold stock to the public before.

Open-Market Sales

Many new stocks and bonds issued in the open market (*open-market sales*) are handled through investment banks such as Goldman Sachs, Citi, J.P. Morgan, and Bank of America Merrill Lynch (see Exhibit 4.4 for a listing of top underwriters). Investment bankers may underwrite the issue themselves or with other investment banks as a syndicate, or they may use their best effort: selling the security on commission at the best prevailing price. The way a company chooses to offer an issue to the public depends, in part, on the size of the issue and the risk of a price decrease during the time the issue is being sold. For relatively strong companies, the investment banker often underwrites the issue: buying the issue at an agreed-upon price and then selling it in the market at, it is hoped, a higher price. Such an agreement is referred to as a *firm commitment*. The issuer may choose the investment banker or syndicate, either individually or by a bid process, selecting the underwriting group with the highest price. With an underwriting arrangement, the selected investment banker will try to profit from the spread between the selling price (retail) and the price paid to the issuer. The spread represents the *floatation cost* to the issuer.

When a new issue is underwritten, the investment banker underwriting the issue bears the risk that the price of the issue could decrease during the time the stocks or bonds are being sold. One way investment banks try to minimize such risk is to solicit

EXHIBIT 4.4   Top Underwriters: U.S. Equity and Bonds, 2013

U.S. Equity 2013			
Underwriter	Rank	Market Share (%)	Amount (Mln of $)
Goldman Sachs & Co.	1	14.1	21,858.52
Citi	2	12.7	19,749.05
JP Morgan	3	11.4	17,720.46
Bank of America Merrill Lynch	4	9.9	15,429.95
Barclays	5	9.8	15,269.41
Morgan Stanley	6	8.7	13,497.18
Credit Suisse	7	6.8	10,501.86
Deutsche Bank AG	8	6	9,336.55
Wells Fargo & Co.	9	4.7	7,294.90
UBS	10	3.1	4,831.58
Jefferies LLC	11	2.1	3,333.52
RBC Capital Markets	12	1.8	2,843.82
Robert W Baird & Co.	13	0.8	1,226.48
Raymond James & Associates	14	0.8	1,226.21
Stifel	15	0.6	955.78

U.S. Bond 2013			
Underwriter	Rank	Market Share (%)	Amount (Mln of $)
JP Morgan	1	12.2	177,111.71
Citi	2	9.5	138,146.87
Bank of America Merrill Lynch	3	8.8	128,402.63
Barclays	4	8.4	122,327.13
Goldman Sachs & Co.	5	8.1	118,627.80
Deutsche Bank AG	6	7.8	113,299.81
Morgan Stanley	7	7.7	112,562.12
Wells Fargo & Co.	8	4.8	69,689.72
Credit Suisse	9	4.1	59,385.43
HSBC Bank PLC	10	3.4	49,991.51
BNP Paribas Group	11	3.3	48,027.30
RBC Capital Markets	12	3	43,027.27
RBS	13	2.5	36,855.00
UBS	14	1.6	22,982.27
Nomura Holdings Inc.	15	1.1	15,882.06

Source: Bloomberg, LTOP Screen

offers (often from the regional offices of the investment bank) to buy the security prior to its sale. A successful solicitation occurs when the issue is *fully subscribed*: All securities being offered are met prior to the issue date. However, it may be that the issue is *undersubscribed* or *oversubscribed*. An undersubscribed issue may be the result of the underwriter setting the price of the security too high, whereas an oversubscribed issue may be the result of him setting the price too low. Alternatively, the investment banker may elect to sell the issue on a best-effort basis or use a combination of underwriting and best effort by using a *standby underwriting agreement*. In this latter agreement, the investment banker sells the issue on a commission, but agrees to buy all unsold securities at a specified price.

Before the issue is sold to the public, the issuer must comply with the SEC Acts of 1933 and 1934 governing disclosure by filing registration statements with the Securities and Exchange Commission. All open market issues of $1.5 million or more and with maturities greater than 270 days must file registration statements. These statements include the relevant business and financial information of the firm, information about the use of the funds, and a risk assessment. Once the company has registered, it must then wait until the SEC verifies the information before it can sell the security issue (usually 20 days). Typically, the investment banker uses this period to advertise the offering and to distribute to potential buyers a preliminary prospectus called a *red-herring*, which details all the pertinent information the official *prospectus* will have except the price. Investment bankers handling the sale often advertise the future offering with a large ad called a *tombstone*. Finally, after the SEC confirms the registration statements or 20 days have passed, the indenture and prospectus become official and the investment banker offers the issue for sale. The SEC requires that most primary issues be accompanied by a prospectus (see Exhibit 4.5 for a listing of disclosure information required by the SEC). For bond issues, the investment banker must also obtain a credit rating from Standard and Poor's, Moody's, or Fetch and select a bond trustee for the bondholder to ensure the issuer meets the obligations specified in the

EXHIBIT 4.5 Disclosure Information Required by SEC for New Issues

1. Article of incorporation.
2. Use of proceeds.
3. Offering price to the public.
4. Offering price to special groups.
5. Underwriter's fee.
6. Information on the issuer: business, history, and location.
7. Indentures associated with the offerings.
8. Officers.
9. Detailed statement of capitalization.
10. Detailed balance sheet.
11. Detailed income and expense statements.
12. Identification of anyone owning more than 10 percent of any class of stock.
13. Copy of underwriting agreement.
14. Copy of the legal opinions on matters related to the issue.

indenture. For an equity issue, the investment bankers may have to arrange for the security to be listed on an exchange or for a market maker to deal the security in the over-the-counter market.

In selling the stock issue, the investment banker often forms a selling group. This group consists of the investment banker who, as an underwriter, acts as a wholesaler (or initial distributor if best-effort is being used) by selling the issue to a number of dealers who, in turn, sell to their clients. The arrangements between the investment banker and the selling group are specified in a *selling group agreement* (described in the prospectus). The agreement defines the period of time the members of the group have to sell their portion of the issue, commissions that they can charge, and restrictions such as prohibiting members from selling below a certain price. Also, the selling group may also include an *e-underwriter* or electronic investment banker. Since the late 1990s, there has been an emergence of e-underwriters, such as DLJdirect. They often operate as part of the syndicate where they distribute part of the issue via the Internet.

Exhibit 4.6 shows several Bloomberg screens describing a 121.43 million shares stock issue by Fifth-Third Bankcorp in January 2011. The major underwriter on the deal was Credit Suisse, with other syndicate members consisting of Deutsche Bank, Goldman Sachs, and J.P. Morgan. The stock was underwritten at an offer price of $14/share, and as specified in the prospectus, the proceeds were used to redeem 136,320 shares of preferred stock sold to the government as part of the Troubled Asset Relief Program (TARP).

In summary, the floating of a stock or bond issue can be quite complex, involving the preparation of registration documents, the selection of an underwriter, and the formation of a selling group. Since 1983, some corporations have been able to shorten this process, as well as reduce the floatation costs of issuing stocks or bonds, by taking advantage of the Securities and Exchange Commission's *Rule 415*. Known as the *shelf registration rule*, Rule 415 allows a firm to register an inventory of securities of a particular type for up to two years. The firm can then sell the securities whenever it wishes during that time—the securities remain on the shelf. To minimize costs, a company planning to finance a number of projects over a period of time could register a large issue, and then sell parts of the issue at different times.

Private Placement

An alternative to selling securities to the public is to sell them directly to institutional investors through a private placement. One of the attractions of privately placed bonds is that they are exempt from SEC registration because they do not involve a public offering. During the 1980s, an increasing proportion of new corporate bonds were sold through *private placement*. Because they are sold through direct negotiation with the buyer, privately placed bonds usually have fewer restrictive covenants than publicly issued ones, and they are more tailor-made to both the buyer's and seller's particular needs.[4] Historically, one of the disadvantages of privately placed bonds was their lack of marketability due to the absence of an active secondary market. Under the SEC Act of 1933, firms could offer securities privately (which did not require SEC registration)

EXHIBIT 4.6   5/3 Stock Issue

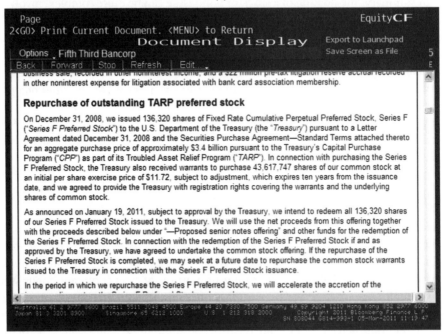

(a)

(b)

only to investors deemed sophisticated—insurance companies, pension funds, banks, and endowments. In 1991, the SEC adopted Rule 144A under SEC Act 1933. Under this rule, issuer could sell unregistered securities to one or more investment bankers who could resell the securities to *qualified investment buyers* (QIBs). QIBs could then sell freely with each other in securities that have not been registered. The adoption of *SEC Rule 144A* eliminated some of the restrictions on the secondary trading of privately placed bonds by institutional investors. As such, it opened up the secondary market for privately placed bonds.

Another reason for the growth in privately placed bonds during the 1980s was their use in financing many of the corporate mergers and takeovers. During this period, many corporations and investment groups sold bonds and borrowed from financial institutions to finance their corporate acquisitions. Because privately placed bonds had less restrictive covenants, they were frequently used to finance these leveraged buyout acquisitions. Moreover, many of these bonds were non-investment grade bonds. By the late 1980s, these bonds accounted for approximately one-third of the new corporate bonds offered, with two-thirds of those bonds being used to finance mergers or corporate restructurings aimed at stopping a corporate takeover.[5] The economic recession of the late 1980s and early 1990s, however, depressed the earning of many leveraged companies to levels that were not sufficient to pay their high interest obligations. Over 250 companies defaulted between 1989 and 1991.

Rights Offering

When a seasonal stock is issued, it may sometimes be sold through a *rights offering* so that the company can adhere to its preemptive rights. As noted previously, a right is a certificate issued to shareholders giving them the right to buy new shares at a subscription price. To maintain ownership proportionality, each share of stock receives one right, and to facilitate the new stock sale, the subscription price is often set below the current stock price. After the company issues rights to its shareholders, the existing shares of stock sell *cum rights* (buyers of the stock are entitled to the right) to a specified ex-rights date, after which the stock sells without the right.

To illustrate, suppose the ABC Corporation is planning to raise $10 million in equity to finance the construction of a new plant. Also, suppose the company currently is worth $100 million, has no debt, and has one million shares of stock outstanding, with each share trading at $100. If ABC uses a rights offering to raise the $10 million, each existing shareholder would be given the opportunity to buy new shares of stock at a subscription price and would be given one right for each share they own. If the subscription price is set at $80 per share, the ABC Corporation would need to sell 125,000 new shares to raise $10 million: Number of New Shares = $10,000,000/$80 = 125,000. Since one right is given for each existing share, eight rights would be needed to purchase one new share: Number of Rights to Buy One Share = 1,000,000/125,000 = 8 Rights. Thus, for this rights offering, shareholders would have to surrender eight rights and $80 to buy one new share. This rights offering, in turn, would provide the ABC company $10 million cash to finance its investment and would create 125,000 additional shares.

Bloomberg LTOP Screen: LTOP <Enter>

LTOP displays top underwriters for the major fixed income, equity, equity-linked securities, and syndicated loan securities markets.

Bloomberg NIM Screens: NIM <Enter>

The Bloomberg NIM identifies new security offerings by security type, period, and region. The NIM screen can be customized to identify certain types of securities and news about announced offerings. Using the screen, you can set alerts for when new issues are announced.

Bloomberg IPO Screen: IPO <Enter>

The IPO screen displays IPOs and seasoned issues in different stages of the underwriting process. Using the screen, you can select type, time period, area, stage, and sector. Clicking the name of the company brings up a screen providing details of the offering.
See Bloomberg Web Exhibit 4.3.

The Markets for Existing Securities

Although a substantial amount of new securities are issued each year to finance corporate investments, most of the trading of these securities still consists of buying and selling existing shares. As noted in Chapter 1, the trading of existing stock in the United States takes place on the organized exchanges (NYSE Euronext and regional exchanges), the OTC, or through an electronic communications network (ECN) or electronic exchange. For a corporation to have its stock traded on an organized exchange or the OTC market, it must be listed. Many companies also have dual listings on several exchanges.

Much of the trading of existing corporate bonds takes place on the OTC market, where the trading is handled by brokers and dealers specializing in certain types of issues. In the OTC market, a core of large dealers dominates the corporate bond market. These dealers buy and sell existing corporate bonds to and from life insurance companies, pension funds, and other institutional investors. They also provide an important wholesale market in which they trade with other dealers and brokers who are executing buy and sell orders from the customers. Although the amount of corporate bonds outstanding is large, the secondary market activity of corporate bonds is less than the activity in the secondary markets for stocks. This is due to the passive investment practices of some large institutions that tend to buy and hold their corporate bonds to maturity.

BLOOMBERG BOND PRICES, TRACE: TRADE RECAP, QR

In 2002, the National Association of Security Dealers, NASD, established mandatory reporting requirement of OTC market transactions to make the secondary market for bonds more transparent. The reporting system that was established was the Trading Reporting and Compliance Engine—TRACE. For a loaded bond, TRACE can be accessed from QR. It can also be accessed from the bond's description page.

Bloomberg Equity Prices: HP and BQ

In addition to each stock's price graph, GP, and intraday price information, GIP, other useful price screens accessible from a stock's equity menu include **HP**, which displays historical price and volume, and **BQ**, which provides a composite overview of key price and trade data, fundamental information, and news for a selected equity.

See Bloomberg Web Exhibit 4.4.

Brokers and Dealers

In the secondary market, the key participants are brokers and dealers. Eighty percent of the secondary market security trades, however, are handled by brokers and dealers of the major investment firms. Some of these companies can be characterized as department stores offering financial services. They act as dealers in some securities, investment bankers for their corporate and government clients, and as brokers.

As brokers, brokerage firms or the brokerage division of large investment firms can buy or sell most securities sold in the world or make arrangements for correspondent firms to do so. They also provide credit to their customers to finance their security acquisitions. In addition to arranging for security purchases, most investment firms also offer their customers safekeeping of their securities. They do this by either providing safe-deposit facilities for their customer's stock and bond certificates, or they hold their securities in *street name*. This means the security will be in the name of the brokerage firm. Accordingly, all dividends and interest and all proxy statements are sent to the brokerage firm, which, in turn, forwards them to the customer/owner. Some *full-service brokerage firms* provide security research, which they communicate to their customers through newsletters, stock recommendation releases, and access to data, information, and analytical retrieval systems. Some firms also buy and sell for their customers by establishing *discretionary accounts*. On the other hand, there are *discount brokerage firms* like Charles Schwab and Company, Fidelity, and Vanguard Brokerage Services who, as part of their discount service, buy and sell securities, maintain records, and provide loans, but who do not provide research or recommendations. Most brokerage firms provide their customers with cash accounts through which any interest, dividends, or gains from their security investments are immediately invested in a money market fund. Finally, there are *electronic brokers* such as E*Trade and Ameritrade who take buy and sell orders over the Internet. Some of these electronic brokers and platforms are associated with the larger investment houses.

Brokers and dealers, combined with the electronic and physical exchanges, create a network whereby investors in almost any part of the world can be linked so that they can buy and sell securities. It is a sophisticated system. However, for most investors the procedures for buying and selling securities is quite simple. It usually takes a phone call to a local broker or a local division of a national brokerage firm or setting up an electronic account on one's computer. The investor is then usually assigned an account executive who sets up an account in which the investor can deposit cash for purchasing the securities and for later receiving cash from the income of the securities that are purchased or when they are sold. After this account is set up, then all an investor has to do to buy or sell a security is to call her account executive or electronically submit an order from her computer.

The investor can instruct her broker to buy or sell the security either at the best prevailing price or at a price she determines. The former instruction is a *market order* and the latter is a *price limit order* to buy or sell. With a market order, the investor simply instructs her broker to buy (or sell) so many shares at the market. The broker will try to execute the order as fast as possible at the best price he can obtain. With a limit order to buy, the investor specifies the maximum price she will pay for the stock. The order then can only be carried out at that price or lower. With a limit order to sell, the investor specifies the minimum price she will accept and the order will then be carried out only at that price or higher.

BLOOMBERG INFORMATION ON BROKERS/DEALERS: RANK AND IBRA

The **RANK** screen displays broker and dealer rankings by volume for a loaded security. **IBRA** is similar to Rank. On IBRA, you select securities from the screen.

Organized Exchanges and the OTC Market

Brokers and dealers serve the function of bringing buyers and sellers together by finding opposite positions or by taking temporary positions in a security. Exchanges and the OTC market, in turn, serve the function of linking brokers and dealers together to buy and sell existing securities that are listed. Exchanges and the OTC market can be described in terms of their listing requirements, the types of trading systems they provide, and whether they are call or continuous markets.

Listing

On the organized exchanges, a corporation that wants to be listed must meet the *listing requirements*, and once listed, it must adhere to its continuous listing requirements. These requirements relate to the company's ability to satisfy sufficient size and ownership distribution requisites and its willingness to divulge its income and balance sheet information. If a listed company fails to maintain these requirements (for example, if the trading of its stock declines below the minimum or if the company merges with another company), then the company may be *delisted* by the exchange, meaning its shares can no longer be traded. The NYSE Euronext listing requirements, for example, are designed to attract large firms based on their market size. Minimum requirements include $100 million market value, earnings of at least $10 million for the last three years, 2,200 shareholders, and monthly trading volume of 100,000 shares. As of 2010, there were over 2,500 companies worldwide that listed their shares on the NYSE.

In contrast, some regional exchanges have less restrictive listing requirements. As such, their lists often include small-cap and microcap companies.[6] Historically, regional exchanges such as Chicago and the Philadelphia-Baltimore-Washington exchange (PBW) began by listing the securities of companies with only a regional interest, making such securities more marketable. However, over time, regional exchanges also provided listings of some popular NYSE stocks (especially those of corporations based in the area). This latter function made it possible for local brokers who were not members of the exchange to broker securities at lower commission costs than member brokers.

Securities not listed on one of the exchanges could be traded in the over-the-counter market. The over-the-counter market is an informal exchange for the trading of stocks, corporate and municipal bonds, investment fund shares, asset-backed securities, and Treasury and federal agency securities. As described in Chapter 1, it is a fragmented market of brokers and dealers linked to each other by computer, telephone, and telex communication systems. The most publicized OTC system is the *National Association of Security Dealers Automatic Quotation System, NASDAQ.* NASDAQ is an information system in which current bid-ask quotes of dealers are offered, and also a system that sends brokers' quotes to dealers, enabling them to close trades. There are over 60,000 NASDAQ computer terminals connected to the NASDAQ mainframe computer. The terminals receive bid-and-ask quotes from dealers making a market in a listed security—a *market maker.* Once an investor's broker identifies a deal, the trade is then executed directly with the dealer. Like the NYSE Euronext, for a company to have its stock listed on the NASDAQ system, it must satisfy requirements related to its net worth and shares outstanding, and it must have at least two dealers/market makers dealing in the security. See Exhibit 4.7 for a brief history of NASDAQ.

For most corporations, listing on the organized exchange or NASDAQ is advantageous, if not imperative: To raise money via stock sales, a corporation needs to provide its investors with assurances that a secondary market for the trading of its stock exists. In addition to providing marketability to a corporation's financial claims, listing also provides advertising (e.g., stock quotes in the newspapers or discussions on financial news shows on radio and TV), and it provides the company with information on how it is doing as reflected by the price investors are willing to pay for its stock. It should be noted that there are companies that qualify for listing on the NYSE Euronext or other exchanges, but choose not to be listed. The reasons for such a decision vary from a desire to control the distribution of the stock to concerns over the disclosure of information.[7] On the other hand, there are those companies who want to be listed

EXHIBIT 4.7   Brief History of NASDAQ

NASDAQ was founded in 1971 by the National Association of Securities Dealers. When it began trading operations, it was the world's first electronic stock market. NASDAQ was also the successor to the OTC system of trading and is still commonly referred to as the OTC.

Over the years, NASDAQ became more of a stock market by adding trade and volume reporting and automated trading systems. NASDAQ was also the first stock market in the United States to start trading online, highlighting NASDAQ-traded companies (usually in technology). Until 1987, most trading occurred via the telephone. The Small Order Execution System (SOES) was established in the late 1980s as one of the first electronic methods for dealers to enter their trades. NASDAQ requires market makers to honor trades over SOES. In 1992, NASDAQ joined with the London Stock Exchange to form the first intercontinental linkage of security markets.

In 2000, NASDAQ went public, forming the NASDAQ Stock Market, Inc. Today, NASDAQ is owned and operated by the NASDAQ OMX Group and listed on its own stock exchange (NDAQ). It is regulated by the Financial Industry Regulatory Authority (FINRA), the successor to the NASD. In 2005, NASDAQ purchased Instinet, and in 2007, it acquired the Philadelphia Stock Exchange (PHLX)—the oldest stock exchange in America (1790).

on more than one exchange—*dual listing*. Some companies, for example, are listed on the NYSE Euronext, as well as security exchanges in other countries and some of the regional exchanges.

Trading Systems — Auction and Dealer Systems

Exchanges are similar in that they provide trading for listed securities. They differ, however, in the types of trading systems they offer. Trading systems can be classified as being an auction system, a dealers system, or a hybrid of each.

In an auction system, security buyers and sellers submit bid and ask prices to a central location where the orders are matched by brokers (or electronically by a computer system). Many auction systems use what is referred to as a *price-driven system*. Here the shares of a security offered by a seller with the lowest ask price is sold to buyers with shares to buy with the highest bid price. For example, suppose on the buy side, Investor A has a bid to buy XYZ stock at $5 or less and Investor B has a bid to buy XYZ at $6 or less, whereas on the sell side, Investor C has an offer to sell XYZ stock at $6 or more and Investor D has an order to sell at $5 or more. In a price-driven system, A's bid to buy at $5 would be matched with D's offer to sell at $5, and B's bid to buy at $6 would be matched with D's offer to sell at $6.

A dealer trading system is one in which dealers take a temporary position in the security. Under a dealer system, an exchange typically assigns a specific stock or security for a dealer to deal, and in the OTC market, dealer requirements are used to set up dealers on a security. Dealers, in turn, act as market makers, buying a security from a seller at a low bid price and selling to a buyer at (they hope!) a higher ask price. Dealers quote a bid price (the maximum price they would be willing to pay) to investors interested in selling the stock and an ask price (price at which they would sell) to investors interested in buying.

Call and Continuous Markets

Security markets can be described as either being a *call market* or a *continuous market*. A call market can be set up so that those investors wishing to trade in a particular security can do so only at that time when the exchange "calls" the security for trading. Once called, sufficient time is usually allowed to accommodate enough buyers and sellers, and market clearing is accomplished through an auction—prices are quoted until the amount demanded is equal to the amount supplied. Call markets can also be set up electronically. Investors wishing to buy or sell a security can submit prices, which are entered into a computer system. They are then allowed to change their order and price until a specified call time, when a price matching the buy and sell order is determined. In such a system, market orders in which investors request that a security be purchased or sold at the best prevailing price are filled at the market-clearing price. Call markets are common on many new exchanges and electronic trading systems. Organized exchanges, like the NYSE Euronext, also use a call market for some stocks at their opening whenever there is an overnight buildup of buy and sell orders that could potentially lead to a significant difference between the previous day's closing price and the opening price. Dealers on the exchange may also use a call market after there is a suspension of trade. For example, suppose ABC stock closed trading at $50 and then overnight significant negative news information was released. If the overnight sell orders were four times greater than the buy orders, then a dealer on the stock might open the market with a call auction on the stock in order to determine a market-clearing price. The motive for implementing a temporary call auction is to minimize potential price volatility in the stock.

In contrast to the call market, in which the time a security is traded is discontinuous, a *continuous market* attempts to have constant trading in a security. To have such a feature, time discrepancies caused by different times when investors want to sell and when others want to buy must be eliminated, or at least minimized. Continuous trading is accomplished with an auction system by having sufficient number of buyers and sellers to ensure that when one wants to buy (sell), there is another investor wanting to sell (buy). Continuous trading is accomplished with a dealer system by having dealers, who are part of the exchange, take temporary positions in a security. On the organized exchanges, these dealers act as either specialists or market makers.

Under a specialist system, the exchange assigns a specific stock or security to a specialist to deal. As dealers, the specialists quote a bid price to investors when selling the stock and an ask price to investors interested in buying, hoping to profit from the bid-ask spread. In addition to dealing, the NYSE Euronext and other exchanges using a specialist system may also require that the specialists maintain the *limit order book* (which appears on their computer screens) on the securities they are assigned. As noted, a limit order is an investor's request to his broker to buy or sell a stock at a given price or better. On the NYSE Euronext, such orders are taken by commission brokers and left with the specialist in that stock for execution. The specialist, in turn, records the order in a limits book with entries. In her role as a dealer, the specialist is constantly being approached at her trading desk by commission and floor brokers wanting to buy and sell. Accordingly, she will use the quotes in the limit books as a reference to establishing her own bid and ask quotes.

As an example, suppose that a commission broker approaches the specialist at the trading post with an order to buy 3,000 shares of the specialist's stock. As is the custom, the commission broker would ask the specialist "How's the Market?" The specialist might then use the limit order prices as a reference if she wanted to trade in her own inventory or she may quote the best figure from the limit book. Suppose, for example, she responds by saying 40 and 41. The commission broker would see that the specialist is offering to buy at 40 and sell at 41. At this point, the commission broker may look around to see if there are any other commission brokers in the area to implement a trade. If he finds one looking to sell, then he and the other broker will approach the trading desk, and after discussing the specialist spread, they will negotiate a price. This type of two-way trading is known as the *double-auction method*. (It should be noted that by the rules of the exchange, the specialist cannot interfere with commission brokers' trading.) Now if the commission broker cannot find an opposite position, then, based on the quoted spread, he will notify the specialist by saying "3,000 bought." The specialist and commission broker will exchange pertinent information. After purchasing 3,000 shares, the specialist will either add to her inventory, which she hopes to sell later at least at 41, or she will use the stock to satisfy one of her limit orders to buy. More importantly, the specialist has made it possible for the commission broker to buy 3,000 shares almost immediately, and by so doing, she has achieved her primary function of ensuring a continuous market.

It should be noted that other security exchanges, as well as some futures and options exchanges, do not use specialists. Instead they use designated market makers (DMMs) and *order book officials*. Similar to specialists, designated market makers are required by the exchange to deal in an assigned security if someone cannot find someone with whom to trade. They do not, however, maintain a limit book; this is the responsibility of the order book official.

BLOOMBERG SITES WITH EXCHANGE INFORMATION

- **EPR or WEXC:** The EPR or WEXC screens can be used to find information on exchanges, including Web sites.
- **MMTK:** MMTK displays a list of market makers and their corresponding codes. You can use MMTK to search for market makers by their name, code, or alternate code. You can also search for a market maker by their registered exchange.
- **HALT:** Halt displays a list of securities or derivatives in which there is a halt or delay in trading. See HELP on HALT screen for more explanation.
- **IMAP:** The IMAP screen can be used to identify stocks that are traded on exchange. On the IMAP screen, select "All Securities," click region and country, and then an exchange (e.g., New York, OTC, or Hong Kong).

See Bloomberg Web Exhibit 4.5.

Convergences of Organized Exchanges, the OTC Market, and the Electronic Communications Networks

Brief History

For many years, stocks were discussed as trading on the organized exchanges, such as the New York Stock Exchange, the Nikkei in Tokyo, the London Stock Exchange, or the DAX in Germany, or as trading over the counter—the OTC market. Since 1990, electronic trading offered by *electronic communications networks* (*ECNs*) such as NASDAQ, Instinet, Wunsch Auction System (later to become the Arizona Stock Exchange), Tradebook, Archipelago, POSIT, Barclay's Stockbrokers, and Tradepoint have transformed the core structure of the organized exchanges and the OTC market.

By definition, an ECN is an electronic network (computer system) that provides a security trading system that brings brokerage firms and traders together so that they can trade among themselves. ECNs are set up to compete with security exchanges, the OTC market, and other ECNs. Many of the early ECNs were created by regional exchanges. Regional exchanges have had a long history of being innovative. For example, in 1981 the Philadelphia Exchange (acquired by NASDAQ) became the first exchange to offer trading in foreign currency options. The Cincinnati Exchange (which discontinued operation in 1995), developed the *National Securities Trading System* (NSTS), which allowed automated purchases and sales from the offices of member brokers and from the floor of the regional exchange. In 1990, the *Arizona Stock Exchange* (AZX) was established as a stock exchange based on a computer system (formerly the Wunsch Auction System).

Operationally, AZX was set up as an automated auction market process that matched the supply and demand for an extensive list of stocks several times during the course of a day. Similarly, the Archipelago Exchange was an electronic exchange that started in Chicago as a system that routed orders to other systems. It was later structured as a holding company owned by a large number of financial institutions, and in 2000, it merged with the Pacific Stock Exchange. Other ECNs were set up through alliances formed with large investment firms and financial information companies. REDBOOK, for example, was an ECN formed from a partnership of Donaldson, Lufkin, and Jenrette; Bank of America; Fidelity; Charles Schwab; and Spear, Leeds, & Kellogg (a large NYSE specialist firms). In Europe, Barclay's, Merrill Lynch, and a number of mutual funds and banks formed E-Crossnet, which was an ECN for institutional investors in Europe. Reuters, the news and information firm, helped formed Instinet, one of the biggest ECNs, providing electronic trading between institutional investors. Bloomberg formed Tradebook for electronic trading of OTC stocks and also later formed an alliance with Investment Technology Group to run POSIT—an ECN that conducted electronic auctions and trades for stocks in the United States, United Kingdom, and Australia.

As ECNs were beginning to emerge in the 1990s, the SEC ruled that such *alternative trading systems* (called *Reg ATS*) could register as stock exchanges. As a result, ECNs such the Wunsch Auction System and Archipelago (after merging with the registered Pacific Stock Exchange), became competing electronic stock exchanges. In 1995, Tradepoint was formed in the United Kingdom as an electronic exchange with a transparent order book showing orders for U. K. stocks. In 2000, *Jiway* launched it electronic platform in which 6,000 European and American stocks were dealt among brokers. In addition to SEC's Reg ATS, the growth in electronic trading systems was also aided by the SEC mandate that the *Consolidated Quotation System* (CQS), which managed the reporting of NYSE information, report current transactions not only from the NYSE, but also the OTC market, American Stock Exchange (AMEX), regional exchanges, and the third market (discussed in the next section) and further that the NYSE create an intermarket trading system (ITS)—an electronic trading network linking markets and facilitating trades. As the NYSE established the ITS, NASDAQ also created an ECN called Primex. The ITS and the Primex system, in turn, were accessible to any registered electronic exchanges—a benefit that turned a number of electronic networks into competing exchanges very quickly.

In response to the emergence of ECNs and electronic stock exchanges, the NYSE began to demutualize—going from owner/member associations to public companies; that is, historically, organized exchanges were structured as mutual or owner/member associations, consisting of member brokers. By exchange rules, only members traded on the exchange. To obtain a membership, also referred to as a *seat* on the exchange, an investment company or individual purchased it from an existing member. By demutualizing and becoming public companies, however, an organized exchange such as the NYSE could issue securities to raise the funds needed to finance the necessary expansion and acquisitions needed to move them into the competing electronic trading market. In 2006, the NYSE merged with Archipelago. It also stopped selling seats representing membership and became a publically traded company with shares traded on the NYSE. Finally, as noted in Chapter 1, in April of 2007 the NYSE became part of NYSE Euronext, a holding company created by combining the NYSE Group, Inc. and Euronext NV. The NYSE Euronext includes six equities exchanges and six derivatives exchanges, providing physical and electronic trading in stocks, bonds, and derivatives. Today, the NYSE is a hybrid physical and electronic exchange, consisting of a physical exchange and also a SuperECN and Electronic Stock Exchange. NASDAQ, in turn, has also become a super ECN with internal order execution capabilities and a centralized order book.

Third Market

The third market is one in which exchange-listed securities are traded on the OTC and regional markets. Before the advent of electronic trading and multiple listings, this market was popular for the trading of a large number of shares of a security, known as a *block trade*. Originally, the market provided institutional investors with a means of avoiding the higher commission cost on their large trades of listed stocks that would have resulted if they had traded through brokers who were members of the exchanges; such brokers, at one time, were required by the rules of the exchange to trade listed securities on the exchange and to charge the relatively high fixed commissions set by the exchange. Thus, brokers who were not members of the exchange, and therefore not bound by exchange rules, found it advantageous to act as block traders, trading blocks of listed stocks on the OTC market. The third market grew until the mid-1970s. In 1975, the elimination of high fixed commission costs, however, served to reduce the activities of the third market, and in 1976 the NYSE began to allow its members to execute orders on NYSE-listed securities on the third market (although it continued to prohibit them from acting as dealers by Rule 390). Finally, in 1979 the SEC ruled that members could act as dealers on securities listed after April 29, 1979.

Today, the third market consists of the OTC market and regional exchanges that offer listed stocks with competitive bid-ask quotes. They, in turn, use the intermarket trading system and the electronic communication network to execute third-market trades. For example, in 1999 the Chicago Stock Exchange (CHX) traded over 90 percent of the NYSE-listed stocks, providing dual listing for those stocks.

Fourth Markets

The fourth market is a market absent of brokers and dealers. It consists of financial institutions, block traders, and market makers who trade listed securities among themselves, dealing directly with each other on price and quantity. Many of the trades making up the fourth market were facilitated by *Instinet* (Institutional Network). Currently, the Instinet system allows participants to input and receive quotations and close trades anonymously. For example, a subscriber to Instinet can enter an order to sell that would be seen by other subscribers. If someone wanted to buy the stock at the seller's quote, he would enter a limit order to buy at that price and the computer would cross both orders and verify the trade. If the buyer wanted to negotiate, however, he could input his own quote and wait for a response. Instinet allows institutional investors to cross-order, matching buy and sell orders directly via computers without using brokers or dealers.

Block Trades

Typically, a block trade is initiated when a financial institution asks a block trader or *block house* to sell or buy a large number of shares (e.g., 100,000 shares of ABC stock). The block trader then acts as a "block positioner" by seeking out other traders interested in taking a position. The custom usually is one of calling other block traders and indicating he is putting together a block on the ABC stock (note that he would not divulge whether the block is to be bought or sold). Once all trading parties had been assembled and their positions identified, the block positioner then matches positions; the block trader might also purchase all or part of the block, hoping to resell the shares at a higher price.

Block positioners often trade in what is referred to as the *upstairs market*—a name used to refer to trading from offices and not on the exchange. Many block trades are also handled electronically via the Instinet system.

National Market System

The 1974 Securities Act Amendment mandated that the security industry move to a national market system in which all investors would have easy access to information and the ability to transact security trading quickly and efficiently. Over the last 30 years, the financial markets have seen the expansion of NASDAQ, the development of the intermarket trading system, the emergence of Electronic Communication Networks and registered electronic exchanges, and the transformation of the NYSE as a physical exchange into the NYSE Euronext—a hybrid physical and electronic exchange providing trading in stocks, bonds, and derivatives. These developments have made it possible for investors to obtain current information on security prices and to buy and sell thousands of securities at the best prices. These developments have also created competition among the exchanges, the OTC, and the third and fourth markets, which has served to reduce commission costs and improve efficiency. As a result, we are much closer today to the goal set forth by the 1974 Securities Act Amendment to establish a national market system.

BLOOMBERG EQUITY PRICES: BID-ASK, BLOCK TRADES: QMC, MBTR, AND SIDE

In addition to the Bloomberg stock price graph, GP, and intraday price information (GIP), other useful price screens accessible from a stock's equity menu include the following:

- **QR:** The QR screen displays individual trades with bid-ask quotes in chronological order for a selected stock and time period.
- **IOIA:** IOIA displays all indications of interest in trades for a select stock (i.e., a broker's announcement that a trade was executed by the respective broker) and ranks all trade advertisements sent from broker-dealers for a selected equity.
- **QMC:** The Bloomberg QMC screen displays all active quotes from all of the exchanges on which a selected equity trades. You can also view volume, historical trends, and arbitrage opportunities.
- **MBTR:** The MBTR monitor screen displays institutional equity transactions of 10,000 shares/lots or more (block trades) on exchanges worldwide. MBTR allows you to monitor block trades based on exchange and to filter them by volume or by using a security list that one defines.
- **SIDE** is used to determine whether an advertising broker/dealer for a specific security was likely a buyer or seller.

See Bloomberg Web Exhibit 4.6.

Trading Securities in the Market

Today existing stocks are traded by individual investors, institutional investors, brokers, dealers, and block traders in the following ways:

- Physically on the organized exchanges (brokers and dealers meeting fact-to-face).

- Through an OTC electronic system consisting of dealers and market makers that make up the over-the-counter market.
- Electronically through electronic matching or order working system (smart systems) on the Electronic Communications Network provided either by an exchange, the OTC market, or an off-exchange company.
- Physically or electronically through ECNs by institutional investors, brokers, dealers, and block traders in the third and fourth markets.

Organized Exchanges — Physical Exchange

Trading in the physical exchange can be described in a two ways. For one, it is a physical exchange, a building where brokers and dealers still go to buy and sell securities on behalf of their investors/clients. Physically, the trading floor of the NYSE exchange is approximately 100 yards long and 50 yards wide, with an annex. On the main floor, there are U-shaped counters, each with windows, known as trading posts. Here exchange specialists and other brokers go to trade securities. Encircling the floor are telephone and communication areas where brokers receive orders from their retail brokerage firms and institutional investors across the country.

A physical exchange can also be described by the functions of its brokers and dealers. Most brokerage firms that have a physical presence on an organized exchange function as commission brokers. *Commission brokers* execute buy and sell orders on behalf of their clients. Before the rise in electronic trading, many exchanges were also populated by *floor brokers*, sometimes referred to as broker's brokers or freelance brokers. They functioned by accepting orders from other brokers (usually commission brokers) and then executing them in return for a share in the commission. The second type of participant is the floor trader. *Floor traders* buy and sell securities only for themselves and not for others. Finally, there are the *specialists* and *market makers* who specialize in the trading of a specific security, and as noted previously, keep trading continuous.

OTC Trading

The OTC market can also be described as a continuous market that functions through market makers. The stocks and other securities traded on the OTC market are those listed ones for which a dealer wishing to make a market decides to take a position. Dealers on the OTC market range from regional brokerage houses making a market in a local corporation's stocks or bonds, to large financial companies, such as Bank of America Merrill Lynch, making markets in Treasury securities, to investment bankers dealing in the securities they had previously underwritten, to dealers in federal agency securities and municipal bonds. Each dealer maintains an inventory in a security and quotes a bid and an ask price at which she is willing to buy and sell.

The *Financial Industry Regulatory Authority* (FINRA) regulates the OTC trading. As noted, communications among brokers and dealers for stocks takes place through the NASDAQ system. This system provides current bid-ask quotes of dealers or sends brokers' quotes to dealers, enabling them to close trades. Price information on NASDAQ that has at least two market makers and a wide trading interest are published on NASDAQ's national daily list, whereas stocks and bonds that are thinly traded are listed with the *National Quotations Bureau* (NQB). NQB's listing included small- or microcap stocks, ADRs for foreign stocks (discussed in Chapter 5) that do not meet U.S. accounting standards, high-yield bonds, and convertible bonds.

Electronic Trading

In the 1980s, the NYSE developed the *Super Designated Order Turnaround System* (SuperDOT or simply DOT, which was an earlier system) to facilitate both small and large orders, as well as multiple-stock orders.[8] Brokers would send orders via a computer directly to this system. The SuperDot was one of the early electronic trading systems and a precursor to today's ECNs. In 2009, SuperDOT was replaced by the NYSE *Super Display Book System* (SDBK) for processing orders. In 2012, NYSE, in turn, replaced Display Book with the *Universal Trade Platform* (UTP).[9]

The NYSE Euronext also expanded its *NYSE Arca* platform, previously known as *ArcaEx*, an abbreviation of *Archipelago Exchange*. Today, the fully electronic NYSE Arca trades more than 8,000 exchange-listed equity securities, including NASDAQ listings. Traders who use this open, direct, anonymous platform are able to make speedy executions in multiple U.S. market centers. As of March 2007, NYSE Arca was the second largest ECN, with approximately one out of every six shares traded on the American financial markets traded on the system.[10]

In the late 1980s, NASDAQ established its electronic system, the *Small Order Execution System* (SOES) for dealers to enter their trades. In 2005, NASDAQ acquired the Instinet platform from Reuters, which had previously merged its platform with Island ECN and renamed it Island technology platform, or Inet (see Exhibit 4.8 for a brief history of Instinet).

Today, individual investors through their brokers, institutional investors, dealers, and block traders can execute trade electronically through electronic trading systems provided by organized exchanges, NASDAQ, or an ECN. Electronic trading systems can be grouped into *order-crossing networks* and *electronic order-working systems* (or smart systems). As noted, such networks can be provided by an electronic exchange that is either separate or part of an organized physical exchange (like NYSE Euronext), or they can be provided by a company or alliance, such as Instinet.

Order-Crossing Networks

Order-crossing networks match buy and sell orders. Such networks provide traders anonymity, but not continuous trading (i.e., it is a call market system devoid of its own market makers). They may do this by an electronic automated auction process or by matching orders rapidly. In an automated call auction system, traders submit orders to buy and sell. The auction system then computes the supply and demand curves for each stock being auctioned, with the intersection of the curve determining the stock's

EXHIBIT 4.8   Brief History of Instinet

Instinet was founded by Jerome M. Pustilnik and Herbert R. Behrens and was incorporated in 1967 as Institutional Networks Corp. The founders aimed to compete with the NYSE by means of computer links between major institutions, such as banks, mutual funds, and insurance companies, with no delays or intervening specialists. Through its Instinet system, the company provided computer services and a communications network for the automated buying and selling of equity securities on an anonymous and confidential basis.

In 1983, Instinet, under the direction of William Lupien, began marketing their system to the broker community, rather than focus exclusively on institutions. Together, they successfully introduced many innovations which made Instinet an integral tool for traders on both the "buy" and "sell" sides of the market.

As a result of Lupien's refocusing of Instinet, the firm grew rapidly in the mid-1980s. In 1987, Reuters acquired the company. Under Reuters, the Instinet platform continued to grow through the late 1980s and into the early 1990s. By the time that the SEC introduced the Order Handling Rules and Alternative Trading Systems (ATS) regulation, Instinet was the dominant ECS. However, these rules also gave rise to new competitors, some of whom employed new pricing schemes. By the early 2000s, these competitors had managed to erode the firm's market share. In 2002, Instinet merged with Island ECN and renamed the platform Island technology platform, Inet. Reuters went on to IPO Instinet in 2001, keeping a 62% ownership stake. In 2005, Instinet was purchased by NASDAQ. NASDAQ retained INET ECN and subsequently sold the agency brokerage business to Silver Lake. In February 2007, Nomura purchased the firm from Silver Lake for a reported $1.2 billion.

Instinet is today operated as an independent subsidiary of Nomura. In May 2012, Nomura announced that it would transfer electronic trading in the United States to Instinet, with the goal of eventually making it the electronic trading arm for all of Nomura. However, in September 2012, Nomura announced that it would instead make Instinet its execution services (cash, program and electronic trading) for all of markets except for Japan.

---

market clearing price. Such systems may also have a reserve book that holds orders back until some part of the open book is met (e.g., a volume or price condition is met). In an auction system, traders are often allowed to change their orders until a specified execution time when the price that best matches the buy and sell orders is determined. Electronic order-crossing systems are often characterized by an allocation system set to address when buy and sell orders do not match. For example, a *first come-first served system* that starts by matching the oldest order to buy with the oldest order to sell. It is possible that one side of a trade may fail to materialize when an order is sent through an order-crossing network, leading to time discrepancy between the time when the order was sent and when it is finally executed. On the other hand, an order-crossing system can have a speedy transaction if the other side of the transaction is already in the system. For example, an order-crossing system may have a reserve book that holds orders back until some part of the open book is met. Rapid trading is also enhanced when there are a number of users of the system, such as block traders, institutional traders, corporations, and market makers from the OTC market or the exchanges.

One of the biggest ECNs operating as an order-crossing network is Instinet (or Inet), which, as noted earlier, initially provided electronic trading for the fourth market. Bloomberg Tradebook system also was set up as a matching system for primarily OTC stocks, and E-Crossnet was set as a cross-ordering ECN for institutional investors.

Electronic Order-Working Systems

Electronic order-working systems are so-called *smart systems* designed to "work an order." These systems work an order by gathering price information from many markets, breaking orders into smaller sizes, simultaneously buying and selling a large number of stocks composing a portfolio, linking global markets, slicing orders to be traded at different times of the day, and evaluating different market maker tendencies. Order-working systems are set up with data inputs about the securities that are traded, such as customer orders, brokerage firm orders, limit orders, and inputs about the markets where the securities are traded. With this information, the order-working system then searches markets where the whole transaction or parts of it can be executed. Often, the system passes the order or parts of it to market makers, order-crossing networks such as Instinet, and other electronic order-working systems. The system takes the information from these systems and markets and uses it to decide whether to execute all or part of trade. If only part is executed, then the order-working system may send the rest of the order to the NYSE's Universal Trade Platform or NASDAQ's order system.

NYSE Universal Trade Platform and NYSE Arca can be best described as order working systems. The Universal Trade Platform accepts market orders, pairs the buy and sell requests, and then sends the net imbalances to the appropriate specialists. The system typically carries out such transactions within a minute. As noted, NYSE Arca is a fully electronic stock exchange, trading more than 8,000 exchange- and NASDAQ-listed securities. NYSE Arca's functions are based on price-time priority system. The system's trading platform electronically links traders to multiple market centers and provides customers with fast electronic execution and open, direct and anonymous market access.

Trade Execution — Example

To see how trades are executed in today's market system consider a simple case in which an investor places a buy market order to purchase 500 shares of P&G stock with her broker. The broker can submit the order either to the brokerage firm's floor broker on the exchange or enter the order into the Universal Trade Platform (based on a prearranged agreement) or to the NYSE Arca platform. If the order goes to the firm's desk, then the firm's broker for P&G will receive the order and go to the trading post for P&G and join the "group" of other brokers with P&G trade orders and also the P&G specialist. The investor's order could be executed in whole or parts with the other traders and the specialist, or with trades against the limit order books.

As a rule, smaller orders such as 500 shares go directly to the specialist display book through the Universal Trade Platform or to Arca. Medium-size orders (under 10,000 shares) are often sent to the firm's booth or possibly "upstairs," where they are traded as part of block trades. Medium-size trades may also be traded over time. Referred to as "working the crowd," trades could be made in increments of, say, 1,000 shares to hide the size of the order.

For large block trades, typically made by institutional investors, execution through the order books by specialists and the trading by the crowd generally cannot be done without significant movement in price. As a result, large trades are often negotiated in the "upstairs market" among block traders. These traders often work via Instinet to match institutional investors interested in taking the other side of the large order. Depending on the activity and interests in the trade, the order may end up being met by some block traders, specialists, and the crowd, and sold over a discrete period of time. A 200,000 order to sell P&G may end up being executed with a block trader setting up 150,000 shares to be purchased by institutional investors, 30,000 traded on the exchange, and 20,000 held by the block trader.

Note on the Secondary Market for Bonds

The secondary market for bonds in the United States and throughout the world is not centralized, but rather it is part of the OTC market. In the OTC market for bonds, market makers provide bid and offer quotes for each issue in which they participate. There are some corporate bonds that are listed on physical exchanges. Such bonds are sometimes said to be trading in the "Bond Room." Although they may be listed, they are more likely to be traded through dealers on the OTC market than on the exchange. There is also a transition to electronic trading. For example, NYSE Euronext recently began offering an all-electronic platform for trading NYSE bonds based on price-time priority system. There are also developing multidealer systems that allow customers to execute bond trades from multiple quotes. The systems display the best bid or offer prices of those posted by all dealers. The participating dealers usually act as the principal in the transaction. There are also developing single-dealer systems that allow investors to execute transaction directly with the specific dealers desired.

Clearinghouse

Once a buyer and seller have agreed on a security trade, the transaction must be settled: cash and security certificates (or other ownership claims such as computer listings) must be properly transferred. Most trades require that settlement be made within five days. Investment firms are engaged in trades with a number of other investment firms. To facilitate settlement, clearing corporations receive all records of the trade; they then notify the investment firm of the net amount of securities to be delivered or received and the net amount of money to be paid or received.

The *National Securities Clearing Corporation* (NSCC), a subsidiary of the Depository Trust Corporation, is the principal clearinghouse for settling security transactions occurring on the exchanges and the OTC market. Members of these exchanges and markets subscribe to this service or use members who do. Those belonging to the exchanges have their daily records of transactions sent to the NSCC, which in turn nets them out. Each member then receives a list of the net amount of security certificates they must deliver, as well as a list of those to be received and the net amount of money to be paid or received. The members then settle with the clearinghouse instead of other brokers and dealers.

In addition to the NSCC, many brokers and dealers also belong to the *Depository Trust Corporation* (DTC). The DTC maintains a record of security ownership of its members and holds all security certificates. Accordingly, if a trade occurs among members, then the transfer is recorded by simply changing the names in the book. Thus, no certificate exchange is necessary.

Finally, to ensure against negligence resulting in a failure to properly transfer ownership after a trade, there exists the *Securities Investor Protection Corporation* (SIPC). Created out of the 1970 Securities Investor Protection Act, SIPC is a government agency that ensures brokers and dealers against any losses resulting in a failure to deliver securities or funds.

Types of Transactions

A security trade usually takes the form of either an order to buy (*long position*) or an order to sell (*short position*). There are, however, other positions to take, such as buying on margin and short sales, and other trade considerations, such as the size of the order and the instructions to the broker regarding the execution of the orders.

Margin Purchases

To purchase securities on margin means that part of the purchase is financed by borrowing, often from the brokerage firm. Accordingly, such a purchase is known as a *margin purchase* or a leveraged position. A margin purchase increases the investor's return-risk opportunities. For example, if an investor buys 100 shares of stock for $100 per share ($10,000), her investment would be worth $20,000 if the stock's price increases to $200, yielding her a 100 percent rate of return if she sold the stock [($20,000 − $10,000)/$10,000], and it would be worth only $5,000, if the stock declines to $50, yielding a 50 percent loss on her investment [($5,000 − $10,000)/$10,000]. Suppose the investor, however, borrows $10,000 and buys 200 shares instead of 100. In this case, her investment would be worth $30,000 if the stock is at $200 [stock value − loan = ($200)(200) − $10,000], and her rate of return from her $10,000 investment would be 200 percent. However, if the stock were at $50, the investor's investment value would be zero [stock value − loan = ($50)(200) − $10,000], and the percentage loss on her investment would be 100 percent. Thus, leveraged or margin purchases, although increasing the potential rate of return that an investor can earn, also increases an investor's risk.

When a margin purchase is handled through a brokerage firm, the firm usually sets up a *margin account* for the investor. In contrast to a *cash account* whereby the investor deposits cash with the brokerage firm in an amount equal to the full cost of the security, a margin account requires only a portion of cash to be deposited in order to cover the acquisition. When such accounts are set up, the customer usually signs a contract known as a *hypothecation agreement*. In this agreement, the customer gives the broker the right to use the securities to be acquired as its collateral for a bank (or other financial institution) loan to the broker that is the source of the loan money. The bank rate to the broker is referred to as the *call money rate*. In addition to the hypothecation agreement, the brokerage firm may also request that the securities purchased be left with the broker or registered in street name so that the brokerage firm can lend out the securities if a short sale opportunity arises (short sales are discussed in the next section).

Given the risk involved in margin purchases, as well as some past abuses, the maximum loan amount a broker can advance toward the purchase of a security is governed by the FRS. Specifically, by *Regulation T* (initiated as part of the 1934 SEC Act) the Fed has the right to limit the initial amount of loans brokers can provide, and by *Regulation U*, they have the power to control the loan amounts of commercial banks to brokers and dealers. The Fed regulations are stated in terms of *initial margin requirements*. A margin (M_0) is defined as the proportion of an investor's equity (cash) to the value of the security:

$$M_0 = \frac{\text{Investor's Cash}}{\text{Market Value of Securities}} = \frac{\text{Market Value} - \text{Loan}}{\text{Market Value of Securities}}$$

Since 1934, the Fed has varied margin requirements from 40 to 100 percent. Usually they change the percentage to control credit in the economy as part of their monetary policy tools.

In addition to initial margin requirements, most brokerage firms also require that the investor adhere to a *maintenance margin requirement* and to rules governing restrictive accounts if the security's price decreases.[11] If a decline in the security's price leads to an actual margin that is lower than the initial margin requirement but higher than the broker-stipulated maintenance margin, then the investor is said to have a *restricted account*. With a restricted account, the investor would be prohibited from acquiring any more shares on margin, but she would not be required to deposit any more cash in her account. However, if the security's price decreases to a level in which the actual margin is below the maintenance margin requirement, then the investor will receive a *margin call* from the brokerage firm instructing her to adjust the margin position to meet the maintenance requirement. The investor could meet the deficiency by either depositing more cash in her cash account, by selling some shares, or both. If the investor did not respond to the margin call, then the brokerage firm could sell the securities and return the proceeds to the investor after loan and commission cost deductions. It should be noted that brokerage firms calculate the customer's actual margin each day based on the previous day's closing prices to see if a margin call is in order. This practice is known as determining which customer is *marked to market*.

To see more specifically how margin requirements work, consider the case of an investor who acquires 100 shares of a stock for $100 per share. Furthermore, suppose that the initial margin requirement is 60 percent and that the maintenance margin is 40 percent. If the investor borrows the maximum amount permitted, she would be able to borrow \$4,000 and her initial and actual margin at the time of the purchase would be 60 percent:

$$M_0 = \frac{\text{Investor's Cash}}{\text{Market Value of Securities}}$$

$$M_0 = \frac{\text{Market Value} - \text{Loan}}{\text{Market Value of Securities}}$$

$$M_0 = \frac{(\$100)(100) - \$4,000}{(\$100)(100)} = 0.60$$

The price at which the investor could receive a maintenance margin call (P_C) would be \$66.67:

$$0.40 = \frac{P_C(100) - \$4,000}{P_C(100)}$$

$$-0.40 P_C(100) + P_C(100) = \$4,000$$

$$P_C(100)(1 - 0.4) = \$4,000$$

$$P_C = \frac{\$4,000}{(100)(1 - 0.4)}$$

$$P_C = \$66.67$$

Thus, if the stock increased to \$120, then the investor's actual margin would rise to 66.67 percent, $[(\$120)(100) - \$4,000]/(\$120)(100) = 0.6667$. At this price, the investor could either liquidate, withdraw the excess margin of 6.67 percent, or purchase more shares on margin until the actual margin equaled the initial requirement. This latter alternative is known as *pyramiding*. In contrast, if the stock declines to a value between \$100 and \$66.67, then the investor would have a restricted account; finally, if it declines to a value below \$66.67, then she would receive a margin call. In the latter case, the investor would have to either put up cash or sell some of the shares for cash in order to maintain her actual margin at 40 percent.

Short Sale

In contrast to the typical investment strategy in which you buy a security now and sell it later, a short sale (also known as *selling short* or *selling under*) involves selling a security now and buying it later. As noted in Chapter 1, to implement this strategy, the investor borrows the security, sells it in the market, and then repays her debt obligation by buying the security later and returning the borrowed share. To profit from a short sale, the security's price must decrease. For example, suppose an investor sells ABC stock short by borrowing one share and selling it in the market for \$100. If the price of ABC stock declines to \$50, then the short seller could repay her obligation (also known as covering the position) by buying back the stock in the market at \$50 and returning the borrowed share, netting a profit of \$50. However, if the price of ABC stock increases to \$150 and the short seller has to cover, then she would lose \$50.

The process involved in executing a short sale for an individual investor involves several steps. First, the investor informs her broker that she wants him to execute a short sale. For example, suppose again an investor wants 100 shares of ABC stock sold short when the market price of ABC is $100. To find a lender of 100 shares of ABC stock, the short seller's broker may use one of the brokerage firm's customers who has the stock held in street name (possibly one who has a margin account), or he may have to contact another brokerage firm. In either case, the *share lender*, also known as the lender of shares, is often unaware of the loan. With the borrowed shares, the broker then will find a buyer of the stock and sell the shares at $100, delivering the 100 shares and receiving $10,000. Once settled, the broker then will hold the short seller's $10,000 as security with no interest paid (known as a flat hold). The short seller also must post collateral in cash or equity.

Both the short seller and the share lender have the right to close their positions at any time. Technically, no time limit exists on a short sale. By definition, it is a *call loan* that is cancelable at any time by either party. If the share lender orders his broker to sell his shares, then the short seller's broker will have to either find another share lender or ask the short seller to cover by buying the shares in the market. If the short seller wants to close because the stock price decreases or because she is fearful of a call, or she has to close because she has been instructed to do so by the share lender's broker, then she simply instructs her broker to buy the 100 shares. If the market price of the stock in our example were $50, then the short seller's broker will use $5,000 of the $10,000 he is holding to buy the shares, then return the 100 shares to the lender and give the short seller both her $5,000 profit and collateral. Of course, if the stock price increases, the broker would have to use $10,000 plus part of the collateral to cover the short sale.

In addition to the mechanics of a short sale, one should also be aware of several other points. First, the SEC has at times required that short sales be executed only on an *up-tick* (when the price at which the borrowed shares are sold exceeds the previous trading day's close) or a *zero-plus-tick* (when the price is equal to the previous trade but higher than the last trade at a different price). Underlying this rule is the hope it will slow down or stop a possible "bear run" on a security. Second, a short seller is expected to cover any dividends that are paid. After the execution of a short sale, the new security buyer is the shareholder of record and thus will receive all dividends from the corporation. The share lender also is entitled to dividends. Accordingly, he will be paid by the short seller.[12] Finally, margin requirements, as noted above, are required on short sales. The short seller's initial margin is the total amount of cash or "investor's assets" that is required. For a short sale, the initial margin requirement (M_0^{SS}) is stated as a proportion of the value of the securities loaned:

$$M_0^{SS} = \frac{\text{Investor's Assets} - \text{Loan}}{\text{Loan}}$$

where:

Investor's Assets = cash from short sale and cash (or security) deposited with the broker.

Loan = market value of securities that were borrowed.

If the initial margin requirement is 0.60, then an investor who sold 100 shares of ABC stock short at $100 would need to add $6,000 to the $10,000 cash obtained from the sale of the borrowed shares to make his margin equal 0.60:

$$M_0^{SS} = \frac{\text{Investor's Assets} - \text{Loan}}{\text{Loan}}$$

$$M_0^{SS} = \frac{(\$10,000 + \text{Cash}) - \$10,000}{\$10,000}$$

$$\text{Cash} = (0.60)(\$10,000) = \$6,000$$

As with margins on long positions, the brokerage house also will require a maintenance margin to protect itself in case the security price increases. In the above example, if the maintenance margin is 40 percent, then the short seller would receive a margin call, asking her to put more cash or securities in her account if the price of the stock increased to $140, causing the actual margin (M^A) to be 0.40:

$$M^A = 0.40 = \frac{P_C(100) - \$10,000}{\$10,000}$$

$$P_C = \frac{(1 + 0.40)(\$10,000)}{100} = \$140$$

BLOOMBERG INFORMATION ON SHORT SALES

Short Interest, SI: Short Interest is the total amount of shares of stock that are sold short and have not been repurchased to close out the position. High levels of short interest indicate that numerous sellers have sold the stock short and are expecting a downturn in the share price.

　The Bloomberg SI Screen displays monthly short interest information for a selected equity security that trades on certain exchanges.

　SSR: The SSR Screen indicates where there are restrictions on short sales.

See Bloomberg Web Exhibit 4.7.

Types of Orders

In addition to the types of transactions (long positions, short positions, and margin positions), an investor also must instruct his broker on the types of orders (unless he wants to give his broker a discretionary order allowing the broker to decide the price and time). The usual instructions involve specifying the size of the order and the price at which the security can be bought or sold.

Size of the Order

The trading on most exchanges occurs as either a *round-lot* or an *odd-lot* order. When an order is a round lot, it is for the standard unit of trading. On the NYSE Euronext and other exchanges, the standard unit for most stocks is 100 shares (referred to as one lot) or a multiple of it, 200, 300, etc. (two, three, etc. lots). An order for less than the standard is defined as an odd lot; thus 3, 50, 75 would be odd lots. Finally, such orders as 162 would be considered as both round (100) and odd (62) lots.[13]

Price Limits of the Order

The investor can instruct her broker to either buy or sell the security at either the best prevailing price—market order—or at a price she determines—limit order. With a market order, the broker will try to execute the order as fast as possible at the best price he can obtain. The advantage of this type of order is the speed at which the trade is executed; the disadvantage is that the investor is unsure of the price she will obtain. The uncertainty over price can be overcome by the investor instructing the broker to execute a limit order to buy or sell the stock. With a limit order to buy, the investor specifies the maximum price he will pay for the stock. The order then can only be carried out at that price or lower. For a limit order to sell, the investor specifies the minimum price he will accept, and the order will then only be carried out at that price or higher. In contrast to market orders, limit orders have the disadvantage of taking time before they can be executed and possibly not being executed if the price limit is not reached.

Time Limits of the Order

In addition to specifying the price limits of an order, the investor must also indicate the *time limit* of the order. Accordingly, she can specify a day order, in which the order remains active only for the trading day during which it is entered, a week order, which expires at the end of the calendar week (Friday), a month order, and so on. Also, there can be either open or specific orders. Often with limit orders, the investors request an *open order or good-till-canceled (GTC) order*, which is open until it is executed or the investor withdraws it. Alternatively, the investor may ask that the order be executed immediately at a limit price or better, or canceled. This order is sometimes referred to as a *fill-or-kill (FOK)* order.

Stop Order

Finally, on the list of investor instructions are *stop orders*. A stop order to sell or *stop loss order* is a market order to sell when the stock hits the specified stop price or below. Stop loss orders are typically used to lock in a gain. For example, if you had bought 100 shares of ABC at $50 and it was presently trading at $100, you would have an unrealized profit of $5,000. To protect some of this profit and at the same time benefit from any further price increase, you could instruct your broker to enter a stop order to sell at $95. If ABC stock hits $95, then the broker would execute a market order to sell. Note that the disadvantage of this order is that a price change could be temporary. For example, the price of ABC might hit $95, then turn around and increase. A stop order to buy or *stop buy* is a market order to buy when the stock hits the stop price. A stop buy order is sometimes used with a short sale. For example, if you had shorted 100 shares of ABC at $50 and it was presently trading at $25, you would have an unrealized profit of $2,500. To protect some of this profit and at the same time benefit from any further price decrease, you could instruct your broker to enter a stop order to buy at $30. If ABC stock were to increase to $30, then the broker would execute a market order to buy 100 shares, allowing you to close your short sale and lock in a profit from the short sale of $2,000.

In addition to a stop order in which a market order is executed when the stop price is reached, an investor can also enter a *stop-limit order*. Like a stop order, this order will be executed when the stop price is reached, but the order also carries the additional instruction that the security must be bought or sold at a price limit. In the above example, if you had requested a stop-limit order to sell at $95, then if the stock hits $95, the broker would enter a limit order to sell at $95. The potential disadvantage of this is that the order might not be executed.

Cost of Trading

Through the exchanges, brokers, dealers, market makers, and specialists have created a network whereby an investor can buy and sell a security in a matter of minutes simply by calling his broker or submitting a request from his computer. The cost of maintaining this complex system is paid for by investors through the commission costs they pay to their brokers, the bid-ask spread investors pay to market makers or specialists when they set up and then later close their positions, and the fees charged by the clearing firms that are usually included in the brokerage commission and paid by their brokers.

Commissions

In accordance with the Securities Act Amendment of 1975, commissions on all security transactions are negotiable between the investor and the broker. However, prior to the enactment of this act on May 1, 1975 (known as *May Day*), the commissions charged by brokers had been fixed. Commission costs differ for discount brokerage firms and full brokerage firms. For institutional investors who trade in blocks, the rates are lower. Note that many brokerage firms require stock buyers to pay a commission when they buy the stock and also when they sell it. Thus, the total *round trip cost* (cost of purchase and sale) would be twice the rate.

Bid-Ask Spread

The primary function of specialists, market makers, and dealers is to ensure a continuous market. To do this, they stand ready to buy and sell securities at their bid and ask prices. The bid-ask spread thus represents their compensation for providing liquidity. To the investor, however, the bid-ask spread represents another transaction cost involved in trading securities. For example, if a dealer's bid price is $4 and her ask price is $4.50, a stock buyer who paid $4.50 for the stock, then immediately sold it for $4.00, would be paying the dealer $0.50 for the services of providing a continuous market. On average, the spread for a typical stock is less than 1 percent per share price. This cost varies depending on the stock's trading price and volume. Interestingly, one change in security market trading that has served to reduce the bid-ask spread is the decimalization that occurred on the NYSE and NASDAQ in 2000. The minimum share price allowed on an exchange is referred to as a tick. The NYSE used to have a tick size of one-eighth and one-sixteenth of a dollar. In 2000, the NYSE and NAS-DAQ changed the tick to one cent, and by so doing, they helped to reduce the bid-ask spread and therefore the cost of trading.

Conclusion

Brokers and dealers operating through organized exchanges, the OTC market, and ECNs have created a sophisticated system in which investors can buy and sell securities easily and quickly. In this chapter, we have examined equity securities, how this trading system operates, and how stocks and corporate bonds are traded in the system. This sophisticated system is global in breadth. In the next chapter, we continue our analysis of security trading by examining investment funds formed with such securities. Since the 1980s, there has also been a globalization of security markets with the openings or expansion of exchanges in Europe, the Middle East, and Asia. In Chapter 5, we will also examine the global trading of securities.

Web Site Information

NYSE Euronext
For information on NYSE Euronext, go to www.nyse.com.

OTC Information
For information on OTC market, go to www.finra.org/index.htm and www.nasdaq.com.

SEC
For information on the laws, regulations, and litigations of the SEC go to www.sec.gov.

For financial information on securities, market trends, and analysis, see:

- www.Finance.Yahoo.com
- http://www.hoovers.com
- http://www.bloomberg.com
- http://www.businessweek.com
- http://www.ici.org
- http://seekingalpha.com
- http://bigcharts.marketwatch.com
- http://www.morningstar.com
- http://free.stocksmart.com
- http://online.wsj.com/public/us

Notes

1. The company's choice of financing with debt or equity, in turn, depends on the return-risk opportunities management wants to provide its shareholders. Because debt instruments have provisions that give creditors legal protection in the case of default, the rate corporations are required to pay creditors for their investments is typically smaller than the rate their shareholders require. As a result, a firm that tends to finance its projects with relatively more debt than equity (i.e., a *leveraged firm*) benefits its shareholders with the relatively lower rates it pays to creditors. In addition, debt financing also has a major tax advantage to corporations: The interest payments on debt are treated as an expense by the Internal Revenue Service (IRS) and are therefore tax deductible, whereas the dividends a corporation pays its shareholders are not tax deductible. The relatively lower rates required by creditors and the tax advantage of debt make debt financing cheaper than equity financing for a corporation, all other things being equal. The lower rates on debt, however, are not without costs. Unlike equity financing, in which funds are paid to shareholders only if they are earned, the obligations of debt instruments are required to be made. Thus, if a company has a period with poor sales or unexpected high costs, it still has to make payments to the bondholders, leaving fewer earnings available for shareholders. Moreover, very low sales or very high costs could lead to the company being unable to meet its interest and/or principal payments. In this case, the creditors can sue the company, forcing them to sell company assets to meet their obligations, or the company can petition the courts to reorganize.

2. Pension fund investments in venture capital firm stated in 1979, after the U.S. Department of Labor clarified the Prudent Man's Rule, making it possible for pensions to make such investments.

3. A number of public companies went private following the passage of the Sarbanes-Oxley Act in 2002.

4. Investment banking firms often assist firms in privately placing securities, often using best effort.

5. With stock prices relatively low and yielding poor returns during the 1970s, Michael Milken of the investment banking firm of Drexel Burnham Lambert was one who saw the potential of selling high-yielding corporate bonds created from financing mergers to institutional investors as a substitute for stock. During the 1980s, some 1,800 corporations issued low-quality, high-yielding junk bonds to finance their acquisitions and to change their capital structure. In underwriting a number of these issues, Drexel Burnham Lambert earned fees as high as 2 percent to 3 percent. In addition, to facilitate the marketability of these bonds, Milken and Drexel Burnham Lambert also improved the credit worthiness of the bonds by standing ready to renegotiate the debt or to loan funds if the company were in jeopardy of default. The investment company also acted as market maker, providing a secondary market for junk bonds.

    Unfortunately, the economic recession of the late 1980s and early 1990s depressed the earning of many leveraged companies. Over 250 companies defaulted between 1989 and 1991, including Drexel Burnham Lambert, who filed for bankruptcy in 1990 due to losses on its holdings of junk bonds. As for Michael Milken, he was convicted of insider trading, resulting from feeding information on target companies to Ivan Boesky, a Wall Street hedge fund player, and others. He was sentenced to three years in prison; his net worth, however, was reported by *Fortune* to be over $400 million in 1993.

6. Until its acquisition by NASDAQ in 2004 (and later the NYSE in 2008), the *American Stock Exchange (AMEX)* represented the other national exchange. AMEX was once called the *curb exchange* (until 1953 when it was named the American Stock Exchange) because its brokers would assemble outside on the curb of Wall Street to take orders phoned into a nearby office. The AMEX historically tended to be more innovative than the NYSE. For example, not only were its listing requirements less stringent than the NYSE, allowing it to attract smaller and usually younger companies, it was also one of the first exchanges to offer a market for warrants and listed options, and it initiated trading in American Depository Receipts (ADR) and exchange-traded funds.

7. For example, for many years commercial banks and life insurance companies had a tradition of not listing on the NYSE (although they were listed on the OTC). In their cases, they did not list out of a concern that a decrease in stock prices, due perhaps to general economic factors, might cause a panic and lead to a deposit withdrawal. In 1965, Chase Manhattan broke that tradition by listing itself on the NYSE, and several other large banks, or their holding companies, followed Chase.

8. SuperDot was the electronic system used by the NYSE to route orders from investors to specialists located on the floor of the exchange. SuperDot was the upgraded form of the previous electronic system used to route orders, known as the Designated Order Turnaround (DOT) system. Since 1976, most of the orders in NYSE had been transmitting electronically to specialists' screens over the DOT or via the upgraded SuperDot.

9. The user, either an investor or a broker, used to enter the order into the system, which immediately reached the specialist and was executed. The users received a confirmation report of the transaction once the order was executed. Most individual investors, however, never had direct access to the SuperDot system. However, they indirectly used the system through software or online services offered by brokerages that in turn placed the client orders into the SuperDot.

10. In late 2006, NYSE Arca was the first one to offer NASDAQ-style fees on NYSE-listed securities, a move that was soon adopted by NASDAQ and other ECNs. NYSE Arca charges traders who remove liquidity from the Arca-book $3.00 per 1,000 shares. Traders who add liquidity receive a $2.00 rebate per 1,000 shares. Traders who route orders out of the NYSE Arca system are charged $1.00 per 1,000 shares.

11. Maintenance margins are set by brokerage firms and not the Fed.

12. Note: Except for commission cost, the payment of dividends should not be a major concern to the short seller, since on the day dividends are paid, the stock price must fall in the market (or abnormal profits would result). The short seller, if she wanted, would therefore be able to buy the stock back, or a percentage of it, at a price low enough to compensate for the dividends she must pay.

13. Up until the 1980s, the distinction between round and odd was important because, by the rules of the exchange, odd lots could only be bought or sold by odd-lot brokers. As a result, the commission per share was higher on odd lots than on round ones.

Selected References

Asquith, P., R. Gertner, and D. Scharfstein. 1994. Anatomy of financial distress: An examination of junk-bond issues. *Quarterly Journal of Economics* 109(3): 625–658.

Battalio, Robert H. 1997. Third-market broker-dealers: Cost competitors or cream skimmers. *Journal of Finance* 52 (March): 341–352.

Bodie, Zvi, Alex Kane, and Alan Marcus. 2011. *Investments*, 9th ed. New York: McGraw-Hill Irwin: 1–59.

Baird, D. G., and T. H. Jackson. 1988. Bargaining after the fall and the contours of the absolute priority rule. *University of Chicago Law Review* 55: 738–789.

Bebchuk, L. A. 1988. A new approach to corporate reorganizations. *Harvard Law Review* 101: 775–804.

Franks, J. R., and W. N. Torous. 1989. An empirical investigation of U.S. firms in reorganization. *Journal of Finance* 44: 747–769.

Johnson, R. Stafford. 2013. *Debt Markets and Analysis*. Hoboken, NJ: John Wiley & Sons: 267–319.

Kim, I. J., K. Ramaswamy, and S. M. Sundaresan. 1993. Valuation of corporate fixed-income securities. *Financial Management* (special issue on financial distress), 22(3): 60–78.

Leland, H. 1994. Risky debt, bond covenants and optimal capital structure. *Journal of Finance* 49: 1213–1252.

Meckling, W. H. 1977. Financial markets, default, and bankruptcy. *Law and Contemporary Problems* 41: 124–177.

Milligan, John W. 1990. Two cheers for 144A. *Institutional Investor* 24 (July): 117–119.

Miller, Merton, and Franco Modigliani. 1961. Dividend policy, growth, and valuation of shares. *Journal of Business* 34 (October): 411–433.

Reilly, Frank, and Keith Brown. 2003. *Investment Analysis and Portfolio Management*, 7th ed. Independence, Kansas: Thomson South-Western: 105–149.

Rogowski, Robert, and Eric Sorensen. 1985. Deregulation in investment banking: Shelf registration, structure, and performance. *Financial Management* 14 (Spring): 5–15.

Warner, J. B. 1977. Bankruptcy, absolute priority, and the pricing of risky debt claims. *Journal of Financial Economics* 4: 239–276.

Wruck, K. H. 1990. Financial distress, reorganization, and organizational efficiency. *Journal of Financial Economics* 27(2): 419–444.

Bloomberg Exercises

1. Select a company of interest and study its size, capital structure (debt/equity ratio), geographical distribution of its products, outstanding bonds, and major equity holders. Screens to examine from its equity menu are as follows:

   - DES   Description; Tabs: Report, Profile, Issue Info, Revenue & EPS, and Ratios
   - RELS   Related securities (e.g., debt, preferred stocks)
   - CF   Company Filings (10-K)
   - HDS   Majors holders of the stock
   - OWN   Equity Ownership
   - SPLC   Supply Chain
   - FA   Tabs: Segments/By Geography, Segments/By Measures, and B/S
   - ISSD   Issuer Description
   - DDIS   Debt Distribution
   - AGGD   Debt Holders
   - BRC   Research on Company
   - RSKC   Risk
   - DRSK   Credit Risk
   - LITI   Litigation

2. Select a stock of interest or the one you selected in Exercise 1 and use its CACS screen to find if it has taken any of the following actions over the last few years:
   - Stock split
   - Stock dividend
   - Acquisitions
   - Divestures
   - New stock offerings

3. Select a stock of interest or the one you selected in Exercise 1 or 2 and use its DVD screen to find when its next ex-dividend and payment dates are.

4. Bloomberg information on corporate actions such as acquisitions and limited partnership deals can be accessed on the CACS screen found on the company's equity menu. Select a company of interest that you know has been active in acquisitions and divestures and use CACS to search for its previous activities.

5. Select a preferred stock of a company of interest (use SECF to find the preferred: SECF <Enter>; FI tab, and Pfd tab; or search by entering: <Pfd> tk <Enter>; if you know the company's ticker, bring up its screen by entering: Ticker <Pfd>). Study the preferred stock using the stock's menu screen. Possible screens to examine from the menus are DES, DVD, and GP.

6. Identify several past acquisitions, IPOs, or divestures using the CACT screen. Set your search for M&A and IPO.

7. Identify several current or recent investment activities of venture capital and private equity holdings companies by using the FLNG screen (click "Venture Capital" and "Private Equity" in "Institution Type" dropdown).

8. Using the FLNG screen, study the past activities of a venture capital and a private equity firm: FLNG <Enter>. On the uploaded screen, select "Venture Capital" or "Private Equity" from the "Institution" dropdown menu. Identify activities to view and activities by sector.

9. Identify several pending corporate deals using EVTS. You can use EVTS for a loaded company: Ticker <Equity>; EVTS. You can also search for events using EVTS and then select an industry or all stocks.

10. Identify and study an IPO using the IPO screen: IPO <Enter>. On the screen, you can access pending IPOs and the deal. To get more information on the company, use its ticker (found on the deal page) and then go to its equity screen: Ticker <Equity>.

11. The LTOP screen displays top underwriters for the major fixed income, equity, equity-linked securities, and syndicated loan securities markets. Using the screen, identify the top underwriters over the past year for U.S. equity and fixed-income issues. Using the dropdown menu, study some of the recent deals for several of the top equity and bond underwriters. To access: LTOP <Enter>. On the LTOP screen, press left click to access a dropdown menu showing descriptions and the underwriter's deals for that period.

12. The Bloomberg NIM screens identify new security offerings by security type, period, and region. The NIM screen can be customized to identify certain types of bonds and securities and news about announced offerings. Using the NIM screen

(Selection dropdown), identify some new or expected offerings in the following security categories:

- U.S. Bonds
- Equity-Linked Securities (Convertibles)
- U.S. Corporate/144A
- Preferred
- Eurobond

13. The IPO screen displays IPO and seasoned issues in different stages in the underwriting process. Use the screen to select several IPOs in the following stages: Announced, Upcoming, Priced, Withdrawn, Postponed, and Lock-Up Expiring. Using the dropdown, get a description of the deal. For a company that has just issued its IPO, get more information on the company by going to its equity screen.

14. Identify and study private equity activities by going to the "Private Equity" menu: PE <Enter>. Bloomberg's Private Equity screen displays a menu of links that provide access to specific Bloomberg private equity analysis functions.

15. Use EPR or WEXC to find the Web site of an exchange of interest.

16. Study the different prices quotes of a stock of interest using the following screens: BQ, QR, QM, and QMC. Determine the interest in the stock using the IOIA screen.

17. Study the different prices quotes of a corporate bond of interest using TRACE: QR and TDH. Determine the interest in the bond using ALLQ.

18. Short Interest is the total amount of shares of stock that are sold short and have not been repurchased to close out the position. High levels of short interest indicate that numerous sellers have sold the stock short and are expecting a downturn in the share price. The SI screen displays monthly short interest information for a selected equity security that trades on the exchanges. Use the SI screen for several stocks of interest to determine whether or not there is a bullish or bearish sentiment regarding the stocks.

19. The MBTR monitor screen displays institutional equity transactions of 10,000 shares/lots or more (block trades) on exchanges worldwide. Set up the screen to monitor the stocks in an index, for example, Russell 3000 (RAY) and the minimum volume (e.g., 100,000 or 500,000). Select one of the stocks that is trading on heavy volume and try to determine if there is an explanation for the size of the trade. Screens to consider from the stock's menu screen: Company News (CN), intraday price graph (GIP), bid and asked spreads and quotes (QR, BQ, and QMC), short interest (SI), dealers' interest (SIDE), and brokers' reported volume (IOIA).

20. The last decade has seen the emergence of electronic trading, exchange consolidation, and global trading. Some of the companies that have been part of this change are NYSE Euronext (NYX <Equity>), NASDAQ OMX Group (NDAQ <Equity>), and Instinet (INNE <Equity>). Study the news, analyst views, and trends of these companies using some of the screens from each company's menu screen: DES, Company News (CN), Company Filings (CF), Supply Chain (SPLC), and Company Research (BRC).

CHAPTER 5

Investment Funds, Intermediate Securities, and Global Equity Markets

Introduction

The intermediary financial market consists of commercial banks, savings and loans, insurance companies, investment funds, and other financial intermediaries. These intermediaries sell financial claims to investors, and then use the proceeds to purchase debt and equity claims or to provide direct loans. Commercial banks, for example, obtain funds from investors by providing deposits and money market accounts, selling securities, and borrowing and then use these funds to provide loans and make investments. Life insurance companies, pensions, trust funds, and investment funds offer financial instruments in the form of insurance policies, retirement plans, and shares in stock or bond portfolios. The proceeds from their premiums, savings plans, and fund shares are used by these institutions to buy stocks, corporate bonds, Treasury securities and other debt instruments, as well as provide corporate, residential, and commercial loans. A major segment of the intermediary market is the market for the intermediary shares created by investment funds. These funds offer financial instruments in the form of shares in portfolios. The proceeds from their fund shares are used by these institutions to buy the stocks, corporate bonds, Treasury securities, and other debt instruments that comprise the portfolios.

In general, financial institutions, by acting as intermediaries, control a large amount of funds and thus have a significant impact on financial markets. For borrowers, intermediaries are an important source of funds; they buy many of the securities issued by corporations and governments and provide many of the direct loans. For investors, intermediaries create a number of securities for them to include in their portfolios. These include negotiable certificates of deposit, banker's acceptances, mortgage- and asset-backed instruments, investment fund shares, annuities, and guaranteed investment contracts. In this chapter, we examine the types and markets for investment funds and intermediate securities.

Investment Funds

Major investment firms and investment banks offer a wide variety of investment funds. For many investors, shares in these funds are an alternative to directly buying stocks and bonds. Fund investment provides several advantages over directly purchasing securities. First, investment funds provide divisibility. An investment company offering shares in a portfolio of negotiable, high-denomination CDs, for example, makes it possible for small investors to obtain a higher rate than they could obtain by investing in a lower yielding, small-denomination CD. Second, an investment in a fund consisting of a portfolio of securities often provides an investor more liquidity than forming his own portfolio; that is, it is easier for an individual investor to buy and sell a share in an investment fund than it is to try to buy and sell a number of securities. Third, the investment companies managing funds provide professional management. They have a team of security analysts and managers who know the markets and the securities available. They buy and sell securities for the fund, reinvest dividends and interest, and maintain records. Finally, since investment companies often buy large blocks of securities, they can obtain lower brokerage fees and commission costs for their investors. In summary, funds provide investors the benefits of divisibility, diversification, and lower transaction costs.

The Markets for Funds

From the end of World War II to the late 1960s, investments in funds grew substantially, boasting as many as 40 million investors in the 1960s. Most of the investment funds consisted of stocks, with their popularity attributed primarily to the general rise in stock prices during that period. In the 1970s, investments in funds declined as stock prices fell due to rising energy prices, inflation, and economic recessions. During this period, a number of funds specializing in debt securities were introduced. In the mid-1980s and in the 1990s, however, the popularity of equity fund investments rebounded. The growth in this period can be attributed to not only the bull market of the 1990s, but also to financial innovations. In addition to the traditional stock funds, investment companies today offer shares in bond funds (municipal bonds, corporate, high-yield bonds, and foreign bonds), *money market funds* (consisting of CDs, commercial paper [CP], Treasury securities, etc.), *index funds* (funds whose values are highly correlated with a stock or bond index), funds with options and futures, *global funds* (funds with stocks and bonds from different countries), and even *vulture funds* (funds consisting of debt securities of companies that are in financial trouble or in Chapter 11 bankruptcy). Exhibit 5.1 displays the Bloomberg Fund Heat

EXHIBIT 5.1   Fund Heat Map, 9/13/2013

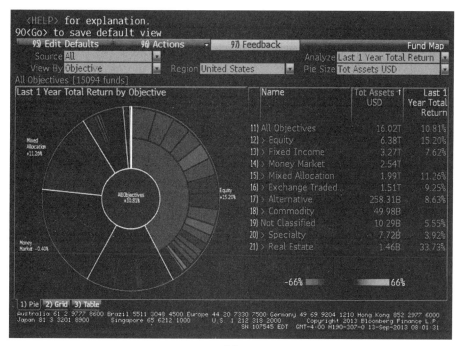

(a)

(b)

Maps (FMAP <Enter>) for the United States and world as it appeared on September 13, 2013. The maps break down the total funds and show their total returns for the past year by type: equity, debt (bond), asset allocation (balanced), money market, and others.

A number of investment companies, such as Fidelity and Vanguard, manage a family of funds. From this family (sometimes referred to as a complex), these investment companies are able to offer investors different funds based on the investor's risk-return preferences. Currently there are over 8,500 funds in the United States—a number that exceeds the number of stocks listed on the major exchanges. Contributing to this large number is the increased percentage of fund investment coming from retirement investments such as individual retirement accounts (IRAs) and 401(k) accounts.

Structure of Funds

There are three types of investment fund structures: open-end funds (also called mutual funds), closed-end funds, and unit investment trusts (UIT's). The first two can be defined as managed funds, whereas the third is an unmanaged one. Exhibit 5.2

EXHIBIT 5.2   Investment Funds by Types, 9/13/2013

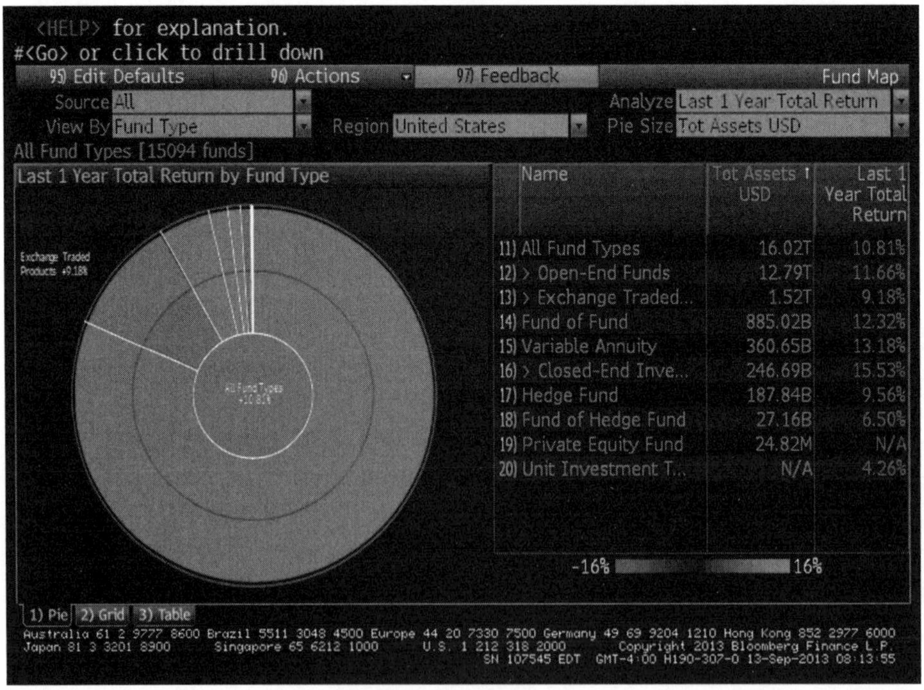

Fund Heat Map, by type: FMAP <Enter>

shows the Bloomberg Fund Heat Map screen for U.S. funds by type as of September 13, 2013.

Open-End Fund

Open-end funds (*mutual funds*) stand ready to buy back shares of the fund at any time the fund's shareholders want to sell, and they stand ready to sell new shares any time an investor wants to buy into the fund. Technically, a mutual fund is an open-end fund. The term *mutual fund,* however, is often used to refer to both open- and closed-end funds. With an open-end fund, the number of shares can change frequently. The price an investor pays for a share of an open-end fund is equal to the fund's *net asset values* (*NAV*). At a given point in time, the NAV of the fund is equal to the difference between the value of the fund's assets (V^A_t) and its liabilities (V^L_t) divided by the number of shares outstanding (N_t): $\text{NAV}_t = (V^A_t - V^L_t)/N_t$. For example, suppose a balanced stock and bond fund consists of a stock portfolio with a current market value $100 million, a corporate bond portfolio with a current market value of $100 million, liquid securities of $8 million, and liabilities of $8 million. The current net worth of this fund would be $200 million. If the fund, in turn, has 4 million shares outstanding, its current NAV would be $50 per share: NAV = ($208 million – $8 million) / 4 million = $50. This value, though, can change if the number of shares, the asset values, or the liability values change.

Open-end funds can be classified as either *load funds* or *no-load funds.* Load funds are sold through brokers or other intermediates; as such, the shares in load funds sell at their NAV plus a commission. The fees are usually charged up-front when investors buy new shares. Some funds charge a redemption fee (also called an exit fee or back-end load) when investors sell their shares back to the fund at their NAV. No-load funds, however, are sold directly by the fund and therefore sell at just their NAV. The fund does charge fees for management and for transferring individual investments from one fund to another. Exhibit 5.3 shows the Bloomberg description screen and price graph (GP) of the Putnam Global Equity Fund. The fund is an open-end fund that focuses on global equity investment in mid- to high-cap companies. The fund charges a 4 percent back load fee, a 0.75 percent management fee, and on September 13, 2013, the fund's NAV was at $10.38 per share.

Closed-End Fund

A *closed-end fund* has a fixed number of nonredeemable shares sold at its initial offering. Unlike an open-end fund, the closed-end fund does not stand ready to buy existing shares or sell new shares. The number of shares of a closed-end fund is therefore fixed. An investor who wants to buy shares in an existing closed-end fund can do so only by buying them in the secondary market from an existing holder. Shares in existing funds are traded on the exchanges and the over-the-counter market. Interestingly, the prices of many closed-end funds often sell at a discount from their NAVs.[1] Exhibit 5.4 shows

EXHIBIT 5.3   Open-End Fund: Putnam Global Equity Fund, 9/13/2013

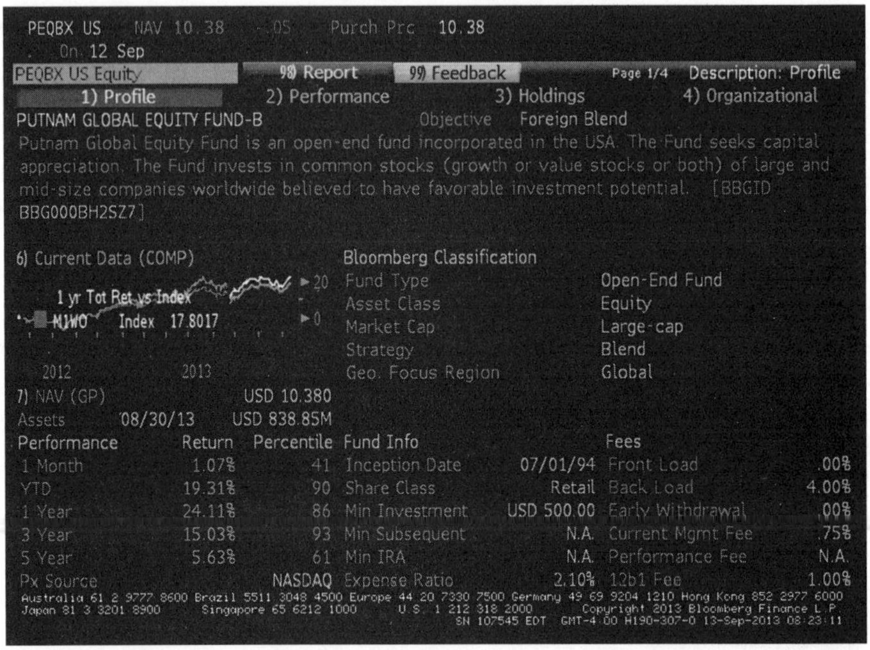

(a)

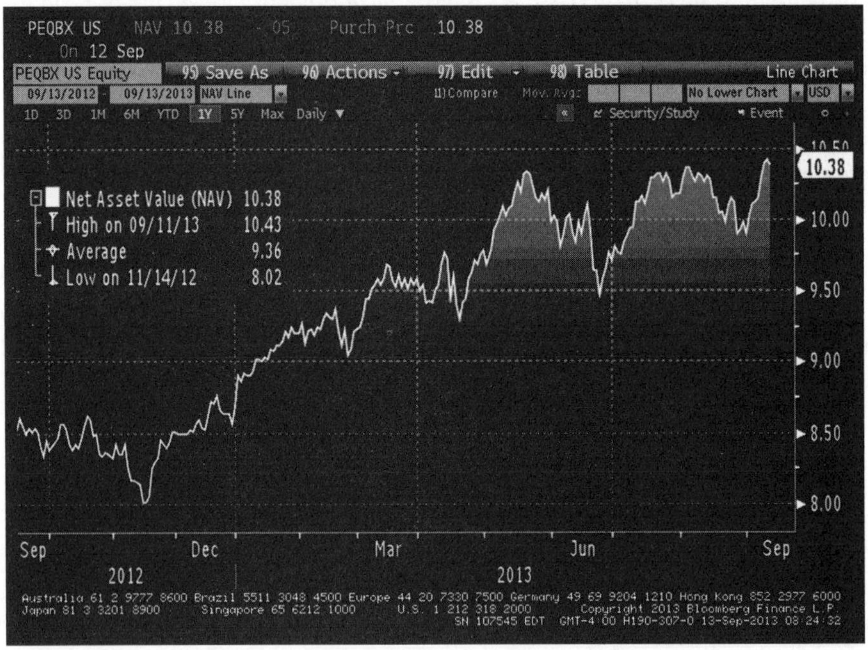

(b)

(a) Putnam: PEQBX US <Equity> <Enter>. (b) Price Graph, GP.

EXHIBIT 5.4   Closed-End Fund, Dividend and Income Fund, 9/13/2013

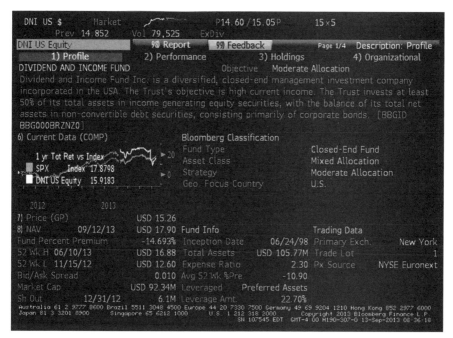

(a)

(b)

(a) Dividend and Income Fund. (b) Price Graph, GP.

the Bloomberg description screen and price graph (GP) of the Dividend and Income Fund. The fund is a closed-end fund that focuses on high current income, with 50 percent of its holdings in stock and the balance in corporate bonds. On September 13, 2013, the fund's shares were trading at $15.26 per share.

Unit Investment Trust

Although the composition of open- and closed-end funds can change as managers buy and sell securities, the funds themselves usually have unlimited lives. In contrast, a *unit investment trust* has a specified number of securities that are rarely changed, and the fund usually has a fixed life. A unit investment trust is formed by a sponsor, such as an investment bank, who buys a specified number of securities, deposits them with a trustee, and then sells claims on the security, known as *redeemable trust certificates,* at their NAV plus a commission fee. These trust certificates entitle the holder to proportional shares in the income from the deposited securities. For example, an investment company might purchase $20 million worth of corporate bonds at an average price of $1,000 per bond, place them in a trust, and then issue 20,000 redeemable trust certificates at $1,025 per share: NAV + Commission = ($20 million / 20,000) + $25 = $1,025. If the investment company can sell all of the shares, it will be able to finance the $20 million bond purchase and earn a 2.5 percent commission of $500,000.

Unit investment trusts are formed with government securities, corporate bonds, municipal bonds, preferred stock, and common stock (often of the firms in a particular sector). The trustee pays all the interest and principal generated from the bonds or dividends from the stocks to the certificate holders. Unlike open- and closed-end funds, the fund has a termination date when the investment trust ceases and the fund is liquidated, with the holders receiving a liquidation dividend. Depending on the types of securities, the maturity on a unit investment trust can vary from 6 months to 20 years. The holders of the securities, however, usually can sell their shares back to the trustee prior to maturity at their NAV plus a load. To finance the purchase of the certificate, the trustee often sells a requisite amount of securities making up the trust. The description screen and dividend screen (DVD) for the First Trust Unit Investment Trust are shown in Exhibit 5.5. The UIT consists of corporate investment-grade bonds, has a termination date of 7/01/2015, a NAV of $920.32 on 9/12/2013, and has paid monthly dividends for the 2011–2013 period ranging between $3.32 and $4.23.

Dual-Purpose Funds

When the tax laws allow capital gains to be taxed at a different rate than income, investors in higher-income tax brackets often prefer stocks that generate more of their return in the form of capital gains, whereas other investors prefer more of their return in the form of dividends and interest income. Given these different objectives, a number of investment companies create *dual-purpose funds.* These funds sell two

EXHIBIT 5.5   Unit Investment Trust, First Trust Corporate Investment Grade, 9/13/2013

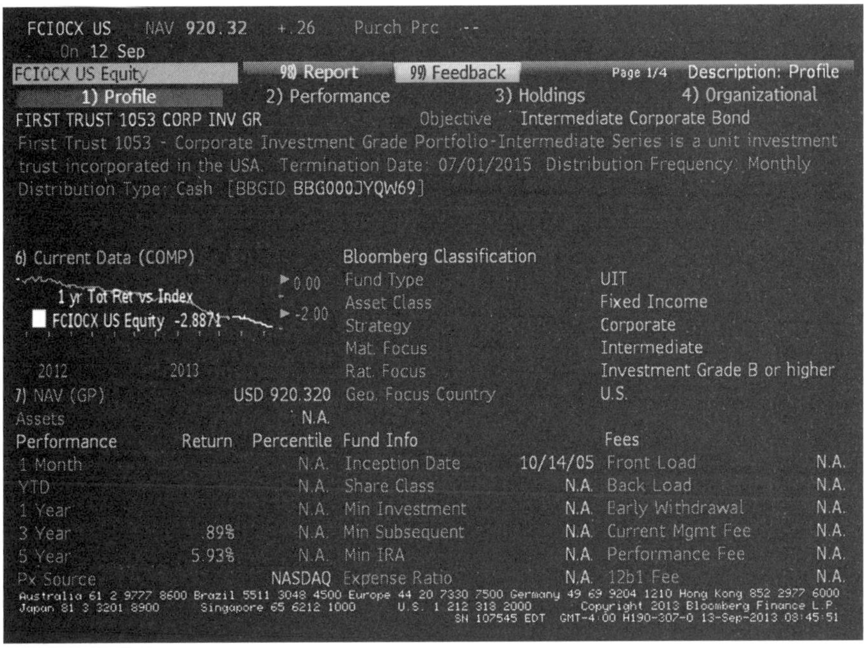

(a)

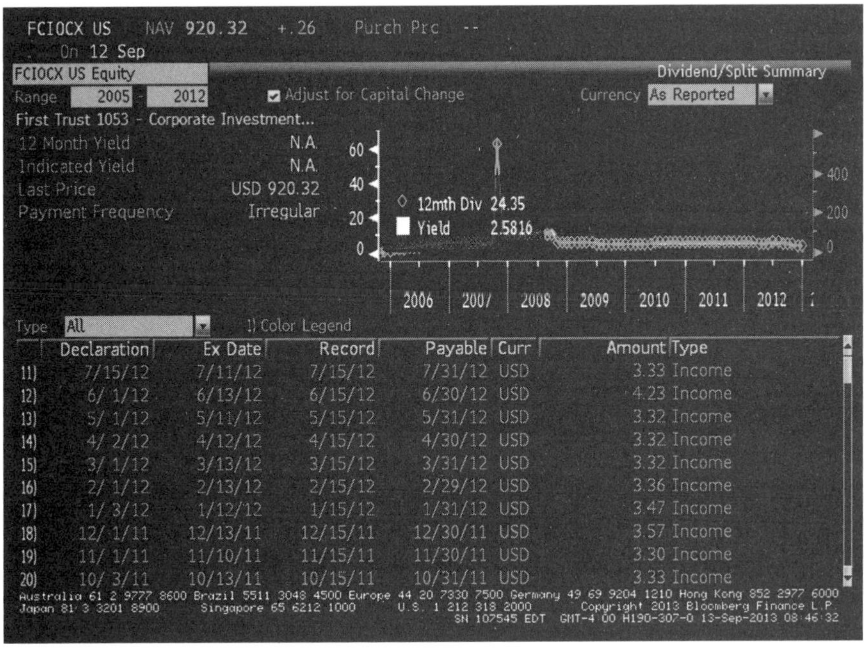

(b)

(a) First Trust: FCIOCX <Equity> <Enter>. (b) Dividend Screen, DVD.

different shares from the same portfolio of stocks: an income share, entitling the holder
to the dividend income from the portfolio, plus cash equal to the initial value of
the share, and a capital share, entitling the holder to any accumulated capital gains
(or losses).

Types of Investment Funds

A board of directors elected by the fund's shareholders determines the general investment policies of the investment fund. Typically, a management or investment advisory
firm, often consisting of those who originally set up the fund, does the actual implementation and management of the policies. Some funds are actively managed, with
fund managers aggressively buying stocks and bonds, whereas others follow a more
passive buy-and-hold investment strategy.

One way of grouping the many types of funds is according to the classifications
defined by Weisenberger's *Annual Investment Companies Manual* for growth funds,
income funds, and balanced funds. *Growth funds* are those whose primary goal is in
long-term capital gains. Such funds tend to consist primarily of those common stocks
offering growth potential. Many of these are diversified stock funds, although there are
some that specialize in certain sectors. *Income funds* are those whose primary goal is
providing income. These funds are made up mainly of stocks paying relatively high dividends or bonds with high coupon yields. Finally, *balanced funds* are those with goals
somewhere between those of growth and income funds. Balance funds are constructed
with bonds, common stocks, and preferred stocks that are expected to generate moderate income with the potential for some capital gains. Similar to balanced funds are
asset allocation funds (or *flexible funds*). These funds consist of both stocks and bonds
but are more actively managed, changing the bond and equity allocation over time in
anticipation of changes in the market or interest rate conditions.

A second way of classifying funds is in terms of their specialization. There are four
general classifications: equity funds, bond funds, hybrid funds (stocks and bonds),
and money market funds. As shown in Exhibit 5.6, each of these fund types can be
broken down further by their specified investment objectives. Equity funds consist
of index funds, sector funds, and funds based on style. An index fund tries to match
the performance of an index (indexes are discussed in the next section). For example,
the Vanguard 500 Index Fund is an open-end fund that tries to replicate the performance of the Standard & Poor's (S&P 500). Sector funds, in turn, focus on a particular sector, such as telecommunications or energy. Finally, style funds form portfolios
that reflect a certain type of investment such as investments in growth stocks or value
stocks or investments based on size, such as large-cap, mid-cap, or small-cap stocks.
Bond funds can be classified as corporate, municipal, government, high-yield, global,
mortgage-backed securities, and tax free. Each category reflects a different investment
objective. Municipal bond funds, for example, specialize in providing investors with
tax-exempt municipal securities; corporate bond funds are constructed to replicate the
overall performance of a certain type of corporate bond, with a number of them formed

EXHIBIT 5.6   Categories of Investment Funds

Equity Funds:
    Value funds
    Growth funds
    Sector funds
    World equity funds
    Emerging market funds
    Regional equity funds
    Small-cap, mid-cap, and large-cap funds

Taxable Bond Funds (short, intermediate, and long term):
    Corporate bond funds
    High yield funds
    Global bond funds
    Government bond funds
    Mortgage-backed securities

Tax-Free Bond Funds (short, intermediate, and long term):
    State municipal bond funds
    National municipal bond funds

Hybrid Funds:
    Asset allocation funds
    Balanced funds
    Income-mixed funds

Money market funds:
    Taxable money market funds
    Tax-exempt money market funds

to be highly correlated with a specific index; money market funds are constructed with money market securities in order to provide investors with liquid investments. Exhibit 5.7 shows examples of the policy statements of an equity fund and bond fund accessed from the Bloomberg description screens.

International Mutual Funds

Instead of buying foreign stocks or bonds, an investor looking for an internationally diversified portfolio may find a more practical alternative is to buy shares in one of many international mutual funds or to invest in a commingled international portfolio offered by a bank trust department or insurance company. Most of these funds provide expertise in foreign security selection and management, and many use currency-hedging tools to minimize exchange-rate risk. The funds differ in terms of the degree of their diversification. Some, for example, offer investments only in certain countries or areas (e.g., Latin American funds), whereas others provide worldwide diversification. For an example, see the description of Pimco Global Bond Fund in Exhibit 5.7.

EXHIBIT 5.7   Examples of Investment Funds, September 13, 2013—Bloomberg Description Files

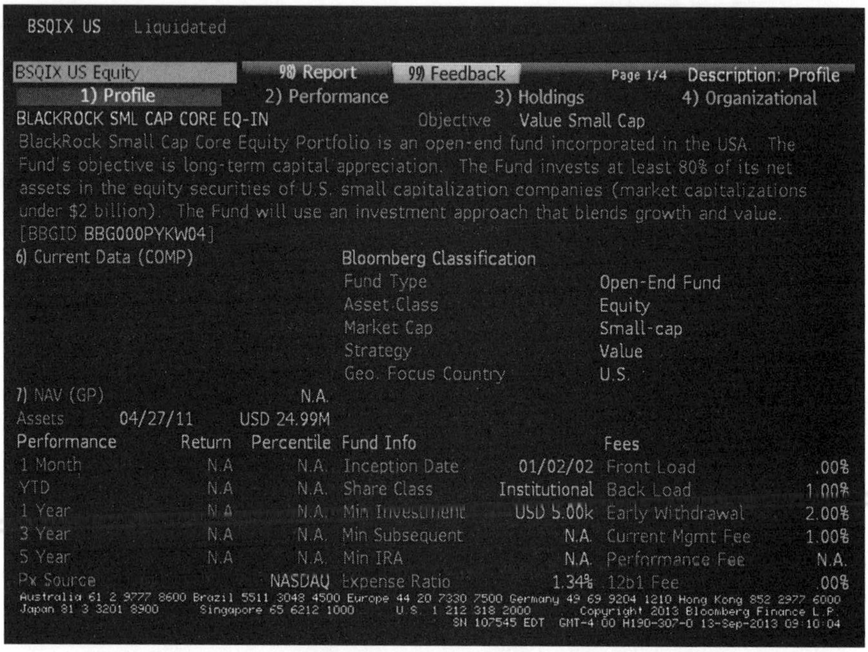

(a)

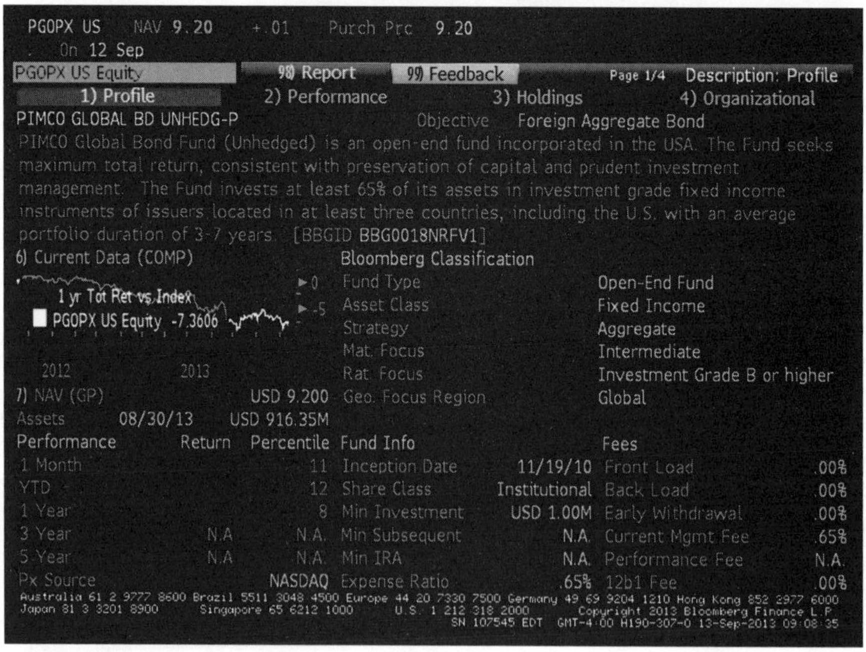

(b)

(a) Blackrock Small Cap. (b) Pimco Global Bond Fund.

Accumulation Plans

Typically, most fund investors buy shares and receive cash from the fund when it is distributed. For investors looking for different cash flow patterns, investment funds also provide voluntary and contractual *accumulation plans* with different types of contributions and withdrawal plans. Included here are automatic reinvestment plans in which the net income and capital gains of the fund are reinvested, with the shareholders accumulating additional shares, and fixed contribution plans in which investors contribute (either contractually or voluntarily) a fixed amount on a regular basis for a set period.

Taxes and Regulations

Most mutual funds make two types of payments to their shareholders: a net income payment from dividends and interest and a realized capital gain payment. If an investment fund complies with certain rules, it does not have to pay corporate income taxes. To qualify for this favorable tax treatment, the company must have a diversified portfolio and it must pay out at least 90 percent of the fund's net income to shareholders. As a result, most investment companies distribute all of the net income from the fund to their shareholders. Investment companies can either distribute or retain their realized capital gains. Most investment companies distribute capital gains. If they retain the gain, they are required to pay a tax equal to the maximum personal income tax rate; the shareholders, in turn, receive a credit for the taxes paid.

Investment funds are regulated under a number of federal laws: The Security Acts of 1933 and 1934 require disclosure of funds and specifies antifraud rules; the Security Act of 1940 requires that all funds be registered; the Investment Advisers Act of 1940 regulates fund advisers. In addition, the Securities and Exchange Commission (SEC) rules require that funds publish detailed information on directors and that there be independence of the directors.[2]

BLOOMBERG INVESTMENT FUND SCREENS

- **FUND** <Enter>: Funds and Holdings Menu.
- **FSRC** <Enter> Fund Search: The FSRC screen searches and screens investment funds by general investment criteria, such as asset class (stock, bonds, or balance), by type (open, closed, unit investment trust, or exchange-traded product), by country, by asset holding criteria (industry, market cap, maturity, and ratings), and by adding fields.
- **PSRT** <Enter>: PSRT searches for companies with specific public portfolio/holder information. You can search by keyword and perform advanced searches based on one's criteria.
- **Fund Ticker** <Equity> <Enter>: Fund menu page.

(Continued)

- **FMAP** <Enter>: FMAP displays and analyzes mutual fund performance by objective, fund type, and region (see Exhibits 5.1 and 5.2).
- **FL** <Enter>: Fund Look-up.
- **SECF** <Enter>, **Funds Tab:** Funds look-up and screener.
- **NI FND**: Fund News.
- **HDC:** Identifies holders of loaded funds.
- **PHDC** searches for institutional and insider holders whose trading activity may influence the price of a selected security: PHDC <Enter>.

See Bloomberg Web Exhibit 5.1.

Note on Indexes

Equity investment funds are often classified by their investment style: S&P 500 index fund, large cap stock fund, small-cap stock funds, emerging market funds, and the like. Similarly, bond funds can be classified as corporate, municipal, government, high-yield, global, mortgage-backed securities, and tax free. Each category reflects a different investment objective. Managers of these various funds, as well as the managers of pension, insurance, and other fixed-income funds, often evaluate the performance of their funds by comparing their fund's return with those of an appropriate index.

A number of stock and bond indexes have been developed in recent years on which funds can be constructed or benchmarked. A number of investment companies also publish a variety of indexes. As noted in Chapter 1, stock indexes can be: broad based, measuring the performance of the overall market; sector specific, measuring the performance of a particular industry or sector; or style specific, measuring the performance of certain type of investment (e.g., investments in small-cap companies or high-yield bond fund). The Dow Jones Industrial Average (DJIA), S&P 500, and Russell 3000 stock indexes, for example, are broad-based indexes measuring the performance of the overall stock market. Stock market indexes are also calculated for a number of stock markets. From these broad-based indexes, there are sub-indexes for the S&P, Russell, or Dow based on size (e.g., small-cap or large-cap) or style (value stocks or growth stocks).

The most cited indexes of the major foreign stock exchanges and world indexes are the Nikkei 225 Index for the Tokyo Stock Exchange and the Financial Times-Stock Exchange Index for the London Stock Exchange, called the "footsie." Some other widely used indexes are the Morgan Stanley and the Dow Jones indexes. Both calculate a number of indexes (in the local currency and in dollars), including national indexes, international industry indexes, a European index, an Asian index, and a world index. Morgan Stanley International computes indexes for more than 20 countries, different geographical areas, and an Aggregate World Index. Finally, a number of bond indexes have been developed by investment companies in recent years on which bond funds can be constructed or benchmarked. The indexes can be grouped into three categories: U.S. investment-grade bonds indexes (including Treasuries), U.S. high-yield bond indexes, and global government bond indexes. Within each category, subindexes are constructed based on sector, quality ratings, or country.[3] Exhibit 5.8 shows the Bloomberg description screens for the S&P 500 index.

Price-Weighted and Market-Based Indexes

The Dow Jones Industrial Average (DJIA) is a *price-weighted index*, calculated by summing the prices of the 30 stocks and dividing by a divisor. In a price-weighted index, the index is constructed initially with a divisor equal to the number of stocks comprising the index. As stock splits and stock dividends occur, the divisor needs to be adjusted. For example, if the index consists of just two stocks, one priced at $30 and the other at $20, then the index would be 25 [= (30 + 20)/2] and the divisor would be 2. If the first stock had a 2-for-1 stock split, changing the price from $30 to $15, then the divisor would need to be changed to reflect an index value of 25. In this case the divisor would have to be changed from 2 to 1.4, for example, (15 + 20)/divisor = 25, divisor = 35/25 = 1.4.

Price-weighted indexes, like the DJIA or the Nikkei 225, weigh each stock in the average only in proportion to its price, with no weight given to the stock's volume or shares outstanding. As a result, the index does not capture the relative values of the larger companies making up the index. To illustrate, suppose you have a price-weighted index of just two stocks: Stock X priced at $50 with 1 million shares outstanding and stock Y at $50, but with 10 million shares outstanding. If Stock X increases by 5 percent to $52.50 and Stock Y increases by 10 percent to $55, then the price-weighted index will increase by 7.5 percent:

$$\frac{[(\$52.50 + (\$55.00)/2] - \$50.00}{\$50.00} = \frac{[(\$52.50 + (\$55.00)/2]}{\$50.00} - 1 = 0.075$$

However, Stock Y is more valuable to the portfolio than Stock X. To capture the relative importance of Y, one needs to construct an index based on market values (price time number of shares). Here, the initial index value would be one and the percentage change would be 9.545 percent:

$$\frac{(\$52.50)(1,000,000) + (\$55.00)(10,000,000)}{(\$50.00)(1,000,000) + (\$50.00)(10,000,000)} - 1 = 0.09545$$

Indexes computed using market values are referred to as *value-weighted index* or *market-based index*. Most indexes, including the S&P 500 are market-based indexes.

EXHIBIT 5.8 S&P 500 Indexes

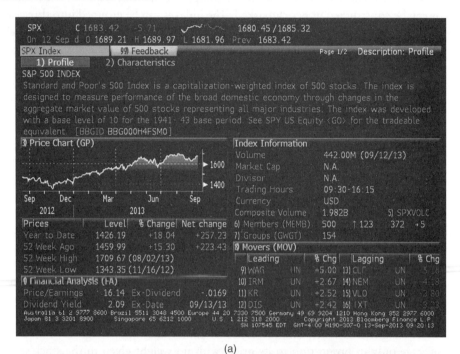

(a)

(b)

(a) S&P 500: SPX <Index> <Enter>. (b) MEMB Screen; Historical Summary Tab.

The S&P 500 is calculated using the total market values of 500 stocks divided by a base value:

$$S\&P\ 500 = \frac{\sum_{i=1}^{500} P_{it}N_{it}}{\sum_{i=1}^{500} P_{ib}N_{ib}}$$

where:

P_{it} = market price per share at time t
N_{it} = number of shares at time t
b = base period

Since market-based indexes are calculated with market values, stock splits and stock dividends are automatically adjusted.

Indexes are used to measure the performance of the market or a segment of the market. Most indexes do not include dividends. As a result, the proportional change in an index over a certain period of time measures the rate of price appreciation of the market or sector the index comprises, but not the total return. The Center for Research in Security Prices (CRSP) does calculate S&P indexes adjusted for dividends.

BLOOMBERG INDEX INFORMATION

- WEI; WEI <Enter>: The World Equity Indexes (WEI) screen monitors world equity indexes. On the WEI screen, you can also see different information about the indexes, such as premarket (futures prices), movers (advance and declines), ratios (e.g., price-to-earnings ratio), and currency. On the screen, click the gray country area (e.g., EMEA) to bring up more indexes for that geographical area.
- **SPX <Enter>:** S&P 500 Index Menu.
- **RUSS <Enter>:** Russell Index Menu.
- **Index Ticker <Index>:** Index Menu Screen.
- **EQS <Enter>:** Select Index from "Indexes" tab (from Country list).
- **SECF <Enter>, Indx/Stats tab.**
- **BI <Enter>:** BI has a comprehensive list of Bloomberg sectors and industries and provides detailed financials and analysis for each. You can find breakdowns of industries by indexes.

See Bloomberg Web Exhibit 5.2.

Exchange-Traded Funds

In 1993, the American Stock Exchange created an S&P 500 index fund called an *exchange-traded fund* (*ETF*) that could be traded continuously like a stock. This first ETF received exemptions from the SEC from various provisions of the Investment Company Act of 1940. The exemptions made it possible for the ETF to be structured so that it could be listed and traded continuously. By 2008, there were over 400 separate ETFs, many with esoteric names such as Spiders (ETF that replicates the S&P 500), Qubes (an ETF indexed to the NASDAQ), Diamonds (an ETF that replicates the DJIA), and Vipers (name for Vanguard ETFs). In 2008, most of the ETFs were designed to track the performance of a specified index or, in some cases, a multiple of or an inverse of their indexes. Today, ETFs include most sectors, commodities, and investment styles. In early 2008, the SEC granted exemptive relief to several fund sponsors to offer actively managed ETFs that met certain requirements. These actively managed ETFs, in turn, led to new exchange-traded products (ETPs) defined by a particular investment objective and policy. By 2010, the total number of index-based and actively managed ETFs had grown to over 728, with total net assets of over $530 billion.

Most ETFs originate with a sponsor, who defines the investment objective of the ETF and the method for tracking the performance. The sponsor of an index-based ETF, for example, defines the index (e.g., large U.S. Bank Sector), and the method of tracking it (e.g., a total replication index method that holds every security in the target index or a sample index-based method that holds a representative sample of securities in the index). Given the fund's objective and tracking method, a *creation basket* is identified that specifies the names and quantities of securities and other assets designed to track the performance of the index portfolio. ETF shares are created after an *authorized participant* (typically an institutional investor) deposits the creation basket and/or cash into the fund—the ETF. In return for the creation basket and/or cash, the authorized participant received the block of ETF shares, referred to as a *creation unit.* The authorized participant can then either keep the ETF shares that make up the creation unit or sell all or part of them on a stock exchange (see Exhibit 5.9).

EXHIBIT 5.9   Creation Process of Exchange-Traded Fund

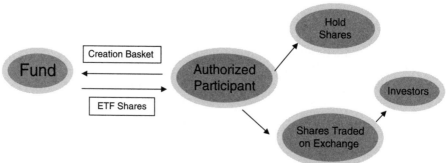

Source: 2009 Investment Company Fact Book: http://www.icifactbook.org/index.html

ETFs are like mutual funds in that their value is derived from the underlying portfolio of securities. Different from mutual funds, ETFs trade like stocks: investors can buy and sell them on a continuous basis and can execute trades with market or limit orders; they can also buy ETFs on margin and sell short. Also different from mutual funds, the price of an ETF is based on market supply and demand conditions. However, because of the disclosure requirements that call for the composition of the ETF's basket to be made public, arbitrageurs are in a position to ensure that the price of an ETF trades close to the underlying net asset value of the securities held in the index basket.[4]

Not surprising, the demand for ETFs has accelerated in recent years with institutional investors increasingly using them to take positions on broad movements in the financial markets. Retail investors and households have also started to add ETFs to their portfolio holdings. According to the Investment Company Institute, an estimated 3 million households owned ETFs in 2009. Although many ETFs are equity based, there are an increasing number of fixed-income ETFs and ETPs being offered. These fixed-income ETPs vary from ETFs that are tied to bond indexes, to those linked to Treasury yields, to ETFs that are tied to a multiple of the Treasury yield. There is also an increasing number of equity, commodity, and fixed-income ETFs and ETPs being offered outside the United States. The ETPs vary from ETFs that are tied to foreign equity and bond indexes to those linked to emerging markets.

BLOOMBERG ETF INFORMATION

- ETF <Enter>.
- SECF <Enter>, Funds tab and ETFs tab.
- FSRC <Enter>: Screen by "Fund Type" and "Exchange-Traded Products."
- Funds <Enter>: Menu of funds information.

See Bloomberg Web Exhibit 5.3.

Other Investment-Type Funds and Securities

In addition to open-end and closed-end investment funds, unit investment trusts, and ETFs, several other investment funds and related intermediary securities of note are hedge funds, real estate investment trusts (REITs), mortgage-backed and asset-backed securities, and collateralized debt obligations (CDOs).

Hedge Funds

Hedge funds can be defined as special types of mutual funds. There are estimated to be as many as 4,000 such funds. They are structured so that they can be largely unregulated. To achieve this, they are often set up as limited partnerships. By federal law, as limited partnerships, hedge funds are limited to no more than 99 limited partners, each with annual incomes of at least $200,000 or a net worth of at least $1 million (excluding home), or to no more than 499 limited partners, each with a net worth of at least $5 million. Many funds or partnerships are set up offshore to circumvent regulations. Hedge funds acquire funds from many different individual and institutional sources; the minimum investments range from $100,000 to $1 billion, with the average investment being $10 million. Because they are lightly regulated, hedge funds often set up investment strategies that use derivatives, short sales, and leveraging, with debt-to-equity ratio in some cases as high as 20 to 1—strategies not open to mutual funds. Some hedge funds use their funds to invest or set up investment strategies reflecting pricing aberrations. One of the most famous is that of Long-Term Capital, which in 1998 set up a fund to profit from an expected narrowing of the default spreads on bonds, which subsequently widened. Other notable hedge fund collapses include Amaranth Advisors, Advanced Investment Management, Bayou Management, and Lipper Convertibles.

One of the fastest-growing sectors in the hedge fund industry is hedge funds that invest in one or more other hedge funds. Such funds are referred to as *funds of funds* or feeder funds. These funds also received considerable attention when it was learned in December 2008 that many large feeder funds were large clients of Bernard Madoff and were hurt by his large Ponzi scheme. Exhibit 5.10 shows Bloomberg description screens for two hedge funds.

BLOOMBERG HEDGE FUNDS INFORMATION

- **HFND** <Enter>: Hedge Fund information and rankings.
- **HFR** <Enter> Hedge Fund Research.
- **Hedge Fund News:** HEDN <Enter>.
- **Hedge Fund News:** BRIEF <Enter> and click "Hedge Fund Newsletter."
- **Best Hedge Fund Player Snapshot:** WHF <Enter>.

Real Estate Investment Trusts

A real estate investment trust (REIT) is a fund that specializes in investing in real estate or real estate mortgages. The trust acts as an intermediary, selling stocks and warrants and issuing debt instruments (bonds, commercial paper, or loans from banks), then using the funds to invest in commercial and residential mortgage loans and other real estate securities. REITs can take the form of an equity trust that invests directly in real estate, a mortgage trust that invests in mortgage loans or mortgage-backed securities, or a hybrid trust that invests in both. Many REITs are highly leveraged, making them more subject to default risks. Most REITs are tax-exempt corporations. To qualify for tax exemptions, the company must receive approximately 75 percent of its income from real estate, rents, mortgage interest, and property sales, and distribute 95 percent

EXHIBIT 5.10   Examples of Hedge Fund

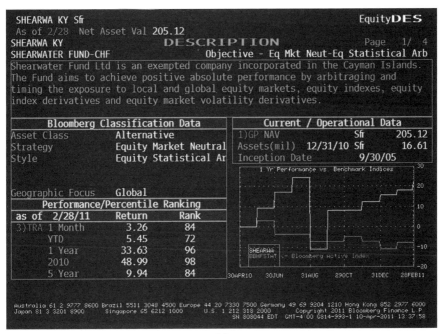

(a)

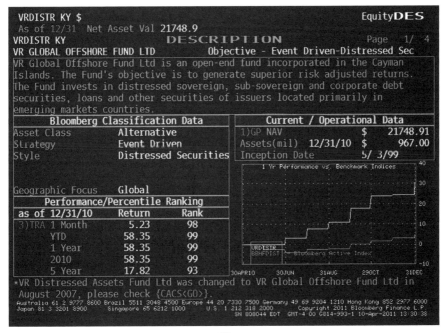

(b)

of its income to its shareholders. The stocks of many existing shares in REITs are listed on the organized exchanges and the OTC market. Exhibit 5.11 shows Bloomberg description screens for two REITs.

BLOOMBERG REIT INFORMATION

- **REIT <Enter>**: REIT platform.
- **REIT Ticker <Equity> <Enter>**: REIT's menu screen.
- **NI REIT <Enter>**: REIT news.
- **RMEN <Enter>**: Real Estate Indexes of the world.
- **HOIN <Enter>**: Housing and construction menu screen.

Mortgage-Backed and Asset-Backed Securities

Up until the mid-1970s, most home mortgages originated when saving and loans, commercial banks, and other thrift institutions borrowed funds or used their deposits to provide loans to home purchasers, possibly later selling the resulting instruments in the secondary market to Fannie Mae or Ginnie Mae. To a large degree, individual deposits financed real estate, with little financing coming from corporations or institutions. In an effort to attract institutional funds away from corporate bonds and other capital market securities, as well as to minimize their poor hedge (short-term deposit liabilities and long-term mortgage assets), financial institutions began to sell mortgage-backed securities in the 1970s. These securities provided them with an instrument that could compete more closely with corporate bonds for inclusion in the portfolios of institutional investors, and it provided the mortgage industry with more liquidity.

By definition, mortgage-backed securities (MBSs) are instruments that are backed by a pool of mortgage loans. Typically, a financial institution, agency, or mortgage banker buys a pool of mortgages of a certain type from mortgage originators (e.g., Federal Housing Administration–insured mortgages or mortgages with a certain minimum loan-to-value ratio or a specified payment-to-income ratio). This mortgage portfolio is financed through the sale of the MBSs, which have a claim on the portfolio. The mortgage originators usually agree to continue to service the loans, passing the payments on to the MBS holders. An MBS investor has a claim on the cash flows from the mortgage portfolio. This includes interest on the mortgages, scheduled payment of principal, and any prepaid principal. Since many mortgages are prepaid early as homeowners sell their homes or refinance their current mortgages, the cash flow from a portfolio of mortgages, and therefore the return on the MBS, can be quite uncertain. To address this type of risk, a number of derivative MBS were created in the 1980s. For example, in the late 1980s Freddie Mac introduced the *collateralized mortgage obligations* (*CMOs*). These securities had different maturity claims and different levels of prepayment risk.

EXHIBIT 5.11   Examples of REITS

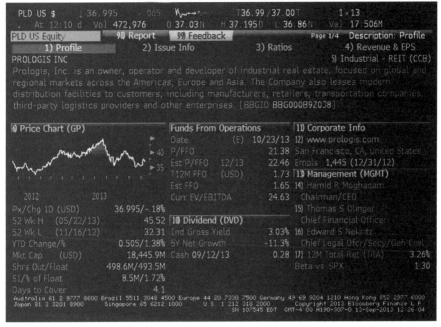

(a)

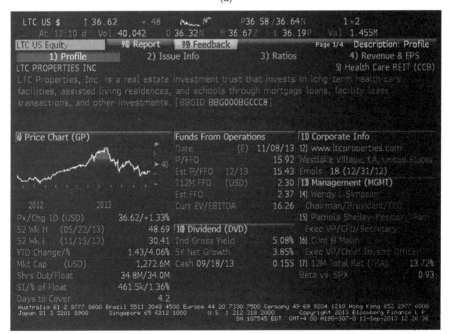

(b)

(a) Prologis: PLD US <Equity> <Enter>. (b) LTC Properties: LTC US <Equity> <Enter>.

An MBS is an asset-backed security created through a method known as *securitization*. As noted in Chapter 1, securitization is the process of transforming illiquid financial assets into marketable capital market instruments. Today, it is applied not only to mortgages, but also to home equity loans, automobile loans, lines of credit, credit card receivables, and leases. Securitization is one of the most important financial innovations introduced in the last two decades; it is examined in detail in many fixed-income texts.

Collateralized Debt Obligations

Collateralized debt obligations (*CDOs*) are securities backed by a diversified pool of one or more fixed-income assets or derivatives. The portfolio of debt obligations underlying the CDO are referred to as the collateral, with the funds to purchase the collateral assets being obtained by the issuance of debt obligations. Assets from which CDOs are formed include investment-grade corporate bonds, high-yield corporate bonds, asset-backed securities, real estate MBSs, commercial loans, commercial MBSs, REITs, municipal bonds, and emerging market bonds. CDOs have a collateral manager who is responsible for managing the portfolio of debt obligations. Restrictions, in turn, are imposed on what the collateral manager can do. The issuance of CDOs grew from the 1990s to 2007, but stopped in 2008 in the aftermath of the 2008 financial crisis. There are still, however, a number of issues outstanding.

Insurance Companies, Pension Funds, and Investment Banks

Insurance companies, pension funds, and investment banks are important financial intermediaries. Insurance companies and pension funds, on the one hand, use the premiums paid on various insurance policies and the investment funds from retirement and savings plans to invest in bonds, stocks, mortgages, and other assets. On the other hand, many individuals use insurance policies and pension plans as their primary investment conduit. Like commercial banks, large investment banks are multifunctional, serving as an important intermediary.

Insurance Companies' Role in the Financial Market

Insurance companies invest billions of dollars into the financial markets each year from the inflows they received from insurance premiums, savings and investment products they offer, and the funds from pension and endowment funds they managed. In 2010, life insurance companies held approximately $6.08 trillion in assets. Since their liabilities tend to be more predictable and long term, life insurance companies tend to invest in long-term assets.[5] In 2010, about 40 percent of their assets were in corporate bonds, followed by equity (22 percent), government securities (11 percent), mortgages (7 percent), and various other assets. In contrast to life insurance companies, property and casualty insurance companies insure against many different types of events, with the amount of potential losses on many of the events they insure more difficult to predict. As a result, property and casualty companies tend to invest in more liquid assets than do life insurance companies.

Life insurance companies provide basic life insurance: protection in the form of income to benefactors in the event of the death of the insurer. They also provide disability insurance, health insurance, annuities, and guaranteed investment contracts. Annuities and guaranteed investment contracts are investment-type instruments. A life insurance company annuity pays the holder a periodic fixed income for as long as the policyholder lives in return for an initial lump-sum investment (coming, for example, from a retirement benefit or insurance cash value). Annuities provide policyholders protection against the risk of outliving their retirement income.[6] They are constructed based on the rates of return insurance companies can obtain from investing an individual's payment for a period equal to the individual's life expectancy (fixed-life annuity) or for a prespecified period (fixed-period annuity).

A guaranteed investment contract (GIC) is an obligation of an insurance company to pay a guaranteed principal and rate on an invested premium. For a lump-sum payment, the insurance company guarantees a specified dollar amount will be paid to the policyholder at a specified future date. For example, a life insurance company for a premium of $1 million, guarantees the holder a five-year GIC paying 8 percent interest compounded annually. The GIC, in turn, obligates the insurance company to pay the GIC holder $1,469,328 [= $1 million $(1.08)^5$]in five years. Pension funds are one of the primary investors in GICs. The GICs provide them not only an investment with a known payment but also an investment that always has a positive value to report; this contrasts with bond investments whose values may decrease if interest rates increase.

Pension Funds

Pension funds are financial intermediaries that invest the savings of employees in financial assets over their working years, providing them with a pool of funds at their retirements. Pension funds are one of the fastest-growing intermediaries in the United States. The total assets of pension funds (private and state and local government) have grown from $700 billion in 1980 to approximately $10 trillion in 2010. Part of this growth reflects a workforce of Baby Boomers making contributions to their pensions. As this generation enters retirement over the next decade and begins to draw from its investments, there is expected to be a marked decline in such growth.

Pension funds can be grouped as public or private plans. The largest public plan is the Federal Old Age and Disability Insurance Program (Social Security). It is a pay-as-you-go system in which current workers' contributions pay for the benefits to the current recipients. The other public pension funds are those sponsored by state and local governments. Private pension plans are those sponsored by employers, groups, and individuals.

There are two general types of pension plans: a defined-benefit plan and a defined-contribution plan. A *defined-benefit plan* promises the employee a specified benefit when they retire. The benefit is usually determined by a formula. Financial problems can arise when pension funds are underfunded and the company goes bankrupt. As a result, over the past two decades most new plans are structured as *defined-contribution plans*. These plans specify what the employee will contribute to the plan instead of what the plan will pay. At retirement, the benefits are equal to the contributions the employee has made and the returns earned from investing them.

To pension contributors, pension funds represent long-term investments through intermediaries. As of 2010, private funds sponsored by employers, groups, and individuals were one of the largest institutional investors in equity, with about 70 percent of their total equity investments going to equity (stock and mutual fund shares). In 2008, public funds sponsored by state and local governments had invested assets valued at over $3 trillion, with 38 percent in equity, 6 percent in mutual funds, 9 percent in corporate bonds, 10 percent in federal agency and Treasury securities, and 26 percent in credit market instruments (see Federal Reserve Flow of Fund Accounts, Table L118; www.federalreserve.gov/releases/z1/Current).[7] In addition to employee and institutional pension plans, retirement plans for U.S. individuals can also be set up through *Keogh plans* and *individual retirement accounts (IRAs)*.[8]

Investment Banks

As discussed in Chapter 4, investment banks are active in the primary market where they underwrite or privately place stock and bond issues, and in the secondary market where they provide brokerage services through their electronic systems or directly through customer relation offices. Investment banks are also important intermediaries. They act as dealers on the OTC market and as position traders on block trades, and many have specialist and market makers that keep the market continuous. Furthermore, as discussed in this chapter, investment banks are active participants in setting up investment funds, structuring and managing collateralized debt obligations and hedge funds.

Two additional areas of note in which investment banks are quite active are mergers, consolidations, and acquisitions and corporate equity sales. Mergers, consolidations, and acquisitions are complicated undertakings. Investment banks are active in serving both the acquirers and the target firms. Acquiring firms use investment bankers to help them identify attractive firms to pursue, to solicit shareholders who might sell, to structure tender offers, to raise financial capital, and to structure the deal. Targeted firms may use investment banks to indicate their interest and commitment or possibly their disinterest and protection, especially when there is a hostile takeover effort.

Investment banks are also active in the sale of not just companies in a merger and acquisition, but also in a division of a company, sometime referred to as an *equity sale*. When a company decides to sell a division or some of its assets, it may come from interest expressed by another company or from a change in the company's strategic plan. The decision to sell a division may also be necessitated by the need to raise funds to finance the acquisition of another company or an investment, or it may be to raise funds to pay off its debt obligations to avoid bankruptcy. Investment banks help in equity sales by providing expertise in determining the value of the business as an ongoing concern and the value of the synergy of a division with other firms. They also help in moving the equity sale forward by initially setting up a bidding process that discretely identifies potential buyers, later procuring letters of intent, and finally obtaining a final contract.

Bloomberg Insurance Information

FLNG <Enter>, select Insurance Company in "Institution Type" tab.

Bloomberg Pension Information

FLNG <Enter>, select Pension Funds in "Institution Type" tab.

Bloomberg Merger and Acquisition Screen, MA

MA: <Enter>: Merger Advisor search engine.

Bloomberg Investment Banker and Underwriter Screens

- **LTOP <Enter>:** The LTOP screen displays top underwriters for the major fixed-income, equity, equity-linked securities, and syndicated loan securities markets. To access: LTOP <Enter>. On the LTOP screen, press the left click to access a dropdown menu showing descriptions and the underwriter's deals for that period.
- **Underwriter's Ticker** (e.g., GS): Ticker <Equity> <Enter>: See DES and CF.
- **LEAG:** <Enter> Underwriter rankings from LTOP.
- **LMX:** <Enter> Underwriter rankings.
- **CACT:** <Enter> CACT screen tracks major corporate moves including mergers and division sales.

Financial Service Industry, the 2008 Financial Crisis, and Regulations

Investment banking firms, commercial banks, insurance companies, and pensions are the key participants in the financial service industry. Prior to the Great Depression, many commercial banks acted as investment bankers by underwriting securities and buying and selling securities for their customer. With over 10,000 commercial banks collapsing during the depression, Congress passed the Glass-Steagall Act in 1932, which separated investment banking from commercial banking. Starting in the 1980s, and later with the passage of the Gramm-Leach-Bliley Act, however, the legal barriers between commercial and investment banking began to diminish. As a result, the financial industry saw many commercial bank holding companies acquiring investment banks, and later investment banks expanding their scope into insurance, real estate, and other financial areas. During this period, Merrill Lynch became an even larger multifunctional financial firm acquiring insurance and real estate companies to combine with its extensive investment banking and brokerage operations. However, large commercial banks such as Citicorp and UBS (formally United Bank of Switzerland) added investment banking to their commercial banking operation. Finally, the industry saw firms such as Goldman Sachs and Lehman Brothers expand the scope of activities in investment banking and developing specializations in stocks, bonds, and derivatives.

In June 2008, the subprime mortgage meltdown that began in August 2007 developed into a global credit crisis. As for the financial industry, the events leading up to the 2008 crisis and the subsequent economic recession led to the passage of the Dodd-Frank Wall Street Reform and Consumer Protection Act, aimed at preventing another financial crisis. Some of the key tenets of the act include those aimed at protecting consumers, constraining large Wall Street bonuses, and ending bailouts to financial institutions in distress (i.e., ending the "Too Big to Fail" bailouts). See Exhibit 5.12 for a summary of some of the provisions related to the investment industry.

BLOOMBERG DODD-FRANK INFORMATION

BLAW: Information on Dodd-Frank can be accessed from the Bloomberg BLAW Platform: BLAW <Enter>; Click "8) PRAC BLAW Practice Areas"; Click "10) Dodd-Frank Legislation" to bring up a menu for accessing information on Dodd-Frank.

Other Dodd-Frank Information Screens
- **Brief <Enter>**: Regulation Newsletter.
- **NI DODDFR <Enter>:** News of Dodd-Frank.

Bloomberg Credit Crisis Screens
- SBPR <Enter> Subprime News.
- STNI Rumor <Enter> Rumors and Speculation.
- HSST <Enter> U.S. Housing and Construction Statistics.
- DQRP <Enter> Rank Deals by Collateral Performance.
- DQSP <Enter> Delinquent Loan Data by Servicer.
- DELQ <Enter> Credit Card Delinquency Rate.
- BBMD <Enter> Mortgage Delinquency Monitor.
- REDQ <Enter> Commercial Real Estate Delinquencies.
- DQLO <Enter> Delinquency Rates by Loan Originators.

See Bloomberg Web Exhibit 5.4.

EXHIBIT 5.12 Dodd-Frank Wall Street Reform and Consumer Protection Act—Select Provisions Related to Investment Banks

Constraints on Size: The Financial Stability Oversight Council can make recommendations to the Federal Reserve for increasingly strict rules for capital, leverage, liquidity, risk management and other requirements as companies grow in size and complexity, with significant requirements on companies that pose risks to the financial system.

Fed Regulation of Nonbank Financial Companies: A 2/3 vote of the Financial Stability Oversight Council and vote of the chair, gives the Federal Reserve the authority to regulate a nonbank financial company if the council believe there would be negative effects on the financial system if the company failed or its activities would pose a risk to the financial stability of the United States.

Break Up Large, Complex Companies: Able to approve, with a 2/3 vote of The Financial Stability Oversight Council and vote of the chair, a Federal Reserve decision to require a large, complex company, to divest some of its holdings if it poses a grave threat to the financial stability of the United States.

Technical Expertise: Creates a new Office of Financial Research within Treasury to be staffed with a highly sophisticated staff of economists, accountants, lawyers, former supervisors, and other specialists to support the council's work by collecting financial data and conducting economic analysis.

Bankruptcy: Most large financial companies that fail are expected to have their reorganization or liquidation resolved through the bankruptcy process.

Limits on Debt Guarantees: To prevent bank runs, the FDIC can guarantee debt of solvent insured banks, but only after meeting serious requirements: 2/3 majority of the Board and the FDIC board must determine there is a threat to financial stability; the Treasury Secretary approves terms and conditions and sets a cap on overall guarantee amounts; the President activates an expedited process for Congressional approval.

Raising Standards and Regulating Hedge Funds: Requires that hedge funds and private equity firms have their advisers register with the SEC as investment advisers and provide information about their trades and portfolios necessary to assess systemic risk. This data will be shared with the systemic risk regulator and the SEC will report to Congress annually on how it uses this data to protect investors and market integrity.

Oversight of Credit Rating Agencies: Creates an Office of Credit Ratings at the SEC with its own compliance staff and the authority to fine agencies. The SEC is required to examine Nationally Recognized Statistical Ratings Organizations at least once a year and make key findings public.

Disclosure: Requires Nationally Recognized Statistical Ratings Organizations to disclose their methodologies, their use of third parties for due diligence efforts, and their ratings track record.

SEC: (1) Gives SEC the authority to impose a fiduciary duty on brokers who give investment advice—the advice must be in the best interest of their customers; (2) Creates a program within the SEC to encourage people to report securities violations; (3) Gives the SEC authority to grant shareholders proxy access to nominate directors; (4) Directs the SEC to clarify disclosures relating to compensation, including requiring companies to provide charts that compare their executive compensation with stock performance over a five-year period; (5) Provides more resources to the chronically underfunded agency to carry out its new duties.

Global Equity Markets and Exchanges

Brokers and dealers operating through organized exchanges, the OTC market, and ECNs have created a sophisticated system in which investors can buy and sell securities easily and quickly. This sophisticated system is global in breadth. Since the 1980s, there has been a globalization of security markets with the openings or expansions of exchanges in London, Frankfort, Singapore, Hong-Kong, Shanghai, Toronto, New Zealand, and Tokyo. The increase in the number of exchanges globally has also led to a number of trading innovations: global electronic trading systems, 24-hour worldwide trading, and alliances between exchanges. The growth in the security trading has also led to consolidations, such as the NYSE Euronext. Today, investors can easily buy and sell securities almost anywhere in the world. In this section, we complete our analysis of security trading by examining the global markets. We begin, however, with a note on the exchange-rate risk that investors face when they diversify their investment globally.

Note on Exchange-Rate Risk

Investors buying foreign securities in national or offshore markets denominated in foreign currency are subject to changes in exchange rates that, in turn, affect the rates of return they can obtain from their investments. For example, suppose a U.S. investor bought one share of a French stock worth €900 per share when the $/€ spot exchange rate was at $1.4717/€. The U.S. investor's total dollar investment would, therefore, be $1,324.53.

$$\text{Dollar Investment} = (\$1.4717/€)(€900) = \$1,324.53$$

Suppose a year later the price of the French stock is trading 11.11 percent higher at €1,000 per share but the $/€ spot exchange rate decreased (a dollar appreciation) by 15 percent from $1.4717/€ to $1.250945/€. If the U.S. investor had to liquidate his investment at that time, then he would lose 5.5 percent in dollars, even though the stock increased in value:

$$\text{Rate} = \frac{(\$1.250945/€)(1,000\ €)}{\$1,324.53} - 1 = -0.055$$

The example illustrates that when investors purchase foreign securities, they must take into account not only the risk germane to the security, but also the risk that exchange rates will move to an unfavorable level. It should be noted that the forward exchange market makes it possible for investors to hedge their investments against exchange-rate risk. In the above case, for example, suppose that when she purchased the French stock, the U.S. investor had entered into a forward contract to sell 1,000 euros one year later at the forward rate of $1.4717/€. At the end of the year, the investor would be sure of converting €1,000 into $1,471.70. Thus, even if the $/€ spot rate fell by 15 percent, the investor would still be able to earn 11.11 percent

[= $1,471.70/$1,324.53) − 1] from her dollar investment. Thus by entering a forward contract to sell foreign currency, the investor is able to profit from her stock investment. There are other ways investors, as well as borrowers, can hedge against exchange risk (future, options, and swaps). Using these tools, in turn, allows investors and borrowers to focus on the choice of securities and the type of funding.

BLOOMBERG SPOT AND FORWARD EXCHANGE RATES SCREENS

Currency Menu Screen: Ticker <Curncy> <Enter>: Screens: ALLQ, Composite Quotes; CQ, Competing Quotes; GP, Price Graph; FXDV, Foreign Exchange Derivative Menu; FXFR (forward and spot quotes).
 FXIP <Enter>: Foreign Exchange Information Portal

Differences in Foreign Security Markets

Foreign investors who buy domestic stocks and bonds will find differences from country to country in how the securities are issued and regulated. In a number of countries, banks, instead of investment bankers, underwrite many new stocks and bonds. In Germany, for example, there had been a long history of no separation between commercial and investment banking. Many banks in Germany acted as security underwriters and as brokers and dealers in the secondary market, trading existing bonds and stocks through an interbank market. In Europe, though, the *Single European Act* did permit banks and financial institutions in the European Economic Community (EEC) to offer a wide variety of the same banking and security services. This act has led to standardization in the EEC. Until 2000, Japan, like the United States, had a history of separating its commercial and investment banking activities. In Japan, brokerage houses such as Nikko, Normura, and Yamaichi underwrite and broker stocks, bonds, and other securities.

A foreign investor buying a domestic security may also be subject to special restrictions. These can include special registrations, exchange controls, and foreign withholding taxes. On some exchanges, trading is conducted electronically or physically only a few times during a day as a call auction. There are also exchanges that have elements of both in which market makers are assigned to actively traded stocks, while thinly traded ones are sold through an open auction.

Security exchanges in the United States, Canada, Japan, Switzerland, and several other countries allow for investors to buy stock on margin. These exchanges are typically spot markets in which the transactions must be settled within a few days. In countries where margin purchases are prohibited, a *futures stock market* for some stocks is provided. An investor buying such a stock on these markets agrees to buy the stock at an agreed-upon price on a specific future date in which the payment of cash is to be made. Typically, futures stock trading is limited to just the major stocks listed on the exchanges, collateral is required, and the future settlement date is often the same for all stocks (e.g., end of the month).

Tax Considerations

Investing in foreign securities often creates different tax considerations than investing domestically. In general, the taxes that an investor may be subject to when investing internationally depend on the tax laws of the investor's country and the country where the investment occurs. The two major cash flows in which taxes may be applied are capital gains and dividend or interest income.[9] In most countries, including the United States, capital gains taxes are based on where the investor lives and not the origin of the investment. Thus, a U.S. investor realizing a capital gain from buying and selling a French stock would only be subject to a U.S. capital gains tax, not a French tax.

On the other hand, for a number of years the dividend or interest income from a security owned by a foreigner was subject to a *foreign withholding tax* in many countries, including the United States. U.S. investors who received dividend income from Heineken stock, for example, would receive a dividend net of a withholding tax paid by the Heineken Company to the Netherlands government. To eliminate or minimize double taxation, many countries established treaties that permitted the investor to receive a tax credit in their home country. Thus, a U.S. investor would report the total foreign dividends on his U.S. tax form, but would be able to subtract the withholding tax paid to the foreign government from his tax liability.[10] In the 1980s, a number of countries repealed this withholding tax, including the United States, which eliminated its tax in 1984.

Global Equity Investments

A U.S. investor who is interested in buying a foreign stock has several alternatives. First, she may be able to buy the stock directly on the foreign company's national market. If the investor buys the stock this way, she will be subject to exchange risk and she may also incur a relatively high transaction cost. Secondly, it may be that the foreign stock is listed on a U.S. stock exchange or the OTC market. Many multinational corporations, as previously noted, are listed not only on their national exchanges, but also on security exchanges in other countries, often where they have subsidiaries or conduct considerable business. If the foreign stock of interest is listed on a U.S. stock exchange, then the U.S. investor could easily purchase the stock there. If she did, she would, in turn, avoid the risk of currency conversions and possibly foreign taxes. Third, the U.S. investor may be able to acquire the stock of a foreign company by buying a special share entitling her to its ownership. In the United States, these special shares are known as *American depository receipts (ADRs)*; deposit receipts offered in any country are referred to as *global depository receipts (GDRs)*. Fourth, the investor may find a market maker on the OTC market or in the Euroequity market who is trading in the foreign stock. Finally, if the U.S. investor is looking to internationally diversify her portfolio, then she may find the easiest way to accomplish this is to buy a share in an international mutual fund.

Foreign Stocks Listed on Domestic Markets

Today, many multinational corporations raise funds to finance their foreign subsidiaries and operations by issuing bonds and selling shares of stock in those countries in which they own a subsidiary or have extensive sales. These security sales provide the corporations with funds denominated in a local currency, which they use to finance their local operations, thus avoiding the currency conversion that would have occurred if they had raised the funds in their own markets. In addition, the cash flows from the subsidiaries often can be used to pay dividends, again allowing the company to avoid currency conversion.

To ensure that the stocks they sell in foreign countries are liquid, companies often decide to list their stock on the country's security exchange. Thus, many companies have stock listings on their own national exchanges and on foreign stock exchanges. Although the primary reason for this multiple listing is to provide liquidity, it also serves to make the company's ownership more diversified, possibly protecting it against takeover bids. However, multiple listing may cause an increase in a stock's volatility since the stock is subject to market conditions in other countries. The major benefit to a domestic investor from buying a stock in a foreign company listed on the investor's national exchange is that she can buy the stock in her local currency. In addition, the investor may also avoid foreign withholding taxes and other fees and regulations that may have resulted if she had purchased the stock on a foreign security market.

Stocks with multiple listings are usually traded at different times and places. A multiple-listed American stock trading on a European exchange, for example, would trade before the U.S. exchange opens. Moreover, if the U.S. market is the dominant market (i.e., a greater proportion of the company's total stock is traded in the U.S. market than on the foreign exchanges), then the price in the European market—the *satellite market*—will probably reflect only the price in the U.S. market the previous day and the exchange rate. However, for some stocks, especially foreign stocks listed on the U.S. exchanges, their home market is not necessarily the dominant one. If this is the case, then the satellite market may lead the home market.

BLOOMBERG FOREIGN SECURITY EXCHANGES

- **EQS** <Enter>: Use EQS to search for exchanges in other countries and their listing.
- **IMAP**: The IMAP screen can be used to identify exchanges and the primary stocks listed on them: IMAP <Enter>; All Securities tab; Click the area from Name list (e.g., Asia Pacific (Emerging); select country (e.g., China); select exchange (e.g., Shanghai).
- **SECF**: SECF <Enter>; Equity Tab; Select Country from Country Tab; Select Exchange from Exchange tab (or leave blank) to get a list of all securities.

(Continued)

- **QMC <Enter>:** Screen displays quotes from all of the foreign exchanges on which a selected stock trades. The screen can be used to identify a stock's primary market and its dual listings.

See Bloomberg Web Exhibit 5.5.

New Exchanges, Consolidation, and Global 24-Hour Trading

Over the last twenty years, the globalization of security exchanges has seen the emergence of new exchanges, the growth in existing exchanges in emerging markets such as China, India, and Brazil, and the consolidation of existing exchanges through mergers and affiliations. For example, since 1995, the market has seen Germany's three exchanges merge into the Frankfort exchange; later, the consolidation of the Frankfort, London, and Paris exchanges into one exchange; and in 2007 the formation of the transatlantic NYSE Euronext, with its six equity and six derivative exchanges. Such consolidation is the result of technology and the emergence of electronic trading systems that today can handle 10,000 stocks as easily as 200. Consolidation has also widened the markets for global investments, providing global access by all traders to most securities. This global access, in turn, has improved the marketability and liquidity of all securities.

Globalization and electronic crossing sessions have also led to 24-hour trading, which can be described as a market in which "investment firms pass-the-book around the world." For example, trading can start in New York where stocks can be traded from 9:30 A.M. to 4:00 P.M. (Eastern time), picked up in Tokyo where stocks can traded with some overlap until 5:00 A.M, then picked up by London where with overlap they can be traded until it is picked back up by New York.

American Depository Receipts

In the 1980s and 1990s, U.S. exchanges began trading American depository receipts (ADRs).[11] As noted, ADRs are dollar-denominated claims on shares of foreign stock kept in safekeeping by U.S. commercial or investment banks. They are formed by a U.S. commercial bank or investment banker who buys foreign shares and then holds them in safekeeping. The intermediary then sells dollar-denominated ADRs to investors. The ADRs thus represent claims to the foreign shares held in safekeeping. Dividends paid on the stocks underlying the ADRs are received by the bank that transfers them to the ADR holders. For U.S. investors, ADRs represent an alternative to buying foreign stock. As of 2010, over 160 foreign stocks were traded as ADRs on the NASDAQ and NYSE Euronext.

Although ADRs are traded like domestic securities, they are similar to foreign stocks in that they are subject to both price risk and exchange-rate risk. The advantage ADRs provide U.S. investors over foreign stocks is convenience: Buying and selling ADRs is like buying and selling any U.S. stock. In addition, companies whose stocks sell as ADRs are required by the SEC to file financial statements similar to those of U.S. companies who are listed. As a result, U.S. investors can obtain information on the foreign companies that is comparable to the information for U.S. companies. Finally, commercial and investment banks in forming ADRs often take into account the exchange rate in determining the number of shares representing an ADR in order to make the prices of ADRs similar to those of U.S. stocks.

BLOOMBERG ADR INFORMATION

- **EQS:** One way to identify ADRs is to use EQS: EQS <Enter>; type "ADR" in "Add Criteria" box.
- **S&P ADR Index: SPADR <Index> <Enter>:** ADRs can also be found looking at ADRs that comprise the S&P ADR index: SPADR <Equity>; MEMB screen.
- **SECF:** ADRs found using SECF: SECF <Enter>; Equity Tab; Select "Receipts" from type; Select country from Country Tab (or leave blank) to get a list; Select exchange from Exchange tab (or leave blank) to get a list.

See Bloomberg Web Exhibit 5.6.

Conclusion

Just like the direct markets for stocks and bonds, the intermediary and global financial markets offer investors a wide array of instruments for financing and investing: from short-term securities, such as CDs, BAs, and shares in money market funds, to intermediate- and long-term instruments, such as MBSs, mutual fund shares, ETFs, pension plans, annuities, and GICs. The investment and commercial banks, insurance companies, investment funds, pension funds and individual investors invest trillions of dollars each year into primary and intermediary securities. The types of securities offered and their trading characterize a financial market of both depth and breadth.

In examining the types of equity and intermediates securities and markets over the last two chapters and in Chapter 1, our focus has been on the markets, with emphasis on equity securities. In the next three chapters, we focus on how investors can evaluate stocks and portfolios in terms of their expected returns and risk.

Web Site Information

1. *Wall Street Journal* site: http://online.wsj.com/public/us
   - Click "Market Data" tab.
   - Click "ETF" tab.
   - Click "Mutual Fund" tab.
   - Use Screener.
2. FINRA: Go to www.finra.org/index.htm, Sitemap, Market Data, and Mutual Funds.
3. Yahoo: Go to http://screen.yahoo.com/funds.html, Fund Screener.

4. Real estate investment trusts: www.nareit.com
   - Price and other information on REITs can be found by going to Yahoo, http://screen.yahoo.com/funds.html; use Stock Screener to find REITs.
5. Investment Company Institute: www.ici.org
6. Investment Company Institute Facts Book: www.icifactbook.org/index.html
7. Investment funds and ratings:
   - www.morningstar.com
   - www.lipper.com
8. Hedge funds:
   - www.thehfa.org
   - www.hedgefund.net
9. Federal Reserve flow-of-fund accounts: www.federalreserve.gov/releases/z1/current/data.htm
   - Go to PDF (2MB) for Flow of Fund Tables by sector and security type.
   - See Table L109-L113 for banks.
   - See Table L121 for mutual funds.
   - See Table L122 for ETFs.
   - See Table L123 for REITs.
   - Go to "Data Download Program" to download series to Excel.
10. Federal Reserve Flow of Fund Accounts: www.federalreserve.gov/releases/z1/current/data.htm
    - Go to PDF (2MB) for Flow of Fund Tables by sector and security type.
    - See Table L115 for life insurance assets.
    - See Table L114 for property and casualty insurance assets.
    - See Table L117-L119 for pension fund assets.
    - Go to "Data Download Program" to download series to Excel.
11. For pension fund information and updates: www.ifebp.org
12. For Social Security Fund information: www.ssa.gov
13. Pension Benefit Guarantee Corporation: www.pbgc.gov
14. Current Currency Quotes: http://online.wsj.com/public/us, Click Market Data Tab; Click FX Tab.
15. Historical foreign exchange rates and balance of payments: www.research.stlouisfed.org/fred2/categories
16. Information on world indexes, exchange rates, and other international data: www.bloomberg.com

Notes

1. Although it is generally true that the number of shares of a closed fund is fixed, such funds occasionally issue new shares either through a public offering or through a share dividend, which is sometimes offered to shareholders who are given an option of receiving either cash or new shares. Also, some funds occasionally go into the market and purchase their own shares.

2. Section 13(f) of the 1934 Securities Exchange Act requires institutional investment managers with investment discretion over $100 million or more of certain equity securities to file quarterly reports disclosing their equity holdings. An institutional investment manager is an entity that either invests in, or buys and sells, securities for its own account, for example, banks, insurance companies, broker/dealers, and corporations and pension funds that manage their own investment portfolios. An institutional investment manager is also a natural person or an entity that exercises investment discretion over the account of any other natural person or entity. Form 13F must be filed within 45 days of the end of each calendar quarter. The Bloomberg's FLNG screen (FLNG <Enter>) displays 13F Filings. From the 13F Filings screen, one can search through a list of companies with 13F Filings status. One can also display aggregated 13F Filings and break down the filings by type: All, Pensions, Banks, Mutual Funds, Venture Capital, and Private Equity.

3. The Barclay, J. P. Morgan, and Merrill Lynch indexes require a subscription to access. The subscription can be made through Bloomberg. With the subscription, one is able to access the indexes from the Bloomberg terminal.

4. Managers of ETFs contract with third parties to calculate a real-time estimate of an ETF's current value, called the *intraday indicative value* (*IIV*). The IIVs are disseminated at regular intervals during the trading day. Investors, in turn, can observe any discrepancies between the ETF's share price and its IIV during the trading day. When a gap exists between the ETF share price and its IIV, investors may decide to trade in either the ETF share or the underlying securities that the ETF holds in its portfolio in order to attempt to capture a profit. This trading helps to narrow any discrepancy between the price of the ETF share and its IIV. For more information on ETFs, see *Investment Company Fact Book*, www.icifactbook.org.

5. Using actuarial tables, life insurance companies can predict with a relatively high degree of accuracy when death benefits would have to be paid.

6. There are three general types of annuities: A *life annuity*, which pays a fixed amount regularly until the investor's death; a *last survivor's annuity*, which pays regular fixed amounts until both the investor and spouse die; and a *fixed-period annuity*, which makes regular fixed payments for a specified period (e.g., 5, 10, or 20 years), with payments made to a beneficiary if the investor dies. These annuities are referred to as fixed annuities. In addition to fixed annuities, insurance companies also offer a *variable annuity* in which regular payments are not fixed, but rather depend on the returns from the investments made by the insurance company (the insurance company sometimes invests in a mutual fund that they also manage). Finally, insurance companies offer *deferred annuities* (variable or fixed) that allow an investor to make a series of payments instead of a single payment.

7. Pension members are not taxed on their contributions, but they do pay taxes on benefits when they are paid out. Pension funds in the United States are governed by the 1974 *Employee Retirement Income Security Act* (*ERISA*). ERISA requires prudent management of the fund's investments and requires that all private plans be fully funded; that is, that the assets and income cover all promised benefits. The act also ensures transferability of plans when employees change jobs, specifies disclosure requirements, and defines the minimum vesting requirements for determining eligibility. In 1974, Congress also created the *Pension Benefit Guaranty Corporation* (*PBGC* or *Penny Benny*) to provide insurance for employee benefits. Similar to the FDIC, Penny Benny is a government agency that insures pension benefit up to a limit if a company goes bankrupt and has an underfunded pension plan. It operates by charging pension plans a premium, and it can borrow funds from the Treasury. In 2008, Penny Benny paid benefits to over 700,000 retirees of failed pension plans.

8. In accordance with the Self-Employed Individual Tax Retirement Act of 1962, self-employed people can contribute up to 20 percent of their net earnings to a Keogh plan (retirement account) with the contribution being tax deductible from gross income. The Pension Reform Act of 1978 updated the 1962 act to permit individual retirement accounts (IRAs). Subsequent legislation in 1981 and 1982, in turn, expanded the eligibility for creating tax-deferred accounts to include most individuals. The Small Business Protection Act of 1996 created simplified retirement plans for businesses with 100 or fewer workers. In addition to company-sponsored and group-sponsored pensions, bank trust departments, insurance companies, and investment companies offer and manage individual retirement accounts and Keogh plans. For small accounts, these institutions often combine the accounts in a *commingled fund,* instead of managing each account separately. A commingled fund is similar to a mutual fund. For accounting purposes, individuals setting up accounts are essentially buying shares in the fund at their NAV, and when they withdraw funds, they are selling essential shares at their NAV. Like mutual funds, insurance companies and banks offer a number of commingled funds, such as money market funds, stock funds, and bond funds.

9. Depending on the country, there also may be a transaction tax levied on the value of the stock purchase.

10. It should be noted that many tax-free investment companies, such as pension funds, were not able to take advantage of this credit, or if they could, they often had to file special exemption forms with the foreign government, which was often costly and time-consuming.

11. ADRs were first introduced in the 1920s. However, it was not until the 1980s that they became popular.

Selected References

Ambachtsheer, K. P. 1998. How should pension funds manage risk? *Journal of Applied Corporate Finance* 11(2): 122–127.

Friedberg, L., and M. T. Owyang. 2002. Not your father's pension plan: The rise of 401(k) and other defined contribution plans. *Review*, Federal Reserve Bank of St. Louis (January–February): 23–34.

Johnson, R. Stafford. 2013. *Debt Markets and Analysis.* Hoboken, Hoboken, NJ: John Wiley & Sons: 319–369.

Madura, Jeff. 2000. *International Financial Management.* 6th ed. Cincinnati, Ohio: South-Western College Publishing, 57–79.

Mishkin, F. S., and S. G. Eakins. 2003. *Financial Markets and Institutions*, 4th ed. Boston: Addison-Wesley.

Mishkin, Frederic S., and Stanley G. Eakins. 2007. *Financial Markets and Institutions*, 6th ed. Boston: Addison-Wesley.

Zirky, E. A., and R. M. Mackey. 1993. Pension plan funding strategies: Defining terms. *Pension World* (August): 40–41.

Bloomberg Exercises

1. Learn more about the different types of funds and their classifications by going to the FUND screen and "Classification" link: FUND <Enter>; click "10".

2. The performances of funds by type (e.g., mutual, hedge funds, ETFs, and unit investment trust) can be found on Bloomberg's Fund Heat Map screen, FMAP. Use the screen to identify the top performers based on total return for several types: FMAP <Enter>, click "Fund Type" in "View By" dropdown.

3. The performances of funds by objective (e.g., equity, debt, asset allocation, money market, and alternative) can be found on FMAP. Use the screen to identify the top performers based on total return for several objectives: FMAP <Enter>, Click "Objective" in "View By" dropdown.

4. Identify several mutual funds (open and closed end) using SECF: SECF <Enter>; Funds Tab, click Open End or Closed End tab or select Open-End fund or Closed-End fund from the Type tab; select Equity, Fixed Income, or Mixed from the Focus tab, and USD from currency tab. Examine one of the funds using the functions on the fund's menu screen (Fund Ticker <Equity> <Enter>). Functions to include are DES, historical fund analysis (HFA) or COMP, fund holdings (MHD), and price graph (GP).

5. Identify several unit investment trusts using SECF: SECF <Enter>; Funds Tab, select Unit Investment Trust from Type tab, Fixed Income from Focus tab, and USD from currency tab. Examine one of the funds using the functions on the fund's menu screen (Fund Ticker <Equity> <Enter>). Functions to include are DES, historical fund analysis (HFA) or COMP, fund holdings (MHD), and price graph (GP).

6. Identify several fund of funds using SECF: SECF <Enter>; Funds Tab; click select F of F tab or select Fund of Funds from Type tab; chose a Focus (e.g., equity, real estate, or all), and currency (e.g., USD). Examine one of the funds using the functions on the fund's menu screen (Fund Ticker <Equity> <Enter>). Functions to include are DES, historical fund analysis (HFA) or COMP, fund holdings (MHD), and price graph (GP).

7. Identify several ETFs using SECF: SECF <Enter>; Funds Tab; click ETFs tab or select ETF from Type tab; chose a focus (e.g., equity, real estate, or all), and currency (e.g., USD). Examine one of the ETFs using the functions on the fund's menu screen (Fund Ticker <Equity> <Enter>). Functions to include are DES, historical fund analysis (HFA) or COMP, fund holdings (MHD), and price graph (GP).

8. Use the Bloomberg fund search screen, FSRC, to search for the following types of open- and closed-end equity funds:
   a. Fund type: Open-End Funds; Classification/Fund Asset Class Focus: Equity; Classification/Fund Market Cap Focus: Small-Cap; Country of Domicile: United States; Analytic criterion: Enter (in amber box) total return for one year of greater than X percent (e.g., 30 percent).
   b. Fund type: Closed-End Investment Funds; Classification/Fund Asset Class Focus: Equity; Country of Domicile: United States.
   Note: To save your searches, click "Save As" in the Actions Tab.

9. Select one of the funds from each of your searches in Exercise 8 and study it using the functions on the fund's menu screen (Fund Ticker <Equity> <Enter>).

10. Use the Bloomberg fund search screen, FSRC, to search for the following types of fixed-income funds and ETFs:
    a. Fund type: Open-End Funds; Classification/Fund Asset Class Focus: Fixed Income; Classification/Maturity band Focus: Long Term; Classification/Fund Rating Class Focus: Investment Grade A or higher; Analytic criterion: Enter (in amber box) total return for one year of greater than X percent (e.g., 4 percent or 10 percent).
    b. Fund type: Open-End Funds; Classification/Fund Asset Class Focus: Fixed Income; Classification/Maturity band Focus: Intermediate Term; Classification/Fund Rating Class Focus: High Yield; Analytic criterion: Enter (in amber box) total return for one year of greater than X percent (e.g., 10 percent).
    c. Fund type: Exchange Traded Products; Country of Domicile: United States; Classification/Fund Asset Class Focus: Fixed Income; Classification/Fund Rating Class Focus: High Yield.
    d. Fund type: Fund of Fund; Classification/Fund Asset Class Focus: Fixed Income; Classification/Fund Rating Class Focus: High Yield.
       Note. To save your searches, click "Save As" in the Action Tab.
11. Select one of the funds from each of your searches in Exercise 10 and study it using the functions on the fund's menu screen (Fund Ticker <Equity> <Enter>).
12. Use the Bloomberg fund search screen, FSRC, to search for the following types of equity funds outside the United States:
    a. Fund type: Open-End Funds or Closed-End; Classification/Fund Asset Class Focus: Equity; Country of Domicile: Select country other than United States (e.g., Netherlands).
    b. Fund type: Open-End Funds or Closed-End; Classification/Fund Asset Class Focus: Fixed-Income; Country of Domicile: Select country other than United States (e.g., Netherlands).
13. Select one of the funds from each of your searches in Exercise 12 and study it using the functions on the fund's menu screen (Fund Ticker <Equity> <Enter>).
14. Use the Bloomberg fund search screen, FSRC, to search for the following types of ETFs:
    a. Fund type: Exchange Traded Product; Classification/Fund Asset Class Focus: Equity or Fixed Income. Consider narrowing your search by entering an analytical criterion: Enter (in amber box) total return for one year of greater than X percent.
    b. Classification/Fund Objective: Select an ETF from the Exchange Traded Product menu. Consider narrowing your search by entering an analytical criterion: Enter (in amber box) total return for one year of greater than X percent.
15. Select one of the funds from each of your searches in Exercise 14 and study it using the functions on the fund's menu screen (Fund Ticker <Equity> <Enter>).

16. Use FSRC to search and screen for different types of government funds: FSRC: FSRC <Enter>; Classification/Fund Objective: Select from a Fixed-Income menu list (e.g., Government Bond, High yield). Funds to consider:
    - Government Bond Long
    - Muni High Yield
    - Muni of a state (e.g., Muni New York Long)

    Select some of the funds from your searches and study them using the functions on the fund's menu screen (Fund Ticker <Equity> <Enter>).

17. Use Bloomberg's SECF screen to find different types of funds: SECF <Enter>, click Funds Tab and then type the fund of interest (municipal, global, or index) in the Search box. You may want to narrow your search by selecting categories from the Focus, Exchange, and Type tabs. Funds to consider:
    - Municipal
    - Global
    - Index

    Study some of funds using the functions on the fund's menu screen (Ticker <Equity> <Enter>).

18. Bloomberg's REIT screen provides a menu for searching for real estate investment trusts by regions: United States, Europe, Asia, Australia, Canada, and other. Using the screens, search and select some REITs from different regions. You can also use the SECF screen: SECF <Enter>, type "REIT" in the Search box. Study the REITs using the functions on the REIT's menu screen (Ticker <Equity> <Enter>).

19. Go to the FUND screen to find news and information on mutual funds, hedge funds, and ETFs: FUND <Enter>, use the "News and Research" link.

20. The hedge fund industry is a leader in creating new investment products. To keep current, go to the BRIEF screen to access the Bloomberg newsletter: "Hedge Fund."

21. Investment banks are an important financial intermediary. Study some of the activities and deals of investment banks by exploring Bloomberg's LTOP and LEAG screens.

22. Keep current on mergers by going to the BRIEF screen to access the Bloomberg newsletter: "Mergers."

23. The LTOP screen displays top underwriters for the major fixed income, equity, equity-linked securities, and syndicated loan securities markets. Using the screen, identify the top underwriters over the past year for global equity issues. Using the dropdown menu, study some of the recent deals for several of the top equity underwriters. To access: LTOP <Enter>.

24. The IMAP screen can be used to identify stocks that are trading on different exchanges around the world. On the IMAP screen, study the securities listed on an exchange outside the United States: IMAP <Enter>, select All Securities, click region, country, and then an exchange.

25. Use WEXC to find the Web site of foreign exchanges of interest.

26. Use SECF to search for ADRS or Global Depository Receipts: SECF <Enter>; Equity tab; select Receipts from Type tab; select country (e.g., United Kingdom); select currency (e.g., USD). Study some of the ADRs using the functions on the fund's menu screen (Ticker <Equity> <Enter>).

27. Use the SECF or EQS screen to search for stocks from countries other than the United States. SECF <Enter>; Equity tab; Common stock from Type tab; select country (e.g., United Kingdom, France, or China). Or, EQS <Enter>; click "Exchange" and then country. Study some of the stocks using the functions on the stock's menu screen (Ticker <Equity> <Enter>).

28. Bloomberg's QMC screen displays quotes from all of the domestic and foreign exchanges on which a selected stock trades. The screen can be used to identify a stock's primary market and its dual listings. Select a stock of interest and study its quotes: Stock Ticker <Equity> <Enter>; QMC. You may want to use the "Exclude" tabs to include or exclude exchanges with quotes in different currencies.

29. Information on Dodd-Frank Financial Regulatory Reform Bill can be accessed from the Bloomberg BLAW Platform: BLAW <Enter>; Click "8) PRAC BLAW Practice Areas," Click "10) "Dodd-Frank Legislation" to bring up a menu for accessing information on Dodd-Frank. Use the portal to learn about some of the legislation and the timetables for implementing some of regulatory changes called for in the bill.

CHAPTER 6

Expected Rate of Return and Risk—Stock

Introduction

Although knowledge of present or past returns is important for security analysts, an investor is more concerned with what a security will yield in the future; that is, she wants to know the expected rate of return, as well as the chance that her expectations might be wrong. For example, after an in-depth analysis, an investor might think a stock would generate a 20 percent rate of return, but she also knows that under certain scenarios she might lose 10 percent or gain as much as 35 percent. Similarly, a bond investor who sees a bond trading to yield 10 percent also knows there is a chance of default in which he might lose 70 percent and also a chance that rates in the market might decrease, causing the bond to sell at a higher price and thus yielding a higher return than the current yield. Whether it is investments in stocks, bonds, investment fund shares, or commodities, investors must deal in a world of uncertainty. As a result, investors have to consider not only the expected rate of return, but also the risk that such a rate may not be attained.

In this chapter, we extend our analysis of security valuation and return presented in Chapter 3 to stock risk and expected return. We begin by first defining a risk-free security and the difference between nominal and real rates of return. We next briefly examine the nature of risk as it relates to stocks. With this background, we then look at a security's expected return and risk statistically by examining return distributions and characteristics—mean, variance, and correlation parameters. Finally, we conclude the chapter by examining the relations between expected return and risk for a stock.

Risk-Free Security, Nominal Rates, and Real Rates

Investment risk is the possibility that the realized return from holding a security will deviate from the expected. Most securities are subject to risk. However, some securities, like a U.S. T-bill, have a future return that is known in advance. For example, an investor who plans to hold a T-bill to its maturity knows with certainty that at that date she will receive the principal. Thus, the rate of return from the time of the investment to maturity is known. Treasury bonds and notes—the Treasury's coupon issues—are, in turn, considered default free with known coupon and principal payments. However, they technically are not risk-free securities since investors are subject to reinvestment risk when they reinvest their coupon income at unknown rates.

Denoted here as R_f, the rate of return on a security whose return is known in advance is defined as the *risk-free rate* (also called the sure rate or riskless rate). An investment in a risk-free security ensures the investor that she will receive a certain amount of cash. Such an investment, however, is not protected against inflation, which can lower the purchasing power of the investment money received. An investor who invested $100 in a one-year, risk-free security paying $105 at maturity, would earn a risk-free rate of 5 percent. If the average price of goods and services increased by 10 percent over the next year, the purchasing power of the $100 would have decreased (i.e., goods that cost $100 at the beginning of the year now cost $110). In this case, the investor would lose approximately 5 percent of purchasing power from the investment as a result of the 10 percent inflation.

Since inflation subjects an investment in a risk-free security to purchasing-power risk, analysts make a distinction between the nominal risk-free rate and the *real risk-free rate*. The nominal risk-free rate is the rate whose future cash is known in advance (i.e., R_f), whereas the real risk-free rate, RR_f, is the rate whose return reflects the investment return's purchasing power. The real rate can be found by discounting the future nominal risk-free return by the inflation rate. That is:

$$RR_f = \frac{1 + R_f}{1 + \text{Inflation rate}} - 1$$

Thus, with a nominal rate from the investment of 5 percent and an inflation rate of 10 percent, the real rate of return in our example is −4.545 percent:

$$RR_f = \frac{1.05}{1.10} - 1 = -0.04545$$

When inflation is expected to be high and the nominal rates on securities low, investors are better off increasing their consumption of goods and services and decreasing their savings and investments. In contrast, when deflation is expected, the real risk-free rate is higher than the nominal, and investors are better off increasing their saving and investment.

Stock Risk: Firm, Industry, and Market Risk

For investments in stocks, realized returns can deviate from expected returns when there are changes in expected dividends, growth rates in dividends, and factors that alter an investor's required returns. In Chapters 11 and 12, we will examine the fundamentals that determine a firm's income and balance sheet and the underlying factors that determine a firm's earnings, dividends, growth rates, and required return. We can, however, categorize the total risk of stock in terms of three general factors that influence a stock's return: factors related to the individual firm, the industry in which the firm competes, and the market in general.

Firm factors are unique to the company under consideration. They include the company's investment and financing decisions, marketing strategies, and competitive position in the industry. For example, an oil company acquiring a refinery and financing the acquisition by selling long-term bonds would be subjecting its equity investors to firm-related factors that would affect not only the expected return on the company's stock, but also the stock's risk. *Industry factors* affect all companies in the same industry. They include economic activities and regulations and laws that affect the industry. For example, the price of Inbev stock is influenced not only by firm factors such as the marketing strategies of the Samuel Adams Brewing Company, but also by industry factors such as consumers' relative taste for wine or other distilled spirits—a consideration that affects all beer companies. Finally, there are *market factors*, which by definition affect all stocks. They include macroeconomic factors, like the growth in the overall economy, the rate of inflation, the general level of interest rates, and the economic growth of emerging markets. For example, an economic recession would be a market factor since it tends to depress the earnings and returns of all companies.

The total risk of a stock can therefore be broken into firm risk, industry risk, and market risk. Total risk of a stock can also be divided into unsystematic risk and systematic risk. As we will examine later in this chapter, *unsystematic risk* is defined as the risk of a security that can be eliminated or reduced when that security is included in a diversified portfolio; it consists of risk due to firm and industry factors. *Systematic risk* is market risk, and in contrast to unsystematic risk, it cannot be eliminated by forming a portfolio of stocks. For example, the industry risk associated with investing in Inbev stock might by eliminated, or at least reduced, by investing in a wine stock, but forming a portfolio with both stocks would probably not eliminate the effect a recession would have on either stock's return. Thus, unlike firm and industry risk, market risk cannot be diversified away by forming a portfolio of stocks.

Statistical Measurements of Expected Return and Risk

In statistics, the term *random variable* describes a variable whose value is uncertain. For most securities, their future cash flows, prices, and rates of return are random variables. Signified with a tilde over the symbol (e.g., $\tilde{R}$), random variables are also called stochastic variables.

An important property of a random variable is its *probability distribution*. A probability distribution assigns probabilities to all possible values of the random variable. The distribution can be objective (as when using past frequencies or simply assuming the distribution takes a specific form) or subjective. Also, the distribution can be continuous, taking on all possible values over the range of the distribution, or discrete,

EXHIBIT 6.1   Probability Distribution for Stock ABC

(1) r_i	(2) p_i	(3) $p_i r_i$	(4) $[r_i - E(r)]$	(5) $[r_i - E(r)]^2$	(6) $p_i[r_i - E(r)]^2$	(7) $[r_i - E(r)]^3$	(8) $p_i[r_i - E(r)]^3$
4%	0.1	0.4	−2	4	0.4	−8	−0.8
5%	0.2	1.0	−1	1	0.2	−1	−0.2
6%	0.4	2.4	0	0	0.0	0	0.0
7%	0.2	1.4	1	1	0.2	1	0.2
8%	0.1	0.8	2	4	0.4	8	0.8
	1	$E(r) = 6\%$			$V(r) = 1.2$		$S_k(r) = 0$

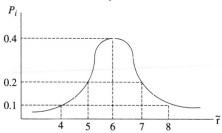

Probability Distribution

where the distribution takes on only a few possible defined values. Exhibit 6.1 shows a probability distribution for next period's rate of return on stock ABC ($\tilde{r}$). This discrete distribution is defined by five possible rates (column 1) and their respective probabilities (column 2) and is shown graphically in Exhibit 6.1. The most common way to describe this distribution is in terms of its expected value, variance, and skewness. The expected value, or mean, is a measure of the central tendency of the distribution and the variance is a measure of the distribution's average squared deviation. The expected value and variance of a security's return distribution are good measures of that security's expected rate of return and risk, respectively.

Expected Value

The expected value of a random variable x, $E(x)$, or its mean, μ, is the weighted average of the possible values, with the weights being the probabilities assigned to each possible value (p_i). The expected value, along with the median and the mode, is a measure of the central tendency of the distribution. For example, the expected rate of return for stock ABC, $E(r)$, shown in Exhibit 6.1 is 6 percent:

$$E(\tilde{r}) = \sum_{i=1}^{T} p_i r_i = p_1 r_1 + p_2 r_2 + \cdots + p_T r_T$$

$$E(\tilde{r}) = (0.1)(4\%) + (0.2)(5\%) + (0.4)(6\%) + (0.2)(7\%) + (0.1)(8\%) = 6\%$$

Like any variable, a random variable can be a function of other variables. The rates of return on many stocks, for instance, are related to the rates of return on a market index (R^M), as measured by the proportional changes in the S&P 500 index or the Dow Jones Average. In such cases, the rate of return on a security can be expressed algebraically as:

$$\tilde{r} = \alpha + \beta \tilde{R}^M$$

where:

α = Interecept

β = Slope = $\frac{\Delta r}{\Delta R^M}$

In this form, the expected value of r is equal to $E[\alpha + \beta R_M]$. The expected value of this equation, in turn, can be simplified by making use of the following expected value operator rules:

1. Expected value of a constant (α) is equal to the constant:

$$\text{EV Rule 1: } E(\alpha) = \alpha$$

2. Expected value of a constant times a random variable is equal to the constant times the expected value of the random variable:

$$\text{EV Rule 2: } E(\beta \tilde{R}^M) = \beta E(\tilde{R}^M)$$

3. Expected value of a sum is equal to the sum of the expected values:

$$\text{EV Rule 3: } E[X + Y] = E(X) + E(Y)$$

By applying these three rules to the equation $E[\alpha + \beta R_M]$, $E(r)$ can be expressed as

$$E(r) = E[\alpha + \beta \tilde{R}^M]$$
$$E(r) = E[\alpha] + E[\beta \tilde{R}^M] \text{ EV Rule 3}$$
$$E(r) = \alpha + \beta E(\tilde{R}^M) \text{ EV Rules 1 and 2}$$

Variance, Standard Deviation, and Coefficient of Variation

Variance

The variance of a random variable ($V(\tilde{r})$) is the expected value of the squared deviation from the mean:

$$V(r) = E[\tilde{r} - E(r)]^2$$

The variance is referred to as the second moment of the distribution. It is a measure of the distribution's dispersion, indicating the squared deviation most likely to occur. As an expected value, the variance can be measured by calculating the weighted average of each squared deviation, with the weights being each squared deviation's probability:

$$V(\tilde{r}) = \sum_{i=1}^{T} p_i [\tilde{r}_i - E(\tilde{r})]^2$$

$$V(\tilde{r}) = p_1 [\tilde{r}_1 - E(\tilde{r})]^2 + p_2 [\tilde{r}_2 - E(\tilde{r})]^2 + \cdots + p_T [\tilde{r}_T - E(\tilde{r})]^2$$

ABC stock described in Exhibit 6.1, in turn, has a variance of 1.2:

$$V(\tilde{r}) = (0.1)[4\% - 6\%]^2 + (0.2)[5\% - 6\%]^2 + (0.4)[6\% - 6\%]^2$$
$$+ (0.2)[7\% - 6\%]^2 + (0.1)[8\% - 6\%]^2$$
$$V(\tilde{r}) = 1.2$$

Standard Deviation

The standard deviation, $\sigma(r)$, is the square root of the variance:

$$\sigma(\tilde{r}) = \sqrt{V(\tilde{r})}$$

The standard deviation provides a measure of dispersion that is on the same scale as the distribution's deviations. The standard deviation for ABC stock is 1.09544; this indicates that the distribution has an average deviation of plus or minus 1.0954451 (± 1.09544).

Coefficient of Variation

As noted, the risk of a security is the uncertainty that the realized return will deviate from the expected return. By definition, the variance and standard deviation of a security's rate of return define a security's risk. That is, the greater a security's variance, the greater the realized return can deviate from the expected return, and thus the greater the security's risk.

Although the variance (or standard deviation) can be used to define and measure a security's risk relative to other securities, using just that parameter can be misleading if there is a large disparity in the expected rates of returns among the securities being evaluated. For example, suppose you are considering an investment in either Stock A or Stock B with the following expected returns and standard deviations:

Stock	A	B
Expected Return	0.05	0.12
Standard Deviation	0.04	0.07

Stock B with a standard deviation of 0.07 appears to be riskier than Stock A, whose standard deviation is only 0.04. However, Stock B's distribution dominates Stock A's distribution; that is, with an expected return of 0.12 and standard deviation of 0.07, Stock B has an average range between 0.05 and 0.19, whereas Stock A, with an expected return of 0.05 and a standard deviation of 0.04, has only an average range of between 0.01 and 0.09. In such cases, the *coefficient of variation* (*CV*) is a better measure of risk than the variance or standard deviation. The coefficient of variation expresses the standard deviation as a proportion of the expected value:

$$CV = \frac{\sigma(r)}{E(r)}$$

In this example, Stock A has a *CV* of 0.80, whereas B has a *CV* of only 0.583:

$$CV_A = \frac{\sigma(r)}{E(r)} = \frac{0.04}{0.05} = 0.80$$

$$CV_A = \frac{\sigma(r)}{E(r)} = \frac{0.07}{0.12} = 0.583$$

Thus, Stock B has less risk per unit of expected return than Stock A.

Skewness

Skewness measures the degree of symmetry of the distribution. A distribution that is symmetric about its mean is one in which the probability of $r = E(r) + x$ is equal to the probability of $r = E(r) - x$, for all values of x. Skewness, $S_k(r)$, is defined as the third moment of the distribution and can be measured by calculating the expected value of the cubic deviation:

$$S_k(\tilde{r}) = \sum_{i=1}^{T} p_i [r_i - E(\tilde{r})]^3$$

$$S_k(\tilde{r}) = p_1 [\tilde{r}_1 - E(\tilde{r})]^3 + p_2 [\tilde{r}_2 - E(\tilde{r})]^3 + \cdots + p_T [\tilde{r}_T - E(\tilde{r})]^3$$

The skewness of the distribution in Exhibit 6.1 is zero, indicating the distribution is symmetrical.

$$S_k(\tilde{r}) = (0.1)[4\% - 6\%]^3 + (0.2)[5\% - 6\%]^3 + (0.4)[6\% - 6\%]^3$$
$$+ (0.2)[7\% - 6\%]^3 + (0.1)[8\% - 6\%]^3$$
$$S_k(\tilde{r}) = 0$$

In investments, security prices are characterized by increasing trends (e.g., a bull market) or decreasing trends (e.g., a bear market). These trends often tend to be characterized statistically by having a negative skewness and positive expected return when there is an increasing trend and positive skewness and negative expected return when there is a decreasing trend.

Normal Distribution

The above example dealt with a discrete probability distribution. Most securities have a large number of possible values at a future date and are better represented by a continuous distribution. The most well-known continuous distribution is the normal distribution. This is a symmetric, bell-shaped distribution extending from $-\infty$ to $+\infty$. The distribution is completely described by two parameters: its mean, μ, and standard deviation, σ. Thus, the only difference between one normal distribution and another is their respective means and standard deviations.

A special type of normal distribution is the standard normal distribution. As shown in Exhibit 6.2, this distribution has a mean (or expected value) of zero, a standard deviation of one, and an area under the distribution equal to one. With the area under the normal distribution equal to one, the probability of an outcome occurring between any two points of a standard normal distribution equals the area between the two points. For example, the probability of an outcome being below the mean (i.e., being between 0 and $-\infty$) is 0.5, and the probability of it being above the mean (i.e., being between 0 and $+\infty$) is also 0.5 (see Exhibit 6.2). Similarly, the probability of an outcome being between one standard deviation below the mean and one standard

EXHIBIT 6.2 Standard Normal Distribution

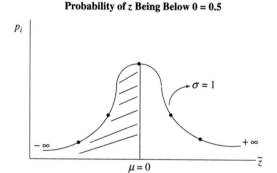

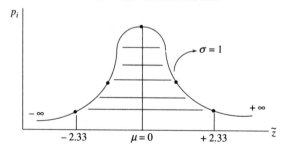

deviation above is 0.68, whereas the probability of an outcome being between 2.33 standard deviations below the mean and 2.33 standard deviations above is 0.99 (see Exhibit 6.2). For the standard normal distribution, the number of standard deviations from the mean (e.g., 1 or 2.33) is referred to as the z-score. The area under a standard normal distribution corresponding to a given z-scores, N(z), can be obtained from a standard normal density table found in most statistics books; the area can also be found using the following formula:

$$n(z) = 1 - 0.5[1 + 0.196854(|z|) + 0.115194(|z|)^2$$
$$+ 0.000344(|z|)^3 + 0.019527(|z|)^4]^{-4}$$

where:
   $|z|$ = absolute value of z.

If z is negative, then the n(z) value obtained from the formula is subtracted from one; if z is positive, then the n(z) obtained from the formula is used:

$$N(z) = 1 - n(z), \text{for } z < 0$$
$$N(z) = n(z), \text{for } z > 0$$

Since other normal distributions differ only in terms of their means and standard deviations, the value of a normally distributed random variable x can be converted into its corresponding z-score by using the following formula:

$$\tilde{z} = \frac{\tilde{x} - \mu}{\sigma} \tag{6.1}$$

and the value of x corresponding to a given z value can be found using the following:

$$\tilde{x} = \mu + \tilde{z}\sigma \tag{6.2}$$

By specifying the z-score needed to achieve a certain probability, a confidence interval for a random variable x can be formed. For example, a 99 percent confidence interval is formed by setting z in Equation (6.2) equal to −2.33 and to 2.33:

$$\text{Probability } [\mu - 2.33\sigma < x < \mu + 2.33\sigma] = 0.99$$

If a security being analyzed has returns that are normally distributed, then given estimates of the security's expected return and standard deviation, a confidence interval for its returns can be formed. For example, a stock with an expected return of 10 percent and a standard deviation of 12 percent would have a 99 percent confidence interval of its return being between −17.96 percent and 37.96 percent (see Exhibit 6.3):

$$\text{Probability } [10\% - 2.33(12\%) < \tilde{r} < 10\% + 2.33(12\%)] = 0.99$$
$$\text{Probability } [-17.96 < \tilde{r} < 37.96] = 0.99$$

EXHIBIT 6.3 Confidence Intervals

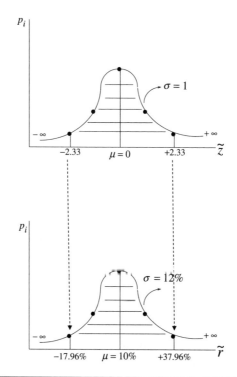

Probability $[\mu - 2.33\,\sigma < x < \mu + 2.33\sigma] = 0.99$

Probability $[10\% - 2.33\,(12\%) < \tilde{r} < 10\% + 2.33\,(12\%)] = 0.99$

Probability $[-17.96 < \tilde{r} < 37.96] = 0.99$

Correlation

Covariance

The covariance is a measure of the extent to which one random variable is above or below its mean at the same time or state that another random variable is above or below its mean. The covariance measures how two random variables move with each other. If two random variables, on average, are above their means at the same time and, on average, are below at the same time, then the random variables would be positively correlated with each other and would have a positive covariance (see Exhibit 6.4). In contrast, if one random variable, on average, is above its mean when another is below and vice versa, then the random variables would move inversely or negatively to each other and would have a negative covariance (see Exhibit 6.5).

The covariance between two random variables, r_1 and r_2, is equal to the expected value of the product of the variables' deviations:

$$Cov(\tilde{r}_1\tilde{r}_2) = E[\tilde{r}_1 - E(\tilde{r}_1)][\tilde{r}_2 - E(\tilde{r}_2)]$$

$$Cov(\tilde{r}_1\tilde{r}_2) = \sum_{i=1}^{T} p_i[\tilde{r}_{1i} - E(\tilde{r}_1)][\tilde{r}_{2i} - E(\tilde{r}_2)]$$

EXHIBIT 6.4   Positive Correlation

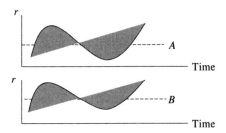

EXHIBIT 6.5   Negative Correlation

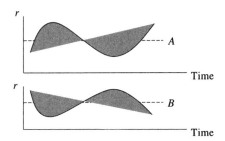

     In Exhibit 6.6, the possible rates of return for securities 1 and 2 are shown for three possible states (A, B, and C), along with the probabilities of occurrence of each state. As shown in the table, $E(r_1) = 18$ percent, $V(r_1) = 36$, $E(r_2) = 16$ percent, and $V(r_2) = 16$ (note the tilde $\tilde{r}$ over the symbol is dropped). In addition, the table also shows that in State A, security 1 yields a return below its mean, whereas security 2 yields a return above its mean. In State B, both yield rates of return equal to their mean, and in State C, security 1 yields a return above its mean whereas security 2 yields a return below. Securities 1 and 2 therefore are negatively correlated and, as shown in Exhibit 6.6, have a negative covariance of −24.

     In contrast, Exhibit 6.7 shows a case of positive correlation. In this case, in State A both securities 1 and 2 have returns below their mean; in State B both have rates of return equal to their mean; in State C both have returns above their means. Securities

EXHIBIT 6.6   Negative Correlation Example

State	p_i	r_{1i}	r_{2i}	$p_i\, r_{1i}$	$p_i\, r_{2i}$	$p_i[r_{1i} - E(r_1)]^2$	$p_i[r_{2i} - E(r_2)]^2$	$p_i[r_{1i} - E(r_1)]\,[r_{2i} - E(r_2)]$
A	1/8	6%	24%	0.75	3.0	(1/8)(144)	(1/8)(64)	(1/8)(−12)(8) = −12
B	6/8	18%	16%	13.5	12.0	(6/8)(0)	(6/8)(0)	(6/8)(0)(0) = 0
C	1/8	30%	8%	3.75	1.0	(1/8)(144)	(1/8)(64)	(1/8)(12)(−8) = −12
				$E(r_1) = 18$	$E(r_2) = 16$	$V(r_1) = 36$	$V(r_2) = 16$	$\mathrm{Cov}(r_1\, r_2) = -24$
						$\sigma(r_1) = 6$	$\sigma(r_2) = 4$	$\rho_{12} = -1$

EXHIBIT 6.7 Positive Correlation Example

State	p_i	r_{1i}	r_{2i}	$p_i\, r_{1i}$	$p_i\, r_{2i}$	$p_i[r_{1i} - E(r_1)]^2$	$p_i[r_{2i} - E(r_2)]^2$	$p_i[r_{1i} - E(r_1)]\,[r_{2i} - E(r_2)]$
A	1/8	6%	8%	0.75	1.0	(1/8)(144)	(1/8)(64)	(1/8)(−12)(−8) = 12
B	6/8	18%	16%	13.5	12.0	(6/8)(0)	(6/8)(0)	(6/8)(0)(0) = 0
C	1/8	30%	24%	3.75	3.0	(1/8)(144)	(1/8)(64)	(1/8)(12)(8) = 12
				$E(r_1) = 18$ $E(r_2) = 16$		$V(r_1) = 36$	$V(r_2) = 16$	Cov($r_1\ r_2$) = 24
						$\sigma(r_1) = 6$	$\sigma(r_2) = 4$	$\rho_{12} = 1$

1 and 2 therefore are positively correlated and, as shown in the exhibit, the securities have a positive covariance of 24.

Correlation Coefficient

The correlation coefficient between two random variables r_1 and $r_2\,(\rho_{12})$ is equal to the covariance between the variables divided by the product of each random variable's standard deviation:

$$\rho_{12} = \frac{Cov(r_1 r_2)}{\sigma(r_1)\rho(r_2)}$$

The correlation coefficient has the mathematical property that its value must be within the range of minus and plus one:

$$-1 \leq \rho_{12} \leq 1$$

If two random variables have a correlation coefficient equal to one, they are said to be perfectly positively correlated; if their coefficient is equal to a minus one, they are said to be perfectly negatively correlated; if their correlation coefficient is equal to zero, they are said to be zero correlated and statistically independent. That is:

$$\text{If } \rho_{12} = -1 \Rightarrow \text{Perfect Negative Correlation}$$
$$\text{If } \rho_{12} = 0 \Rightarrow \text{Uncorrelated}$$
$$\text{If } \rho_{12} = 1 \Rightarrow \text{Perfect Positive Correlation}$$

Correlation and Portfolio Risk

Correlation is important in measuring the risk of a portfolio of securities. If the returns of two stocks are perfectly negatively correlated, then a zero risk portfolio can be formed with the two stocks. Consider the two stocks described in Exhibit 6.6 that are perfectly negatively correlated with a covariance of −24. The negative correlation suggests that when stock 1's return (r_1) is above its mean, $E(r_1)$, stock 2's return (r_2) is below its mean, $E(r_2)$, and when r_2 is above $E(r_2)$, r_1 is below $E(r_1)$. If an investor were holding these securities in a portfolio with 40 percent of her investments in stock 1 and 60 percent in stock 2, her portfolio rate of return (R_p) would be 16.8 percent in each of the three possible states shown in Exhibit 6.6. For example, in State A, the return on stock 1 is 6 percent, and the return on stock 2 is 24 percent. With allocation of 40 percent in stock 1 and 60 percent in stock 2, the investor would earn only 2.4 percent [=(0.40)(6%)] from her investment in stock 1 but would earn a 14.4 percent rate of return [=(0.60)(24%)] from her investment in stock 2. Combined, the investor's portfolio return would be 16.8 percent [=(0.40)(6%) + (0.60)(24%)]. In State B, her return from stock 1 would be 7.2 percent [=(0.40)(18%)] and her return from stock 2 would be 9.60 percent [=(0.60)(16%)], yielding again a portfolio return of 16.80 percent [=(0.40)(18%) + (0.60)(16%)]. Finally, in State C, the return from stock 1 would be 12 percent [=(0.40)(30%)] and the return from stock 2 would be 4.8 percent [=(0.60)(8%)], yielding again a portfolio return of 16.8 percent [=(0.40)(30%) + (0.60)(8%)]. In summary:

State	Stock 1	Stock 2	Proportional Investment in Stock 1	Proportional Investment in Stock 2	Portfolio Rate of Return
A	6%	24%	0.4	0.6	0.168
B	18%	16%	0.4	0.6	0.168
C	30%	8%	0.4	0.6	0.168

Thus, the investor would find for each of the three possible states that her portfolio rate of return is always 16.8 percent. Thus, since the investor can always attain a 16.8 percent rate of return, there is no portfolio risk. It is interesting that both stocks 1 and 2 are risky $[\sigma(r_1) = 6]$ and $[\sigma(r_2) = 4]$, but the portfolio formed with them has rate of return of 16.8 percent for all states and therefore a portfolio variance of zero. Again, this is due to the perfect negative correlation.

In contrast, the two stocks described in Exhibit 6.7 are perfectly positively correlated with a covariance of 24. Portfolios formed with these stocks will always be subject to risk. For example, a portfolio with allocations of 40 percent in stock 1 and 60 percent in stock 2, generates a portfolio return of 7.2 percent in State A, 16.8 percent in State B, and 26.4 percent in State C. The returns from different portfolio allocations would all be characterized by lower returns in State A, moderate returns in State B, and higher returns in State C.

Parameter Estimates: Historical Averages

In most cases, we do not know the probabilities associated with the possible values of the random variable and must therefore estimate the parameter characteristics. The simplest way to estimate the mean, variance, skewness, and covariance is to calculate the parameters' historical average values from a sample. The historical averages also provide analysts with important descriptive information about a security's past performance. For the rate of return on a security, the average rate of return per period can be calculated using the security past holding period yields, HPY_t (stock $HPY = [(P_t - P_{t-1}) + \text{dividend}]/P_{t-1}) + \text{coupon})$ over N historical periods:

$$\bar{r} = \frac{1}{N} \sum_{t=1}^{N} HPY_t$$

Similarly, the variance of a security can be estimated by averaging the security's squared deviations, and the covariance between two securities can be estimated by averaging the product of the securities' deviations. Note, in estimating the variance and covariance, averages usually are found by dividing by $N - 1$ instead of N in order to obtain better unbiased estimates:

$$\bar{V}(r) = \frac{1}{N-1} \sum_{t=1}^{N} (HPY_t - \bar{r})^2$$

$$\overline{Cov}(r_1 r_2) = \frac{1}{N-1} \sum_{t=1}^{N} (HPY_{1t} - \bar{r}_1)(HPY_{2t} - \bar{r}_2)$$

An example of estimating parameters is shown in Exhibit 6.8, in which the average HPY, variances, and covariance are computed for a stock and a hypothetical stock index (S_m).

Geometric Mean and Arithmetic Mean

In computing historical averages, there are two ways to measure a security's average HPY: the arithmetic mean and the geometric mean. The arithmetic mean is simply the sum of the periodic HPYs divided by the number of periods (N):

$$\text{Arithmetic Mean} = \frac{1}{N} \sum_{t=1}^{N} HPY_t$$

The geometric mean is the Nth root of the products of one plus the HPYs for each of the N periods minus one:

$$\text{Geometric Mean} = \left[\prod_{t=1}^{N} (1 + HPY_1) \right]^{1/N} - 1$$

$$\text{Geometric Mean} = \left[(1 + HPY_1)(1 + HPY_2) \cdots (1 + HPY_N) \right]^{1/N} - 1$$

Different from the arithmetic mean, the geometric mean takes into account the compounding effect. For example, if a stock yields a 5 percent rate in one period, then

EXHIBIT 6.8 Historical Averages and Regression Estimates

Time	S	Dividend	HPY	(HPY − Av.)	(HPY − Av.)^2
1	100	0			
2	105	0	0.050000	0.032324	0.0010448
3	110	1	0.057143	0.039467	0.0015576
4	115	0	0.045455	0.027779	0.0007716
5	110	1	−0.034783	−0.052459	0.0027519
6	105	0	−0.045455	−0.063131	0.0039855
7	100	1	−0.038095	−0.055771	0.0031104
8	105	0	0.050000	0.032324	0.0010448
9	110	1	0.057143	0.039467	0.0015576
			0.141408		0.0158244

Av. = 0.017676   Var = 0.0022606

Stan. Dev. = 0.0475457

Time	S_m	R_m = HPY	$(R_m - Av.)$	$(R_m - Av.)^2$	$(R_m - Av.)(HPY - Av.)$
1	300				
2	315	0.050000	0.035583	0.001266	0.0011502
3	333	0.057143	0.042726	0.001825	0.0016863
4	346	0.039039	0.024622	0.000606	0.0006840
5	334	−0.034682	−0.049099	0.002411	0.0025757
6	319	−0.044910	−0.059327	0.003520	0.0037454
7	306	−0.040752	−0.055169	0.003044	0.0030769
8	320	0.045752	0.031335	0.000982	0.0010129
9	334	0.043750	0.029333	0.000860	0.0011577
		0.115339		0.014514	0.0150888

Av. = 0.014417   Var = 0.0020735   Cov = 0.002156

$$\hat{\alpha} = \bar{r} - \hat{\beta}\bar{R}_m$$
$$= 0.017676 - 1.04(0.014417) = 0.00268$$
$$\hat{\beta} = \frac{\hat{Cov}(r\ R_m)}{\hat{V}(R_m)} = \frac{0.002156}{0.002073} = 1.04$$
$$V(\varepsilon) = V(R) - \hat{\beta}^2 V(R_m)$$
$$= 0.0022606 - (1.04)^2 0.002073 = 0.0000184$$

$$E(r) = \alpha + \beta E(R_m)$$
$$= 0.00268 + 1.04E(R_m)$$
$$V(r) = \beta^2 V(R_m) + V(\varepsilon)$$
$$= (1.04)^2 V(R_m) + 0.0000184$$

the return for the second period would reflect the return earned in that period based on the compounded investment value at the beginning. As a result, the geometric mean is a better estimate of the rate at which the investment grew over the historical period.

To see the difference in the two average measures, consider the following three annual HPYs:

Year	0	1	2	3
XYZ Stock Price	$100	$200	$100	$150

Period	Beginning Value	Ending Value	HPY
1	$100	$200	1.00
2	$200	$100	−0.50
3	$100	$150	0.50

The *HPYs* represent the annual rates earned over a three-year period from investing in XYZ stock (assume no dividends). As shown, the *HPYs* of 100 percent, −50 percent, and 50 percent, reflect XYZ's value going from $100 to $200 in the first year, $200 to $100 in the second year, and $100 to $150 in the third year. The arithmetic mean of these three *HPYs* is 33.33 percent, whereas the geometric mean is 14.47 percent:

$$\text{Arithmetic Mean} = \frac{1}{N} \sum_{t=1}^{N} HPY_t$$

$$\text{Arithmetic Mean} = \frac{1.00 + (-0.50) + 0.50}{3} = 0.3333$$

$$\text{Geometric Mean} = \left[(1 + HPY_1)(1 + HPY_2) \cdots (1 + HPY_N)\right]^{1/N} - 1$$

$$\text{Geometric Mean} = \left[(1 + 1)(1 - 0.50)(1 + 0.50)\right]^{1/3} - 1 = 0.1447$$

Since the geometric mean takes into account the compounding of interest each period, it provides a measure of the rate at which the investment grows to equal its end-of-period value. The arithmetic mean, however, tends to overshoot the end-of-the period value. In this example, using the geometric mean of 14.47 percent, a $100 investment would grow annually at that rate of 14.47 percent to equal its correct value of $150 at the end of year three:

$$\$100(1.1447)^3 = \$150$$

In contrast, using the arithmetic rate of 33.33 percent as the average annual rate, the $100 investment would grow to equal a value of $237 at the end of three years:

$$\$100(1.3333)^3 = \$237$$

Similarly, looking at the *HPYs* for the first two years, the geometric mean is zero, correctly reflecting the fact that the investment of $100 is still worth $100 at end of year two; the arithmetic mean, on the other hand, is 25 percent even though there is no gain in value:

$$\text{Arithmetic Mean} = \frac{1.00 + (-0.50)}{2} = 0.25$$
$$\text{Geometric Mean} = [(1 + 1)(1 - 0.50)]^{1/2} - 1 = 0$$

Thus, unless the *HPYs* are the same in each period, the geometric mean will be less than the arithmetic mean and will correctly value the end-of-the period value, whereas the arithmetic mean will tend to overvalue the end-of-the period value.

Cumulative Returns

In addition to averages, analysts often look at how the past returns from an investment cumulate over time. Cumulative returns can be computed by either adding periodic *HPYs* starting from a base of zero or from a $1 investment or by calculating the compounded return each period. The cumulative *HPY* returns and compounded returns for the past *N* periods are:

$$\text{Cumulative return} = HPY_t + HPY_{t-1} + \cdots + HPY_{t-N}$$
$$\text{Compounded return} = \left[(1 + HPY_t)(1 + HPY_{t-1}) \cdots (1 + HPY_{t-N})\right] - 1$$

Cumulative *HPY* and compounded returns, in turn, allow an investor to evaluate the performance of the investment over time. Furthermore, by comparing the cumulative and compounded returns of different stocks or indexes, one can also evaluate the relative performance of an investment over time. Exhibit 6.9 shows graphically and in a table the cumulative *HPYs* and compounded returns starting from time period 0 to period 10. The cumulative and compounded returns are generated from the end-of-the period stock prices shown in Column 1 and the corresponding *HPYs* (assume no dividends). In examining the graphs, note that an investor who purchased the stock in time period 0 and sold it in period 6 would have realized a cumulative *HPY* of 20 percent and a compounded return of 20.06 percent. From period 6 to 7, however, the stock price declines by 20 percent, lowering the cumulative *HPY* to zero and the cumulative compounded return to −3.95 percent. Thus, if the investor had maintained the investment to year 7, she would have lost 3.95 percent of her initial investment. With the stock increasing in periods 8 through 10, the investor would have regained some of the loss with the cumulative *HPY* for the 10 periods being 20 percent and the compounded return being 16.48 percent.

Note that the compounded return captures the actual rate at which the stock grows over time to equal its ending value and is therefore a more accurate measure of the investor's return over time than the cumulative *HPYs*.

EXHIBIT 6.9 Cumulative and Compounded Returns

Period	Price	HPY	Cumulative HPY	1 + Cumulative HPY	1 + Compound Return	Compounded Return
t	P_t	$(P_t/P_{t-1}) - 1$	$HPY_t + HPY_{t-1} + \cdots + HPY_{t-n}$		$[(1 + HPY_t)(1 + HPY_{t-1}) \cdots (1 + HPY_{t-n})]$	$[(1 + HPY_t)(1 + HPY_{t-1}) \cdots (1 + HPY_{t-n})] - 1$
0	$100.00	0.0000	0.0000	1.0000	1.0000	0.0000
1	$110.00	0.1000	0.1000	1.1000	1.1000	0.1000
2	$115.50	0.0500	0.1500	1.1500	1.1550	0.1550
3	$103.95	-0.1000	0.0500	1.0500	1.0395	0.0395
4	$114.35	0.1000	0.1500	1.1500	1.1435	0.1435
5	$114.35	0.0000	0.1500	1.1500	1.1435	0.1435
6	$120.06	0.0500	0.2000	1.2000	1.2006	0.2006
7	$96.05	-0.2000	0.0000	1.0000	0.9605	-0.0395
8	$105.65	0.1000	0.1000	1.1000	1.0565	0.0565
9	$110.94	0.0500	0.1500	1.1500	1.1094	0.1094
10	$116.48	0.0500	0.2000	1.2000	1.1648	0.1648

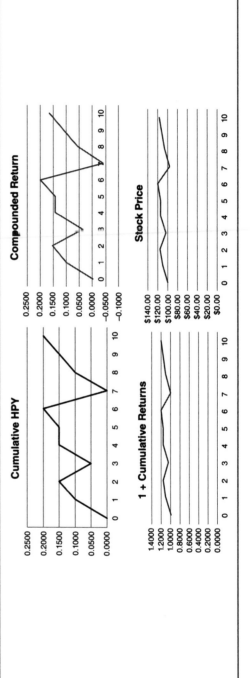

Cumulative HPY

1 + Cumulative Returns

Compounded Return

Stock Price

BLOOMBERG STATISTICS

Statistical calculations of the prices and returns for stocks, bonds, indexes, and portfolios are common on many Bloomberg screens. Screens of note include Comparative Total Returns (COMP), Graph Volatility (GV), Historical Volatility Table (HVT), Company Risk (RSKV), CORR, and PC.

> **Total Return, COMP**: The COMP screen shows the cumulative holding period returns for a selected stock, bond, portfolio, or index.
>
> **Graph Volatility Screen**: The GV screen charts historical prices, volatility, and other volatility measures for up to four securities.
>
> **CORR:** The CORR screen can be used to create and save a number of correlation matrices for securities, indexes, currencies, interest rates, and commodities. The matrix also shows a variance-covariance matrix (Cov), correlation coefficient matrix (Correlation), beta, and other correlation and regression parameters. A correlation matrix allows you to compare a maximum of 500 peers. The number of peers that can appear depends on the type of matrix you create. A symmetric matrix displays a maximum of 10 rows and 10 columns (10x10). A nonsymmetric matrix displays a maximum of 500 rows and 10 columns (500x10). An additional column may be inserted as the first column for any security in the matrix to see its correlation to other instruments in the matrix.

Bloomberg Excel Add-In

There are a number of Bloomberg Excel Add-in templates that calculate returns and volatility, as well as screen securities by volatility and return. See the DAPI screen and click "Excel Template Library." One useful template for calculating cumulative returns for different securities and for different periods is the XTOT Template. To access: DAPI <Enter>, click "Excel Template Library" and look for "Multiple Security Total Return Applications" in the "Equity" and "Other" category.

See Bloomberg Web Exhibit 6.1.

Parameter Estimates: Regression

Linear Regression

Historical averages provide analysts with important descriptive information about a security's past performance, but as noted, they are not usually good estimates of future values. Another approach to estimating expected returns and variances is to use regression analysis to estimate the behavioral relationship between the returns on a security and an identified explanatory variable such as the economy or the overall market. Given the estimated relation, the expected return, variability, and covariance can be estimated by independently projecting the future values of the explanatory variable.

Regression involves estimating the coefficients of an assumed algebraic equation. A *linear regression* model has only one explanatory variable, whereas a *multiple regression* model has more than one independent variable. As an example, consider a linear regression model relating the rate of return on a stock (dependent variable) to the market rate of return, R^M (independent variable), where R^M is measured by the proportional change in a stock index:

$$r_j = \alpha + \beta R_j^M + \varepsilon_j$$

where:

α = intercept
β = slope = $\Delta r / \Delta R^M$
j = observation
ε = error

In the above equation, ε_j is referred to as the error term or stochastic disturbance term. Thus, the model assumes that for each observation j, errors or deviations in the relationship between r and R^M can exist, causing r to deviate from the algebraic relation defined by $\alpha + \beta R^M$. Since, a priori, the errors are not known, the regression model needs to provide assumptions about ε. The standard assumptions are:

$$E(\varepsilon_j) = 0$$
$$V(\varepsilon_j) \text{ is constant}$$
$$Cov(\varepsilon, R^M) = 0$$

This regression model is depicted graphically in Exhibit 6.10. The regression line shown in the figure is referred to as the *characteristic line*. As shown in the figure, for each observation (R_1^M and R_2^M), there are corresponding values for r, given α and β (r_1 and r_2), and there are possible errors, ε, that can cause r to be greater or less than the values determined by the intercept and slope. The assumption $E(\varepsilon_j) = 0$,

EXHIBIT 6.10   Characteristic Line

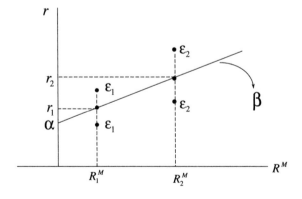

however, indicates that, on average, the errors cancel each other out, causing the $E(r_j)$ for observation R_j^M to equal $E[\alpha + \beta R_j^M]$. The second assumption of a constant $V(\varepsilon)$, in turn, implies that the distribution of errors is the same at each observation; the third assumption indicates that ε and R_j^M are independent.

Using the above assumptions and the expected value operator rules, the expected value and variance can be defined in terms of the regression model as follows (see Exhibit 6.11 for the derivation of the equations):

$$E(r) = E[\alpha + \beta R^M + \varepsilon]$$
$$E(r) = \alpha + \beta E(R^M) + E(\varepsilon) \tag{6.3}$$
$$E(r) = \alpha + \beta E(R^M)$$

$$V(r) = E[r - E(r)]^2$$
$$V(r) = \beta^2 V(R^M) + V(\varepsilon) \tag{6.4}$$

If two securities (1 and 2) both are related to R^M such as

$$r_1 = \alpha_1 + \beta_1 + \varepsilon_1$$
$$r_2 = \alpha_2 + \beta_2 + \varepsilon_2$$

(where the j subscript indicating observation is deleted) and ε_1 and ε_2 are independent $(Cov(\varepsilon_1, \varepsilon_2) = 0)$, then the equation for the $Cov(r_1\ r_2)$ is

$$Cov(r_1 r_2) = \beta_1 \beta_2 V(R_m) \tag{6.5}$$

See Exhibit 6.11 for the derivations of Equation (6.4) and (6.5).

Estimating the Regression Coefficients

The intercept and slope of a linear regression model can be estimated by the ordinary least squares (OLS) estimation procedure. This technique uses sample data for the dependent and independent variables (time series data or cross-sectional data) to find the estimates of α and β that minimize the sum of the squared errors. Graphically, OLS estimation can be described as finding the line (α and β) that cuts through a scatter diagram of data coordinates of the dependent and independent variables that minimizes the errors (or sum of squared errors). The estimating formulas for α and β that best cut through the scatter diagram in which the errors are minimized are:

$$\hat{\alpha} = \bar{r} - \hat{\beta}\bar{R}^M \tag{6.6}$$

$$\hat{\beta} = \frac{\hat{Cov}(r, R^M)}{\hat{V}(R^M)} \tag{6.7}$$

EXHIBIT 6.11   Math Derivation of $V(R)$ and $Cov(R_1, R_2)$ in Terms of the Regression Model

Variance

  Assume:

  $E(\varepsilon) = 0$

  $Cov(R^M \varepsilon) = 0$

  $Cov(R^M \varepsilon) = E[R^M - E(R^M)][\varepsilon - E(\varepsilon)]$

  $V(\varepsilon) = E[\varepsilon - E(\varepsilon)]^2 = E[\varepsilon - 0] = E[\varepsilon^2]$

  $V(r) = E[r - E(r)]^2$

  $V(r) = E[\alpha + \beta R^M + \varepsilon - \alpha - \beta E(R^M)]^2$

  $V(r) = E[\beta[R^M - E(R^M)] + \varepsilon]^2$

  $V(r) = E[\beta^2[R^M - E(R^M)]^2 + \varepsilon^2 + 2\beta[R^M - E(R^M)]\varepsilon$

  $V(r) = \beta^2 E[R^M - E(R^M)]^2 + E(\varepsilon^2) + 2\beta E[R^M - E(R^M)]\varepsilon$

  $V(r) = \beta^2 V(R^M) + V(\varepsilon)$

Covariance

  Given:

  $r_1 = \alpha_1 + \beta_1 R^M + \varepsilon_1$

  $r_2 = \alpha_2 + \beta_2 R^M + \varepsilon_2$

  $Cov(\varepsilon_1 \varepsilon_2) = E[\varepsilon_1 - E(\varepsilon_1)][\varepsilon_2 - E(\varepsilon_2)] = E[\varepsilon_1 - 0][\varepsilon_2 - 0] = E[\varepsilon_1 \varepsilon_2] = 0$

  Assume :

  $E(\varepsilon) = 0$

  $Cov(\varepsilon_1 \varepsilon_2) = E[\varepsilon_1 \varepsilon_2] = 0$

  $Cov(\varepsilon R^M) = 0$

  $Cov(r_1 r_2) = E[r_1 - E(r_1)][r_2 - E(r_2)]$

  $Cov(r_1 r_2) = E[\alpha_1 + \beta_1 R^M + \varepsilon_1 - \alpha_1 - \beta_1 E(R^M)][\alpha_2 + \beta_2 R^M + \varepsilon_2 - \alpha_2 - \beta_2 E(R^M)]$

  $Cov(r_1 r_2) = E[\beta_1 \beta_2[R^M - E(R^M)]^2 + \varepsilon_1 \varepsilon_2 + \beta_1[R^M - E(R^M)]\varepsilon_2 + \beta_2[R^M - E(R^M)]\varepsilon_1$

  $Cov(r_1 r_2) = \beta_1 \beta_2 E[R^M - E(R^M)]^2 + E(\varepsilon_1 \varepsilon_2) + \beta_1 E[R^M - E(R^M)]\varepsilon_2 + \beta_2 E[R^M - E(R^M)]\varepsilon_1$

  $Cov(r_1 r_2) = \beta_1 \beta_2 V(R^M) + Cov(\varepsilon_1 \varepsilon_2) + \beta_1 Cov(R^M \varepsilon_2) + \beta_2 Cov(R^M \varepsilon_1)$

  $Cov(r_1 r_2) = \beta_1 \beta_2 V(R^M) + 0 + 0 + 0$

  $Cov(r_1 r_2) = \beta_1 \beta_2 V(R^M)$

where:

  $C\hat{o}v(r, R_m), \hat{V}(R_m), \bar{r},$ and $\bar{R}_m$ = estimates (averages)

  $\wedge$ = sign for estimate

An estimate of the $V(\varepsilon)$, can be found using Equation (6.4) for $V(r)$. That is:

$$\hat{V}(\varepsilon) = \hat{V}(r) - \hat{\beta}^2 V(\hat{R}^M) \tag{6.8}$$

where: $V(r)$ and $V(R^M)$ can be estimated using the sample averages, and β can be estimated using the ordinary least squares estimating Equation (6.7).

Exhibit 6.8 shows how to estimate a regression model relating the rate of return on a stock to the market rate using quarterly data on the stock and the stock index. In the example in the exhibit, the estimated β is 1.04, α is 0.00268, and $V(\varepsilon)$ is 0.0000184. Using these estimates, the expected return and risk of the stock in term of this regression model are:

$$E(r) = \hat{\alpha} + \hat{\beta} E(R^M)$$
$$E(r) = 0.00268 + 1.04 E(R^M)$$
$$V(r) = \hat{\beta}^2 V(R^M) + \hat{V}(\varepsilon)$$
$$V(r) = (1.04)^2 \ V(R^M) + 0.0000184$$

Regression Qualifiers

The coefficients between any variable can be estimated with a regression model. Whether the relationship is good or not depends on the quality of the regression model. All regression models therefore need to be accompanied by information about the quality of the regression results. Two commonly used regression qualifiers are the coefficient of determination (R^2) and the t-statistic (or t-test).

The coefficient of variation measures how much of the variation in the dependent variable can be explained by the variation in the explanatory variables. The variance of a security's return defined in terms of the above regression model, Equation (6.4), measures how much variation in return can be attributed to the market, $\beta^2 V(R^M)$ and how much variation can be attributed to other factors, $V(\varepsilon)$:

$$V(r) = \beta^2 V(R^M) + V(\varepsilon)$$

The variability can also be expressed as proportions of total variability by dividing Equation (6.4) by $V(r)$:

$$1 = \frac{\beta^2 V(R^M)}{V(r)} + \frac{V(\varepsilon)}{V(r)}$$
$$1 = R^2 + \frac{V(\varepsilon)}{V(r)} \tag{6.9}$$

The first term on the right-hand side of Equation (6.9) measures the proportion of variation in r that can be attributed to the market, and the second term measures the proportion due to other factors. Statistically, the first term on the right side of the equation is defined as the coefficient of variation, R^2:

$$R^2 = \frac{\beta^2 V(R^M)}{V(r)} \tag{6.10}$$

Note: Since both terms are positive, R^2 must be between 0 and 1:

$$0 \leq R^2 \leq 1$$

Thus, the higher the R^2, the more the variability is explained by the explanatory variables and the less by other factors, and therefore the better is the statistical quality of the regression model. If the R^2 coefficient is 0.9, for example, it indicates that 90 percent of the fluctuations in the security's return can be attributed to the market and 10 percent to other factors.

The other qualifier, a t-test or t-statistic, is equal to the ratio of the estimated slope coefficient (e.g., β) to standard deviation in the coefficient estimates, $\sigma_{\hat{\beta}}$. For our regression example, the t-statistic is

$$t = \frac{\hat{\beta}}{\sigma_{\hat{\beta}}}$$

Explanations of the t-distribution, t statistics, and distributions of estimates can be found in most statistics texts. For our purposes, the t-statistic provides a test of the null hypothesis of the coefficient being equal to zero. A t-statistic greater than 2.5 in absolute value, indicates that one can reject the null hypothesis, H_0, that the coefficient is equal to zero (i.e., H_0: $\beta = 0$), whereas a relatively low t-statistic— that is, less than 2.5 in absolute value—indicates that one cannot reject the null hypothesis. Since the hypothesis of $\beta = 0$ implies there is no relation between the dependent and independent variable (i.e., between a security's return and the market return), a high t-value (one greater than 2.5 in absolute value) indicates the relation between the dependent, and independent variable is significant (at the 5 percent level).

Regression Examples

Linear regressions for the Disney Corporation and General Electric are shown in Exhibit 6.12. Both regression analyses were done on Bloomberg's "Beta" screen. In each regression, the stock's daily percentage returns are regressed against the percentage changes in the S&P 500 (SPX) for the period from 9/8/2008 to 9/5/2013. The Beta screen shows the scatter diagram, regression estimates, and qualifiers. From this regression, Disney has a beta 1.106, alpha of 0.034, $\sigma(\varepsilon)$ of 1.153 ($V(\varepsilon) = 1.33$), t-statistic = $\beta/\sigma(\beta) = 54.494$, and R^2 of 0.703:

$$E(r) = \hat{\alpha} + \hat{\beta}E(R^M)$$
$$E(r) = 0.034 + 1.106E(R^M)$$

$$V(r) = \hat{\beta}^2 V(R^M) + \hat{V}(\varepsilon)$$
$$V(r) = (1.106)^2 V(R^M) + 1.33$$

EXHIBIT 6.12   Disney and GE Regressions

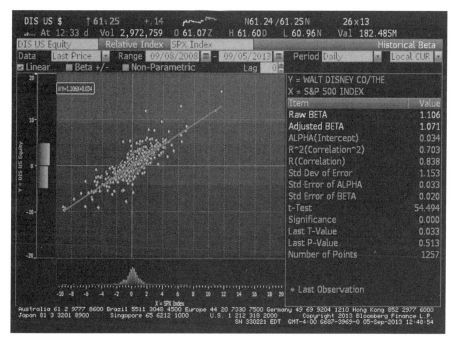

(a)

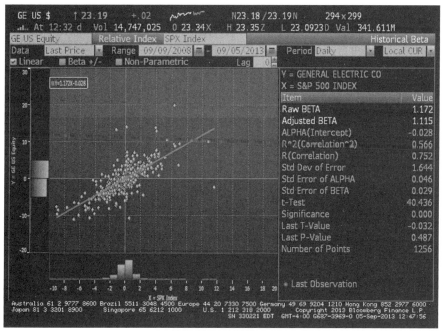

(b)

EXHIBIT 6.13   Statistical Analysis in Excel of Disney: Regression Commands

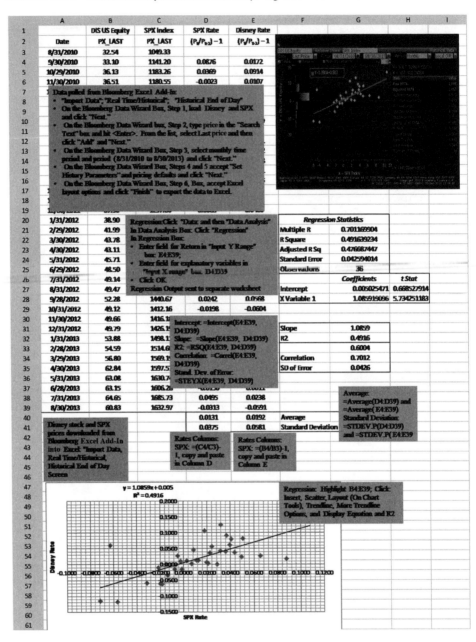

	A	B	C	D	E	F	G	H	I
1		DIS US Equity	SPX Index	SPX Rate	Disney Rate				
2	Date	PX_LAST	PX_LAST	$(P_t/P_{t-1})-1$	$(P_t/P_{t-1})-1$				
3	8/31/2010	32.54	1049.33						
4	9/30/2010	33.10	1141.20	0.0876	0.0172				
5	10/29/2010	36.13	1183.26	0.0369	0.0914				
6	11/30/2010	36.51	1180.55	-0.0023	0.0107				
7		Data pulled from Bloomberg Excel Add-in:							
8		• "Import Data"; "Real Time/Historical"; "Historical End of Day"							
9		• On the Bloomberg Data Wizard Box, Step 1, load Disney and SPX							
10		and click "Next."							
11		• On the Bloomberg Data Wizard box, Step 2, type price in the "Search							
12		Text" box and hit <Enter>. From the list, select Last price and then							
13		click "Add" and "Next."							
14		• On the Bloomberg Data Wizard Box, Step 3, select monthly time							
15		period and period (8/31/2010 to 8/30/2013) and click "Next."							
16		• On the Bloomberg Data Wizard Box, Steps 4 and 5 accept "Set							
17		History Parameters" and pricing defaults and click "Next."							
18		• On the Bloomberg Data Wizard Box, Step 6, Box, accept Excel							
19		layout options and click "Finish" to export the data to Excel.							
20	1/31/2012	38.90		Regression Click "Data" and then "Data Analysis"			*Regression Statistics*		
21	2/29/2012	41.99		In Data Analysis Box Click "Regression"		Multiple R	0.701169904		
22	3/30/2012	43.78		In Regression Box:		R Square	0.491639234		
23	4/30/2012	43.11		• Enter field for Return in "Input Y Range"		Adjusted R Sq	0.476687447		
24	5/31/2012	45.71		box: E4:E39;		Standard Error	0.042594014		
25	6/29/2012	48.50		• Enter field for explanatory variables in		Observations	36		
26	7/31/2012	49.14		"Input X range" box: D4:D39			Coefficients	t Stat	
27	8/31/2012	49.47		Regression Output sent to separate worksheet		Intercept	0.005025471	0.668527914	
28	9/28/2012	52.28	1440.67	0.0242	0.0568	X Variable 1	1.085919096	5.734251183	
29	10/31/2012	49.12	1412.16	-0.0198	-0.0604				
30	11/30/2012	49.66	1416.18			Intercept =Intercept(E4:E39,			
31	12/31/2012	49.79	1426.19			D4:D39)	Slope	1.0859	
32	1/31/2013	53.88	1498.11			Slope: =Slope(E4:E39, D4:D39)	R2	0.4916	
33	2/28/2013	54.59	1514.68			R2: =RSQ(E4:E39, D4:D39)		0.6004	
34	3/29/2013	56.80	1569.19			Correlation: =Correl(E4:E39,	Correlation	0.7012	
35	4/30/2013	62.84	1597.57			D4:D39)	SD of Error	0.0426	
36	5/31/2013	63.08	1630.74			Stand. Dev. of Error: =STEYX(E4:E39, D4:D39)			
37	6/28/2013	63.15	1606.28						
38	7/31/2013	64.65	1685.73	0.0495	0.0238		Average: =Average(D4:D39) and =Average(E4:E39)		
39	8/30/2013	60.83	1632.97	-0.0313	-0.0591				
40				0.0131	0.0192	Average	Standard Deviation: =STDEV.P(D4:D39) and =STDEV.P(E4:E39)		
41		Disney stock and SPX prices downloaded from Bloomberg Excel Add-In into Excel: "Import Data, Real Time/Historical, Historical End of Day Screen		0.0375	0.0581	Standard Deviation			
42				Rates Columns: SPX: =(C4/C3)-1, copy and paste in Column D	Rates Columns: SPX: =(B4/B3)-1, copy and paste in Column E				
43									
44									
45									
46									
47				y = 1.0859x + 0.005		Regression: Highlight B4:E39; Click: Insert, Scatter, Layout (On Chart Tools), Trendline, More Trendline Options, and Display Equation and R2			
48				R² = 0.4916					

y = 1.0859x + 0.005
R² = 0.4916

GE has a beta 1.172, alpha of -0.028, $\sigma(\varepsilon)$ of 1.644 ($V(\varepsilon) = 2.7027$), t-statistic $= \beta/\sigma(\beta) = 40.436$, and R^2 of 0.566:

$$E(r) = \hat{\alpha} + \hat{\beta}E(R^M)$$
$$E(r) = -0.028 + 1.172E(R^M)$$

$$V(r) = \hat{\beta}^2 V(R^M) + \hat{V}(\varepsilon)$$
$$V(r) = (1.172)^2\ V(R^M) + 2.7027$$

Given the betas of GE and Disney, the covariance formula for these stocks based on the estimated regression equation is

$$Cov(r_1 r_2) = \beta_1 \beta_2 V(R^M)$$
$$Cov(r_1 r_2) = (1.106)(1.172)V(R^M)$$

Regression analysis can be done using Excel spreadsheets and Excel regression commands. Exhibit 6.13 shows the regression of monthly returns of Disney stock against the S&P 500 for the period from 8/31/2010 to 8/30/2013. The data were downloaded from the Bloomberg Excel Add-in (described in the Bloomberg Exhibit Box). The exhibit shows three Excel commands for generating the regression parameters: "Data Analysis" Excel Add-in, Scatter diagrams, and Excel Regression Commands.

BLOOMBERG REGRESSION AND CORRELATION SCREENS

HRA: Bloomberg's Linear Regression Screen

The HRA screen is an analytical screen that estimates linear regression of a selected security (or the loaded security) to a change in the value of a second selected security or index. On the HRA screen, you can select (1) the dependent variable (e.g., IBM stock) and independent variable (S&P 500, SPX); (2) Data (e.g., last price or mid-price); (3) Period (e.g., daily, weekly, or monthly); regression time periods: two time periods for the regressions can be analyzed (e.g., two-year regression period and three-year period); (4) Regression analysis: regress values, differences in values, or percentage change in values.

The screen displays a scatter diagram of the data points (moving your curser to the diamond coordinate brings up the date and each security's return), the estimated regression parameters, alpha and beta, and qualifiers (R^2), standard error ($\sigma(\varepsilon)$), and t-statistic $\beta/\sigma(\beta)$.

Other features: (1) Beta +/− (check box) calculates Beta+ when the independent variable is increasing, the Beta− when it is decreasing, and the difference or convexity. (2) The Non-Param check box converts the data to logs. (3) There is also a calculation of the security's adjusted beta (Adj Beta). The security's adjusted beta is derived from historical data but modified by moving the regression beta (raw beta) toward the market average.

(Continued)

Beta: Bloomberg's Linear Regression Screen

The Beta screen is similar to the HRA screen, estimating a linear regression of a selected security (or the loaded security) to a change in value of a second selected security or index. See Exhibit 6.12.

PC, Peer Correlation: Stock and Peer Correlation and Regression Parameters

- The PC platform shows correlation and regression parameters of a selected stock with its peers and related indexes: S&P 500, Dow Jones, Sector Index, and other indexes.
- You can select different peers, indexes, portfolios, and securities from searches from the "Peer Source" dropdown, select different parameters (correlation, beta, covariance, or *t*-statistics) from the "Calculation" tab, different regression periods, and frequencies (e.g., daily, weekly, or monthly).
- From the red "Edit" tab, you can also change the securities (rows) and indexes (columns). Each security's information (e.g., price graphs) can also be accessed by clicking the cell associated with that security and index.
- The PC screen can be saved to the Correlation Matrix from the red "Save to CORR" tab, where it can be accessed for later study by bringing up the CORR screen (CORR <Enter>). See Exhibit 6.15.

Bloomberg Add-In for Excel

Data for conducting time-series analysis also can be done using the Bloomberg Add-in for Excel (see Chapter 2 for a description on the Bloomberg Excel Add-in). On the Bloomberg Add-in, click "Import Data" and "Real-Time/Historical" dropdowns and follow the "Data Wizard" steps. Linear regression and other statistical analysis can be done in Excel by using Excel Commands. See Exhibit 6.13 for an illustration.

See Bloomberg Web Exhibit 6.2.

Using β as a Measure of Market Risk

In the regression model $r = \alpha + \beta R^M + \varepsilon$, the slope in that equation, β, measures the change in the stock's rate of return per change in the market rate of return:

$$\beta = \Delta r / \Delta R^M$$

β, in turn, is a measure of an individual security's response to the market. If r and R^M are linearly related, β also measures the proportional relation between r and R^M. Thus, a stock with $\beta > 1$ would have rates of return that changes more than the market changes. For example, a stock with $\beta = 1.5$ would have a rate of return that changes by 15 percent for a 10 percent change in the market. A stock with $\beta = 1$, in turn, would have a change in its rate that matches the changes is the market, a stock with a $\beta < 1$

would have a smaller change than the market, and one with a $\beta < 0$ would have rates that change inversely to the market:

$\beta > 1$: Example $\beta = 2$: 10% ↑ in R^M ⇒ 20% ↑ in r
   10% ↓ in R^M ⇒ 20% ↓ in r
$\beta = 1$: Example $\beta = 1$: 10% ↑ in R^M ⇒ 10% ↑ in r
   10% ↓ in R^M ⇒ 10% ↓ in r
$\beta < 1$: Example $\beta = 0.5$: 10% ↑ in R^M ⇒ 5% ↑ in r
   10% ↓ in R^M ⇒ 5% ↓ in r
$\beta = 0$: Example $\beta = 0.0$: 10% ↑ in R^M ⇒ 0% ↑ in r
   10% ↓ in R^M ⇒ 0% ↓ in r
$\beta < 0$: Example $\beta = -0.5$: 10% ↑ in R^M ⇒ 5% ↓ in r
   10% ↓ in R^M ⇒ 5% ↑ in r

Systematic and Unsystematic Risk

As previously discussed, the total risk of a stock can be broken into firm risk, industry risk, and market risk. It can also be broken into unsystematic risk and systematic risk. Unsystematic risk is a stock's risk due to firm and industry factors, whereas systematic risk is market risk. Since β measures how a security's rate of return relates to the market, it can be used to measure the security's systematic risk. Thus, a stock with a $\beta > 1$ would have greater risk than the market and one with a $\beta < 1$ would have less.

The regression model also can be used to decompose the total risk of a security into systematic risk and unsystematic risk. Specifically, Equation (6.8) for the variance of a security's return measures how much variation in return can be attributed to the market, $\beta^2 V(R^M)$, and how much variation can be attributed to other (firm and industry) factors, $V(\varepsilon)$. Thus, the first term measures a security's systematic risk and the second term measures its unsystematic risk:

$$V(r) - \beta^2 V(R^M) + V(\varepsilon)$$

$$\boxed{\frac{\text{Total}}{\text{Risk}}} = \boxed{\frac{\text{Systematic}}{\text{Risk}}} + \boxed{\frac{\text{Unsystematic}}{\text{Risk}}}$$

Systematic and unsystematic risk can also be expressed as proportions of total risk by dividing Equation (6.8) by $V(r)$:

$$1 = \frac{\beta^2 V(R^M)}{V(r)} + \frac{V(\varepsilon)}{V(r)}$$

$$1 = R^2 + \frac{V(\varepsilon)}{V(r)}$$

$$\boxed{1} = \boxed{\frac{\text{Systematic}}{\text{Risk}}} + \boxed{\frac{\text{Unsystematic}}{\text{Risk}}}$$

The first term on the right-hand side of the equation measures the proportion of variation in r that can be attributed to the market, and the second term measures the proportion due to unsystematic factors. As noted, the first term is defined as the coefficient of variation, R^2. If this coefficient is 0.9, for example, it implies that 90 percent of the fluctuations in the security's return can be attributed to the market, and 10 percent to other factors.

A Note on Adjusting Betas

A number of empirical studies have reported evidence that historically estimated betas for stocks are generally not good predictors of future betas. Marshall Blume found low R^2's on the regressions of randomly selected stocks (average R^2 of 0.36) and low correlations between stock betas in one period and the next (average correlation coefficient of 0.60). This study and others have pointed to the need to adjust the beta of a stock, especially if it is to be used to measure a stock's market risk.[1]

Observing a tendency for the forecast beta to move from the historical beta toward a portfolio beta, Oldrich Vasicek proposed adjusting betas using a Bayesian estimation technique. This technique calls for calculating the forecast beta as a weighted average of the historical beta and the average beta across a sample of stocks. In the Bayesian approach, the weights are estimated by using the square of the standard error of an estimate of beta and the variance of the betas over the sample of stocks. An adjusted beta is also given on the Bloomberg BETA screen (Adj Beta). The security's adjusted beta shown is derived using a Bayesian approach in which the historical beta is modified by moving the regression beta (raw beta) toward the market average. For example, the adjusted beta for Disney is 1.071 compared to its historical or raw beta of 1.106, and the adjusted beta for GE is 1.115 and its raw beta is 1.172 (see Exhibit 6.12).

Beta⁺ and Beta⁻ and Convexity

Some stocks are observed to change differently when the market is increasing than when it is decreasing. One way to statistically estimate whether this may or may not be the case is to divide the data in a regression analysis into increasing market rates and decreasing market rates and then run two regressions. The beta for the increasing rate data is referred to as Beta⁺ and the beta for the decreasing rate data is referred to as Beta⁻. If the Beta⁺ does not equal the Beta⁻, then there is an asymmetrical gain/loss relation. For example if Beta⁺ were equal to 1.25 and Beta⁻ were equal to 0.75, then for a 10 percent increase in the market, the stock would increase by 12.5 percent, and for a 10 percent decrease in the market, the stock would decrease only by 7.5 percent. If two stocks have the same betas, but one has in absolute value a Beta⁺ greater than a Beta⁻, whereas the other has equal Beta⁺ and Beta⁻, then the former would be more valuable; that is, it provides greater gains if the market increases and smaller losses if the market decreases. The asymmetrical gain/loss relation defined by Beta⁺ and Beta⁻

is referred to a stock's *convexity*, where convexity is measured as the difference between Beta$^+$ and Beta$^-$ divided by two.

The Beta$^+$, Beta$^-$ and convexity for Disney and GE calculated from the previous regression period are shown in Exhibit 6.14. As shown, Disney has a Beta$^+$ of 1.192, Beta$^-$ of 1.026, and convexity of 0.083. The stock is more responsive when the market increases than when it decreases, increasing 1.192 percent for a 1 percent increase in the market, while decreasing by 1.026 percent for a 1 percent decrease in the market. Thus, it has greater gain-to-loss relation or a positive convexity. In contrast, GE has a Beta$^+$ of 1.088, a Beta$^-$ of 1.250, and a convexity of −0.081. The stock is more responsive when the market decreases than when it increases, decreasing 1.250 percent for a 1 percent decrease in the market, while increasing by 1.088 percent for a 1 percent increase in the market. It has greater loss to gain relation, or a negative convexity.

Alpha

From the regression, the intercept term, alpha, can be used as a measure of the stock's return above or below its risk-adjusted return. That is, if the intercept is positive, it suggests the stock is generating a return in excess of the market risk premium. For example, a stock with a beta of one and an alpha of zero would increase by 10 percent when the market is up by 10 percent and decrease by 10 percent when the market is down by 10 percent. Its return matches the return in the market. If the stock had a beta of one and an alpha of 0.02 (or 2 percent), then it would increase by 12 percent when the market increases by 10 percent and decrease by only 8 percent when the market decreases by 10 percent. Its return is always 2 percent better than the market return. The alpha for the Disney stock shown in Exhibit 6.12 is a positive 0.034, whereas the alpha for GE is −0.028. It should be noted that with a portfolio it is possible to diversify away firm and industry risk. If this is the case, then a portfolio with a positive alpha would be providing its investors with an excess or abnormal return. Using the intercept as a portfolio performance measure was first introduced by Jensen and is often referred to as the Jensen index. This measure of excess return for evaluating portfolios is discussed in more detail in Chapter 7.

Exhibit 6.15 shows a comparison of the R^2 or systematic risk measures and alphas for GE and related companies in its industry taken from Bloomberg's PC screen. Based on its R^2, approximately 55 percent of GE's variability is explained by market factors. This is similar to the R^2's of many of its peers. GE, however, is one of only five in the peer group with a negative alpha.

Multiple Regression Analysis

The return on many stocks are better explained (higher R^2) in terms of a multiple regression model in which there are more than one explanatory variable. In terms of

EXHIBIT 6.14 B⁺ and B⁻

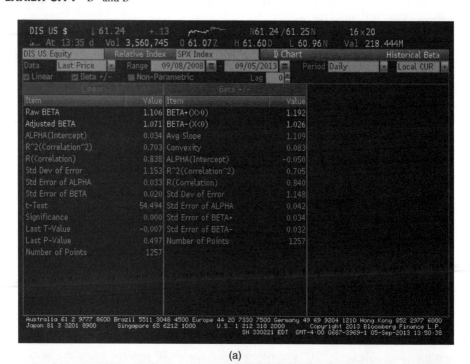

(a)

(b)

BETA Screen, Beta⁺ and Beta⁻ and Convexity. Bloomberg Beta Screen shows the stocks Beta⁺ and Beta⁻ and convexity. To access: Ticker <Equity>; Beta; click Beta +/− box; click "Show Detailed Statistics" in the Actions tab. Beta⁺ and Beta⁻ and convexity can also be accessed from the HRA screen.

EXHIBIT 6.15 Peer Comparison of Alpha and R^2

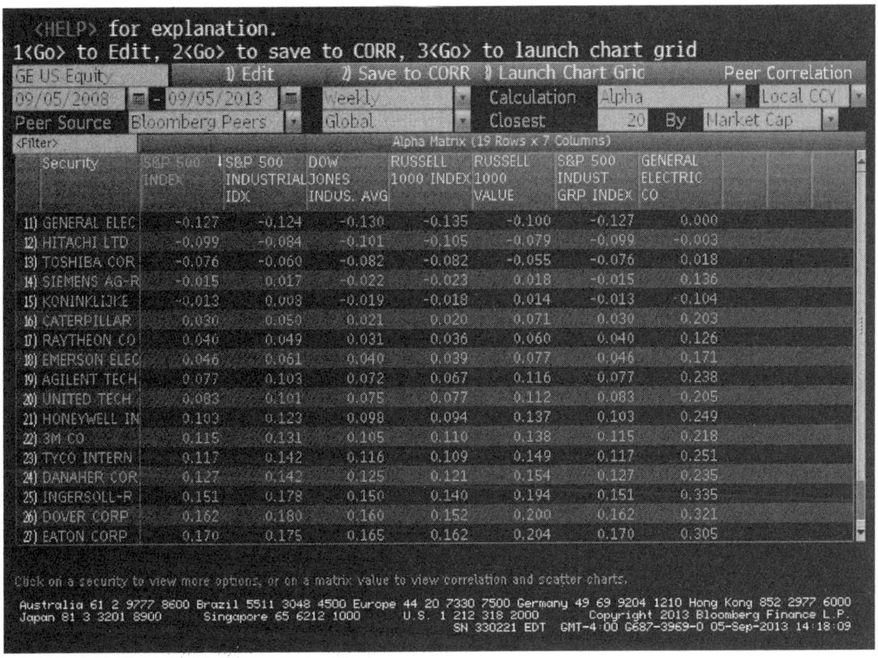

<HELP> for explanation.
1<Go> to Edit, 2<Go> to save to CORR, 3<Go> to launch chart grid

GE US Equity | 1) Edit | 2) Save to CORR | 3) Launch Chart Gric | Peer Correlation
09/05/2008 - 09/05/2013 | Weekly | Calculation | Alpha | Local CCY
Peer Source | Bloomberg Peers | Global | Closest | 20 | By | Market Cap
<Filter> Alpha Matrix (19 Rows x 7 Columns)

Security	S&P 500 INDEX	S&P 500 INDUSTRIAL IDX	DOW JONES INDUS. AVG	RUSSELL 1000 INDEX	RUSSELL 1000 VALUE	S&P 500 INDUST GRP INDEX	GENERAL ELECTRIC CO
11) GENERAL ELEC	-0.127	-0.124	-0.130	-0.135	-0.100	-0.127	0.000
12) HITACHI LTD	-0.099	-0.084	-0.101	-0.105	-0.079	-0.099	-0.003
13) TOSHIBA COR	-0.076	-0.060	-0.082	-0.082	-0.055	-0.076	0.018
14) SIEMENS AG-R	-0.015	0.017	-0.022	-0.023	0.018	-0.015	0.136
15) KONINKLIJKE	-0.013	0.008	-0.019	-0.018	0.014	-0.013	0.104
16) CATERPILLAR	0.030	0.050	0.021	0.020	0.071	0.030	0.203
17) RAYTHEON CO	0.040	0.049	0.031	0.036	0.060	0.040	0.126
18) EMERSON ELEC	0.046	0.061	0.040	0.039	0.077	0.046	0.171
19) AGILENT TECH	0.077	0.103	0.072	0.067	0.116	0.077	0.238
20) UNITED TECH	0.083	0.101	0.075	0.077	0.112	0.083	0.205
21) HONEYWELL IN	0.103	0.123	0.098	0.094	0.137	0.103	0.249
22) 3M CO	0.115	0.131	0.105	0.110	0.138	0.115	0.218
23) TYCO INTERN	0.117	0.142	0.116	0.109	0.149	0.117	0.251
24) DANAHER COR	0.127	0.142	0.125	0.121	0.154	0.127	0.235
25) INGERSOLL-R	0.151	0.178	0.150	0.140	0.194	0.151	0.335
26) DOVER CORP	0.162	0.180	0.160	0.152	0.200	0.162	0.321
27) EATON CORP	0.170	0.175	0.165	0.162	0.204	0.170	0.305

Click on a security to view more options, or on a matrix value to view correlation and scatter charts.

Australia 61 2 9777 8600 Brazil 5511 3048 4500 Europe 44 20 7330 7500 Germany 49 69 9204 1210 Hong Kong 852 2977 6000
Japan 81 3 3201 8900 Singapore 65 6212 1000 U.S. 1 212 318 2000 Copyright 2013 Bloomberg Finance L.P.
SN 330221 EDT GMT-4:00 G687-3969-0 05-Sep-2013 14:18:09

(a)

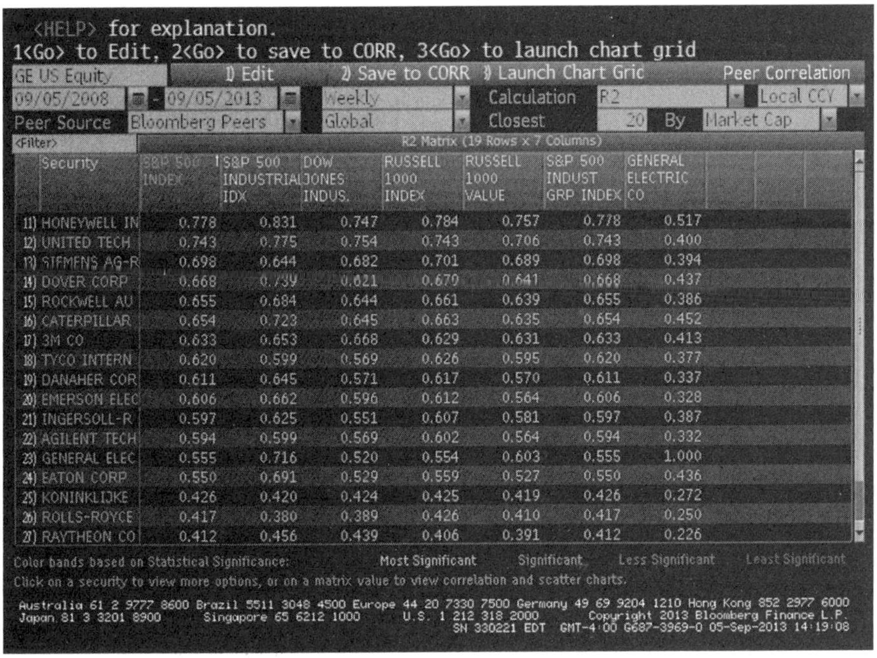

<HELP> for explanation.
1<Go> to Edit, 2<Go> to save to CORR, 3<Go> to launch chart grid

GE US Equity | 1) Edit | 2) Save to CORR | 3) Launch Chart Gric | Peer Correlation
09/05/2008 - 09/05/2013 | Weekly | Calculation | R2 | Local CCY
Peer Source | Bloomberg Peers | Global | Closest | 20 | By | Market Cap
<Filter> R2 Matrix (19 Rows x 7 Columns)

Security	S&P 500 INDEX	S&P 500 INDUSTRIAL IDX	DOW JONES INDUS.	RUSSELL 1000 INDEX	RUSSELL 1000 VALUE	S&P 500 INDUST GRP INDEX	GENERAL ELECTRIC CO
11) HONEYWELL IN	0.778	0.831	0.747	0.784	0.757	0.778	0.517
12) UNITED TECH	0.743	0.775	0.754	0.743	0.706	0.743	0.400
13) SIEMENS AG-R	0.698	0.644	0.682	0.701	0.689	0.698	0.394
14) DOVER CORP	0.668	0.739	0.621	0.679	0.641	0.668	0.437
15) ROCKWELL AU	0.655	0.684	0.644	0.661	0.639	0.655	0.386
16) CATERPILLAR	0.654	0.723	0.645	0.663	0.635	0.654	0.452
17) 3M CO	0.633	0.653	0.668	0.629	0.631	0.633	0.413
18) TYCO INTERN	0.620	0.599	0.569	0.626	0.595	0.620	0.377
19) DANAHER COR	0.611	0.645	0.571	0.617	0.570	0.611	0.337
20) EMERSON ELEC	0.606	0.662	0.596	0.612	0.564	0.606	0.328
21) INGERSOLL-R	0.597	0.625	0.551	0.607	0.581	0.597	0.387
22) AGILENT TECH	0.594	0.599	0.569	0.602	0.564	0.594	0.332
23) GENERAL ELEC	0.555	0.716	0.520	0.554	0.603	0.555	1.000
24) EATON CORP	0.550	0.691	0.529	0.559	0.527	0.550	0.436
25) KONINKLIJKE	0.426	0.420	0.424	0.425	0.419	0.426	0.272
26) ROLLS-ROYCE	0.417	0.380	0.389	0.426	0.410	0.417	0.250
27) RAYTHEON CO	0.412	0.456	0.439	0.406	0.391	0.412	0.226

Color bands based on Statistical Significance: Most Significant Significant Less Significant Least Significant
Click on a security to view more options, or on a matrix value to view correlation and scatter charts.

Australia 61 2 9777 8600 Brazil 5511 3048 4500 Europe 44 20 7330 7500 Germany 49 69 9204 1210 Hong Kong 852 2977 6000
Japan 81 3 3201 8900 Singapore 65 6212 1000 U.S. 1 212 318 2000 Copyright 2013 Bloomberg Finance L.P.
SN 330221 EDT GMT-4:00 G687-3969-0 05-Sep-2013 14:19:08

(b)

explaining the relation between a security's return and multiple explanatory variables, a multiple regression model takes the following form:

$$r = \alpha + \beta_1 \tilde{F}_1 + \beta_1 \tilde{F}_1 + \cdots + \beta_1 \tilde{F}_1 + \tilde{\varepsilon}$$

where:

α = intercept
F_i = explanatory variable
β_i = slope = $\Delta r / \Delta F_i$
ε = error

When a number of stocks are explained by the same set of factors, the model is known as a factor model. A linear regression model is known as a *single-factor model*, and a multiple regression model is referred to as a *multifactor model*. Typically, a single-factor model is explained by the market return and is referred to as the market model. For multifactor models, the challenge is identifying the explanatory variables. One of the early studies using specified factors was done by William Sharpe. In his study, he estimated the relationship between a stock's return and the market rate, the long-term bond rate, and the stock's dividend yield. He estimated this relationship for over 2,000 stocks using data covering 1931 through 1979. In comparing several regression models, Sharpe found that models with two or more coefficients had better regression results than the linear regression market model explained by just R^M. This finding provided some support for a multifactor model. A more recent study of multifactor models was done by Chen, Roll, and Ross. They found a relatively strong statistical relation between a stock's return and four factors measuring unanticipated changes in inflation, the term structure of rates (differences in long-term and short-term bond rates), industrial production, and risk premiums (differences in yields on low-quality and high-quality bonds). Thus, like the Sharpe study, the Chen, Roll, and Ross study provided evidence in support of the multifactor model as an explanation of what determines a stock's returns. These and other multifactor models are examined in more detail in Chapter 10.

MRA: BLOOMBERG'S MULTIPLE REGRESSION SCREEN

Multiple regression analysis can be done using the Bloomberg MRA screen. On the screen, one selects a set for inputting information or editing a previous set. The dependent and independent variables are inputted by their ticker and <Equity> or Index ticker <Index>. Economic information such as that found in ECOF or ECST has a ticker; to input into MRA, one types in its Ticker and presses the <Index> key. Once the variables are selected, the user can save the set by typing 1 and hitting <Enter> and can select the time period and frequency (daily, weekly, etc.) by hitting 2 <Enter>. The MRA output shows the coefficient estimates, t-tests, R^2, and F-Statistic.

Multiple Regression Using Bloomberg Excel Add-In and Data Analysis Excel Add-In

Using Bloomberg data pulled from the Bloomberg's Excel Add-in or other data sources, multiple regressions can be done in Excel by using the "Data Analysis" Add-in.

See Bloomberg Web Exhibit 6.3.

Cross-Sectional Regression Analysis

The data used in the regression example (Exhibit 6.8) was time-series data. In estimating a security's expected return, risk, and other features, analysts often use cross-sectional data in which the rates of return on a number of securities are used. Cross-sectional regression analysis can be used to explain how the market prices securities or to identify market factors that are important to determining an investment's return. Some analysts use a cross-sectional regression model to estimate how the market prices a stock, P, relative to its earnings per share (e)—its price-to-earnings ratio, P/e. The cross-sectional models differ in terms of the explanatory variables used to explain P/e. Elton and Gruber, for example, regressed the P/e ratios of 150 stocks against their historical growth rates to estimate the following simple linear relation between the P/e of any stock i and its growth rate, g_i. For one given year, they estimated the following relation:

$$\frac{P}{e_i} = 3 + 1.6\, g_i$$

In an earlier study, Malkiel and Cragg regressed 150 stocks' P/e ratios against three variables: dividends-to-earnings ratio (d/e), historical growth rates, g, and betas. For the relation for one of the years in their study, they found:

$$\frac{P}{e_i} = 15.52 + 1.82\, g_i + 1.75(d/e)_i - 1.53\, \beta_i$$

The coefficients in the cross-sectional regression equations are estimates of the relative importance the market places on the explanatory variable to determine how much a stock's price trades relative to its earnings-per-share (eps). For example, the slope coefficient of the Elton-Gruber regression of 1.6 indicates that for each 1 percent of growth, the market prices a stock $1.60 more per its eps. Thus, a stock with a 5 percent growth rate the market would price at $11 per dollar of eps (P/e = 11) and a stock with a 6 percent growth rate the market would price at $12.60 per dollar of eps (P/e = 12.6). The cross-sectional regression model of Malkiel and Cragg shows not only the relative importance the market places on the growth rate in determining P/e, but also the positive impact dividend/earnings have on P/e and the negative impact a stock's beta has on P/e.

EXHIBIT 6.16 Cross-Sectional Regression Analysis Using Excel and Data Downloaded from Bloomberg Excel Add-In

	A	B	C	D	E	F	G
1		P/e	β	g	d/e		
2		Current Price to	Adjusted Beta	Implied Growth	Dividend Payout		
3		last 12 Mo EPS	Bloomberg	Bloomberg DDM (%)	Bloomberg DDM (%)		
4	AAPL UW Equity	12.37	0.97	9.52	29.33		
5	ABT UN Equity	21.39	0.73	8.59	28.07		
6	ACN UN Equity	17.03	1.10	14.60	38.60		
7	AEP UN Equity	12.23	0.70	3.54	61.66		
8	AIG UN Equity	13.32	1.51	19.73	4.21		
9	ALL UN Equity	10.53	0.97	8.15			
10	AMGN UW Equity	18.45	0.75	8.34	Data pulled from Bloomberg Excel Add-In:		
11	APA UN Equity	9.91	1.44	17.58	• On the Bloomberg Add in, click "Real/Current" from		
12	APC UN Equity	21.04	1.39	22.85	the "Import Data" and "Real-Time/Historical"		
13	AXP UN Equity	16.04	1.04	13.57	dropdowns.		
14	BA UN Equity	19.69	1.06	13.58	• On the Bloomberg Data Wizard Box, Step 1, click		
15	BAC UN Equity	11.24	1.55	18.76	"indices" in the "From" dropdown and the name of		
16	BAX UN Equity	15.11	0.90	8.98	index (S&P 100) from the "Indices" dropdown, and		
17	BK UN Equity	12.21	1.36	15.89	then click "Add All." This will bring up the stocks		
18	C UN Equity	11.40	1.76	21.46	for the index. Once loaded, click "Next."		
19	CAT UN Equity	12.25	1.31	13.00	• On the Bloomberg Data Wizard box, Step 2, search		
20	CL UN Equity	20.85	0.69	8.51	and then add stock returns (e.g., Price-to-earning		
21	CMCSA UW Equity	19.83	1.06	13.09	(P/e), DDM implied growth rates, DDM dividend		
22	COF UN Equity	8.54	1.20	12.61	payout ratio in growth stage, adjusted beta.		
23	COP UN Equity	11.55	1.01	7.87	• After loading variables, click "Next."		
24	CSCO UW Equity	15.26	1.08	9.20	• On the Bloomberg Data Wizard Box, Step 3, click		
					Finish.		
25	CVS UN Equity	16.46	0.76	8.02	23.04		
26	CVX UN Equity	9.95	1.12	9.75	32.24		
27	DD UN Equity	18.41	1.15	11.27	46.94		
87	VZ UN Equity	19.15	0.73	3.27	74.55		
88	WAG UN Equity	19.97	0.75	7.36	35.36		
89	WFC UN Equity	11.13	1.13	10.89	29.89		
90	WMT UN Equity	14.14	0.63	4.21	35.91		
91	XOM UN Equity	11.27	0.96	8.78	32.53		
92							
93		Coefficients	Standard Error	t Stat	Regression: Click "Data" and then "Data Analysis."		
94	Intercept	16.2737	2.5750	6.3199	In Data Analysis Box: Click "Regression."		
95	X Variable 1	−20.5913	2.4786	−8.3078	In Regression Box:		
96	X Variable 2	1.5091	0.1747	8.6371	• Enter field for Return in "Input Y Range"		
97	X Variable 3	0.1220	0.0336	3.6308	box: B4:E91;		
98		Regression Statistics			• Enter field for explanatory variables in		
99		Multiple R	0.7090		"Input X range" box: C4:E91.		
100		R Square	0.5026		• Click OK.		
101		Adjusted R Sq	0.4849		Regression Output sent to separate worksheet.		
102		Standard Error	3.6581		Note: Not all data is shown here.		
103		Observations	88				
104							

Regression analysis can be done using Excel spreadsheets and Excel regression commands. Exhibit 6.16 shows the regression of the P/e ratios of 80 stocks taken from the S&P 100 against their betas, growth rates, and dividend payout ratio. Different from the Malkiel and Craig study, the growth rates and payout ratios for each stock were the estimated value used in Bloomberg's DDM (described in Chapter 3), and for beta, the stocks' adjusted betas were used instead of historical betas. The data were downloaded from the Bloomberg Excel Add-in (described in the Bloomberg Exhibit Box). The exhibit shows the data and regression results from using the Excel Add-in: Data Analysis:

$$\frac{P}{e_i} = 16.27 + 1.509\, g_i + 0.122(d/e)_i - 20.583\, \beta_i$$

BLOOMBERG EXCEL ADD-IN: CROSS-SECTIONAL MULTIPLE REGRESSION

Data for conducting cross-sectional analysis can be pulled from Bloomberg's database using the Bloomberg Add-in for Excel and then pulling in stocks from an index or portfolio (see Chapter 2 for a description on Bloomberg Excel Add-in):

- On the Bloomberg Add-in, click "Real-Time/Current" from the "Import Data" and "Real-Time/Historical" dropdowns.
- On the Bloomberg Data Wizard Box, Step 1, click "Indexes" in the "From" dropdown and the name of index (e.g., S&P 100) from the "Indexes" dropdown, and then click "Add All." This will bring up the stocks for the index. Once loaded, click "Next."
- On the Bloomberg Data Wizard box, Step 2, search and then add stock returns (e.g., Price-to-earning (P/e), growth rates, DDM implied growth rates, DDM dividend payout ratio in growth stage, or Altman Z-Score).
- After loading variables, click "Next."
- On the Bloomberg Data Wizard Box, Step 3, click "Finish" to export the data to Excel.

Multiple-Regression in Excel

- Multiple-regression can be done in Excel by using the "Data Analysis" Add-in. For an example, see Exhibit 6.16.

Relationship between Return and Risk

In general, there is a direct relationship between the expected return and risk among securities available in the market. That is, the greater a security's risk, the greater its rate of return. This positive return-risk relationship is simply the result of rational investment decisions. For example, if there were two stocks available in the market that had the same expected returns but different risks, rational investors would obviously want only the lower risk security. This preference would increase the demand and price of that security (causing its rate to decrease) and lower the demand and price of the higher risk security (causing its rate of return to increase). After this market adjustment, the higher risk security's price would reflect a higher rate of return than the lower risk security.

Security Market Line

In the finance literature, the relationship between return and risk has been described by the *Capital Asset Pricing Model* (CAPM). The CAPM postulates that most investors hold portfolios and therefore are not exposed to unsystematic risk; that is, with a portfolio investors can diversify away firm and industry risk. As a result, a security's *equilibrium rate of return* is determined only by its systematic risk, which, in turn, can be measured by its beta. In terms of the CAPM, a stock with a $\beta > 1$ has more risk than the market, and therefore, in equilibrium it should be priced so that its equilibrium expected rate, $E(r)^*$, is greater than the expected market rate of return: $E(r)^* > E(R^M)$. In contrast, a security with a $\beta < 1$ should be priced so that, in equilibrium, its expected rate is less than the expected market rate: $E(r)^* < E(R^M)$. By the same reasoning, a security with a $\beta = 1$, would have the same risk as the market (if there is no unsystematic risk) and therefore should be priced such that its expected rate is equal to the expected market rate: $E(r)^* = E(R^M)$. Moreover, if systematic risk is the only determining factor, then a security with a $\beta = 0$ should be priced in equilibrium such that its rate of return is equal to the rate on a risk-free security: $E(r)^* = R_f$. Finally, if investors make decisions in a portfolio context, then a stock with a negative beta would be negatively correlated with the market. Its inclusion in a portfolio would serve to reduce the portfolio's risk more than a risk-free security, and as a result, it would be priced to yield a return less than the risk-free rate.

The relation between beta and a security equilibrium return is summarized in Exhibit 6.17. The direct relationship between an investment's equilibrium rate of return and β is also shown graphically in Exhibit 6.18. The line depicted in the figure is known as the *security market line*, SML. The equation of the SML is:

$$E(r_i)^* = R_f + [E(R^M) - R_f]\,\beta_i \tag{6.11}$$

where:
i = any investment (stock or portfolio) i
*signifies equilibrium

EXHIBIT 6.17   Equilibrium Return and Beta Relation

		In equilibrium, security is priced so that:
$\beta > 1 \Rightarrow$	Security has greater risk *(fluctuations) than the market*	$\Rightarrow E_i^* > E(R^M)$
$\beta = 1 \Rightarrow$	Security has the same risk *(fluctuations) as the market*	$\Rightarrow E_i^* = E(R^M)$
$\beta < 1 \Rightarrow$	Security has less risk *(fluctuations) than the market*	$\Rightarrow E_i^* < E(R^M)$
$\beta = 0 \Rightarrow$	Security has no systematic risk	$\Rightarrow E_i^* = R_f$
$\beta < 0 \Rightarrow$	Security reduces portfolio risk more than R_f Security	$\Rightarrow E_i^* < R_f$

EXHIBIT 6.18 SML

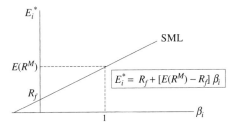

- CAPM: Relation
- Security Market Line (SML): Depicts the equilibrium relationship between any investment's equilibrium return and its beta.

$$E_i^* = R_f + [E(R^M) - R_f]\beta_i$$

The SML represents a cross-sectional model; it shows the equilibrium rate for any security given that security's beta. (Note that the characteristic line shown in Exhibit 6.10 is a time-series model, showing the relationship between a security's return and the market.) The slope of the SML, $E(R^M) - R_f$, is the market risk premium, RP^M:

$$RP^M = E(R^M) - R_f$$

It measures the additional return over the risk-free rate investors require in order to invest in the market.[2]

Equation (6.11) is often used by analysts to determine a stock's required return, k, or to determine the required equity return in a capital budgeting problem. For example, if the risk-free rate were 6 percent and the market risk-premium were 4 percent, a stock with a β of 1.5 would have a required return of 12 percent using the SML equation:

$$k = R_f + [E(R^M) - R_f]\beta_i$$
$$k = 0.06 + [0.04]1.5 = 0.12$$

If the stock were expected to generate dividends of $10 each year for three years and be worth $100 at the end of year three, then it would be valued at $95.20 given the required return of 12 percent:

$$V_0^S = \frac{\$10}{(1.12)} + \frac{\$10}{(1.12)^2} + \frac{\$10}{(1.12)^3} + \frac{\$100}{(1.12)^3} = \$95.20$$

The return-risk relationship depicted by the SML is not static. Changes in the SML occur as a result of either a change in the risk-free rate or a change in the market risk-premium. A change in the risk-free rate leads to a parallel shift in the SML: An increase in R_f causes an increase in the required returns for any β; a decrease in R_f

causes a decrease in the required returns for any β. The risk-free rate, in turn, is influenced by macroeconomic factors such as changes in monetary policy, fiscal policy, international balance of payments, real economic growth, and inflation. Changes in the market risk premium, on the other hand, cause changes in the slope of the SML. Such changes occur as a result of changing investor attitudes toward risk. For example, if investors were to become more timid (perhaps because of information indicating an economic recession), they would require a greater risk premium to invest in stock. Under such conditions, investor actions would cause the market risk premium to increase and the SML to become steeper. The CAPM and other models for determining the equilibrium return on investments are examined in more detail in Chapter 9 and Chapter 10.

EQRP: BLOOMBERG'S EQUITY RISK PREMIUM SCREEN

The EQRP screen shows a stock's risk premium. The premium is equal to the forecasted market risk premium $E(R^M) - R_f$ times the stock's beta. The forecasted market risk premium is based on a projected market rate and risk-free rate. The risk-free rate is the 10-year Treasury for the country. Beta is the historical beta. The user can change the market risk-premium and beta. The screen also shows the historical premiums and betas.

See Bloomberg Web Exhibit 6.4.

Return-Risk Preferences

What return-risk combination an investor chooses depends on her risk-return preference. Risk-return preference of investors in general—the market's risk-return preference—has an impact on the risk premium. To see the relation between risk-return preferences and the risk premium, suppose there are only two securities available in the market: a risk-free security and a risky bond. Suppose the risk-free security is a zero-coupon bond promising to pay $1,000 at the end of one year and that it currently is trading for $909.09 to yield a one-year risk-free rate, R_f, of 10 percent:

$$P_0 = \frac{\$1,000}{1.10} = \$909.09$$

$$R_f = \frac{\$1,000}{\$909.09} - 1 = 0.10$$

Suppose the risky bond is also a one-year zero coupon bond with a principal of $1,000, but there is a chance it could default and pay nothing. In particular, suppose there were a 0.8 probability the bond would pay its principal of $1,000 and a 0.2 probability it would pay nothing. The expected dollar return from the risky bond is therefore $800:

$$E(\text{return}) = 0.8(\$1,000) + 0.2(0) = \$800$$

Given the choice of two securities, suppose that the market were characterized by investors who are willing to pay $727.27 for the risky bond, in turn yielding them an expected rate of return of 10 percent:

$$E(R) = \frac{E(\text{return})}{P_0} - 1$$

$$E(R) = \frac{\$800}{\$727.27} - 1 = 0.10$$

By paying $727.27, investors would have a 0.8 probability of attaining a rate of return of 37.5 percent [($1,000/$727.27) − 1] and a 0.2 probability of losing their investment. In this case, investors would be willing to receive an expected return from the risky investment that is equal to the risk-free rate of 10 percent, and the risk premium, $E(R) - R_f$, would be equal to zero. In finance terminology, such a market is described as *risk neutral*. Thus, in a risk neutral market, the required return is equal to the risk-free rate and the risk premium is equal to zero.

Instead of paying $727.27, suppose investors like the chance of obtaining returns greater than 10 percent (even though there is a chance of losing their investment), and as a result they are willing to pay $750 for the risky bond. In this case, the expected return on the bond would be 6.67 percent, and the risk premium would be negative:

$$E(R) = \frac{\$800}{\$750} - 1 = 0.0667$$

$$RP = E(R) - R_f = 0.0667 - 0.10 = -0.033$$

By definition, markets in which the risk premium is negative are called *risk loving*. Risk-loving markets can be described as ones in which investors enjoy the excitement of the gamble and are willing to pay for it by accepting an expected return from the risky investment that is less than the risk-free rate. Even though there are some investors who are risk loving, a risk-loving market is an aberration, with the exceptions being casinos, sports gambling markets, lotteries, and racetracks.

Whereas risk-loving and risk-neutral markets are rare, they do serve as a reference for defining the more normal behavior toward risk—*risk aversion*. In a risk-averse market, investors require compensation in the form of a positive risk premium to pay them for the risk they are assuming. Risk-averse investors view risk as a disutility, not a utility, as risk-loving investors do. In terms of our example, suppose most of the investors making up our market were risk averse and as a result were unwilling to pay $727.27 or more for the risky bond. In this case, if the price of the risky bond were $727.27 and the price of the risk-free were $909.09, there would be little demand for the risky bond and a high demand for the risk-free one. Holders of the risky bonds who wanted to sell would therefore have to lower their price, increasing the expected return. On the other hand, the high demand for the risk-free bond would tend to increase its price and lower its rate. For example, suppose the markets cleared when the price of the risky bond dropped to $701.75 to yield 14 percent, and the price of the risk-free bond increased to $917.43 to yield 9 percent:

$$E(R) = \frac{\$800}{\$701.75} - 1 = 0.14$$

$$R_f = \frac{\$1,000}{\$917.43} - 1 = 0.09$$

In this case, the risk premium would be 5 percent and the market is defined as being risk averse.

In a risk-averse market, the positive risk premium required by an investor to hold the riskier bond is partly the result of uncertainty and partly due to liquidity. For example, if investors knew that the probability of default was in fact 0.8, then they would know that by buying a portfolio of such bonds (e.g., 100 bonds like B), 80 percent of the portfolio would pay $1,000 at the end of the year and 20 percent would pay nothing. Alternatively, if investors buy Bond Bs over time, then they would find that in eight out of 10 years, they would receive a $1,000 principal and two out of 10 years, they would receive nothing. Thus, if the price of Bond B were the risk-neutral price of $727.27, then investors' average portfolio return or their average return over time would be 10 percent. It would appear that provided the 0.8 probability is known, investors would be indifferent between a portfolio of B bonds and Bond A or a strategy of buying B bonds or A Bonds over time. However, to obtain the certain portfolio return of 10 percent would require that investors buy a portfolio of B bonds or buy such bonds over an extended period to realize the 10 percent rate. This would require more funds or time than simply buying the risk-free Bond A. As a result, investors would demand less of B because of these marketability or liquidity requirements. The liquidity concern would, in turn, push the price of the B Bond down and increase its yield above the risk-free rate.

Historically, security markets such as the stock and corporate bond markets have generated rates of return that on average have exceeded the rates on Treasury securities. This would suggest that such markets are risk averse. Since most markets are risk averse, a relevant question is the degree of risk aversion. The degree of risk aversion can be measured in terms of the size of the risk premium. The greater an investor's risk aversion, the greater the demand for risk-free securities and the lower the demand for risky ones, and thus the larger the risk premium.

Conclusion

Although securities can be described and evaluated in terms of their common characteristics, for most investors the most important security characteristics are the expected rate of return and risk. The risk of a security is the possibility that the realized return will deviate from the expected return. By definition, the variance, standard deviation, and coefficient of variation of a stock's rate of return define such risk. That is, the greater a security's variance, the greater the realized return can deviate from the expected return, and thus the greater the security's risk. In this chapter, we examined the expected return and risk of stock statistically by examining return distributions and characteristics—mean, variance, and correlation parameters. In the next chapters, we continue our analysis of return and risk by examining the return and risk of a portfolio of stocks.

Web Site Information

1. For financial information on stocks see:
   - www.Finance.Yahoo.com
   - http://www.hoovers.com
   - http://www.bloomberg.com
   - http://www.businessweek.com
   - http://www.ici.org
   - http://seekingalpha.com
   - http://bigcharts.marketwatch.com
   - http://www.morningstar.com
   - http://free.stocksmart.com
2. FINRA
   - Go to http://www.finra.org/index.htm, "Sitemap," "Market Data," and "Equity & Options."
   - *Wall Street Journal.*
   - Go to http://online.wsj.com/public/us, Market Data and U.S. Stocks.
3. Yahoo.com
   - Go to http://finance.yahoo.com.
4. Stock Screener: Go to http://screener.finance.yahoo.com/newscreener.html, enter "name of issuer," and for click "Search."
5. Market Browser: Stocks and other security data.
6. Download program for Market Browser: http://www.marketbrowser.com

Notes

1. Blume proposed adjusting betas by using a cross-sectional model in which the betas of a sample set of stocks estimated in one period (period 2) are regressed against those stocks' betas estimated from the preceding period (period 1). That is:

$$\beta_{i2} = \gamma_0 + \gamma_1 \beta_{i1} + \varepsilon_i$$

In estimating this relationship for two five-year periods, Blume found:

$$\beta_{i2} = 0.343 + 0.677 \beta_{i1}$$

Using Blume's estimated equation, a stock with a five-year historical beta of 2, would have a forecasted beta for the next five-year period of 1.697, and a stock with a beta of 0.5 would have a forecast beta of 0.682.

Observing a tendency for the forecasted beta to move from the historical beta toward a portfolio beta, Oldrich Vasicek proposed adjusting betas using a Bayesian estimation technique. This technique calls for calculating the forecast beta as a weighted average of the historical beta, β_{i1}, and the average beta across a sample of stocks, β_{ip}:

$$\beta_{i2} = w_i \beta_{i1} + w_p \beta_{ip}$$

In the Bayesian approach, the weights are estimated by using the square of the standard error of an estimate of beta, $\sigma_{\beta_i}^2$, and the variance of the betas over the sample of stocks, $\sigma_{\beta_p}^2$ such that:

$$w_i = \frac{\sigma_{\beta_i}^2}{\sigma_{\beta_p} + \sigma_{\beta_i}^2}$$

$$w_p = \frac{\sigma_{\beta_p}^2}{\sigma_{\beta_p} + \sigma_{\beta_i}^2}$$

Another approach is to simply use equal weights; that is, make $w_i = 0.5$ and $w_p = 0.5$.

The Blume approach and a Bayesian approach have been tested. Studies by Klemkosky and Martin and Elton, Gruber, and Urich, for example, found that both approaches led to more accurate forecasts of future betas than did the unadjusted historical betas. Elton, Gruber, and Urich also found that adjusted betas were better predictors of future correlation coefficients.

2. Studies by Ibbotson and Associates have found that the market risk premium has varied from 4 percent to 7 percent over time, given different economic conditions.

Selected References

Blume, Marshall. 1975. Betas and their regression tendencies. *Journal of Business* 39 (June): 3–19.

Fisher, Lawrence, and James Lorie. 1970. Some studies of variability of returns on investments in common stocks. *Journal of Business* 43 (2): 99–134.

Friedman, Milton, and Leonard Savage. 1948. The utility analysis and choices involving risk. *Journal of Political Economy* (August): 279–304.

Markowitz, Harry 1959. *Portfolio Selection*. Hoboken, NJ: John Wiley & Sons: Chapters 3–5.

Sharpe, W. F. 1964. Capital asset price: a theory of market equilibrium under conditions of risk (September): 425–442.

Tobin, James. 1958. Liquidity preference and behavior towards risk. *The Review of Economic Studies* 26 (January): 65–86.

Vasicek, Oldrich. 1973. A note on using cross-sectional information in Bayesian estimation of security betas. *Journal of Finance* 8 (December): 1233–1239.

Bloomberg Exercises

1. Select a stock of interest and examine its total returns for different periods and frequencies (daily, weekly, etc.) relative to the S&P 500 using the COMP screen: Stock Ticker <Equity> <Enter> and then click COMP.

2. Select a stock of interest and examine its price and volatility for different periods and frequencies using the GV screen. Stock Ticker <Equity> <Enter> and then click GV and select the following:

   a. Select: Price; Period: Daily; Select: Statistics check box to show Histogram window.

   b. Select: Historical Volatility; Level: 30 Days; Period: Daily; Select: Statistics to show Histogram window.

3. Select a stock of interest and compare its historical volatility for different periods (30-day, 60-day, etc.) using the HVT screen.

4. Study the historical correlation over different periods of the top 10 stocks by market cap of the Dow Jones Average, the S&P 100, or some other index using the CORR screen. CORR <Enter>; click the red "Create New" tab; click "Symmetric Matrix" box; click "Add from Source"; select "Equity Indexes (e.g., INDU, OEX, or SPX) under "Name" tab; Select "All," and click "Add."

5. Select a stock of interest and examine its historical regression with the S&P 500 over different periods and frequencies using the Beta screen: Stock Ticker <Equity> <Enter> and click BETA. In your examination, note the stock's regression parameters, qualifiers, and adjusted beta. Find the stocks $\beta+$, $\beta-$, and convexity by clicking Beta $+/-$ checkbox.

6. Select a stock of interest and compare its beta, alpha, and systematic risk (R^2) with its peers using the PC screen.

7. Use Bloomberg's Excel Add-in to download price data for a stock of interest and the S&P 500. Using Excel, run a regression of the stock's rates of return against the S&P 500 rates.

   - "Import Data"; "Real-Time/Historical"; "Historical End of Day."
   - On the Bloomberg Data Wizard Box, Step 1, load Stock and SPX and click "Next."
   - On the Bloomberg Data Wizard Box, Step 2, type price in the "Search Text" box and hit <Enter>. From the list, select Last Price and then click "Add" and "Next."
   - On the Bloomberg Data Wizard Box, Step 3, select periodicity (e.g., monthly) and time period; click "Next."
   - On the Bloomberg Data Wizard Box, Steps 4 and 5, accept "Set History Parameters" and pricing defaults and click "Next."
   - On the Bloomberg Data Wizard Box, Step 6, Box, accept Excel layout options and click "Finish" to export the data to Excel.
   - In Excel, calculate period rates (as proportional price changes) from your price data.
   - Use Excel regression commands to run your regressions.
     See Exhibit 6.13 for an example.

8. Use the MRA screen to run a multiple regression of the returns of a stock or index of interest. For your explanatory variables, consider the S&P 500 (SPX <Index>) and long-term Treasury yields (USGG30YR <Index>): MRA <Enter>; select a set for inputting information; on the set screen select dependent and independent

variables; save the set by typing 1 and hitting <Enter> and select the time period and frequency (daily, weekly, etc.) by hitting 2 <Enter>. For an example, see Bloomberg box: "MRA: Bloomberg's Multiple Regression Screen."

9. In early studies of factors determining a stock's P/e ratio, Elton and Gruber and Malkiel and Craig found the growth rates in DPS, beta, and dividend payout ratios to be significant in explaining stock P/e ratios. Using Bloomberg's Excel Add-in for data and Excel regressions (found on Excel's "Data Analysis" Add-in) conduct a cross-section regression of stock P/e ratios against past or forecasted growth rates, betas, and dividend payout.

   - On the Bloomberg Add-in, click "Real/Current" from the "Import Data" and "Real-Time/Historical" dropdowns.
   - On the Bloomberg Data Wizard Box, Step 1, click "Indexes" in the "From" dropdown and the name of index (S&P 100) from the "Indexes" dropdown, and then click "Add All." This will bring up the stocks for the index. Once loaded, click "Next."
   - On the Bloomberg Data Wizard Box, Step 2, search and then add, stock returns (e.g., price-to-earning (P/e), DDM implied growth rates, DDM dividend payout ratio in growth stage, and adjusted beta.
   - After loading variables, click "Next."
   - On the Bloomberg Data Wizard Box, Step 3, click "Finish" to export the data to Excel.

     To run you regression, use the Bloomberg Excel Add-in: Click "Data" and then "Data Analysis"; in Data Analysis Box: Click "Regression"; in the Regression Box: enter field for the return in "Input Y Range" box and enter field for explanatory variables in "Input X range" box; Click OK.

     See Exhibit 6.16 for an example.

10. The EQRP screen shows a stock's risk premium. The premium is equal to a forecasted market risk premium $E(R^M) - R_f$ times the stock's beta. The market risk premium on the EQRP screen is based on a forecasted market rate and a risk-free rate equal to the 10-year Treasury for the country, and the beta is the stock's historical beta. Using the screen, examine the risk premium for a stock of interest. Also examine the stock's historical premiums and betas.

CHAPTER 7

Portfolio Evaluation

Introduction

In the last chapter, we examined how to measure the return and risk of stocks. In an efficient market, investors, however, either individually or through an investment fund, can attain better return-risk opportunities by investing in a portfolio. In this chapter, we analyze portfolios, with the emphasis being on stock portfolios.

Portfolio analysis consists of the evaluation and selection of the financial assets that makeup the portfolio. As with individual security evaluation, stock portfolio evaluation entails measuring the characteristics of the portfolio, with the most important properties being the portfolio expected rate of return and risk. Portfolio selection, in turn, involves finding what proportion of investment funds to allocate to each security to give the portfolio either the maximum expected return for a given risk or the minimum risk given a specified return. In this chapter, we evaluate portfolios of risky stocks in terms of their expected portfolio return and risk, and in Chapter 8, we focus on portfolio selection. We begin by examining the relationship between portfolio return and risk and the relationship between portfolio risk and number of securities in the portfolio. Next, we introduce a risk-free security and show how investors can obtain different return-risk combinations with different allocations of their investment funds to the risk-free security and a portfolio of risky stocks.

Portfolio Return and Risk

A portfolio can be described by the proportion of investment funds allocated to each security in it. For example, suppose an individual invested $1,000 in three stocks, denoted X_1, X_2, and X_3. Her stock portfolio would be described by the proportion of investment funds ($1,000), denoted as w_i, that she allocates to each stock:

$$w_i = \frac{\text{Stock } i \text{ Investment}}{\text{Total Investment}}$$

Thus, if she buys \$200 worth of X_1, \$300 of X_2, and \$500 of X_3, then her portfolio would be described in terms of her proportional allocations of $w_1 = 0.20$, $w_2 = 0.30$, and $w_3 = 0.5$.

In describing a portfolio, two points should be noted. First, the whole must equal the sum of the parts; that is, the proportion of investment funds allocated to each security must sum to one. Thus:

$$\sum_{i=1}^{n} w_i = 1$$

where n = number of stocks in the portfolio.

Second, the allocation or weights, w_i, can take on any value. If $w_i < 0$, then there would be a negative investment in security i. A negative investment is the opposite of investment, which is borrowing or selling the stock short. In the case of a negative investment in a risky security, such as stock, the negative weight can be interpreted as a short sale in which the investor uses the proceeds from the sale to invest in the other securities in the portfolio. For example, suppose an investor with \$1,000 of investment funds also sells \$500 worth of Stock 1 short (i.e., borrows shares of the stock and sells them in the market for \$500) and uses the proceeds along with his \$1,000 to invest in Stock 2. His portfolio can be described as consisting of two stocks with allocations of $w_1 = -0.5$ and $w_2 = 1.5$:

$$w_1 = \frac{\text{Stock 1 Investment}}{\text{Total Investment}} = \frac{-\$500}{\$1,000} = -0.5$$

$$w_1 = \frac{\text{Stock 2 Investment}}{\text{Total Investment}} = \frac{\$1,500}{\$1,000} = 1.5$$

$$w_1 + w_2 = -0.5 + 1.5 = 1$$

Most stock portfolios constructed by investment companies do not include negative investments or short positions. In our analysis, we will focus on risky stock portfolios with no short positions; that is, all the stocks have positive weights.

Portfolio Expected Return

The portfolio rate of return is the sum of the weighted rates of return of the securities making up the portfolio, with the weights being the proportion of investment funds allocated to each security:

$$R_p = \sum_{i=1}^{n} w_i r_i = w_1 r_1 + w_2 r_2 + \cdots + w_n r_n \tag{7.1}$$

where:

R_p = portfolio rate of return
r_i = rate of return on security i for the period (holding period yield)

Thus, if the above investor who allocated 20 percent, 30 percent, and 50 percent of her $1,000 in stocks X_1, X_2, and X_3, attained rates of return of 10 percent, 5 percent, and 15 percent, respectively, for holding these stocks for one year, then her portfolio rate of return (or *HPY*) would be 11 percent:

$$R_p = (0.20)10\% + (0.30)5\% + (0.50)15\% = 11\%$$

Note that in Equation (7.1) the rate of return on the security is defined as a return for the period (total return, *TR*, or holding period yield, *HPY*). Using *HPY* as the measure of return implies an analysis that is static; that is, it applies to only one period in time. The length of time used for portfolio analysis is difficult to determine. Generally, portfolio analysis excludes very short periods (often characterized by speculative trading), and extremely long periods (often subject to greater uncertainty). Static portfolio analysis is therefore restricted to a period between the very short and long run, anywhere between six months and three years. A static analysis of portfolios does not require that the length of time be defined, only that the analysis be constrained to one period instead of multiple periods.

As we noted in our discussion of security return and risk, investors are concerned not with past returns, but with expected returns. The expected portfolio rate of return is the sum of the weighted expected rates of return of the securities making up the portfolio. That is:

$$E(R_p) = \sum_{i=1}^{n} w_i E(r_i) = w_1 E(r_1) + w_2 E(r_2) + \cdots + w_n E(r_n) \qquad (7.2)$$

Equation (7.2) is obtained by treating r_i in Equation (7.1) as a random variable and w_i as a constant and then taking the expected value of Equation (7.1) (i.e., apply expected value operator rules).

Portfolio Risk

Investment risk can be measured by the variance or standard deviation in the security's rate of return. This measure of risk is also appropriate in measuring the risk of a portfolio. From our statistics discussion in Chapter 6, we noted that a portfolio's variance (risk) should depend not only on the variances of the individual stocks that make up the portfolio, but also on the correlation between the stocks composing the portfolio. Recall, the correlation between the rates of return of two securities can be measured by the covariance between their rates or by their correlation coefficient. The covariance is a measure of the extent to which one random variable is above or below its mean at the same time or state that another random variable is above or below its mean. If two random variables, on average, are above their means at the same time, and, on average, below at the same time, then the random variables will be positively correlated with each other and their covariance would be positive. In contrast, if one random variable, on average, is above its mean when another is below, and vice versa, then the random variables would move inversely or negatively to each other and their covariance would be negative.

The covariance between two random variables (e.g., security rates of return), r_1 and r_2, is equal to the expected value of the product of the variables' deviations. Like any expected value, the covariance can be defined as a weighted sum, with the weights being probabilities associated with each possible product of deviation. That is:

$$Cov(r_1 r_2) = E[r - E(r_1)][r_2 - E(r_2)]$$

$$Cov(r_1 r_2) = \sum_{j=1}^{T} p_j [r_{1j} - E(r_1)][r_{2j} - E(r_2)]$$

Recall from Chapter 6, the correlation coefficient between two random variables such as r_1 and r_2 (ρ_{12}) is equal to the covariance between the variables divided by the product of each random variable's standard deviation, σ:

$$\rho_{12} = \frac{Cov(r_1 r_2)}{\sigma(r_1)\sigma(r_2)} \qquad (7.3)$$

The correlation coefficient has the mathematical property that its value must be within the range of minus and plus one. If two random variables have a correlation coefficient equal to one, they are said to be perfectly positively correlated; if their coefficient is equal to a minus one, then they are perfectly negatively correlated; if their correlation coefficient is equal to zero, then they are uncorrelated and statistically independent:

The covariance or correlation coefficient between two security returns can be estimated using historical averages or a regression model similar to the one described in Chapter 6. An average can be calculated using holding period yields over N historical periods:

$$Cov_{avg} = \frac{1}{N-1} \sum_{t=1}^{N} [HPY_{1t} - \bar{r}_{1t}][HPY_{2t} - \bar{r}_{2t}]$$

The covariance also can be estimated by using a regression model. If we assume two stocks (1 and 2) that are both related to the market, R^M, such that

$$r_1 = \alpha_1 + \beta_1 R^M + \varepsilon_1$$
$$r_2 = \alpha_2 + \beta_2 R^M + \varepsilon_2$$

and assume the error terms, ε, are uncorrelated ($Cov(\varepsilon_1 \ \varepsilon_2) = 0$), then $Cov(r_1 \ r_2)$ simplifies to:

$$Cov(r_1 r_2) = \beta_1 \beta_2 V(R^M)$$

This says that if each stock's unsystematic risk is independent of every other stock's unsystematic risk, then unsystematic risk in the portfolio would average out to zero, and the covariance between any two securities in the portfolio would depend only on each security's systematic risk. A model in which all securities are related just to one factor, such as the market, and their error terms are uncorrelated is referred to as the Single Index Model. It is examined in more detail in the next chapter.

Importance of the Covariance

The importance of including the covariance between securities' rates of return in measuring portfolio risk can be seen in Exhibit 7.1. The figure is derived from the observations that appear in the exhibit table. The estimated parameters at the bottom of the table are based on the assumption that next period's returns can be obtained from past observations (i.e., on averages). Both the figure and table show the rates of return of two stocks, X_1 and X_2, over time. Both stocks X_1 and X_2 have an expected rate of return of 18%, a risk factor as measured by their individual variances of 36%, a covariance of –36, and a correlation coefficient of –1.

An examination of the figure in Exhibit 7.1 shows that when X_1's return (r_1) is above its mean, $E(r_1)$, X_2's return (r_2) is below its mean, $E(r_2)$, and when r_2 is above $E(r_2)$, r_1 is below $E(r_1)$; r_1 and r_2 in this example are perfectly negatively correlated ($\rho_{12} = -1$). If an investor, holding these securities in equal proportion, computed his portfolio rate of return (R_p) in time period 3, he would have obtained a rate of return of 18 percent. Similarly, if the investor computed the return for time period 6, he would likewise find an 18 percent rate of return; in fact, with equal weights, the investor would find for any time period that his portfolio rate of return always would be 18 percent. Thus, since the investor can always attain an 18 percent rate of return, there is no portfolio risk. This example therefore illustrates what we first broached in Chapter 6, that the measurement of portfolio risk must take into account not only the risk of each security in the portfolio, but also the correlations that exist between the securities in the portfolio. If we measure the risk of a portfolio by the variance, then both of these factors explicitly are taken into account.

Derivation of Portfolio Variance Equation

To derive the equation for the variance of portfolio, $V(R_p)$, we start with the definition of $V(R_p)$. That is:

$$V(R_p) = E[R_p - E(R_p)]^2 \tag{7.4}$$

If, for simplicity, we assume a two-security portfolio:

$$R_p = w_1 r_1 + w_2 r_2$$

then the portfolio variance expression (7.4) is

$$V(R_p) = E[w_1 r_1 + w_2 r_2 - w_1 E(r_1) - w_2 E(r_2)]^2 \tag{7.5}$$

EXHIBIT 7.1 Correlation between Stock X_1 and Stock X_2

Period	Stock X_1 Rate of Return, r_1	Stock X_2 Rate of Return, r_2
1	18%	18%
2	18	18
3	6	30
4	18	18
5	18	18
6	30	6
7	18	18
8	18	18

r_{1i}	P_i	$P_i\, r_{1i}$	$P_i\,[r_{1i} - E(r_1)]^2$	R_{2i}	P_i	$P_i\, r_{2i}$	$P_i\,[r_{2i} - E(r_2)]^2$
18%	6/8	13.50%	(6/8)(0)	18%	6/8	13.50%	(6/8)(0)
6%	1/8	0.75	(1/8)(144)	30%	1/8	3.75	(1/8)(144)
30%	1/8	3.75	(1/8)(144)	6%	1/8	0.75	(1/8)(144)
		18.00%	$V(r_1)=36$			18.00%	$V(r_1) = 36$
			$\sigma(r_1) = 6$				$\sigma(r_1) = 6$

P_i	r_1	R_2	$[r_{1i} - E(r_1)]$	$[r_{2i} - E(r_2)]$	$P_i\,[r_{1i} - E(r_1)]\,[r_{2i} - E(r_2)]$
6/8	18%	18%	0	0	(6/8)(0)(0) = 0
1/8	6%	30%	−12	12	(1/8)(−12)(12) = −18
1/8	30%	6%	12	−12	(1/8)(12)(−12) = −18
					$Cov(r_1 r_2) = -36$
					$\rho_{12} = -1$

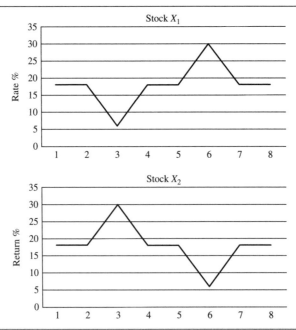

272

Second, we collect the variables in terms of w_1 and w_2; this yields:

$$V(R_p) = E[w_1[r_1 - E(r_1)] + w_2[r_2 - E(r_2)]]^2 \qquad (7.6)$$

Equation (7.6) is similar to $[ab + cd]^2$, which is equal to $a^2b^2 + c^2d^2 + 2abcd$. As a third step, we take the square of Equation (7.6). Similar to $(ab + cd)^2$, this yields:

$$V(R_p) = E[w_1^2[r_1 - E(r_1)]^2 + w_2^2[r_2 - E(r_2)]^2 \\ + 2w_1w_2[r_1 - E(r_1)][r_2 - E(r_2)]] \qquad (7.7)$$

The fourth step in the derivation is to apply the expected value operator rules. Applying the rules to Equation (7.7) yields:

$$V(R_p) = w_1^2E[r_1 - E(r_1)]^2 + w_2^2E[r_2 - E(r_2)]^2 \\ + 2w_1w_2E[r_1 - E(r_1)][r_2 - E(r_2)] \qquad (7.8)$$

Finally, by definition we know:

$$V(r_1) = E[r_1 - E(r_1)]^2 \\ V(r_2) = E[r_2 - E(r_2)]^2 \\ Cov(r_1r_2) = E[r_1 - E(r_1)][r_2 - E(r_2)]$$

Substituting these expressions into Equation (7.8) yields the desired two-security portfolio variance equation:

$$V(R_p) = w_1^2V(r_1) + w_2^2V(r_2) + 2w_1w_2Cov(r_1r_2) \qquad (7.9)$$

The portfolio standard deviation, $\sigma(R_p)$, also can be used as the measure of risk and is obtained simply by taking the square root of (7.9):

$$\sigma(R_p) = \sqrt{V(R_p)} = \sqrt{w_1^2V(r_1) + w_2^2V(r_2) + 2w_1w_2Cov(r_1r_2)} \qquad (7.10)$$

Equations (7.9) and (7.10) measure the risk of a two-security portfolio. Note that the portfolio variance includes both the weighted variances of the individual securities' rates of return and the covariance between the securities' returns; hence, the correlation among securities explicitly is taken into account in the equations for the portfolio variance and standard deviation. Moreover, if we substitute into Equation (7.9) the parameter values in Exhibit 7.1 used in the preceding example, we can confirm our graphical interpretation that the risk of that portfolio is indeed zero

$$V(R_p) = w_1^2V(r_1) + w_2^2V(r_2) + 2w_1w_2Cov(r_1r_2) \\ V(R_p) = (0.5)^2(36) + (0.5)^2(36) + 2(0.5)(0.5)(-36) = 0$$

If the securities in the preceding example had not been perfectly negatively corre-lated, then the portfolio risk would not have been zero. For example, if X_2 had a 6% return in time period 3 and a 30% return in period 6, its expected return and variance would still be 18% and 36%. The covariance between X_1 and X_2, however, would be a positive 36 instead of a negative 36, and therefore $\rho_{12} = +1$ instead of -1; the two securities therefore would be perfectly positively correlated in this case. Calculating $V(R_p)$ with the $Cov\,(r_1 r_2) = 36$, we obtain a portfolio variance of 36:

$$V(R_p) = w_1^2 V(r_1) + w_2^2 V(r_2) + 2w_1 w_2 Cov(r_1 r_2)$$
$$V(R_p) = (0.5)^2(36) + (0.5)^2 + 2(0.5)(0.5)(36) = 36$$

Although Equation (7.9) is only for a two-security portfolio, the variance for a larger portfolio necessarily takes the same form, the only difference being the number of inputs (variances and covariance) included. For example, if we have a three-security portfolio, then our variance expression would consist of three security variances and three covariances; that is, the covariances for all combinations between stock returns:

$$\begin{aligned} V(R_p) = {}& w_1^2 V(r_1) + w_2^2 V(r_2) + w_3^2 V(r_3) \\ & + 2w_1 w_2 Cov(r_1 r_2) \\ & + 2w_1 w_3 Cov(r_1 r_3) \\ & + 2w_2 w_2 Cov(r_2 r_3) \end{aligned}$$

If we had a four-security portfolio, then there would be four variances and six covariances, and so on. Equation (7.11) gives a general portfolio variance formula for an n-security portfolio.

$$\begin{aligned} V(R_p) = {}& w_1^2 V(r_1) + w_2^2 V(r_2) + \cdots + w_n^2 V(r_n) \\ & + 2w_1 w_2 Cov(r_1 r_2) + \cdots + 2w_1 w_n Cov(r_1 r_n) \\ & + 2w_2 w_3 Cov(r_2 r_3) + \cdots + 2w_2 w_n Cov(r_2 r_n) \\ & + 2w_3 w_4 Cov(r_3 r_4) + \cdots + 2w_3 w_n Cov(r_3 r_n) + \cdots \cdot \quad (7.11) \end{aligned}$$

For large portfolios, the number of inputs and thus the size of the portfolio expres-sion can be quite substantial. For example, if we were to compute the variance of a 100-security portfolio, as inputs we would need to compute 100 variances and 4,950 covariances. In general, the number of inputs for any n-security portfolio variances is:

- n expected returns.
- n variances.
- $[n^2 - n]/2$ covariances.

Alternative Portfolio Variance Expressions

The portfolio variance equation also can be expressed in terms of the correlation coefficients by substituting $\rho_{ij} \, \sigma_i \, \sigma_j$ for $Cov(r_i, r_j)$ in Equation (7.11):

$$
\begin{aligned}
V(R_p) = {} & w_1^2 V(r_1) + w_2^2 V(r_2) + \cdots + w_n^2 V(r_n) \\
& + 2w_1 w_2 \rho_{12} \sigma(r_1)\sigma(r_2) + \cdots + 2w_1 w_n \rho_{1n} \sigma(r_1)\sigma(r_n) \\
& + 2w_2 w_3 \rho_{23} \sigma(r_2)\sigma(r_3) + \cdots + 2w_2 w_n \rho_{2n} \sigma(r_2)\sigma(r_n) \\
& + 2w_3 w_4 \rho_{34} \sigma(r_3)\sigma(r_4) + \cdots + 2w_3 w_n \rho_{3n} \sigma(r_3)\sigma(r_n) + \cdots \cdot \quad (7.12)
\end{aligned}
$$

Equation (7.12) highlights the direct relationship between the degree of correlation among securities in the portfolio and the portfolio's risk: the lower the correlation, the lower the portfolio risk.

The portfolio variance expression can be written compactly with summation signs. If we denote the variance of a security's return as its standard deviation squared and represent it as

$$
\sigma(r_i)^2 = \sigma_i^2
$$

and we denote the covariance of securities i and j as

$$
Cov(r_i r_j) = \sigma_{ij} \quad \text{where} \quad i \neq j
$$

then $V(R_p)$ can be expressed as

$$
V(R_p) = \sum_{i=1}^{n} w_i^2 \sigma_i^2 + \sum_{i=1}^{n} \sum_{\substack{j=1 \\ j \neq i}}^{n} w_i w_j \sigma_{ij} \qquad (7.13)
$$

Note how the double summation of covariances does yield the two $w_i w_j \sigma_{ij}$ terms. For example, in a three-security case, the double summation term is

$$
\sum_{i=1}^{3} \sum_{\substack{j=1 \\ j \neq i}}^{3} w_i w_j \sigma_{ij} = w_1 w_2 \sigma_{12} + w_1 w_3 \sigma_{13} + w_2 w_1 \sigma_{21}
$$

$$
+ w_2 w_3 \sigma_{23} + w_3 w_1 \sigma_{31} + w_3 w_2 \sigma_{32}
$$

Since, $\sigma_{ij} = \sigma_{ji}$, this expression is

$$
\sum_{i=1}^{3} \sum_{\substack{j=1 \\ j \neq i}}^{3} w_i w_j \sigma_{ij} = 2w_1 w_2 \sigma_{12} + 2w_1 w_3 \sigma_{13} + 2w_2 w_3 \sigma_{23}
$$

In summary, the portfolio expected return Equation (7.2) and the portfolio variance Equation (7.11) or Equation (7.12) are the important formulas needed to evaluate portfolios. They allow us to quantify any portfolio in terms of its return and risk. By changing the allocations (w_i), we change the portfolio's return and risk. The return-risk equations also show that an investor constructing a portfolio based on the criteria of return and risk must search not only for securities with high expected returns and low risks, but also for ones that are uncorrelated and ideally negatively correlated with each other.

Example

Consider the case of an investor with two stocks, A and B, with the following characteristics:

Stock A	$E(r_A) = 10\%$
	$V(r_A) = 36\%$
Stock B	$E(r_B) = 10\%$
	$V(r_B) = 36\%$
	$Cov(r_A\ r_B) = 18$
	$\rho_{AB} = 0.5$

Suppose the investor currently has half of her investment funds allocated to each of the stocks, yielding her a portfolio expected rate of return and variance of

$$E(R_p) = (0.5)(10\%) + (0.5)(10\%) = 10\%$$
$$V(R_p) = (0.5)^2(36) + (0.5)^2(36) + 2(0.5)(0.5)(18) = 27$$

Suppose that the investor, however, would like to add a third stock to her portfolio and is considering either stock C, stock D, or stock E, each with the following characteristics:

Stock C	$E(r_C) = 10\%$	$Cov(r_A\ r_C) = 18$
	$V(r_C) = 36\%$	$Cov(r_B\ r_C) = 18$
Stock D	$E(r_D) = 10\%$	$Cov(r_A\ r_D) = 0$
	$V(r_D) = 72$	$Cov(r_B\ r_D) = 0$
Stock E	$E(r_E) = 10\%$	$Cov(r_A\ r_E) = -36$
	$V(r_E) = 144$	$Cov(r_B\ r_E) = -36$

If she adds stock C to her portfolio and allocates one-third of her investment funds to each stock, her new portfolio expected return and variance would be:

$$E(R_p) = (1/3)(10\%) + (1/3)(10\%) + (1/3)(10\%) = 10\%$$
$$\begin{aligned} V(R_p) = &(1/3)^2(36) + (1/3)^2(36) + (1/3)^2(36) \\ &+ 2(1/3)(1/3)(18) + 2(1/3)(1/3)(18) \\ &+ 2(1/3)(1/3)(18) = 24 \end{aligned}$$

If the investor selects stock D instead of stock C, and again allocates one-third of her funds to each stock, then her portfolio expected return and variance would be:

$$E(R_p) = (1/3)(10\%) + (1/3)(10\%) + (1/3)(10\%) = 10\%$$
$$\begin{aligned} V(R_p) = &(1/3)^2(36) + (1/3)^2(36) + (1/3)^2(72) \\ &+ 2(1/3)(1/3)(18) + 2(1/3)(1/3)(0) \\ &+ 2(1/3)(1/3)(0) = 20 \end{aligned}$$

Finally, if the investor selects stock E as her third security and again uses an equal allocation strategy, then her expected portfolio return and variance would be:

$$E(R_p) = (1/3)(10\%) + (1/3)(10\%) + (1/3)(10\%) = 10\%$$
$$\begin{aligned} V(R_p) = &(1/3)^2(36) + (1/3)^2(36) + (1/3)^2(144) \\ &+ 2(1/3)(1/3)(18) + 2(1/3)(1/3)(-36) \\ &+ 2(1/3)(1/3)(-36) = 12 \end{aligned}$$

Given the choice of adding only one of the stocks to form an equally allocated portfolio, what stock should she choose? If she bases her selection on a portfolio return-risk criterion, stock E would be her best choice. That is, since the same portfolio expected return of 10 percent is attained whether she adds C, D, or E, stock E must be the best since it gives a lower portfolio variance than C or D. What is interesting, however, is that when we measure individual security risk by the variance, stock E is twice as risky as stock D and four times as risky as stock B, yet when we add stock E to the portfolio, it yields the smallest portfolio variance. The reason, of course, is the lower correlation stock E has with stocks A and B compared to the correlations stocks D and E have with A and B:

Portfolio A, B, C	Portfolio A, B, D	Portfolio A, B, E
$\rho_{AB} = 0.5$	$\rho_{AB} = 0.5$	$\rho_{AB} = 0.5$
$\rho_{AC} = 0.5$	$\rho_{AD} = 0$	$\rho_{AE} = -0.5$
$\rho_{BC} = 0.5$	$\rho_{BD} = 0$	$\rho_{BE} = -0.5$

The example shows the importance of including the correlation in measuring portfolio risk. In addition, if we compare the different portfolio variances obtained with stocks C, D, and E, we confirm our earlier point that the portfolio risk will be lower, the smaller the correlation.

BLOOMBERG CORRELATION MEASURE SCREENS

CORR: The CORR screen can be used to create and save a number of correlation matrices for securities, indexes, currencies, interest rates, and commodities. As noted in Chapter 6, the matrix also shows a variance-covariance matrix (Cov), correlation coefficient matrix (Correlation), beta, and other correlation and regression parameters.

PC: The PC platform shows correlation and regression parameters of a selected stock with its peers and related indexes: S&P 500, Dow Jones, sector indexes, and others. One can select different peers, indexes, portfolios, and securities from searches from the "Bloomberg Peer" dropdown, select different parameters (correlation, beta, covariance, or t statistics) from the "Calculation" tab, different regression periods, and frequencies (e.g., daily, weekly, or monthly).

The PC screen can be saved to the Correlation Matrix from the red "Save to CORR," where it can be accessed for later study by bringing up the CORR screen (CORR <Enter>).

Portfolio Risk and Size Relation

It can be shown mathematically that as the size of a portfolio increases, the portfolio standard deviation (risk) decreases at a decreasing rate to a point (asymptote) where any additional increase in portfolio size has no impact on portfolio risk. Appendix 7A (text Web site) presents the mathematical derivation of portfolio risk-size relation.

The portfolio risk and size relation has also been examined empirically. Evans and Archer were the first to examine this relationship. In their 1968 study, they calculated the average standard deviations of randomly selected portfolios of different sizes. Specifically, they formed a database of the semi-annual returns of 470 NYSE-listed stocks for the period from 1958 to 1967. Securities were then selected using a random number generator and formed into equally weighted portfolios. They first randomly selected 60 two-stock portfolios and calculated the average standard deviation. Evans and Archer then repeated this process: randomly selecting 60 3-security portfolios, 60 4-security portfolios, and so on up to 60 40-security portfolios, then calculating the average standard deviations for each size portfolio:

$$\bar{\sigma}_n = \frac{1}{60} \sum_{i=1}^{60} \sigma_{ni}, \qquad \text{where: } n = 2, 3, \dots, 40$$

EXHIBIT 7.2 Evans and Archer: Risk-Size Relation

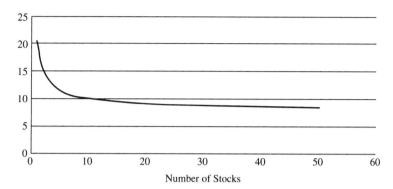

Number of Stocks

The result of the Evans and Archer study are shown in Exhibit 7.2. The graph in the exhibit shows the average portfolio standard deviations that Evans and Archer calculated plotted against their size. This empirically generated portfolio risk and size graph, in turn, shows that as the portfolio size increases, the portfolio risk decreases at a decreasing rate to a point where any additional increase in portfolio size has no impact on portfolio risk. In the Evans and Archer study, the maximum risk reduction is realized with a portfolio of approximately 25 stocks, with the portfolio risk being 0.09.

Recall that in Chapter 6 we defined the unsystematic risk of a security or portfolio as the industry and firm risk that could be diversified away, and we defined a security's or portfolio's systematic risk as the market risk that could not be diversified away. In the context of our discussion here, the Evans and Archer study suggests that a portfolio of approximately 25 to 30 stocks would be needed to eliminate unsystematic risk.

Return and Risk of a Portfolio of Risky Stocks and a Risk-Free Security

In Chapter 6, we defined a risk-free security as one whose rate of return is known in advance. If we let R_f be the rate of return on the risk-free security, then by definition the variance of R_f is equal to zero: $V(R_f) = 0$. In addition to a zero variance, the risk-free security also is characterized by having a zero covariance with the returns of any other security or portfolio. That is, there is no correlation between a random variable and a constant:

$$Cov(rR_f) = 0$$

Given the opportunity to invest in a risk-free security, investors also want to be able to evaluate a portfolio in which a risk-free security is included with a portfolio of risky stocks. In terms of portfolio evaluation, the inclusion of a risk-free security to a portfolio of risky stocks simply means that we are adding to a stock portfolio a security with a rate of return of R_f, a variance of zero, and a covariance with the other securities in the portfolio of zero. However, to highlight the impact of including a riskless security, let us treat the portfolio as a two-security portfolio, with one of the securities being the risk-free one and the other being the portfolio of risky securities with a return of $E(R_p)$ and risk of $V(R_p)$. Denoting R_I as the rate of return on this two-security portfolio, its expected rate of return would be:

$$E(R_I) = w_R R_f + w_p E(R_p) \qquad (7.14)$$

where:

w_R = proportion of investment funds allocated to the risk-free security
w_p = proportion of investment funds allocated to the portfolio of risky securities

As with all portfolios, Equation (7.14) is constrained by the condition that the weights sum to one:

$$w_R + w_p = 1$$

Given this constraint, Equation (7.14) can be expressed in terms of just one of the weights, w_p, by substituting $1 - w_p$ for w_R in (7.14):

$$E(R_I) = (1 - w_p)R_f + w_p E(R_p)$$
$$E(R_I) = R_f + [E(R_p) - R_f]w_p \qquad (7.15)$$

Using the two-security portfolio variance equation, the variance of a portfolio of risky securities and a risk-free security can be expressed as

$$V(R_I) = w_p^2 V(R_p) + w_R^2 V(R_f) + 2w_p w_R Cov(R_f R_p)$$

Given $V(R_f) = 0$ and $Cov(R_f R_p) = 0$, this variance expression simplifies to

$$V(R_I) = w_p^2 V(R_p) \qquad (7.16)$$

Finally, taking the square root of (7.16), we obtain the standard deviation of this portfolio:

$$\sigma(R_I) = \sqrt{w_p^2 V(R_I)}$$
$$\sigma(R_I) = \sqrt{w_p^2 \sigma(R_p)^2}$$
$$\sigma(R_I) = w_p \sigma(R_p) \qquad (7.17)$$

Equations (7.14) and (7.17) measure the expected return and risk of a portfolio consisting of risky securities and a risk-free security. Note that these equations measure the expected return and standard deviation of returns of the investor's funds. If an investor places all her funds in the portfolio ($w_p = 1$), then her risk would be equal to the portfolio's risk, $\sigma(R_p)$; if she places half of her funds in the risky portfolio and half in the risk-free security, then her investment risk would be equal to half of the portfolio's risk: $(0.5)[\sigma(R_p)]$.

Borrowing and Lending Portfolios

Equations (7.14) and (7.17) can be used to determine the different return-risk opportunities obtainable by changing the allocations of investment funds between the risk-free security and the risky portfolio. For example, suppose an investor is considering investing in a risky stock portfolio with an expected return of $E(R_p) = 10\%$ and a risk (as measured by the standard deviation) of $\sigma(R_p) = 4$. Suppose, however, that the investor is willing to accept a lower expected return for less risk. The investor could change the allocation of the securities in the risky portfolio, with more funds allocated to the less risky stocks. A simpler approach, however, would be to invest only a proportion of funds in the portfolio, the remaining proportion being invested in the risk-free security. For example, suppose the rate on the risk-free security is 5 percent, and the investor decides to place half of his funds in the risk-free security and half in the stock portfolio. Using Equations (7.14) and (7.17), his expected return and risk would be $E(R_I) = 7.5\%$ and $\sigma(R_I) = 2$:

$$E(R_I) = (0.5)(10\%) + (0.5)(5\%) = 7.5\%$$
$$\sigma(R_I) = (0.5)(4) = 2$$

Thus, although the investor's expected return is lower, he has reduced his risk by investing part of his funds in the risk-free security. Moreover, if the investor were still not satisfied with his return-risk opportunity, he could use another allocation strategy. In fact, from a minimum return-risk combination of $E(R_I) = R_f = 5\%$ and $\sigma(R_I) = 0$, in which $w_R = 1$ to a maximum combination of $E(R_I) = E(R_p) = 10\%$, and $\sigma(R_I) = \sigma(R_p) = 4$, in which $w_p = 1$, there are an infinite number of return-risk combinations available to the investor. A portfolio consisting of an investment in a portfolio of risky securities and a risk-free security is referred to as a *lending portfolio*. In a lending portfolio, the allocation to the risk-free security is positive, $w_R > 0$, implying an investment in that security.

Recall from our earlier discussion, that the weights can also be negative. As we noted, a negative weight implies a short position. A short position in a risk-free security ($w_R < 0$) could be implemented by borrowing a risk-free security and selling it in the market at a discount rate of R_f, then at maturity either buying the bond back at its face value and returning it to the security lender so she can collect the principal or simply paying the principal to her. In this case, the short seller of the risk-free security uses the funds from the short sale to invest in the portfolio of risky securities, and she would pay a rate on those proceeds equal to the risk-free rate. A short position can also be implemented by issuing a risk-free security or by borrowing funds from a financial institution at a rate of R_f. In either case, a portfolio of risky securities that is financed in part with funds borrowed at a risk-free rate is referred to as a *borrowing* or *leveraged portfolio*.

In contrast to a lending portfolio, a leveraged portfolio allows an investor to increase his expected return, but at the expense of assuming a higher risk position. For example, suppose the investor in our preceding case wanted an expected return greater than the 10 percent portfolio return and was willing to assume a risk greater than the risky portfolio's risk of $\sigma(R_p) = 4$. The simplest way to accomplish this would be to leverage the portfolio investment by borrowing additional funds to invest in the portfolio. For example, suppose the investor had $1,000 of his own funds to invest, plus he borrowed an additional $1,000 at $R_f = 5\%$ to also invest in the stock portfolio. The proportion of his funds allocated to the stock portfolio would therefore be 2, and the proportion of his funds allocated to the risk-free security would be −1 (i.e., negative investment or borrowing):

$$w_p = \frac{\text{Stock Portfolio Investment}}{\text{Total Investment}} = \frac{\$2,000}{\$1,000} = 2$$

$$w_R = \frac{\text{Borrowed Funds}}{\text{Total Investment}} = \frac{-\$1,000}{\$1,000} = -1$$

$$w_p + w_R = 2 + (-1) = 1$$

Using Equations (7.14) and (7.17), the expected return and risk of this leveraged portfolio would be $E(R_l) = 15\%$ and $\sigma(R_l) = 8$:

$$E(R_l) = (2)(10\%) + (-1)(5\%) = 15\%$$
$$\sigma(R_l) = (2)(4) = 8$$

For the investor to actually attain a 15 percent return, the portfolio expected return of 10 percent would have to be realized. If it is, then the investor would receive $200 from the $2,000 invested in the stock portfolio, but he would have to pay $50 on the borrowed funds. His net return would therefore be $150, yielding a rate of return of 15 percent from his $1,000 investment, $150/$1,000:

$$E(R_l) = \frac{0.10(\$2,000) - 0.05(\$1,000)}{\$1,000} = 0.15$$

The risk of $\sigma(R_p) = 8\%$ suggests that if the portfolio were to yield a return of only 6 percent (i.e., 4 percent less than its expected return or one standard deviation below its mean: $R_p = E(R_p) - \sigma(R_p) = 10\% - 4\% = 6\%$), the investor's return would be 7 percent (i.e., 8 percent less than its expected return or one standard deviation below its mean: $R_l = E(R_l) - \sigma(R_l) = 15\% - 8\% = 7\%$); that is, he would receive only

EXHIBIT 7.3 Return Distributions of Risk Portfolio and Leveraged Portfolio

z	-2	-1	0	1	2
$R_p = 10 + z4$	2%	6%	10%	14%	18%
$R_I = 15 + z8$	-1%	7%	15%	23%	31%

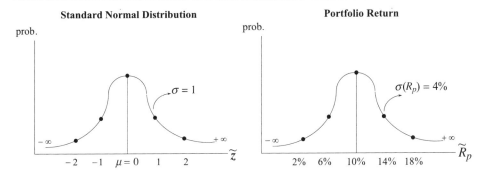

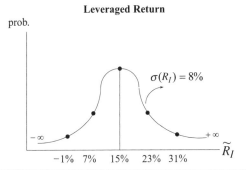

$120 from portfolio [(0.06)($2,000) = $120] and would have to pay $50 on the borrowed funds, for a net return of $70, and a rate of return of 7 percent ($70/$1,000):

$$R_I = \frac{0.06(\$2,000) - 0.05(\$1,000)}{\$1,000} = 0.07$$

Note that the assumption that the portfolio's return distribution is normal (i.e., it depends on only the mean and variance) implies that the actual portfolio return of 6 percent and the leveraged return of 7 percent correspond to one deviation below the standard normal distribution, that is, a z score of -1 (see Exhibit 7.3). Thus:

$$R_p = E(R_p) + z\sigma(R_p)$$
$$R_p = 10\% + (-1)(4\%) = 6\%$$

$$R_I = E(R_I) + z\sigma(R_I)$$
$$R_I = 15\% + (-1)(8\%) = 7\%$$

If the actual portfolio return were two standard deviations below the mean, $z\sigma\ (R_p) = (2)(4\%) = 8\%$, then the portfolio return would be 2% (i.e., $R_p = E(R_p)$ $- z\sigma\ (R_p) = 10\% - (2)(4\%) = 2\%$), and the return on the leveraged investment would be -1%:

$$R_I = \frac{0.02(\$2,000) - 0.05(\$1,000)}{\$1,000} = -0.01$$

$$R_I = E(R_I) + z\sigma(R_I)$$
$$R_I = 15\% + (-2)(8\%) = -1\%$$

On the other hand, if the realized portfolio returns were above the expected return, then the returns on the leveraged portfolio will be even higher: For a $z = +1$, $R_p = 14\%$ and $R_I = 23\%$, and for $z = +2$, $R_p = 18\%$, and $R_I = 31\%$. Exhibit 7.3 summarizes the different returns obtained from the portfolio and the leveraged portfolio given different z scores.

In summary, given the opportunity to borrow and lend at a risk-free rate, an investor can attain an unlimited number of return-risk combinations, ranging from a minimum return-risk combination of R_f and zero when $w_R = 1$, to a $E(R_p)$ and $\sigma(R_p)$ combination when $w_p = 1$, to a return-risk combination that is greater than the portfolio's when $w_p > 1$ and $w_R < 0$. Thus, the opportunity to borrow and lend at a risk-free rate, gives the investor a tool for changing his return-risk opportunities without forcing him to change his portfolio's composition of risky securities.

Return-Risk Relation

Exhibit 7.4 summarizes the return-risk combinations from the preceding example. To reiterate, we assumed our investor could hold a risky portfolio yielding an expected return of 10 percent and a risk of $\sigma(R_p) = 4$, and could borrow and lend at the risk-free rate of 5 percent. Given this portfolio, we generated different return-risk combinations the investor could obtain with different allocations in the risk-free security and the portfolio. Line ABCDE in Exhibit 7.4 is a plot of the return-risk combinations that we obtained. The graph is defined here as the *borrowing-lending line*. The line shows that when the investor places all his funds in the risk-free security, he is on the vertical axis with $\sigma(R_I) = 0$ and $E(R_I) = R_f = 5\%$. By contrast, when the investor places all of his investment funds in the portfolio ($w_p = 1$), he is at point C on the borrowing-lending line where he obtains the portfolio's expected return and risk. Point B lies halfway between points A and C and shows the return-risk combination of $E(R_I) = 7.5\%$ and $\sigma(R_I) = 2$, obtained when the investor places half his investment fund in the portfolio and half in the risk-free security. Finally, point D shows the investor's return-risk combination obtained when he borrows an amount equal to 50 percent above his investment funds ($w_R = -0.5$ and $w_p = 1.5$). The borrowing-lending line, in turn, can be divided into two segments: one segment showing lending portfolios and the other borrowing (or leveraged) portfolios. In particular, the segment to the left of

EXHIBIT 7.4 Borrowing and Lending Line

Portfolio	w_R	w_p	$E(R_I)$	$\sigma(R_I)$
A	1	0	$R_f = 5\%$	0
B	0.5	0.5	7.5%	2
C	0	1	$E(R_p) = 10\%$	$\sigma(R_p) = 4$
D	−0.5	1.5	12.5%	6
E	−1	2	15%	8

Borrowing-Lending Line: Graph showing the return-risk combinations obtainable by varying funds between risk-free security and portfolio of risky stocks.

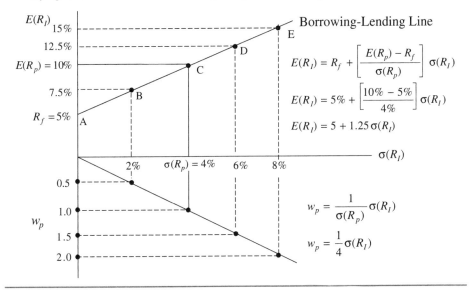

C delineates all the various lending portfolios, whereas the segment to the right of C shows all the borrowing portfolios.

The equation for the borrowing-lending line is

$$E(R_I) = R_f + \left[\frac{E(R_p) - R_f}{\sigma(R_p)}\right]\sigma(R_I)$$

$$E(R_I) = R_f + \lambda\sigma(R_I) \qquad (7.18)$$

where:

R_f = the intercept of the line ABCDE

$\lambda = \left[\dfrac{E(R_p) - R_f}{\sigma(R_p)}\right]$ is the slope of the line ABCDE

Equation (7.18) is obtained by solving Equations (7.15) and (7.17) simultaneously. Specifically, solving Equation (7.17) for w_p yields

$$w_p = \frac{\sigma(R_I)}{\sigma(R_p)} \tag{7.19}$$

and then substituting $\sigma(R_I)/\sigma(R_p)$ for w_p into Equation (7.15), we obtain Equation (7.18).

Substituting the numerical values of our example for R_f, $E(R_p)$, and $\sigma(R_p)$ into Equation (7.18), we obtain the borrowing-lending line equation for ABCDE of

$$E(R_I) = R_f + \left[\frac{E(R_p) - R_f}{\sigma(R_p)} \right] \sigma(R_I)$$

$$E(R_I) = 5\% + \left[\frac{10\% - 5\%}{4\%} \right] \sigma(R_I)$$

$$E(R_I) = 5\% + 1.25\sigma(R_I)$$

Thus, for a specified risk level (e.g., $\sigma(R_I) = 2$), one can determine the expected return $[E(R_I) = 5\% + 1.25\ (2) = 7.5\%]$. In addition, using Equation (7.19), one can also determine the allocation needed to attain the specified risk-return combination $[w_p = \sigma(R_I)/\sigma(R_p) = 2\%/4\% = 0.5$, and $w_R = 1 - w_p = 1 - 0.5 = 0.5]$. The allocations needed to attain the return-risk combinations described by ABCDE are shown by the line in the lower quadrant of the figure in Exhibit 7.4. The line comes from Equation (7.19) and shows w_p plotted against $\sigma(R_I)$, with the slope of the line equal to $1/\sigma(R_p) = 1/4$.

Equation (7.18) is the equation for any borrowing-lending line. It shows the different return-risk combinations that are obtainable by varying one's investment funds between a risk-free security and a given portfolio of risky securities. A special borrowing-lending line is the *Capital Market Line* (*CML*). The CML is formed with the risk-free security and the market portfolio—the portfolio consisting of all securities in the market. Given the market portfolio's expected rate of $E(R^M)$ and its risk of $\sigma(R^M)$, the equation for the CML is

$$E(R_I) = R_f + \left[\frac{E(R^M) - R_f}{\sigma(R^M)} \right] \sigma(R_I)$$

$$E(R_I) = R_f + \lambda^M \sigma(R_I) \tag{7.20}$$

As shown in Exhibit 7.5, the CML shows the different return-risk combinations investors can obtain from different allocations in the risk-free security and the market portfolio.

Before ending our discussion on the return-risk relationship obtained from borrowing and lending portfolios, we should note that throughout the discussion we have

EXHIBIT 7.5 Capital Market Line

- **Capital Market Line (CML)**: The CML is formed with the risk-free security and the market portfolio. The CML shows the different return-risk combinations investors can obtain from different allocations in the risk-free securities and the market portfolio.

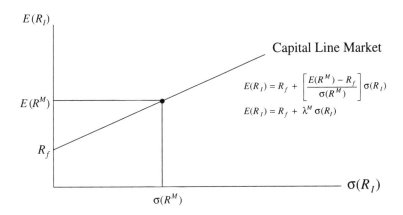

assumed that the risk-free rate that applied to borrowing and lending was the same. Obviously, it is more realistic to assume that the borrowing rate, R_B, exceeds the lending rate, R_L. If we assume this to be the case, then our borrowing and lending line will no longer be continuous, but rather will exhibit a kink at the return-risk combination where $w_p = 1$; That is, we basically have two lines as shown in Exhibit 7.6, a steeper lending line segment $R_L E$ with a slope of $\lambda_L = [E(R_p) - R_L]/\sigma(R_p)$, and a borrowing segment EF with a slope of $\lambda_B = [E(R_p) - R_B]/\sigma(R_p)$.

EXHIBIT 7.6 Borrowing and Lending Line with Different Borrowing and Lending Rates

- Borrowing-Lending Line with borrowing rate greater than lending rate. The steeper lending line segment $R_L E$ with a slope of $\lambda_L = [E(R_p) - R_L]/\sigma(R_p)$, and a borrowing segment EF with a slope of $\lambda_B = [E(R_p) - R_B]/\sigma(R_p)$.

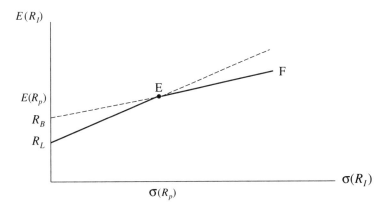

Portfolio Ranking

The return-risk opportunities described by a borrowing-lending line are generated by changing the allocation of investment funds between the risk-free security and the portfolio of risky securities. This return-risk analysis summarized by the borrowing-lending line can be extended to the ranking of different portfolios of risky securities. To see this, suppose the investor in our preceding example was considering an investment in one of two portfolios: portfolio A (the one we just analyzed) or portfolio B. The characteristics of each portfolio are:

Portfolio A	$E(R_p) = 10\%$
	$\sigma(R_p) = 4\%$
Portfolio B	$E(R_p) = 20\%$
	$\sigma(R_p) = 8\%$

Given the choice of selecting one portfolio, which portfolio should the investor choose?

Because portfolio B yields twice the return and twice the risk as portfolio A, it might appear at first that the investor's decision would depend on his return-risk preference. If he is very risk averse, he would select portfolio A; but if he is less risk averse, then he would select portfolio B. Selecting securities or portfolios based on an investor's risk-return preference is sometimes referred to as the *interior decorator view*. According to this view, an investment advisor would try to match the return-risk characteristic of an investment to the investor's return-risk preferences. In terms of this case, the choice of portfolio would be subjectively based on preference: A timid investor should select portfolio A, and an aggressive investor should select portfolio B.

Given that the investor can borrow and lend at a risk-free rate, however, he is not constrained to the specified return-risk characteristics of the portfolios. That is, he can combine portfolio A with a risk-free security to obtain a set of return-risk combinations (depicted by the borrowing-lending line), as well as combine portfolio B with the riskless security to obtain another set of return-risk combinations (depicted by a different borrowing-lending line). Exhibit 7.7 shows the borrowing-lending lines generated for each of the portfolios given a risk-free rate of 5 percent. The equations for each of the lines are

Portfolio A:

$$E(R_I) = 5\% + \left[\frac{10\% - 5\%}{4\%}\right]\sigma(R_I)$$
$$E(R_I) = 5\% + 1.25\sigma(R_I)$$

Portfolio B:

$$E(R_I) = 5\% + \left[\frac{20\% - 5\%}{8\%}\right]\sigma(R_I)$$
$$E(R_I) = 5\% + 1.875\sigma(R_I)$$

EXHIBIT 7.7 Ranking Portfolios with Borrowing and Lending Lines

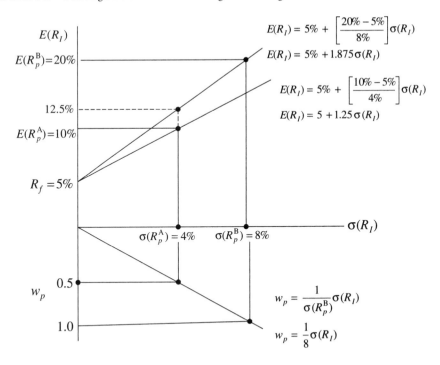

$$E(R_I) = 5\% + \left[\frac{20\% - 5\%}{8\%}\right]\sigma(R_I)$$

$$E(R_I) = 5\% + 1.875\sigma(R_I)$$

$$E(R_I) = 5\% + \left[\frac{10\% - 5\%}{4\%}\right]\sigma(R_I)$$

$$E(R_I) = 5 + 1.25\sigma(R_I)$$

$$w_p = \frac{1}{\sigma(R_p^B)}\sigma(R_I)$$

$$w_p = \frac{1}{8}\sigma(R_I)$$

The borrowing-lending line formed with portfolio B is steeper than the line formed with portfolio A; that is, the slope of portfolio B's borrowing-lending line is $\lambda_B = 1.875$, whereas portfolio A's borrowing-lending line slope is $\lambda_A = 1.25$. Given the same intercepts (R_f), portfolio B's steeper slope implies that for any risk level, the investor can obtain a greater expected return from an investment in portfolio B and risk-free security than he can from an investment in portfolio A and a risk-free security. For example, suppose the investor was timid, and following the interior decorator view, placed all of his investment funds in portfolio A with the lower expected return and risk of 10 percent and 4 percent. Alternatively, for the same risk of 4 percent, the investor could obtain a higher expected return of 12.5 percent by placing half of his funds in portfolio B and half in the risk-free security:

$$E(R_I) = 5\% + 1.875\sigma(R_I)$$
$$E(R_I) = 5\% + 1.875(4\%) = 12.5\%$$
$$w_p = \frac{\sigma(R_I)}{\sigma(R_p)} = \frac{4\%}{8\%} = 0.5$$

Thus, with the borrowing-lending line formed with B dominating the line formed with A, we can conclude that for any risk, investments formed with portfolio B and the risk-free security yield higher expected returns than those formed with portfolio A and the risk-free security. Portfolio B is therefore the best portfolio.

EXHIBIT 7.8 Stochastic Dominance

z	-2	-1	0	1	2
A: $R_p = 10 + z4$	2%	6%	10%	14%	18%
B: $R_p = 20 + z8$	4%	12%	20%	28%	36'%

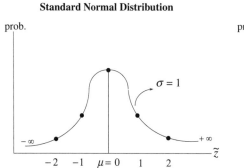

Standard Normal Distribution

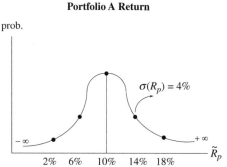

Portfolio A Return

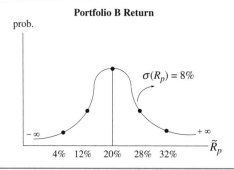

Portfolio B Return

Mathematically, the only difference between the borrowing-lending lines for portfolio A and B is their slope, λ. The slope coefficient therefore provides a useful index for ranking portfolios: the greater a portfolio's λ, the greater its return-risk opportunities, or equivalently, the greater its risk premium, $E(R_p) - R_f$, per level of risk, $\sigma(R_p)$.

The dominance of portfolio B over A also can be seen by comparing its distribution of returns to A's distribution. As shown in Exhibit 7.8, for all z-scores covering the distribution, portfolio B's returns are always greater than portfolio A's return. When a random variable has a distribution that dominates another random variable's distribution, it is said to be *stochastically dominant*. Thus, another way to rank portfolios would be to compare their distributions to see which one dominates.

Note that the choice of portfolio B over A is based on an objective criterion of comparing return-risk opportunities or distributions, not on the investor's subjective return-risk preference. This, in turn, suggests that an investor in selecting portfolios (or any asset) based on return and risk should separate the investment decision concerning the choice of portfolios (or assets) from her return-risk preference decision. In finance, the separation of the investment decision from the risk-return preference decision is known as the separation theorem. In terms of our example, the *separation theorem* says that the investor should first select the best portfolio (the one with dominant borrowing-lending line or λ), regardless of her return-risk preference. Once the best portfolio is determined, the investor can then combine that portfolio with a risk-free security to obtain her desired risk-return preference (i.e., desired point on the borrowing-lending line).

Portfolio Performance Measures

Sharpe Index

Ranking portfolios by the slopes of their borrowing-lending lines has been a commonly used technique in evaluating the performances of mutual funds, pensions, and other large portfolios. This ranking index is sometimes referred to as the reward-to-variability ratio. The first study to use the slope coefficient to evaluate portfolios was done by William Sharpe. In his study, he evaluated the performance of 34 mutual funds over the decade from 1954 to 1965 using historical return data from *Wiesenberger*. Sharpe calculated each fund's average return and standard deviation and then ranked each in terms of their average risk premium per level of risk using a risk-free rate of 3 percent:

$$\lambda_S = \frac{\bar{R}_p - R_f}{\bar{\sigma}_p}$$

As a standard of comparison, Sharpe also calculated the same ratio for the Dow Jones Industrial Average (DJIA). The data and indexes of the mutual funds are shown in Exhibit 7.9. Sharpe found that the average reward-to-volatility index of the 34 funds was 0.633, which was below the 0.667 index for the DJIA. In fact, of the 34 funds, only 11 had index values higher than the DJIA. Moreover, a study by Lorie and Fisher found that, statistically, the returns from the DJIA were not significantly different from a randomly selected portfolio. Thus, the Sharpe study suggests that many investors during that period would have been better off forming their own portfolios by random selection (e.g., using a random number generator, throwing darts, or having a way for their pets to select stocks) instead of buying mutual fund shares.

Treynor Index

As an index, the slope of the borrowing-lending line ranks portfolios in terms of their risk premium per unit of risk. A variation on this index is to use the portfolio's beta, β_p, as the measure of risk:

$$\lambda_T = \frac{\bar{R}_p - R_f}{\beta_p}$$

EXHIBIT 7.9   Sharpe Mutual Fund Ranking

Mutual Fund	Average Annual Return, %	Standard Deviation of Annual Return, %	Risk Premium* to Standard Deviation Ratio = S_i
Affiliated Fund	14.6	15.3	0.75896
American Business Shares	10.0	9.2	0.75876
Axe-Houghton, Fund A	10.5	13.5	0.55551
Axe-Houghton, Fund B	12.0	16.3	0.55183
Axe-Houghton, Stock Fund	11.9	15.6	0.56991
Boston Fund	12.4	12.1	0.77842
Broad Street Investing	14.8	16.8	0.70329
Bullock Fund	15.7	19.3	0.65845
Commonwealth Investment Co.	10.9	13.7	0.57841
Delaware Fund	14.4	21.4	0.53253
Dividend Shares	14.4	15.9	0.71807
Dow Jones Industrial Average (DJIA)	16.3	19.9	0.66700
Eaton and Howard, Balanced Funds	11.0	11.9	0.67399
Eaton and Howard, Stock Fund	15.2	19.2	0.63486
Equity Fund	14.6	18.7	0.61902
Fidelity Fund	16.4	23.5	0.57020
Financial Industrial Fund	14.5	23.0	0.49971
Fundamental Investors	16.0	21.7	0.59894
Group Securities, Common Stock Fund	15.1	19.1	0.63316
Group Securities, Fully Administered Fund	11.4	14.1	0.59490
Incorporated Investors	14.0	25.5	0.43116
Investment Company of America	17.4	21.8	0.66169
Investors Mutual	11.3	12.5	0.66451
Loomis-Sales Mutual Fund	10.0	10.4	0.67358
Massachusetts Investors Trust	16.2	20.8	0.63398
Massachusetts Investors - Growth Stock	18.6	22.7	0.68687
National Investors Corporation	18.3	19.9	0.76798
National Securities - Income Series	12.4	17.8	0.52950
New England Fund	10.4	10.2	0.72703
Putnam Fund of Boston	13.1	16.0	0.63222

EXHIBIT 7.9 (*Continued*)

Mutual Fund	Average Annual Return, %	Standard Deviation of Annual Return, %	Risk Premium* to Standard Deviation Ratio = S_i
Scudder, Stevens & Clark Balanced Fund	10.7	13.3	0.57893
Selected American Shares	14.4	19.4	0.58788
United Funds - Income Funds	16.1	20.9	0.62698
Wellington Fund	11.3	12.0	0.69057
Wisconsin Fund	13.8	16.9	0.64091

* S_i = (average return − 3 percent)/std. dev. The ratios shown were computed from original data and thus differ slightly from ratios obtained from the rounded data shown in the table.
Source: William F. Sharpe 1966. Mutual fund performances. *Journal of Business* (January, Suppl.): 125.

Recall that in Chapter 6 we defined beta as a measure of systematic risk. Thus, a portfolio with a beta of two would have twice the fluctuations as the market and would be considered to have twice the systematic risk as a portfolio with a beta of one. A portfolio's beta can be estimated by regressing the portfolio's return against the market:

$$R_p = \alpha_p + \beta_p R^M + \varepsilon_p$$

Ranking portfolios in terms of their risk premium per level of systematic risk was first introduced by Treynor in a study of how to rate investment funds. Accordingly, the index is often referred to as the Treynor index.

Jensen Index

A third way of ranking portfolios is to estimate a portfolio's risk-adjusted return. This can be done by first regressing a portfolio's risk premium ($R_p - R_f$) against the market risk premium ($R^M - R_f$):

$$R_p - R_f = \alpha_p + \beta_p [R^M - R_f] + \varepsilon_p$$

From the regression, the intercept term, α_p, can be used to measure the portfolio's risk-adjusted return. If the intercept is positive, for example, it suggests the portfolio is generating a return in excess of the risk premium. Using the intercept as a portfolio performance measure was first introduced by Jensen and is often referred to as the Jensen index:

$$\lambda_J = \alpha_p$$

Because the intercept measures only a portfolio's risk-adjusted return, to be used as a reward-to-risk ranking measure in evaluating different portfolios, it needs to be divided by the portfolio risk (as measured by either the portfolio beta or standard deviation).

Portfolio Performance Evaluation Using Bloomberg

The historical returns and risk of a portfolio can be analyzed using Bloomberg's Portfolio Risk & Analytics Screen, PORT. Exhibit 7.10 shows several PORT performance screens for the Xavier Student Investment Fund (XSIF). The top screen in the exhibit shows the total return of the fund relative to the Russell 1000 index (RIY). The Russell 1000 index consists of the largest 1,000 companies of the Russell 3000. For the period from 9/6/2006 to 9/6/2013, the XSIF fund outperformed the Russell with a total return of 68.30 percent compared to 51.17 percent for the index. The lower screen in Exhibit 7.10 also shows for the seven-year period a lower annualized standard deviation of 25.92 for the XSIF fund compared to 27.80 for the Russell (last two columns). With the higher return and lower risk, the XSIF fund has a larger Sharpe index, 0.50, than the index, 0.40. Note, however, that over the more recent periods of six months and YTD, the XSIF underperformed the Russell and had a lower Sharpe index. Over the three-month period, however, the fund rebounded, outperforming the Russell 1000 with higher returns, lower standard deviations, and a higher Sharpe index.

In addition to performance, Bloomberg's PORT screen can also be used to analyze other features of a portfolio, such as the portfolio composition, sector breakdowns, and attributes. Bloomberg portfolio construction using the PRTU screen and portfolio analysis using screens on the PMEN menu and PORT are described in Chapter 2 and in the Bloomberg exhibit box in this chapter: "Bloomberg Portfolio Screens for Evaluating Portfolios: PRTU and PORT." The box in this chapter and the Bloomberg screens in Bloomberg Web Exhibit 7.1 found on the text Web site show more of the features of the XSIF fund.

Conclusion

In this chapter, we started our analysis of portfolios by examining how to evaluate portfolios of risky securities in terms of their expected returns and risk. In contrast to individual securities, a portfolio's risk characteristics depend on the correlations of the security returns. If two securities are perfectly negatively correlated, a portfolio can be constructed with zero risk. We then introduced a risk-free security and showed how investors can obtain different return-risk opportunities by varying their investment funds between the risk-free security and a portfolio of risky stocks. In the next chapter, we continue our analysis of portfolios by examining Markowitz portfolio selection for determining the allocation of securities making up the portfolio.

EXHIBIT 7.10   Return Performances of the XSIF Fund and the Russell 1000—Bloomberg
PORT Screen

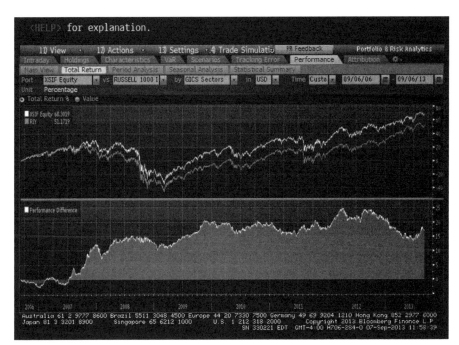

(a)

(b)

BLOOMBERG PORTFOLIO SCREENS FOR EVALUATING PORTFOLIOS: PRTU AND PORT

PRTU

On the Bloomberg PRTU screen, you can set up a stock or fixed-income portfolio. Once loaded, you can analyze the portfolio using screens from the PMEN menu. See Chapter 2 for a description on how to construct portfolios using PRTU.

Historical Portfolio Returns

To analyze the past return performances of a portfolio, a history of portfolio rates of return needs to be created in PRTU. With history, the historical performance of the portfolio can then be analyzed from the performance tab on the PORT screen.

Steps for Creating Historical Data for Portfolios in PRTU

Bring up the PRTU screen for your portfolio. On the screen, change the date in the amber "Date" box (e.g., Month/Day/2006). Click the "Edit" tab (if it appears) and then the "Actions" tab. From the "Actions" dropdown, select "Import" to bring up the import box. On the import box, select "Portfolio" from the "Source" dropdown, the name of your portfolio from the "Name" dropdown, change the date (e.g., back to the current period), hit the "Import" tab, and then click "Save." You should now have a portfolio with historical data.

PORT

On the Bloomberg "Portfolio Risk & Analytics Screen (PORT)," you can evaluate portfolios in depth. By using the screen tabs (e.g., "Holdings," "Characteristics," "Performance," and "Attributions"), you can evaluate the features, drivers, and historical performances of the portfolio, securities in the portfolio, and the portfolio's index. (Note: Many of these same functions can be accessed directly: PORT HD to access holdings, PORT CH to access characteristics, and PORT PA to access performance attributes.)

PORT Tabs:
1. For portfolio securities: Holdings tab, "by none."
2. For Sector breakdown: Holdings tab, "by GIC Sectors."
3. For Size: Holdings tab, "by Market Cap."
4. For portfolio features: Characteristics tab, "Main View," "Portfolio vs Index" (e.g., INDU), "by GIC Sectors."
5. For performance: Performance tab, "Main View," "Portfolio vs None."
6. For performance: Performance tab, "Total Return," "Portfolio vs Index" (e.g., INDU), Time = MTD, YTD, and Custom (for Custom, the select time period must be within the period history of the portfolio created in PRTU).
7. For performance: Performance tab, "Statistical Summary," "Portfolio vs Index" (e.g., INDU).

8. For performance: Performance tab, "Seasonal Analysis."
9. Performance tab, "Period Analysis."
10. For portfolio features: Attribution tab, "Main View," "Portfolio vs None," Time = MTD, YTD, and Custom.
11. For portfolio features: Attribution tab, "Main View," "Portfolio vs None," Time = MTD, YTD, and Custom.
12. For portfolio features: Attribution tab, "Attribution Summary," "Portfolio vs None," Time = MTD, YTD, and Custom.
13. For portfolio features: Attribution tab, "Attribution Summary," "Portfolio vs Index" (e.g., INDU), Time = MTD, YTD, and Custom.

Other PMEN Screens for Portfolio Analysis

Other screens of note on the PMEN menu screen are Portfolio Display (PDSP), Portfolio News (NPH), Events Calendar (EVTS), Expected Cash Flow (PCF), and Summary Reports (PRTS). (Some of these screens can be found from the PMEN screen by clicking a white heading (e.g., "Performance & Attributions"). Many of these screens have tabs for accessing different information, sending information to Excel, and downloading information to PDF and Excel reports.

Importing PRTU Portfolios to Other Screens

As noted in Chapter 2, once a portfolio is created, you can export it to other screens or import your portfolio if you are on another screen. For example, if you want to analyze a portfolio created in PRTU using relative valuation, you could select a stock in the portfolio (e.g., Apple), access the stock's menu (AAPL <Equity> <Enter>), and then bring up the stock's RV menu. On the RV menu of the stock, you can then import the portfolio by selecting "Portfolio" from the dropdown "Comp Source" tab and the name of the portfolio from the dropdown "Name" menu. Similarly, you can also import the portfolio from other screens, such as CORR, PC, CACT, MOST, FMAP, EVTS, MRR, and MMAP screens, and also from Excel using the Bloomberg Excel Add-In.

Bloomberg Screens for Investment Funds

The portfolio of an investment fund can be analyzed using PORT, as well as other screens found on the fund's menu. See Bloomberg exhibit box in Chapter 5: Bloomberg Investment Fund Screens.

Bloomberg Material on Funds

- **FSRC**: FSRC generates a list of funds based on specific search criteria. See Chapter 5.
- **PSRT** searches for companies with specific public portfolio/holder information. You can search by keyword and perform advanced searches based on one's criteria.

(Continued)

Other Screens for Evaluating Investment Fund Portfolios

RV: The RV screen on a fund's menu screen (Fund Ticker <Equity> <Enter>) can be used to rank a fund relative to its peers using the portfolio ranking indexes of Sharpe, Treynor, and Jensen.

   FSCO: The FSCO screen scores and ranks funds belonging to the same peer group based on a combination of weighted indicators.

   See Bloomberg Web Exhibit 7.1.

Web Site Information

1. For financial information on stocks, see:
   - http://seekingalpha.com
   - http://bigcharts.marketwatch.com
   - http://www.morningstar.com
2. Market Browser: Stock and other security data: Download program for Market Browser: http://www.marketbrowser.com

Selected References

Brennan, Michael J. 1975. The optimal number of securities in a risky asset portfolio when there are fixed cost of transacting: theory and some empirical results. *Journal of Financial and Quantitative Analysis* 10 (September): 483–496.

Cahart, Mark M. 1997. On persistence in mutual fund performance. *Journal of Finance* 52 (March): 57–82.

Francis, Jack C., and S. H. Archer. 1979. *Portfolio Analysis*. Englewood Cliffs, NJ: Prentice-Hall.

Goetzman, William, and Roger G. Ibbotson. 1994. Do winners repeat? *Journal of Portfolio Management* 20 (Winter): 9–18.

Jensen, Michael. 1968. The performance of mutual funds in the period 1945–1964. *Journal of Finance* (May): 389–416.

Malkiel, Burton G. 1995. Return from investing in equity mutual funds, 1971–1991. *Journal of Finance* 50: 549–572.

Markowitz, Harry. 1959. *Portfolio Selection: Efficient Diversification of Investments*. Hoboken, NJ: John Wiley & Sons.

Sharpe, William F. 1966. Mutual fund performance. *Journal of Business* 39 (January): 118–138.

Tobin, James. 1958. Liquidity preference and behavior towards risk. *The Review of Economic Studies* 26 (January): 65–86.

Treynor, Jack L. 1973. How to rate management of investment funds. *Harvard Business Review* 43 (January): 63–75.

Bloomberg Exercises

1. Select an equity investment fund of interest (use SECF and click Funds tab) and examine its price and volatility for different periods and frequencies using the

GV screen. Fund Ticker <Equity> <Enter> and then click GV and select the following:

- Historical volatility and price from "Type" dropdown.
- Statistics check box to show Histogram window.

2. Select a stock of interest and compare its correlation with the market, systematic risk (use R^2), alpha, and beta with its peers using the PC screen: Stock ticker <Equity> <Enter>; PC.

3. Study the historical correlation over different periods of the top 10 stocks by market cap making up the S&P 500 using the CORR screen. CORR <Enter>; click the red "Create New" tab; click "Add from Source"; select Equity Index under "Source" tab and SPX under "Name" tab; Select "All," and click "Add."

4. Use EQS to find stocks making up the S&P 500 or the Russell 3000 with a market cap greater than $15 billion and then import your stocks into PRTU to form a portfolio.

   - EQS <Enter>; select Standard and Poor's 500 or Russell 3000 from the Indexes tab; in the yellow ribbon box, type Market Cap and enter $15B; save your screen.
   - PRTU <Enter>; click red "Create;" click "Actions" tab and then import stocks (on the settings screen, enable history; see Bloomberg exhibit box: Bloomberg Portfolio Screens for Evaluating Portfolios: PRTU and PORT).

     a. Examine the betas, alphas, systematic risk (R^2) of the stocks in your portfolio using the PC screen: Bring up the equity screen for one of the stocks in the portfolio (Stock Ticker <Equity> <Enter>); type in PC; on the PC screen, import your portfolio from the "Peer Source" yellow dropdown tab. On the PC screen, choose a time period for your analysis and then select alpha, beta, and R^2 from the Calculation dropdown tab.

     b. Evaluate your portfolio's past performance relative to an index (e.g., Dow Jones (INDU)) using the PORT screen over different time periods: Performance tab, "Total Return," "Portfolio vs Index" (e.g., INDU), Time = MTD, YTD, and Custom (for Custom, the select time period must be within the period history of the portfolio created in PRTU).

     c. Evaluate your portfolio's performance relative to your index using PORT: Performance tab, "Statistical Summary," "Portfolio vs Index" (e.g., INDU).

     d. Examine the top news related to the stocks in your portfolio using the "Portfolio News Screen" (NPH) to see if there is any news to explain a stock's performance.

     e. Examine the top movers and laggers in your portfolio for different periods using the MRR screen: MRR <Enter>; select "Portfolio" from "Source" tab and select time period.

     f. Check current prices and news for the stock in your portfolio using MOST: MOST <Enter>; load the stocks of your portfolio from the amber tab (left side of screen).

     g. Using MMAP, study some of the features of the stocks in your portfolio such as P/e, eps growth, beta, and total returns for different periods: MMAP

<Enter>; select Portfolio from "Source" dropdown, the name of your port-folio from "Name" dropdown, and characteristic from "Analyze" dropdown.

   h. Use CACT and EVTS screen to see if there were any corporate actions and events that could explain the performances of some of the stocks in your portfolio: CACT <Enter>, select Portfolio from "Source" dropdown, the name of your portfolio from "Name" dropdown, and select time period.

5. The performances of funds by type can be found on the Bloomberg Fund Heat Map Screen, FMAP.

   a. Use the screen to identify several equity funds: FMAP <Enter>, click "Objec-tive" in "View By" dropdown and United States in "Region" dropdown, and then click "Equity" and type (e.g., Growth). Select one of the funds and study it (the fund's ticker can be found on the description page) using the functions on the fund's menus screen (Fund Ticker <Equity> <Enter>). Functions to include: DES, historical fund analysis (HFA), and price graph (GP).

   b. Evaluate the fund using the Holdings, Performance, and Characteristics tabs on the fund's PORT screen.

   c. Examine the fund's total returns for different periods and frequencies relative to the S&P 500, Russell 3000, other indexes, and other funds using the COMP screen: Fund Ticker <Equity> <Enter> and then click COMP.

   d. Using the HRA or Beta screen, determine the fund's characteristic line with the S&P 500, its systematic risk (R^2), and unsystematic risk.

   e. Using your selected fund's RV screen, compare the fund with other similar funds in terms of Sharpe, Treynor, and Jensen ranking indexes. On the RV screen, type in Sharpe, Treynor, and Jensen in the amber box to find those indexes or select Return/Risk from the Theme dropdown.

6. The FSCO screen scores and ranks funds belonging to the same peer group based on a combination of weighted indicators. Select a fund style using FSCO, select a fund style and category (e.g., open-end, growth, large cap fund domiciled in the United States), and then score them in terms of indexes (e.g., Sharpe, Treynor, and Jensen indexes).

7. Select one of the top-ranked funds you identified in Exercise 6 (or another fund of interest) and evaluate it using PORT. In your evaluation, use some of the following PORT tabs:

   a. Holdings tab, "by none."

   b. Holdings tab, "by GIC Sectors."

   c. Holdings tab, "by Market Cap."

   d. Characteristics tab, "Main View," "Portfolio vs Index" (e.g., Dow (INDU)), "by GIC Sectors."

   e. Characteristics tab, "Main View," "Portfolio vs Index" (e.g., Dow (INDU)), "by GIC Sectors."

   f. Performance tab, "Main View," "Portfolio vs None."

   g. Performance tab, "Total Return," "Portfolio vs Index" (e.g., INDU), Time = MTD, YTD, and Custom.

    h. Performance tab, "Statistical Summary," "Portfolio vs Index" (e.g., Dow (INDU)).

    i. Performance tab, "Seasonal Analysis."

    j. Performance tab, "Period Analysis."

    k. Attribution tab, "Main View," "Portfolio vs None," Time = MTD, YTD, and Custom.

    l. Attribution tab, "Main View," "Portfolio vs None," Time = MTD, YTD, and Custom.

    m. Attribution tab, "Attribution Summary," "Portfolio vs None," Time = MTD, YTD, and Custom.

    n. Attribution tab, "Attribution Summary," "Portfolio vs Index" (e.g., Dow (INDU)), Time = MTD, YTD, and Custom.

8. Use the Bloomberg fund search screen, FSRC, to search for the following open-end equity fund: Fund Type: Open-End; Classification/Fund Asset Class Focus: Equity; Classification/General Attribute: Index Fund; Country of Domicile: United States; Screening Criteria (enter in amber box): total return for one year of greater than X% (e.g., 20%). You may want to save the search. To do so, go to the "Action" tab and click "Save As."

    a. Using this screen, examine several of the funds. Select one of the funds and study it using the functions on the fund's menus screen (Fund Ticker <Equity> <Enter>). Functions to include are DES, fund holdings (MHD), Beta or HRA, relative valuation (RV), and price graph (GP).

    b. Examine the fund's total returns for different periods and frequencies relative to the S&P 500 using the COMP screen: Fund Ticker <Equity> <Enter> and then click COMP.

    c. Evaluate the fund's performance using PORT: Performance tab, "Total Return," "Portfolio vs Index" (e.g., Dow (INDU)), Time = MTD, YTD, and Custom; Performance tab, "Statistical Summary," "Portfolio vs Index" (e.g., Dow (INDU)).

    d. Using your selected fund's RV screen, compare the fund with other similar funds in terms of Sharpe, Treynor, and Jensen ranking indexes. On the RV screen, type in Sharpe, Treynor, and Jensen in the amber box to find those indexes.

9. Use the Bloomberg advanced PSRT screen to search for an equity mutual fund in a particular area (country or city) and then analyze the fund using PORT: PSRT <Enter>; Mutual Funds (Source); Click "Metro Area"; click fund's name; click portfolio analytics to bring up the PORT screen.

10. Construct your own equity portfolio and then analyze it using PORT. In constructing you own portfolio, consider using the equity search screen (EQS), FMAP to identify stocks that make up different types of funds, or the stocks making up indexes. In your PORT analysis, include some of the following tabs:

    a. Holdings tab, "by none."

    b. Holdings tab, "by GIC Sectors."

    c. Holdings tab, "by Market Cap."

d. Characteristics tab, "Main View," "Portfolio vs Index" (e.g., Dow (INDU)), "by GIC Sectors."
e. Characteristics tab, "Main View," "Portfolio vs Index" (e.g., Dow (INDU)), "by GIC Sectors."
f. Performance tab, "Main View," "Portfolio vs None."
g. Performance tab, "Total Return," "Portfolio vs Index" (e.g., Dow (INDU)), Time = MTD, YTD, and Custom (for Custom, the select time period must be within the period history of the portfolio created in PRTU).
h. Performance tab, "Statistical Summary," "Portfolio vs Index" (e.g., Dow (INDU)).
i. Performance tab, "Seasonal Analysis."
j. Performance tab, "Period Analysis."
k. Attribution tab, "Main View," "Portfolio vs None," Time = MTD, YTD, and Custom.
l. Attribution tab, "Main View," "Portfolio vs None," Time = MTD, YTD, and Custom.
m. Attribution tab, "Attribution Summary," "Portfolio vs None," Time = MTD, YTD, and Custom.
n. Attribution tab, "Attribution Summary," "Portfolio vs Index" (e.g., Dow (INDU)), Time = MTD, YTD, and Custom.

Create a Launchpad view with pages for one of the portfolios you created in this chapter or for a fund or index. See Chapter 2 for a guide in setting up a Launchpad.

- BLP <Enter>.
- On Launchpad toolbar, click "View" to bring up the toolbar showing the tabs with Views, Pages, Setting, and Tools.
- To import a portfolio, index, or search: Click the "Browser" tab, "Monitor," and the "Launch Component" to bring up a stock monitor screen. This will bring up a box where you can select from a source: portfolios (PRTU), equity searches (EQS), equity indexes, fund screens (FSCR), Bloomberg peers, and other sources.

CHAPTER 8

Portfolio Selection – Markowitz Model

Introduction

In his 1952 seminal article, Harry Markowitz stated that the objective of portfolio selection is to determine the allocation of securities in a portfolio such that it yields the maximum expected return given a specified risk or, alternatively, the minimum portfolio risk given a specified portfolio expected return. Given Equation (7.2) for the portfolio's expected return and Equation (7.11) for the portfolio variance, the Markowitz portfolio selection objective therefore involves determining the weights (w_i) for those equations that yield either the maximum $E(R_p)$ given a specified $V(R_p)$ or the minimum $V(R_p)$ given a specified $E(R_p)$. In this chapter, we examine the Markowitz portfolio selection model for determining optimum portfolio allocations. We begin our analysis by first examining the importance of correlation in determining the different return-risk combinations attainable by varying the security allocations of a two-stock portfolio. With this background, we next examine Markowitz portfolio selection and define an efficiency frontier in terms of that process. We conclude the chapter by extending the selection process to the single-index and multi-index models that were introduced in Chapter 6.

Two-Security Portfolio Return-Risk Relation

As we change the allocation of securities, we change both the portfolio's expected return and risk. How portfolio return and risk change in relation to each other depends on the correlations between the securities. This can be seen by examining the return-risk relationship of a two-security portfolio. Consider first a portfolio formed from two perfectly positively correlated stocks A and B with the following expected returns and variances:

Stock A	Stock B
$E(r_A) = 12\%$	$E(r_B) = 18\%$
$V(r_A) = 16\%$	$V(r_B) = 36\%$
$\sigma(r_A) = 4\%$	$\sigma(r_B) = 6\%$
Correlation:	$Cov(r_A\ r_B) = 24$
	$\rho_{AB} = +1$

The return-risk relation of portfolios formed with these two stocks can be seen by varying the allocations of investment funds between the two stocks. For example, if all investment funds are placed in A ($w_A = 1$, $w_B = 0$), the portfolio return and standard deviation would be equal to A's expected return and standard deviation of 12 percent and 4 percent, respectively. If half of the funds are invested in A and half in B, then the portfolio expected return would be 15 percent and the portfolio standard deviation would be 5 percent:

$$E(R_p) = (0.5)(12\%) + (0.5)(18\%) = 15\%$$

$$\sigma(R_p) = \sqrt{(0.5)^2(16) + (0.5)^2(36) + 2(0.5)(0.5)(24)} = 5\%$$

Finally, if all funds are place in B, then the portfolio return and risk would equal stock B's expected return and standard deviation of 18 percent and 6 percent, respectively. Exhibit 8.1 shows these and other portfolio return-risk combinations obtained by varying funds between A and B, and the figure in Exhibit 8.1 shows a graph of the relationship (note: the relation does not include any short positions; that is, all the weights are nonnegative).

The figure in Exhibit 8.1 shows a positive linear relationship between portfolio return and risk. The linear relationship suggests that the portfolio's return and risk are simply linear combinations of the return and risk of the two securities and do not depend on the correlation between securities. That is, when the correlation coefficient is one, the portfolio variance (or standard deviation) depends only on the securities' variances (or standard deviations). That is:

$$V(R_p) = w_1^2 V(r_1) + w_2^2 V(r_2) + 2w_1 w_2 Cov(r_1 r_2)$$
$$V(R_p) = w_1^2 V(r_1) + w_2^2 V(r_2) + 2w_1 w_2 \rho_{12} \sigma(r_1) \sigma(r_2)$$
$$V(R_p) = w_1^2 \sigma(r_1)^2 + w_2^2 \sigma(r_2)^2 + 2w_1 w_2 (1) \sigma(r_1) \sigma(r_2)$$
$$V(R_p) = [w_1 \sigma(r_1) + w_2 \sigma(r_2)]^2$$
$$\sigma(R_p) = [w_1 \sigma(r_1) + w_2 \sigma(r_2)]$$

EXHIBIT 8.1   Portfolio Return and Risk with Perfect Positive Correlation

Portfolio	w_A	w_B	$E(R_p)$	$\sigma(R_p)$
1	1	0	$E(R_A) = 12\%$	$\sigma(R_A) = 4$
2	0.75	0.25	13.5%	4.5
3	0.5	0.5	15.0%	5.0
4	0.25	0.75	16.5%	5.5
5	0	1	$E(R_B) = 18$	$\sigma(R_B) = 6$

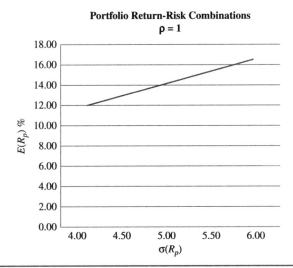

Intuitively, if two securities move in perfect unison with each other, there is no correlation benefit, and therefore the different portfolio return and risk combinations are linear combinations of the two securities' returns and risks.

Consider next the portfolio return-risk relation shown in Exhibit 8.2 where the returns of stocks A and B are assumed to be perfectly negatively correlated (−24 covariance). In this case, the portfolio return-risk relationship is characterized by two linear segments: a negatively sloped segment and a positively sloped segment. The negatively sloped segment extends from the 12 percent and 4 percent return-risk combination obtained by placing all funds in the low return-risk stock A to the 14.4 percent return and zero risk combination on the vertical axis obtained by investing 60 percent in A and 40 percent in B. The positively sloped segment extends from the vertical intercept to the 18 percent and 6 percent return-risk combination obtained by investing all funds in the high return-risk stock B. The positive-sloped portion of the figure includes all efficient portfolios and the negatively sloped portion consists of inefficient portfolios. *Efficient portfolios* are defined as those that yield the maximum return for a given risk, whereas inefficient portfolios are those that yield the minimum return for a given risk. Thus, at the 12 percent, 4 percent coordinate the return of 12 percent

EXHIBIT 8.2 Portfolio Return and Risk with Perfect Negative Correlation

Portfolio	w_A	w_B	$E(R_p)$	$\sigma(R_p)$
1	1	0	$E(R_A) = 12\%$	$\sigma(R_A) = 4$
2	0.8	0.2	13.2%	2
3	0.6	0.4	14.4%	0
4	0.4	0.6	15.6%	2
5	0.2	0.8	16.8%	4
6	0	1	$E(R_B) = 18\%$	$\sigma(R_B) = 6$

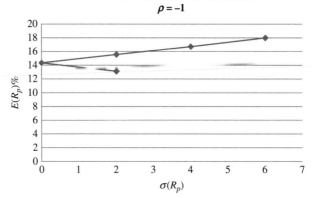

is the lowest return an investor can obtain for assuming a risk of 4. By changing the allocation from $w_A = 1$ and $w_B = 0$, to $w_A = 0.20$ and $w_B = 0.80$, the investor can move up to the positively sloped segment where for a risk of 4 percent the maximum return of 16.8 percent is obtained. Finally, note that the vertical intercept represents a zero risk portfolio. Whenever securities are perfectly negatively correlated, a graph of the portfolio's return-risk relation will always touch the vertical axis.[1]

In Exhibit 8.3, the return-risk relationships for both correlation cases are plotted on the same graph. The two curves define the limits within which all portfolios of these two securities must lie for any intermediate correlation coefficient between $\rho_{AB} = -1$ and $\rho_{AB} = +1$. To fit into the triangle ACB, the curve depicting the return-risk relation for an intermediate correlation has to be convex. This convex relation is illustrated in Exhibit 8.4, where the portfolio return-risk combinations are shown for the case in which the correlation coefficient for stocks A and B is zero. The convex shape of the portfolio return-risk curve means that for equal increases in the portfolio return, the portfolio risk as measured by the standard deviation will increase at an increasing rate. For example, as the portfolio return increases by equal increments of 1.2 percent, the portfolio standard deviation goes from 3.39 percent to 3.93 (change of 0.54), from 3.93 to 4.86 (change of 0.93), and from 4.86 to 6 (change of 1.14).

EXHIBIT 8.3   Portfolio Return and Risk with Different Correlations

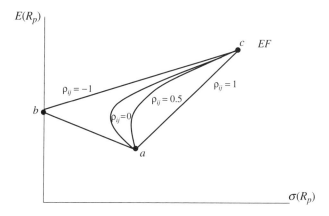

EXHIBIT 8.4   Portfolio Return and Risk with Zero Correlation

Portfolio	w_A	w_B	$E(R_p)$	$\sigma(R_p)$
1	1	0	$E(R_A) = 12\%$	$\sigma(R_A) = 4$
2	0.8	0.2	13.2%	3.42
3	0.6	0.4	14.4%	3.39
4	0.4	0.6	15.6%	3.93
5	0.2	0.8	16.8%	4.86
6	0	1	$E(R_B) = 18\%$	$\sigma(R_B) = 6$

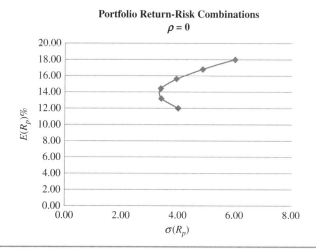

Intuitively, the convex return-risk relation implies that as you move up from the middle of the return-risk graph, you become more specialized in the high return-risk stock. As a result, the portfolio risk takes on progressively more and more of the risk of the high-risk security. In addition, as the portfolio becomes more specialized (and therefore less diversified) it loses the covariance effect. Combined, the increasing proportion allocated to the risky security and the loss of the covariance effect due to specialization causes the portfolio risk to increase at an increasing rate. Since the correlations among many securities are less than one, many portfolio return-risk relations are characterized by this convex relation.

In examining Exhibit 8.3, several additional points should be noted. First, the lower the correlation coefficient, the more dominant the portfolio's return-risk combinations. Thus, for a given risk, over the positively sloped portion of the curves portfolio returns are greater for lower correlation coefficients. Secondly, note that each of the return-risk curves with intermediate correlations has a vertical point (inflection point) where the slope of the curve is zero. This point represents the minimum variance portfolio. For a two-security portfolio, this portfolio can be found with calculus by taking the derivative of the portfolio variance equation with respect to one of the weights, setting the derivative equal to zero, and solving the resulting equation for the weight. Doing this, we obtain:

$$w_A = \frac{\sigma(r_B)^2 - \sigma(r_A)\sigma(r_B)\rho_{AB}}{\sigma(r_B)^2 + \sigma(r_A)^2 - 2\sigma(r_A)\sigma(r_B)\rho_{AB}}$$

Finally, note that each of the return-risk combinations is unique; that is, each return-risk combination is associated with one allocation. This is because we have limited our analysis to two securities. If we expand our portfolio to more than two securities, then we will find that there are a number of allocations that can yield the same portfolio return and a number of allocations that can yield the same portfolio risk; that is, when the number of securities in a portfolio exceeds two, then the portfolio selection problem is one of determining the allocation that will yield an efficient portfolio—Markowitz portfolio selection.

Markowitz Portfolio Selection

Math Approach

There are several approaches that can be used to solve for the security allocations that satisfy the Markowitz portfolio selection objective. One of these is the mathematical approach and another is quadratic programming. The math approach uses differential calculus to find the allocation that will minimize the portfolio variance subject to the constraints that the weights sum to one and a specified portfolio return is attained, or the allocation that will maximize the portfolio return subject to the constraints that the weights sum to one and a specified portfolio variance is attained.

Thus, for a three-stock portfolio, the objective of portfolio variance minimization would be to solve for the w_1, w_2, and w_3 allocations that would yield the minimum portfolio (Min V_p), subject to the constraints that w_1, w_2, and w_3 sum to one and yield a specified portfolio return, $E_p{}^*$:

Portfolio Inputs:

$$\text{Given Estimates: } V_1, V_2, V_3, C_{12}, C_{13}, C_{23}$$

Objective Function:

$$\text{Minimize } V_p = w_1^2 V_1 + w_2^2 V_2 + w_3^2 V_3 + 2w_1 w_2 C_{12} + 2w_1 w_3 C_{13} + 2w_2 w_3 C_{23}$$

where:

$$V_p = V(R_p)$$
$$V_i = V(r_i)$$
$$C_{ij} = Cov(r_i r_j)$$

First constraint:

$$w_1 + w_2 + w_3 = 1$$

Second constraint:

$$w_1 E_1 + w_2 E_2 + w_3 E_3 = E_p{}^*$$

where:

$$E_i = E(r_i)$$

The math approach for portfolio maximization given a specified portfolio variance is similar to the variance minimization approach. In this case, the objective function is the portfolio expected return, and the constraint is the portfolio variance. The portfolio return maximization approach is consistent with the portfolio variance minimization approach, yielding the same allocations as the portfolio variance approach.

This constrained optimization problem can be solved mathematically using the Lagrangian technique. The approach is presented in Appendix 8A (text Web site) along with an example. The approach requires using matrix algebra to solve a set of equations simultaneously. The Bloomberg Exhibit box, "Using the Bloomberg CORR Screen and Excel to Solve for Markowitz Efficient Portfolios," explains how to download a variance-covariance matrix for a portfolio from its CORR screen to Excel and then explains how to use Excel matrix multiplication commands to solve for a Markowitz efficient portfolio using the math approach. See the supplemental Appendix B (text Web site) on matrix algebra and for a listing of matrix algebra commands in Excel.

The math approach for solving for Markowitz efficient portfolios is capable of handling large portfolios. Its limitation is that the solutions do not necessarily exclude negative weights. Thus, it is possible to obtain an optimum portfolio that requires taking a short position in a poor security and using the proceeds to invest in other securities in the portfolio. Since most investors do not consider shorting poor securities, the mathematical approach may not be practical.

USING THE BLOOMBERG CORR SCREEN AND EXCEL TO SOLVE FOR MARKOWITZ EFFICIENT PORTFOLIOS

1. The CORR screen can be used to create and save a number of correlation matrices for securities, indexes, currencies, interest rates, and commodities. As noted in Chapter 6, the matrix also shows a variance-covariance matrix (Cov) for portfolios up to 10 stocks.
2. A portfolio created in PRTU can be imported into CORR. To import: (1) Click "Create New" tab; (2) Select dates and period for statistical analysis (e.g., Date Range: 8/5/2006 to 8/8/2013 and weekly periods); (3) in Matrix Securities Box, click "Symmetric Matrix box," and "Add from Sources" tab, Select "Portfolio," Name of Portfolio (e.g., Blue Rock), click "Select All," and click "Update."
3. On the CORR screen, you can obtain the variance-covariance matrix by selecting "Covariance" from the dropdown "Calculations" tab.
4. Matrices in CORR can be exported to Excel by clicking "Export to Excel" in the dropdown "Export" tab in the far right corner of the screen.
5. A *coefficient matrix*, **A**, formed from a variance-covariance matrix and its inverse, $\mathbf{A}^{-1}$, can be used to solve for the Markowitz efficient portfolio; these matrices can be created in Excel.

See Appendix 8A for an explanation of the math approach and Appendix B for a primer on matrix algebra and matrix Excel commands.

See Bloomberg Web Exhibit 8.1.

BLOOMBERG SCREENS FOR THE STOCK RETURNS OF A PORTFOLIO

PORT Screen, Performance Tab

The PORT screen can used to find historical returns of the portfolio and the returns on the stock:

- For portfolio: Performance tab, "Total Return," "Portfolio vs Index" (e.g., Dow (INDU)).
- For stocks: Performance tab, "Main View," "By" dropdown: None, "Portfolio vs None."

- Time = MTD, YTD, and Custom (for Custom, the select time period must be within the period history of the portfolio created in PRTU).
- Note: The Heat Map for the portfolio and stocks can be uploaded by clicking the "Chart" icon on the right.

MRR Screen

The MRR can be used to find average returns for stocks for different time periods. MRR <Enter>; select "Portfolio" from Source tab and your portfolio from the "Name" tab; select the time period for your analysis.

DDM Screen

The DDM estimates a stock's intrinsic value using a three-stage growth model. You can input different values for the lengths of each growth period, growth rates, and discount rates. The DDM also calculated an IRR that can be used as an estimate of expected rate. See Bloomberg exhibit box in Chapter 3.
    See Bloomberg Web Exhibit 8.2.

Quadratic Programming Approach

An alternative to the mathematical approach is quadratic programming (QP). QP is an algorithm that iteratively solves for the security weights that yield the minimum portfolio variance subject to three constraints: The weights sum to one, they yield a specified portfolio expected return, and each weight is nonnegative. For a three-stock portfolio, the QP approach can be defined as follows:

Portfolio Inputs:

$$\text{Given Estimates: } V_1, V_2, V_3, C_{12}, C_{13}, C_{23}$$

Objective Function:

$$\text{Minimize: } V_p = w_1^2 V_1 + w_2^2 V_2 + w_3^2 V_3 + 2w_1 w_2 C_{12} + 2w_1 w_3 C_{13} + 2w_2 w_3 C_{23}$$

First constraint:

$$w_1 + w_2 + w_3 = 1$$

Second constraint:

$$w_1 E_1 + w_2 E_2 + w_3 E_3 = E_p^*$$

Third constraint of nonnegative weights:

$$w_1 \geq 0; \quad w_2 \geq 0; \quad w_3 \geq 0$$

With the nonnegative weight constraints, quadratic programming provides a more practical approach to constructing portfolios that satisfy the Markowitz objective.

Excel Solver Approach: Bloomberg's Asset Allocation Optimizer Template

In Excel, efficient portfolios (maximum E_p^* given V_p or minimum V_p^* given E_p) with nonnegative weight constraints can be generated using the Excel Solver Add-In. Such programs yield results similar to QP-generated portfolios. A Bloomberg Excel program that uses Excel Solver for solving for such portfolios, "Asset Allocation Optimizer," can be downloaded from the Bloomberg Excel Template library found on the DAPI screen (DAPI <Enter>; Click Excel Template Library and Portfolios topic and then select "Asset Allocation Optimizer.") The template is shown in Exhibit 8.5. To use the program, the user:

1. Inputs the stock tickers (for stocks, ticker with the "Equity" moniker, for indexes, ticker with "Index" moniker, etc.).
2. Inputs average returns or expected returns.
3. Selects the time period for calculating the variance-covariance matrix (the template in Exhibit 8.5 shows the correlation matrix).
4. Selects minimum weight and maximum weight constraints for each stock; here the user can set the minimum weights to zero and the maximum weights at 99 percent (or another specified constraint).
5. Inputs the risk-free rate and values for the optimization programs: the portfolio standard deviation for portfolio maximization optimization and portfolio return for portfolio variance minimization.
6. Clicks "Optimize Weights" tab to run the program.

Exhibit 8.5 shows the optimum solutions for the 10 stocks making up the Blue Rock Fund. The variance-covariance matrix is calculated for the time period from 8/5/2006 to 8/8/2013 (weekly prices are used), the expected stock returns are based on averages over a more recent time period, the specified portfolio return is 15.5 percent, and the specified annualized portfolio standard deviation is 17 percent.[2] As shown at the bottom of the table in Exhibit 8.5, the optimum portfolio weights for the variance minimization are 30.7 percent in CVS, 21.4 percent in Disney, 22 percent in Johnson & Johnson, and 25.9 percent in Kroger.

The ex-post total returns from the one-year period from 8/13/12 to 8/13/13 and for the three-year period from 8/13/10 to 8/13/13 for the Markowitz efficient portfolio and the S&P 500 are shown in Exhibit 8.6 (Bloomberg's PORT screen, Performance tab, and Total Return tab). As shown in the exhibit, the back testing results show the portfolio out-performs the market for both the one-year period (total return of 44.82 percent compared to 16.11 percent total return for S&P 500) and the three-year period (total return of 96.22 percent compared to 56.03 percent total return for S&P 500). Using the Bloomberg PORT screen (Performance tab and Statistics Summary tab) the

EXHIBIT 8.5 Markowitz Efficient Portfolios Generated Using the Asset Allocation Optimizer Excel Program

(a)

Risk	Return	ADM	AFL	CVS	Dis	Duke	J&J	Kroger	Microsoft	PG	Exxon
13.8%	9.8%	0.0%	0.0%	14.6%	0.0%	13.9%	38.6%	5.4%	0.2%	27.3%	0.0%
13.9%	10.5%	0.0%	0.0%	18.3%	0.0%	10.2%	39.5%	9.7%	0.0%	22.8%	0.0%
14.1%	11.2%	0.0%	0.0%	22.2%	0.0%	6.4%	39.5%	13.1%	0.0%	18.8%	0.0%
14.4%	11.9%	0.0%	0.0%	24.4%	2.5%	4.2%	38.4%	15.3%	0.0%	15.1%	0.0%
14.8%	12.6%	0.0%	0.0%	25.6%	5.8%	2.1%	37.6%	17.5%	0.0%	11.4%	0.0%
15.3%	13.4%	0.0%	0.0%	27.4%	9.7%	0.0%	35.8%	19.5%	0.0%	7.7%	0.0%
15.8%	14.1%	0.0%	0.0%	28.3%	13.2%	0.0%	33.8%	21.8%	0.0%	2.9%	0.0%
16.3%	14.8%	0.0%	0.0%	29.7%	17.2%	0.0%	29.8%	23.2%	0.0%	0.0%	0.0%
17.0%	15.5%	0.0%	0.0%	30.7%	21.4%	0.0%	22.0%	25.9%	0.0%	0.0%	0.0%
17.7%	16.2%	0.0%	0.0%	31.9%	25.6%	0.0%	14.3%	28.2%	0.0%	0.0%	0.0%
18.5%	16.9%	0.0%	0.0%	33.1%	29.8%	0.0%	6.6%	30.4%	0.0%	0.0%	0.0%
19.3%	17.6%	0.0%	0.0%	33.4%	36.1%	0.0%	0.0%	30.4%	0.0%	0.0%	0.0%
20.9%	18.3%	0.0%	0.0%	28.3%	55.3%	0.0%	0.0%	16.4%	0.0%	0.0%	0.0%
23.5%	19.0%	0.0%	0.0%	23.2%	74.2%	0.0%	0.0%	2.6%	0.0%	0.0%	0.0%
27.4%	19.8%	0.0%	0.0%	1.0%	99.0%	0.0%	0.0%	0.0%	0.0%	0.0%	0.0%

(b)

(Continued)

EXHIBIT 8.5 (*Continued*)

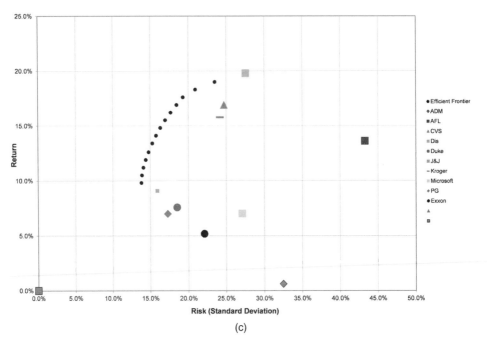

(c)

Markowitz portfolio has a beta close to one based on year-to-date calculation, as well as a very large alpha, suggesting abnormal returns.

Elton, Gruber, and Padberg also have developed an algorithm based on the single-index model (examined later) for determining the best efficient portfolio. The technique they derive for generating efficient portfolios, in turn, can also be constrained so that the weights are nonnegative. The technique is presented in Appendix 8B (text Web site) and its application is presented later in this chapter.

Efficiency Frontier

The Markowitz portfolio selection objective can be restated as one of deriving an efficiency frontier, EF. An efficiency frontier is a graph showing the portfolio expected return, $E(R_p)$, and standard deviation, $\sigma(R_p)$, combinations that are Markowitz efficient; that is, satisfy the Markowitz objective of maximum $E(R_p)$ given a specified $V(R_p)$, or minimum $V(R_p)$ given a specified $E(R_p)$.

There are three steps involved in generating an efficiency frontier. The first step is to estimate the portfolio inputs: $E(r_i)$, $V(r_i)$, and $Cov(r_i\ r_j)$. These parameters can be estimated using either historical averages or a regression model. There are several regression models that can be used. The simplest is the single-index model in which each security's return is regressed against the market return. As discussed in the next section, the single-index model reduces the number of estimates needed to generate

EXHIBIT 8.6 Ex-Post Performance, 8/13/2012–8/12/13 Markowitz Portfolio (Blue Rock Equity) and S&P 500

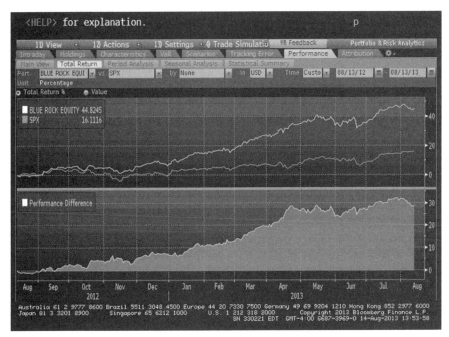

(a)

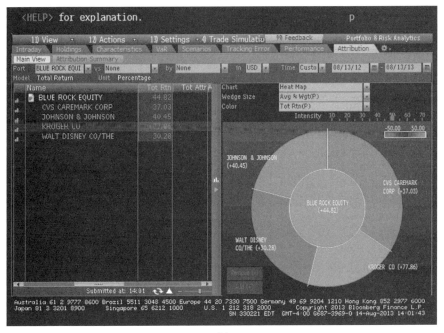

(b)

(*Continued*)

EXHIBIT 8.6   (*Continued*)

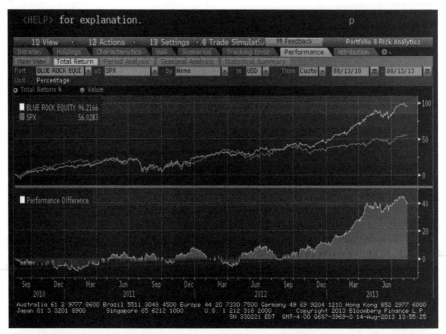

(c)

Portfolio Statistics	3 Months Port	Bench	6 Months Port	Bench	Year To Date Port	Bench	3 Year(s) Port	Bench
5. Return								
Total Return	5.56	5.19	24.28	10.50	34.63	15.17	96.22	56.03
Maximum Return	2.09	1.60	2.34	1.60	2.34	2.40	4.40	4.31
Minimum Return	-4.01	-2.42	-4.01	-2.42	-4.01	-2.42	-4.79	-6.23
Mean Return (Annualized)	37.32	33.33	87.69	33.77	98.83	38.85	39.14	25.33
Mean Excess Return (Annualized)	3.01		40.35		43.08		11.03	
6. Risk								
Standard Deviation (Annualized)	18.94	12.75	17.18	12.95	16.23	12.77	17.72	19.04
Downside Risk (Annualized)	14.65	9.83	13.10	9.98	12.29	9.56	12.90	13.88
Skewness	-1.01	-.80	-.84	-.75	-.80	-.48	-.34	-.40
VaR 95% (ex-post)	-1.31	-1.02	-1.34	-1.09	-1.22	-1.04	-1.34	-1.57
Tracking Error (Annualized)	10.97		11.05		10.64		11.36	
7. Risk/Return								
Sharpe Ratio	1.96	2.60	5.10	2.60	6.08	3.03	2.20	1.32
Jensen Alpha	-3.88		53.31		61.29		19.96	
Information Ratio	.27		3.65		4.05		.97	
Treynor Measure	.30		.86		1.03		.52	
Beta (ex-post)	1.24		1.02		.96		.76	
Correlation	0.8306		0.7658		0.7560		0.8112	

(d)

EXHIBIT 8.7 Efficiency Frontier

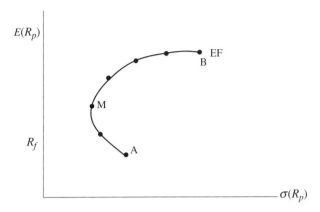

efficient portfolios, and it has been shown to lead to better estimates of the portfolio inputs than historical averages. Some practitioners also use a multi-index model in which each security's return is regressed against several explanatory variables.

Once the expected returns, variances, and covariances of the securities included in the portfolio are estimated, the next step is to generate Markowitz efficient portfolios. As noted above, this can be done using either the math approach, quadratic programming, or with Excel Solver. With any of these approaches, one would first specify a number of portfolio expected returns (or variances), then solve for the weights that would yield the minimum portfolio variance (or maximum portfolio return) for each return (or variance). Each portfolio return and variance would be either a Markowitz efficient or inefficient portfolio. The last step is to plot each portfolio's expected return and standard deviation (not portfolio variance) to generate the efficiency frontier.

The EF curve shown in Exhibit 8.7 depicts a typical efficiency frontier. The curve has features similar to the return-risk graph for a two-security portfolio previously discussed. First, like the two-security return-risk graph, EF is characterized by both a negatively sloped portion and positively sloped portion. The negatively sloped portion of EF represents the inefficient portfolios [minimum $E(R_p)$, given $\sigma(R_p)$], whereas the positively-sloped portion shows the efficient portfolios. Second, the efficiency frontier, like the portfolio return and risk curve for a two-security portfolio, is convex from below, except for cases in which the securities are perfectly positively or negatively correlated. As discussed with the two-security portfolio, the convexity of the efficiency frontier is explained by the increase specialization in the high-risk security and the loss of the covariance effect that occurs as one moves up the efficiency frontier. Finally, the efficiency frontier has a vertical segment (inflection point) that defines the minimum variance portfolio. The efficiency frontier and table for the portfolio in Exhibit 8.5 generated by using the Bloomberg "Asset Allocation Optimizer" is shown in Exhibit 8.5c.

EXHIBIT 8.8   Best Efficiency Portfolio

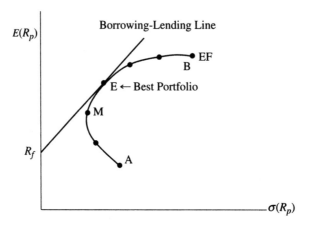

Best Efficient Portfolio

All portfolios along the positively sloped portion of the efficiency frontier are Markowitz efficient; that is, all have the maximum $E(R_p)$ given $V(R_p)$, or minimum $V(R_p)$ given $E(R_p)$. From this set of efficient portfolios, it is possible to determine the best portfolio by using the concept of portfolio ranking examined in Chapter 7. This can be seen in Exhibit 8.8, in which portfolio E represents the best portfolio. This is because the borrowing and lending line constructed with portfolio E has the steepest slope (largest λ). Thus, the return-risk combinations available with portfolio E and a risk-free security dominate the return-risk opportunities available from any other efficient portfolio and the risk-free security. If the efficiency frontier is convex (as we expect for many portfolios), then the best portfolio, such as E, can be determined at the point of tangency of the efficiency frontier and the borrowing and lending line. Furthermore, if the efficiency frontier is convex, then the best portfolio would be defined as one of the middle points on EF (not at a corner), implying that the best portfolio would be diversified.

Efficiency Frontiers for Stocks with Perfect Positive and Negative Correlations

It should be noted that if the securities in the portfolio are perfectly positively correlated, then the efficiency frontier is linear and the best portfolio will be one that is at one of the corners. Since the corner points of an efficiency frontier define a one-security portfolio (either the low return-risk security or the high return-risk security), the best portfolio therefore consists of only one security (see Exhibit 8.9). Thus, if the securities in the portfolio are perfectly positively correlated, then there is no benefit to diversification and the best portfolio consists of either the low return-risk security or the high return-risk security. This observation confirms a previously stated observation that if securities are moving in unison, there is no diversification benefit and

EXHIBIT 8.9 Efficiency Frontier with Perfect Positive Correlation

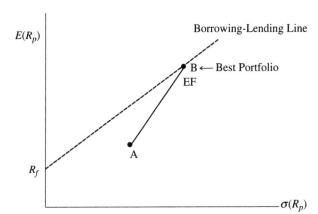

a portfolio with a large number of perfectly positively correlated securities would be superfluous.

Finally, note that if the securities are perfectly negatively correlated, then the best portfolio (i.e., the one with the steepest borrowing-lending line) would be the zero risk portfolio obtained with limited diversification in two securities that are perfectly negatively correlated (see Exhibit 8.10). In this case, if the securities are in fact perfectly negatively correlated, or if two perfectly negatively correlated positions are formed (e.g., long stock position and a short stock position formed with stock option positions), then an arbitrage opportunity would exist if the risk-free rate were different than the portfolio rate associated with the zero risk portfolio. For example, if the risk-free rate were less than the zero-risk portfolio's rate, then an arbitrageur would borrow as much as she could to invest in the portfolio. By doing this, the arbitrageur would realize a free lunch: a future dollar return with no risk and no investment—an arbitrage.

EXHIBIT 8.10 Efficiency Frontier with Perfect Negative Correlation

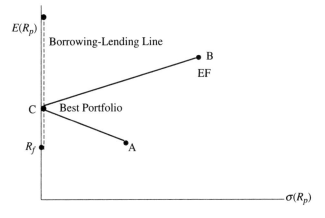

BLOOMBERG'S ASSET ALLOCATION OPTIMIZER

To access Asset Allocation Optimizer Excel template go to the template library found on the DAPI screen (DAPI <Enter>) and click "Excel Template Library," "Equity," and "Portfolios." The template is shown in Exhibit 8.5.

As described in the Template's "Help" sheet, the optimization program uses historical returns or user-customized forecasted returns to generate optimal portfolios. You can customize beginning and ending dates for the historical returns, standard deviation, and correlation matrix data. The spreadsheet uses Microsoft Excel's Solver Add-in to solve portfolio equations to find optimal portfolios. Instructions are provided in Help for uploading the Add-in if it is not already on your Excel spreadsheet. The program generates an optimal portfolio in the "Optimizer tab" and builds an efficient frontier in the "Efficient Frontier" tab. For an example of how to use the template, see Exhibit 8.5, "Markowitz Efficient Portfolios Generated Using the Asset Allocation Optimizer Excel Program."

See Bloomberg Web Exhibit 8.3.

Single-Index Model

Markowitz Portfolio Theory was introduced over 60 years ago. Since then most of the academic research on Markowitz portfolio analysis has focused on how to implement the theory. One area that initially drew the interest of researchers was the simplification of the computational process. Recall that a portfolio with 100 stocks would require estimates of 4,950 covariances, 100 variances, and 100 expected returns. Two models that reduce the number of calculations needed to generate efficient portfolios are the *single-index model* and the *multi-index model*.

Developed by William Sharpe, the single-index model (also called the *diagonal model*) assumes that all securities in a portfolio are related just to the market return and that there is no correlation between the unsystematic risks of securities. Combined, these assumptions imply that comovements between securities in a portfolio are related to a single factor—the market return. As a result, in the single-index model one does not have to estimate the correlations between stocks in the portfolio; instead, one only has to estimate each security's relation to the common factor. In Chapter 6, we examined this model when we looked at estimating stock's expected return, variance, and covariance. Formally, the single-index model assumes that each security i in the portfolio being evaluated is only related to the market as described by the regression model:

$$r_i = \alpha_i + \beta_i R^M + \varepsilon_i \qquad (8.1)$$

The model also assumes that the standard regression assumptions hold for each security in the portfolio and that there is no correlation between the error terms of the stocks; that is, the covariance between the errors of any two securities j and k is zero:

1. Each stock's ε is normally distributed.
2. $E(\varepsilon_i) = 0$, for all securities.
3. Each stock's $V(\varepsilon)$ is constant over all observations.
4. $Cov(R^M, \varepsilon) = E(R^M \varepsilon) = 0$, for all securities.
5. $Cov(\varepsilon_j \varepsilon_k) = 0$.

From these assumptions, the expected returns, variances, and covariances of the stocks in the portfolio are:

$$E(r_i) = \alpha_i + \beta_i E(R^M) \tag{8.2}$$

$$V(r_i) = \beta_i^2 V(R^M) + V(\varepsilon) \tag{8.3}$$

$$Cov(r_j r_k) = \beta_j \beta_k V(R^M) \tag{8.4}$$

As discussed in Chapter 6, Equation (8.3) shows that the variance of each stock in the portfolio depends on its sensitivity to the market as measured by β_i, the variability of the market, $V(R^M)$, and the stock's unsystematic risk as measured by $V(\varepsilon_i)$. Equation (8.4) shows that the comovement of securities is related just to the movement of the market. This result follows directly from the assumption that ε_j is independent of ε_k. This, in turn, implies that when there is no correlation between industry and firm factors among securities, then the comovement of securities is explained only in terms of each security's relative movements to the market. By contrast, if we do assume that the errors are correlated, then each covariance term in the portfolio would include a $Cov(\varepsilon_j \varepsilon_k)$. Such a model that assumes each security in the portfolio is related only to the market but does not assume $Cov(\varepsilon_j \varepsilon_k) = 0$ is known as the *market model*.

Equations (8.2), (8.3), and (8.4) define the expected return, variance, and covariance for the single-index model. To estimate this model requires estimating an α_i, β_i, and $V(\varepsilon_i)$ for each security and then estimating the expected return and variance of the market, $E(R^M)$ and $V(R^M)$. These parameters can be estimated either through a regression analysis using historical data or they can be provided independently. For an n-security portfolio, the number of parameters to estimate is $3n + 2$. In contrast, to estimate the portfolio inputs using historical averages would require $([n^2 - n]/2) + 2n$ estimates. Thus, for a 100-security portfolio, the single-index model would require 302 estimates, and for a 200-security portfolio, it would require 602 estimates. Using averages, on the other hand, would require estimating 5,150 parameters for the 100-security portfolio and 20,300 parameters for the 200-security portfolio. Thus, the single-index model greatly simplifies the computation for generating portfolio inputs.

> **BLOOMBERG REGRESSION SCREENS**
> _____
>
> **HRA and Beta: Bloomberg's Linear Regression Screen**
>
> The Bloomberg HRA and Beta screens show the linear regression of a loaded security and an index or other security. See the Bloomberg exhibit box in Chapter 6: "Bloomberg Regression and Correlation Screens."

Portfolio Return and Risk in Terms of the Single-Index Model

In the single-index model, the portfolio expected return and portfolio variance can be expressed in forms similar to a stock's expected return and variance: Equations (8.2) and (8.3). The simplest way to derive the portfolio return and risk equations is to substitute Equation (8.1) into the expression for portfolio return. Doing this we obtain:

$$R_p = \sum_{i=1}^{n} w_i r_i$$

$$R_p = \sum_{i=1}^{n} w_i [\alpha_i + \beta_i R^M + \varepsilon_i]$$

$$R_p = \sum_{i=1}^{n} w_i \alpha_i + \left[\sum_{i=1}^{n} w_i \beta_i \right] R^M + \sum_{i=1}^{n} w_i \varepsilon_i$$

$$R_p = \alpha_p + \beta_p R^M + \varepsilon_p \tag{8.5}$$

where the portfolio coefficients α_p, β_p, and ε_p are equal to the weighted sum of the stock's parameters.

Equation (8.5) for the portfolio return has the same form as the regression equation for a stock. Thus, by analogy, the portfolio expected return and variance are

$$E(R_p) = \alpha_p + \beta_p E(R^M) \tag{8.6}$$

$$V(R_p) = \beta_p^2 V(R^M) + V(\varepsilon_p) \tag{8.7}$$

where:

$$V(\varepsilon_p) = \sum_{i=1}^{n} w_i^2 V(\varepsilon_i)$$

Equations (8.6) and (8.7) for the portfolio expected return and variance are similar in form to the regression equations for a stock's return and variance. In practice, analysts often regress a portfolio's rate return against the market. When a portfolio's return is regressed against the market, then the intercept and slope of the regression equation (α_p and β_p) can be interpreted as being the weighted α's and β's of the stocks making up the portfolio.

Like the variance equation for an individual security, Equation (8.7) decomposes the portfolio's risk into its systematic and unsystematic risk components. As with a security, the systematic risk of a portfolio is that risk that can be explained by market factors (those factors that affect all securities), whereas unsystematic risk is risk that can be explained by the industry and firm factors affecting each security that makes up the portfolio. In our Chapter 7 discussion of portfolio risk and size, we noted that unsystematic risk can be diversified away with a portfolio consisting of approximately 30 stocks. If the portfolio under consideration is of this size or more, then $V(\varepsilon_p)$ would approach zero.[3] Thus for a portfolio consisting of approximately 30 stocks, the portfolio variance and standard deviation would be:[4]

$$V(R_p) = \beta_p^2 V(R^M)$$
$$\sigma(R_p) = \beta_p \sigma(R^M)$$

Example

Exhibit 8.11(a) shows the α_i, β_i, and $V(\varepsilon_i)$ for the 10 stocks presented in our earlier example. The parameters values were pulled from Bloomberg's RV screen. The Bloomberg values for alpha, beta, and the standard deviation of the error term for the 10 stocks are based on the more recent 2012–2013 time period rather than the 2006–2013 time period used to calculate the average returns, variances, and covariances in our earlier example; the parameter values are also calculated from daily observations compared to weekly that were used in the earlier example. As a result, the expected returns, variances, and covariances for the 10 stocks differ in these examples.

The expected returns and variances for each stock are shown, respectively, in columns (6) and (9). These estimates were generated using Equations (8.2) and (8.3) and by assuming an expected market return, $E(R^M)$, of 16 percent and a market variance, $V(R^M)$ of 20. The stocks are ranked in the order of their Treynor index:

$$\lambda_T = [E(r) - R_f]/\beta.$$

The 45 covariances between the 10 stocks were calculated using Equation (8.4) and are shown in the variance-covariance matrix in Exhibit 8.11(b). For an equally allocated portfolio ($w_i = 1/10$) formed with these 10 stocks, the portfolio beta is

EXHIBIT 8.11 Single-Index Model

$E(r_i) = \alpha_i + \beta_i E(R^M)$, $V(r_i) = \beta_i^2 V(R^M) + V(\epsilon)$, $Cov(r_j r_k) = \beta_j \beta_k V(R^M)$

$E(R^M) = 16\%$, $V(R^M) = 20$, $R_f = 5\%$

(a) Portfolio Inputs

	Stock	Ticker	α_j	β_j	$E(r_j)$	$\beta_j^2 V(R^M)$	$V(\epsilon_j)$	$V(r_j)$	$\sigma(R_j)$	λ_T
1	Archer-Daniels-Midland	ADM	0.0717	1.146	18.41	26.28	5.79	32.07	5.66	11.70
2	Walt Disney	DIS	0.0418	1.121	17.98	25.14	3.71	28.85	5.37	11.58
3	Kroger	KR	0.1523	1.007	16.27	20.29	4.48	24.76	4.98	11.19
4	CVS Caremark	CVS	0.0516	1.005	16.14	20.21	3.41	23.62	4.86	11.08
5	Aflac Inc	AFL	0.0465	0.947	15.20	17.93	7.51	25.44	5.04	10.77
6	Exxon Mobil	XOM	−0.0503	0.826	13.17	13.66	1.68	15.34	3.92	9.89
7	Procter & Gamble	PG	0.0285	0.801	12.85	12.83	3.64	16.47	4.06	9.79
8	Microsoft	MSFT	−0.0408	0.800	12.76	12.80	6.79	19.59	4.43	9.70
9	Johnson & Johnson	JNJ	0.0742	0.696	11.21	9.70	1.73	11.43	3.38	8.93
10	Duke Energy	DUK	−0.0273	0.666	10.62	8.86	3.23	12.09	3.48	8.45
	Sum		0.3483	9.016	144.61		41.9651			
	Portfolio ($w_i = 1/10$)		α_p	β_p	$E(R_p)$	$\beta_p^2 V(R^M)$	$V(\epsilon_p)$	$V(R_p)$	$\sigma(R_p)$	
			0.03483	0.9016	14.46	16.26	0.41965	16.68	4.08	
	Market		0.00	1.00	16.00	1.00	0.00	20.00	4.47	

$\lambda_T = (E(r_j) - R_f)/\beta_j$

$R_f = 5\%$

(b) Variance-Covariance Matrix

		ADM	DIS	KR	CVS	AFL	XOM	PG	MSFT	JNJ	DUK
		1	2	3	4	5	6	7	8	9	10
ADM	1	32.07	25.70	23.09	23.05	21.71	18.95	18.37	18.34	15.96	15.26
DIS	2		28.85	22.58	22.54	21.24	18.53	17.96	17.94	15.61	14.92
KR	3			24.76	20.25	19.07	16.65	16.14	16.11	14.02	13.41
CVS	4				23.62	19.04	16.62	16.11	16.09	14.00	13.38
AFL	5					25.44	15.65	15.17	15.15	13.19	12.60
XOM	6						15.34	13.24	13.22	11.51	11.00
PG	7							16.47	12.82	11.16	10.66
MSFT	8								19.59	11.14	10.65
JNJ	9									11.43	9.27
DUK	10										12.09

0.9016, the portfolio alpha is 0.0348, and the portfolio's unsystematic risk, $V(\varepsilon_p)$, is 0.41965:

$$\sum_{i=1}^{n} w_i \alpha_i = (1/10) \sum_{i=1}^{n} \alpha_i = (1/10)(0.348) = 0.0348$$

$$\sum_{i=1}^{n} w_i \beta_i = (1/10) \sum_{i=1}^{n} \beta_i = (1/10)(9.016) = 0.9016$$

$$V(\varepsilon_p) = \sum_{i=1}^{n} w_i^2 V(\varepsilon_i) = (1/10)^2(41.965) = 0.41965$$

For an expected market return of $E(R^M) = 16$ percent and market variance of $V(R^M) = 20$ ($\sigma(R^M) = 4.47$), the portfolio expected return is 14.46 percent, its variance is 16.68, and its standard deviation is 4.084.

$$E(R_p) = \alpha_p + \beta_p E(R^M)$$
$$E(R_p) = 0.0348 + 0.9016(16\%) = 14.46\%$$

$$V(R_p) = \beta_p^2 V(R^M) + V(\varepsilon_p)$$
$$V(R_p) = (0.9016)^2(20) + 0.419651 = 16.68$$
$$\sigma(R_p) = 4.084$$

PORTFOLIO REGRESSION/BLOOMBERG CIXB SCREEN AND CORR SCREEN

CIXB

The returns of a portfolio in EQS or PRTU can be evaluated using historical regression by putting the portfolio into a CIXB basket, creating historical data, and then treating the portfolio as an index.

Steps

1. CIXB <Enter>.
2. On the CIXB screen, name the ticker and the portfolio in the ".Ticker" and "Name" yellow box and hit <Enter> to update (.XSIF13 for ticker and XSIF 2013 for Name.
3. Click "Import" from the Actions dropdown tab.
4. On the "Import from Excel" box, click "Import from List" tab at bottom to bring up "Import from List" tab.
5. On "Import from List" tab: Select Portfolio (or EQS search or index) from the "Source" dropdown and the name of the portfolio (search, or index) from the "Name" dropdown, and then click the "Import" tab. These steps will import the portfolio's stocks, shares, and prices to the CIXB screen.

6. On CIXB screen, click the "Create" tab to bring up a time period box for selecting the time period for price and return data. After selecting the time period, hit "Save." This will activate a Bloomberg program for calculating the portfolio's daily historical returns.
7. The data will be sent to a report, RPT. To access this report, type "RPT" and hit<Enter>.
8. To access the menu screen for your portfolio: Ticker <Index> <Enter>. For regression, bring up HRA.

Bloomberg's CORR Screen to Compute R^2, Alphas, and Betas for Stocks in a Portfolio

To create a CORR screen for the stocks of a portfolio created in PRTU:

- Enter CORR <Enter>.
- Click "Create New" tab; select data time period.
- In the "Matrix Securities" box, unclick "Symmetric Matrix" button, import portfolio from "Add from Source" tab, and click update.
- In Column Securities Box, add stock index (e.g., S&P 500) by typing index ticker and index moniker (e.g., SPX <Index>), and then click the "Next" tab; name your CORR Screen.
- On your portfolio's CORR screen, select the data time period for analysis and then use the Calculation tab to find each stock's R^2, alphas, and betas.

   See Bloomberg Web Exhibit 8.4.

Elton, Gruber, and Padberg

Technique for Determining the Best Efficient Portfolio

In a 1976 article, Elton, Gruber, and Padberg showed how the single-index model can be extended to determine the best efficient portfolio (tangency point of the borrowing-lending line with the efficiency frontier). The technique they derive for generating efficient portfolios, in turn, is much simpler than using the calculus minimization approach or quadratic programming. Moreover, the approach can be set up with a constraint that weights are nonnegative.

   The Elton, Gruber, and Padberg (EGP) algorithm starts by ranking each stock in the portfolio by its Treynor index, $\lambda_{\beta j}$ (stock j's risk premium per level of systematic risk as measured by the stock's beta). Next calculating an index C_i for a set of portfolios starting first with a one-security portfolio ($i = 1$) consisting of the security with the highest rank, $\lambda_{\beta 1}$, then a two-security portfolio ($i = 2$) consisting of the first two securities with the highest ranks, $\lambda_{\beta 2}$, and so on, with the final C_i calculation consisting of a portfolio of all the securities. Columns 2 and 7 of Exhibit 8.12 show respectively

EXHIBIT 8.12 Elton, Gruber, and Padberg Technique for Determining Allocations

| Stock | Portfolio i | $\lambda_{\beta_j} = \dfrac{E(r_j) - R_f}{\beta_j}$ | $\dfrac{(E(r_j) - R_f)\beta_j}{V(\varepsilon_j)}$ | $\dfrac{\beta_j^2}{V(\varepsilon_j)}$ | $\displaystyle\sum_{j=1}^{i} \dfrac{(E(r_j) - R_f)\beta_j}{V(\varepsilon_j)}$ | $\displaystyle\sum_{j=1}^{i} \dfrac{\beta_j^2}{V(\varepsilon_j)}$ | $C_i = \dfrac{V(R^M)\displaystyle\sum_{j=1}^{i} \dfrac{[E(r_j) - R_f]\beta_j}{V(\varepsilon_j)}}{1 + V(R^M)\displaystyle\sum_{j=1}^{i} \dfrac{\beta_j^2}{V(\varepsilon_j)}}$ |
		1	2	3	4	5	6	7
Archer-Daniels-Midland	1	11.70	2.6533	0.2268	2.6533	0.2268	9.5868
Walt Disney	2	11.58	3.9268	0.3392	6.5801	0.5659	10.6832
Kroger	3	11.19	2.5327	0.2264	9.1127	0.7923	10.8185
CVS Caremark	4	11.08	3.2845	0.2965	12.3972	1.0888	C* = 10.8860
Aflac Inc	5	10.77	1.2864	0.1195	13.6836	1.2083	10.8749
Exxon Mobil	6	9.89	4.0236	0.4069	17.7073	1.6152	10.6340
Procter & Gamble	7	9.79	1.7268	0.1763	19.4341	1.7915	10.5536
Microsoft	8	9.70	0.9150	0.0943	20.3491	1.8858	10.5119
Johnson & Johnson	9	8.93	2.4988	0.2800	22.8478	2.1658	10.3114
Duke Energy	10	8.45	1.1569	0.1370	24.0047	2.3027	10.2029

1		2	3	4	5	6	7
Stock j		$\dfrac{\beta_j}{V(\varepsilon_j)}$	$\lambda_{\beta_j} = \dfrac{E(r_j) - R_f}{\beta_j}$	C^*	$\text{Max}(\text{Col}(3) - \text{Col}(4), 0)$	Z_j Col(2) X Col(5)	$w_j = Z_j/\sum Z_j$ Col(6)/0.4946
Archer-Daniels-Midland	1	0.1978	11.7005	10.8860	0.8146	0.1612	0.3258
Walt Disney	2	0.3025	11.5779	10.8860	0.6919	0.2093	0.4232
Kroger	3	0.2248	11.1865	10.8860	0.3006	0.0676	0.1366
CVS Caremark	4	0.2949	11.0777	10.8860	0.1917	0.0565	0.1143
Aflac Inc	5	0.1261	10.7691	10.8860	0.0000	0.0000	0.0000
Exxon Mobil	6	0.4923	9.8890	10.8860	0.0000	0.0000	0.0000
Procter & Gamble	7	0.2201	9.7940	10.8860	0.0000	0.0000	0.0000
Microsoft	8	0.1179	9.6993	10.8860	0.0000	0.0000	0.0000
Johnson & Johnson	9	0.4021	8.9253	10.8860	0.0000	0.0000	0.0000
Duke Energy	10	0.2058	8.4463	10.8860	0.0000	0.0000	0.0000

$$\sum Z_j = 0.4946$$

329

the $\lambda_{\beta j}$ and the C_i formula and calculations for the portfolios formed with the 10 stocks in the example presented in Exhibit 8.11. Note that as you increase the size of the portfolio by adding the next higher ranked security to the portfolio, the C_i values increase until you get to portfolio $i = 4$. After that point, adding each successive higher ranked stock reduces the value of C_i. The highest C_i is defined as the *cutoff index* and is denoted as C^*. In this example, the cutoff index is $C^* = 10.8860$. Given the cutoff index, the next step is to select all securities with $\lambda_{\beta j} > C^*$ for inclusion in the portfolio. With $C^* = 10.8860$, there are four stocks in our example with $\lambda_{\beta j}$ values exceeding C^*. The final step is to determine the portfolio allocations of each of the selected securities, w_j. Each security's w_j is determined as a proportion of an index Z_j for the security to the sum of indexes for all securities in the portfolio. That is:

$$w_j = \frac{Z_j}{\sum\limits_{j=1}^{n} Z_j}$$

where:

$$Z_j = \frac{\beta_j}{V(\varepsilon_j)} \left[\frac{E(r_j) - R_f}{\beta_j} - C^* \right]$$

The second panel of Exhibit 8.12 shows the Z_i calculations for the four stocks included in the portfolio and their allocations. The Elton, Gruber, and Padberg technique is described in more detail in Appendix 8B. An Excel program, "Elton-Gruber Optimum Portfolio," which calculates the optimum weights using the algorithm, can be accessed from the text's Web site.

The ex-post total returns from the one-year period from 8/8/12 to 8/8/13 for the Markowitz efficient portfolio using the EGP algorithm and the S&P 500 are shown in the figure in Exhibit 8.13 (Bloomberg's PORT screen, Performance tab, and Total Return tab). The back testing results show the portfolio outperforms the market for the one-year period (total return of 42.24 percent compared to 16.44 percent for S&P 500). A one-year regression of the portfolio against the S&P 500 (generated using the Bloomberg CIXB and HRA screens), shows the Markowitz portfolio has a beta close to one but a relatively large alpha of 0.059, indicating abnormal returns.

Note also that this efficient portfolio invested 32.58 percent in Archer-Daniels. In contrast, the portfolio shown in Exhibit 8.5 generated using the Asset Allocation template has a zero allocation to this stock. The difference can be explained in terms of the time periods. In the template example, the portfolio input averages were calculated over the seven-year period from 2006 to 2013. By contrast, in this case the averages were based on the more recent period from 2011 to 2013. For the longer period, Archer-Daniels has a relatively lower alpha of 2.7 percent (compared to 7.7 percent for the 2011–2013 period) and a beta of only 0.421. Several other stocks, such as Aflac,

EXHIBIT 8.13 Performance of Markowitz Efficient Portfolio Using the EGP Algorithm and the S&P 500

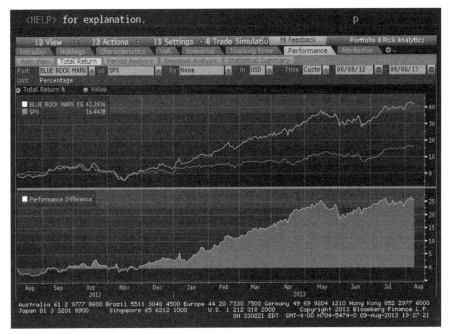

(a)

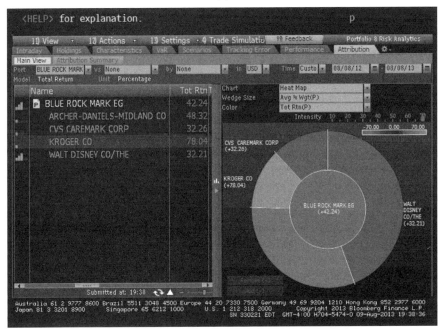

(b)

(Continued)

EXHIBIT 8.13 (*Continued*)

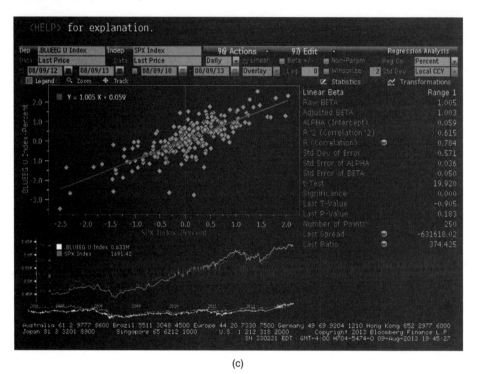

(c)

also have alphas and betas that differ significantly given the time period analyzed. These differences in the portfolios do highlight the problem of using historical averages to estimated portfolio inputs.

BLOOMBERG: FINDING ELTON, GRUBER, AND PADBERG PORTFOLIO INPUTS USING BETA, RV, AND PC SCREENS

The portfolio inputs for solving for the best efficient portfolio using the Elton, Gruber, and Padberg algorithm are each stocks' α_i, β_i, and $V(\varepsilon_i)$. Estimates of these parameters can be generated from a number of Bloomberg screens: Stock beta, HRA, PC, and RV screens.

See Bloomberg Web Exhibit 8.5.

Bloomberg/Markowitz Excel Program

A Markowitz Excel Program that determines portfolio allocations using the Elton, Gruber, and Padberg technique for a portfolio imported from the Bloomberg PRTU screen can be downloaded from the text's Web site. Using the "Markowitz" Excel program, one can import the names of the stocks from a portfolio created in PRTU into the program (see Bloomberg Exhibit Box: "Markowitz Excel Program"). The user can then select a risk-free rate from a dropdown, an index (e.g., S&P 500 or Dow Jones), a regression time period, and a length of period (daily or weekly). The program then calculates α_i, β_i, and $V(\varepsilon_i)$, and then each stock's $E(r_i)$ and $V(r_i)$, and $\lambda_{\beta j}$ based on the index's average market return and variability: $E(R^M) = \text{Av}R^M$ and $V(R^M) = \text{Av}V(R^M)$. The user can also elect to use either Bloomberg's adjusted beta or the regression beta (raw beta). Calculation Sheet 2 of the Excel program shows each stock's parameter values in the order of their $\lambda_{\beta j}$'s and the Elton, Gruber, and Padberg parameter calculations of C_i, and optimum weights. Exhibit 8.14 shows (1) the Bloomberg PRTU slide of the illustrative 10-stock portfolio; (2) the input page of the Excel program where the S&P 500, 10-year Treasury, and a weekly time period from 8/5/2006 to 8/8/2013 were selected for the regressions (note that this a different time period than the previous example in Exhibit 8.12 but similar to Exhibit 8.5 generated from the Asset Allocation Optimizer program); and (3) the Calculation Sheet 2, where the allocations for the portfolio are shown. The portfolio consists of the same stocks as the Optimizer program with high (but not identical) allocations to CVS, Disney, Kroger, and Johnson & Johnson. Exhibit 8.15 shows the ex-post performance of the portfolio (named Blue Mark Bloom) relative to the S&P 500 for the 8/8/2006–8/19/2013 period. The fund dramatically outperforms the market during this period with a total return for the period of 127.82 percent compared to a return of 78.01 for the S&P 500, with the most significant gains occurring in 2013.

BLOOMBERG: THE MARKOWITZ EXCEL PROGRAM

The Markowitz Excel Program can be downloaded from the text Web site. The program uses the Elton, Gruber, and Padberg Technique for determining the allocation for the best efficient portfolio. The user imports the stocks of a portfolio created in PRTU into the program by typing in the portfolio's ID number found on the top left corner of the PRTU screen. The user then selects a risk-free rate from a dropdown, an index (S&P 500 or Dow Jones), a regression time period, and a length of period (daily or weekly). The program then calculates α_i, β_i, and $V(\varepsilon_i)$, and then each stock's $E(r_i)$, $V(r_i)$, and $\lambda_{\beta j}$ based on the average market return and variability. The user can also elect to use Bloomberg's adjusted beta or the regression beta (raw beta). Calculation Sheet 2 of the Excel program shows each stocks parameter values in the order of their $\lambda_{\beta j}$'s and the Elton, Gruber, and Padberg parameter calculations of C_i, C^*, and the optimum weights. See Exhibit 8.14.

Multi-Index Models

The single-index model assumes that all stocks in the portfolio are related to only one factor, with that factor typically being the market return. In a multi-index model, the number of factors affecting each security in the portfolio is extended to include more

EXHIBIT 8.14 Bloomberg and Markowitz Excel Program Using Elton, Gruber, and Padberg Technique for Determining Allocation

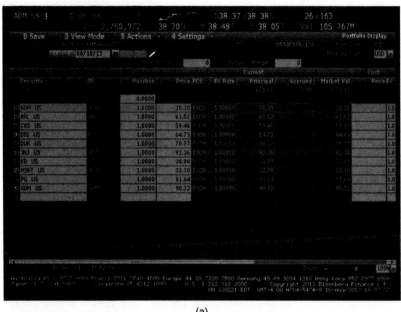

(a)

Rf		10 yr treas
Rm	Index	SPX
	Start date	8/5/2006
	Ending date	8/8/2013
	Daily or weekly	W
Beta	Type	raw beta
	Relativev Index	SPX
	Start date	8/5/2006
	Ending date	8/8/2013
	Daily or weekly	W

Import Data Type	Portfolio
ID or Name	u5945505-128

(b)

Name	$E(r_i)$	β_i	$V(\varepsilon_i)$	Rf	$V(R^M)$	λ_s	C_i	W_i
KROGER CO	15.77	0.56	8.70	2.58	2.84	23.73	2.1750	22.5%
CVS CAREMARK CORP	16.91	0.61	8.71	2.58	2.84	23.44	4.2959	24.3%
WALT DISNEY CO	19.78	1.08	5.08	2.58	2.84	15.99	8.3425	35.7%
JOHNSON & JOHNSON	9.07	0.50	2.89	2.58	2.84	12.92	8.8792	16.6%
DUKE ENERGY CORP	7.57	0.55	4.43	2.58	2.84	9.09	8.8967	0.5%
PROCTER & GAMBLE CO	6.99	0.49	3.87	2.58	2.84	9.04	8.9068	0.4%
AFLAC INC	13.61	1.51	17.61	2.58	2.84	7.33	8.7041	0.0%
MICROSOFT CORP	7.01	0.80	8.98	2.58	2.84	5.56	8.4977	0.0%
EXXON MOBIL CORP	5.15	0.78	4.45	2.58	2.84	3.30	7.9118	0.0%
ARCHER-DANIELS-MIDLAND CO	- 0.61	0.88	13.88	2.58	2.84	- 3.62	7.4022	0.0%

(c)

EXHIBIT 8.15 Ex-Post Performance of Markowitz Fund and S&P 500, 8/8/2006–8/9/2013

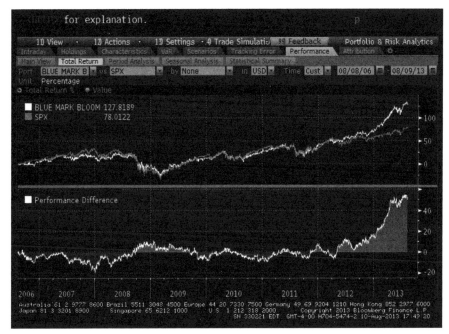

(a)

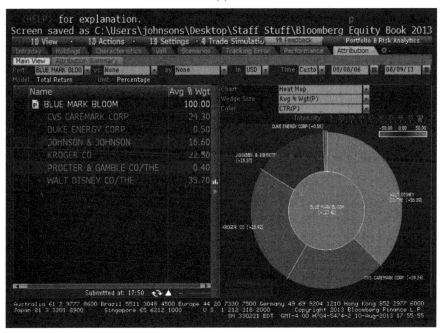

(b)

than one explanatory variable. Specifically, the model assumes that the return of each stock i in the portfolio being evaluated is related to the same set of factors, I_{ij}:

$$r_i = \alpha_i + \beta_{i1}I_1 + \beta_{i2}I_2 + \cdots + \beta_{in}I_n + \varepsilon_i \tag{8.8}$$

This model also assumes that the standard regression assumptions hold for each security (ε is normally distributed with $E(\varepsilon) = 0$, $Cov(\varepsilon_i\, I_j) = 0$, and $V(\varepsilon)$ is constant over observations), and that there is no correlation in the error terms for securities ($Cov(\varepsilon_j\, \varepsilon_k) = 0$).

There are three potential problems in applying multi-index models to explain what determines a stock's return. The first is identifying those factors that are statistically significant in explaining the returns. Multi-index models vary in terms of the factors used to explain returns. For example, there are *industry models* that explain stock returns in terms of the market and the average returns of the stock's industry; *pseudo industry models* in which the indexes are formed from stocks grouped into categories such as growth, cyclical, and stable; and *macroeconomic models* in which factors such as the market return, inflation, and bond returns explain each stock's return. As noted in Chapter 6, empirical research has provided evidence that provides some support for the construction of multi-index models based on macroeconomic factors that affect the value of stock as measured by the present value of the stock's future cash flows. These models are discussed further in Chapter 10 in conjunction with the testing of equilibrium models.

The second problem in applying multi-index models relates to their manageability and statistical accuracy. In a multi-index model, the number of computations needed to determine an optimal portfolio is greater than the computations needed for the single-index model but less than the requirements needed using historical averages.

The third problem relates to the possibility that the explanatory variables in a multiple regression model could be linearly related—a condition referred to as multicollinearity. When multicollinearity exists, one of the variables is redundant (i.e., it is simply a linear transformation of the other), and the regression qualifiers (t-test and F-test) are biased. As a result, the quality of the regression cannot be determined. Procedures for converting multi-index models into ones with uncorrelated indexes are presented in a number of statistics books.[5]

The latter two problems (number of computations and multicollinearity) can be eliminated (or minimized) by converting the multi-index model into another multi-index model in which the indexes, I^*, are uncorrelated.

MRA: BLOOMBERG'S MULTIPLE REGRESSION SCREEN

Multiple regression analysis can be done using the Bloomberg MRA screen. See the Bloomberg exhibit box in Chapter 6: "MRA: Bloomberg's Multiple Regression Screen."

Conclusion

Harry Markowitz introduced his model for determining portfolios in a 1952 article in the *Journal of Finance*. Even though the model is over 60 years old, it is still referred to as *modern portfolio theory*. Such persistence, in part, reflects the number of years it took to appreciate the importance and subtleties of his theory and in part the time it has taken the discipline to learn how to use the theory. Perhaps the most significant contribution of Markowtiz's work is that it introduced a statistical and mathematical methodology for approaching investment decisions. In 1989, Harry Markowitz, along with Merton Miller and William Sharpe, was awarded the Noble Prize in Economics for his contribution to Economics and Finance.

BLOOMBERG CASE: CONSTRUCTING AND BACK TESTING MARKOWITZ PORTFOLIOS IN BLOOMBERG

Steps for Constructing and Analyzing

Step 1: Construct a portfolio in PRTU consisting of one share in each of the DJIA stocks: PRTU <Enter>; click "Create;" from Settings Screen, click "Import"; from "Actions" tab, select "Equity Index" from "Source" dropdown and INDU from "Name" dropdown.

Step 2: Use the Markowitz Excel program to determine the best efficient portfolio using the Elton, Gruber, and Padberg algorithm box: "Markowitz Excel Program."

Step 3: Create your Markowitz portfolio in PRTU. In constructing the portfolio, use fixed weights:

- PRTU <Enter>.
- Click "Create" tab.
- From Settings Screen click "Fixed Weight" in the "Position Type" dropdown.
- Enter the Markowitz weights.

Step 4: Create history for the Markowitz portfolio:

Step 5: Analyze the portfolio's performance relative to an index (e.g., Dow) in PORT: PORT <Enter>, select "INDU" for comparison, click Performance tab, Total Return tab, and select time period for analysis.

See Bloomberg Web Exhibit 8.6.

OTHER BLOOMBERG PORTFOLIO SCREENS

PORT's Trade Simulation Tab allows you to select and edit hypothetical trading positions for your portfolio in order to assess the impact these moves may have on your portfolio.

(Continued)

PORT's VAR Tab: Value-at-Risk: VAR displays value at risk analytics for a portfolio. One can select from the tabs Absolute VAR/Relative VAR (relative to a benchmark) from the toolbar to display the desired data. The VAR calculation is based on the following methodologies: Historical 1 year, Historical 2 years, Historical 3 years, Monte Carlo, or Parametric. VAR is based on a given confidence interval (95 percent, 97.5 percent, or 99 percent), and a given time horizon (between 1 day and 1 quarter) and shows the range of possible values of the portfolio, industry, stocks, and index.

Notes

1. For a two-security portfolio, the allocation that yields a zero risk portfolio can be found by setting $V(R_p)$ equal to zero and then solving for one of the weights. For this example, in which there is perfect negative correlation:

$$V(R_p) = w_1^2 \sigma(r_1)^2 + w_2^2 \sigma(r_2)^2 + 2w_1 w_2 \rho_{12} \sigma(r_1) \sigma(r_2)$$
$$V(R_p) = w_1^2 \sigma(r_1)^2 + w_2^2 \sigma(r_2)^2 + 2w_1 w_2(-1) \sigma(r_1) \sigma(r_2)$$
$$V(R_p) = [w_1 \sigma(r_1) - w_2 \sigma(r_2)]^2$$
$$0 = [w_1 \sigma(r_1)^2 - w_2 \sigma(r_2)^2]^2$$
$$w_1 = \frac{\sigma(r_1)}{\sigma(r_1) + \sigma(r_2)}$$
$$w_1 = \frac{4}{4+6} = 0.4$$

2. The annualized variance is equal to the periodic variance (e.g., weekly) times the number of periods of that length (week) in a year (52). The annualized standard deviation is equal to the square root of the annualized variance.
3. More formally, given

$$V(\varepsilon_p) = \sum_{i=1}^{n} w_i^2 V(\varepsilon_i)$$

and assuming an equal allocation strategy such that $w_i = 1/n$ and

$$V(\varepsilon_p) = \sum_{i=1}^{n} \left(\frac{1}{n}\right)^2 V(\varepsilon_i)$$

the larger the portfolio (i.e., the greater n), the smaller $V(\varepsilon_p)$.

$$V(\varepsilon_p) = \sum_{i=1}^{n} \left(\frac{1}{n}\right)^2 V(\varepsilon_i) \to 0 \text{ as } n \to \infty$$

Thus for portfolio consisting of approximately 30 stocks, the portfolio variance and standard deviation simplify to:

$$V(R_p) = \beta_p^2 V(R^M)$$
$$\sigma(R_p) = \beta_p \sigma(R^M)$$

4. Note that if the portfolio consists of all securities in the market and the allocations reflect each security's proportional value to the market, then the portfolio represents the market portfolio and $E(R_p)$ will be equal to $E(R_M)$. To ensure that $E(R_p) = E(R^M)$, α_p must be equal to zero and β_p must be equal to one.
5. Elton and Gruber have derived a simplified technique for generating the best efficient portfolio using a multi-index model. See: Elton, Gruber, Brown, and Goetzmann (2003).

Selected References

Alexander, Gordon. 1976. The derivation of efficient sets. *Journal of Financial and Quantitative Analysis* (December): 817–830.

Ali, Mukhart. 1975. Stochastic dominance and portfolio analysis. *Journal of Financial Economics* 2 (June): 205–230.

Ali, Mukhtart, and Cramelo Giaccotto. 1982. Optimum distribution-free tests and further evidence of heteroscedasticity in the Market Model. *Journal of Finance* 37 (December): 1495–1511.

Blume, Marshall. 1970. Portfolio theory: A step toward its practical application. *Journal of Business* 43 (April): 152–173.

Chen, Nai-fu. 1983. Some empirical tests of the theory of arbitrage pricing. *Journal of Finance* 38 (December): 1392–1414.

Diamond, Peter, and Joseph Stiglitz. 1974. Increases in risk and risk aversion. *Journal of Economic Theory* 8 (July): 337–360.

Elton, Edwin, and Martin Gruber. 1971. Dynamic programming applications in finance. *Journal of Finance* 24 (May): 473–505.

Elton, Edwin, and Martin Gruber. 1977. Risk reduction and portfolio size: An analytical solution. *Journal of Business* 50 (October): 415–437.

Elton, Edwin J., Martin Gruber, Stephen Brown, and William Goetzmann. 2003. *Modern Portfolio Theory and Investment Analysis*. Hoboken, NJ: John Wiley & Sons, Inc., Chapters 6–11.

Elton, Edwin J., Martin Gruber, and Manfred Padberg. 1976. Simple criteria for optimal portfolio selection. *Journal of Finance* 11 (December): 1341–1357.

Elton, Edwin J., Martin Gruber, and Manfred Padberg. 1978. Simple criteria for optimal portfolio selection: Tracing out the efficiency frontier. *Journal of Finance* 13 (March): 296–302.

Elton, Edwin J., Martin Gruber, and Manfred Padberg. 1978. Optimum portfolios from simple ranking devices. *Journal of Portfolio Management* 4 (Spring): 15–19.

Evans, L. John, and Stephen Archer. 1968. Diversification and reduction of dispersion: An empirical analysis. *Journal of Finance* 23 (December): 761–767.

Fabozzi, Frank, and Jack Clark Francis. 1977. Stability tests for alphas and betas over bull and bear condition. *Journal of Finance* 22 (September): 1093–1099.

Francis, Jack C., 1975 Skewness and investors' decisions. *Journal of Financial and Quantitative Analysis* 10 (March): 163–172.

Francis, Jack C., and S. H. Archer. 1979. *Portfolio Analysis*. Englewood Cliffs, NJ: Prentice-Hall.

Hamada, Robert S. 1971. The effect of the firm's capital structure on the systematic risk of common stocks. *Journal of Finance* 8 (May): 435–452.

Jacob, Nancy. 1971. The measurement of systematic risk for securities and portfolios: Some empirical results. *Journal of Financial and Quantitative Analysis* 6 (March): 815–833.

Jean, William H. 1980. The geometric mean and stochastic dominance. *Journal of Finance* 35 (March): 151–158.

Johnson, K., and D. Shannon. 1974. A note on diversification and the reduction of diversification. *Journal of Financial Economics* 1 (December): 365–371.

Johnson, R., C. Hultman, and R. Zuber. 1979. Currency cocktails and exchange-rate risk. *Columbia Journal of World Business*, 14 (Winter): 117–127.

Latane, Henry, Don Tuttle, and Allan Young. 1971. How to choose a market index. *Financial Analysts Journal* 27 (September–October): 75–85.

Lintner, John. 1965. The valuation of risk assets and the selection of risky investments in stock portfolios and capital budgets. *Review of Economics and Statistics* 46 (February): 13–37.

Markowitz, Harry. 1952. Portfolio Selection. *Journal of Finance* 89 (March): 77–91.

Markowitz, Harry. 1959. *Portfolio Selection: Efficient Diversification of Investments*. Hoboken, NJ: John Wiley & Sons, Inc.

Markowitz, Harry. 1970. Markowitz revisited. *Financial Analyst Journal* 32 (September–October): 47–52.

Merton, Robert. 1972. An analytic derivation of the efficient portfolio frontier. *Journal of Financial and Quantitative Analysis* 7 (September): 1851–1872.

Sharpe, William. 1971. Mean absolute-deviation characteristic lines for securities and portfolios. *Management Science* 18 (October): B1–B13.

Sharpe, William, and Bernell Stone. 1973. A linear programming foundation of general portfolio selection model. *Journal of Financial and Quantitative Analysis* 8 (September): 621–636.

Roll, Richard. 1973. Evidence on the "Growth-Optimum" model. *Journal of Finance* 28 (June): 551–556.

Roy, A.D. 1952. Safety first and the holding of assets. *Econometrics* 10 (July): 432–449.

Samuelson, Paul. 1958. The fundamental approximation theorem of portfolio analysis in terms of means, variance, and higher moments. *Review of Economic Studies* 25 (February): 65–86.

Solnik, Bruno. 1974. Why not diversify internationally? *Financial Analysts Journal* 20 (July/August): 48–54.

Solnik, Bruno. 1988. *International Investments*. Reading, Mass.: Addison-Wesley.

Solnik, Bruno, and B. Noetzlin. 1982. The performance of international asset allocation. *Journal of Portfolio Management* 2 (Fall): 11–21.

Bloomberg Exercises

CREATING HISTORICAL DATA FOR PORTFOLIOS IN PRTU

Bring up the PRTU screen for your portfolio. On the screen, change the date in the amber "Date" box (e.g., Month/Day/2006). You may see the stocks disappear from the screen. Click the "Edit" tab (if needed) and then the "Actions" tab. From the "Actions" dropdown, select "Import" to bring up the import box. On the import box, select "Portfolio" from the "Source" dropdown, the name of your portfolio from the "Name" dropdown, change the date (e.g., back to the current period), hit the "Import" tab, and then click "Save." You should now have a portfolio with historical data.

1. Using the some of the stocks comprising the Dow, generate an efficiency frontier using Bloomberg's Asset Allocation Optimizer Template. To download the program you may want to use DAPI: DAPI <Enter> and click "Excel Template Library," "Equity," "Portfolios," and "Asset Allocation Optimizer." For the DJIA stocks, select no more than 12 stocks, set each stock's minimum weight to zero and maximum weight to 99 percent, and use the average risk-free rate for the period.

2. Study the characteristics of some the stocks composing the DJIA or the stocks of the Markowitz portfolio you constructed in Exercise 1 in terms of their R^2's, alphas, betas, and $V(\varepsilon)$'s using Bloomberg's PC screen (PC <Enter>). On the PC screen, examine the R^2's, alphas, betas, and $V(\varepsilon)$'s over different time periods. Note: $V(\varepsilon) = V(r)(1 - R^2)$.

To create a PC screen for the DJIA (or your portfolio), use the PC screen for one of the stocks in the DJIA (portfolio) (e.g., IBM) and then type: IBM <Equity> PC <Enter>. On the PC screen, you can import the index (portfolio) from the "Peer Source" tab by clicking "Equity Index" ("Portfolio") and then INDU (name of your portfolio) from the "Name Source" tab. You may want to use the edit screen to delete some of the indexes. Use the edit screen to also add an index (e.g., S&P 500) to the rows for stocks in order to have its variance. After saving your edited screen, you can set the time period for your analysis. Alphas and betas for each stock for the selected time period can be accessed from the "Calculation" tab and exported to Excel from the "Export" tab (upper right corner). Each stock's variance of the error, $V(\varepsilon)$, can be calculated from the stock's R^2 and its variance using the stock variances (found by clicking "Covariance" and R^2 from the "Calculation" tab).

3. Stock rankings:
   a. Estimate the expected returns for each of the stocks you analyzed in Bloomberg Exercise 2 using the Bloomberg DDM model (see Bloomberg Exhibit in Chapter 3: "Bloomberg DDM Screen").
   b. Given your expected return estimates for each stock, estimate their betas and then determine the risk free rate (e.g., current 10-year Treasury yield; see Bloomberg FIT screen). For beta, you may want to use the stock's adjusted beta (found on the stock's beta screen) or a beta from one of the PC screen calculations you made in Exercise 2.
   c. Given your stocks' expected returns and betas and the risk-free rate, rank the stocks using the Treynor index.
      Exercise 4 is based on material presented in Appendix 8A (text Web site).

4. Using Bloomberg's CORR screen, select 10 stocks to analyze from the DJIA: CORR <Enter>; click "Create New" tab; select data time periods (e.g., daily, last seven years); on the "Matrix Securities" box, click the "Add from Sources" tab and then click "Equity Indexes" from "Source" dropdown and INDU from the "Name" dropdown; add 10 of the DJIA stocks from the list appearing in the right box; click "Update."
   a. On the CORR screen for your 10 stocks, select a data time period for analysis and then select "Covariance" from the "Calculation" tab to bring up the

variance-covariance matrix. Export the matrix to Excel (click "Export to Excel" from the "Export" tab in upper right corner).

   b. In Excel, create a coefficient matrix **A** from the variance-covariance matrix that you exported from Bloomberg. For your stock expected returns, use averages or formulate you own expected returns.

   c. Using the math approach for portfolio variance minimization, solve for the allocations for several efficient portfolios. Use Excel and the Excel matrix multiplication commands (see Appendix 8A (text Web site) and the Bloomberg Box: "Using the Bloomberg CORR Screen and Excel to Determine Markowitz Efficient Portfolios").

   d. Comment on your results and the limitations of using the math approach to solve for Markowitz efficient portfolios.

5. Use EQS to find stocks making up the S&P 500 with a market cap greater than $30 billion and then import your stocks into PRTU to form an equally allocated portfolio.

- EQS <Enter>; select Standard and Poor's 500 from the Indexes tab; in the amber ribbon box, type Market Cap, and enter $30B; save your screen.
- PRTU <Enter>; On the Settings Screen, click "Actions" and "Import," and then select "Equity Search (EQS)" from the Source dropdown and the Name of your search from the Source dropdown.
- Create history for your portfolio (see the box in the exercises, "Creating Historical Data for Portfolios in PRTU").

   a. Examine the correlation of the stocks in your portfolio using the PC screen: Bring up the equity screen for one of the stocks in the portfolio (Stock Ticker <Equity> <Enter>); type in PC; on the PC screen, import your portfolio from the "Peer Source" yellow dropdown tab.

   b. Evaluate your portfolio using tabs on the PORT screen.

   c. Evaluate the performance of your portfolio using the "Performance" tab on the PORT screen.

   d. Examine the top movers and laggers in your portfolio for different periods using the MRR screen: MRR <Enter>; select "Portfolio" from the "Source" dropdown and find your portfolio from the "Name" dropdown.

   e. Examine your portfolio's regression relation with the S&P 500, its historical total return relative to the S&P 500, and its price graph by importing your portfolio to a basket using CIXB and then using the HRA, COMP, and GP screens. See Bloomberg Exhibit Box: Portfolio Regression, Bloomberg CIXB Screen.

6. Bloomberg's FMAP screen provides information on investment funds by category, areas, performance, and type.

   a. Using FMAP, examine several equity funds in different categories.

   b. Select a U.S. equity fund with a certain investment style (e.g., Value and Large Cap) and study it using the functions on the fund's menus screen: FMAP <Enter>; select "Objective" from "View by" dropdown and United States from "All Region" dropdown; click equity from the listing on the right-side of

FMAP box, and then select type and the fund. To examine the fund go to the fund's menu screen: Fund Ticker <Equity> <Enter>. Screens on the fund's menu screen to consider: DES, historical fund analysis (HFA), fund holdings (MHD), price graph (GP), and comparative returns (COMP).

   c. Examine the fund you selected in 6b in more detail using the PORT screen.

7. Form a portfolio in PRTU consisting of some of the stocks of your selected fund in Exercise 6. For an easy way to load securities of the fund into PRTU, see the Bloomberg box in this exercise section: Dragging and Dropping Securities from MHD into PRTU. Your portfolio could consist of one share or 1,000 shares of each stock or you can determine an equal allocation for each. In forming your portfolio in PRTU, be sure to also create history (see Bloomberg Box in this exercise section: Creating Historical Data for Portfolios in PRTU).

   a. Using PORT, evaluate the historical performance of your portfolio relative to an index.

   b. Using the CORR screen, create a CORR screen by importing the portfolio: CORR <Enter>; click "Create New" tab; select data time period; in the "Matrix Securities" unclick "Symmetric Matrix" button, import portfolio from "Add from Source" tab and click update; in Column Securities Box, add stock index (e.g., S&P 500) by typing index ticker and index moniker (e.g., SPX <Index>) and then click the "Next" tab; name your CORR Screen.

   c. On your portfolio's CORR screen, evaluate the stocks' R^2, alphas, and betas.

DRAGGING AND DROPPING SECURITIES FROM MHD INTO PRTU

The Security holding of a fund appearing on the fund's MHD screen can be dragged and dropped into the PRTU setting screen. To do this: (1) open the MHD screen for a fund and the PRTU setting screen for inputting securities; (2) drag the green icon in the upper right corner of the MHD screen and drop it in the blank security input box in PRTU. You will then see the fund's securities in PRTU with each security holding consisting of one share.

---

8. The following list shows 20 equity investment funds with different equity styles.

   a. Study the policy statements for several of the funds found on the fund's description page: Ticker <Equity>; DES.

   b. Create a portfolio of the funds in PRTU and analyze it using the PORT screen.

   c. Create a basket of portfolio returns and make it an index using CIXB. As an index, use HRA to determine the portfolio's regression relation with the S&P 500.

   d. Examine each fund's alpha, beta, and R^2 using the CORR Screen: Enter CORR <Enter>; click "Create New" tab; select data time period; in the "Matrix Securities" unclick "Symmetric Matrix" button, import portfolio from "Add from

Source" tab and click update; in Column Securities Box, add stock index (e.g., S&P 500) by typing index ticker and pressing the index moniker (e.g., SPX <Index>) and then click the "Next" tab; name your CORR Screen. On your portfolio's CORR screen select the data time period for analysis and then use the Calculation tab to find the stocks' R^2, alphas, and betas.

Ticker	Name
BTO US Equity	JOHN HANCOCK FINANCIAL OPPOR
CHN US Equity	CHINA FUND INC
CISGX US Equity	TOUCHSTONE SANDS CAP INC GRW
EISMX US Equity	EATON VANCE-ATLANTA SMID-I
FCPVX US Equity	FIDELITY SMALL CAP VALUE-I
FEN US Equity	FIRST TRUST ENERGY INCOME AN
FMFAX US Equity	FIDELITY ADVISOR MATERIAL-A
FRIFX US Equity	FIDELITY REAL ESTATE INCOME
FSGRX US Equity	FRANKLIN SMALL CAP GRW FD-A
HCPIX US Equity	PROFUNDS HEALTH CARE ULTR-IV
JCE US Equity	NUVEEN CORE EQUITY ALPHA FUN
JTIVX US Equity	JPMORGAN INTL VALUE SMA
MAPCX US Equity	BLACKROCK PACIFIC FUND-I
MERDX US Equity	MERIDIAN GROWTH FUND INC
MFVSX UQ Equity	MASSMUTUAL SEL FOC VALUE-S
OSMAX US Equity	OPPENHEIMER INTL SMALL CO-A
PEUGX US Equity	PUTNAM EUROPE EQUITY FUND-A
RYZAX US Equity	RYDEX LARGE CAP VALUE FUND-H
VINAX US Equity	VANGUARD INDUSTRIALS IDX-ADM
VUIAX US Equity	VANGUARD UTILITIES INDEX-ADM

9. Create your own fund of funds portfolio:
   a. Using the FMAP screen, select funds with different styles: FMAP <Enter>; View by = Objective; Region = United States; Analyze by = Last 3-Year Total Return.
   b. Create a portfolio of your funds in PRTU and analyze the portfolio using PORT.
   c. Create a basket of your portfolio returns and make it an index in CIXB. As an index, use HRA to determine its regression relation with the S&P 500.

d. Examine each fund's alpha, beta, and R^2 using the CORR Screen: Enter CORR <Enter>; click "Create New" tab; select data time period; in the "Matrix Securities" unclick "Symmetric Matrix" button, import portfolio from "Add from Source" tab and click update; in Column Securities Box, add stock index (e.g., S&P 500) by typing index ticker and pressing the index moniker (e.g., SPX <Index>), and then click the "Next" tab; name your CORR Screen. On your portfolio's CORR screen, select the data time period for analysis and then use the Calculation tab to find the stocks' R^2, alphas, and betas.

10. Examine a portfolio you formed in one of the exercises (or some other portfolio you have formed) in terms of the portfolio's regression relation with the S&P 500, its historical total return relative to the S&P 500, and its price graph. Import your portfolio to a basket and make it an index using CIXB; then use the HRA, COMP, and GP screens on the index menu created for your portfolio. Comment on the portfolio's systematic and unsystematic risk and its alpha.

Create a CORR screen for your portfolio to evaluate each stock's relationship to the market (S&P 500): CORR <Enter>; click "Create New" tab; select data time period; in the "Matrix Securities" unclick "Symmetric Matrix" button, import portfolio from "Add from Source" tab and click update; in Column Securities Box, add S&P 500 index by typing index ticker and pressing the index moniker (SPX <Index>) and then click the "Next" tab; name your CORR Screen.

On your portfolio's CORR screen, evaluate the stocks' R^2, alphas, and betas.

CHAPTER 9

The Capital Asset Pricing Model

Introduction

Like supply-and-demand models of economics, models for determining the equilibrium return on a security or a portfolio involve finding that unique return toward which the return naturally tends. The two most widely used models for determining the equilibrium return on an investment are the Capital Asset Pricing Model (CAPM), which was first discussed in Chapter 6, and the Arbitrage Pricing Theory (APT). The CAPM was the first general equilibrium model for determining an investment return, and it is based on the single-index model discussed in Chapter 8. The APT, on other hand, is based on a multifactor model. As we will see, both models are rooted in portfolio theory. In this chapter, we examine the CAPM, and in Chapter 10 we look at APT.

Overview[1]

One of the implications of portfolio analysis is that in an efficient market rational investors would prefer portfolio investments to individual security investments because unsystematic risk can be diversified away with a portfolio. In the 1960s, Sharpe (1964), Lintner (1965), and Mossin (1966) showed that if investors make their investment decisions in a portfolio context, then the selection of individual securities would be based solely on that security's contribution to the overall portfolio's expected return and risk. As a result, a security's undiversified or unsystematic risk would not affect the security's equilibrium price and return.

The idea that a security is important only in a portfolio context is the foundation of CAPM. CAPM can be stated in terms of the following proposition:

> The equilibrium return on an investment is determined by its systematic risk as measured by its beta and not by unsystematic factors that investors can diversify away with a portfolio.

Recall that beta is the slope of the characteristic line: $r = \alpha + \beta R^M$. It is a measure of the change in a security's rate of return to a change in the market rate of return: $\beta = \Delta r / \Delta R^M$. If r and R^M are linearly related, then beta also measures the proportional relationship between r and R^M. Thus, a security with a $\beta = 1.5$ would change by 15 percent for a 10 percent change in the market. Statistically, beta measures a security's variability relative to the market's variability. Thus, a security with a $\beta = 1$ has the same variability as the market; one with a $\beta > 1$ has greater variability than the market, and one with a $\beta < 1$ has less variability.

In terms of the CAPM, a stock with a $\beta > 1$ has more risk than the market and therefore, in equilibrium, should be priced so its equilibrium expected rate of return, $E(r)^*$, is greater than the expected market rate of return: $E(r)^* > E(R^M)$. If such a stock were priced such that its expected rate of return were equal to or less than the market, then there would be little if any demand for the security. The lack of demand would cause the stock's price to drop and its expected rate of return to increase until the equilibrium condition of $E(r)^* > E(R^M)$ was satisfied. In contrast, a stock with a $\beta < 1$ in equilibrium should be priced so its expected rate of return is less than the market rate. $E(r)^* < E(R^M)$. If such a security were priced such that its expected rate equaled or exceeded the market rate, then there would be a high demand for this security with relatively low risk. This demand, in turn, would increase the price of the security and lowers its return until $E(r)^* < E(R^M)$. A security with $\beta = 1$ by definition has the same risk as the market and therefore should be priced such that its expected rate is equal to the expected market rate: $E(r)^* = E(R^M)$. Finally, if investors hold portfolios that diversify away unsystematic risk, then a security with a beta equal to zero should be priced in equilibrium such that its rate of return is equal to the risk-free rate: $E(r)^* = R_f$.

It should be noted that a security with a negative beta would in equilibrium have an expected return less than the risk-free rate: $E(r)^* < R_f$. That is, for investors who make decisions based on the security's contribution to their portfolio, a negative beta security yielding at least the same rate of return as the risk-free security would be considered more valuable than the risk-free security since its addition to the portfolio would serve to reduce the portfolio's risk more than the addition of a risk-free security. Thus, if a security with a $\beta < 0$ were priced such that $E(r) \geq R_f$, then there would be a high demand for the security, causing its price to increase and its return to decrease until $E(r)^* < R_f$.

The relationships between beta and a security's equilibrium return are graphically depicted in Exhibit 9.1. The line in the exhibit shows the relation between any security's equilibrium return and its beta. As noted in Chapter 6, this line is known as the *security market line* (*SML*). The line has an intercept of R_f (i.e., when $\beta = 0$, $E(r)^* = R_f$) and a slope equal to the market risk premium $E(R_M) - R_f$. The equation for the SML is

$$E(r_i)^* = R_f + [R(R^M) - R_f]\beta_i \qquad (9.1)$$

where: i represents any investment i.

EXHIBIT 9.1   Security Market Line

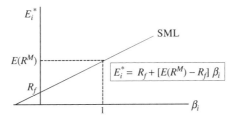

- CAPM: Relation
- Security Market Line (SML): Depicts the equilibrium relationship between any investment's equilibrium return and its beta.

$$E_i^* = R_f + [E(R^M) - R_f]\, \beta_i$$

β	Risk	In equilibrium, the security is priced such that
$\beta > 1$	Security has more risk than the market	$E(r)^* > E(R^M)$
$\beta = 1$	Security has the same risk as the market	$E(r)^* = E(R^M)$
$\beta < 1$	Security has less risk than the market	$E(r)^* < E(R^M)$
$\beta = 0$	Security has no systematic risk	$E(r)^* = R_f$
$\beta < 0$	Security lowers portfolio risk	$E(r)^* < R_f$

The CAPM as depicted by the SML represents a cross-sectional model showing the equilibrium return and beta combinations for any security or portfolio. For example, if the risk-free rate were 6 percent and the market risk premium were 4 percent, then a security with a $\beta = 0.5$ would have an equilibrium return of 8 percent; another security with a $\beta = 1$ would have an equilibrium return of 10 percent; and another security with a $\beta = 1.5$ would have an equilibrium return of 12 percent. It should be emphasized that in the CAPM, systematic risk is the only factor determining a security's equilibrium return, or equivalently, unsystematic risk (industry risk and firm risk) is unimportant. This feature is based on the assumption that investors make decisions in a portfolio context; that is, since investors can eliminate unsystematic risk through simple diversification, there are no additional returns to them for bearing such risk.

Derivation of the CAPM

The above overview of the CAPM is not a derivation, but rather an explanation of the model. A formal derivation of the model is presented in Appendix 9A (text Web site). In general, the model assumes:

1. Ideal market conditions in which all investors are assumed to have similar expectations with respect to each investment's expected return, variance, and covariance,

and where there are no transaction costs, securities are perfectly divisible and marketable, and there are no taxes that would make investors differentiate between returns in the form of capital gains and income.
2. Investors make decisions solely in terms of each investment's contribution to their portfolio's expected return and risk.

The first assumption of ideal market implies that the optimum portfolio of risky securities held by any investor will be identical to the optimum portfolio held by any other investor. If all investors have the same portfolio, then in equilibrium that portfolio must be the market portfolio: The portfolio of all risky securities, with each security's weight equal to the proportion of its market value to the market value of all securities:

$$w_i = \frac{\text{Market Value of Security } i}{\text{Market Value of All Securities}}$$

The CAPM is often described by the borrowing-and-lending line that is tangent to the efficiency frontier constructed for all securities and associated with the equilibrium risk-free rate. This special borrowing and lending line is known as the *capital market line (CML)*. In equilibrium, all investors will end up somewhere along the CML with a portfolio yielding an expected return and risk of $E(R_I)$ and $\sigma(R_I)$ obtained by investing in the market portfolio (defined as the best Markowitz efficient portfolio) with a return and risk of $E(R^M)$ and $\sigma(R^M)$ and by going long or short in a risk-free security. As shown in Exhibit 9.2, the CML's intercept is the equilibrium risk-free rate, R_f, and its slope is the market portfolio's risk-premium per risk: $[E(R^M) - R_f]/\sigma(R^M)$:

$$E(R_I)^* = R_f + \left[\frac{E(R^M) - R_f}{\sigma(R^M)}\right] \sigma(R_I)$$

Note that not all security or portfolio return-risk combinations lie along the CML; that is, the CML shows only the Markowitz return-risk combinations that investors hold in equilibrium. The SML, on the other hand, shows the equilibrium return-risk combinations of all investments (securities, efficient portfolios, and nonefficient portfolios). The SML, in turn, can be derived from the equilibrium risk-free rate and market portfolio defined by the CML using an arbitrage argument.

The second CAPM assumption, that investors make decisions in a portfolio context, implies that they diversify away unsystematic risk. As a result, the only risk relevant for investors in evaluating securities to include in their portfolios would be systematic risk, and the only relevant factors for investors in evaluating any security would be its expected rate of return, $E(r_i)$ and its β_i. Interestingly, if all securities and investments are explained by just two factors ($E(r_i)$ and β_i), then all of the equilibrium return and beta combinations available in the market can be generated from the return and beta combinations formed from a portfolio of the market portfolio (with an expected

EXHIBIT 9.2   Capital Market Line

- **Capital Market Line (CML):** The CML is formed with the risk-free security and the market portfolio. The CML shows the different return-risk combinations investors can obtain from different allocations in the risk-free securities and the market portfolio.

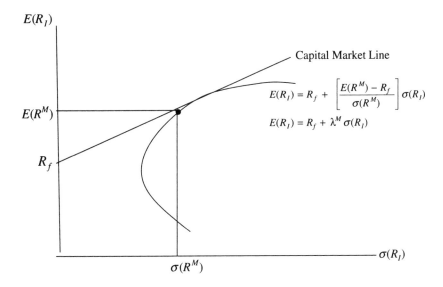

return of $E(R^M)$ and beta of one) and the risk-free security (with a rate of R_f and beta of zero).

To see this, first consider any two investments, A and C, with the following features:

Investments	$E(r)$	β
A	10%	0.5
C	15%	1.5

By forming a portfolio with these two investments, we can generate an unlimited number of expected return and beta combinations. All of the portfolio return and beta combinations formed with these securities will lie along the straight line RABCD shown in Exhibit 9.3. Points A and C on the line consist of investments only in A and C, respectively; point B, in turn, shows the portfolio return and beta combination of $E(R_p) = 12.5\%$ and $\beta_p = 1$ constructed from an equally weighted portfolio:

$$E(R_p) = w_A E(R^A) + w_C E(R^C) = (0.5)(10\%) + (0.5)(5\%) = 12.5\%$$
$$\beta_p = w_A \beta_A + w_C \beta_C = (0.5)(0.5) + (0.5)(1.5) = 1$$

EXHIBIT 9.3 Portfolio Return and Beta Combinations Formed with Stocks A and C

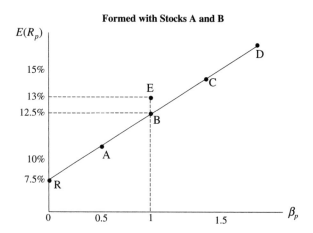

In addition, by taking short positions in C and long positions in A, return and beta combinations extending from point A to the vertical axis and beyond can also be generated. For example, by going short in C by an amount equal to 50 percent of one's investment funds ($w_C = -0.5$) and by investing in A by an amount equal to 150 percent ($w_A = 1.5$), the return and beta combination of 7.5 percent and 0 defining the vertical intercept R is obtained. In contrast, by taking short positions in A and long positions in C, one can obtain a higher return and beta combination than C's.

Given the linearly related return and beta combinations formed with securities A and C, consider now a third security E with a beta of one and an expected return of 13 percent. This security's return and beta combination lies above the line RABCD. If investors are rational and informed, this investment opportunity would not last long. That is, since this security yields the same risk as the equally allocated portfolio of A and C, but has a greater return, it would pay investors to short the equally allocated portfolio of A and C and then use the proceeds from the short sale to invest in security E. Investors executing this strategy would earn a positive cash flow with no risk and no investment—an arbitrage:

	Investment	Expected Return	Beta
Long Security E	$100	$13.00	1
Short Portfolio A and B	-$100	-$12.50	-1
Arbitrage Portfolio	0	$0.50	0

Eventually, efforts to go short in A and C and long in security E would change the prices and returns on these securities until E yielded the same return as the portfolio of A and C. This equilibrium condition would be met when security E's return and beta combination was on the return and beta line generated from securities A and C.[2] Moreover, this same arbitrage argument can be applied to any security or portfolio investment with return and beta combinations not on line RABCD. The line RABCD in Exhibit 9.3 therefore depicts the equilibrium return and beta combination for any investment (stock or portfolio), not just for portfolios formed with A and C. Thus, in equilibrium all investments must lie along a straight line in return-beta space.

Since the line RABCD can be formed with any two securities or investments, consider the straight line in return and beta space that is generated with the market portfolio and the equilibrium risk-free security as defined by the CML. The market portfolio has a return of $E(R^M)$ and a beta of one; the risk-free security has a return of R_f and a beta of zero. Just as we did with securities A and C, we can generate an infinite number of return and beta combinations with portfolios formed with the market portfolio and the risk-free security, and we can argue again that arbitragers would ensure that any investment's return and beta combination would have to be on that line. For example, if there was an investment with beta of one and return less than the market rate, then arbitrageurs could earn a riskless return by going short in the investment and long in the market (e.g., index fund). Furthermore, investors would have no demand for the investment. Arbitrageurs and investors would therefore drive the price of the security down and its return up until its return is equal to the market return, $E(R^M)$. Thus, the line in return-beta space formed with the market portfolio and the risk-free security defines the equilibrium return-beta combinations for all investments. Moreover, this line, which has an intercept of R_f and a slope of $E(R^M) - R_f$, is the SML that we defined earlier (see Exhibit 9.4).

Summary

The CAPM can be described in terms of the SML equation:

$$E(r_i)^* = R_f + [R(R^M) - R_f]\beta_i$$

The equation shows that an investment's equilibrium return is linearly and positively related to the investment's systematic risk, as measured by its beta —the greater an investment's systematic risk, the greater its equilibrium return. The SML shows that an investment's equilibrium return depends only on its systematic risk. The omission of other explanatory factors is based on the CAPM assumption that investors make security decisions based on a portfolio return-risk criterion. To recapitulate, this assumption means that since investors can diversify away unsystematic risk by forming portfolios, the market will not reward any investor for bearing such risk.

EXAMPLE USING BLOOMBERG INFORMATION TO GENERATE AN EX-POST SML

A graph of return and beta combinations with portfolios formed with the S&P 500 (SPX) and the risk-free security is shown in Bloomberg Web Exhibit 9.1 (text Web site).

EXHIBIT 9.4   Portfolios Formed with Market Portfolio and Risk-Free Security Market Line

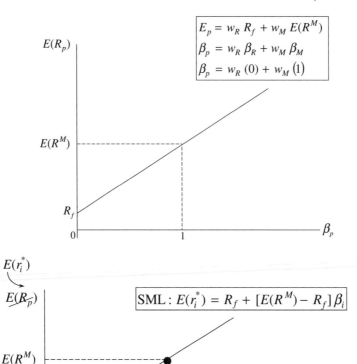

Empirical Tests of the CAPM

There has been an extensive amount of empirical testing of the CAPM. The objective in many of these tests is to empirically estimate the SML to see how it compares with the theoretical SML. In estimating the SML, many researchers use first- and second-pass tests. In the first pass, time-series regressions are used to estimate the betas of securities or portfolios, and in the second pass, a cross-sectional regression is used to estimate the SML.

One of the first studies using a first- and second-pass methodology was done by Lintner. Using the average annual returns for 301 stocks over a sample period, Lintner first estimated each stock's beta by regressing its yearly return, r_{it}, against the average return for all the stocks in the sample, R_t^M; that is:

$$r_{it} = \alpha_i + \beta_i R_t^M + \varepsilon_{it}$$

In the second pass, Lintner regressed the average returns of the 301 stocks against their estimated betas and their residual variances, $V(\varepsilon_i)$, obtained from the first pass:

$$\bar{r}_i = \gamma_0 + \gamma_1 \beta_i + \gamma_2 V(\varepsilon_i) + \varepsilon_i$$

For the CAPM to be valid, the regression intercept, γ_0, should be equal to the risk-free rate, the slope coefficient γ_1 should be equal to the market risk premium, $R_M - R_f$, and the coefficient γ_2 should be zero, indicating that unsystematic risk as measured by $V(\varepsilon)$ has no impact on an investments' equilibrium return. Compared to the estimated market rate and risk-free rate for that period, Lintner's regression intercept, γ_0, was considered too large and his estimated risk premium, γ_1, was considered too small. In addition, Lintner's regression also showed that unsystematic risk as measured by the residual variance was statistically significant. Thus, Lintner's statistical results questioned the validity of the CAPM.

Empirical tests of equilibrium models constructed similar to those of Lintner are often subject to two types of errors: *measurement errors* and *stochastic errors*. In the Lintner study, measurement errors could have occurred as a result of using unadjusted betas. That is, Lintner's estimated betas were obtained from historical regressions. Given the results of the Blume study (discussed in Chapter 6) that showed the poor statistical quality of regressions of stock returns against the market, the betas used in Lintner's study were considered poor estimates of the stocks' true betas. The measurement errors resulting from using historically estimated betas can be redressed by using either adjusted betas or using betas of portfolios instead of stocks. Stochastic errors, on the other hand, occur when the model is incorrectly specified. In Lintner's test of the CAPM, the form of the cross-section regression test implied that the risk-free rate was constant. If the risk-free rate changes and is correlated with the market rate, then Lintner's first-pass regressions would be subject to biases. One way to rectify this problem, is to regress the security's risk-premium, $r_i - R_f$ against the market risk premium, $R^M - R_f$.

The measurement and stochastic errors germane to the Lintner study were redressed in an early study conducted by Black, Jensen, and Scholes (BJS). Instead of using stock returns in their first-pass test, BJS regressed the risk premiums of portfolios, grouped in the order of their betas, against the market risk premium:[3]

$$R_{pt} - R_{ft} = \alpha + \beta[R_t^M - R_{ft}] + \varepsilon$$

In their second-pass tests, BJS regressed the average excess returns of the portfolios against their betas:

$$\bar{R}_{pi} - R_f = \gamma_0 + \gamma_1 \beta_i + \varepsilon_i$$

BJS found a relatively high correlation between the portfolio risk premiums and their beta and a slope coefficient, γ_1, that was consistent with the market risk premium.

Similar to the BJS study, Fama and MacBeth also used portfolio returns in their first- and second pass-tests. The cross-sectional equation they tested was of the form

$$\bar{R}_{pi} = \gamma_0 + \gamma_1 \beta_{pi} + \gamma_2 \beta_{pi}^2 + \gamma_3 \sigma(\varepsilon_{pi}) + \varepsilon_i$$

Fama and MacBeth found γ_1 significant and consistent with the size of the market risk premium. Furthermore, they found that over the sample period the coefficients γ_2 and γ_3 were small and not significantly different from zero, indicating that residual errors and β^2 were not significant explanatory variables.[4] Thus, in contrast to the Lintier study, the Fama and MacBeth study provides support that there is a linear relation between investment returns and systematic risk and that systematic risk is the only relevant factor in determining an investment's equilibrium return.

BLOOMBERG: AN APPLICATION OF FIRST- AND SECOND-PASS TESTS

The average returns and betas for stocks, portfolios, or investment funds can be generated in RV.

Example

1. Create a portfolio in PRTU of stocks or funds (e.g., 20 investment funds with different investment styles selected using FMAP).
2. Bring up the RV screen for one of the securities and type RV.
3. On the security's RV screen, import the portfolio into RV (Comp Source: Portfolio; Name).
4. Customize the RV screen (e.g., creating new columns for beta and returns by typing adjusted beta or beta and total returns in the amber box).
5. Click "Excel" in the Output dropdown to export the RV information to Excel.
6. In Excel, use the Excel commands to find the intercept and slope and other regression statistics (see Exhibit 6.13).

Data for conducting cross-sectional analysis also can be done using the Bloomberg Add-In for Excel (see Chapter 2 for a description on Bloomberg Excel Add-In). On the Bloomberg Add-In, click "Real/Current" from the "Import Data" and "Real-Time/Historical" dropdowns (see the Bloomberg exhibit box in Chapter 6: Bloomberg Excel Add-In: Cross-Sectional Multiple Regression).

Bloomberg HRA and Beta Applied to Portfolios and Funds

The regression of a diversified portfolio (put in a CIXB basket) or a diversified investment fund against the S&P 500 often shows a regression with a high R^2 and t-statistic, suggesting that portfolios often diversify away the unsystematic risk. In contrast, examining stocks regressed against the market using HRA or Beta, often shows low R^2 and high t-statistics.

See Bloomberg Web Exhibit 9.2.

Application of CAPM: Wells Fargo Stock Selection Approach

Today, many practitioners estimate betas or use estimated betas found in several investment publications to determine the required returns on capital investment projects and stocks they are evaluating. Several years ago Wells Fargo used as one of its investment strategies a first and second test empirical model as part of their stock investment approach. The Wells Fargo stock selection approach consisted of four steps:

Step 1: An analyst estimates the rate of return on a stock using the three-period discounted cash flow valuation model (see Chapter 3). This requires estimating dividends per share for next year, D_1, the growth rate in dividends, g, for the next five years, determining the length of the transitional period, and estimating the steady state growth rate. Given this model, the analyst then solves for the discount rate, k_e, given the current market price of the stock. The table in Exhibit 9.5 shows an example of an estimated dividend flow for a stock using the three-stage growth model. The rate of return on the stock

EXHIBIT 9.5   Wells Fargo

Period	Year	Earnings per Share	Earnings per Share	Dividend/ Earnings	Dividends per Share
	1	$2.00	$2.00	0.4	$0.80
	2	$2.00(1.08)	$2.16	0.45	$0.97
Growth = 8%	3	$2.14(1.08)	$2.33	0.5	$1.17
	4	$2.29(1.08)	$2.52	0.55	$1.39
	5	$2.45(1.08)	$2.72	0.6	$1.63
Transitional	6	$2.93(1.07)	$2.91	0.6	$1.75
Growth = 7%, 6%, and 5%	7	$6.38(1.06)	$3.09	0.6	$1.85
	8	$6.89(1.05)	$3.24	0.6	$1.94
Steady State: Growth Rate = 4%	9	$7.38(1.04)	$3.37	0.6	$2.02

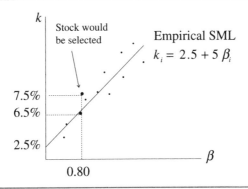

is $k = 7.5\%$ given the stock is trading in the market at \$40.40. This rate is obtained by solving for the discount rate k that equates the present value of the estimated dividend flow to the price of \$40.40:

$$P_0 = \$40.40 = \frac{\$0.80}{(1+k)^1} + \frac{\$0.97}{(1+k)^2} + \frac{\$1.17}{(1+k)^3} + \frac{\$1.39}{(1+k)^4} + \frac{\$1.63}{(1+k)^5}$$

$$+ \frac{\$1.75}{(1+k)^6} + \frac{\$1.85}{(1+k)^7} + \frac{\$1.94}{(1+k)^8} + \frac{\frac{\$2.02}{k-0.04}}{(1+k)^8} \Rightarrow k = 0.075$$

Step 2: The analyst estimates the beta of the stock. This could be the stock's historical beta, adjusted beta, or a forecasted one. For the above stock, suppose the analyst estimates its beta to be 0.80.

Step 3: Wells Fargo takes the estimated k and beta combinations for all stocks being analyzed and runs a cross-sectional regression to generate an ex-ante SML. See the figure in Exhibit 9.5.

Step 4: Wells Fargo includes stocks in the portfolio with positive excess returns (stocks with k and beta coordinates above the estimated SML) and rejects stocks with negative excess returns (those with coordinates below the line). The stock in this example would be accepted.

APPLYING THE WELLS FARGO APPROACH USING BLOOMBERG'S DDM MODEL AND ADJUSTED BETAS

The Bloomberg's DDM model estimates the intrinsic value of a selected equity using a three-stage growth model. The model also estimates the IRR: The discount rate that equated the present value of the stock's dividends and terminal value at beginning of the maturity stage. The model is similar to the methodology used by Wells Fargo analysts to estimate a stock's return (k).

- On 8/30/2013, the Bloomberg DDM screen for Procter & Gamble showed P&G with a market price of 77.89 and an IRR of 8.614%. The Beta screen for P&G on 8/30/2013 showed P&G with an adjusted beta of 0.706 for the regression period from 8/30/2006 to 8/30/2013.
- If an analyst concurred with the default assumptions underlying the DDM model and the adjusted beta as the best estimate of P&G's true beta, then she could include them as one-return beta stock.

Bloomberg Excel Add-In

Data for conducting cross-sectional analysis can be done using the Bloomberg Add-In for Excel (see Chapter 2 for a description on Bloomberg Excel Add-In). Steps to run a cross-sectional regression of DDM returns against betas are as follows:

- On the Bloomberg Add-In, click "Real/Current" from the "Import Data," "Real-Time/Historical," and "Historical/Current" dropdowns.

- On the Bloomberg Data Wizard Box, Step 1, click "indexes" in the "From" dropdown and "Dow Jones Average" from the "Indexes" dropdown, and then click "Add All." This will bring up the Dow stocks. Once loaded, click "Next."
- On the Bloomberg Data Wizard Box, Step 2, search for DDM by typing DDM in "Search Text" box and hit <Enter>. From the list, select "DDM Internal Rate," and then click "Add."
- On the Bloomberg Data Wizard Box, Step 2, search for the adjusted beta by typing beta in "Search Text" box and hit <Enter>. From the list, select "Overridable Adjusted Beta," and click "Add."
- After loading DDM and beta, click "Next."
- On the Bloomberg Data Wizard Box, Step 3, click "Finish" to export the data to Excel.

Bloomberg RVC Screen—Return-Beta Space

The RVC displays scatter data for a security (stock or fund) and its peer group. The screen allows you to select from a variety of analysis criteria and peer group types and sizes. By selecting return and beta combinations for stocks or funds and their peers you can create an ex-post return and beta space for identifying stocks or funds with abnormal returns.

See Bloomberg Web Exhibit 9.3.

Conclusion

The empirical work examining the validity of the CAPM is not definitive. Although studies by Fama and MacBeth, as well as some more recent studies, provide some support for the standard form of the CAPM, there are other studies (some discussed in the next chapter) suggesting that factors other than systematic risk are important in determining a security's equilibrium return. There is also some empirical evidence supporting nonstandard forms of the CAPM, that is, CAPMs derived from relaxing some of the model's assumptions: different borrowing and lending rates, tax impacts, nonmarketable securities, and heterogeneous expectations. The empirical evidence supporting the nonstandard forms of the CAPM are also nonconclusive. Finally, there has been strong criticism directed at the empirical methodology used to test the CAPM. In a 1977 article in the *Journal of Financial Economics*, Richard Roll argued that the CAPM may not be amendable to testing. He contended that tests using any portfolio other than the true market portfolio are not appropriate tests of the CAPM; rather, they are simply tests of whether the portfolio being used is a good proxy for the market portfolio.

Although the evidence in support of CAPM may not be conclusive, and Roll's criticism has merit, the CAPM is still an important model in finance. Since its introduction in the 1960s, the CAPM has been used by analysts and academics to determine required returns on stock investment and to solve capital budgeting problems.

Today, many practitioners estimate betas or use estimated betas found in several investment publications to determine the required returns on capital investment projects and stocks they are evaluating. In addition to determining required returns for valuation, the CAPM has also been used in many academic studies to determine whether abnormal returns (returns significantly different from the CAPM's equilibrium return) can be earned from certain types of investments. Some of these studies will be discussed in Chapter 15, when we examine the efficient market hypothesis. Finally, the CAPM has been used to define and justify investment strategies, such as the construction of index funds with a portfolio beta of one, and market timing in which active investors move into high beta stocks in anticipation of a bull market or low beta stock in anticipation of a bear market.

EQRP: BLOOMBERG'S EQUITY RISK PREMIUM SCREEN

The EQRP screen shows a stock's risk premium. The premium is equal to the forecasted market risk premium $E(R^M) - R_f$ times the stock's beta. The forecasted market risk premium forecast the market rate based on a projected market rate and risk-free rate. The risk-free rate is the 10-year Treasury for the country. Beta is the historical beta. The user can change the market risk-premium and beta. The screen also shows the historical premiums and betas.

Notes

1. This section is based on our earlier discussion of the security market line. See Chapter 6.
2. For a security with a return and beta combination below line RABCD, arbitrageur would short the security and use the proceeds to invest in a portfolio of A and C with the same beta as the security.
3. In constructing portfolios, BJS began by using the first five years of monthly data in their sample to estimate the betas of each stock. They next ranked the stocks in the order of their betas, formed 10 descile portfolios, and then calculated the monthly rates of returns for the portfolios for the sixth year. BJS then took the stock return data for years two through six in the sample to estimate betas, rank stocks, and form the descile portfolios; they then calculated the monthly rates of returns for portfolios for year seven. BJS repeated this process until they obtained 35 years of data for each descile portfolio.
4. The β^2 term makes the regression equation nonlinear if its coefficient is significantly different from zero. Fama and MacBeth found the coefficient was not significantly different from zero, supporting a linear relationship.

Selected References

Black, Fisher, N. Jensen, and M. Scholes. 1972. The capital asset pricing model: Some empirical tests. In *Studies in the Theory of Capital Markets*. Edited by M. Jensen. New York: Praeger.

Elton, Edwin, and Martin Gruber (eds). 1979. *Portfolio Theory 25 Years Later*. Amesterdam: North Holland.

Elton, Edwin J. 1999. Presidential address: Expected return, realized return, and asset pricing tests. *Journal of Finance* 54 (August): 1199–1220.

Fama, Eugene. 1973. Risk, return, and equilibrium: Empirical test. *Journal of Political Economy* 79 (January/February): 30–55.

Fama, Eugene. 1976. *Foundations of Finance*. New York: Basic Books.

Fama, Eugene, and James MacBeth. 1973. Risk, return, and equilibrium: Empirical test. *Journal of Political Economy* 38: 607–636.

Grossman, S., and R. Shiller. 1987. Estimating the continuous-time consumption-based asset-pricing model. *Journal of Business and Economic Statistics* 5: 315–328.

Jarrow, Robert, and Andrew Rudd. 1983. A comparison of the APT and SML. *Journal of Banking and Finance* 7 (June): 295–303.

Kroll, Yoram, and Haim Levy. 1992. Further tests of the Separation Theorem and the Capital Asset Pricing Model. *The American Economic Review* 82 (June): 664–670.

Lintner, John. 1965. Security prices, risks, and maximum gains from diversification. *Journal of Finance* (December): 587–615.

Mossin, J. 1966. Equilibrium in a capital asset market. *Econometrika* 34 (October): 768–783.

Roll, Richard. 1973. Evidence on the "Growth-Optimum" Model. *Journal of Finance* 28 (June): 551–556.

Ross, Stephen. 1978. A simplified approach to the valuation of risky streams. *Journal of Business* 51 (July): 453–475.

Roy, A. D. 1952. Safety first and the holding of assets. *Econometrics* 10 (July): 432–449.

Sharpe, William F. 1963. A simplified model for portfolio analysis. *Management Science* (January): 277–293.

Sharpe, W.F. 1964. Capital asset price: A theory of market equilibrium under conditions of risk. *Journal of Finance* (September): 425–442.

Bloomberg Exercises

1. Use Bloomberg FMAP, FSRC, or SECF (see "Bloomberg Funds Search Box" in this exercise section) to select a number of different types of equity funds, such as, index, value, growth, small-cap, and large-cap fund: See Bloomberg Box: "Bloomberg: An Application of First- and Second-Pass Tests."

   a. Conduct a first-pass test for each fund using the HRA screen by regressing the fund's returns against market returns. Use S&P 500 (SPX) or Russell 3000 (RAY) and select a data time period you think is appropriate.

   b. Comment on your regression findings. Based on your findings, comment on the CAPM premise: "Investors with a portfolio can diversify away unsystematic risk."

   c. Using the Fund's COMP screen as a guide, determine each fund's total return. On the COMP screen, specify the data time period and then use the annualized return appearing in the upper right corner of the screen.

   d. Using Excel, conduct a second-pass test with the returns and betas you found in 1a and 1b. See Bloomberg Exhibit Box: "Bloomberg: An Application of First- and Second-Pass Tests."

Bloomberg Funds Search
- FMAP <Enter>.
- FSRC Search: Use FSRC to search for funds.
  Click Results tab.
  Create a portfolio of the funds in PRTU.
- SECF: Click Funds Tab.
- RUSS <Enter>; Click "Russell Index Ticker" to bring up a PDF with Ticker listing.
- SPX <Enter> to bring up screen for identifying S&P indexes and tickers.

2. Create a portfolio of different types of indexes. To find a listing of different types of Russell indexes go to the Russell page (RUSS) <Enter> and click "Russell Index" to bring up a PDF with a listing of Russell indexes. For S&P indexes, enter: SPX <Enter>. Indexes can also be found using the SECF screen.
   a. Use the CORR screen to create a nonsymmetrical matrix of your indexes: CORR <Enter>; click Create tab; enter data time period; enter index's ticker in the row matrix and the S&P 500 (SPX) in the column matrix. Compare the R^2's, betas, and alphas of the indexes. Comment on the systematic and unsystematic risk you observe for the indexes.
   b. Examine several of your indexes using the HRA or beta screen: Fund Ticker <Index> <Enter>; HRA. You may want to consider the period from 2008 to the present.
   c. Find the total returns for the indexes you analyzed in 2b using the fund's COMP screen. The annualized return appears in the right corner of the screen. Consider the period from 2008 to the present.
3. Generate a graph of the portfolio return and beta combination obtained from the market portfolio and the risk-free security. For the market portfolio, calculate the average return for the S&P 500 (SPX), and for the risk-free rate, use the average yield for 10-year U.S. Treasury (USGG10yr). For the S&P 500, you may want to use the S&P 500 COMP screen (SPX <Index> <Enter>; COMP) and consider the period from 2008 to the present. For the 10-year Treasury yield, you may want to use the average yield for the same period (USGG10yr <Index>; GP screen; Ask yield, and look for average in the screen's summary box).
   a. Are the return and beta combinations of the indexes you analyzed in 2 above or below the line you generated? Explain the arbitrage portfolio you would construct if an index is not on the line.
   b. Comment on the following statement: "If all securities and investments are explained by just two factors—expected return and beta—then all of the equilibrium return and beta combinations available in the market can be generated from the return and beta combinations formed from any two investments."

4. The RVC displays scatter data for a security (stock or fund) and its peer group. The screen allows you to select from a variety of analysis criteria and peer group types and sizes. Select a stock or investment fund and then use its RVC screen to create an ex-post return and beta space for identifying stocks or funds with abnormal returns. For an example, see the Bloomberg Web Exhibit 9.3 (text Web site).

5. Select a number of stocks to analyze using the Wells Fargo Stock Selection Approach. In selecting your stocks, you may want to consider some of the stocks that make up an index or all the stocks that are included in the Dow.

   a. Use Bloomberg's DDM model to estimate each of your stock's returns (IRR). You can use Bloomberg's default assumptions used in their DDM model or change them.

   b. Use the Bloomberg's Beta screen for each of your stocks to estimate their betas. Select a time period you think is appropriate and use either the raw beta or adjusted beta.

   c. Estimate an ex-ante SML relation by running a cross-sectional regression of the returns and betas of your stocks. To use Excel for your regressions, see Exhibit 6.16 and Bloomberg Exhibit Box: "Bloomberg: An Application of First- and Second-Pass Tests."

   d. Calculate the excess return of each stock to determine which stock you would include in your portfolio.

6. Use the Bloomberg Excel Add-in to run a second-pass test in Excel. Consider: for your stocks, the stocks composing the DJIA or the S&P; for rates of return, the internal rates of return calculated from Bloomberg's DDM model; and for betas, the stocks' adjusted betas. See Bloomberg Exhibit Box, "An Application of First- and Second-Pass Tests," for an example of using regression analysis in Excel. For a guide to using the Bloomberg Excel Add-in, see Bloomberg Web Exhibit 9.2 (text Web site) and Bloomberg box: "Applying the Wells Fargo Approach Using Bloomberg's DDM Model and Adjusted Betas."

CHAPTER 10

The Arbitrage Pricing Theory

Introduction

The CAPM is based on a single-index model in which all security returns depend only on the market return. In Chapter 8, we examined this model, as well as the multi-index model in which all security returns are assumed to be a function of more than one factor. Just as the CAPM can be viewed as an extension of the single-index model, the arbitrage pricing theory (APT) can be viewed as an extension of the multi-index model. In fact, the contribution of the APT to the finance literature is in showing how an equilibrium model can be extended from one determining factor to multiple factors. The APT also differs from the CAPM in that it is more general. That is, it is based on fewer assumptions than the CAPM, and unlike the CAPM, which considers systematic risk as the determining factor, APT does not specify what factors determine a security's equilibrium returns, leaving this to empirical inquiry. What APT does do is delineate how arbitrage determines equilibrium returns. In this chapter, we examine APT.

Derivation of the Model

In Chapter 9, the SML was derived by demonstrating that in the absence of arbitrage all securities must be on a line in return and beta space. The APT applies this same arbitrage argument to establish the equilibrium state for cases in which investment returns are determined by a number of factors. The model starts by assuming that the returns on any security or portfolio are linearly related to a common set of factors (F_j). That is:

$$r_i = \alpha_i + b_{i1}F_1 + b_{i2}F_2 + \cdots + b_{in}F_n + \varepsilon_i$$

Such factors could be the market return, an industry return, aggregate output, inflation, or the difference between long-term and short-term bond rates. As

365

we noted above, the model does not specify the factors, it only requires that there be a common set of factors determining investment returns. The APT model also assumes that the standard regression assumptions hold ($E(\varepsilon_i) = 0$; $V(\varepsilon_i)$ is constant over observations; $\text{cov}(\varepsilon_i F_j) = 0$), and that there is no correlation between the error terms for different securities and portfolios and no correlation between factors: $\text{cov}(F_j F_k) = 0$.

According to the APT, if we assume that investors hold portfolios such that they can diversify away unsystematic risk (i.e., the residual error, ε), then the only relevant characteristics or attributes needed by an investor in evaluating a security or portfolio would be its expected return and its sensitivities to each common factor, b_{ij}. If all securities are described in terms of their expected returns and b_{ij}'s, then an equilibrium relationship (analogous to the SML) can be obtained by generating the portfolio expected return and portfolio b_{ij} combinations obtained from a set of selected securities.

To see how the equilibrium relation is obtained, assume that all security returns are determined by just two factors:

$$r_i = \alpha_i + b_{i1}F_1 + b_{i2}F_2 + \varepsilon_i$$

Assuming that investors can diversify away ε, there would be only three security attributes that investors would be concerned with in making their investment decisions: the security's $E(r_i)$, its sensitivity to the first factor, b_{i1}, and its sensitivity to the second factor, b_{i2}. If securities can be evaluated in terms of only three attributes, one can take any three securities (or portfolios) and generate all of the equilibrium expected return, b_1 and b_2 combinations available in the market. For example, suppose we select stocks A, B, and C with the following expected returns, b_{i1}'s, and b_{i2}'s:

Security	$E(r_i)$	b_{i1}	b_{i2}
A	8%	0.5	0.3
B	6%	0.25	0.5
C	4%	0.15	0.1

Any portfolio formed with these stocks would have expected returns, b_1, and b_2 values equal to:

$$E(R_p) = w_A E(r_A) + w_B E(r_B) + w_C E(R_C)$$
$$b_{p1} = w_A b_{A1} + w_B b_{B1} + w_C b_{C1}$$
$$b_{p2} = w_A b_{A2} + w_B b_{B2} + w_C b_{C2}$$

In addition, any portfolio formed with these stocks would also have to lie on a plane in $E(R_p)$, b_{p1}, and b_{p2} space. The plane showing all combinations of the

EXHIBIT 10.1   APT Plane

FROM PORTFOLIOS FORM WITH SECURITIES A, B, AND C
$E(R)$, b_1, and b_2 Space

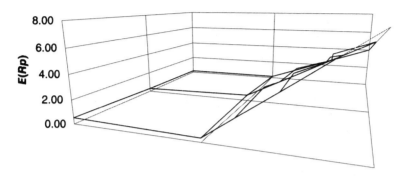

portfolio return, b_{p1}, and b_{p2} formed with stocks A, B, and C is shown in Exhibit 10.1. The equation of any plane in $E(R_p)$, b_{p1}, and b_{p2} space is:

$$E(R_p) = \lambda_0 + \lambda_1 b_{p1} + \lambda_2 b_{p2}$$

Mathematically, the equation of the plane formed with stocks A, B, and C is derived by first substituting the $E(r_i)$, b_{i1}, and b_{i2} values of our three stocks into the above equation for the plane to form three equations with three unknowns, λ_0, λ_1, and λ_3:

$$8\% = \lambda_0 + 0.5\lambda_1 + 0.3\lambda_2$$
$$6\% = \lambda_0 + 0.25\lambda_1 + 0.5\lambda_2$$
$$4\% = \lambda_0 + 0.15\lambda_1 + 0.1\lambda_2$$

The three equations can then be solved simultaneously for λ_0, λ_1, and λ_3 using matrix algebra. The matrix solution is shown in Exhibit 10.2 (for a primer on matrix algebra, see supplemental Appendix B). Solving this equation system simultaneously for these coefficients, we obtain $\lambda_0 = 2.25$, $\lambda_1 = 10$, and $\lambda_2 = 2.5$. The equation for the plane shown in Exhibit 10.1 is therefore:

$$E(R_p) = 2.25 + 10b_{p1} + 2.5b_{p2}$$

Any portfolio formed with stocks A, B, and C would lie on the plane in Exhibit 10.1. For example, an equally allocated portfolio formed with stocks A, B, and C would yield an expected portfolio return of 6 percent, a sensitivity to the first

EXHIBIT 10.2   Solving for λ_0, λ_1, and λ_3 Using Matrix Algebra

The unknowns in an equation system can be expressed in matrix form with the unknowns solved using either the inverse matrix approach or Cramer's rule. Given the equation system:

$$8\% = \lambda_0 + 0.5\lambda_1 + 0.3\lambda_2$$

$$6\% = \lambda_0 + 0.25\lambda_1 + 0.5\lambda_2$$

$$4\% = \lambda_0 + 0.15\lambda_1 + 0.1\lambda_2$$

Expressing the system in matrix form: $\mathbf{E} = \mathbf{A}\,\lambda$

$$
\begin{array}{ccc}
\mathbf{E} & \mathbf{A} & \lambda \\
\begin{pmatrix} 8 \\ 6 \\ 4 \end{pmatrix} = & \begin{pmatrix} 1 & 0.5 & 0.3 \\ 1 & 0.25 & 0.5 \\ 1 & 0.15 & 0.1 \end{pmatrix} & \begin{pmatrix} \lambda_0 \\ \lambda_1 \\ \lambda_2 \end{pmatrix}
\end{array}
$$

Using the inverse matrix approach to solve for λ:
$\lambda = \mathbf{A}^{-1}\,\mathbf{E}$

$$
\begin{array}{ccc}
\lambda & \mathbf{A}^{-1} & \mathbf{E} \\
\begin{pmatrix} \lambda_0 \\ \lambda_1 \\ \lambda_2 \end{pmatrix} = & \begin{pmatrix} -0.4167 & -0.04147 & 1.4583 \\ 3.333 & -1.6667 & -1.6667 \\ -0.8333 & 2.9167 & -2.0833 \end{pmatrix} & \begin{pmatrix} 8 \\ 6 \\ 4 \end{pmatrix}
\end{array}
$$

Multiplying $\mathbf{A}^{-1}\,\mathbf{E}$:

$$
\begin{array}{cc}
\lambda & \mathbf{A}^{-1}\mathbf{E} \\
\begin{pmatrix} \lambda_0 \\ \lambda_0 \\ \lambda_0 \end{pmatrix} = & \begin{pmatrix} (-0.4167)(8) + (-0.04167)(6) + (1.4583)(4) = 2.25 \\ (3.333)((8) + (-1.6667)(6) + (-1.6667)(4) = 10 \\ (-0.8333)(8) + (2.9167)(6) + (-2.0833)(4) = 2.5 \end{pmatrix}
\end{array}
$$

Or in algebraic form:

$$\lambda_0 = (-0.4167)(8) + (-0.04167)(6) + (1.4583)(4) = 2.25$$

$$\lambda_1 = (3.333)((8) + (-1.6667)(6) + (-1.6667)(4) = 10$$

$$\lambda_2 = (-0.8333)(8) + (2.9167)(6) + (-2.0833)(4) = 2.5$$

The equation for the plane is therefore:

$$E(R_p) = \lambda_0 + \lambda_1 b_{p1} + \lambda_2 b_{p2}$$

$$E(R_p) = 2.25 + 10 b_{p1} + 2.5 b_{p2}$$

Solving Equations Simultaneously in Excel with Matrix Multiplication Commands:
1. Form a coefficient matrix $\mathbf{A}$ in Excel (e.g., in cells A1:C3)
2. Generate the inverse matrix, $\mathbf{A}^{-1}$, by highlighting the cells for the matrix (e.g., E1:G3), entering the command "=minverse ((a1:a3), and then pressing CTrl + shift + Enter.
3. Generate the value for the λ vector by creating a column vector for E (e.g., cells B5:B7) and then multiplying the $\mathbf{A}^{-1}$ matrix by vector $\mathbf{E}$. In Excel, the product matrix is generated by highlighting an Excel column (E5:E7), entering the command: "=mmult (E1:G3, B5:B7)," and then pressing CTrl + shift + Enter.

EXHIBIT 10.2 (*Continued*)

	A	B	C	D	E	F	G	
1	1	0.5	0.3		−0.41667	−0.04167	1.458333	**A⁻¹:** The inverse matrix, A^{-1}, is generated by
2	1	0.25	0.5		3.333333	−1.66667	−1.66667	highlighting the cells for the matrix (e.g., E1:G3),
3	1	0.15	0.1		−0.83333	2.916667	−2.08333	entering the command "=minverse ((A1:A3),
4		E			$\lambda = A^{-1} E$			and then pressing CTrl + shift + Enter.
5		8			2.25			$\lambda = A^{-1}E$: The product matrix is generated by
6		6			10			highlighting (E5:E7), entering the command:
7		4			2.5			"=mmult (E1:G3, B5:B7)",
8								and then pressing CTrl + shift + Enter.

factor of $b_{p1} = 0.3$, and a sensitivity to the second factor of $b_{p2} = 0.3$, and the portfolio's coordinate $(E(R_p), b_{p1}, b_{p2}) = (6\%, 0.3, 0.3)$ would lie on the plane:

$$E(R_p) = (1/3)(0.08) + (1/3)(0.06) + (1/3)(0.04) = 0.06$$
$$b_{p1} = (1/3)(0.5) + (1/3)(0.25) + (1/3)(0.15) = 0.3$$
$$b_{p2} = (1/3)(0.3) + (1/3)(0.5) + (1/3)(0.10) = 0.3$$

$$E(R_p) = 2.25 + 10b_{p1} + 2.5b_{p2}$$
$$E(R_p) = 2.25 + 10(0.3) + 2.5(0.3) = 0.06$$

Finally, using the same arbitrage argument we used to derive the SML, we can establish that in equilibrium any security or portfolio would also have to be on the plane defined by stocks A, B, and C. For example, consider a stock D with attributes of $b_{D1} = 0.3$, $b_{D2} = 0.3$, and $E(r_D) = 4\%$. Stock D's $E(r)$, b_1, and b_2 coordinate is below the plane formed with A, B, and C. In this case, arbitragers would be able to profit by going short in stock D and long in an equally allocated portfolio of A, B, and C, with the portfolio investment financed from the proceeds from the short position. This arbitrage portfolio would yield a positive cash flow at the end of the period, with no risk and no investment—a "free lunch."

	Investment	Expected Return	b_{i1}	b_{i2}
Short Security D	−$100	−$4.00	−0.3	−0.3
Long Portfolio of A,B,C	$100	$6.00	0.3	0.3
Arbitrage Portfolio	0	$2.00	0	0

With this opportunity, arbitrageurs would pursue this strategy, causing the price of stock D to fall and its expected return to increase (and possibly the prices of A, B, and C to increase and their returns to fall) until stock D was on the plane formed with securities A, B, and C. Moreover, this same arbitrage argument can be applied to any security or investment with an expected return, b_1, and b_2 combinations not on the plane formed with A, B, and C. The plane in Exhibit 10.1 therefore depicts the equilibrium return, b_1, and b_2 combinations for any security or portfolio, not just for portfolios formed with securities A, B, and C. Thus, if all securities are determined by just two factors, then in equilibrium all investments must be on a plane in return, b_1, and b_2 space, with the equilibrium return for any security or portfolio being determined by the investment's attributes b_{i1} and b_{i2}; that is:

$$E(r_i)^* = \lambda_0 + \lambda_1 b_{i1} + \lambda_2 b_{i2}$$

λ Coefficient Values

The λ values defining the equilibrium return relation were obtained by solving the three-equation system simultaneously. Alternatively, these coefficients can be found by examining particular portfolios. For example, consider a portfolio formed with zero sensitivity to both factors, $b_{p1} = b_{p2} = 0$. Such a portfolio would have an equilibrium return equal to λ_0.[1] With securities A, B, and C, this portfolio can be formed with an allocation of $w_A = -0.41667$, $w_B = -0.04167$, and $w_C = 1.458333$ and would yield an expected return of 2.25 percent, which is equal to the λ_0 value we calculated. Since investors can eliminate systematic risk with this portfolio, this portfolio would be riskless. Using the arbitrage argument, the rate on a riskless security, in equilibrium, would have to be equal to the rate on the portfolio formed with zero sensitivity to the factors; thus, a priori the intercept should be equal to the risk-free rate:

$$\lambda_0 = R_f$$

Next, consider a portfolio formed with unit sensitivity to the first factor and zero sensitivity to the second: $b_{p1} = 1$ and $b_{p2} = 0$. With securities A, B, and C, this portfolio is formed with an allocation of $w_A = 2.92$, $w_B = -1.71$, and $w_C = -0.21$ and would yield an expected return of 12.25 percent. If the value of the first factor is $E(R_1)$, then in equilibrium the coefficient λ_1 would be equal to $E(R_1) - R_f$; that is, solving for λ_1 for a portfolio with unit sensitivity to the first factor and zero to the second and with a return in equilibrium of $E(R_1)$, we obtain:

$$E(r_i)^* = \lambda_0 + \lambda_1 b_{i1} + \lambda_2 b_{i2}$$
$$E(R_1) = R_f + \lambda_1(1) + \lambda_2(0)$$
$$\lambda_1 = E(R_1) - R_f$$

This is consistent with the λ_1 value we solved for in our equation for the plane:

$$\lambda_1 = E(R_1) - R_f = 12.25\% - 2.25\% = 10\%$$

If the first factor, in turn, were the market return, then in equilibrium a portfolio formed with unit sensitivity to the market and zero sensitivity to the other factor would have to have a return equal the market return and λ_1 would have to be equal to $E(R^M) - R_f$.

Finally, consider a portfolio formed with unit sensitivity to the second factor and zero sensitivity to the first: $b_{p2} = 1$ and $b_{p1} = 0$. With securities A, B, and C, this portfolio is formed with an allocation of $w_A = -1.25$, $w_B = 2.875$, and $w_C = -0.625$ and would yield an expected return of 4.75 percent. If the value of the second factor is $E(R_2)$, then in equilibrium the coefficient λ_2 would be equal to $E(R_2) - R_f$:

$$E(r_i)^* = \lambda_0 + \lambda_1 b_{i1} + \lambda_2 b_{i2}$$
$$E(R_2) = R_f + \lambda_1(0) + \lambda_2(1)$$
$$\lambda_2 = E(R_2) - R_f$$

This result is also consistent with our example, where the λ_2 value we solved for in our equation for the plane was 2.5 percent:

$$\lambda_2 = E(R_2) - R_f = 4.75\% - 2.25\% = 2.5\%$$

Thus, if the second factor were the expected return on the average bond investment, $E(R_B)$ (e.g., bond index return), then in equilibrium a portfolio formed with unit sensitivity to the bond market return and zero sensitivity to the other factor would have to have a return equal the bond market return and λ_2 would have to be equal to $E(R_B) - R_f$.

Given the a priori values of the coefficients, the equilibrium relation for any investment i can alternatively be defined as

$$E(r_i)^* = \lambda_0 + \lambda_1 b_{i1} + \lambda_2 b_{i2}$$
$$E(r_i)^* = R_f + [E(R_1) - R_f]b_{i1} + [E(R_2) - R_f]b_{i2}$$

As noted, this equation is consistent with our numerical example:

$$E(R_p) = \lambda_0 + \lambda_1 b_{p1} + \lambda_2 b_{p2}$$

$$E_i^* = 2.25 + 10b_{p1} + 2.5b_{p2}$$

It should be highlighted that the equilibrium APT equation is similar in form to the SML equation, which is also defined in terms of risk-free rate, factor (market) premium, and the investment's sensitivity to the factor.

General APT Model

The equilibrium return in the above case is based on a two-factor model. The equilibrium relation was obtained by generating a plane from the return, b_1, and b_2 characteristics of three securities, then using an arbitrage argument to establish that in equilibrium all securities should lie on that plane. This methodology is the same approach we used in Chapter 9 to derive the SML. For the SML, we had a single-factor model, with the one factor being the market return, and we generated a line from the return and beta combinations of two investments; we then used an arbitrage argument to establish that in equilibrium all securities would be on that line. See Exhibit 10.3 for a summary comparison of CAPM and APT. In general, the APT is defined by the multifactor model (sometimes referred to as the multifactor return-generating process) and the resulting equilibrium return relation:

$$r_i = \alpha_i + b_{i1}F_1 + b_{i2}F_2 + \cdots + b_{in}F_n + \varepsilon_i$$
$$E(r_i)^* = \lambda_0 + \lambda_1 b_{i1} + \lambda_2 b_{i2} + \cdots + \lambda_2 b_{i2}$$
$$E(r_i)^* = R_f + [E(R_1) - R_f]b_{i1} + [E(R_2) - R_f]b_{i2} + \cdots$$
$$+ [E(R_n) - R_f]b_{in}$$

Empirical Tests of the APT

Like the CAPM, the empirical testing of the APT lends itself to a first- and second-pass methodology. The problem in applying first- and second-test methods to the APT, however, is that unlike the CAPM where the factor is known (the market rate), the factors are not identified in the APT. Because of this problem, researchers in testing the APT have used two approaches. The first is to use a statistical approach known as *factor analysis* that does not specify specific factors; the second is to use a specified factor approach in which factors are identified.

Unspecified Approach: Factor Analysis

Factor analysis is a complex statistical procedure used to create proxy factors that explain correlations among observations from a set of variables. The procedure involves gathering data on a large number of variables and trying to statistically identify underlying forces that could explain the observed trends. For example, suppose a statistician collected information such as weight, height, eye color, hair color, and length of hair from a sample of people. Applying factor analysis to the data, the statistician might find that there is a correlation among height, weight, and hair length, but not hair color, that could be explained by some common factor. We know a priori that the factor is gender. Looking just at the data, however, the statistician would not know this. She would be able to create a proxy variable or factor based on the sample that reflects gender (e.g., an index equal to the 30th percentile of hair length, 40th percentile of weight, and 40th percentile of height). This proxy factor would not be able to identify the correlation in hair color with other characteristics. By analyzing the data further, however, the statistician might observe that 10 percent of the sample has gray hair, which she might define as an index or proxy factor that we know would describe the factor of "age over 50." From this factor analysis, the statistician might conclude that there are two proxy factors that explain the correlations among the observations.

EXHIBIT 10.3 Comparison of CAPM and APT

CAPM	APT
Based on Single-Index Model:	**Based on Multi-Index Model**
Assumes all investments (i) are related to the market:	Assumes all investments (i) are related to a common set of factors:
$$r_i = \alpha_i + \beta_i R^M + \varepsilon_i$$	$$r_i = \alpha_i + b_{i1}F_1 + b_{i2}F_2 + \cdots + b_{in}F_n + \varepsilon_i$$
The explanatory factor is the market return, R^M	Common set of explanatory factors are not specified
ε_i is Diversified Away	**ε_i is Diversified Away**
Investors make their investment decisions in a portfolio context. With a portfolio, investors can diversify away unsystematic risk, ε_i. Thus, a security's undiversified or unsystematic risk would not affect the security's equilibrium price and return.	Investors make their investment decisions in a portfolio context. With a portfolio, investors can diversify away unsystematic risk, ε_i. Thus, a security's undiversified or unsystematic risk would not affect the security's equilibrium price and return.
Equilibrium Return	**Equilibrium Return**
The equilibrium return on an investment is determined by its systematic risk as measured by its beta and not by unsystematic factors that investors can diversify away.	The equilibrium return on an investment is determined by its sensitivity to each factor, b_1, $b_2, \ldots b_n$ and not by unsystematic factors that investors can diversify away.
Equilibrium Return Relation:	**Equilibrium Return Relation:**
With unsystematic risk diversified away, the only relevant factors for investors in evaluating any security would be its expected rate of return, $E(r_i)$, and its β_i.	With unsystematic risk diversified away, the only relevant factors for investors in evaluating any security would be its expected rate of return, $E(r_i)$, and its sensitivity to each factor $b_1, b_2, \ldots b_n$.
If all securities and investments are explained by just two factors, then all of the equilibrium return and beta combinations available in the market can be generated from the return and beta combinations formed from a portfolio of the market portfolio with an expected return of $E(R^M)$ and beta of one and the risk-free security with a rate of R_f and beta of zero. Arbitrage would ensure that all equilibrium return and beta combinations would be on a line in $E(r)$, β space.	If all securities and investments are explained by two factors, for example, then all of the equilibrium return and b_1 and b_2 sensitivity combinations available in the market can be generated from the return and b_1 and b_2 combinations formed from a portfolio of three investments. Arbitrage would ensure that all equilibrium return and b_1 and b_2 combinations would be on a plane in $E(r)$, b_1 and b_2 space.
The equilibrium relation is depicted by the SML and SML equation:	For two factors, the equilibrium relation is depicted by a plane and the equation for the plane.
	$$E(r_i)^* = R_f + [E(R_1) - R_f]b_{i1} + [E(R_2) - R_f]b_{i2}$$

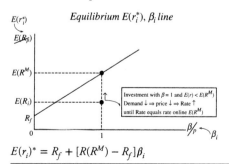

Equilibrium $E(r_i^*)$, β_i line

$E(r_i^*)$, $E(R_p)$, $E(R^M)$, $E(R_i)$, R_f

Investment with $\beta = 1$ and $E(r) < E(R^M)$
Demand $\downarrow \Rightarrow$ price $\downarrow \Rightarrow$ Rate $\uparrow$
until Rate equals rate online $E(R^M)$

$$E(r_i)^* = R_f + [R(R^M) - R_f]\beta_i$$

$E(R)$, b_1, and b_2 Space

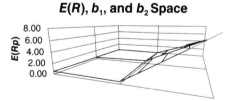

For n-securities, the equilibrium relation is

$$E(r_i)^* = R_f + [E(R_1) - R_f]b_{i1} + [E(R_2) - R_f]b_{i2}$$
$$+ \cdots + [E(R_n) - R_f]b_{in}$$

(Continued)

EXHIBIT 10.3   (*Continued*)

CAPM	APT
Empirical Relation:	**Empirical Relation:**

Empirical Relation:

Empirically the SML is estimated by using a first-pass and second-pass methodology. In the first pass, time-series regressions are used to estimate the betas of securities (or portfolios):

$$r_{it} = \alpha_i + \beta_i R_t^M + \varepsilon_{it}$$

In the second pass, a cross-sectional regression is used in which the average returns or risk premiums of the securities (or portfolios) are regressed against their betas to estimate a SML relation:

$$\bar{R}_{pi} - \bar{R}_f = \gamma_0 + \gamma_1 \beta_i + \varepsilon_i$$

Explanatory Factors

Market Return

Empirical Relation:

Empirically APT is estimated by using a first-pass and second-pass methodology: In the first pass, time-series regressions are used to estimate the factor sensitivities of securities (or portfolios), $b_1, b_2, \ldots b_n$

$$r_i = c_0 + c_1 F_{i1} + c_2 F_{i2} + c_3 F_{i3} + \cdots + c_n F_{in} + \varepsilon_i$$

In the second pass, a cross-sectional regression is used in which the average returns or risk premiums of the securities (or portfolios) are regressed against their sensitivity factors $b_1, b_2, \ldots b_n$ to estimate the APT relation:

$$\bar{r}_i - \bar{R}_f = \gamma_0 + \gamma c_{11} + \gamma_2 c_2 + \gamma_3 c_{31} + \cdots + \gamma_4 c_n + \varepsilon_i$$

Explanatory Factors

Chen, Roll, and Ross: Unanticipated changes in inflation, the term structure of rates (differences in long-term and short-term bond yields), industrial production, and risk spreads (differences in yields on low quality and high quality bonds.

Burmeister and McElroy: Unexpected changes in default risk, changes in term structure, inflation, changes in growth rate in real aggregate, and independent market return factor.

Fama and French: Market return, return of a portfolio of small stocks over a portfolio of large stocks, and excess return as measured by return of a portfolio of high book-to-market value in excess of the return of a portfolio of low book-to-market value.

When factor analysis is applied to security returns, the data usually consists of time-series rates of return from a large sample of securities. Factors are then constructed that best explain the correlations of returns within the sample. After the factors have been formed, the time-series data on each security's return is often regressed against the factors (first-pass test) to estimate each security's sensitivity attributes, b_{ij}. Finally, each security's average return is regressed against its b_{ij}'s (second-pass test). In a classic study examining the validity of the APT, Roll and Ross used factor analysis techniques on 42 groups of 30 stocks over a sample period from 1962 to 1972. They found between four and six factors that were significant in explaining the correlations among investment returns. Their study provided early support for the multifactor/APT models.

Specified Factor Approach

From factor analysis, equilibrium returns are explained in terms of factors that are manufactured from the data. Studies using a specified factor approach to test the validity of the APT begin by identifying the common factors important in determining a security's equilibrium returns. Given those factors, many studies then apply a first-pass test to estimate each security's sensitivity (either its return, r_i or risk premium) to the identified factors:

$$r_i = c_0 + c_1 F_{i1} + c_2 F_{i2} + c_3 F_{i3} + \cdots + c_n F_{in} + \varepsilon_i$$

A second-pass test in which the average returns on each security (or average risk premium) are regressed against their sensitivity factors is then used to estimate the market relation:[2]

$$\bar{r}_i = \gamma_0 + \gamma c_{i1} + \gamma_2 c_{i2} + \gamma_3 c_{i3} + \cdots + \gamma_n c_{in} + \varepsilon_i$$

Sharpe Study

One of the early studies using specified factors was done by William Sharpe. In his first-pass test, he estimated the relationship between a stock's return and the market rate, long-term bond rate, and the stock's dividend yield. He estimated this relationship for over 2,000 stocks using data covering 1931 through 1979. In his second pass, Sharpe regressed the average returns of each stock against the coefficients estimated from the first-pass tests. He made several second-pass tests, varying the number of coefficients used as explanatory variables and the time periods. In comparing several regression models, Sharpe found that models with two or more coefficients had better regression results than did the linear regression model explained by just beta. This finding provided some support for a multifactor/APT model.

Chen, Roll, and Ross

A more recent study of multifactor/APT models was done by Chen, Roll, and Ross (CRR). They argued that equilibrium returns on investments should be related to macroeconomic factors that affect the present value of an investment's future cash flows (e.g., real gross domestic product, interest rates, market risk, and inflation). In addition, CRR argued that investors respond to unanticipated changes in these factors. To test this empirically, CRR first estimated the relationship between the returns on portfolios grouped in terms of the size of their betas (Fama and MacBeth approach) and four factors measuring unanticipated changes in inflation, the term structure of rates (differences in long-term and short-term bond yields), industrial production, and risk spreads (differences in yields on low-quality and high-quality bonds). Finding a relatively strong statistical relation between the portfolio returns and the unanticipated macroeconomic factors, CRR next estimated the cross-sectional relationship between the average portfolio returns and the estimated coefficients from the time-series regressions. They found the coefficients of the macroeconomic factors to be significant. They also found that when they included the portfolio's beta as an explanatory variable along with the other macro variable coefficients, it was insignificant. Thus, like the Sharpe study, the CRR study provided evidence in support of the multifactor/APT model as an explanation of what determines equilibrium returns.

Burmeister and McElroy

Following the lead of CRR, Burmeister and McElroy (BM) also tested multifactor models using unexpected macroeconomic variables. In their time-series regressions, the monthly returns of 70 stocks were regressed against the following five variables:

1. F_1 = unexpected changes in default risk as measured by the average difference between corporate and government monthly rates (0.5 percent) minus the observed difference: $F_1 = 0.5\% - (R_{corp} - R_{gov})$.
2. F_2 = unanticipated changes in term structure as measured by the average difference between the monthly rates on long-term Treasury bonds and short-term Treasury bills (which they assumed to be zero) minus the observed differences: $F_2 = R_{LT} - R_{ST}$.
3. F_3 = unanticipated inflation as measured by the forecast inflation for the beginning of the month (using trend analysis) and the actual inflation rate at the end of the month.
4. F_4 = unanticipated changes in the growth rate in real aggregate output as measured by the forecast growth rate in real aggregate expenditures at the beginning of the month (using trend analysis) and the actual rate at the end of the month.
5. F_5 = independent market return factor. To minimize statistical bias (problems related to multicollinearity), the market return factor was measured by the error term, ε_M, obtained by first regressing the market risk premium $(R^M - R_f)$ against the above four factors and then taking the difference between the observed market premium and the estimated one using observed values of the factors, F^{Obs}:

$$R^M - R_f = \gamma_0 + \gamma_1 F_1 + \gamma_2 F_2 + \gamma_3 F_{31} + \gamma_4 F_4 + \varepsilon_M$$
$$F_5 = \varepsilon_M = [R^M - R_f] - [\gamma_0 + \gamma_1 F_1^{Obs} + \gamma_2 F_2^{Obs} + \gamma_3 F_3^{Obs} + \gamma_1 F_4^{Obs}]$$

From the 70 regressions, BM found that 215 out of the 350 coefficients estimated were significant and that on average the five factors explained approximately 50 percent of the variation in a security's return. BM also regressed portfolio returns against the above factors. The portfolios consisted of stocks grouped into growth, cyclical, stable, utility, transportation, and finance categories. BM found the results from these regressions were better than from stock regression: More coefficients were significant and the five factors explained about 80 percent of the variation in returns. Thus, like the Sharpe and CRR studies, the BM study also supports a multifactor model.

Fama and French

Fama and French proposed a three-factor model using (1) the market return, (2) corporate capitalization or size as measured by the difference in the return of a portfolio of small stocks over a portfolio of large stocks, and excess returns as measured by the return of a portfolio of high book-to-market value stocks in excess of the return of a portfolio of low book-to-market value stocks. (Firms with high ratios of book-to-market value are likely to be in more financial stress than firms with low ratios.) The Fama-French model was tested by Davis, Fama, and French, who formed nine portfolios with different ranges in size and book-to-market value. The statistical results for each of the nine portfolios had R^2 over 0.90 and large t-statistics, providing support for the explanatory power of this three-factor model.

Summary of Empirical Models

In studies using factor analysis, equilibrium returns are explained in terms of factors that are manufactured from the data. Because the APT does not specify the determining factors, factor analysis is a proper and sufficient empirical test of the theory. In the financial and economic literature, however, there is a ubiquitous debate over whether or not models should be prespecified on the basis of theory or whether models should be generated empirically. Without theory, the empirical results are often difficult to interpret and are not as insightful.[3] The empirical studies of Sharpe; Chen, Roll, and Ross; Burmeister and McElroy and others avoid this problem by first specifying the factors and then applying first- and second-pass regression tests to empirically estimate the equilibrium relationship. A problem with this approach is that poor statistical results could be the effect of selecting the wrong factors and would therefore not necessarily invalidate the APT. Many of the studies using a specified factor approach, however, are consistent with the Roll and Ross factor analysis study in their support of the multifactor/APT model. In addition, the more recent studies using a specified factor approach provide some evidence in support of equilibrium returns being determined by macroeconomic factors.

MRA: BLOOMBERG'S MULTIPLE REGRESSION SCREEN

Multiple regression analysis can be done using the Bloomberg MRA screen. On the screen, one selects a set for inputting information or editing a previous set. The dependent and independent variables are inputted by their tickers and <Equity> or Index ticker <Index>. The MRA output shows the coefficient estimates, t-tests, R^2, and F-Statistic.

BLOOMBERG EXCEL ADD-IN: SECOND-PASS TEST FOR MULTIFACTOR MODELS

French and Fama argue that firms with high ratios of book-to-market value are likely to be in more financial stress than firms with low ratios, and that such risk is important in explaining equilibrium returns. Altman's Z score is a measure of a company's likelihood of default and possibly a good proxy for financial risk.

(Continued)

Test of Relationship: Conduct a second-pass test of stock returns explained in terms of their betas and Altman's Z-scores.

Data for conducting cross-sectional analysis can be found using the Bloomberg Add-In for Excel (see Chapter 2 for a description of Bloomberg Excel Add-In). Steps to run a cross-sectional regression of returns against betas and Altman Z-Score are as follows:

- On the Bloomberg Add-in, click "Real-Time Current" from the "Import Data" and "Real-Time/Historical" dropdowns.
- On the Bloomberg Data Wizard Box, Step 1, click "indexes" in the "From" dropdown and the name of index (e.g., S&P 100) from the "Indexes" dropdown, and then click "Add All." This will bring up the stocks for the index. Once loaded, click "Next."
- On the Bloomberg Data Wizard Box, Step 2, search and then add stock returns (e.g., DDM Internal Return, betas, and Altman Z-Score).
- After loading variables, click "Next."
- On the Bloomberg Data Wizard Box, Step 3, click "Finish" to export the data to Excel.
- Multiple-regression can be done in Excel by using the "Data Analysis" Add-in. See Exhibit 6.16.
- Example: The S&P 100 stocks' DDM internal rates regressed against their betas and Altman Z-scores and instruction on running multiple regression:

	A	B	C	D	E	F	G
1	Stocks	DDM IRR	Adjusted Beta	Altman Z-Score	Multiple Regression: Click "Data"		
2	AAPL UW Equity	13.3363	0.9657	5.4980	and then "Data Analysis"		
3	ABBV UN Equity	9.0815	1.0720	4.2521			
4	ABT UN Equity	9.1800	0.7351	3.5552	In Data Analysis Box: Click "Regression"		
5	ACN UN Equity	10.1505	1.0978	6.6480	In Regression Box:		
6	AEP UN Equity	8.1879	0.7068	0.8991	• Enter field for Return in "Input Y Range"		
7	AMGN UW Equity	8.5779	0.7446	2.8591	box: B2:B86;		
8	AMZN UW Equity	11.7587	1.1792	6.2581	• Enter field for explanatory variables in		
9	APA UN Equity	10.9999	1.4378	1.6732	"Input X range" box: C2:D86		
10	APC UN Equity	10.2836	1.3811	1.8056	• Click OK		
11	BA UN Equity	10.0843	1.0591	1.9648	Regression Output sent to separate worksheet		
12	BAX UN Equity	9.7470	0.9038	3.0687			
13	BMY UN Equity	7.4564	0.6493	4.1850	Multiple R	0.66456058	
14	BRK/B UN Equity	7.5869	0.8904	2.2908	R Square	0.44164077	

Data Pulled from Bloomberg Excell Add-In:
- "Import Data"; "Real Time/Historical"; "Real Time Current"

- Bloomberg Data Wizzard Box - Step 1 of 3: Loaded S&P 100 stocks

- Bloomberg Data Wizzard Box - Step 2 of 3, Select Fields: DDM IRR, Override adjusted beta, Altman Z-Score

- Bloomberg Data Wizzard Box - Step 3 of 3: click Finish

Adjusted R Sq	0.42802225	
Standard Error	1.08295894	
Observations	85	

	Coefficients	t Stat
Intercept	5.81697563	10.615359
X Variable 1	3.91311396	8.008853
X Variable 2	0.09510728	2.1482794

Application of APT: Factor Models

Portfolios constructed by practitioners from multifactor/APT analysis are called factor models. Three general types of multifactor models are statistical factor models, fundamental models, and macro model. Statistical factor models are based on explaining security and portfolio returns based on artificial factors created from factor analysis. Fundamental models, in turn, use a cross-sectional approach similar to the Wells Fargo model examined in Chapter 9, but with more than one explanatory variable. Macroeconomic factor models are portfolios that are constructed based on macroeconomic factors. A number of these models are rooted in the works of Chen, Roll, and Ross and Burnmeister and McElroy.

Most of the factor models are proprietary models. One published model was the Salomon-Smith-Barney's Risk Attributes Model (RAM). The model consists of four steps:

1. **Step 1:** Stock returns are explained by a set of macroeconomic variables:
   1. Investors' Confidence: $R^{corp} - R^{govt}$.
   2. Interest Rates: Δ(LT Rate – ST Rate)
   3. Inflation Shock: Actual minus expected inflation rate.
   4. Aggregate Business Fluctuations: Δ (Industrial Production).
   5. Foreign Variables: Δ(Exchange Rate).
   6. Market Factors: Residual Market Beta.
2. **Step 2:** Time-series regressions of the stock returns against the six macroeconomic variables: Salomon-Smith-Barney model regressed the returns of 3,500 stocks against the above macroeconomic factors:

$$r_i = a_i + b_{i1}F_1 + b_{i2}F_2 + \cdots + b_{i6}F_6 + \varepsilon_i$$

3. **Step 3:** Standardization of the coefficients: For each coefficient, the average coefficient and average standard deviation are computed. For example, for b_1:

$$\bar{b}_1 = \frac{\sum_{i=1}^{3,500} b_{i1}}{3,500}$$

$$\sigma_{b_1} = \left[\frac{\sum_{i-1}^{3,500} (b_{i1} - \bar{b}_1)^2}{3,500} \right]^{1/2}$$

For stock i, its adjusted standardized coefficient is calculated as:

$$\hat{b}_{i1} = \frac{b_{i1} - \bar{b}_1}{\sigma_{b_1}}$$

If a stock has an adjusted beta equal to zero, then the stock's sensitivity to factor 1 is no different from the average. If its adjusted beta exceeds zero, then the stock has an above average responsiveness to factor 1. Finally, if the adjusted beta is less than zero, then the stock has a below average responsiveness to factor one.

4. **Step 4:** For each stock, its score, S_i, is determined. The score is obtained by multiplying the stock's adjusted coefficients by an estimate of the macroeconomic factors, then summing the products:

$$S_i = a_i + \hat{b}_{i1}(E(F_1)) + \hat{b}_{i2}(E(F_2)) + \cdots + \hat{b}_{i6}(E(F_6))$$

5. **Step 5:** A portfolio is constructed consisting of the stocks with the highest scores.

Conclusion

Since its introduction in the 1960s, the CAPM has been used by analysts and academics to determine required returns on stock investment and solve capital budgeting problems. Today, many practitioners estimate betas, or use estimated betas found in several investment publications, to determine the required returns on capital investment projects and stocks they are evaluating. The newer multifactor/APT model has not been used as extensively as the CAPM. However, it can be applied in many of the same ways as the CAPM: determining required returns for valuation, estimating abnormal returns, and defining investment and portfolio strategies. One of the advantages of the multifactor/APT model over the CAPM is that one can generate portfolios with more than one attribute. For example, a pension fund manager wanting a portfolio that is both invariant to inflation and highly correlated with the market could use a multifactor model similar to the one estimated by Burmeister and McElroy to find stocks with relatively small coefficients associated with the inflation factor (F_3) and coefficients that are approximately equal to one for the independent market factor (F_5). Similarly, by selecting stocks based on their sensitivities to a set of factors such as inflation, interest rates, and the market, an investor may be able to speculate on not only the market's future performance but also on inflation and interest rate changes.

As we conclude this chapter on equilibrium models, it is important to keep in mind that we are dealing with theory, and not a definitive explanation of what determines security returns. This, of course, is not comforting to portfolio and investment managers who can't afford to be too dogmatic or theoretical, but rather must find out what works. As theories supported by some empirical work, however, both the CAPM and the APT give us important insights into how the capital market functions: the importance of portfolio decisions, how diversification reduces the importance of firm and industry factors, how returns can be determined by certain factors, and the importance of macroeconomic factors. As the noted economist John Maynard Keynes said, "half-baked theory may not be much value in practice, but it may be halfway towards final perfection."

Notes

1. The allocations needed to obtain portfolios that have a sensitivity to the first factor of b^*_{p1} and sensitivity to the second of b^*_{p2} can be found by substituting $1 - w_A - w_B$ for w_C in the

equations for b_{p1} and b_{p2}, setting the equations equal to b_{p1}^* and b_{p2}^*, then solving the two equations simultaneously for w_A and w_B. That is:

$$b_{p1}^* = w_A b_{A1} + w_B b_{B1} + (1 - w_A - w_B) b_{C1}$$
$$b_{p2}^* = w_A b_{A2} + w_B b_{B2} + (1 - w_A - w_B) b_{C2}$$

2. The Fama and MacBeth study discussed in Chapter 9 could be viewed as an empirical test of the multifactor/APT model. Recall that Fama and MacBeth estimated the relation between the equilibrium return of portfolios and beta, beta squared, and the variance of the residual error.
3. Note that this was not the problem in the CAPM where we started with a theory that identified market return as the relevant factor to explain a security's equilibrium return.

Selected References

Arnott, Robert D., and Chris G. Luck. 2003. The many elements of equity styles: Quantitative management of core, growth, and value styles. *Handbook of Equity Style Management*. Edited by T. D. Coggin, F. J. Fabozzi, and R. D. Arnott. Hoboken, NJ: John Wiley & Sons.

Burmeister, Edwin, and Marjorie McElroy. 1988. Joint estimation of factor sensitivities and risk premia for the Arbitrage Pricing Theory. *Journal of Finance* 43 (July): 721–733.

Chen, Nai-fu. 1983. Some empirical tests of the theory of arbitrage pricing. *Journal of Finance* 38 (December): 1392–1414.

Chen, Nai-fu, Richard Roll, and Stephen Ross. 1986. Economic forces and the stock market. *Journal of Business* 59 (July): 386–403.

Cho, D. Chinhyung, Edwin Elton, and Martin Gruber. 1984. On the robustness of the Roll and Ross Arbitrage Pricing Theory. *Journal of Financial and Quantitative Analysis* 24 (March 1984): 1–10.

Fama, Eugene, and Kenneth French. 1992. The cross section of expected stock returns. *Journal of Finance* 47 (June): 427–466.

Fama, Eugene, and James MacBeth. 1973. Risk, return, and equilibrium: Empirical test. *Journal of Political Economy* 38: 607–636.

Gibbons, M. 1982. Multivariate tests of financial models: A new approach. *Journal of Financial Economics* 10 (March): 3–27.

Huberman, G. 1982. A simple approach to Arbitrage Pricing Theory. *Journal of Economic Theory* 28 (October): 183–191.

Ingersoll, Jonathan E. 1984. Some results in the theory of arbitrage pricing. *Journal of Finance* 19: 1021–1039.

Jarrow, Robert, and Andrew Rudd. 1983. A comparison of the APT and SML. *Journal of Banking and Finance* 7 (June): 295–303.

Joreskog, K. J. 1963. *Statistical Estimation in Factor Analysis*. Stockholm: Almqvist & Wiksell.

Kim, Dongcheol. 1995. The errors-in-variables problem in the cross-section of expected stock returns. *Journal of Finance* 50: 1605–1634.

Lawley, D., and M. A. Maxwell. 1963. *Factor Analysis as a Statistical Method*. London: Butterworths.

McElroy, Marjorie, and Edwin Burmeister. 1988. Arbitrage Pricing Theory as a restrictive non-linear multivariate regression model: ITNLSUR estimate. *Journal of Business and Economics Statistics* 6 (January): 29–42.

Reinganum, M. 1981. The Arbitrage Pricing Theory: Some empirical results. *Journal of Finance* 36 (May): 313–321.

Roll, Richard. 1977. A critique of the asset-pricing theory's tests; Part I: On past and potential testability of the theory. *Journal of Financial Economics* 4 (March): 129–176.

Roll, Richard, and Stephen Ross. 1980. An empirical investigation of the Arbitrage Pricing Theory. *Journal of Finance* 35 (December): 1073–1103.

Ross, Stephen. 1976. The arbitrage pricing theory of capital asset pricing. *Journal of Economic Theory* 13 (December): 341–360.

Sharpe, W. F. 1970. *Portfolio Theory and Capital Markets.* New York: McGraw-Hill.

Sharpe, William. 1984. Factor models, SMLs, and the APT. *Journal of Portfolio Management* 11 (Fall): 21–25.

Sharpe, W. F., and G.M. Cooper. 1972. Risk-return class of New York Stock Exchange common stocks, 1931–1967. *Financial Analysts Journal* 28 (March–April): 46–52.

Bloomberg Exercises

1. French and Fama argue that firms with high ratios of book-to-market value are likely to be in more financial stress than firms with low ratios. Altman's Z-score) is a measure of a company's likelihood of default. Examine the significance of financial stress in determining equilibrium returns by conducting a second-pass test of stock returns explained by their betas and Altman's Z-scores.

   To run your regression, use the Bloomberg Excel Add-In to run the second-pass test in Excel. Consider the following: for your stocks, consider the stocks composing the DJIA or the S&P 100 or 500; for rates of return, the internal rates of return calculated from Bloomberg's DDM model; for betas, the stocks' adjusted betas; for risk, Altman's Z-score. For an example on using multiple regression analysis in Excel, see the Excel table in the Bloomberg exhibit box, "Bloomberg Excel Add-In: Second-Pass Test for Multifactor Models."

2. In an early study of the CAPM, Fama and MacBeth found the market risk premium to be significant in explaining equilibrium returns but found residual errors not significant. Their study provided support that systematic risk is the only relevant factor in determining an investment's equilibrium return. Using a second-pass test, reexamine Fama and MacBeth's findings.

   To run your regression, use the Bloomberg Excel Add-In to run the second-pass test in Excel. Consider: for your stocks, the stocks composing the DJIA, the S&P 100 or S&P 500; for your rates of return, the internal rates of return calculated from Bloomberg's DDM model; for your betas, the stocks' adjusted betas; and for your unsystematic risk, the standard deviation of the errors. For an example of using multiple regression analysis in Excel, see the Excel table in the Bloomberg exhibit box, "Bloomberg Excel Add-In: Second-Pass Test for Multifactor Models."

3. William Sharpe in a 1970s study identified market returns and long-term bond rates as being significant in explaining equilibrium returns. Using Bloomberg's MRA screen, conduct a multiple regression analysis for several stocks using proportional changes in the S&P 500 (SPX) as a measure of the market rate and proportional changes in the yields on 30-year Treasuries (USGG30YR).

To use MRA:

- MRA <Enter>; Click MRA Run.
- Fill in fields in the "Multiple Regression Creation Box:" for dependent variable stock ticker <Equity>; for independent variables: SPX <Index> and USGG30YR <Index>; for Column fields: Percent (P) for Data, Close (C) for Value, and None (N) for Log Type; Click Menu or Enter 1 <Go> to save.
- Click your saved MRA run to bring up the Multiple Regression Analysis Box.
- In the Multiple Regression Box, enter data range and period (e.g., Month), and hit <Enter> to see regression results.

CHAPTER 11

The Financial Anatomy of a Company—Fundamental Analysis

Introduction

The two most common approaches to evaluating and selecting stocks are fundamental analysis and technical analysis. The goal of fundamental analysis is to determine a stock's equilibrium price or intrinsic value. Fundamentalists (those practicing fundamental analysis) hope to profit by purchasing stocks they estimate to be underpriced (whose market price is below the equilibrium value they have determined) and selling or shorting stocks they determine to be overpriced. Thus, the real objective of the fundamentalist is to earn abnormal returns by being able to identify mispriced securities. Technical analysis, on the other hand, involves studying trends in security prices. Technicians search for patterns such as a stock trading low on one day of the week and high on another, a stock that increases only after another security has increased, or a stock whose price decreases after it trades away from an average level. As we will discuss in Chapter 14, technical analysis uses measures such as moving averages or confidence indexes and theories such as the Dow theory or the theory of contrary opinion. In this chapter, we focus on fundamental analysis. We begin by examining the anatomy of a company and the fundamental factors that determine the value of a company and its equity. In Chapter 12, we extend our examination of fundamental analysis by looking at different quantitative approaches that are used to estimate the intrinsic value of security. Finally, in Chapter 13, we look at aggregate economic and industry factors and look at the valuation of the overall market and industries.

Stock Value

As we discussed in Chapter 3, the value of a stock is the present value of its future dividends. Thus, the stock value of a company expected to last N periods can be expressed as:

$$V_0^S = \sum_{t=1}^{N} \frac{d_t}{(1 + k_e)^t} = \frac{d_1}{(1 + k_e)^1} + \frac{d_2}{(1 + k_e)^2} + \cdots + \frac{d_N}{(1 + k_e)^N}$$

where:

d_t = dividend per share (DPS) in period t
k_e = required rate

If dividends were expected to grow at a constant rate, g, over the entire life (N) of the stock, then the value of the stock would be:

$$V_0^S = \sum_{t=1}^{N} \frac{d_0(1 + g)^t}{(1 + k_e)^t} = \frac{d_0(1 + g)^1}{(1 + k_e)^1} + \frac{d_0(1 + g)^2}{(1 + k_e)^2} + \cdots + \frac{d_0(1 + g)^N}{(1 + k_e)^N}$$

Many companies have an indefinite life, with many expected to last many years. As shown in Chapter 3, as N gets large, the valuation equation approaches a maximum value equal to $d_1/(k_e - g)$ at a discrete N value such as 30 to 50 years (see Exhibit 3.4 in Chapter 3 for the proof). Thus, for a company expected to have a constant growth rate in dividends for the next 40 to 50 years—a profile that describes many large companies—the value of its stock would be:

$$V_0^S = \sum_{t=1}^{N} \frac{d_0(1 + g)^t}{(1 + k_e)^t} = \frac{d_0(1 + g)^1}{k_e - g} = \frac{d_1}{k_e - g} \quad \text{for large } N$$

Thus, investors requiring a 10 percent rate on a stock currently paying a $5 dividend and expected to grow at an annual rate of 3 percent for a long time would value the stock at $73.57:

$$V_0^S = \frac{d_0(1 + g)^1}{k_e - g} = \frac{d_1}{k_e - g} = \frac{\$5(1.03)}{0.10 - 0.03} = \$73.57$$

Note that the value of the stock would still be $73.57 even if an investor planned to sell it at a future horizon date, provided that the expected selling price at the investor's horizon is equal to the present value of the stock's future dividends. For example, if an investor's horizon were three years, then dividends in year four would be $5.63 [= $5(1.03)^4] and the value of the stock at year three would be $80.39. Discounting this value and the dividends back to the present yields a current value of the stock of $73.57:

$$V_0^S = \frac{d_0(1+g)^1}{(1+k_e)^1} + \frac{d_0(1+g)^2}{(1+k_e)^2} + \frac{d_0(1+g)^3 + V_3^e}{(1+k_e)^3}$$

$$V_0^S = \frac{\$5(1.03)}{1.10} + \frac{\$5(1.03)^2}{(1.10)^2} + \frac{\$5(1.03)^3 + \$80.39}{(1.10)^3} = \$73.57$$

where:

$$V_3^S = \frac{d_4}{k_e - g} = \frac{d_0(1+g)^4}{k_e - g} = \frac{\$5(1.03)^4}{0.10 - 0.03} = \frac{\$5.63}{0.10 - 0.03} = \$80.39$$

As discussed in Chapter 3, companies and industries may be in different stages of industrial development and as a result have different growth rates over time instead of a constant growth rate. For example, a company could be characterized by a three-stage growth process where it is expected to have an extraordinary growth rate of g_1, a transitional period in which the growth rate moves from the extraordinary rate to the steady-state rate, and then to a steady-state period in which the stock dividend grows at the steady-state rate. In terms of the above example, suppose investors expect the dividends to initially grow at an annual rate of 6 percent for three years, then steadily decline with growth rates of 5 percent, 4 percent, and 3 percent in years four, five, and six, respectively, and in year six to grow at a constant steady-state rate of 3 percent. Given these assumptions, the investor would value the stock at $81.66:

$$V_0^S = \frac{d_0(1+g_1)^1}{(1+k_e)^1} + \frac{d_0(1+g_1)^2}{(1+k_e)^2} + \frac{d_0(1+g_1)^3}{(1+k_e)^3} + \frac{d_0(1+g_1)^3(1+g_2)}{(1+k_e)^4}$$

$$+ \frac{d_0(1+g_1)^3(1+g_2)(1+g_3)}{(1+k_e)^5} + \frac{d_0(1+g_1)^3(1+g_2)(1+g_3)(1+g_4)}{(1+k_e)^6}$$

$$+ \frac{\dfrac{d_0(1+g_1)^3(1+g_2)(1+g_3)(1+g_4)(1+g_4)}{k_e - g_4}}{(1+k_e)^6}$$

$$V_0^S = \frac{\$5(1.06)^1}{(1.10)^1} + \frac{\$5(1.06)^2}{(1.10)^2} + \frac{\$5(1.06)^3}{(1.10)^3} + \frac{\$5(1.06)^3(1.05)}{(1.10)^4}$$

$$+ \frac{\$5(1.06)^3(1.05)(1.04)}{(1.10)^5} + \frac{\$5(1.06)^3(1.05)(1.04)(1.03)}{(1.10)^6}$$

$$+ \frac{\dfrac{\$5(1.06)^3(1.05)(1.04)(1.03)(1.03)}{0.10 - 0.03}}{(1.10)^6} = \$81.66$$

$$V_0^S = \frac{\$5.30}{(1.10)^1} + \frac{\$5.62}{(1.10)^2} + \frac{\$5.96}{(1.10)^3} + \frac{\$6.25}{(1.10)^4}$$

$$+ \frac{\$6.50}{(1.10)^5} + \frac{\$6.70}{(1.10)^6} + \frac{98.56}{(1.10)^6} = \$81.66$$

In practice, estimating a stock's future dividend growth is very challenging, requiring knowledge of the company's operations, the external factors that affect the company, and the company's investment opportunities. The two most important factors influencing the equity value of a company, however, are its potential earnings from current operations and its potential investments. To see how these two factors affect value, we first need to examine how a company's operations and investment decisions determine its dividends and dividend growth rates. We start with the simple case of a company that does not make any corporate investments and is expected to last a long time.

Equity Valuation of a Firm

Consider the case of an investor who is planning to buy stock in the Zuber Oil Company. Zuber is a small company that owns and operates a producing crude oil well. The company has five million shares of stock outstanding (n), long-term debt of $250 million in which it pays 8 percent interest (Int) each year, no short-term debt or cash position, no depreciation or depletion allowances, and an effective corporate tax rate (t) of 40 percent. Suppose after studying geological reports, long-term forecasts of crude oil price trends, and the cost of operating oil wells, the investor estimates that Zuber's oil well reserves will produce a constant annual output of 1.8 million barrels for a long time—the next 100 years—that the price of crude oil will average $100/barrel, and that the annual operating cost (TOC) of the well will be $60 million.[1] Based on these estimates, the investor determines that Zuber's expected total revenue (TR) will be $180 million per year and the company's annual earnings before interest and taxes ($EBIT$) will be $120 million (see Exhibit 11.1):

$$E(EBIT) = E(TR) - E(TOC)$$

$$E(EBIT) = \$180 \text{ million} - \$60 \text{ million} = \$120 \text{ million}$$

With long-term debt of $250 million and an interest rate on the debt, k_d, of 8 percent, Zuber will pay $20 million in interest each year, which under federal corporate tax laws is deductible. The investor therefore estimates that Zuber's expected earnings before taxes (EBT) will be $100 million, its tax liability (T) will be $40 million, and its expected earnings after taxes (EAT) will be $60 million:

$$E(EBT) = E(EBIT) - Int$$

$$E(EBIT) = \$120 \text{ million} - \$20 \text{ million} = \$100 \text{ million}$$

$$E(EAT) = E(EBT) - T = E(EBT) - E(EBT)t$$

$$E(EAT) = \$100 \text{ million}(1 - 0.4) = \$60 \text{ million}$$

EXHIBIT 11.1   Zuber Oil Company Expected Annual Income Statement

Total Revenue (TR)	$180 million
− Total Operating Cost (TOC)	$60 million
= Earnings Before Interest and Taxes (EBIT)	$120 million
− Interest (Int = (.08)($250 million) = $20 million	$20 million
= Earnings Before Taxes (EBT)	$100 million
− Taxes (T) (Effective Corporate Tax Rate = t = 40%)	$40 million
= Earnings After Taxes (EAT)	$60 million
− Retained Earnings (RE)	0
= Total Dividends (D)	$60 million
÷ Number of Shares (n)	5 million
= Dividends per Share (d)	$12

Finally, suppose that the investor does not expect Zuber to make any corporate investments in the future; that is, Zuber is a no-growth company. As a result, the investor would expect Zuber's retained earnings (*RE*) to be zero (since the company plans no investments) and its expected annual total dividend (*D*) each year to be equal to its earnings of $60 million:

$$E(D) = E(EAT) - RE$$
$$E(D) = \$60 \text{ million} - 0 = \$60 \text{ million}$$

With 5 million shares, the investor would expect Zuber's dividend per share (*d* or *DPS*) to be $12.00:

$$E(d) = \frac{E(D)}{n} = \frac{\$60 \text{ million}}{5 \text{ million}} = \$12$$

In summary:

$$E(d) = \frac{[E(EBIT) - Int)](1 - t) - RE}{n}$$

$$E(d) = \frac{[120 \text{ million} - \$20 \text{ million}](1 - 0.4) - 0}{5 \text{ million}} = \frac{\$60 \text{ million}}{5 \text{ million}} = \$12$$

Note, in this and subsequent chapters dealing with fundamental stock valuation, we will adopt the nomenclature often used in finance of denoting firm values with upper case symbols and per share values with lower case symbols.

Since the oil well is expected to produce at a constant rate of 1.8 million barrels per year for 100 years, and the investor does not expect the company to make any future investments, the value of Zuber's stock can be determined by using the constant growth rate model, with an assumed growth rate in dividends (g) of zero:

$$\text{Total Equity Value: } V_0^E = \frac{E(D_1)}{k_e}$$

$$\text{Per Share Value: } V_0^e = \frac{E(d_1)}{k_e}$$

The investor's required return can be determined by using an equilibrium model such as the CAPM or APT described in Chapter 9 and Chapter 10. In this case, suppose the investor determines her required return based on the CAPM, estimating the beta of Zuber to be two, the risk-free rate to be 4 percent, and the market risk premium ($E(R^M) - R_f$)) to be 10 percent. Thus, using the CAPM, her required return would be 24 percent:

$$k_e = R_f + [E(R^M) - R_f]\beta$$
$$k_e = 0.04 + [0.14 - 0.04](2) = 0.24$$

Given a 24 percent required return, the investor would therefore value Zuber stock to be worth $50 per share:

$$V_0^e = \frac{E(d_1)}{k_e}$$

$$V_0^e = \frac{\$12}{0.24} = \$50$$

Thus, if the investor were able to buy the stock at $50, then based on her projected *DPS* of $12.00, her expected return would be 24 percent [$E(R^E) = \$12.00/\$50$], which would equal her required return:

$$E(R^E) = \frac{E(d_1)}{V_0^e}$$

$$E(R^E) = \frac{\$12}{\$50} = 0.24$$

The investor, of course, would hope that Zuber were priced below $50—underpriced—yielding her an expected return exceeding her required return.

Note that with 5 million shares outstanding, the investor would value Zuber's total equity, V_0^E, at $250 million:

$$V_0^E = \frac{E(D_1)}{k_e} = \frac{\$60 \text{ million}}{0.24} = \$250 \text{ million}$$

$$V_0^E = V_0^e n = (\$50)(5 \text{ million}) = \$250 \text{ million}$$

Value of Assets

The value of a firm's asset, V^A (i.e., the value of the firm) is equal to the value of its equity plus the value of its debt, V^D. With a debt of $250 million, the total value of Zuber's would be $500 million:

$$V_0^A = V_0^E + V_0^D$$
$$V_0^A = \$250 \text{ million} + \$250 \text{ million} = \$500 \text{ million}$$

Recall, from corporate finance, the *value of the asset* can also be calculated by discounting the expected earnings that flow to both shareholders, $E(EAT)$, and creditors, *Int*, at the investor's *weighted average cost of capital*, k_C:

$$V_0^A = \frac{E(EAT) + Int}{k_C}$$

where:

$k_C = f_E k_e + f_D k_d$
f_E = the proportion of the firm financed by equity (V_E/V_A)
f_D = the proportion financed by debt (V_E/V_A)

If the equity-to-asset and debt-to-asset ratios reflect the ex-ante equity values of $250 million and debt of $250 million, then f_E would be 0.5 [= (V_E/V_A) = $250 million/$500 million] and f_D would be 0.5 [= (V_D/V_A) = $250 million/$500 million]. Given the cost of debt, k_d, equals the interest rate of 8 percent, then with a firm financed with half debt and half equity, the overall cost of capital would be 16 percent and the total value would be $500 million, matching the sum of the value of equity and the value of debt:

$$k_C = f_E k_e + f_D k_d$$
$$k_C = (0.5)(0.24) + (0.5)(0.08) = 0.16$$

$$V_0^A = \frac{E(EAT) + Int}{k_C}$$

$$V_0^A = \frac{\$60 \text{ million} + \$20 \text{ million}}{0.16} = \$500 \text{ million}$$

Thus, if Zuber can generate $80 million per year—a 16 percent return from a total asset valued at $500 million—it would be able to take care of equity investors who are financing half the firm (the oil well) and require a 24 percent return, that is, (0.24)(0.5)($500 million) = $60 million, and take care of creditors who are financing half the asset and require an 8 percent return, that is, (0.08)(0.5)($500 million) = $20 million.

It should be noted that the $80 million of earnings flowing to investors takes into account the interest tax deduction benefits of the debt. If the total asset value is calculated based on the net *EBIT* of $72 million [= ($120 million) (1 − 0.4)], then the earnings flowing to investors would be underestimated by $8 million. To correct for this in valuing the asset, the cost of capital for debt needs to be calculated net of taxes [$k_d(1 − t)$]:

$$k_C^T = f_E k_e + f_D k_d (1 - t)$$

$$k_c^T = (0.5)(0.24) + (0.5)(0.08)(1 - 0.4) = 0.144$$

$$V_0^A = \frac{E(EBIT)(1 - t)}{k_C^T}$$

$$V_0^A = \frac{\$120 \text{ million}(1 - 0.4)}{0.144} = \$500 \text{ million}$$

BLOOMBERG WACC SCREEN

The Bloomberg WACC screen calculates the WACC for a loaded stock. The cost of equity is determined by the CAPM model, and the cost of debt is determined by the after-tax rate on debt, with the rate on debt adjusted to reflect the company's quality ratings. You can click the Equity, Debt Cost, and Preferred Equity tabs to bring up screens showing calculations.

See Bloomberg Web Exhibit 11.1.

Comparative Analysis

If all investors formulate the same expectations about the Zuber Oil Company as our investor did, then the equilibrium market price of Zuber would be $50. The market share price of Zuber would change if investors change their expectations about dividends or the required return by investors. For example, if new geological estimates indicated greater crude oil reserves or new information on oil demand indicated higher prices than the expected price of $100/barrel, then investors would expect Zuber's earnings and dividends to be greater than $60 million or $12 per share and accordingly would value the stock higher. Similarly, if long-term interest rates were expected to decline with no change in the market risk premium, investors would also value the stock higher; that is, an interest rate decrease would have two impacts on the value of stock. First, it would lower the company interest payments on its debts if the company refinances, thereby increasing the company earnings and value. Second, lower interest rates would decrease investors' required return, k_e, provided the risk premium, $E(R^M) - R_f$, did not increase. For example, suppose in our above case investors expected long-term interest rates to decrease with the risk-free rate decreasing from its 4 percent level to 3 percent and with the risk premium staying at 10 percent, and furthermore they expected Zuber to refinance its 8 percent, $250 million debt at 6 percent. Based on that scenario, investors would expect Zuber's DPS to increase from $12 to $12.60 because of the lower interest expenses:

$$E(d) = \frac{[E(EBIT) - k_d V_D)](1 - t)}{n}$$

$$E(d) = \frac{[\$120 \text{ million} - (0.06)(\$250)](1 - 0.4)}{5 \text{ million}} = \frac{\$63 \text{ million}}{5 \text{ million}} = \$12.60$$

the required return to decrease from 24 percent to 23 percent:

$$k_e = R_f + [E(R^M) - R_f]\beta$$

$$k_e = 0.03 + [0.10](2) = 0.23$$

and the value of Zuber's stock to increase by 9.57 percent from $50 to $54.78:

$$V_0^e = \frac{E(d)}{k_e} = \frac{\$12.60}{0.23} = \$54.78$$

In general, stock prices are quite sensitive to changes in interest rate, the growth rate in the economy, and inflation. As we saw in Chapter 10, the study by Roll, Ross, and Chen provided some statistical support for the importance of macroeconomic factors in determining a stock's equilibrium return and value. Such factors can be described as exogenous to the company. That is, they are factors over which the company has no control, even though they impact the company and its stock. For stock analysts, exogenous factors are market factors—factors that affect all stocks; the analyst's job is to determine the impact such factors have on the stock's value. In contrast, factors that the company has control over are referred to as endogenous. Two important endogenous factors affecting the value of a company's stock are its capital structure decisions related to how much its assets are financed with debt and how much with equity (that is, the company's debt-to-equity ratio), and the investments the company makes or is expected to make in the future.

BLOOMBERG FA SCREEN, IS TAB

Company income statements can be found on Bloomberg's FA screen, IS tab. You can use the graph icon to see multiple items graphically.

(Continued)

Bloomberg EEO Screen

The Bloomberg EEO screen provides current and estimated growth rates for EPS and DPS. The estimates are provided by broker/contributors. As such, they represent the consensus estimate of the market. You can select forecast based on standard consensus, contributor estimates that have been weighted based on past accuracy, estimates that factor in the last month's adjustments, and the like. See the screen's "Help" page for more information on forecast.

Bloomberg EEB Screen:

The Bloomberg EEB shows projections of earnings, sales, and other income statement items from a consensus of Bloomberg contributors. You can view how the consensus has changed over time and the estimates of individual contributors.

Other Bloomberg Earnings Screens:

- **ERN**: Earnings History.
- **EE**: Earnings and Estimates.
- **EM**: Earnings Trends.
- **EE SURP**: Earnings Surprises.
- **EE Z**: Zach's Earnings Estimates.

See Bloomberg Web Exhibit 11.2.

Capital Structure

The amount of debt a company has relative to its equity is often determined by the way in which it finances its investments over time. A company with a propensity to finance its investment projects with debt would in time have a higher debt-to-equity ratio than a company that tends to finance its investment by selling new stock or by retaining its earnings. Sometimes, however, changes in a company's capital structure occur as a result of a merger. Many companies are acquired by private equity or leverage buyout companies or other corporations that financed the acquisition by issuing bonds. In many of those cases, the major difference between the old company and the new one is that the later company just had more debt. Finally, some companies change their capital structure as part of a corporate policy. A company such as the Zuber Company that we assumed did not make any corporate investments might decide that it wants a higher debt-to-equity ratio than its current ratio of one in order to take advantage of tax laws (discussed below). To realize this, the company could borrow funds to finance the purchase of some of its stock. Alternatively, if the company wanted to lower its debt-to-equity ratio, it could do so by selling new stock and using the proceeds to retire some of its debt.

Whether a company's capital structure changes by the way in which it finances its investments, by a corporate merger, or through a change in corporate policy, any change in the company's debt-to-equity ratio will have an impact on the value of the company's stock. Generally, changes in capital structure influence stock prices by altering the company's risk exposure on its equity and by changing the stock's expected earnings-per-share.

Capital Structure, Risk, and Stock Price

If the interest payments on debt are fixed, then a change in capital structure will lead to changes in the risk that equity investors are assuming. This change in risk exposure is due to the debt's contractual obligation in which the corporation is required to pay creditors interest and principal regardless of the earnings of the company. Companies with high debt-to-equity ratios find that they are able to provide their shareholders with more earnings per share (*EPS*) in good economic states when their earnings before interest and taxes are high and their payments to creditors are fixed, but less *EPS* in poor economic states when *EBIT* are low and yet the fixed interest must still be paid. Thus, the larger a company's debt-to-equity ratio, the greater its fluctuations in *EPS* and the greater the fluctuations in the return on equity to investors. The increased fluctuations in the returns on equity resulting from an increase in a company's debt-to-equity ratio, also serves to increase the stock's beta; that is, an increase in the debt-to-equity ratio increases the stock's fluctuations relative to the market's fluctuations. In a 1969 seminal article in the *Journal of Finance*, Robert Hamada derived an equation showing this positive relationship between a stock's beta and its debt-to-equity ratio. The Hamada equation is derived in many corporate finance texts. The equation is

$$\beta_L = \beta_u[1 + (1 - t)\phi]$$

where:
β_L = levered beta; beta of a company with debt
β_u = unlevered beta; beta of the company if it has no debt
t = corporate tax rate
ϕ = debt-to-equity ratio

Recall that according to the CAPM, the greater a stock's beta, the greater its required return, k_e. Thus, a company that increases its debt-to-equity ratio, ϕ, will find both the beta of its stock and the rate of return required by investors to be greater. All other things equal, an increase in leverage will cause an increase in the required return causing the stock to decrease. The direct relation between ϕ and k_e is depicted graphically in Exhibit 11.2. The upper quadrant of the figure in the exhibit shows the relation between k_e and β as defined by the security market line (SML) with a risk-free rate of 4 percent and a market risk premium of 10 percent, and the lower quadrant shows the Hamada relationship between ϕ and β as defined by the Hamada equation for a

EXHIBIT 11.2   SML and Hamada Relation

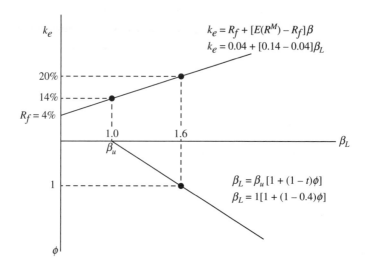

company with an unlevered beta of one and an effective corporate tax rate of 40 percent. Thus, if the company were unlevered ($\beta_u = 1$), then its required return would be
14 percent; if it changed its debt-to-equity ratio to $\phi = 1$, then its beta would increase
to 1.6 and its required return would increase to 20 percent.

Capital Structure, EPS, and Stock Price

In addition to changing a stock's risk, changes in capital structure also can change
shareholders' expected *EPS*. For U.S. companies, the change in *EPS* resulting from a
change in capital structure is due to corporate tax laws. Specifically, federal tax codes
allow corporations to deduct the interest they pay on debt before determining the
earnings that are taxable. Thus, with interest being tax deductible and dividends not,
companies with greater debt-to-equity ratios, will, with other factors equal, have more
of their earnings going to investors (creditors and shareholders) and less to the government. This can be seen in Exhibit 11.3 where the income statements are shown for the
Zuber Company for the case in which the company has zero debt and one where it has
$250 million in debt. In the no-debt case, Zuber provides its investors (shareholders)
with $72 million, whereas in the leverage case, investors receive a total of $80 million
($20 million to creditors and $60 million to shareholders).

The law allowing interest to be tax deductible suggests that it makes a difference
whether a company calls its investors either shareholders or creditors. Many of the
leverage buyout companies (LBOs) that emerged in the 1980s to acquire corporations
were formed to take advantage of this tax law. These LBOs would issue lower quality,
high-yielding junk bonds to finance their corporate acquisition. After the acquisition,
the resulting company was more highly leveraged, often with a greater proportion of
its investors now being creditors. With interest tax deductible, however, the newly

EXHIBIT 11.3 Zuber Earnings Given Different Debt Levels

Items	Zuber Company with no debt	Zuber Company with $250 million debt, paying 8% interest
E(EBIT)	$120 million	$120 million
− Interest	0	$20 million
= *E(EBT)*	$120 million	$100 million
− Taxes (*t* =0.04)	$48 million	$40 million
= *E(EAT)*	$72 million	$60 million
Earnings to Investors: *E(EAT)* + Interest	$72 million + 0 = $72 million	$60 million + $20 million = $80 million

structured company was able to pay less in corporate taxes, enabling it to pay the higher interest to creditors, as well as leaving the company with the ability to earn a greater *EPS* for its stockholders. Thus, an increase in the debt-to-equity ratio, often leads to a greater expected *EPS*, and with all other factors constant, an increase in the value of the company's stock.

It should be noted that a change in capital structure can also change the number of shares outstanding. If a company increases its debt-to-equity ratio by borrowing funds and buying up shares, then the number of shares would decrease, and if the company lowers the ratio by selling new stock in order to retire some of its debt, then the number of shares would increase.

In summary, a change in capital structure has two opposite effects on a company's stock. On the one hand, when there is an increase (decrease) in the debt-to-equity ratio, the stock's risk increases (decreases), causing the required return to increase (decrease) and the price of the stock to decrease (increase). On the other hand, because of the interest tax deduction and the change in the number of shares, an increase (decrease) in the debt-to-equity ratio increases (decreases) *EPS*, causing the stock price to increase (decrease). If this latter effect of an increase in *EPS* dominates the first effect of an increase in risk and required return, then the price of the stock would increase; if the first effect of an increase in risk and required return dominates the *EPS* effect, then the stock price would decrease.

BLOOMBERG FA SCREEN: FA LEV

The Bloomberg FA screen can be used to analyze a company's capital structure. On FA, click "Ratios" and "Credit" tabs to bring up leverage ratios. You can also bring up the screen by entering FA LEV.

    See Bloomberg Web Exhibit 11.3.

Corporate Investments

A U.S. food-processing company expanding its markets to Europe, a multinational electric company developing a new technology, a pharmaceutical company developing and marketing a new drug, or an oil company drilling for new wells are all examples of investments that corporations undertake each year. For many analysts, a corporation's current and future investments are the most important factors to consider in determining the company's value.

Case 1: Zuber Oil Company

To most large corporations, investments are an ongoing activity. To see the impact of investments on a stock's value, however, let us start with a simple case in which our illustrative Zuber Oil Company is expected to make a one-time-only investment. To simplify our analysis, assume that Zuber has no debt (an all-equity or unleveraged company) and is expected to generate annual EAT from its oil well of $60 million. The EAT of $60 million can be viewed as the company's earnings from its existing assets (in this case the producing oil well). Also, assume Zuber's beta is again two, the risk-free rate is 4 percent, and the market risk premium is 10 percent, yielding a required return of 24 percent:

$$k_e = R_f + [E(R^M) - R_f]\beta$$
$$k_e = 0.04 + [0.14 - 0.04](2) = 0.24$$

Given our assumption that Zuber's oil well is expected to last a long time, the total equity value of Zuber, as well as asset value (since it is an all-equity company), would be $250 million, and given five million shares, its EPS would be $12 and its share price would be $50:

$$V_0^E = \frac{E(EAT_1)}{k_e} = \frac{\$60 \text{ million}}{0.24} = \$250 \text{ million}$$

$$E(EPS) = \frac{E(EAT_1)}{n} = \frac{\$60 \text{ million}}{5 \text{ million}} = \$12$$

$$V_0^e = \frac{V_0^E}{n} = \frac{\$250 \text{ million}}{5 \text{ million}} = \$50$$

$$V_0^e = \frac{E(EPS_1)}{k_e} = \frac{\$12}{0.24} = \$50$$

To illustrate the impact that corporate investments have on a stock's value, suppose Zuber announced that in year one it will make a one-time-only investment (I) of $60 million by purchasing a new oil well ($I_1 = \$60$ million). After evaluating the investment, suppose that security analysts, as well as Zuber management, estimate that the investment will generate an annual investment rate of return (i) of 24 percent

EXHIBIT 11.4   Zuber Company's Earnings and Investment Case

	Assumptions
1.	All Equity Company
2.	EAT = Earnings from Existing Asset $60 million
3.	Beta of Existing Asset $\beta = 2$
4.	Number of Shares $n = 5$ million
5.	SML: $k_e = 0.04 + [0.10]\beta = 0.24$
6.	Investment Expenditure in Year 1: $I_1 = \$60$ million
7.	Expected Return on Investment: $i = 0.24$
8.	Beta of Investment: $\beta_p = 2$
9.	Required Return on Investment: $k_e^p = 0.24$

($i = 0.24$), that the risk of the investment project, as measured by its beta, β_p, would be two ($\beta_p = 2$)—the same risk as the existing asset—and like the current oil well, the new one is expected to have a very long life. Note, that with a beta of two, the investment would have a required return equal to Zuber's preinvestment required return of 24 percent, implying that the investment would not change the risk or required return of the company; also note that the investment return is equal to the required return: $i = k_e = 0.24$. Exhibit 11.4 summarizes the information on the Zuber Oil Company and its investment expenditure.

The impact of the investment on the company can be analyzed by determining its impact on either the equity value of the company or its share price. The total equity value can be measured in terms of the present value of the cash flows that go to existing shareholders. Since there is only one investment, the current equity value can be defined in terms of the cash flow over two years, with the cash flow in the second year being the dividends received by *existing* shareholders and the estimated stock value (V_2^E):

$$V_0^E = \frac{D_1}{(1 + k_e)^1} + \frac{D_2}{(1 + k_e)^2} + \frac{V_2^E}{(1 + k_e)^2}$$

Before we can estimate the impact of Zuber's proposed investments on its current equity value, we need to know how the firm plans to finance the investment.

That is, every investment decision has a related financing decision. In this context, the *financing decision* facing the firm is one of whether they should finance the investment internally through retained earnings (i.e., existing shareholders financing the investment by giving up their dividends) or externally by selling new stock or borrowing.

Suppose that investors expect Zuber to finance internally. To do this, Zuber would have to retain $60 million in earnings in year one to finance the investment expenditure. Since the estimated earnings from its existing assets are just $60 million, dividends to shareholders in the first year would be zero under an internal financing case:

$$D_1 = EAT_1 - RE_1$$
$$D_1 = EAT_1 - I_1$$
$$D_1 = \$60 \text{ million} - \$60 \text{ million} = 0$$

In year two, shareholders would expect to receive dividends totaling $74.4 million. This would include $60 million from the existing asset (old oil well) and 14.4 million $[(i)(I_1) = (0.24)(\$60 \text{ million}) = \$14.4 \text{ million}]$ from the new asset (new oil well):

$$D_2 = EAT_1 + iI_1$$
$$D_2 = \$60 \text{ million} + (0.24)(\$60 \text{ million})$$
$$D_2 = \$60 \text{ million} + \$14.4 \text{ million} = \$74.4 \text{ million}$$

Since both oil wells (current and proposed) are expected to last a long time, the total equity value in year 2 would be equal to the value of perpetuity, paying an annual dividend of $74.4 million. With both assets having a beta of two, the required return by investors would still be 0.24; thus the total equity value of Zuber in year two would be $310 million:

$$V_2^E = \frac{D_3}{k_e} = \frac{EAT_1 + iI_1}{k_e}$$
$$V_2^E = \frac{\$60 \text{ million} + \$14.4 \text{ million}}{0.24} = \frac{\$74.4 \text{ million}}{0.24} = \$310 \text{ million}$$

Discounting each year's cash flows by $k_e = 0.24$, the current value of equity is $250 million:

$$V_0^E = \frac{D_1}{(1 + k_e)^1} + \frac{D_2}{(1 + k_e)^2} + \frac{V_2^E}{(1 + k_e)^2}$$
$$V_0^E = \frac{0}{1.24} + \frac{\$74.4 \text{ million}}{(1.24)^2} + \frac{\$310 \text{ million}}{(1.24)^2} = \$250 \text{ million}$$

Recall that the value of Zuber's equity without the investment was also $250 million. Thus, the investment financed internally has no impact on the equity value of the company. Note that we can also reach the same conclusion if we value Zuber on a per share basis. That is, dividing each cash flow by the number of shares ($n = 5$ million), we end up with the price per share of $50—the same per share price of Zuber's stock without the investment:

$$V_0^e = \frac{D_1/n}{(1 + k_e)^1} + \frac{D_2/n}{(1 + k_e)^2} + \frac{V_2^E/n}{(1 + k_e)^2}$$

$$V_0^e = \frac{d_1}{(1 + k_e)^1} + \frac{d_2}{(1 + k_e)^2} + \frac{V_2^e}{(1 + k_e)^2}$$

$$V_0^e = \frac{0/5 \text{ million}}{1.24} + \frac{\$74.4 \text{ million}/5 \text{ million}}{(1.24)^2} + \frac{\$310 \text{ million}/5 \text{ million}}{(1.24)^2}$$

$$V_0^e = \frac{0}{(1.24)^1} + \frac{\$14.88}{(1.24)^2} + \frac{\$62}{(1.24)^2} = \$50$$

Suppose Zuber is expected to finance its $60 million new oil well investment in year one externally. Zuber could externally finance the project by selling new shares or borrowing (issuing bonds or borrowing from a financial institution), or some combination of the two. If Zuber borrows, then the stock value could be affected by not only the investment, but also by the change in capital structure. To isolate just the investment impact, let us assume that, since Zuber is an all-equity firm, it decides to finance its investment by selling new stock. If Zuber can sell new shares in year one at the current price of $50, it would need to sell 1.2 million new shares (n_N) in order to raise the requisite $60 million:

$$n_N = \frac{I_1}{V_0^e} = \frac{\$60 \text{ million}}{\$50 \text{ per share}} = 1.2 \text{ million shares}$$

The total value of equity to *existing* shareholders under this external financing case would be equal to the present value of the total dividends of $60 million that existing shareholders receive in year one and the present value of the existing shareholder's claim on the cash flows in year two. After the sale of 1.2 million new shares in year one, the total number of shares outstanding in year two would be 6.2 million shares. As a result, existing shareholders would have an 80.645 percent claim (= 5 million/6.2 million) on the estimated $74.4 million dividends and $310 million equity value expected to occur in year two. Discounting these cash flow claims by 24 percent yields a current equity value to existing shareholders of $250 million—the same as the internal financing case and the no investment case:

$$V_0^E = \frac{D_1}{(1 + k_e)^1} + \frac{D_2}{(1 + k_e)^2} + \frac{V_2^E}{(1 + k_e)^2}$$

$$V_0^E = \frac{\$60 \text{ million}}{1.24} + \frac{\$74.4 \text{ million } (5M/6.2M)}{(1.24)^2}$$

$$+ \frac{\$310 \text{ million } (5M/6.2M)}{(1.24)^2} = \$250 \text{ million}$$

Finally, dividing the cash flow in each year by the number of shares ($n = 5$ million in year 1 and $n + n_N = 6.2$ million in year 2), we obtain the dividend per share of $12 in both years 1 and 2 and a value per share in year 2 of $50. Discounting those values by 24 percent, we obtain a current value per share of $50:

$$V_0^e = \frac{D_1/n}{(1 + k_e)^1} + \frac{D_2/(n + n_N)}{(1 + k_e)^2} + \frac{V_2^E/(n + n_N)}{(1 + k_e)^2}$$

$$V_0^E = \frac{\$60 \text{ million}/5 \text{ million}}{1.24} + \frac{\$74.4 \text{ million}/6.2 \text{ million}}{(1.24)^2}$$

$$+ \frac{\$310 \text{ million}/6.2 \text{ million}}{(1.24)^2}$$

$$V_0^E = \frac{\$12}{1.24} + \frac{\$12}{(1.24)^2} + \frac{\$50}{(1.24)^2} = \$50$$

Inferences from the Case

Two important inferences can be drawn from the above case. First, the equity value of Zuber is $250 million under both the internal and external financing cases. This suggests that the choice of financing (internal or external) is irrelevant.[2] The irrelevance in the choice of financing is due to offsetting tradeoffs between the two types of financing. With internal financing, shareholders give up early earnings in return for greater earnings in the future with no dilution in the value of their claims; with external financing, shareholders receive early earnings but give up part of the total amount of future earnings, allowing for dilution. Since these two tradeoffs exactly offset each other, there is no gain in value by financing either internally or externally.

It should be noted that the argument for the irrelevance of financing (sometimes referred to as dividend policy) is based on purely financial grounds. Arguments for one form of financing over another can be made, however, for nonfinancial reasons. For example, in order to avoid sending the wrong signals to the market or to change the cash flows it normally provides to its shareholders, a company as a matter of policy may pay a constant dividend each period, often deciding to finance its investments externally instead of through retaining earnings to achieve this goal. In contrast, an argument for internal financing could be made based on tax considerations. Given that the tax rate on capital gains is less than income, a company that provides its shareholders with more of a return in the form of capital gains could be more valuable than one that provides more of its return in the form of dividends. That is, if the markets are inefficient in the sense that such differences in dividend and capital gain returns are not reflected in security prices, then investors who hold stocks that generate more return in the form of capital gains would obtain higher after-tax returns than investors who received more of their returns in the form of dividends. This can be seen by examining the per share value of Zuber for both internal and external financing cases. If the market price of Zuber stock were $50 in both cases, then an investor purchasing the stock would expect to receive an annual before-tax rate of return of 24 percent. However, in the internal case, the 24 percent return would consist of a $14.88 dividend and a capital gain of $12 (= $62 − $50) in year 2, whereas in the external case, the 24 percent return would consist exclusively of the $12 in dividends received in years one and two:

$$\text{External: } \$50 = \frac{0}{(1+R)^1} + \frac{\$14.88}{(1+R)^2} + \frac{\$62}{(1+R)^2} \Rightarrow \text{Before} - \text{Tax } R = 0.24$$

24% return comes from $14.88 dividend and $12 capital gain

$$\text{Internal: } \$50 = \frac{\$12}{(1+R)^1} + \frac{\$12}{(1+R)^2} + \frac{\$50}{(1+R)^2} \Rightarrow \text{Before} - \text{Tax } R = 0.24$$

24% return comes from $24 dividends and zero capital gains

With the capital gains tax rate less than the personal, the internal financing case would therefore yield a greater after-tax rate of return than the external case (assuming the stock sells for $50 in both cases). Thus, for tax reasons an argument could be made that in an effort to take care of their shareholders, corporations should finance their investments internally; this argument is often referred to as the *clientele effect*.

The second inference to be drawn from the above case is that Zuber's investment did not change the equity value. That is, the company was valued at $250 million with or without the investment:

Without investment:

$$V_0^E = \frac{D_1}{(1+k_e)^1} + \frac{D_2}{(1+k_e)^2} + \frac{V_2^E}{(1+k_e)^2}$$

$$V_0^E = \frac{\$60M}{1.24} + \frac{\$60M}{(1.24)^2} + \frac{\$60/0.24}{(1.24)^2}$$

$$V_0^E = \frac{\$60M}{1.24} + \frac{\$60M}{(1.24)^2} + \frac{\$250}{(1.24)^2} = \$250 \text{ million}$$

With investment (internal case):

$$V_0^E = \frac{D_1}{(1+k_e)^1} + \frac{D_2}{(1+k_e)^2} + \frac{V_2^E}{(1+k_e)^2}$$

$$V_0^E = \frac{0}{1.24} + \frac{\$60M + (0.24)(\$60M)}{(1.24)^2} + \frac{(\$60 + \$14.4)/0.24}{(1.24)^2}$$

$$V_0^E = \frac{0}{1.24} + \frac{\$74.4M}{(1.24)^2} + \frac{\$310M}{(1.24)^2} = \$250 \text{ million}$$

The reason for this is that Zuber is expected to obtain the same risk-adjusted rate of return from its new oil well investment that its shareholders can obtain in the market. That is, for a beta of two on the investment project, Zuber and its investors expect to obtain an investment return of $i = 24$ percent, which is the same rate (given our CAPM assumption) that its shareholders or any investor can obtain in the market. Recall that the method of valuing stock by discounting the stock's cash flows by the required return takes into account not only the returns from dividends and capital gains, but also the reinvestment of cash flows at the discount rate. Thus, the $250 million value of Zuber without the investment captures the annual dividends of $60 million and also the value that shareholders have from reinvesting their dividends in the market at 24 percent for investments with a beta of two. The corporate investment case, in turn, shows management reinvesting shareholders' $60 million dividend at the same rate of 24 percent in a project with a beta of two. Since management is expected to obtain the same risk-adjusted rate that its shareholders can obtain for themselves in the market, the corporation's investment does not change the equity value of the company.

If Zuber management could obtain a risk-adjusted return on its investments that exceeded the returns that investors could obtain in the markets, then the value of Zuber's equity would be greater than $50 if investors believed that Zuber was going to pursue the investments. For example, if the new oil well was expected to generate a rate of 30 percent instead of 24 percent and the investment still had a beta of two, then the value of Zuber's equity would be $262.10 million and the share price would be $52.42:

$$V_0^E = \frac{D_1}{(1+k_e)^1} + \frac{D_2}{(1+k_e)^2} + \frac{V_2^E}{(1+k_e)^2}$$

$$V_0^E = \frac{0}{1.24} + \frac{\$60M + (0.30)(\$60M)}{(1.24)^2} + \frac{(\$60M + \$18M)/0.24}{(1.24)^2}$$

$$V_0^E = \frac{0}{1.24} + \frac{\$78M}{(1.24)^2} + \frac{\$325M}{(1.24)^2} = \$262.10 \text{ million}$$

and

$$V_0^e = \frac{d_1}{(1+k_e)^1} + \frac{d_2}{(1+k_e)^2} + \frac{V_2^e}{(1+k_e)^2}$$

$$V_0^e = \frac{0}{1.24} + \frac{\$78M/5M}{(1.24)^2} + \frac{\$325M/5M}{(1.24)^2}$$

$$V_0^e = \frac{0}{1.24} + \frac{\$15.60}{(1.24)^2} + \frac{\$65}{(1.24)^2} = \$52.42$$

It is important to note that if the market priced the stock at $54.42, then investors would realize an expected return of 24 percent given expected dividends of $15.60 and an expected year two stock price of $65. This 24 percent is the same rate investors could obtain in the market for an investment with a beta of two:

$$\$52.42 = \frac{0}{(1+R)^1} + \frac{\$15.60}{(1+R)^2} + \frac{\$65}{(1+R)^2} \Rightarrow R = 0.24$$

If the market priced Zuber stock above $52.42—overpriced the stock—then the expected return would be less than the 24 percent return that could be obtained in the market. In this case, an investor would obtain a risk-adjusted return less than the return obtained in the market; that is, for a beta of two, a return less than 24 percent—a bad investment to make. If the market, however, priced Zuber less than $52.42 (underpriced), then the risk-adjusted return would be above the returns obtained in the market—an abnormal return—for a beta of two, a return greater than 24 percent and a good investment to make.

In contrast, if the risk-adjusted return on Zuber's investment were less than what investors could obtain in the market, then the value of their stock would be less than $50 if investors believed that Zuber was going to undertake the investment. For example, if the investment return were expected to be only 20 percent, then the value of Zuber's equity would be $241.94 million and the share price would be $48.39:

$$V_0^E = \frac{D_1}{(1+k_e)^1} + \frac{D_2}{(1+k_e)^2} + \frac{V_2^E}{(1+k_e)^2}$$

$$V_0^E = \frac{0}{1.24} + \frac{\$60M + (0.20)(\$60M)}{(1.24)^2} + \frac{(\$60M + \$12M)/0.24}{(1.24)^2}$$

$$V_0^E = \frac{0}{1.24} + \frac{\$72M}{(1.24)^2} + \frac{\$300M}{(1.24)^2} = \$241.94 \text{ million}$$

and

$$V_0^e = \frac{d_1}{(1 + k_e)^1} + \frac{d_2}{(1 + k_e)^2} + \frac{V_2^e}{(1 + k_e)^2}$$

$$V_0^e = \frac{0}{1.24} + \frac{\$72M/5M}{(1.24)^2} + \frac{\$300M/5M}{(1.24)^2}$$

$$V_0^e = \frac{0}{1.24} + \frac{\$14.40}{(1.24)^2} + \frac{\$60}{(1.24)^2} = \$48.39$$

If the market prices the stock at $48.39, then investors would still realize an expected return of 24 percent given the expected dividends of $14.40 and year two stock price of $60. Again, 24 percent is the same rate investors could obtain in the market for an investment with a beta of two:

$$\$48.39 = \frac{0}{(1 + R)^1} + \frac{\$14.40}{(1 + R)^2} + \frac{\$60}{(1 + R)^2} \Rightarrow R = 0.24$$

If the market priced Zuber stock below $48.39—underpriced the stock—then the expected return would exceed the 24 percent expected return that could be obtained in the market. In this case, an investor could obtain a risk-adjusted return better than the return obtained in the market; that is, for a beta of two, a return greater than 24 percent, this is an abnormal return and a good investment. If the market, however, priced Zuber above $48.39 (overpriced), then the risk-adjusted return would be below the returns obtained in the market; for a beta of two, this would be a return less than 24 percent and a bad investment.

It should be noted that in these cases we are assuming an investment project with the same beta as the current asset of the company. The same conclusions, however, would be reached if we evaluated Zuber undertaking an investment with a different beta.

In summary, a firm that can obtain a risk-adjusted return on its investments that exceeds the return investors can obtain in the market is referred to as a *growth firm*; a firm that earns investment returns that are less than what investors can obtain in the market is called a *declining firm*; and a firm that obtains investment returns that are equal to the returns investors can obtain in the market is referred to as a *normal firm*. In term of the CAPM, a growth company is one whose corporate investments have return (i) and risk (β_p) combinations that are above the SML; this was the case for Zuber when $i = 30\%$. A declining company, in turn, would be one with an i and β_p combination below the SML; for Zuber, that would be when its $i = 20\%$. Finally, a normal firm is one with the i and β_p combination on the line; in the Zuber case, it is when $i = 24\%$. If the market prices normal, growth and declining firms that capture their abilities to earn returns equal, above, or below the market rates, then the equilibrium returns of their stocks will match their market rates.

In practice, analysts evaluate companies that they know will be making numerous investments now and into the future. The idea of a growth firm can be better defined as one in which investors view management as being capable of obtaining returns on their investments that exceed the returns investors can obtain in the market. The definitions of firms as growth, declining, and normal based on their return relative to the market return was first introduced by Robert Gordon. The valuation of the Zuber Company in terms of the Gordon-Williams model is discussed in the next section.[3]

Gordon-Williams Model

In the Zuber case, we had a company that made a one-time only investment. As a result, the company earnings grew by 24 percent from year one to year two: $EAT_1 = \$60$ million to $EAT_2 = \$74.4$ million $[= EAT_1 + iI_1 = \$60$ million $+ (0.24)(\$60$ million$)]$:

$$g = \frac{EAT_2 - EAT_1}{EAT_1} = \frac{EAT_2}{EAT_1} - 1 = \frac{\$74.4\text{M}}{\$60\text{M}} - 1 = 0.24$$

The 24 percent growth in earnings was equal to Zuber's investment return of $i = 0.24$. If Zuber's investment expenditures had been \$30 million instead of \$60 million—half of its earnings $(I_1/EAT_1 = \$30\text{M}/\$60\text{M})$ instead of 100 percent—then its earnings would have grown by 12 percent from year one to year two: $EAT_2 = \$67.2$ million $[= EAT_1 + iI_1 = \$60$ million $+ (0.24)(\$30$ million$)]$:

$$g = \frac{EAT_2 - EAT_1}{EAT_1} = \frac{EAT_2}{EAT_1} - 1 = \frac{\$67.2\text{M}}{\$60\text{M}} - 1 = 0.12$$

By definition, a company's *sustainable growth rate* is equal to its return on its investments times its investment policy, where the investment policy is defined as the proportions of its investment expenditures (I) to earnings (EAT).

$$g = \frac{I_t}{EAT_t} i$$

Thus, if Zuber were to make an investment in year one equal to 100 percent of its earnings $(I_1/EAT_1 = 1)$ with a 24 percent rate of return on the investment, then its growth rate from year one to year two would be 24 percent $[= (1)(0.24)]$; if Zuber were to make an investment equal to 50 percent of its earnings $(I_1/EAT_1 = 0.5)$, then its growth rate would be 12 percent $[= (0.5)(0.24)]$.

The growth rate in dividends, in turn, depends on the growth rate in earnings and the dividend payout ratio (dividends/earnings). If Zuber were to finance its investments internally through retained earnings, then its investment policy (I/EAT) would be equal to retention ratio (f): the ratio of retained earnings to earnings (RE/EAT);

and its dividend-payout ratio would be equal to one minus its retention ratio:

Internal Financing:

$$\textit{Investment Policy:} \ \frac{I}{EAT} = \frac{RE}{EAT} = f$$

$$\textit{Dividend Payout:} \ \frac{D}{EAT} = 1 - \frac{RE}{EAT} = 1 - f$$

Thus, with an investment policy equal to 50 percent of earnings ($I/EAT = 0.50$), a return on investment of 24 percent ($i = 0.24$), and internal financing ($RE/EAT = f = I/EAT = 0.5$), Zuber would grow at 12 percent ((I/EAT)(i) $= fi = (0.5)(0.24) = 0.12$), and would have a dividend payout of 0.5 ($= D/EAT = 1 - f = 0.5$). Given k_e of 24 percent, Zuber would be valued at \$250 million, or \$50 per share, given its one-time only investment:

$$V_0^E = \frac{D_1}{(1 + k_e)^1} + \frac{D_2}{(1 + k_e)^2} + \frac{V_2^E}{(1 + k_e)^2}$$

$$V_0^E = \frac{\$30}{1.24} + \frac{\$60M + (0.24)(\$30M)}{(1.24)^2} + \frac{(\$60M + \$7.2M)/0.24}{(1.24)^2}$$

$$V_0^E = \frac{\$30M}{1.24} + \frac{\$67.2M}{(1.24)^2} + \frac{\$280M}{(1.24)^2} = \$250 \text{ million}$$

With the Zuber Company not expected to make any new investments after year one, the expected growth rate is zero after year two, with the company expected to generate a constant dividend of \$67.2 million. As discussed previously, the Gordon-Williams model is a constant growth model that assumes dividends grow at a constant rate for a very long time. Dividends will grow at a constant rate if a corporation's investments over time are equal to a constant proportion of the company's earnings, if the investment rate of return is the same over time, and if the dividend payout ratio is constant. Such a profile fits many well-established companies in mature industries. Suppose that Zuber was a company that was expected to make investments every year for a long time—a perpetual investment machine. Given the same investment policy of 50 percent and return on investment of 24 percent, Zuber's earnings would grow at a constant rate of 12 percent over time. In addition, if it financed its investments internally, then its dividend payout ratio would also be constant over time and its dividends would also grow at a constant rate of 12 percent. In this case, the Gordon-Williams model could be applied to determine the value of Zuber:

$$V_0^E = \sum_{t=1}^{\infty} \frac{D_0(1 + g)^t}{(1 + k_e)^t} = \frac{D_0(1 + g)^1}{k_e - g} = \frac{D_1}{k_e - g}$$

$$V_0^e = \sum_{t=1}^{\infty} \frac{d_0(1 + g)^t}{(1 + k_e)^t} = \frac{d_0(1 + g)^1}{k_e - g} = \frac{d_1}{k_e - g}$$

For an internally financed firm like Zuber, dividends each year, the growth rate, and value would be:

$$\text{Investment Policy: } \frac{I_t}{EAT_t}$$

$$\text{Internal Financing: } \frac{RE_t}{EAT_t} = f = \frac{I_t}{ERT}$$

$$\text{Growth Rate in Earnings: } g = fi$$

$$\text{Payout Ratio: } \frac{D_t}{EAT_t} = 1 - \frac{RE_t}{EAT_t} = 1 - f$$

$$\text{Dividend: } D_t = (1 - f)EAT_t = (1 - f)(1 + g)EAT_{t-1}$$
$$= (1 - f)(1 + fi)EAT_{t-1}$$

$$V_0^E = \sum_{t=1}^{\infty} \frac{D_t}{(1 + k_e)^t} = \sum_{t=1}^{\infty} \frac{(1 - f)(1 + g)^t EAT_0}{(1 + k_e)^t} \rightarrow \frac{(1 - f)EAT_1}{k_e - g} = \frac{D_1}{k_e - g}$$

$$V_0^E = \frac{D_1}{k_e - g} = \frac{(1 - f)EAT_0(1 + fi)}{k_e - fi}$$

Given $f = 0.5$ and $i = 0.24$ and a current *EAT* of \$60 million, the total equity value of Zuber as a perpetual investment company would be \$280 million:

$$V_0^E = \frac{D_1}{k_e - g} = \frac{(1 - f)EAT_0(1 + fi)}{k_e - fi}$$

$$V_0^E = \frac{(1 - 0.5)\$60M(1 + (0.5)(0.24))}{0.24 \quad 0.12} = \frac{\$33.60M}{0.24 - 0.12} = \$280 \text{ million}$$

or

$$V_0^E = V_0^E = \sum_{t=1}^{\infty} \frac{D_0(1 + g)^t}{(1 + k_e)^t} = \frac{\$30M(1.12)^1}{(1.24)^1} + \frac{\$30M(1.12)^2}{(1.24)^2}$$

$$+ \frac{\$30M(1.12)^3}{(1.24)^3} + \cdots + \frac{\$30M(1.12)^{20}}{(1.24)^{20}} + \cdots$$

$$V_0^E = \frac{\$33.60M}{(1.24)^1} + \frac{\$37.63M}{(1.24)^2} + \frac{\$42.15M}{(1.24)^3} +$$

$$\cdots + \frac{\$289.39M}{(1.24)^{20}} + \cdots \rightarrow \frac{\$33.60M}{0.24 - 0.12} = \$280 \text{ million}$$

Normal, Growth, and Declining Firms

Like our previous case, the Gordon-Williams model also can be used to define growth, declining, and normal firms. To see this, consider again the Zuber Company: an all-equity company with EAT of $67.20 million expected in year one $[= (1 + g)EAT_0 = (1.12)\$60\text{ million}]$, 5 million shares outstanding, investment policy of investing 50 percent of its earnings $(I/EAT = 0.5)$, and investments financed internally $(f = I/EAT)$. As before, assume Zuber's expected rate of return on its investment is 24 percent, and the beta on its project is equal to the firm's beta of two, the risk-free rate is 4 percent, and the market risk premium is 10 percent. Using the Gordon-Williams model, the company's expected growth rate in earnings (and dividends) would be $g = fi = (0.5)(0.24) = 0.12$, and the value of the company would be $280 million with a per share value of $56:

$$V_0^e = \frac{d_1}{k_e - g} = \frac{(1 - f)(EAT_1/n)}{k_e - fi}$$

$$V_0^e = \frac{(1 - 0.5)(\$67.20M/5M)}{0.24 - 0.12} = \frac{\$6.72}{0.24 - 0.12} = \$56$$

$$V_0^e = \frac{V_0^E}{n} = \frac{\$280M}{5M} = \$56$$

Since this company is expected to earn the same rate of return on its investments that investors can earn in the market $(i = k_e)$, any investment policy the company pursues will not change the value of the company. This is illustrated in Exhibit 11.5. As shown, if the company were to eliminate all future investments after year one and instead distribute all of its $67.20 million earnings in year one to its shareholders $(D/EAT = 1$ and $RE/EAT = f = 0)$, the company would still be worth $280 million and $56 per share:

$$V_0^E = \frac{E_1}{k_e} = \frac{\$67.20}{0.24} = \$280$$

$$V_0^e = \frac{V_0^E}{n} = \frac{\$280M}{5M} = \$56$$

In contrast, if the company were to invest 75 percent of its earnings each year $(f = 0.75)$, yielding a growth rate in earnings of 18 percent $[= fi = (0.75)(0.24)]$, or invest nearly all of its earnings $(f = 0.999$; note the model is undefined at $f = 1)$, then its value would still be $280 million and $56 per share:

$$V_0^E = \frac{D_1}{k_e - g} = \frac{(1 - f)(EAT_1)}{k_e - fi}$$

$$V_0^E = \frac{(1 - 0.75)\$67.20M}{0.24 - (0.75)(0.24)} = \frac{\$16.8M}{0.24 - 0.18} = \$280 \text{ million}$$

$$V_0^e = \frac{V_0^E}{n} = \frac{\$280M}{5M} = \$56$$

EXHIBIT 11.5   Equity Value, Growth, and Investment Policy

Growth	$i > k_e$	$\Delta V^E_0 / \Delta f > 0$
Normal	$i = k_e$	$\Delta V^E_0 / \Delta f = 0$
Declining	$i < k_e$	$\Delta V^E_0 / \Delta f < 0$

$f = RE/EAT$	i	$g = fi$	EAT_1	$Div_1 = (1-f)EAT_1$	k_e	$V^E = Div_1/(k_e - g)$	V^s
Normal			in millions	in millions		in millions	
0	0.24	0	$67.20	$67.20	0.24	$280.00	$56.00
0.5	0.24	0.12	$67.20	$33.60	0.24	$280.00	$56.00
0.75	0.24	0.18	$67.20	$16.80	0.24	$280.00	$56.00
Growth							
0	0.3	0	$67.20	$67.20	0.24	$280.00	$56.00
0.5	0.3	0.15	$67.20	$33.60	0.24	$373.33	$74.67
0.75	0.3	0.225	$67.20	$16.80	0.24	$1,120.00	$224.00
Declining							
0	0.2	0	$67.20	$67.20	0.24	$280.00	$56.00
0.5	0.2	0.1	$67.20	$33.60	0.24	$240.00	$48.00
0.75	0.2	0.15	$67.20	$16.80	0.24	$186.67	$37.33

As stated earlier in the case of the one-time-only investment, the reason the stock's value is invariant to the company's investments is because its management is expected to obtain the same risk-adjusted return on its investments that investors can obtain in the market. As previously noted, such a firm is known as a normal firm. If the company were able to obtain rates of return on its investments exceeding the required return, then its value would increase the more investments it undertakes (i.e., the greater f). This can be seen in middle panel of Exhibit 11.5, where the company's return on investments is expected to be 30 percent. In this case, if the company's investment expenditures are equal to 50 percent of its earnings, then its growth rate in earnings would be 15 percent; its equity value, $373.33 million; and its per share value, $74.67:

$$V^E_0 = \frac{D_1}{k_e - g} = \frac{(1-f)(EAT_1)}{k_e - fi}$$

$$V^E_0 = \frac{(1 - 0.50)\$67.20M}{0.24 - (0.50)(0.30)}$$

$$= \frac{\$33.60M}{0.24 - 0.15}$$

$$= \$373.33 \text{ million}$$

$$V_0^e = \frac{V_0^E}{n}$$

$$= \frac{\$373.33M}{5M}$$

$$= \$74.67$$

If the company does not pursue its investment opportunities ($f = 0$), then its stock value would be only \$280 million and \$56 per share:

$$V_0^E = \frac{D_1}{k_e} = \frac{(EAT_1)}{k_e} = \frac{\$67.20M}{0.24} = \$280 \text{ million}$$

$$V_0^e = \frac{V_0^E}{n} = \frac{\$280M}{5M} = \$56$$

and if it increased its investment so that $f = 0.75$, then its growth rate would be 22.5 percent, its equity value would be \$1,120 million, and its per share value would be \$224.

$$V_0^E = \frac{D_1}{k_e - g} = \frac{(1-f)(EAT_1)}{k_e - fi}$$

$$V_0^E = \frac{(1 - 0.75)\$67.20M}{0.24 - (0.75)(0.30)} = \frac{\$16.80M}{0.24 - 0.225} = \$1,120 \text{ million}$$

$$V_0^e = \frac{V_0^E}{n} = \frac{\$1,120M}{5M} = \$224$$

As we defined previously, such a firm is a growth firm: one that can obtain returns on its investments that exceed the returns obtainable in the market. The value of such a firm will increase if investors see the company as pursuing its investment opportunities. It is possible, however, for a growth firm to decline in value. This would occur if investors in the market believe that such a firm was not pursing its investment opportunities.

Finally, if the company obtained returns on its investments that were less than the returns its shareholders could obtain in the market, then its equity value would decrease if the company pursued (or was expected to pursue) its investments. This can be seen in the lower panel of Exhibit 11.5, where the company's return on investments is expected to be 20 percent. In this case, if the company's investment expenditures are equal to 50 percent of its earnings, its growth rate in earnings would be 10 percent, its equity value, \$240 million, and its per share value, \$48:

$$V_0^E = \frac{D_1}{k_e - g} = \frac{(1 - f)(EAT_1)}{k_e - fi}$$

$$V_0^E = \frac{(1 - 0.50)\$67.20M}{0.24 - (0.50)(0.20)} = \frac{\$33.60M}{0.24 - 0.10} = \$240 \text{ million}$$

$$V_0^e = \frac{V_0^E}{n} = \frac{\$240M}{5M} = \$48$$

If this declining company increased its investment so that $f = 0.75$, then its total equity value would decrease to \$186.67 million and \$37.33 per share.

$$V_0^E = \frac{D_1}{k_e - g}$$

$$= \frac{(1 - f)(EAT_1)}{k_e - fi}$$

$$V_0^E = \frac{(1 - 0.75)\$67.20M}{0.24 - (0.75)(0.20)}$$

$$= \frac{\$16.80M}{0.24 - 0.15}$$

$$= \$186.67 \text{ million}$$

$$V_0^e = \frac{V_0^E}{n}$$

$$= \frac{\$186.67M}{5M}$$

$$= \$37.33$$

In contrast, if the company does not undertake its investment opportunities ($f = 0$), then its stock value would increase to \$280 million and \$56 per share:

$$V_0^E = \frac{D_1}{k_e} = \frac{(EAT_1)}{k_e} = \frac{\$67.20M}{0.24} = \$280 \text{ million}$$

$$V_0^e = \frac{V_0^E}{n} = \frac{\$280M}{5M} = \$56$$

Hence, in this case of a declining firm, management can increase the equity value of the company by eliminating investments and paying all earnings to its shareholders who can obtain greater returns than management by investing the cash flows themselves.

Good and Bad Investments

If investors in our example pay the equilibrium price for the stock, their expected return will be 24 percent regardless of whether the company is a normal, growth, or declining firm—their investment return and beta combination will be on the SML. The 24 percent return can be seen in Exhibit 11.6, where the annual price and dividend patterns are shown for the normal, growth, and declining firms for which the investment policy for each is assumed to be 50 percent of earnings ($f = 0.5$). Thus, in the case of the growth firm [$g = fi = (0.50)(0.30) = 0.15$], for example, if investors pay the a market price equal to the equilibrium value of $74.67 [$= E(DPS_1)/(k_e - g) = \$6.72/(0.24 - 0.15)$], then their expected annual gain in price would be 15 percent based on an expected price of $85.87 in year one and their expected annual dividend yield would be 9 percent [$= E(Div_1)/P_0 = \$6.72/\$74.67$], yielding a total return of 24 percent. As shown in the Exhibit 11.6, these yield patterns hold true for each year, if investors in the market price the stock equal to the equilibrium value.

As an investment principle, an investment can be a good or bad one, depending on whether it underpriced or overpriced in the market. Just because a firm is a declining company does not mean it is a bad investment–that is, the stock could be underpriced. On the other hand, just because a firm is a growth company does not mean it is a good investment—that is, the stock could be overpriced. As we discussed previously, a good investment would be one in which the market price is below the equilibrium value. Buying underpriced stocks, in turn, provides investors with returns above the risk-adjusted return. In terms of the example shown in Exhibit 11.6, an investor who purchased the normal firm below its equilibrium value of $56 would earn a rate greater than the 24 percent rate provided in the market for stocks with a beta of two. Similarly, an investor who purchased the growth firm below its equilibrium of $74.67 or the declining firm below its equilibrium value of $48 would expect to receive a return greater than the risk-adjusted return of 24 percent. Thus, by buying underpriced stocks, an investor can obtain an investment return and beta combination above the SML. In contrast, an investor who purchased either the normal firm above its equilibrium value of $56, the growth firm above its equilibrium of $74.67, or the declining firm above $48 would earn a rate less than the 24 percent rate provided in the market for stocks with a beta of two. Thus, the purchase of overpriced securities can provide an investor with a return and beta combination below the SML.

In summary, the Gordon-Williams constant growth rate model is very restrictive. Obviously, companies pursue investments over time that differ in terms of their life, risk characteristics, and cash flow patterns. The contribution of the Gordon-Williams model, however, is not in its practicality, but rather in establishing that the criterion for evaluating stocks should be based on determining whether a company's investment returns exceed the returns available in the market.

EXHIBIT 11.6 Price, Dividend, and Return Patterns

Year	EAT (millions)	DIV (millions)	DPS	Share Price E(d)/ ($k_e - g$)	Expected Capital Gain	Expected Price Yield	Expected Dividend Yield	Total Yield
Normal	$f = 0.5$, $i = 0.24$, $g = 0.12$							
0				$56.00				
1	$67.20	$33.60	$6.72	$62.72	$6.72	0.12	0.12	0.24
2	$75.26	$37.63	$7.53	$70.25	$7.53	0.12	0.12	0.24
3	$84.30	$42.15	$8.43	$78.68	$8.43	0.12	0.12	0.24
4	$94.41	$47.21	$9.44	$88.12	$9.44	0.12	0.12	0.24
5	$105.74	$52.87	$10.57	$98.69	$10.57	0.12	0.12	0.24
6	$118.43	$59.21	$11.84	$110.53	$11.84	0.12	0.12	0.24
7	$132.64	$66.32	$13.26	$123.80				
8	$148.56	$74.28	$14.86					
Growth	$f = 0.5$, $i = 0.30$, $g = 0.15$							
0				$74.67				
1	$67.20	$33.60	$6.72	$85.87	$11.20	0.15	0.09	0.24
2	$77.28	$38.64	$7.73	$98.75	$12.88	0.15	0.09	0.24
3	$88.87	$44.44	$8.89	$113.56	$14.81	0.15	0.09	0.24
4	$102.20	$51.10	$10.22	$130.59	$17.03	0.15	0.09	0.24
5	$117.53	$58.77	$11.75	$150.18	$19.59	0.15	0.09	0.24
6	$135.16	$67.58	$13.52	$172.71	$22.53	0.15	0.09	0.24
7	$155.44	$77.72	$15.54	$198.61				
8	$178.75	$89.38	$17.88					
Declining	$f = 0.5$, $i = 0.20$, $g = 0.10$							
0				$48.00				
1	$67.20	$33.60	$6.72	$52.80	$4.80	0.1	0.14	0.24
2	$73.92	$36.96	$7.39	$58.08	$5.28	0.1	0.14	0.24
3	$81.31	$40.66	$8.13	$63.89	$5.81	0.1	0.14	0.24
4	$89.44	$44.72	$8.94	$70.28	$6.39	0.1	0.14	0.24
5	$98.39	$49.19	$9.84	$77.30	$7.03	0.1	0.14	0.24
6	$108.23	$54.11	$10.82	$85.03				
7	$119.05	$59.52	$11.90					

EAT, DIV, and DPS for year 1 are assumed to be the same for Normal, Growth, and Declining firms
Price Yield = Expected Capital Gain/Price; Div. Yield = E(DPS)/P; Total Yield = Price Yield + Dividend Yield

BLOOMBERG: CACS, CACT, AND SUSTAINABLE GROWTH RATE

CACS

The Bloomberg CACS screen is a good screen to use to identify a company's past and pending investments. On the screen, you can click M&A and IPO/ADDL screen, and set dates to bring up corporate investments, divestments, and other corporate actions.

CACT

The Bloomberg CACT screen is a good screen for investment activities for cross-sectional listings (e.g., stocks composing an index, portfolio formed in PRTU, or a search saved in EQS).

Bloomberg Sustainable Growth

The sustainable growth rate is equal to the investment policy (I/E) times the rate of return on its investments (i). For internally financed companies, the investment policy is equal to the retention ratio ($f = 1 - d/e$). The rate of return on corporate investments is highly correlated with the return on equity (ROE), and the retention ratio is considered a good measure of a company's long-run investment policy. Sustainable growth is often measured as the product of the retention ratio times the ROE: fROE.

- Sustainable growth rates measured as the retention ratio times ROE for companies, industry indexes, and market indexes can be accessed from Bloomberg's FA, GF, and FA screens.
- The RV screen can be used to compare sustainable growth rates for a company and its peers. Use the Custom tab to search for sustainable growth, return on equity, and retention ratio.

    See Bloomberg Web Exhibit 11.4.

Case 2: Two-Dollar General Store

Two-Dollar General Store Inc. franchises discount stores nationally. Suppose the company has the following features:

- All equity company.
- Current $EAT_0 = \$24$ million.
- Corporate investment policy in which its annual investments equal 75 percent of its *EAT*.
- Investment financing done internally.
- Estimated rate of return on its investments $= i = 0.20$.
- Beta of the firm and beta of the company's investments $= 2$.

- SML: $k_e = 0.05 + [0.10]\beta$.
- The above features are expected to characterize this company for a long time.
- Number of shares = 5 million.

If we expect the company to maintain its investment policy, internal financing, and investment returns for a many years, then the value of Two-Dollar General Store could be determined by the Gordon-Williams model. Specifically, based on the above features, Two-Dollar's growth rate would be 15 percent [= (0.75)(0.20)], its investment policy would equal its retention ratio of 0.75, and its dividend payout ratio would be 0.25. With a growth rate of 15 percent, Two-Dollar's EAT_1 would be $27.6 million [= $EAT_0(1 + g)$ = $24 million (1.15)] and its Div_1 would be $6.90 million [= $(1 - f)EAT_1$ = (1 − 0.75)$27.6 million], and *DPS* would be $1.38. The total equity value of Two-Dollar General Store would therefore be $69 million, and the share value would be $13.80.

$$V_E = \frac{D_1}{k_e - g} = \frac{\$6.9M}{0.25 - 0.15} = \$69 \text{ million}$$

$$V_e = \$69M/5M = \$13.80$$

If investors were to price Two-Dollar at $13.80 per share and over time the assumptions underlying this scenario regarding investment returns, investment policy, and internal financing were realized, then investors would earn a 25 percent return. As shown in Exhibit 11.7, the 25 percent return would consist of a 15 percent price yield and a 10 percent dividend yield, the price of the stock would increase over five years from $13.80 to $27.76, and its dividends per share would increase from $1.20 to $2.78 over that period—again if these assumptions hold.

Suppose an analyst reports that Two-Dollar's managers have indicated that they do not see the growth in its store expansion to be as great as first forecasted and have revised their long-term investment policy to be equal to 50 percent of its *EAT*. Based on this report, Two-Dollar's growth rate would be 10 percent [− (0.50)(0.20)], it investment policy and retention ratio would be 0.50, and its dividend payout ratio would be 0.50. With a growth rate of 10 percent, Two-Dollar's EAT_1 would, in turn, be $26.4 million [= $EAT_0(1 + g)$ = $24 million (1.10)], its Div_1 would be $13.2 million [= $(1 - f)EAT_1$ = (1 − 0.50)$26.4 million], and its DPS_1 would be $2.64. The total equity value of Two-Dollar General Store based on this report would be $88 million, and the share value would be $17.60:

$$V_E = \frac{D_1}{k_e - g} = \frac{\$13.2M}{0.25 - 0.10} = \$88 \text{ million}$$

$$V_e = \$88M/5M = \$17.60$$

The lower panel in Exhibit 11.7 shows the prices, dividends, and yields over several years based on this investment return, investment policy, and internal financing.

EXHIBIT 11.7   Prices, Dividends, and Yields for Two-Dollar General Store

Year	EAT (millions)	DIV (millions)	DPS	Share Price E(d)/ ($k_e - g$)	Expected Capital Gain	Expected Price Yield	Expected Dividend Yield	Total Yield
	$f = 0.75$, $i = 0.20$, $g = 0.15$							
0	$24.00	$6.00	$1.20	$13.80				
1	$27.60	$6.90	$1.38	$15.87	$2.07	0.15	0.10	0.25
2	$31.74	$7.94	$1.59	$18.25	$2.38	0.15	0.10	0.25
3	$36.50	$9.13	$1.83	$20.99	$2.74	0.15	0.10	0.25
4	$41.98	$10.49	$2.10	$24.14	$3.15	0.15	0.10	0.25
5	$48.27	$12.07	$2.41	$27.76	$3.62	0.15	0.10	0.25
6	$55.51	$13.88	$2.78					
	$f = 0.50$, $i = 0.20$, $g = 0.10$							
0	$24.00	$12.00	$2.40	$17.60				
1	$26.40	$13.20	$2.64	$19.36	$1.76	0.1	0.15	0.25
2	$29.04	$14.52	$2.90	$21.30	$1.94	0.1	0.15	0.25
3	$31.94	$15.97	$3.19	$23.43	$2.13	0.1	0.15	0.25
4	$35.14	$17.57	$3.51	$25.77	$2.34	0.1	0.15	0.25
5	$38.65	$19.33	$3.87	$28.34	$2.58	0.1	0.15	0.25
6	$42.52	$21.26	$4.25					

There are two inferences to draw from this case. First, note the wide difference in prices as a result of investment opportunities. With the optimistic investment opportunity characterized by a 75 percent investment policy, investors would price Two-Dollar at $13.80 using the Gordon-Williams model, and with the conservative investment opportunity projection of 50 percent, they would price the stock at $17.60. The market price of the stock would eventually move to where the consensus position is on Two-Dollar's growth. Moreover, this is a position that could change with new information.

The second inference to draw from this case is that Two-Dollar's stock value was lower under the scenario of reduced future investments in new stores. This can be explained by the fact that Two-Dollar is a declining firm. It has a beta of two and return on its investments of 20 percent compared to its required return of 25 percent. The equity value of Two-Dollar would increase if investors expected the company to reduce its futures investments and pay more of its earnings to shareholders who could obtain greater returns than management by investing the cash flows in the market.

Two-Stage and Three-Stage Growth Models

The assumption that a company can maintain a constant growth rate for a long time is unrealistic for many companies, especially those in early stages of development. As we examined in Chapter 3, a two-stage growth or three-stage growth model may be more applicable.

In the case of Two-Dollar General Store, suppose that in addition to an investment policy of 50 percent of its *EAT* the analyst also reports that Two-Dollar's management believes that the company will experience an investment return in each of its first three years of $i = 30\%$ and then afterward will obtain a 20 percent return. Based on this report, Two-Dollar's growth rate would be 15 percent [$= fi = (0.50)(0.30)$] for three years and 10 percent thereafter [$= fi = (0.50)(0.20)$]. The total equity value of Two-Dollar General Store using two growth rates would be $99.07 million, and its per share value would be $19.81:

$$V_E = \frac{\$12M(1.15)}{1.25} + \frac{\$12M(1.15)^2}{(1.25)^2} + \frac{\$12M(1.15)^3}{(1.25)^3}$$

$$+ \frac{\$12(1.15)^3(1.10)/(0.25 - 0.10)}{(1.25)^3}$$

$$V_E = \frac{\$13.8M}{1.25} + \frac{\$15.87M}{(1.25)^2} + \frac{\$18.25M}{(1.25)^3} + \frac{\$133.84M}{(1.25)^3} = \$99.07 \text{ million}$$

$$V_0^e = \frac{V_0^E}{n} = \frac{\$99.07M}{5M} = \$19.81$$

Finally, suppose that an analyst believes Two-Dollar's future dividend flow will follow the three-stage growth model similar to Bloomberg's DDM discussed in Chapter 3 with the following features:

1. *EPS* will be $4.80 for FY1, $5.52 for FY2, and $6.35 for FY3 based on consensus estimates.
2. The length of the initial growth stage will be seven years with the annual growth rate estimated to be 15 percent for that period.
3. The length of the transitional stage will be 10 years.
4. The mature growth period will start in year 20 with an assumed dividend-payout ratio of 75 percent and with a growth rate of 6.25 percent. The mature growth rate will be equal to the discount rate of 25 percent times the retention ratio (0.25).
5. The transition period starts in year 11, with the growth rate decreasing by increments of 0.875 percent per year [$= (15\% - 6.25\%)/10$] from 15 percent to 6.25 percent. Column 2 in the table in Exhibit 11.8 shows the growth rates for each year (starting in year 4) and its corresponding *EPS* ($EPS_t = EPS_{t-1}(1+g_t)$).
6. The dividend-payout ratio for the first 10 years (FY1–FY3 plus the seven-year growth period) will be equal to the dividend-payout ratio for FY1 of 0.25 ($= DPS_{FY1}/EPS_{FY1} = \$1.20/\$4.80$).

7. Starting in year 11 (the first year of the transition period), the payout ratios start to increase by annual increments of 5 percent [= (75% − 25%)/10] to reach the model's assumed payout rate of 75 percent at year 20, the last year of the transition period.
8. From year 20 on, the dividend payout stays at 25 percent.
9. The dividends-per-share each year will be equal to the *EPS* times the payout ratio.
10. The value of Two-Dollar's equity in year 20 will be equal to Gordon's constant growth model value ($V = d/(k − g)$).

Exhibit 11.8 shows the cash flow calculations of Two-Dollar General Store. Discounting each *DPS* and the terminal value by the discount rate of 25 percent (Column 6), we obtain an intrinsic value for Two-Dollar General Store of $13.87.

Determining which growth-rate model an analyst should use depends on the type of the company being evaluated. Companies in emerging industries such as new technologies, for example, are typically characterized by multistage growth periods. For such companies, there is often an initial period of extraordinary growth in which the companies in the new industry are expanding their manufacturing and marketing base to meet the immense domestic and possible world demand for their products. The length of this initial period can vary depending on capital requirements, the ease of entry of new firms into the industry, the emergence of subsequent technology, and the potential demand. The initial growth stage for General Motors, Ford, and Chrysler arguably lasted as long as 50 years (from 1920 to 1970). In contrast, companies in more mature industries, such as steel manufacturing, food processing, or mining, may be better characterized by a constant growth rate model in which their dividends and earnings are expected to grow at a steady state rate. However, it is important to remember that such companies can be influenced by external factors, both good and bad, which can transform them into an emerging industry again. For example, many analysts who considered the banking industry to be mature and stable in the 1960s saw it transformed into a growth industry as a result of the liberalization of banking laws and the emergence of new technology. Similarly, the fall of communism in the 1980s and the emergence of China, India, and Brazil in the last 20 years has led to new markets for the product of many companies in mature industries.

BLOOMBERG DDM SCREEN

Bloomberg's DDM model estimates the intrinsic value of a selected equity using a three-stage growth model. The screen also can be used to calculate the IRR, expected return, and implied growth rate based on a series of assumptions. Estimates for *EPS* for FY1–FY3, dividend payout ratio, growth rates, length of years for stage 1 growth and transition years, and discount rates appear in the amber boxes. You can change any of the assumptions. See Bloomberg exhibit box in Chapter 3: Bloomberg DDM Screen and Exhibit 3.15 for the DDM screen for Disney. You can change the DDM model to reflect your own assumptions.

See Bloomberg Web Exhibit 11.5.

EXHIBIT 11.8 Value of Two-Dollar General Store Using Three-Stage DDM Model

1	2	3	4	5	6
Year	Growth Rate	EPS	Dividend Payout Ratio	DPS	PV at $k = 0.25$
1		$4.80	0.250	$1.200	$0.96
2		$5.52	0.250	$1.380	$0.88
3		$6.35	0.250	$1.588	$0.81
4	0.1500	$7.30	0.250	$1.826	$0.75
5	0.1500	$8.40	0.250	$2.099	$0.69
6	0.1500	$9.66	0.250	$2.414	$0.63
7	0.1500	$11.11	0.250	$2.777	$0.58
8	0.1500	$12.77	0.250	$3.193	$0.54
9	0.1500	$14.69	0.250	$3.672	$0.49
10	0.1500	$16.89	0.250	$4.223	$0.45
11	0.1413	$19.28	0.300	$5.783	$0.50
12	0.1325	$21.83	0.350	$7.641	$0.53
13	0.1238	$24.53	0.400	$9.813	$0.54
14	0.1150	$27.35	0.450	$12.309	$0.54
15	0.1063	$30.26	0.500	$15.130	$0.53
16	0.0975	$33.21	0.550	$18.266	$0.51
17	0.0888	$36.16	0.600	$21.695	$0.49
18	0.0800	$39.05	0.650	$25.383	$0.46
19	0.0713	$41.83	0.700	$29.283	$0.42
20	0.0625	$44.45	0.750	$33.336	$0.38
20	0.0625	$47.23	0.75	$188.90	$2.18
				V_{20}	**Intrinsic Value**
					$13.87

Growth Years

Growth Rate = 0.15

Dividend Payout Rate = 0.75

Transitional Years

Annual Growth Rate Decrease = 0.00875

Annual Payout Rate Increase = 0.05

Maturity

Dividend Payout Rate = 0.75

Growth Rate = (1 − Payout Rate)(Discount Rate)

Growth Rate = (0.25)(0.25) = 0.0625

$EPS_{21} = EPS_{20}(1 + g) = 44.4479(1.0625) = 47.2259$

$DPS_{21} = $ (Payout Rate)$EPS_{21} = (0.75)(47.2259) = 35.42$

$V_{20} = DPS_{21}/(k − g) = 35.42/(0.25 − 0.0625) = \$188.90$

Mergers and Acquisitions

As perpetual investment machines, blue-chip companies not only invest in new endeavors, but they also buy the assets and divisions of other companies, frequently sell their own assets and divisions (divestments and equity sales), acquire companies in which they gain control (acquisition), absorb the assets and liabilities of other businesses (merger where the acquired company loses its independent existence), and consolidate with two or more firms to form an entirely new company (consolidation).

Mergers, consolidations, acquisitions, and equity sales are complicated undertakings. Consideration of such activities—both real and potential—is an important part of the valuation of a company. As noted in Chapter 5, investment banks are very active in mergers, consolidations, acquisitions, and equity sales, serving both the acquirers and the target firms. Acquiring firms use investment bankers to help them identify attractive firms to pursue, to solicit shareholders who might sell, to structure tender offers, to raise financial capital, and to structure the deal. Targeted firms may use investment banks to indicate their interest and commitment or possibly their disinterest and protection, especially when there is a hostile takeover effort. The decision to buy or sell assets, divisions, and other companies also necessitates the need to raise funds to finance the acquisition of another company or an investment, or as in the case of an equity sale, it may be necessitated by the need to raise funds to pay off debt obligations to avoid bankruptcy or to acquire another company. Exhibit 11.9 defines some of terms and identifies some of the technical points related to corporate acquisitions.

Every year there are thousands of mergers, acquisitions, and consolidations. To see the complexities of such deals, consider a merger in which one company acquires another corporation. Often, when a merger is being proposed, one company will make a *tender offer* to the shareholders of the targeted company offering to buy their shares at a specified price if they will agree to give up all existing shares. To induce shareholders to give up their shares, the tender offer has to be attractive. A targeted company with its stock trading for $20 might be offered cash or shares of the acquiring company worth $30 per share if the shareholders will agree to the merger. As a result, many analysts have investment strategies in which they try to identify companies they believe will be merger targets. Such strategies often involve evaluating certain industries, such as banking, airlines, or communications, in which technology or regulatory changes have made consolidation in such industries more profitable. Another strategy is to follow companies that have either implicit or explicit policies of acquiring companies.

Although the tender offer will serve to increase the stock price of the acquired company, the price of the acquiring company's stock often decreases, at least in the short run. In the long run, the value of the acquiring company will increase if there is *synergy* in combining the two companies. Synergy occurs when the combined value of the two companies, V^{XY}, is greater than the sum of the values of the companies:

$$V_A^{XY} > V_A^X + V_A^Y$$

EXHIBIT 11.9   List of Merger and Acquisition Terms

Terms

- **Acquisition:** One firm gains control of another firm.
- **Merger:** One company absorbs the assets and liabilities of another company and assumes the company's business. The acquired company loses its independent existence.
- **Consolidation:** Two or more firms combine to form an entirely new entry. Shares of each of the consolidated firms are exchanged for shares of the new firm. Both of the consolidated firms lose their independence, often becoming subsidiaries of a new firm or becoming a new firm.
- **Stock Acquisition:** Company purchases another company's stock (in the open market or via a tender offer). The acquiring firm can still obtain the target company's assets and liabilities, but no shareholder meeting is required.
- **Tender offer** is an offer to purchase.
- **Asset Acquisition:** An acquirer purchases only the assets of another firm (liabilities remain the responsibility of the selling firm).
- **Horizontal Merger:** Merger of two firms in the same line of business.
- **Vertical Merger:** Merger that either integrates a firm forward toward the consumer (manufacturing company buying a retailer) or backward toward the source of supply (manufacturing company buying a mineral extracting company).
- **Conglomerate Merger:** Merger of two firms in unrelated businesses.

Technical Points

- **Shareholder Approval:** A merger or consolidation must comply with each corporation's charter. Many corporation charters require a simple majority vote of the firm's shareholders for approval; some require 2/3.
- **Tax Treatment:** The IRS will treat the acquisition as tax-free if the targeted shareholders are treated as having exchanged their old shares for substantially new ones. Each acquiree who receives stock does not have to pay any tax on the gain until the shares are sold. The acquirer's tax base in each asset that is transferred is the same as the acquiree's (as it relates to depreciation, tax carry forwards, etc.)
- **Accounting Issues:** Acquisitions involve difficult accounting issues. In a pooling of interest, the assets, liabilities, and operating statements of the firms are added together without any adjustment to values.
- **Antitrust Considerations:** A merger or consolidation must comply with federal antitrust laws, state anti-takeover statutes, corporate charters, and federal and state security laws. The Clayton Act, Section 7, forbids a firm to purchase the assets or stock of another firm if the purchase substantially lessens competition or creates a monopoly in any line commerce or any section of the country.
- **Tender Offer:** A tender offer is an offer to purchase shares at a stated price from shareholders of the target firm who are willing to tender shares at that price. Tender offers are usually cash offers. With a cash tender offer, the acquirer does not have to register new securities. SEC rules do require the acquirer to file a notice of the offer and to keep the offer open for at least 20 days. The acquirer usually sets conditions in the offer so that it does not have to buy any shares unless the required minimum number is tendered. The tender offer usually specifies the purchases of just enough shares so that it can effectively control the company (20% to 40%). Once the acquirer has purchased shares via the tendered offer, then it can effect a merger structured to achieve 100% ownership and organize so as to realize a tax-free acquisition. Once the potential acquirer has made a tender offer, it may follow the offer by purchasing the target firm's stock in the open market. This is done if the potential acquirer believes other company will also make offers. If a higher bidder emerges, then the initial company who put the target company into 'play' will profit from owning the stock.
- **Proxy Contest:** Tender offers are expensive because the bidder must purchase enough shares to secure control. Alternatively, one or more parties can initiate a proxy contest. The dissidents solicit SH's proxies to vote their shares in favor of their slate of directors.

(Continued)

EXHIBIT 11.9   *(Continued)*

Anticipatory Defensive Tactics

- *Dual-Class Recapitalization:* Firm distributes a special class of common stock that possesses superior voting rights (e.g., 10 votes per share).
- *Employee Stock Ownership Plan:* The firm sells shares to employee groups and then uses the funds to acquire outstanding shares in the market.
- *Super Majority:* Firm's charter is amended to require a super majority (e.g., 80%) to be voted in favor of a merger.
- *Flip-in Poison Pill:* Firm issues rights to its shareholders (often one right per share) that give the holder the right to purchase, at say half the market price, shares of the firm's stock if a potential acquirer acquires more than a specified percentage of the firm's shares.
- *Flip-out Poison Pill:* Firm issues rights to its SHs that give the holders the right to purchase at a lower price shares of the acquirer's firm's stock if a potential acquirer acquires more than a specified percentage of the firm's shares. Note: The acquiree's board usually has the right to redeem the rights for a nominal fee (e.g., $0.05/right) if it approves the acquisition.

Responsive Defensive Tactics

- *Asset Purchase or Sale:* The firm purchases assets that the bidder does not want or would create antitrust problems. The firm sells assets the acquirer may want—sells the crown jewels.
- *Leveraged Recapitalization:* Firm borrows large sums and distributes the proceeds as cash or repurchases its stock.
- *Pac-Man Defense:* The firm makes a counter bid for the stock of the potential acquirer.
- *Golden Parachute:* The firm's board approves generous payment to managers who lose their jobs as a result of a takeover.

In practice, synergy is often the result of economies of scale. Economies of scale can be defined as the output and input (labor and capital) relation of a firm. If there are increasing (decreasing) returns to scale, then a proportional increase in the scale of operation will lead to a greater (smaller) proportional increase in output. When increasing returns to scale exist, a firm can reduce its average cost of producing and thereby increase its profit by simply increasing its scale of operation.[4] In many mergers involving companies in the same industry, the economic justification of the merger is based on an argument that increasing returns to scale exist. Synergy may also be realized by combining companies with different competitive advantages, for example, the merger of one company with production and engineering proficiencies with a company with marketing expertise, or the merger of one company with a strong market in one geographical area with a company with a strong market in another. Synergy could also come from potential tax benefits in which the acquired firm has a tax loss carry forward of which it cannot take full advantage. Similarly, synergy could come from an excessive cash position in which the targeted firm has a substantial cash position but few capital investment opportunities. Finally, it may be that the company can gain by buying the company and selling its assets and division—buying the company and stripping it. This would be feasible if the sum of the values of the assets to be stripped were greater than the price for acquiring the company—the sum of the values of assets was greater than the combined value.

Merger Case

In evaluating mergers from the perspective of the acquiring company, a valuation approach can be used to determine the new value of the company resulting from the merger and whether or not the tender offer is correctly priced. This approach requires that the analyst estimate the synergy effect. To see this, suppose an analyst is evaluating a targeted merger in which Company X, a $600 million company (value of its assets), is targeting Company Y, a $610 million company. Suppose both companies being analyzed are expected to last a long time, each has only long-term debt, neither has depreciation and depletion allowances or future investment plans, and each has an effective tax rate of 40 percent, a cost on debt of 10 percent, and a dividend-payout ratio of one.

Suppose the analyst estimates that Company X will generate an annual *EBIT* of $80 million, $30 million annual interest payments on its debt of $300 million [$= (0.10)(\$300$ million)], taxes of $20 million, *EAT* of $30 million, 5 million shares, and an *EPS* and *DPS* of $6.00:

$$E(d) = \frac{(\text{Div Payout})[E(EBIT) - k_d V_D)](1 - t)}{n}$$

$$E(d) = \frac{(1)[\$80 \text{ million} - (0.10)(\$300)](1 - 0.4)}{5 \text{ million}} = \frac{\$30 \text{ million}}{5 \text{ million}} = \$6.00$$

She, in turn, estimates that Company Y will generate an annual *EBIT* of $100 million, interest payments of $25 million on its $250 million debt [$= (0.10)(\$250$ million)], taxes of $30 million, *EAT* of $45 million, 5 million shares, and an *EPS* and *DPS* of $9.00:

$$E(d) = \frac{(\text{Div Payout})[E(EBIT) - k_d V_D)](1 - t)}{n}$$

$$E(d) = \frac{(1)[\$100 \text{ million} - (0.10)(\$250)](1 - 0.4)}{5 \text{ million}} = \frac{\$45 \text{ million}}{5 \text{ million}} = \$9.00$$

Based on revenue and earnings, company Y is larger than Company X. Suppose the analyst sees Company Y as being riskier than X, estimating Y's beta to be 1.5 and X's beta to be one. Using the CAPM and determining a risk-free rate of 5 percent and market risk-premium of 5 percent, she estimates the required return on X's equity to be 10 percent and the required return on Y's equity to be 12.5 percent:

$$k_e = R_f + [E(R^M) - R_f]\beta$$
$$k_e^X = 0.05 + [0.05](1) = 0.10$$
$$k_e^Y = 0.05 + [0.05](1.5) = 0.125$$

Given her assessment that both companies are expected to last a long time and not make any investments, the analyst would value X's equity at $300 million and Y's at $360 million:

$$V_X^E = \frac{D_1}{k_e} = \frac{\$30M}{0.10} = \$300 \text{ million}$$

$$V_Y^E = \frac{D_1}{k_e} = \frac{\$45M}{0.125} = \$360 \text{ million}$$

With X having $300 million in debt, the market value of its assets would be $600 million, and based on market values, X's overall cost of capital, k_C, would be 10 percent and its tax-adjusted cost of capital $k_C{}^T$, 8 percent:

$$V_X^A = V_X^E + V_X^D = \$300M + \$300M = \$600M$$

$$k_C = f_E k_e + f_D k_d == \left(\frac{\$300M}{\$600M}\right)(0.10) + \left(\frac{\$300M}{\$600M}\right)(0.10) = 0.10$$

$$V_X^A = \frac{EAT + Int}{k_C} = \frac{\$30M + \$30M}{0.10} \$600 \text{ million}$$

$$k_C^T = f_E k_e + f_D k_d(1 - t) = (0.5)(0.10) + (0.5)(0.10)(1 - 0.4) = 0.08$$
$$V_X^A = \frac{EBIT(1 - t)}{k_C^T} = \frac{\$80M(1 - 0.4)}{0.08} \$600 \text{ million}$$

With debt of $250 million, Y's asset, in turn, would be valued at $610 million, its overall cost of capital, k_C, would be 11.4754 percent, and its tax-adjusted cost of capital, $k_C{}^T$, 9.8361 percent:

$$V_Y^A = V_Y^E + V_Y^D = \$250M + \$360M = \$610M$$

$$k_C = f_E k_e + f_D k_d = \left(\frac{\$250M}{\$610M}\right)(0.10) + \left(\frac{\$360M}{\$610M}\right)(0.125) = 0.114754$$

$$V_X^A = \frac{EAT + Int}{k_C} = \frac{\$45M + \$25M}{0.114754} = \$610 \text{ million}$$

$$k_C^T = f_E k_e + f_D k_d(1 - t) = k_C = f_E k_e + f_D k_d$$

$$k_C^T = \left(\frac{\$250M}{\$610M}\right)(0.10)(1 - 0.04) + \left(\frac{\$360M}{\$610M}\right)(0.0125) = 0.098361$$

$$V_X^A = \frac{EBIT(1 - t)}{k_C^T} = \frac{\$100M(1 - 0.4)}{0.098361} \$610 \text{ million}$$

The financial information on the two companies is summarized in Exhibit 11.10.

EXHIBIT 11.10 Merger Case: Pre-Merger Values of X and Y

Company	Pre-Merger Valuation	
	X	Y
EBIT	$80,000,000	$100,000,000
Interest ($k_d = 0.10$)	$30,000,000	$25,000,000
EBT	$50,000,000	$75,000,000
tax ($t = 0.4$)	$20,000,000	$30,000,000
EAT	$30,000,000	$45,000,000
β	1.00	1.50
$k_e = 0.05 + (0.05)$ Beta	0.10	0.125
k_d	0.10	0.10
$k_C{}^T = (V_E/V_A)k_e + (V_D/V_A)\,k_d\,(1-t)$	0.08	0.0984
Value of Equity: $V^E = EAT/k_e$	$300,000,000	$360,000,000
Value of Debt: $V_D = \text{Interest}/k_D$	$300,000,000	$250,000,000
Value of Asset: $V_A = V_E + V_D = EBIT(1-t)/k_C{}^T$	$600,000,000	$610,000,000
Number of Shares = n	5,000,000	5,000,000
Equity value per share: $V^e = V^E/n = EPS/k_e$	$60	$72
Debt/Equity = V_D/V_E	1.00	0.694

Synergy and Merger Premium

Finally, suppose the analyst estimates that if the two firms merge, then their combined *EBIT* will be $200 million, which exceeds the sum of their *EBITs* of $180 million. Thus, she estimates a synergy between the firm in which:

$$EBIT_t^{XY} > EBIT_t^{X} + EBIT_t^{Y}$$
$$\$200M > \$80M + 100M$$

The weighted beta of the merged companies using each company's pre-merger market values is 1.2727, the cost of equity is 11.3636 percent, and the overall cost of capital adjusted for taxes is 8.926 percent:

$$\beta_{XY} = \frac{V_E^X}{V_E^X + V_E^Y}\beta^X + \frac{V_E^Y}{V_E^X + V_E^Y}\beta^Y$$

$$\beta_{XY} = \frac{\$300M}{\$660M}(1) + \frac{\$360M}{\$660M}(1.5) = 1.2727$$

$$k_e^{XY} = 0.05 + [0.05](1.2727) = 0.113636$$

$$k_C^{XY} = \frac{V_E^X + V_E^Y}{V_A^X + V_A^Y} k_e^{XY} + \frac{V_D^X + V_D^Y}{V_A^X + V_A^Y}(1-t)k_d^{XY}$$

$$k_C^{XY} = \frac{\$300M + \$360M}{\$1,210M}(0.113636) + \frac{\$300M + \$250M}{\$1,210M}(1-0.4)(0.10)$$

$$k_C^{XY} = 0.089256$$

The value of assets of the merged company given $200 million *EBIT* and a cost of capital of 8.9256 percent is therefore$1,344.44 million:

$$V_A = \frac{EBIT_{XY}(1-t)}{k_c^{XY}} = \frac{\$200M(1-0.4)}{0.089256} = \$1,344.44M$$

Subtracting, the combined debt of $550 million of X and Y from the $1,344.44 million asset, the equity value of the merged companies would be $794.44 million·

$$V_D^{XY} = V_D^X + V_D^Y = \$300M + \$250M = \$550M$$

$$V_E^{XY} = V_A^{XY} - V_d^{XY} = \$1,344.44M - \$550M = \$794.44M$$

Note that the value of the combined assets without synergy (i.e., using *EBIT* = $180 million), is $1,210 million and the combined value of equity is $660, which is equal to the sum of the X and Y's asset and equity values:

$$V_A = \frac{EBIT_{XY}(1-t)}{k_c^{XY}} = \frac{\$180M(1-0.4)}{0.089256} = \$1,210M$$

$$V_D^{XY} = V_D^X + V_D^Y = \$300M + \$250M = \$550M$$

$$V_E^{XY} = V_A^{XY} - V_d^{XY} = \$1,210M - \$550M = \$660M$$

If the analyst believes that the synergy exists, then she would see the merger as leading to a gain in equity value or *merger premium* of $134.44 million:

$$\text{Merger premium} = V_E^{XY} - V_E^X - V_E^Y$$

$$\text{Merger premium} = \$794.44M - \$300M - \$360M = \$134.44M$$

Tender Offer, Exchange Ratio, and Post-Merger Stock Value

As an investment in Stock X, an analyst would consider X to be a good investment (i.e., the stock price increasing as a result of the merger) if X was able to purchase Company

Y's five million shares for less than $494.44 million—the value of Y's equity plus the merger value—or $98.89 per share.

$$\text{Maximum Tender Offer} = V_E^Y + \text{Merger premium}$$

$$\text{Maximum Tender Offer} = \$360M + \$134.44M = \$494.44 \text{ million}$$

$$\text{Per Share Maximum Tender Offer} = \frac{V_E^Y + \text{Merger premium}}{n^Y}$$

$$\text{Per Share Maximum Tender Offer} = \frac{\$494.44M}{5M} = \$98.89$$

In a merger, the acquiring company may pay for the acquisitions in cash (perhaps selling an asset or a division to raise the cash needed to purchase the company). Company X, for example, might offer to buy Y's five million shares for $98.89 per share in cash. The total acquisition cost would be $494.44 million. Note this cost does not include the transaction costs nor does it take into account the debt. It may be that after acquiring Y, X could refinance Y's $250 million debt for less than 10 percent, making the actual acquisition cost less.

For many mergers, the acquiring firm buys the targeted company by exchanging shares of their stock for the acquired company's shares; they also might buy the company with a combination of cash and shares. In a stock-for-stock acquisition, it is customary for the acquiring company to negotiate an exchange ratio with the target company: the number of shares of the acquiring company's stock for one share of the target company. In the example, X's stock has a premerger value of $60/share, and X's maximum offer value to buy Y is $98.89/share. The equivalent of X buying stock Y for $98.89 per share would be to exchange 1.6481 (= $98.89/$60) shares of X for one share of Y—an exchange ratio of 1.6481.

As an investment in Stock X, our analyst would consider X to be a good investment (i.e., the stock price increasing as a result of the merger) if X were able to purchase Y at an exchange ratio less than 1.6481. At an exchange ratio of 1.6481 (which reflects the maximum offer price of $98.89) the postmerger value of X would be equal to premerger value of $60 per share. In this case, X would have to create 8.241 million new shares [$(n_N = (1.6481$ Shares of X/Shares of Y$)(5$ million shares of Y$) = 8.241$ million] to exchange for the five million share of Y. Company X's postmerger number of shares of X would therefore be 13.241(= 5 million premerger share of X plus 8.241 million new shares). With the analyst's estimate of $794.44 million for the value of equity of the merged company (which reflects the synergy), the postmerger value per share of X would be $60:

$$\text{Postmerger } V_E^X = \frac{V_E^{XY}}{n + n_N} = \frac{\$794.44M}{5M + 8.241M} = \$60$$

If the exchange ratio were less than 1.6481 (reflecting an offer price less than the maximum offer price of $98.89), then the postmerger value would exceed the premerger value of $60. For example, if the ratio were 1.5 (reflecting an offer price of $90), then X would need 7.5 million new shares to acquire Y and the postmerger value would be $63.56.

$$\text{Postmerger } V_E^X = \frac{V_E^{XY}}{n + n_N} = \frac{\$794.44M}{5M + 7.5M} = \$63.56$$

Inference

Mergers can be quite complex as well as challenging to evaluate. In trying to determine the impact a merger would have on a company's value, the preceding case suggests that two factors that are important in evaluating a merger are synergy and the price paid or the exchange ratio.

In terms of the preceding case, if there was no synergy from merging X and Y, then the equity value of X and Y would be $660 million. If this were the case, the merger premium would be zero, the maximum offer price would simply be the value of Y's stock of $72, and the maximum exchange ratio would be 1.20 ($= \$72/\$60$). Thus, in a stock-for-stock exchange, X would have to create six million new shares [($n_N = (1.2$ shares of X/shares of Y)(5 million shares of Y) = 6 million] to exchange for Y's five million. If the exchange ratio were 1.2 and there is no synergy, then the postmerger value would be $60.

$$\text{Postmerger } V_E^X = \frac{V_E^{XY}}{n + n_N} = \frac{\$660M}{5M + 6M} = \$60$$

Thus, for a merger to increase the acquiring company's stock, there has to be either synergy (increase in V_E^{XY}), an exchange ratio that is less than the ratio that reflects the maximum tender offer, or some combination to increase the stock price from its $60 premerger value. The expected postmerger values of the X and Y merger for different scenarios are presented in Exhibit 11.11.

In the financial markets, mergers often lead to a decrease in the stock price. If the markets are efficient, the decrease would suggest that the acquiring company pays too much for the target stock.

It should be noted that not all mergers are based on synergy. Sometimes a buyout company is formed through an investment company to acquire another company and then strip it; that is, sell its assets. Such acquisitions were prevalent in the 1980s, and they have often been portrayed in movies (such as *Wall Street* and *Other People's Money*) and in the press as sinister. Moreover, the financial scandals of the 1980s that led to the convictions of Ivan Boesky and Michael Milken certainly gave credence to such views. Nevertheless, there are cases in which a company is worth less than the sum of the values of the assets that compose it. In such cases, economic efficiency is realized by a buyout company acquiring such a company and then selling its assets. Similarly, a buyout company may be formed to take advantage of leverage. As noted earlier,

EXHIBIT 11.11 Merger Case: Expected Post-Merger Values of Merged XY Companies—Different Scenarios

XY	Synergy with Maximum Exchange Ratio	Synergy with Exchange Ratio less than Maximum (1.5)	No Synergy with Maximum Exchange Ratio	No Synergy with Exchange Ratio less than Maximum (1.1)
$EBIT^{XY}$	$200,000,000	$200,000,000	$180,000,000	$180,000,000
$Interest^{XY}$	$55,000,000	$55,000,000	$55,000,000	$55,000,000
$EBIT^{XY}$	$145,000,000	$145,000,000	$125,000,000	$125,000,000
Tax ($t = 0.4$)	$87,000,000	$87,000,000	$75,000,000	$75,000,000
EAT^{XY}	$58,000,000	$58,000,000	$50,000,000	$50,000,000
β^{XY}	1.2727	1.2727	1.2727	1.2727
$k_e^{XY} = 0.05 + (0.05)\beta^{XY}$	0.1136	0.1136	0.1136	0.1136
k_d^{XY}	0.1000	0.1000	0.1000	0.1000
k_C^{TXY}	0.0893	0.0893	0.0893	0.0893
Value of Asset: $V_A^{XY} = EBIT^{XY}(1-t)/k_C^{TXY}$	$1,344,444,444	$1,344,444,444	$1,210,000,000	$1,210,000,000
Value of Debt $= V_D^{XY} = V_D^X + V_D^Y$	$550,000,000	$550,000,000	$550,000,000	$550,000,000
Value of Equity: $V_E^{XY} = V_A^{XY} - V_D^{XY}$	$794,444,444	$794,444,444	$660,000,000	$660,000,000
Merger Premium: $V_E^{xy} - (V_E^X + V_E^Y)$	$134,444,444.44	$134,444,444.44	$0.00	$0.00
Maximum Offer Price $= V_E^Y + $ Merger Premium	$494,444,444	$494,444,444	$360,000,000	$360,000,000
Per share Maximum Tender offer $=$ Max Offer Price/n^Y	$98.89	$98.89	$72.00	$72.00
Exchange ratio $=$ Per share Max Tender offer/V_e^X	1.6481	1.5000	1.2000	1.1000
$n_N = $ Total number of shares	8,240,741	7,500,000	6,000,000	5,500,000
Post-merger number of shares of $X = n^X + n_N$	13,240,741	12,500,000	11,000,000	10,500,000
Post-merger value per share $= V_E^{XY}/(n^x + n_N)$	$60.00	$63.56	$60.00	$62.86

$k_C^{TXY} = (V_C^X + V_C^Y)/(V^X + V^Y)k_e^{XY} + (V_d^Y + V_D^Y)/(V_A^X + V_A^Y)k_d^{XY}$.

$\beta^{XY} = (V_E^X/(V_E^X + V_E^Y))\beta^X + (V_E^Y/(V_E^X + V_E^Y))\beta^Y$.

$n_N = $ Total number of new shares of $X = $ (Exchange Ratio)(n^Y).

many leverage buyout companies were formed in the 1980s. These companies would issue low-quality, higher yielding bonds and use the proceeds to acquire companies. As we noted earlier, because of the interest tax deduction, the emerging, more highly leveraged company often was able to realize greater earnings to its investors, although it was often a riskier company than the one that existed before the takeover.

BLOOMBERG M&A SCREEN

The Bloomberg MA screen allows you to analyze previous mergers and acquisitions, as well as new or pending deals. You can drill into a deal by clicking the entry and then using the tabs. MA <Enter>; On the MA screen, enter company name in the "Company Search" box to find company; click the deal to bring up screens for analysis of the deal.

Other Bloomberg Merger and Acquisition Screens

- **MARB**: Merger and Arbitrage Differentials.
- **MADL**: Merger and Acquisition Deal list.
- **CACS**, Click M&A.
- **CACT**, Click M&A.

See Bloomberg Web Exhibit 11.6.

Conclusion

Fundamental stock analysis involves determining whether stocks are correctly priced in the market. As we noted, in practice the ability to earn abnormal returns by finding mispriced stocks is a difficult task, requiring not only an understanding of the company and its current operations, but also the ability to forecast where the company is headed in both the near and long term. In this chapter, we have provided a foundation for fundamental analysis by examining at a theoretical level how factors such as corporate investment, capital structure, and mergers affect stock value.

In the next chapter, we introduce several empirical approaches that have been used by analysts to estimate stock value. The two most common approaches used by fundamentalists to select stocks are the discounted cash flow (DCF) method and the multiplier approach. The DCF approach is the valuation approach we have examined in this chapter. It involves either determining the present value of the stock's future cash flows or estimating the stock's expected rate of return by solving for the rate that equates the present value of the stock's cash flows to its market price. The multiplier approach involves estimating the stock's price to earnings-per-share ratio and its expected earnings next year to determine its value.

Notes

1. Geologists can estimate the annual production of crude oil based on the estimated size of the well's reserves and the pressure in the well (which is a function of the size of the well and its rate of output). The output of most oil wells decreases over time, rather than staying constant.

2. The irrelevance of financing argument was first introduced by Modiglini and Miller. It is also referred to as the dividend irrelevance argument.

3. Note that the definitions of growth, declining, and normal firms are consistent with acceptance rules applied to capital budgeting techniques. That is, if an investment project has a net present value exceeding zero, then the risk-adjusted return on the investment exceeds the required return, and an acceptance of the investment project will increase the equity value of the company.

4. In economics, economies of scale are often depicted by a long-run U-shaped average cost curve where long-run average cost is plotted against output. The negatively sloped portion of the curve represents the range of increasing returns to scale and the positively sloped portion defines the range of decreasing returns to sale. A company operating on the negatively sloped portion could reduce its average cost by increasing its output.

Selected References

Arditti, Fred, and John Pinkerton. 1978. The valuation and cost of capital of the levered firm with growth opportunities. *Journal of Finance* 33 (March): 54–73.

Black, Fisher. 1980. The magic in earnings: Economic earnings verses accounting earnings. *Financial Analysts Journal* (November–December): 19–24.

Black, Fisher, and M. Scholes. 1974. The effects of dividend yield and dividend policy on common stock prices and returns. *Journal of Financial Economics* 1 (May): 4–22.

Brealey, Richard. 1969. *An Introduction to Risk and Return from Common Stocks*. Cambridge, Mass.: MIT Press.

Copeland, T.E., Tim Koller, and Jack Murrin. 2001. *Valuation: Measuring and Managing the Value of Companies*, 3rd ed. Hoboken, NJ: John Wiley & Sons.

Cottle, Sidney, Roger McMurray, and Frank E. Block. 1988. *Security Analysis*, 5th ed. New York: McGraw-Hill.

Elton, Edwin, and Martin Gruber. 1968. The effect of share repurchases on the value of the firm. *Journal of Finance* 28 (May): 373–380.

Elton, Edwin, and Martin Gruber. 1970. Marginal stockholder tax rates and the clientele effect. *Review of Economics and Statistics* 52 (February): 68–74.

Elton, Edwin, and Martin Gruber. 1973. Asset selection with changing structure. *Journal of Financial and Quantitative Analysis* 8 (June): 459–473.

Graham, B., D. Dodd, and S. Cottle. 1962. *Security Analysis Principles and Techniques*, 4th ed. New York: McGraw-Hill.

Gordon, Myron J. 1962. *The Investment, Financing, and Valuation of the Corporation*. Homewood, Illinois: Irwin.

Gordon, J., and Myron Gordon. 1997. The finite horizon expected return model. *Financial Analysts Journal* 53 (May–June): 52–61.

Hamada, Robert S. 1971. The effect of the firm's capital structure on the systematic risk of common stocks. *Journal of Finance* 8 (May): 435–452.

Miller, Merton. 1993. *The Modigliani-Miller propositions after 30 years.* In *The New Corporate Finance: Where Theory Meets Practice.* Edited by D. Chew. New York: McGraw-Hill.

Miller, Merton, and Franco Modigliani. 1961. Dividend policy, growth, and valuation of shares. *Journal of Business* 34 (October): 411–433.

Modigliani, Franco, and Merton Miller. 1958. The cost of capital, corporation finance, and the theory of investments. *American Economic Review* (June): 261–297.

Modigliani, Franco, and Merton Miller. 1963. Corporate income taxes and the cost of capital: A correction. *American Economic Review* (June): 433–443.

Myers, S. C. 1976. A framework for evaluating mergers. In *Modern Developments in Financial Development.* Edited by S. C. Myers. New York: Praeger.

Niederhoffer, V., and P. Regan. 1972. Earnings changes, analysts forecasts, and stock prices. *Financial Analysts Journal* 28 (May–June): 65–71.

Shiller, Robert J., and John Campbell. 1988. Stock prices, earning, and expected dividends. *Journal of Finance* 43: 661–676.

Solt, Michael, and Meir Statman. 1989. Good companies, bad stocks. *Journal of Portfolio Management* 15 (Summer): 39–44.

Williams, John Burke. 1938. *The Theory of Investment Value.* Cambridge, Mass.: Harvard University Press.

Bloomberg Exercises

1. Select a stock of interest and study its size, capital structure (debt/equity ratio), WACC, growth rates, payout ratios, and return on equity. Screens to examine from its equity menu are as follows:
   - DES   Description.
   - WACC   Weight Average Cost of Capital.
   - FA   Tabs: Ratios and Credit or Enter: FA LEV.
   - FA   Tabs: Ratios and Growth.
   - FA   Tabs: Ratios and Profitability.

2. Select a stock of interest or the one you selected in Exercise 1 and use its FA screen to study its income statement. Use FA and "I/S" tab and "As Reported" tab. Click the Bloomberg graphic icon to view the income items together. Items in the income statement to consider are revenue, cost of products sold, selling and general administration expenses, operating income, income before taxes, profit after taxes, and basic *EPS*. Comment on what drives the profits of the company.

3. Select a stock of interest or one you already selected in one of the exercises and use its FA screen to study its revenues and operating income: FA and "I/S" tab and "Standardized" tab. Click the Bloomberg graphic icon for revenue and operating income to view the income items together. Examine the company's operating margin separately (click Operating Margin). Comment on what drives the profits of the company.

4. Select a stock of interest or one you already selected in one of the exercises and use its FA screen to study its capital structure: FA and "Ratios" tab and "Credit" tab. Click the Bloomberg graphic icon for debt-equity ratio, debt-to-total assets,

and other leverage ratios. Click the item to bring up a definition and to see how the ratio is calculated.

5. Select a stock of interest or one you already selected in one of the exercises and use its FA screen to study its balance sheet items. Use FA and "B/S" tab and "Standardized" tab. Click the Bloomberg graphic icon for different items to compare. Click the item to bring up a definition and to see how the item is calculated. Some possible comparisons to consider are as follows:
   a. Total current assets, total long-term assets, and total assets.
   b. Long-term investments, long-term receivables, and total long-term assets.
   c. Total current liabilities, total long-term liabilities, and total liabilities.
   d. Long-term borrowing, other-long-term liabilities, and total long-term liabilities.
   e. Total assets, total liabilities, and total equity.

6. Select a company and do a comparative analysis of it with its peers using the Bloomberg RV screen. Tabs to consider are as follows:
   a. "Comp Sheets" tab and "Balance Sheets" tab.
   b. "Comp Sheets" tab and "Profitability" tab.

7. Select a company and do comparative analysis of it with its peers using the Bloomberg RV screen. Use the custom tab to enter names of items for your comparison. You may want to save your custom screens. Consider the following screens to customize:
   a. Leverage: Debt-to-assets, common-equity-to-assets, and debt-to-equity.
   b. Income-Statement: Sales growth and earnings growth.

8. Bloomberg has a number of earnings screens that provide history, consensus forecast, surprises, and Zach earnings forecast. Study some of the following earnings screens for a company of interest:
   a. EEO   Current Consensus.
   b. EEB   Best Consensus Detail.
   c. ERN   Earnings History.
   d. EE   Earnings and Estimates.
   e. EM   Earnings Trends.
   f. EE SURP   Earnings Surprises.
   g. EE Z: Zach's   Earnings Estimates.

9. Select a stock of interest or one you already selected in one of the exercises and its DVD screen to study trends in the company's dividend payments.

10. Bloomberg's measure of sustainable growth is the company's retention ratio times its return on equity. Do a relative analysis of company's sustainable growth using the RV screen. Customize your screen by creating columns for sustainable growth, the retention ratio, and the return on equity.

11. Bloomberg information on corporate actions such as acquisitions and limited partnership deals can be accessed on the CACS screen found on the company's equity menu. Select a company of interest that you know has been active in acquisitions and divestures and use CACS to search for its previous activities.

12. Value several stocks of interest using the DDM model using a three-stage growth model, constant-growth model, and two-stage model: Ticker <Equity> <Enter>; DDM. For a guide, see Bloomberg exhibit box: "Bloomberg DDM Screen" and Bloomberg Web Exhibit 11.5 (text Web site).

   a. For several of your stocks, examine the impact on the stock's value when you change the discount rate, the growth rate for the growth years, and the growth rate for the mature stage.

   b. Given the current prices of your stocks, compare their IRR's to their required returns. Comment on what stocks you believe would be good investments and which would be bad.

13. Excel Exercise: Create an Excel spreadsheet for determining the intrinsic value of a stock you analyzed in Exercise 12 using the DDM model (for a guide, see Bloomberg Web Exhibit 11.5 (text Web site) and Bloomberg exhibit box: "Bloomberg DDM").

14. The Bloomberg MA screen allows you to analyze previous mergers and acquisitions. Select a stock of interest (enter company name in "Company Search" on the MA screen) and review one of its completed acquisitions. On the MA Deal screen, analyze the deal using the following tabs. "Summary," "Timeline," "Parties," "Structure," "Approvals," "Financials," and "Arbitrage." Study the impact the acquisition had on the stock price of the acquiring firm and the target firm. Use the GP graphs for each company and set the time period to include time before and after the announcement and acquisition. For a guide, see Bloomberg Web Exhibit 11.6 (text Web site).

15. The Bloomberg MA screen allows you to analyze and track possible and pending deals. Select one of the proposed or pending deals identified on the MA screen and study the current proposal.

CHAPTER 12

Applied Fundamental Analysis

Introduction

In the last chapter, we examined how such factors as a firm's investments, choice of financing, and capital structure decisions determine the value of its stock. In this chapter, we extend our examination of fundamental analysis by looking at different quantitative approaches that are used to estimate the intrinsic value of a stock. The two most common approaches used by fundamentalists to value stocks are the discounted cash flow (DCF) method and the *multiplier approach*. The DCF approach is the valuation approach we discussed in preceding chapters. The important variables to estimate in the DCF are earnings per share (*EPS*) next year, the growth rate in EPS, the dividend-payout ratio, the discount rate, and the type of growth—constant, two-stage, or three-stage. The multiplier approach involves estimating the stock's price-to-earnings ratio and its expected earnings next year to determine its value. For years, the multiplier approach was the most popular method used by analysts to estimate a stock's value. It and other similar multiplier approaches using different multipliers (e.g., price-to-sales or price-to-earnings before interest, taxes, depreciation, and amortization, *EBITDA*) are referred to as relative valuation analysis. Quantitative stock analysis, however, always needs to be complemented with qualitative analysis of the strengths, weakness, opportunities, and threats (SWOT) facing a company. Combining the quantitative with qualitative engenders a conviction regarding whether a stock merits a buy or a sell recommendation.

In this chapter, we examine the multiplier and DCF models for evaluating stocks, as well as identify qualitative factors that analysts consider when evaluating stock. In Chapter 13, we will extend our examination of fundamental analysis by showing how the models are applied to valuing the overall market and industries.

Valuation Using the Multiplier Approach

The multiplier approach involves valuing a stock by multiplying the stock's price-earnings ratio by the stock's forecasted earnings per share for the next period.

$$V_t = \frac{P}{e}E(EPS_{t+1})$$

The *EPS* (*e* also signifies EPS) for the price-to-earnings ratio, *P/e*, multiplier is the expected *EPS* with *EPS* generally measured as an annualized *EPS*.

Estimating the P/e Multiplier

The *P/e* is defined as the stock's equilibrium *P/e* value. Riskier stocks, for example, trade with higher discount rates and lower prices relative to their earnings than do less risky stocks. Stocks with higher expected growth rates trade with higher prices relative to their earnings than do stocks with lower rates. Analysts vary in how they estimate the equilibrium *P/e* ratio. Some simply use an historical *P/e* ratio as an estimate of the equilibrium *P/e* ratio. Others divide the current price or an average price by a consensus estimate of next period's *EPS* made by analysts.

One simple approach for estimating the multiplier is to use the Gordon-Williams constant-growth model: Divide the model's value *V* (or price, *P*) by *EPS* (or *e*).

$$V = P = \frac{d}{k_e - g}$$
$$\frac{V}{e} = \frac{P}{e} = \frac{d/e}{k_e - g}$$

Using this approach, *P/e* is estimated by estimating the model's three parameters, d/e, k_e, and g. For example, consider our Two-Dollar General Store that we evaluated in Chapter 11:

- All equity company.
- Current EAT_0 = $24 million.
- Corporate investment policy in which its annual investments equal 75 percent of its *EAT*.
- Dividend payout = 25%.
- Investment financing done internally.
- Estimated rate of return on its investments = i = 0.20.
- Beta of the firm and beta of the company's investments = 2.
- Security market line (SML): $k_e = 0.05 + [0.10]\beta = 0.25$.
- The above features are expected to characterize this company for a long time.
- Number of shares = 5 million.
- g = (retention ratio) (i) = (0.75)(0.20) = 0.15.
- $E(EAT_1) = EAT_0(1 + g)$ = $24 million (1.15) = $27.6 million.

- Total Dividends $= D_0 =$ (dividend-payout ratio) $EAT_0 = (0.25)$ ($24 million) = $6 million.
- $E(D_1) = D_0 (1 + g) = 6 million $(1.15) = 6.9 million.
- $EPS_0 = EAT_0/n = 24 million/5 million $= $4.80.
- $DPS_0 = D_0/n = 6 million/5 million $= $1.20.
- $E(EPS_1) = EPS_0 (1 + g) = $4.80 (1.15) = $5.52.
- $E(DPS_1) = DPS_0 (1 + g) = $1.20 (1.15) = $1.38.
- $V_E = E(D_1)/(k_e - g) = 6.9 million$/(0.25 - 0.15) = 69 million.
- $V_e = E(d_1)/(k_e - g) = $1.38/(0.25 - 0.15) = $13.80.

The *P/e* for Two-Dollar General store would be 2.5, and its value using the multiplier would be $13.80 (the same value we obtained directly):

$$\frac{P}{e} = \frac{E(DPS_1)/E(EPS_1)}{k_e - g} = \frac{(\$1.38/\$5.52)}{0.25 - 0.15} = \frac{0.25}{(0.25 - 0.15)} = 2.5$$

$$V_e = \frac{P}{e} E(EPS_1) = (2.5)(\$5.52) = \$13.80$$

Estimating the Multiplier

The multiplier is quite sensitive to changes in k_e and g. For example, suppose analysts estimated the return on investments for Two-Dollar to be 30 percent instead of 20 percent. The growth rate for the company would then be 22.5 percent and Two-Dollar's *P/e* ratio would increase from 2.5 to 10 [= 0.25/(0.25 – 0.225)]. Or suppose the company's beta was reassessed by analysts and estimated to be 1.5 instead of 2. The required return would be 20 percent instead of 25 percent, and the *P/e* would increase from 2.5 to 5 [= 0.25/(0.20 – 0.15)]. Note also that the *P/e* value using the Gordon-Williams model is undefined when g is equal to or greater than k_e.

Instead of a direct approach, some analysts use a cross-sectional regression model to estimate the multiplier. Cross-sectional models differ in terms of the explanatory variables used to explain *P/e*. As discussed in Chapter 6, Elton and Gruber regressed the *P/e* ratios of 150 stocks against their historical growth rates to estimate the relation between the *P/e* of any stock and its growth rate. In an earlier study, Malkiel and Cragg regressed 150 stocks' *P/e* ratios against three variables: dividends-to-earnings ratio, historical growth rates, and betas.

Finally, Bloomberg provides a number of *P/e* measures for stocks and indexes. Their ratios vary from *P/e* ratios based on the current year or period values, *P/e* ratios based on estimated *EPS* for next year, to *P/e* ratios calculated using moving averages for *EPS*. Some of the Bloomberg *P/e* ratios are defined in Exhibit 12.1, and their different values are shown for the Dow stocks in Exhibit 12.2. In examining the *P/e* ratios in Exhibit 12.2, note the wide variation in the different *P/e* values on the same stock. This suggests that finding the equilibrium *P/e* ratio is a challenge facing analysts using the multiplier approach.

EXHIBIT 12.1   Selected Bloomberg *P/e* Measures

- **Price Earnings, PE_Ratio**: Ratio of the price of a stock and the company's earnings per share. It is calculated as last price divided by trailing 12 month EPS before XO items or Basic EPS before XO.
- **Estimated PE Next Year, EST_PE_NXT_YR**: Price earnings ratio calculated based on next year's earnings per share estimates provided by BEst (Bloomberg Estimates).
- **Estimated PE Current Year, EST_PE_CUR_YR**: Price earnings ratio calculated based on current year earnings per share estimates provided by BEst(Bloomberg Estimates).
- **Best PE Ratio, BEST_PE_RATIO**: Ratio calculated by dividing the price of the security by BEst (Bloomberg Estimates) earnings per share. The periodicity of the default denominator is dependent on the user settings. If default is set to Quarterly, the consensus estimates for the next four quarters is used. If BEst EPS for the next four upcoming quarters are not available, BEst P/E Ratio will return N.A. If user default is set to Semi-Annual or Yearly, the semiannual or annual BEst EPS will be used in the denominator instead.
- **Price/Earning – Five-Year Average, 5_YR_AVE_PRICE_EARNINGS**: The simple five-year average of the price/earnings ratio. If the quarterly or semiannual periodicity is selected the ratio will return the average of the last five periods (quarters or semiannuals).
- **BEst P/E Next Year, BEST_PE_NXT_YR**: The company's price/earnings ratio using the BEst next year estimated earnings per share.
- **Cons Est P/E Curr Year, CONS_EST_PE_CUR_YR(Consolidated Estimated P/E current year)**: Price Earnings ratio calculated based on current year earnings per share estimates provided on consolidated basis. Estimates provided by Bloomberg Estimates (BEst).
- **Best P/E Ratio Market Convention, BEST_PE_RATIO_MARKET**: Bloomberg Estimates ratio calculated by dividing the current price of the security by the earnings per share estimate provided by the requested broker or consensus.
- **Ten-Year Moving Average P/E: 10_YEAR_MOVING_AVERAGE_PE**: Ratio of the price of a stock to the company's average annual earnings per share (EPS) in the past 10 years.
- **BEst Est P/E Next 4 Quarters, BEST_EST_PE_4Q**: The price/earnings ratio using the BEst earnings per share estimate for the next four quarters.
- **Long-Term Price Earnings Ratio, LONG_TERM_PRICE_EARNINGS_RATIO**: Long-term price to earnings ratio using the company's Last Price and ten-year average real earnings per share (EPS). Real EPS is computed by adjusting earnings per share for ratios by the company's country's Consumer Price Index (CPI). Ten-year average real EPS is computed using 40 quarters, or 20 semiannual periods or 10 annual figures.

Example: Macy's *P/e* Ratio

The department store industry in North America consists of companies such as Macy's, Belk, Kohl's, and Sears. Macy's is one of the largest companies in that industry. Exhibit 12.3 summarizes some of the key points and drivers identified in Macy's 2012 10-K Report, and Exhibit 12.4 shows annual data on sales-per-share (*SPS*), *EPS*, *DPS*, profit margins, and *P/e* ratios for the company. The data were pulled from Bloomberg's FA and GP screens.

Macy's *P/e* multipliers from 2000 to 2013 fluctuated. The *P/e* ratio based on actual price and the trailing 12-month *EPS* increased from 8.33 in 2000 to 21.49 in 2009 and then decreased to 11.27 in 2012. The five-year average *P/e* from 2000 to 2013 fluctuated within a more narrow range between 13.912 and 11.2017. Using the

EXHIBIT 12.2 *P/e* Ratios for Dow Jones Stocks, 8/10/2013

	PE_RATIO	EST_PE_ NXT YR	EST_PE_ CUR_YR	BEST_PE _RATIO	FIVE_YR_AVG _PRICE _EARNINGS	BEST_PE_ NXT YR	CONS_EST _PE _CUR_YR	BEST_PE_ RATIO _MARKET	10_YEAR MOVING_ AVERAGE_ PE	BEST_EST _PE_ 4QTRS	LONG_TERM_ _PRICE_ EARNINGS RATIO	Average	Standard Deviation	Coefficient of Variation
American Express Co	15.700	13.509	14.839	14.261	16.858	13.509	14.839	14.261	25.057	14.261	21.346	16.222	3.675	0.227
Boeing Co/The	21.134	15.907	17.736	17.198	16.148	15.907	17.736	17.198	30.452	17.198	26.855	19.406	4.856	0.250
Caterpillar Inc	12.337	11.652	13.329	12.416	16.192	11.652	13.329	12.416	17.705	12.416	15.440	13.535	2.011	0.149
Cisco Systems Inc	14.515	9.921	10.684	10.694	14.997	9.921	10.684	10.694	18.379	10.694	17.024	12.564	3.082	0.245
Chevron Corp	9.520	9.432	9.728	9.575	9.619	9.432	9.728	9.575	13.818	9.575	12.036	10.185	1.416	0.139
El du Pont de Nemours	18.772	13.276	14.980	13.606	13.366	13.276	14.980	13.606	20.660	13.606	17.881	15.274	2.611	0.171
Walt Disney Co/The	19.333	16.251	18.869	16.899	14.853	16.251	18.869	16.899	34.947	16.899	28.838	19.901	6.228	0.313
General Electric Co	15.331	13.116	14.346	14.046	12.609	13.116	14.346	14.046	14.523	14.046	12.890	13.856	0.824	0.059
Goldman Sachs Group Inc/The	8.980	9.994	10.275	10.811	12.178	9.994	10.275	10.811	11.556	10.811	10.018	10.518	0.859	0.082
Home Depot Inc/The	21.325	16.958	20.092	18.595	17.396	16.958	20.092	18.595	32.552	18.595	28.138	20.845	4.989	0.239
International Business Machines	12.000	9.910	10.760	10.322	12.419	9.910	10.760	10.322	21.133	10.322	18.410	12.388	3.785	0.306

(*Continued*)

EXHIBIT 12.2 (*Continued*)

	PE_RATIO	EST_PE_ NXT YR	EST_PE_ CUR YR	BEST_PE _RATIO	FIVE_YR_AVG _PRICE _EARNINGS	BEST_PE NXT YR	CONS_EST _PE_ CUR YR	BEST_PE_ RATIO_ MARKET	10_YEAR _MOVING_ AVERAGE_ PE	BEST_EST _PE_ 4QTRS	LONG_TERM_ _PRICE_ EARNINGS RATIO	Average	Standard Deviation	Coefficient of Variation
Intel Corp	12.293	11.340	11.908	11.278	12.190	11.340	11.908	11.503	15.674	11.278	14.170	12.266	1.403	0.114
Johnson & Johnson	16.334	14.777	15.738	15.550	13.562	14.777	15.738	15.550	21.149	15.550	18.608	16.121	2.072	0.129
JPMorgan Chase & Co	7.949	8.397	8.868	8.883	13.597	8.397	8.868	8.883	13.820	8.883	11.970	9.865	2.165	0.219
Coca-Cola Co/The	18.257	16.487	17.657	17.271	17.540	16.487	17.657	17.271	25.663	17.271	22.620	18.562	2.886	0.155
McDonald's Corp	17.094	15.298	16.673	16.023	16.916	15.298	16.673	16.023	27.633	16.023	24.418	18.006	4.072	0.226
3MCo	18.385	15.940	17.566	16.726	14.502	15.940	17.566	16.726	24.334	16.726	21.252	17.788	2.762	0.155
Merck & Co Inc	13.624	13.015	13.595	13.444	10.277	13.015	13.595	13.444	14.776	13.444	13.260	13.226	1.085	0.082
Microsoft Corp	12.133	11.153	12.317	12.386	11.708	11.153	12.317	12.386	17.294	12.386	15.857	12.826	1.938	0.151
NIKE Inc	24.626	20.168	23.227	22.562	19.555	20.168	23.227	22.562	39.912	22.562	35.802	24.943	6.630	0.266
Pfizer Inc	13.439	12.220	13.073	12.720	9.046	12.220	13.073	12.720	13.582	12.720	11.816	12.421	1.238	0.100
Procter & Gamble Co/The	19.011	16.485	17.920	17.966	17.097	16.485	17.920	17.966	23.735	17.966	21.564	18.556	2.205	0.119
AT&T Inc	14.277	12.579	13.653	13.163	13.085	12.579	13.653	13.163	16.032	13.163	14.329	13.607	0.991	0.073

Travelers Cos Inc/The	11.179	10.317	9.829	10.292	11.007	10.317	9.829	10.292	17.632	10.292	14.913	11.446	2.496	0.218
UnitedHealth Group Inc	13.570	12.214	12.966	12.751	9.596	12.214	12.966	12.751	21.835	12.751	18.944	13.869	3.441	0.248
United Technologies Corp	18.184	14.844	16.708	16.129	14.044	14.844	16.708	16.129	24.685	16.129	21.657	17.278	3.190	0.185
Visa Inc	22.408	20.602	24.248	21.655	20.469	20.602	24.248	21.655	NA	21.655	NA	21.949	1.452	0.066
Verizon Communications Inc	18.974	13.306	16.435	14.913	16.201	13.306	16.435	14.913	19.643	14.913	17.420	16.042	2.064	0.129
Wal-Mart Stores Inc	14.202	12.758	14.020	13.459	13.929	12.758	14.020	13.459	21.524	13.459	18.879	14.770	2.791	0.189
Exxon Mobil Corp	10.984	10.658	11.239	10.868	11.900	10.658	11.239	10.868	14.057	10.868	12.325	11.424	1.016	0.089

- **PE_Ratio**: Price Earnings: Calculated as last price divided by trailing 12-month EPS before XO items
- **EST_PE_NXT_YR, Estimated PE Next Year**: P/e based on next year's EPS estimates provided by BEst (Bloomberg Estimates)
- **EST_PE_CUR_YR, Estimated PE Current Year**: Based on current year EPS estimates provided by BEst
- **BEST_PE_RATIO, Best PE Ratio**: Based on BEst EPS
- **5_YR_AVE_PRICE_EARNINGS, Price/Earnings – 5 year Average**: 5-year average
- **BEST_PE_NXT_YR, BEst P/E Next Year**: Based on BEst next year estimated EPS
- **CONS_EST_PE_CUR_YR, Consolidated Estimated P/E current year)**: Based on current year EPS estimates provided on consolidated basis
- **BEST_PE_RATIO_MARKET, Best P/E Ratio Market Convention**: Based on EPS estimates provided by the requested broker or consensus
- **10_YEAR_MOVING_AVERAGE_PE, 10-Year Moving Average P/E**: Based on average annual EPS for the past 10 years
- **BEST_EST_PE_4Q, BEst Est P/E Next 4 Quarters**: Based on BEst EPS for the next four quarters
- **LONG_TERM_PRICE_EARNINGS_RATIO, Long Term Price Earnings Ratio**: Based on last Price and 10-year average real EPS

BLOOMBERG EXCEL ADD-IN

The data in many of the exhibits in this chapter were imported into Excel using Bloomberg's Excel Add-In and the "Import Data" tab.

To create cross-section exhibits like Exhibit 12.2, 12.6, and 12.11, do the following:

- On the Bloomberg Add-In in Excel, click "Real-Time/Current" from the "Import Data" dropdown.
- On the Bloomberg Data Wizard Box, Step 1, click "Indexes" in the "From" dropdown and the name of index (e.g., DOW JONES INDUS. AVG.) from the "Indexes" dropdown, and then click "Add All." This will bring up the stocks for the index. Once loaded, click "Next."
- On the Bloomberg Data Wizard Box, Step 2, search and then add stock returns, for example, price-to-earnings, growth rates, and DDM implied growth rates. Note, the definitions for the variable appear at the bottom.
- After loading variables, click "Next."
- On the Bloomberg Data Wizard Box, Step 3, click "Finish" to export the data to Excel.

To create time-series exhibits like Exhibit 12.4 do the following:

- On the Bloomberg Add-In in Excel, click "Historical End of Day" from the "Import Data" and then follow the Wizard's steps.

Gordon-Williams model, the author, in turn, estimated Macy's *P/e* ratio to be 13.14. This estimate is closer to the high range of the five-year average *P/e*. The author's P/e was based on an estimated growth rate of 12.5 percent in *EPS*, payout ratio of 23 percent, and a required return of 14.25 percent. The growth rate reflected Macy's recent high returns on equity and sustainable growth rates (see Exhibit 12.4). The required return was based on the estimated SML relationship found on Bloomberg's EQRP screen on 12/31/2012 and using Macy's adjusted beta of 1.428 (Bloomberg's HRA screen):

$$k_e = R_f + [E(R^M - R_f] \beta$$
$$k_e = 0.0175 + [0.0875] \, 1.428$$
$$k_e = 0.1425$$

Given these estimated values, the *P/e* value for Macy's using the Gordon-Williams model was 13.14:

$$\frac{P}{e} = \frac{d/e}{k_e - g} = \frac{0.23}{0.1425 - 0.125} = 13.14$$

EXHIBIT 12.3   Macy's 2012 10-K Information

Company
- The Company is a corporation organized under the laws of the State of Delaware in 1985. The Company's executive offices are located at 7 West Seventh Street, Cincinnati and New York, New York.
- The Company and its predecessors have been operating department stores since 1830.
- As of February 2, 2013, the operations of the Company included approximately 840 stores in 45 states, the District of Columbia, Guam and Puerto Rico under the names "Macy's" and "Bloomingdale's" as well as macys.com and bloomingdales.com.
- The Company operates twelve Bloomingdale's Outlet stores.
- Bloomingdale's in Dubai, United Arab Emirates, is operated under a license agreement with Al Tayer Insignia, a company of Al Tayer Group, LLC.
- The Company is an omnichannel retail organization operating stores and Web sites under two brands (Macy's and Bloomingdale's) that sell a wide range of merchandise, including apparel and accessories (men's, women's and children's), cosmetics, home furnishings and other consumer goods in 45 states, the District of Columbia, Guam and Puerto Rico.
- In 2012, the Company's subsidiaries provided various support functions to the Company's retail operations on an integrated, company-wide basis: The Company's bank subsidiary, FDS Bank provides credit processing and collections; Macy's Systems and Technology, Inc. provides operational electronic data processing and management information services to all of the Company's operations; Macy's Merchandising Group, Inc. a wholly-owned direct subsidiary of the Company, and its subsidiary Macy's Merchandising Group International, LLC., is responsible for the design, development and marketing of Macy's private label brands and certain licensed brands; Macy's Logistics and Operations, a division of a wholly-owned indirect subsidiary of the Company, provides warehousing and merchandise distribution services for the Company's operations.
- As of February 2, 2013, the Company had approximately 175,700 regular full-time and part-time employees.

Industry Features
- Seasonality: The retail business is seasonal in nature with a high proportion of sales and operating income generated in the months of November and December.
- Purchasing: The Company purchases merchandise from many suppliers.
- Competition: The retailing industry is intensely competitive. The Company's operations compete with many retailing formats, including department stores, specialty stores, general merchandise stores, off-price and discount stores, manufacturers' outlets, the Internet, mail order catalogs and television shopping, among others.
- Comparative Advantage: The Company seeks to attract customers by offering superior selections, obvious value, and distinctive marketing in stores that are located in premier locations, and by providing an exciting shopping environment and superior service through an omnichannel experience.

Risk
- The Company's pension funding could increase at a higher than anticipated rate.
- The Company's expenses relating to employee health benefits are significant. Unfavorable changes in the cost of such benefits could negatively affect the Company's financial results and cash flow.
- Inability to access capital markets could adversely affect the Company's business or financial condition. A decrease in the ratings that rating agencies assign to the Company's short and long-term debt may negatively impact the Company's access to the debt capital markets and increase the Company's cost of borrowing.
- The Company depends on its ability to attract and retain quality employees.

(Continued)

EXHIBIT 12.3 (*Continued*)

- The Company depends upon designers, vendors and other sources of merchandise, goods and services. The Company's relationships with established and emerging designers have been a significant contributor to the Company's past success. The Company's ability to find qualified vendors and access products in a timely and efficient manner is often challenging, particularly with respect to goods sourced outside the United States.
- The Company's procurement of goods and services from outside the United States is subject to risks associated with political or financial instability, trade restrictions, tariffs, currency exchange rates, transport capacity and costs and other factors relating to foreign trade.
- The Company's sales and operating results could be adversely affected by product safety concerns.
- The Company depends upon the success of its advertising and marketing programs.

Notables
- Macy's MAGIC Selling program is an approach to customer engagement that helps Macy's to better understand the needs of customers, as well as to provide options and advice.
- In fiscal 2010, the Company piloted a new Bloomingdale's Outlet store concept. Bloomingdale's Outlet stores are each approximately 25,000 square feet and offer a range of apparel and accessories, including women's ready-to-wear, men's, children's, women's shoes, fashion accessories, jewelry, handbags and intimate apparel.
- Additionally, in February 2010, Bloomingdale's opened in Dubai, United Arab Emirates.
- During 2011, the Company opened three new Bloomingdale's Outlet stores and reopened one Macy's store that had been closed in 2010 due to flood damage.
- During 2012, the Company opened two new Macy's stores and five new Bloomingdale's Outlet stores. Also during 2012 the Company opened its new 1.3 million square foot fulfillment center in Martinsburg, WV.
- The Company has announced that in 2013 it intends to open three new Macy's stores.
- Comparable sales increased 3.7% which represents the third consecutive year of comparable sales growth in excess of 3.5%.
- Operating income for fiscal 2012 was $2.666 billion or 9.6% of sales, excluding impairments, store closing costs and gain on sale of leases, an increase of 12% and 60 basis points as a percent of sales over 2011 on a comparable basis. See pages 16 to 18 for a reconciliation of this non-GAAP financial measure to the most comparable GAAP financial measure and other important information.
- Diluted earnings per share, excluding certain items, grew 20% to $3.46 in 2012.
- Adjusted *EBITDA* (earnings before interest, taxes, depreciation and amortization, excluding premium on early retirement of debt and impairments, store closing costs and gain on sale of leases) as a percent to net sales reached 13.4% in 2012, reflecting steady improvement toward the Company's goal of a 14%.
- Return on invested capital reached 21.2%, continuing an improvement trend over the past four years.
- The Company repurchased 35.6 million shares of its common stock for $1,350 million in 2012, and doubled its annualized dividend rate to 80 cents per share.

Estimating *EPS*

In addition to estimating *P/e*, the multiplier model also requires the analyst to make a forecast of *EPS* for next period. *EPS* measures can vary depending on the inclusion or exclusion of income statement items. There are also forecasts of *EPS* made by analysts. Exhibit 12.5 shows the definitions of some of the Bloomberg measures of *EPS*, and Exhibit 12.6 shows the different *EPS* values for the Dow stocks as of 10/10/2013.

EXHIBIT 12.4 Macy's: Sales, EPS, DPS, Profit Margin, Payout, and P/e

Date	Sales Sales per Share	Proportional Change	EPS	Proportional Change	Profit Margin EPS/Sales	DPS	Dividend Payout DPS/EPS	P/e Current Price to Trailing 12 Month EPS	P/e 5-Year Average P/e Ratio	Share Price	Proportional Change	Personal Consumption Expend. PCE (billions)	Proportional Change
12/29/00	$40.620		-$0.45		-0.01108	$0.000	0.0000	$8.33	$13.52	$17.50		$6,989	
12/31/01	$39.987	-0.0156	$0.71	0.3667	-0.01763	$0.000	0.0000	$13.37	$13.12	$20.45	0.1686	$7,190	0.02180
12/31/02	$39.116	-0.0218	$2.08	-3.9433	0.05305	$0.000	0.0000	$8.43	$11.37	$14.38	-0.2968	$7,549	0.04322
12/31/03	$41.388	0.0581	$1.88	-0.0940	0.04542	$0.188	0.0997	$12.74	$11.20	$23.57	0.6387	$7,970	0.04753
12/31/04	$44.632	0.0784	$1.97	0.0452	0.04403	$0.265	0.1349	$13.13	$11.41	$28.90	0.2262	$8,514	0.05537
12/30/05	$52.559	0.1776	$3.30	0.6794	0.06279	$0.385	0.1167	$12.98	$11.93	$33.17	0.1478	$9,021	0.03326
12/29/06	$49.944	-0.0497	$1.84	-0.424	0.03684	$0.508	0.2758	$15.13	$12.58	$38.13	0.1497	$9,508	0.04923
12/31/07	$58.919	0.1797	$2.00	0.870	0.03395	$0.518	0.2588	$11.10	$13.46	$25.87	-0.3215	$9,941	0.03580
12/31/08	$59.098	0.0030	-$11.40	-6.7000	-0.19290	$0.528	-0.0463	$7.00	$12.10	$10.35	-0.5999	$9,737	0.01681
12/31/09	$55.701	-0.0575	$0.78	-1.0684	0.01400	$0.200	0.2564	$21.49	$13.67	$16.76	0.6193	$10,001	-0.00324
12/31/10	$59.067	0.0604	$2.00	1.5641	0.03386	$0.200	0.1000	$11.94	$13.19	$25.30	0.5095	$10,438	0.03066
12/31/11	$62.203	0.0531	$2.96	0.4300	0.04759	$0.350	0.1182	$11.20	$12.22	$32.18	0.2719	$10,887	0.03263
12/31/12	$68.276	0.0976	$3.29	0.1115	0.04819	$0.800	0.2432	$11.27	$12.10	$39.02	0.2126	$11,301	0.04597
Average	$51.655	0.04695	$0.73	-0.7262	0.01524	$0.303	0.1198	$12.16	$12.45	$25.04	0.1438	$9,157	0.03409
Standard Deviation	$9.749	0.07944	$3.85	2.3.47	0.06697	$0.242	0.1115	$3.62	$0.87	$9.03	0.3811	$1,414	0.01637

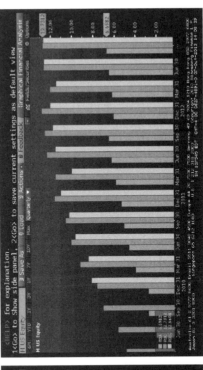

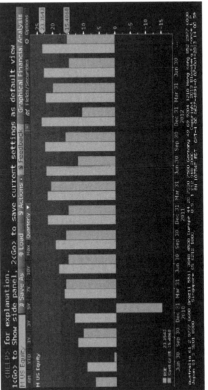

447

EXHIBIT 12.5   Selected Bloomberg EPS Measures

- **Trailing 12-Month EPS, TRAIL_12MO_EPS**: The trailing 12-month diluted EPS from continuing operations.
- **BEst EPE, BEST_EPS: The BEst (Bloomberg Estimates)**: Earnings per share (EPS adjusted) estimate returns earnings per share from continuing operations, which may exclude the effects of one-time and extraordinary gains/losses.
- **BEst LTG EPS, BEST_LTG_EPS: The BEst (Bloomberg Estimates)**: LTG EPS is the estimated compounded annual growth rate (CAGR) of the operating earnings per share (EPS) over the company's next full business cycle (typically three to five years).
- **Trailing 12-Month Estimate Comparable EPS Adjusted, TRAIL_12M_EST_COMP**: Trailing 12-month estimate comparable EPS adjusted, calculated by adding estimate comparable EPS adjusted for the most recent four quarters.
- **Best EPS Excludes Stock Compensation Expense, BEST_EPS_EXCLUDES**: Indicates the company excludes stock compensation expense and may exclude the effects of one-time and extraordinary gains/losses. One-time charges include: realized investment gains/losses, restructuring charges, nonrecurring charges/gains, unusual charges/gains, special charges/gains, reserve charges, large writedowns, spin-off/sell-off expenses, merger expenses, acquisition charges, sale of subsidiary expenses, forgiveness of debt, writedown of goodwill, ESOP charges, and acquired research and development costs.
- **Basic Earnings per Share, IS_EPS**: Bottom-line earnings per share. Includes the effects of all one-time, non-recurring and extraordinary gains/losses. Uses Basic Weighted Average Shares excluding the effects of convertibles. Computed as Net Income Available to Common Shareholders divided by the Basic Weighted Average Shares outstanding.
- **Est EPS Curr Year, EEPS_CURR_YR**: Estimated EPS Current year: Current year earnings per share estimates provided by BEst.
- **BEst EPS GAAP, BEST_EPS_GAAP**: The BEst (Bloomberg Estimates) GAAP earnings per share (EPS) estimate returns reported earnings per share (Before Extraordinary Items OR Bottom Line). Available for Broker estimates and Consensus: Standard, Re-Set Consensus, and 4 Week.
- **Est EPS Next Year, EEPS_NXT_YR**: Estimated EPS Next year: Next year earnings per share estimates provided by BEst.

Analysts vary in their approaches to forecasting earnings. Some analysts, for example, use regression models to estimate the relationship between a company's *EPS* or its growth rate and macroeconomic factors such as inflation, gross domestic product (*GDP*), and interest rates. Given the estimated equation, they then try to forecast the macroeconomic variables for next year to determine the company's *EPS* for next year. For many stocks, however, there is often a low correlation between *EPS* and macroeconomic variables such as *GDP*. Given this common problem, many analysts forecast the individual components defining *EPS*, instead of forecasting *EPS* directly in terms of *GDP* or some other economic aggregate.

EPS, Sales-per-Share, and Profit Margins

One *EPS* forecast model is to forecast sales per share (*SPS*) for the stock, *S*, based on an estimated regression relationship between *SPS* and macroeconomic variables, such

EXHIBIT 12.6   EPS Measures for Dow Jones Stocks, 8/10/2013

Name	TRAIL_ 12M_EPS	BEST_ EPS	TRAIL_12M_ EST_COMPARA BLE_ EPS_ ADJ	IS_EPS	EEPS_ CURR _YR	EEPS_ NXT _YR	BEST_ EEPS_ CUR_YR
American Express Co	4.60	1.22	4.60	3.91	4.87	5.35	4.87
Boeing Co/The	5.42	1.52	6.03	5.15	6.45	7.20	6.45
Caterpillar Inc	6.77	1.72	6.35	8.71	6.27	7.17	6.27
Cisco Systems Inc	1.55	0.51	1.89	1.87	2.11	2.27	2.11
Chevron Corp	11.69	2.89	11.31	13.42	11.92	12.31	11.92
El du Pont de Nemours	3.03	0.41	3.27	2.98	3.80	4.29	3.80
Walt Disney Co/The	3.29	0.76	3.29	3.17	3.37	3.91	3.37
General Electric Co	1.54	0.35	1.51	1.29	1.64	1.80	1.64
Goldman Sachs Group Inc/The	17.20	2.46	16.44	14.63	15.03	15.45	15.03
Home Depot Inc/The	3.48	0.89	3.48	3.03	3.69	4.37	3.69
International Business Machines	15.11	3.95	15.92	14.53	16.85	18.30	16.85
Intel Corp	1.84	0.54	1.92	2.20	1.90	1.99	1.90
Johnson & Johnson	5.26	1.32	5.36	3.94	5.46	5.82	5.46
JPMorgan Chase & Co	6.38	1.31	6.19	5.22	5.72	6.04	5.72
Coca-Cola Co/The	2.03	0.53	2.05	2.00	2.10	2.25	2.10
McDonald's Corp	5.46	1.51	5.45	5.41	5.59	6.10	5.59
3M Co	6.39	1.76	6.38	6.40	6.69	7.38	6.69
Merck & Co Inc	3.47	0.87	3.47	2.03	3.48	3.63	3.48
Microsoft Corp	2.73	0.55	2.67	2.61	2.69	2.97	2.69
NIKE Inc	2.88	0.58	2.92	2.77	3.05	3.51	3.05
Pfizer Inc	2.11	0.56	2.10	1.96	2.17	2.31	2.17
Procter & Gamble Co/The	4.05	1.06	4.06	4.04	4.29	4.67	4.29
AT&T Inc	2.36	0.65	2.37	1.25	2.47	2.68	2.47
Travelers Cos Inc/The	7.37	1.93	7.38	6.35	8.38	7.98	8.38
UnitedHealth Group Inc	5.26	1.52	5.26	5.38	5.51	5.84	5.51
United Technologies Corp	5.66	1.54	5.50	5.73	6.16	6.93	6.16
Visa Inc	8.20	1.85	7.16	3.17	7.58	8.92	7.58
Verizon CommLinications Inc	2.43	0.74	2.43	0.31	2.81	3.47	2.81
Wal-Mart Stores Inc	5.14	1.13	5.14	5.04	5.21	5.72	5.21
Exxon Mobil Corp	7.75	1.88	7.76	9.70	7.58	7.99	7.58

Source: Bloomberg

as *GDP*, inflation, personal consumption expenditures, world economic growth, or energy prices, P^{EN}:

$$S_t = a + b_1\, GDP_t + b_2\, \text{Inflation}_t + P_t^{EN}$$

Given the regression relation, an analyst would next forecast the explanatory variables and then use the regression relation to estimate next period sales. Given an *SPS* forecast, *EPS* is estimated by first estimating the profit margin for the company, *m*. Profit margins are generally explained in terms of factors that influence profitability: industrial production (*IP*), production capacity (*Cap*), labor cost (*LCost*), exchange rates (*ER*), inflation, and advertising expenditures (*Adv*):

$$m = \frac{EPS_t}{S}$$

$$m_t = c_0 + c_1 IP_t + c_2 Cap_t + c_3 ER_t + c_4 \text{Inflation}_t + c_5 Adv + c_6 LCost$$

As a methodology, an analyst could forecast these explanatory variables and then use an estimated regression relation to estimate the company's profit margin for next period.

Finally, given the multiplier estimate, expected *EPS* for the next period is obtained by multiplying the estimated margin by our forecasted sales:

$$EPS_t = m_t S_t$$

To see the relations between *EPS*, *SPS*, and profit margins, consider the case of the Zuber Oil Company that was presented in Chapter 11. The company's income statement is shown in Exhibit 12.7. The exhibit shows two forecasts of the company's income. The first shows the company expected to generate $180 million in total revenue (*TR*) next year from the sale of its crude oil from its oil well. As shown, the company also expects to pay $60 million in operating cost, $20 million in interest (that is tax deductible), and $40 million in taxes. The Zuber Company's expected profit margin based on these expectations is 33.33 percent, and with five million shares, its expected *SPS* (*S*) is $12 and its expected *EPS* is $12.

$$S_1 = \frac{TR_1}{n} = \frac{\$180\,\text{million}}{5\,\text{million}} = \$36$$

$$m_1 = \frac{E(EAT_1)}{TR_1} = \frac{\$60\,\text{million}}{\$180\,\text{million}} = 0.3333$$

$$E(EPS_1) = m_1 E(S_1) = (0.33333)(\$36) = \$12$$

The second forecast shown in Exhibit 12.7 projects lower revenues of $175 million based on an expectation of lower world oil prices, and projects higher operating costs of $65 million based on an expectation of greater labor costs and health costs. With these projections, the Zuber Company's expected profit margin is 30.86 percent, its

EXHIBIT 12.7 Zuber Oil Company Expected Annual Income Statement, Margins, and Sales Per Share

Total Revenue (*TR*)	$180 million	$175 million
−Total Operating Cost (*TOC*)	$60 million	$65 million
= Earnings Before Interest and Taxes (*EBIT*)	$120 million	$110 million
− Interest (*Int* = (0.08)($250 million) = $20	$20 million	$20 million
= Earnings Before Taxes (*EBT*)	$100 million	$90 million
− Taxes (*T*) (Effective Corporate Tax Rate = *t* = 40%)	$40 million	$36 million
= Earnings After Taxes (*EAT*)	$60 million	$54 million
− Retained Earnings (*RE*)	0	0
= Total Dividends (*D*)	$60 million	$54 million
÷ Number of Shares (*n*)	5 million	5 million
= Dividends per Share (*d*)	$12	$10.80
Sales per Share (*S*) = *TR/n*	$36	$35
Profit Margin: *m* = *EAT/TR*	0.33333	0.3086
EPS = *m S*	$12	$10.80
Operating Margin = m^O = *EBIT/TR*	0.66667	0.6286
Interest Expense per Share = *I* = *Int/n*	$4	$4
EBIT/n = m^O *S*	$24	$22
EPS = [*EBIT/n* − *I* − *Dep/n*](1 − 0.4)	$12	$10.80

expected *SPS* is $35, and its expected *EPS* is $10.80:

$$S_1 = \frac{TR_1}{n} = \frac{\$175 \text{ million}}{5 \text{ million}} = \$35$$

$$m_1 = \frac{E(EAT_1)}{TR_1} = \frac{\$54 \text{ million}}{\$175 \text{ million}} = 0.3086$$

$$E(EPS_1) = m_1 E(S_1) = (0.3086)(\$35) = \$10.80$$

For a simple company like Zuber it may be easier to estimate each item in the income statement as was done in the exhibit. For complicated companies or for indexes and industries, forecasting the margins may lead to better statistical relations.

Estimating Macy's EPS, Intrinsic Value, and Expected Return

Exhibit 12.8 shows the author's forecast of Macy's *EPS* for 2013 based on sales and profit margin estimates, an estimate of the company's intrinsic value on 12/31/2012

EXHIBIT 12.8   2013 Forecast of Macy's Intrinsic Value *EPS* and Expected Rate

	2012 12/31/12	2013 12/31/13	Reason
(1) Sales (*S*)	$68.276	$72.07	2013 Forecast: $\Delta PCE/PCE = 0.05$ $\Delta S/S = 1.11192(\Delta PCE/PCE) = 0.0556$ $S_{13} = (1 + \Delta S/S)S_{12}$ $S_{13} = (1 + 0.0556)(\$68.276) = \$72.07$
(2) Profit Margin, *m* = *EPS/S*	4.819%	4.819%	Macy's strong competitive position and innovation will more than offset expected increases in cost, enabling the company to sustain its relatively high profit margin.
(3) EPS	$3.29	$3.47	$EPS_{13} = m_{13} S_{13}$ $EPS = (0.04819)(\$72.07) = \$3.47$
(4) Payout Ratio (*d/e*)	0.2432	0.23	Macy's reported in their 2012 10-K Report that they planned to target *DPS* at $0.80. Given a project *EPS* of $3.47, a *DPS* of $0.80 would equate to a projected payout ratio of 23% (= $0.80/$3.47).
(5) *DPS*	$0.80	$0.80	$DPS_{13} = (d/e)_{13} EPS_{13}$ $DPS_{13} = (0.23)(\$3.47) = \$0.80$
(6) *g*		12.5%	The growth reflects Macy's recent high returns on equity and sustainable growth rates.
(7) k_e		14.25%	$k_e = R_f + [E(R^M - R_f]\beta$ $k_e = 0.0175 + [0.0875]1.428 = 0.1425$
(8) *P/e*	13.14	13.14	Estimated based on Gordon-Williams model and the estimate of *d/e*, *g*, and k_e: $\frac{P}{e} = \frac{d/e}{k_e - g} = \frac{0.23}{0.1425 - 0.125} = 13.14$
(9) Value, *V*	$45.60	$51.30 or $48.13	$V_{12} = (P/e)E(EPS_{13}) = (13.14)(\$3.47) = \$45.60$ $V_{13} = (P/e)E(EPS_{13})(1 + g) = (13.14)(\$3.47)(1.125) = \$51.30$ $V_{13} = (P/e)E(EPS_{13})(1 + g) = (13.14)(\$3.47)(1.0556) = \$48.13$
(10) Market Price, *P*	$39.02		Macy's is underpriced by 14.43% (=($45.60/$39.02) − 1)
(11) Expected Rate		33.52% or 24.50%	$E(\text{Rate}) = [(\$51.30 + \$0.80)/\$39.02] − 1 = 0.3352$ $E(\text{Rate}) = [(\$48.13) + \$0.80)/\$39.02] − 1 = 0.2540$

Buy Recommendation: With expected rates exceeding the required rate of 14.25%, Macy's merits a buy recommendation.

given the estimated *P/e* ratio of 13.14, and a forecast of Macy's expected rate of return for 2013. The estimates and forecasts were made by the author on 12/31/2012 using data on *SPS*, *EPS*, *DPS*, profit margins (*m*), *P/e* ratios, and personal consumption expenditures that are shown in Exhibit 12.4.

EPS and Intrinsic Value

1. **Sales:** The forecast projects that Macy's *SPS* will increase 5.56 percent from its $68.276 per share level on 12/30/2012 to $72.07 per share on 12/30/2013. The sales projection is based on a projected 5 percent increase in disposable personal

consumption expenditures and on the following estimated relationship between the proportional change in *SPS* for Macy's and the proportional change in personal consumption expenses (*PCE*):

$$\Delta S/S = 1.11192(\Delta PCE/PCE)$$

The sales and PCE relation was estimated by regressing annual data on the proportional change in *SPS* of Macy's against the proportional changes in *PCE*. The forecast of a 5 percent increase, in turn, was based on recent trends in *PCE*.

$$\Delta S/S = 1.11192(\Delta PCE/PCE)$$
$$\Delta S/S = 1.11192(0.05) = 0.0556$$
$$S_{13} = S_{12}(1 + \Delta S_t/S)$$
$$S_{13} = \$68.276\,(1 + 0.0556) = \$72.07$$

2. **Profit Margin**: The forecast projects no change in the Macy's profit margin from its 2012 level of 4.819 percent. Macy's projected profit margin of 4.819 percent is significantly higher than the department store industry's margin of 0.821 percent. The industry's low margins were due to high commodity and labor costs, higher exchange rates, and increased competition from outlet stores and online retailing. In contrast, Macy's had experienced an increase in its market share resulting from its marketing strategies. (See Exhibit 12.3 for a summary of the drivers identified in Macy's 2012 10-K Report). The forecast, in turn, projects that Macy's strong competitive position will more than offset the expected cost increases, enabling the company to sustain its high profit margin.

3. **EPS**: Given a projected profit margin of 4.819 percent and the forecasted *SPS* of $72.07, the projected 2013 *EPS* for Macy's was $3.47. This represents a 5.56 percent increase in *EPS* from the *EPS* of $3.29 (= $3.47305/$3.29 − 1) on 12/31/2012:

$$EPS_{13} = m_{13}\,S_{13}$$
$$EPS_{13} = (0.04819)(\$72.07)$$
$$EPS_{13} = \$3.47$$

4. **DPS**: Macy's reported in their 2012 10-K Report that they planned to target *DPS* at $0.80 (see Exhibit 12.3). Given a project *EPS* of $3.47, the *DPS* of $0.80 equates to a payout ratio of 23 percent (= $0.80/$3.47):

$$DPS_{2013} = EPS_{2013}\,(d/e)_{2013}$$
$$DPS_{2013} = \$3.47(0.23)$$
$$DPS_{2013} = \$0.80$$

5. **P/e**: As noted previously, Macy's five-year average *P/e* from 2000 to 2013 ranged between 13.912 and 11.2017. The author's estimated *P/e* was 13.14 based on a

growth rate of 12.5 percent in *EPS*, an estimated payout ratio of 23 percent, and a required return of 14.25 percent:

$$\frac{P}{e} = \frac{d/e}{k_e - g} = \frac{0.23}{0.1425 - 0.125} = 13.14$$

6. **Intrinsic Value**: Using the *P/e* of 13.14 and the projected *EPS* for the next year of $3.47, the intrinsic value of the Macy's on 12/31/2012 was $45.60:

$$V_{12} = \frac{P}{e}E(EPS_{13})$$
$$V_{12} = (13.14)(\$3.47) = \$45.60$$

Given the share price of Macy on 12/30/2012 of $39.02, the stock was underpriced by 16.86% [= ($45.60/39.02) – 1].

Macy's Expected Intrinsic Value and Expected Rate of Return

Macy's estimated intrinsic value on 12/31/2012 is based on the expected *EPS* for 2013. Using the multiplier approach, the estimated intrinsic value for the next year (12/31/2013) should be based on the expected *EPS* for 2014. Using the estimated growth rate in *EPS* of 12.5 percent, *g*, the projection for *EPS* in 2014 would be $3.90 [= $3.47(1.125)]. If we assume no change in the equilibrium *P/e* ratio of 13.14, the projected intrinsic value for 2013 is $51.30:

$$V_{13} = \frac{P}{e}E(EPS_{14}) = \frac{P}{e}E(EPS_{13})(1 + g)$$
$$V_{13} = (13.14)(\$3.47)(1.125) = \$51.30$$

Note that if Macy's had been trading at the estimated intrinsic value of $45.60 on 12/31/2013 instead of $39.02, then with a projected *DPS* of $0.80 and an estimated 2013 intrinsic value of $51.30, its expected rate of return would have equaled its required rate of 14.25 percent:

$$E(\text{Rate}) = \frac{\$51.30 + \$0.80}{\$45.60} - 1 = 0.1425$$

The 14.25 percent expected return would consist of an expected price yield of 12.5 percent and an expected dividend yield of 1.75 percent:

$$\frac{\Delta P}{P} = \frac{\$51.30}{\$45.60} - 1 = 0.125$$
$$\frac{E(d)}{P} = \frac{\$0.80}{\$45.60} = 0.0175$$

Given the lower market price of $39.02 on 12/30/2012, the expected rate would be 33.52 percent given the projected *DPS* of $0.80 and an expected price equal to the estimated intrinsic value of $51.30:

$$E(\text{Rate}) = \frac{\$51.30 + \$0.80}{\$39.02} - 1 = 0.3352$$

This 33.52 percent rate consists of an expected price yield of 31.47 percent [= ($51.30/$39.02) − 1] and an expected dividend yield of 2.05 percent (= $0.80/$39.02).

With an expected rate of 33.52 percent exceeding the required rate of 14.24 percent, a portfolio manager confident in this forecast would take a strong bullish position on Macy's. The assessment, however, is based on the projection that *EPS* will grow in 2014 at the projected equilibrium growth rates of 12.5 percent. The 12.5 percent growth rate in *EPS* represents an equilibrium rate used to estimate the equilibrium *P/e* multiplier. This rate, in turn, was predicated on Macy's increasing its market share. Realizing that such changes may take time, an analyst would more likely want to use a more recent growth rate in *EPS* or the current project *EPS* growth rate of 5.56 percent for her forecast of 2014 *EPS*. If we use the projected 2013 *EPS* growth of 5.56 percent for 2014, then *EPS* in 2014 would be only $3.66 and the estimated 2013 value of Macy's would be $48.13:

$$V_{13} = \frac{P}{e}E(EPS_{14}) = \frac{P}{e}E(EPS_{13})(1+g)$$
$$V_{13} = (13.14)(\$3.47)(1.0556) = \$48.13$$

If an analyst expected Macy's to be priced at the end of 2013 at $48.13, then her expected rate of return would be only 25.40 percent:

$$E(\text{Rate}) = \frac{\$48.13 + \$0.80}{\$39.02} - 1 = 0.2540$$

The two expected rates of return shown in Exhibit 12.8 are the rates where Macy's *EPS* are projected to grow in 2014 at 5.56 percent and at 12.5 percent. Both these scenarios are based on an assessment that Macy's is underpriced now but would be equal to its equilibrium value one year later. It is quite possible that Macy's could continue to be underpriced one year later. If we assume, however, that Macy's stock would increase from its market price of $39.02 by the 12.5 percent growth rate and that the expected dividend yield would be equal to 1.75 percent of the current price, then on 12/31/2013 the projected price of Macy's would be $43.90 [= $39.02(1.125)], dividends would be $0.68 [= (0.0175)($39.02)], and the expected return would be equal to Macy's required rate of 14.25 percent:

$$E(\text{Rate}) = \frac{\$43.90 + \$0.68}{\$39.02} - 1 = 0.1425$$

Thus, for an investor to obtain an expected rate greater than the required rate, a combination of expected price yield and dividend yield would have to exceed 14.25 percent. For example, if the estimated intrinsic value of $45.60 was the projected value for 12/31/2013 and dividends were expected to be $0.80, then the expected price yield would be 16.86 percent [= ($45.60/$39.02) − 1]; the expected dividend yield would equal 2.05 percent ($0.80/$39.02); and the expected rate of return would be 18.91 percent, exceeding the 14.5 percent required return:

$$E(\text{Rate}) = \frac{\$45.60 + \$0.80}{\$39.02} - 1 = 0.1891$$

Ex-Post Analysis

An ex-post analysis of the buy recommendation for the period from 12/30/2012 to 10/4/2013 shows the stock hitting a high for the period of $50.37 on 7/9/2013—a price increase of 29.09 percent (see Exhibit 12.9). This return exceeded the required return of 14.25 percent. However, on 10/3/2013 Macy's was trading at $44.10, reflecting an increase of only 13.02 percent. The company had also made three dividend payments for the year totaling $0.60. The periodic rate for the period from 12/30/2012 to 10/3/2013 was 14.56 percent [= ($44.10+$0.60)/$39.02) − 1] and the approximate annualized rate was 19.41 percent [= (4/3)(14.56%)]—greater than the required rate of 14.25 percent. At that point, an analyst would be happy (for the moment) with her buy recommendation of Macy's, but also be concerned with its price drop from it $50.37 high. The total return for the period based on weekly returns was 23.31 percent, close to the total return of the S&P 500 of 24.3 percent and significantly greater than industry index return of 11.85 percent (see lower screen in Exhibit 12.9).

Note

In trying to determine the intrinsic value of Macy's using this multiplier approach, several points should be noted. First, there are some statistical issues. Specifically, the data sample was relatively small in estimating the regression equations. Thus, the simple regression analysis applied here should be considered only preliminary. Second, the estimated P/e ratio as explained in terms of d/e, k_e, and g is quite sensitive to changes in those parameters. Alternatively, one should also consider using one of the Bloomberg's P/e values or conducting a cross-sectional regression to estimate P/e. Finally, the valuation should also be done using other approaches to see if there is consistency and whether or not similar conclusions are reached.

EPS, Sales, and Operating Profit Margins

Next period's *EPS* were estimated by forecasting sales and profit margins (*EPS/S*). A more disaggregate approach is to estimate sales, the operating profit margin instead of

EXHIBIT 12.9   Macy's: GP and COMP Screens

(a)

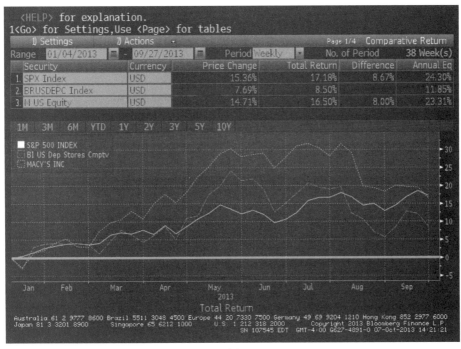

(b)

the profit margin ($m^O = EBDIT/TR$), depreciation per share (Dep/n), interest expense per share ($I = Int/n$), and the effective tax rate (t). For an index or industry, this is done on a per share basis, and for a company, it can be done on per share basis or with total firm value:

$$m_t^O = \frac{EBDIT_t}{S}$$

$$EBDIT_t/n = m_t^O S_t$$

$$EPS_t = [(EBDIT_t/n - Dep_t/n) - I_t](1 - t)$$

The first forecast of the Zuber Oil Company (Exhibit 12.7) shows an expected *EBIT* of \$120 million, interest costs of \$20 million or \$4 per share, and no depreciation. The Zuber Company's expected operating profit margin is 66.67 percent, and again its expected *EPS* is \$12:

$$S_1 = \frac{TR_1}{n} = \frac{\$180 \text{ million}}{5 \text{ million}} = \$36$$

$$m_1^O = \frac{E(EBDIT_1)}{TR_1} = \frac{\$120 \text{ million}}{\$180 \text{ million}} = 0.66667$$

$$\text{Interest Expense per Share} = I_1 = \frac{Int}{n} = \frac{\$20 \text{ million}}{5 \text{ million}} = \$4$$

$$\text{Depreciation Expense per Share} = \frac{Dep_1}{n} = \frac{0}{5 \text{ million}} = 0$$

$$E(EBDIT_1/n) = m_1^O E(S_1) = (0.66667)(\$36) = \$24$$

$$E(EPS_1) = [E(EBDIT_1/n) - I_1 - (Dep_1/n)](1 - t)$$

$$= [\$24 - \$4 - 0](1 - 0.4) = \$12$$

It is important to note that using this approach requires that one estimate operating margins, interest expenses, depreciation, and taxes. Depending on the type of company, the operating profit margin can depend on the company's capacity utilization rate, labor cost, cost of goods sold, material costs, administrative cost, and exchange rates (if inputs and goods are imported). Labor costs, in turn, depend on not only wages, salaries, and the cost of benefits, but also on productivity, which can be impacted by technology. The costs of goods sold, inputs costs, and material costs can be influenced by inflation and by the exchange rate. For companies that import their goods to be sold or the materials they use for manufacturing, exchange rate considerations are important. Operating costs also depend on the efficiency of the company's supply chain.

Depreciation expenditures relate primarily to the amount and types of corporate investments companies make. For manufacturing companies, depreciation is often related to capacity utilization. Annual percentage increases in depreciation expenses have tended to range between 5 percent and 8 percent, with the higher end of the percentage increases occurring when the economy is at a high level of capacity utilization (leading to a need for greater capital expenditures on new equipment and plant expansion). Interest expenses depend not just on interest rates but also on the company's capital structure. In the 1990s, for example, interest costs were decreasing not just because of the decline in interest rates but also because companies were reducing their debt levels following the highly leveraged period of the 1980s. Finally, tax changes are the result of changes in tax codes. Estimating corporate taxes often require that an analyst conduct a detailed analysis of possible congressional and executive tax initiatives at the federal, state, and municipal levels, as well as international considerations for multinational companies.

EPS Forecasted in Term of Projected Income Statement Items

A third approach is to estimate *EPS* by forecasting the accounting income statement items as reported by companies. Reported income statement items can be found on Bloomberg's FA screen ("IS" and "As Reported" tab). To forecast *EPS* based on reported items, an analyst needs to make a projection of each income statement item:

- Operating Income = Revenue (*S*) – Cost of Goods Sold (*CGS*) – Selling and General Administrative Expenses (*SGS*).
- Pretax Income = Operating Income – Interest Expenses (*Int*) – Net Foreign Exchange Losses – Net Nonoperating Losses.
- Income Before XO Items = Pretax Income – Income Tax.
- Net Income = Income before XO Item – Net XO Loss – Net Tax Effect of XO Loss – Minority Interest.

Based on the current reported income and expense items, an analyst could make estimates of the proportional changes (*g*) in revenue (*S*), cost of goods sold, *SGA*, interest expenses (*Int*), net FX losses, and income taxes and then multiply the reported level by $(1 + g)$ to obtain a forecast for next period:

$$S_1 = (1 + g)S_0$$
$$CGS_1 = (1 + g)CGS_0$$
$$Int_1 = (1 + g)Int_0$$

As an example, a one-year forecast of Macy's *EPS* based on projected proportional changes in these income-statement items is shown in Exhibit 12.10. The forecast was made on 10/8/2013 using the Excel program: EPE_PE_Estimator. This program can be downloaded from the text's web site. The program pulls financial data on the selected company from Bloomberg. The forecast of *EPS* is based on the inputted proportional changes expected in sales, cost of goods sold, and other income statement items. These proportional changes are applied to the last four quarters of the income statement item to forecast out the item for the next four quarters.

EXHIBIT 12.10 Macy's *EPS* 2014 Forecast and Value: 10/8/2013 EPS_PE_Estimator Excel Program

Estimated EPS	4.23	9.75862069
Estimated PE = (d/e)/(k-g)	13.14	V = (BB PE)E(EPS)
Estimated Price (PE)	$ 55.59	$ 41.27
Current Price	42.45	

| Date | 7/28/2012 | 10/27/2012 | 2/2/2013 | 5/4/2013 | 8/3/2013 | Trailing | Next |
Period	FQ2 2013	FQ3 2013	FQ4 2013	FQ1 2014	FQ2 2014	Four Quarters	Full Year
Revenue	6,118	6,075	9,350	6,387	6,066	27,878	28,993
Sales Growth	-0.41%	-0.70%	53.91%	-31.69%	-5.03%	3.88%	4.00%
Cost of Goods Sold (Revenue)	3,555	3,672	5,554	3,911	3,533	16,670	17,837
% Δ in COGS	-5.38%	3.29%	51.25%	-29.58%	-9.67%	4.14%	7.00%
COGS/Revenue	58.11%	60.44%	59.40%	61.23%	58.24%	59.80%	61.52%
Selling, General & Administrative Expense	2,009	2,078	2,400	2,041	1,999	8,518	9,114
% Δ in S,G,&A	0.70%	3.43%	15.50%	-14.36%	-2.06%	2.18%	7.00%
S,G,&A/Revenue	32.84%	34.21%	25.67%	31.96%	32.95%	30.55%	31.44%
Operating Income	554	325	1,396	435	534	2,690	2,042
Operating Margin	9.06%	5.35%	14.93%	6.81%	8.80%	9.65%	7.04%
Interest Expense	105	104	106	97	97	404	424
% Δ in Interest	-7.08%	-0.95%	1.92%	-6.49%	0.00%	-7.13%	5.00%
Foreign Exchange Loss (G)	–	–	–	–	–	–	–
Net Non-Operating Loss (G)	–	(1)	138	–	(1)	136	–
Pretax Income	449	222	1,152	338	438	2,150	1,618
Income Tax Expense	170	77	422	121	157	777	–
Effective Tax Rate	37.86%	34.68%	36.63%	35.80%	35.84%	36.14%	0.00%
Income Before XO Items	279	145	730	217	281	1,373	1,618
XO Loss (Gain) Pretax	–	–	–	–	–	–	–
Tax Effect on XO Items	–	–	–	–	–	–	–
Minority Interest	–	–	–	–	–	–	–
Net Income	279	145	730	217	281	1,373	1,618
EPS	0.68	0.36	1.86	0.56	0.73	3.51	4.23
Number of Shares	411.20	401.30	392.30	388.20	382.50		382.50
						*Forecast uses	
						last quarter's	
						# of shares*	

460

For Macy's the forecast made on 10/8/2013 projects its *EPS* for next full year to be $4.23. The $4.23 forecast represents a 20.51 percent increase from the $3.51 level of the preceding four quarters. The *EPS* increase is based on a projected 4 percent increase in sales, 7 percent increase in the costs of goods sold and selling and administrative expenses, and 5 percent increase in interest cost. The program also allows the user to input a discount rate and growth rate to estimate the *P/e* ratio based on the Gordon-Williams model. The program then calculates the value of the stock based on the projected *EPS* and *P/e* ratio. The program also shows Bloomberg's best *P/e* estimates and determines the value based on that *P/e* and the forecasted *EPS*. Using our estimated multiplier of 13.14, the intrinsic value of Macy's on 10/8/2013 was $55.58. Using Bloomberg's best *P/e* estimate of 9.758, the value was $41.28, which was closer to the market price of $42.45 on 10/8/2013.

In summary, forecasting *EPS* in terms of a company's projected sales, operating cost, cost of goods sold, interest expenses, depreciation, and taxes is a challenge facing all analysts. By doing so, an analyst develops a methodology for better understanding the company, what determines its stock value, and whether it is a good investment. In the process of estimating earnings, one becomes a better analyst—one who has an understanding of the breadth and the depth of a company.

BLOOMBERG: EPS_PE_ESTIMATOR EXCEL PROGRAM

The EPS_PE_Estimator Excel Program can be downloaded from the text web site. The program calculates the *EPS* for the next four quarters forward based on the user's inputted projections of the proportional changes in sales, cost of goods sold, interest expenses, and other income statement items. The program uses the company's reported income statement that can be found on the "IS" tab and "As Reported" tab on the FA screen for the stock. The program also calculates the value of the stock based on the projected *EPS* and a *P/e* ratio: A *P/e* ratio based on the Gordon-Williams model ($P/e = (d/e)/(k_e - g)$) and one based on Bloomberg's best *P/e* estimates. See Exhibit 12.10 for an example.

- To load a stock in EPS_PE_Estimator Excel Program, enter the stock's ticker from the "BB Data" tab.
- Historical data on each income statement item, input box for inputting projections, and projections are found in the "Model" tab.
- Graphs of income-statement items can be accessed from the "Graphs" tab.
- Note: Cells are not protected in this Excel worksheet.

See Bloomberg Web Exhibit 12.1.

Other Multipliers

Instead of *EPS*, the multiplier approach can be extended by using different denominators, such as free cash flow, *EBITDA*, *EBIT*, sales, or book value. Similar to the

P/e approach, the income or balance sheet item used as the denominator is defined as the expected value for next period. The value of the stock or index, in turn, is equal to the product of estimated equilibrium multiplier and the expected value of the denominator:

$$\frac{P}{EBITDA_t} = \frac{P}{Expected\ EBITDA\ per\ share}$$

$$V = \frac{P}{EBITDA}E(EBITDA_t)$$

$$\frac{P}{S_t} = \frac{P}{Expected\ Sales\ per\ Share}$$

$$V = \frac{P}{S}E(S_t)$$

$$\frac{P}{BV_t} = \frac{P}{Expected\ Book\ Value}$$

$$V = \frac{P}{BV}E(BV_t)$$

The choice of multiplier depends on the type or stock or index being valued. Moreover, in the case of foreign stocks, a *P/S* multiplier may be a better multiplier than *P/e* or *P/EBIT* when there is suspected accounting manipulations. Like *P/e*, the equilibrium multiplier can be estimated using historical averages, the current values, or a consensus forecast of the values of the variables next period. Exhibit 12.11 shows Bloomberg measures for *P/EBITDA*, *P/S*, and *P/e* multipliers for the Dow Jones stocks.

One can also use a cross-sectional regression model to estimate the relation between the multiplier and identified explanatory factors, or the Gordon-Williams constant growth model (value divided by sales per share, *EBIT* per share, *EBITDA* per share, or *BV* per share) and estimate the multiplier directly in term of g, k_e, and $d/EBITDA$, d/S, or $d/EBIT$:

$$V = P = \frac{d}{k_e - g}$$

$$\frac{V}{S} = \frac{P}{S} = \frac{d/S}{k_e - g}$$

Macy's Valuation Using the P/S Multiplier

On 12/30/2012, the *P/S* ratio for Macy's was 0.536 (Bloomberg's BEst *P/S*). Multiplying this ratio by the projected sales for 2013 of $72.07, we obtain an intrinsic value for Macy's of $38.63, slightly less than the market price of 39.02. If we project the same sales growth in 2014 of 5.56 percent that was projected for 2013, then expected sales for 2014 would be $76.08. Furthermore, if we assume the same *P/S* multiplier

EXHIBIT 12.11 P/S, P/EBITDA, P/e Ratios for Dow Jones Stocks, 8/10/2013

Name	Price to EBITDA	Price to Sales	Price to Sales 5-Year Av	Best Price to Sales	P/e Current Year	Sales per Share	EBITDA per Share	Book Value per Share	Best EPS
American Express Co	7.6741	2.3962	1.5583	2.3698	14.839	29.0148	2.5128	17.5590	1.2170
Boeing Co/The	10.9167	1.0833	0.6623	0.9922	17.736	108.7743	2.8264	9.9810	1.5180
Caterpillar Inc	5.5583	0.9152	0.9724	0.9414	13.329	92.3535	3.5667	27.2091	1.7150
Cisco Systems Inc	8.9640	2.5178	2.7002	2.4185	10.684	9.1212	0.6344	10.9705	0.5060
Chevron Corp	5.1543	1.0480	0.8713	0.9654	9.728	112.4085	5.1728	73.3760	2.8850
El duPont de Nemours	9.6440	1.5377	1.1642	1.4404	14.980	37.7735	2.8894	14.1434	0.4080
Walt Disney Co/The	10.2586	2.6505	1.6627	2.4760	18.869	24.6709	1.9828	24.1867	0.7580
General Electric Co	10.4036	1.7604	1.2232	1.6499	14.346	14.0157	0.5948	12.0298	0.3540
Goldman Sachs Group Inc/The	3.5532	1.7402	1.4219	2.2365	10.275	75.3117	10.0338	151.2124	2.4590
Home Depot Inc/The	10.6374	1.4096	0.8910	1.3385	20.092	53.2620	2.4128	10.7861	0.8940
International Business Machines	8.5740	2.0037	1.7871	1.9453	10.760	91.4742	4.5781	16.2092	3.9530
Intel Corp	5.6815	2.1915	2.4523	2.1342	11.908	10.5223	0.9462	10.8091	0.5510
Johnson & Johnson	11.0920	3.4792	2.7628	3.4006	15.738	25.0172	2.1554	24.7549	1.3210
JPMorgan Chase & Co	NA	1.8126	1.3303	1.9491	8.868	26.6481	NA	52.4755	1.2880

(*Continued*)

463

EXHIBIT 12.11 (*Continued*)

Name	Price to EBITDA	Price to Sales	Price to Sales 5-Year Av	BEst Price to Sales	P/e Current Year	Sales per Share	EBITDA per Share	Book Value per Share	Best EPS
Coca-Cola Co/The	13.3477	3.5357	3.7386	3.5057	17.557	10.6430	0.8360	7.2673	0.5340
McDonald's Corp	9.2854	3.4009	3.2885	3.2521	16.673	27.6489	2.5850	15.1768	1.5100
3M Co	10.5189	2.7084	2.1034	2.5593	17.566	43.8111	2.9599	26.1548	1.7580
Merck & Co Inc	9.5363	3.1706	2.6426	3.1102	13.595	14.8207	1.0961	16.2311	0.8740
Microsoft Corp	9.2224	3.6152	3.4480	3.3655	12.317	9.2969	0.8455	9.4793	0.5480
NIKE Inc	17.8233	2.5255	1.9068	2.3101	22.227	28.9008	1.1584	12.6714	0.5780
Pfizer Inc	8.5887	3.7238	2.5740	3.7352	15.073	7.6589	0.8510	11.8591	0.5590
Procter & Gamble Co/The	11.9478	2.5229	2.1784	2.4774	17.920	30.6870	1.3600	24.4052	1.0580
AT&T Inc	6.2130	1.4864	1.4118	1.3896	13.653	22.8545	1.9855	16.1155	0.6530
Travelers Cos Inc/The	NA	1.2266	1.0680	1.2114	9.829	68.4671	NA	66.6399	1.9300
UnitedHeath Group Inc	7.0793	0.6432	0.4544	0.5723	12.966	114.4558	2.7166	31.1938	1.5230
United Technologies Corp	9.3732	1.5273	1.1603	1.4689	16.708	68.8663	3.2693	29.4133	1.5380
Visa Inc	15.9267	10.1636	7.0540	9.5048	24.248	18.5181	2.9616	34.3113	1.8530
Verizon Communications Inc	4.2213	1.1302	0.9812	1.0890	16.435	41.3125	3.7368	11.9026	0.7420
Wal-Mart Stores Inc	6.7517	0.5232	0.4858	0.4932	14.020	142.4336	2.7505	21.9415	1.1320
Exxon Mobil Corp	6.1758	0.9714	1.0242	0.8515	11.239	95.4363	3.0774	37.6299	1.8830

Source: Bloomberg

for 2013 that we used in 2012, then the estimated 2013 value for Macy's would be $40.78 and the expected rate with an $0.80 DPS would be just 6.56 percent:

$$S_{13} = S_{12}(1 + \Delta S_t / S)$$

$$S_{13} = \$68.276(1 + 0.0556) = \$72.07$$

$$V_{12} = \frac{P}{S}E(S_{13})$$

$$V_{12} = (0.536)(\$72.07) = \$38.63$$

$$S_{14} = S_{13}(1 + \Delta S_t / S)$$

$$S_{14} = \$72.07(1.0556) = \$76.08$$

$$V_{13} = \frac{P}{S}E(S_{14})$$

$$V_{13} = (0.536)(\$76.08) = \$40.78$$

$$E(\text{Rate}) = \frac{\$40.78 + \$0.80}{\$39.02} - 1 = 0.0656$$

Based on the valuation using the Bloomberg's *P/S* multiplier, Macy's would be overpriced by 1.01 percent [= ($39.02/$38.63) – 1] and the expected rate of return using the 2013 estimated intrinsic value of $40.78 as our estimated price would only be 6.56 percent, considerably less than the required return. An analyst relying on this evaluation would likely recommend a sell or no buy. The different conclusions reached with the *P/S* model are the result of not including the strong long-run growth rate that was captured in *P/e* multiplier valuation. It could also be owing to the selection of the *P/S* multiplier.

Valuation Using the Discounted-Cash Flow Model and Bloomberg's DDM Model

In valuing Macy's using the *P/e* multiplier approach, we estimate the *P/e* multiplier using the Gordon-Williams model. This model is a constant growth rate model. As a result, our valuation was based on the assumption that Macy's *EPS* would grow at constant growth rate of 12.5 percent, have a fixed dividend-payout ratio of 0.23, and its required rate would be 14.25 percent. If we value Macy's based on the values using the constant growth valuation model, we obtain our intrinsic value of $45.60 (allow for slight rounding differences):

$$V = \frac{E(d_1)}{k_e - g} = \frac{(d/e)E(EPS)}{k_e - g} = \frac{0.23(\$3.47)}{0.1425 - 0.125} = \$45.60$$

An approximate value of $46.73 is also obtained using the Bloomberg DDM screen. This can be seen in Exhibit 12.12, which shows the valuation of Macy's using DDM. The DDM screen shown in the exhibit was adjusted to reflect our constant growth model assumptions: $g = 12.5\%$, $\beta = 1.428$, $k_e = 0.142 = 0.0171 +$

EXHIBIT 12.12   Macy's Constant Growth Model Using Bloomberg DDM Screen, 10/12/2013

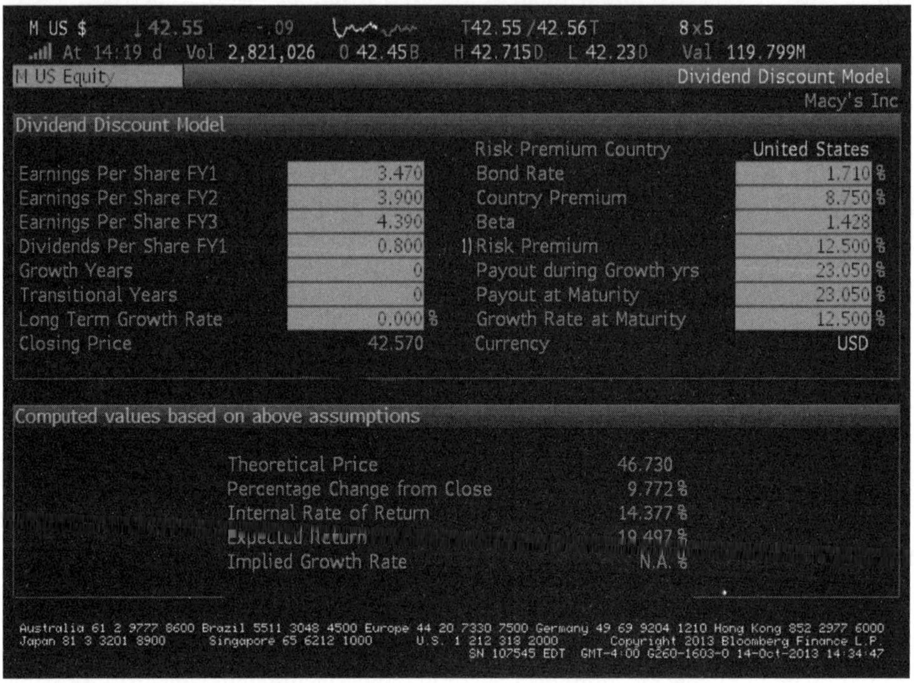

$(0.08755)\beta$, $E(\text{EPS}_{FY1}) = 3.47$, $E(\text{EPS}_{FY2}) = 3.47(1.125) = \$3.90$, and $E(\text{EPS}_{FY3}) = 3.47(1.125)^2 = \$4.39$, $\text{DPS}_{FY1} = 0.80$, dividend payout $= 0.23$, and no growth or transition period.

One of the limitations of the Gordon-Williams model is that the assumption of a constant growth rate is not applicable to many stocks and sectors. In one of our scenarios of Macy's, we assumed an expected growth rate in *EPS* to be relatively low (5.062 percent) for at least two years and then take on a rate of 12.5 percent. As discussed in previous chapters, Bloomberg's DDM determines the value of a stock using a three-stage growth model. The program defaults to one of four growth stage scenarios: explosive growth, high growth, average growth, and slow/mature growth. The classification is based on the normalized distribution of the forecasted growth rate for all equities. Explosive growth firms are at the high end of the distribution, with growth rates significantly above the normalized mean or median, while low/mature growth firms are those at the low end of the distribution. The Bloomberg DDM model initially sets the length of the growth stage to three years for explosive growth, five years for high growth, seven years for average growth, and nine years for slow growth. The growth rate defaults to the mean secular growth rate. The other default assumptions of the DDM include:

- A growth rate in the mature stage equal to the retention rate times the stocks required rate.

- The growth rates in the transition period decrease annually from the rate in the growth stage period to the rate in the mature stage.
- *EPS* for FY1, FY2, and FY3 equal the consensus earnings projections.
- The *EPS* for the remaining years in the initial growth period reflect the long-term growth rate assumption.
- *DPS* are FY2 and FY3, and the growth year periods are based on the current dividend-payout ratio.
- The payout ratio in the mature stage is 45 percent.
- The discount rate is equal to the risk-free rate of the 10-year Treasury bond plus a risk premium.

The upper DDM screen shown in Exhibit 12.13 shows the DDM value of Macy's on 10/8/2013. The screen shows a $50.426 value of Macy's and an internal rate of 11.105 percent. The value is based on Bloomberg's default assumptions: EPS_{FY1} = $3.822, EPS_{FY2} = $4.350, EPS_{FY3} = $4.976, DPS_{FY1} = $0.951, long-term growth rate of 10.52 percent, β = 1.032, k_e = 10.44 percent, and mature growth rate = 5.742 percent. The lower screen in the exhibit shows a $45.036 value for the stock and an internal rate of 11.852 percent; this value reflects assumptions that are closer to our preceding analysis: EPS_{FY1} = $3.90 (= (1.125)($3.47)), EPS_{FY2} = $4.39, EPS_{FY3} = $4.94, DPS_{FY1} = $0.80, long-term growth rate of 12.5 percent, β = 1.2, k_e = 11.65 percent, and mature growth rate = 6 percent. Both scenarios value Macy's higher than the current prices of $42.55 and $42.99 and both have internal rates of return exceeding their required returns. Thus, the DDM analysis would merit a buy recommendation by an analyst based on these projections, but perhaps not a strong buy.

Exhibit 12.14 shows the market prices on 10/10/2013, *EPS*, *P/e* ratios, and DDM values of each stock composing the Dow Jones Average. The Bloomberg's DDM model reflects the Bloomberg DDM default assumptions. As a first pass, a comparison of market prices with DDM values shows 12 of the 30 Dow stocks were underpriced as of 10/10/2013.

Growth Duration Model

Finding how long a company will grow at an extraordinary rate or equivalently how long it will take to reach the transitional or steady-state period is important if one is to estimate the values of stock using 2-stage and 3-stage models. As a general rule, companies with extraordinary growth rates will not grow at those rates for an extended time. They will eventually run out of potentially high-return investments. As noted, Bloomberg's DDM determines the length of stages by classifying stocks based on a normalized distribution of the forecasted growth rates for all equities. Explosive growth firms are at the high end of the distribution, with growth rates significantly above the normalized mean or median, while low/mature growth firms are those at the low end of the distribution.

EXHIBIT 12.13   Macy's Three-Stage Growth Model Value Using Bloomberg's DDM Model, 10/8/2013

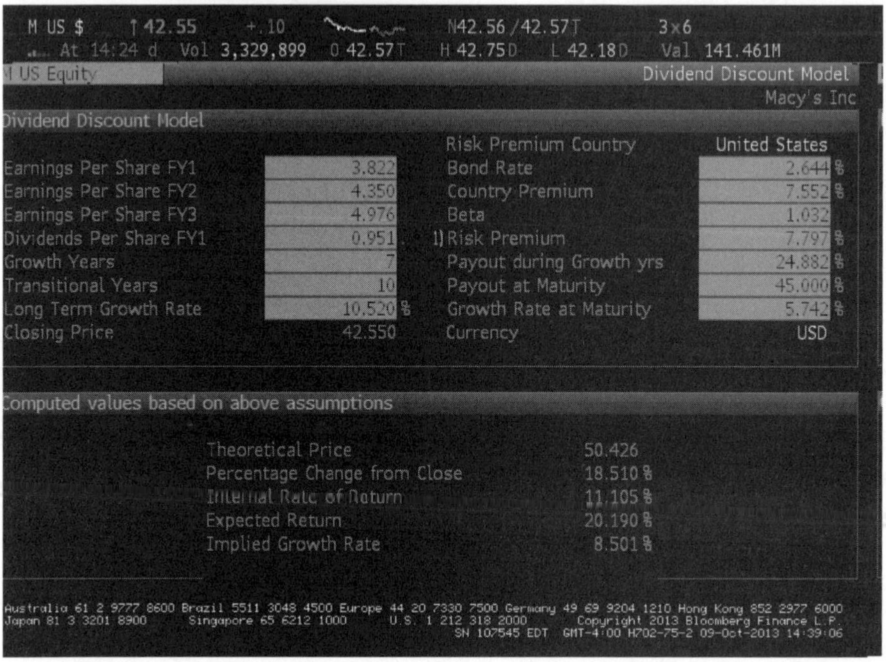

(a)

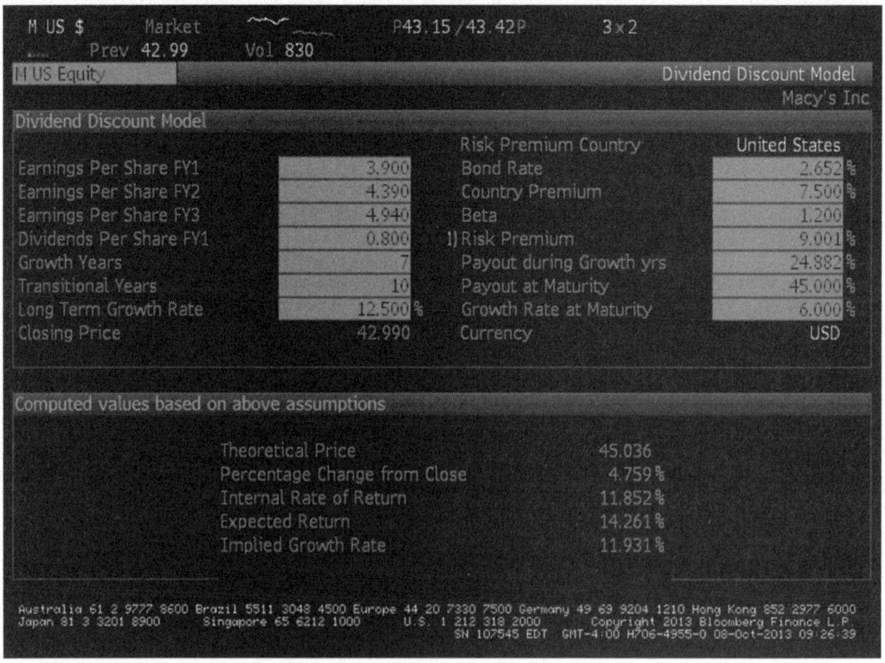

(b)

(a) 10/9/2013: Bloomberg Default Assumptions.
(b) 10/8/2013

EXHIBIT 12.14 DDM Value, Market Price and Economic Value Added, Dow Jones Stocks, 8/10/2013

Name	BEst EPS:Y	BEst P/E:Y	Market Price	DDM Value	Proportion mispriced: (Mkt Price/ DDM) − 1	EVA
DJIA Stocks						
GENERAL ELECTRIC CO	1.641	14.360	23.570	21.866	0.078	2,088.52
EXXON MOBIL CORP	7.577	11.239	85.160	147.604	−0.423	2,407.45
MICROSOFT CORP	2.685	12.317	33.070	37.759	−0.124	896.29
JOHNSON & JOHNSON	5.462	15.737	85.960	83.327	0.032	3,583.62
WAL−MART STORES INC	5.207	14.020	73.000	120.125	−0.392	−4,919.51
CHEVRON CORP	11.921	9.742	116.130	80.253	0.447	704.51
PROCTER & GAMBLE CO/THE	4.294	17.921	76.950	98.833	−0.221	165.65
INTL BUSINESS MACHINES CORP	16.851	10.760	181.320	228.601	−0.207	−9,750.13
JPMORGAN CHASE & CO	5.723	8.867	50.750	30.904	0.642	−7,109.32
PFIZER INC	2.166	13.064	28.290	27.542	0.027	2,470.54
AT&T INC	2.472	13.653	33.750	39.728	−0.150	8,775.17
COCA−COLA CO/THE	2.100	17.657	37.080	36.607	0.013	3,678.26
MERCK & CO. INC.	3.477	13.595	47.270	39.725	0.190	9,900.97
VERIZON COMMUNICATIONS INC	2.811	16.438	46.200	61.242	−0.246	−11,157.43
CISCO SYSTEMS INC	2.106	10.682	22.500	23.281	−0.034	3,260.02
VISA INC-CLASS A SHARES	7.582	24.250	183.850	225.184	−0.184	3,803.19
WALT DISNEY CO/THE	3.370	18.869	63.590	40.237	0.580	2,514.24
INTEL CORP	1.896	11.913	22.590	21.022	0.075	45.87
HOME DEPOT INC	3.690	20.092	74.140	116.178	−0.362	13,395.34
UNITED TECHNOLOGIES CORP	6.155	16.709	102.840	92.895	0.107	1,119.45
MCDONALD'S CORP	5.594	16.674	93.270	125.172	−0.255	5,520.29
BOEING CO/THE	6.454	17.735	114.470	88.656	0.291	4,256.30
3M CO	6.693	17.566	117.570	105.636	0.113	375.02
AMERICAN EXPRESS CO	4.867	14.840	72.220	58.764	0.229	−4,613.26
UNITED HEALTH GROUP INC	5.505	12.966	71.380	85.482	−0.165	3,190.17
GOLDMAN SACHS GROUP INC	15.031	10.274	154.440	48.860	2.161	2,822.49
NIKE INC–CLB	3.050	23.243	70.890	65.689	0.079	666.14
CATERPILLAR INC	6.266	13.329	83.520	53.585	0.559	5,970.78
DU PONT (E.I.) DE NEMOURS	3.801	14.981	56.940	43.013	0.324	12,914.22
TRAVELERS COS INC/THE	8.378	9.829	82.350	73.725	0.117	2,554.99

Source: Bloomberg

Growth duration models can also be used to estimate the implied time it would take to move to steady state. One duration model is based on assuming that the current P/e of a stock will eventually converge to a value that is proportional to the market P/e, with the proportion being based on earnings and the market's steady-state growth. The formula for the model is:

$$T = \frac{ln\left[\dfrac{P/e}{P/e_M}\right]}{ln\left[\dfrac{(1+g+DY)}{1+g_M+DY_M}\right]}$$

where:

P/e = Current price-to-earnings ratio
g = Estimated growth rate in earnings (sustained)
DY = Dividend yield
M = Market

Exhibit 12.15 shows the years, T, to steady state using the growth duration model for nine Dow stocks. The calculations are based on the stocks' P/e, dividend yields, and sustainable growth rates as of 8/10/2013. The company with the longest duration is Pfizer.

EXHIBIT 12.15 Times to Steady State, Duration Growth Model of Nine Dow Jones Stocks, 8/10/2013

Name	P/e	Dividend Yield, DY (%)	Sustained Growth Rate, g (%)	Time to Steady State, T (Years)
S&P 500	16.40	2.0800	9.0112	
WALT DISNEY CO	17.58	1.1101	11.9403	3.9624
GENERAL ELECTRIC	14.54	3.1639	5.6712	5.8635
HOME DEPOT INC	19.14	2.0558	15.6524	2.6723
JOHNSON & JOHNSON	16.18	2.9111	6.9645	1.2533
COCA-COLA CO/THE	17.60	2.9494	13.7367	1.4374
MERCK & CO	13.49	3.6329	1.8505	3.7680
NIKE INC–CL B	23.35	1.2320	16.2696	6.2982
PFIZER INC	12.84	3.3182	5.5454	12.0868
AT&T INC	13.36	5.2895	−3.0357	2.4738

Source: Bloomberg; P/e = Bloomberg BEst P/e
$$T = ln\left[\frac{P/e}{P/e_{S\&P}}\right] / ln\left[\frac{1+g+DY}{1+g_{S\&P}+DY_{S\&P}}\right]$$

Economic Value Added

Economic Value Added (*EVA*, also referred to as economic profit) is a measure of a company's residual wealth. It is calculated by deducting the cost of capital from the company's operating profit.

$$EVA = \text{Net Operating Profit After Taxes} - \text{Cost of Capital}$$
$$EVA = EBDIT(1 - t) - (WACC)(\text{Value of Assets})$$

Companies that can obtain risk-adjusted returns on their investments (i) that exceed the returns obtained in the market will have positive *EVA*s. For example, consider our illustrative Zuber Oil Company. Recall that the company had bought an oil well reserve for $500 million financed by the equity investors raising $250 million and the company borrowing $250 million at 8 percent. Suppose Zuber Oil Company was expected to generate $120 million in *EBIT*, with $20 million going to creditors, $40 million to the government in taxes, and $60 million to equity investors in dividends (see Exhibit 12.7). Zuber has a cost of equity capital of 24 percent ($\beta = 2$; SML: $k_e = R_f + (RP)\beta = 0.04 + (0.10)(2) = 0.24$), cost of debt of 8 percent (k_d), and WACC of 14.4 percent ($WACC = f_d\,k_d\,(1 - t) + f_e\,k_e = (0.5)(0.08)(1 - 0.4) + (0.5)(0.24) = 0.144$). Given these rates, the value of Zuber's assets is $500 million and its *EVA* is zero.

$$k_C^T = WACC = f_E k_e + f_D k_d(1 - t)$$
$$WACC = (0.5)(0.24) + (0.5)(0.08)(1 - 0.4) = 0.144$$
$$V_0^A = \frac{E(EBIT)(1 - t)}{k_C^T}$$
$$V_0^A = \frac{\$120\,\text{million}\,(1 - 0.4)}{0.144} = \$500\,\text{million}$$
$$EVA = EBIT(1 - t) - WACC(V_0^A)$$
$$EVA = \$120M\,(1 - 0.4) - (0.144)(\$500M) = 0$$

The zero *EVA* for Zuber indicates that the company is generating (or is expected to generate) an after-tax return of 14.44 percent from its $500 million oil well assets—$72 million:

$$\frac{EBIT(1 - t)}{V_0^A} = \frac{\$72M}{\$500M} = 0.144$$

A 14.4 percent return from $500 million of invested capital equals the return the company required in order to take care of its shareholders who are financing half the asset and require a return of 24 percent and its creditors who are financing half the asset and require an 8 percent rate that is tax deductible.

Zuber would have a positive *EVA* if it generates a rate of return greater than its required return. For example, suppose the company generated $130 million in *EBIT* and \$78 million in net operating profit $[EBIT(1 - t) = \$130M\ (1 - 0.4) = \$78M]$. If the market values the company at \$500 million, then the company's return on its \$500 asset would be 15.60 percent $[= EBIT(1 - t)/V^A = \$130M(1 - 0.4)/\$500M)]$, exceeding its $WACC$ of 14.4 percent, and its EVA would be \$6 million:

$$EVA = EBIT(1 - t) - WACC(V_0^A)$$
$$EVA = \$130M\ (1 - 0.4) - (0.144)\ (\$500M) = \$6M$$

Companies with positive $EVAs$ are growth firms—those capable of generating risk-adjusted rates on their investments that exceed the rates investors can obtain in the market. Suppose Zuber made a \$60 million investment in a new oil well with an investment return of 30 percent ($i = 0.30$) and beta of two, and financed the new investment by raising \$30 million in new debt and \$30 million in equity (either by retained earnings or issuing stock). With this investment, Zuber's $WACC$ would still be 14.4 percent, its total asset would be \$560 million, and its $EBIT$ would be \$138 million: \$120 million from its old oil well and \$18 million from its new oil well $[= iI - (0.30)(\$60M) = \$18M]$ With the new investment, Zuber's EVA would be \$2.16 million:

$$EVA = [EBIT + iI_1](1 - t) - WACC(V_0^A + I_1)$$
$$EVA = [\$120M + (0.30)(\$60M)]\ (1 - 0.4) - (0.144)(\$500M + \$60M)$$
$$EVA = \$138M\ (1 - 0.4) - (0.144)\ (\$560M) = \$2.16M$$

If Zuber's investment return on the new oil well were 24 percent—the same rate investors can get in the market for a β of two—then Zuber's EVA would be equal to zero.

$$EVA = [EBIT + iI_1](1 - t) - WACC(V_0^A + I_1)$$
$$EVA = [\$120M + (0.24)(\$60M)](1 - 0.4) - (0.144)(\$500M + \$60M)$$
$$EVA = \$134.40M\ (1 - 0.4) - (0.144)\ (\$560M) = 0$$

$EVAs$ are often measured in terms of book values for assets. These EVA values can be pulled from Bloomberg. The last column of Exhibit 12.14 shows the $EVAs$ for the Dow stocks as of 8/10/2013. Note just five of the Dow stocks have negative $EVAs$.

Relative Analysis

Stock valuation can be done on a stock-by-stock basis, with the objective of determining if a stock is underpriced and meriting a buy recommendation or overpriced and deserving a sell or no buy recommendation. Stock and portfolio investment decisions, however, also require relative analysis. This entails conducting a comparative analysis of the companies in the same industry or with the same style (e.g., growth stocks or small-cap stocks) and then applying the same type of analysis and forecast for each company.

A relative analysis of the larger cap companies that make up the department store industry is shown in the top panel of Exhibit 12.16. The exhibit shows the *SPS, EPS, DPS*, profit margin, and *P/e* ratios based on Bloomberg's best consensus estimates as of 10/9/2013. The screen also shows the market prices on 10/9/2013, adjusted betas, sustainable growth rates, and the intrinsic values for each stock based on Bloomberg's DDM model (with Bloomberg DDM default assumptions). Based on the company DDM values relative to their market prices, Macy's was underpriced by 16.49 percent [(Market Price/DDM Value) − 1 = ($42.45/$50.83) − 1 = −0.1649], Dillards by 19.28 percent [= ($76.97/$95.36) − 1], Nordstrom by 0.52 percent [= ($55.62/$55.91) − 1], and Kohl's by 34.65 percent [= ($50.77/$77.69 − 1]. In contrast, Saks was overpriced by 348 percent [= ($15.98/$3.53) − 1] and both J.C. Penney and Sears had negative *EPS* and zero sustainable growth rates, making their DDM values zero. As a first pass, an analyst would take a bearish position on Saks, J.C. Penney, and Sears (although each might warrant a different analysis later) and bullish positions on Macy's, Dillards, and Kohl's.

In evaluating the buy recommendations, the DDM values for Macy's and Nordstrom are based on both having relatively high projected growth rates of 10.52 percent and 11.86 percent, respectively, and large discount rates because of their higher betas (see top DDM screen in Exhibit 12.13a for Macy's, and see Exhibit 12.17a for Nordstrom's DDM screen). In contrast, the DDM values for Kohl's and Dillards reflect lower growth rates of 8.76 percent and 9.4 percent and lower discount rates because of their lower betas of 0.71 and 0.719 (see Exhibit 12.17b and Exhibit 12.17c).

The second panel in Exhibit 12.16 shows various ratios related to sustainable growth and risk: business, financial, bankruptcy, liquidity, and external market risks. The ratios were pulled from Bloomberg's RV screens. In evaluating the companies with the initial buy recommendations in term of sustainable growth rates and return on equity (*ROE*). Nordstrom has the highest *ROE* (39.26 percent), followed by Macy's (23.35 percent), Dillards (18.04 percent), and Kohl's (15.86 percent). Nordstrom, in turn, has the highest sustainable growth rate. *ROE*s are often analyzed in terms of the financial ratios that define the DuPont model for measuring ROE:

$$ROE = \left[\frac{\text{Net Income}}{\text{Sales}}\right]\left[\frac{\text{Sales}}{\text{Assets}}\right]\left[\frac{\text{Assets}}{\text{Equity}}\right]$$

The second panel of Exhibit 12.16 shows each company's DuPont ratios, ROEs, and return on assets (*ROA*). Note that each of the four companies have relatively high net income-to-sales ratios, with the highest being Kohl's (10.51 percent), followed by Nordstrom (10.48 percent), Macy's (8.80 percent), and Dillards (4.75 percent). Macy's and Nordstrom, however, have higher asset-to-equity ratios (3.49 and 4.21) than do Kohl's and Dillards (2.33 and 2.04). The higher asset-to-equity ratios for Macy's and Nordstrom help to explain why their *ROE*'s (23.35 percent and 39.26 percent) exceed those of Kohl's and Dillard (15.86 percent and 18.03 percent). All of

EXHIBIT 12.16 RV Analysis of Department Store Industry, 10/9/2013

Department Store Industry Name	Market Cap	Sale per Share 12 Month Trailing	Best EPS	Best Profit Margin	Best CPS	Best P/E	DDM Value	Market Price	Adjusted Beta	Sustainable Growth Rate
MACY'S INC	15907.43	71.28	3.82	0.0253	0.5511	11.106	50.83	42.450	1.032	16.866
DILLARDS INC-CL A	3550.44	143.30	7.35	0.0326	0.2400	10.479	95.36	76.970	0.721	5.138
KOHLS CORP	11104.71	85.62	4.25	0.0414	1.5150	11.945	77.69	50.770	0.710	10.927
J.C. PENNEY CO INC	2396.92	55.09	-5.72	-0.1407	0.0000	15.107	0.00	7.770	1.482	0.000
NORDSTROM INC	10872.69	62.99	3.68	0.0461	1.3989	15.107	55.91	55.620	1.021	26.622
SAKS INC	2404.33	21.88	0.37	0.0229	0.0000	43.357	3.53	15.980	1.190	5.337
SEARS HOLDINGS CORP	6365.83	362.64	-5.88	-0.0382	0.0000		0.00	63.050	1.729	0.000

Department Store Industry	Dupont Ratios				Growth Rate and ROE and ROA				
Name	Operating Income to Net Sales: Q (%)	Sales to Total Asset	Assets to Equity	ROE	Retention Ratio	Sustainable Growth Rate	ROA	Debt/ Equity	Adjusted Beta
MACY'S INC	8.8032	0.2969	3.4895	23.354	65.970	15.407	6.197	114.527	1.032
DILLARDS INC-CL A	4.7455	0.3693	2.0427	18.035	93.650	16.890	8.042	41.825	0.721
KOHLS CORP	10.5153	0.3042	2.3289	15.865	67.965	10.783	7.030	75.281	0.710
J.C. PENNEY CO INC	-13.0680	0.2285	5.0233	-53.714		0.000	-9.290	94.040	1.482
NORDSTROM INC	10.4819	0.3739	4.2088	39.255	68.478	26.881	8.866	163.670	1.021
SAKS INC	-4.3263	0.3368	1.8196	3.7679		0.000	2.981	31.273	1.190
SEARS HOLDINGS CORP	-3.2916	0.4602	6.8265	-42.960		0.000	-4.568	98.361	1.729

	Financial Risk				Business Risk			Bankruptcy Risk	
Name	Long-Term Debt to Total Equity	Debt-to-Equity 5 Yr Geo Growth Rate	EBIT to Total Interest	Operating Profit Margin	Gross Margin	Profit Margin	Pretax Margin	Altman Z	Bloomberg Default Probability
MACY'S INC	112.48	2.280	6.059	8.803165	40.265839	4.821932	7.59229	3.724	0.000576
DILLARDS INC-CL A	41.74	-6.345	7.583	4.745529	37.094746	4.976039	7.49293	3.835	0.000348
KOHLS CORP	73.54	18.012	5.710	10.515272	36.257069	5.114373	8.09689	3.219	0.000528
J.C. PENNEY CO INC	93.22	28.381	-4.478	-13.067968	31.313053	-7.585676	-11.829	0.747	0.079948
NORDSTROM INC	163.30	-7.574	8.302	10.481852	38.821205	6.050379	9.75469	3.528	0.000152
SAKS INC	22.66	-10.011	3.844	-4.326272	40.592789	1.997805	3.15785	3.506	
SEARS HOLDINGS CORP	61.25	34.893	-3.642	-3.291624	26.381292	-2.333517	-3.70854	1.738	0.007389

	Liquidity Risk				External Market Risk				
Name	Quick Ratio LF	Cash Ratio LF	Inventory Turnover LF	Ace. Rec. Turnover LF	Short Interest Ratio	Average Volume	Bid-Ask Spread	Market Cap	DDM Value
MACY'S INC	0.3425	0.2754	3.208	78.97	1.6341	5127780	0.01	15907.43	50.832
DILLARDS INC-CL A	0.1755	0.1426	2.989	226.20	6.0865	551857	0.06	3550.44	95.361
KOHLS CORP	0.2206	0.2206	3.345		10.1128	2257518	0.02	11104.71	77.694
J.C. PENNEY CO INC	0.4353	0.4353	2.809		3.1339	52559280	0.01	2396.92	0.000
NORDSTROM INC	1.1810	0.3810	5.351	5.34	4.8177	1855050	0.02	10872.69	55.908
SAKS INC	0.0185	0.0185	2.401		5.5650	6178331	0.01	2404.33	3.532
SEARS HOLDINGS CORP	0.1464	0.0749	3.506	63.54	8.0239	770519	0.15	6365.83	0.000

Source: Bloomberg RV Screens

475

EXHIBIT 12.17 Nordstrom, Kohl's and Dillards DDM Values, 10/9/2013

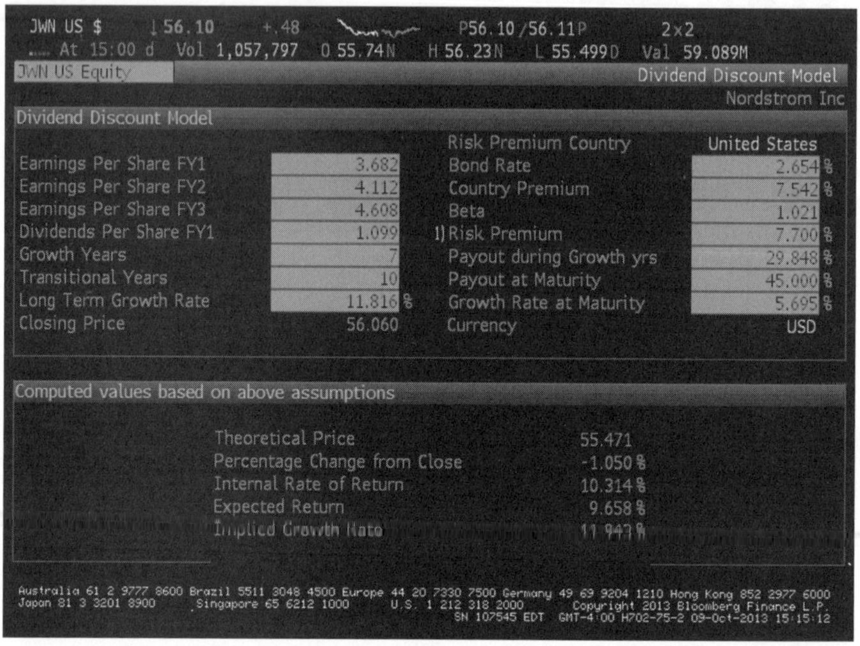

(a)

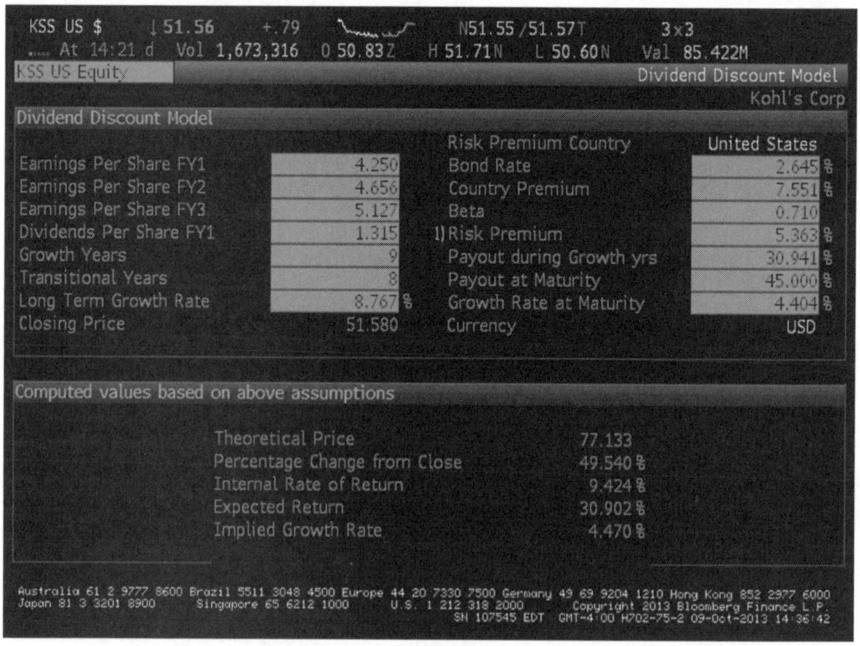

(b)

EXHIBIT 12.17 (*Continued*)

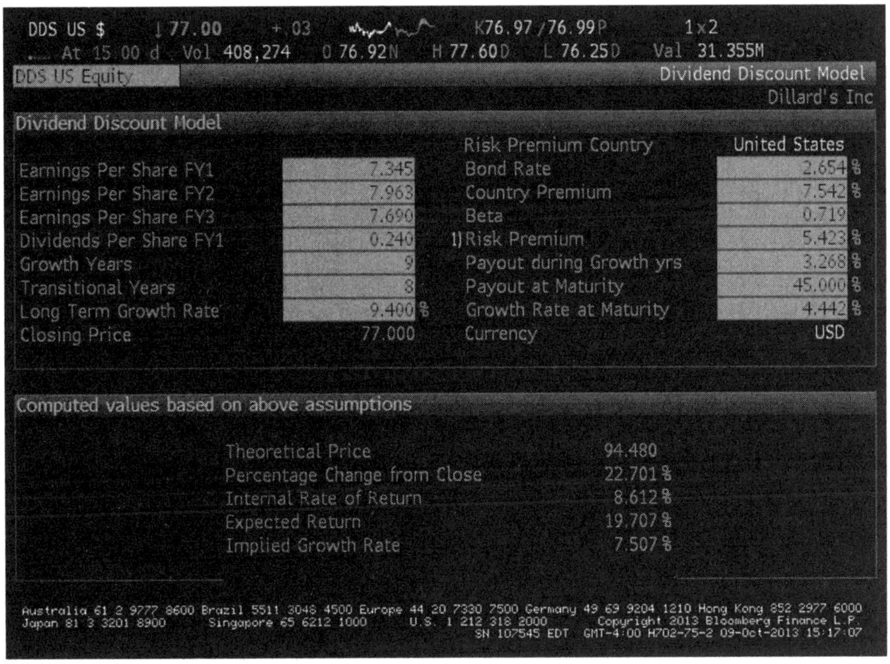

(c)

(a) Nordstrom
(b) Kohl's
(c) Dillards

the companies, however, have comparable ROAs, with Nordstrom having the highest (8.87 percent) followed by Dillards (8.04 percent), Kohl's (7.03 percent), and Macy's (6.197 percent). The high asset-to-equity ratios of Macy's and Nordstrom show that both are more leveraged than Kohl's and Dillard (Note: A further financial risk analysis of companies in this industry would require looking at their leases.) This is also reflected by the leverage ratios of the companies shown in the exhibit. Comparing Macy's and Nordstrom to Kohl's and Dillards, we find Macy's and Nordstrom with debt-to-equity ratios of 114.5 percent and 163.67 percent, compared to Kohl's and Dillards with ratios of only 75.28 percent and 41.82 percent. The higher leverage ratios for Macy's and Nordstrom would explain, in part, their higher *ROE* and why they have higher betas and discount rates.

In general, difference in betas among companies can be explained in terms of business risk (unleveraged beta) and financial risk. Companies with a high operating leverage tend to have high operating profit margins. As a result, their earnings vary more with sales, and as a result they tend to have higher unleveraged betas. Operating leverage relates to the mix of fixed (capital) and variable inputs (labor) used to produce the product. High operating leverage companies tend to have higher earnings in economic expansion and lower in economic slowdowns. Steel companies, for example, have high operating leverages and operating margins. Retail companies tend to have lower operating leverages and margins. Sales of cyclical sectors, such as auto or steel, tend to be more volatile than noncyclicals, such as hospital services. A relative analysis of business risk would look at a company's operating margins and profit margins or the volatility in operating income or in sales. In comparing the four companies' operating margins, Macy's, Kohl's, and Nordstrom have comparable operating margins, ranging between 8.8 percent for Macy's and approximately 10.5 percent for Kohl's and Nordstrom. Dillards had the lowest operating margin of 4.74 percent. An analyst would conclude that three of the four companies have similar business risk.

It should be noted that risk may not be limited just to business and financial risk. Financial and business risk may lead to bankruptcy risk, and there may also be liquidity risk where companies are in a cash-poor situation, reflecting possible future financial distress. Measures of bankruptcy risk include the Altman's Z-score, bond spreads, and spreads on credit default swaps. Liquidity risk, in turn, can be measured in terms of liquidity ratios (current ratio, quick ratio, and cash ratio) and turnover ratios for accounts receivable and inventory. Altman's Z-scores, Bloomberg default probability, and several liquidity ratios for the department stores are shown in Exhibit 12.16. The low Z-score, high default probability, and negative operating margin for J.C. Penney are red flags for the company. Sears and Saks both have relatively low cash ratios, as well as negative operating profits. Business risk may also be reflected in exchange-rate risk. Companies such as department stores that buy products from foreign suppliers or companies that have large foreign sales are subject to exchange-rate risk. Finally, independent of business and financial risk, is external liquidity risk. This risk is related to the marketability of the company's stock. Recall that marketability refers to the speed of trading a security with little change in price. External liquidity measures include the stock's trading volume, trading turnover (proportion of outstanding shares traded during a period of time), its bid-ask spread, and its proportion of institutional ownership.

In summary, the first-pass analysis of the companies making up the department store industry shows Macy's, Dillards, and Kohl's merit strong buy recommendations and Nordstrom a buy recommendation. Macy's and Nordstrom have more financial risk and therefore higher discount rates than do Kohl's and Dillards, but also a higher ROE and expected growth rates in EPS. Sears, J.C. Penney, and Saks appear to be overpriced, with negative profit margin. At certain prices, these stocks could be good values, plus given the industry's past tendency for consolidation, one of them could be the target for acquisition. The next step for an analyst would be to conduct a valuation analysis similar to the one we examined for Macy's.

Qualitative Analysis

The quantitative approach to valuing equity requires estimating EPS, growth rates, capitalization rates, and growth stages. Estimating these values, in turn, requires one to breakdown these variables in term of their components and the factors that determine them: sales, operating cost, interest, depreciation, business risk, and financial risk. It is important to keep in mind that behind these numbers are tangible and intangible real assets—corporate investment machines—that create the next new

EXHIBIT 12.18   SWOT Analysis

1. **Strengths:** What is company's competitive advantage?
   - Strong R&D, strong financial resources, strong buy image, low-cost producers, high quality producer.
2. **Weaknesses:** What are the exploitable advantages of the company's competitors? Is the company doing anything about its weaknesses?
   - Foreign competition, poor financial resources, etc.
3. **Opportunities:** What are the external and internal factors that favor the company?
   - Shrinking competition, favorable exchange rates, new products, new markets, etc.
4. **Threats:** What are the external and internal factors that could hurt the company?
   - Slow economy, government regulations, new entrants, new technology that makes company's product obsolete, etc.

Competitive Strategy Considerations
1. Brand names.
2. Investment in technology to lower cost.
3. Investment in delivery systems.
4. Low-cost leader: Economies of scale, proprietary technology, access to raw material, etc.
5. Differentiated products: Unique marketing, distribution system.

miracle drug, smart phone, computer chip, financial information platform, online store, jumbo plane, energy source, blockbuster movie, sports franchise, consumer product, and skyscraper. Collectively, these companies add value to our lives. An important part in analyzing and valuing a company is to examine the qualitative factors underlying the company's value.

Qualitative analysis of a stock can be done by conducting a SWOT analysis of the company: strengths, weaknesses, opportunities, and threats. The analysis will vary depending on the company and its industry. SWOT can be on the revenue side, such as new markets or patents, or on the cost side, such as improved supply chains. SWOT can be internal, related to the company's management or the quality of its engineers, scientists, and strategic planners, or it can be external, such as the state of the economy, changing taste, or changes in exchange rates. Exhibit 12.18 lists some of the considerations analysts consider when they do SWOT analysis. Bloomberg also provides detailed analysis by industry on its BI screen. This screen provides not only quantitative analysis, but also qualitative assessments of industry drivers and trends provided by some of the top analysts for the industry. Exhibit 12.19 shows BI screens for the pharmaceutical and department store industries.

One of the most respected and successful investor is the well-known Warren Buffett. Exhibit 12.20 summarizes some of Warren Buffett's tenets for investing. Examining these tenets shows his appreciation of both quantitative and qualitative analysis, as well common sense, when it comes to equity investing.

When to Sell

The valuation of stock is generally associated with stock purchases. Once a stock is purchased, however, it needs monitoring and analysis to determine if investors should sell the stock or buy more.

EXHIBIT 12.19   Bloomberg BI Screens

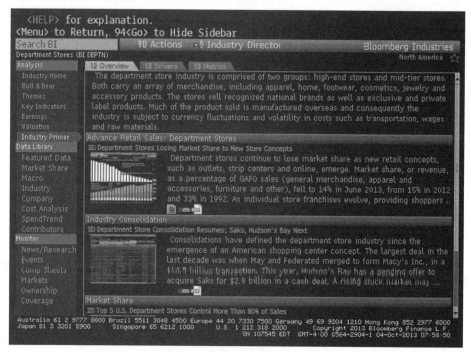

(a)

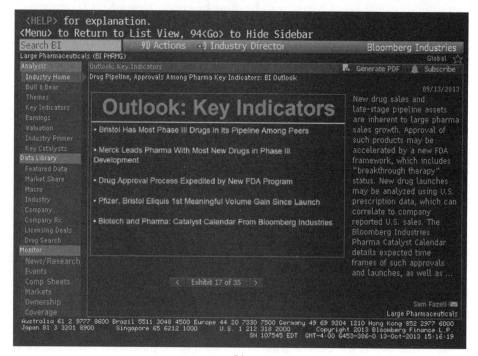

(b)

EXHIBIT 12.20 Warren Buffett Investment Tenets

1. **Business Tenets:**
   - Business is simple.
   - Consistent operating history.
   - Favorable long-run prospects (e.g., the product is needed).
2. **Management Tenets:**
   - Management is rationale.
3. **Financial Tenets:**
   - Focus on ROE
   - Look for good ROE with little or no debt.
   - Look for high profit margins.
   - Look at free cash flow.
4. **Market Tenets:**
   - What is the value of the business?
   - Look at economic value-added model.

As a general rule, the answer to when to sell should be based on the analysis, research, and convictions that convinced the investor to buy the stock in the first place. The key drivers that were identified for buying the stock, such as competitive advantage, reduced cost, or new opportunities, need to be monitored. When they change or weaken, it is time to reevaluate and possibly sell. In general, when a stock approaches its intrinsic value, it may be time to sell and reinvest the funds in another underpriced stock. Macy's, for example, may not continue to pick up market share as we forecasted, or the market may start to value Macy's as we do, driving up its price. These considerations would cause us to reevaluate and possibly change a hold position to a sell one. As a rule, if an investor knows why she bought the stock, she will be able to recognize when to sell it.

Conclusion

In this chapter, we extended our examination of fundamental analysis by looking at the multiplier and DCF approaches to valuing stock. With both models, the important variables to estimate are expected *EPS*, the growth rate in *EPS*, the dividend-payout ratio, the discount rate, and the type of growth: constant, two stage, or three stage. Moreover, quantitative approaches are important because they help us identify the correct questions that need to be asked and answered: What is the required return? What is the *ROE*? What is the investment policy? What are the expected sales? What is the profit margin? We also noted the importance of qualitative stock analysis as a complement to qualitative analysis. Ultimately, the fundamental evaluation of stock requires forming a vision about where the company is headed. Unfortunately, there is no unique approach or analysis of stocks that can give one a crystal ball for predicting where a company will be in the future. What fundamental analysis can do is try to identify the important factors and criteria that are needed in order to make a good assessment. In Chapter 13, we will complete our examination of fundamental analysis by examining the aggregate market and industries.

BLOOMBERG RV AND FA SCREENS AND EXCEL TEMPLATES

Bloomberg RV Screen

- The Bloomberg RV screen can be used to do a relative analysis of companies in terms of valuation, ratios, and earnings. From the Comp source dropdown, you can pull the stocks from indexes, portfolios formed in PRTU, and stocks in the loaded stock's industry or sector. The RV screen can also be customized (Custom Tab, "Create Templates," and click "Save as" tab to save the screen).

Bloomberg FA Screen

- Company income statements, balance sheets, valuation, and other information can be accessed on Bloomberg's FA screen. You can also create customized screens.

Bloomberg: Excel Templates

Bloomberg has a number of Excel templates for conducting fundamental analysis. Use DAPI to see a listing and to download: DAPI <Enter>; Click "Excel Template Library"; Click "Fundamentals." Templates of note include the following:

- Discounted Cashflows Analysis, XDCF.
- Bloomberg Company in Depth Analysis, XIDA.XLS.
- Financial Statements for Equity Indexes, XFAI.XLS.
- Banks Comparison Sheet, XBS.XLS.
- Company Snapshot with Financial Analysis, XCSF.XLS.
- Company In-Depth Fundamentals, XIDS.XLS.
- Company Snapshot with Transparency, XCS4.XLS.
- Fundamental Scoring, XPFS.
- Financial Analysis, XFA.XLS.
- Company Comparison Sheet, XCS.XLS.

     See Bloomberg Web Exhibit 12.2.

Web Site Information

For financial information on securities, market trends, and analysis, see:

- www.Finance.Yahoo.com
- http://www.hoovers.com
- http://www.bloomberg.com
- http://www.businessweek.com

- http://seekingalpha.com
- http://bigcharts.marketwatch.com
- http://www.morningstar.com
- http://free.stocksmart.com
- http://online.wsj.com/public/us

Selected References

Beaver, W., and D. Morse. 1978. What determines price-earnings ratios? *Financial Analysts Journal* 34 (July/August): 65–76.

Copeland, T. E., Tim Koller, and Jack Murrin. 2001. *Valuation: Measuring and Managing the Value of Companies*, 3rd ed. Hoboken, NJ: John Wiley & Sons.

Cottle, Sidney, Roger McMurray, and Frank E. Block. 1988. *Security Analysis*, 5th ed. New York: McGraw-Hill.

Elton, Edwin J., and Martin J. Gruber. "Modern portfolio theory and investment analysis, 1995."

Fama, Eugene, and Kenneth French. 1992. The cross section of expected stock returns. *Journal of Finance* 47 (June): 427–466.

Fairfield, Patricia M. 1994. P/E, P/B, and the present value of future dividends. *Financial Analysts Journal* 50 (July–August): 23–31.

Foster, Earl. 1970. Price-earnings ratios and corporate growth. *Financial Analysts Journal* 26 (January–February): 96–99.

Holt, Charles C. 1962. The influence of growth duration on share prices. *Journal of Finance* 7 (September): 465–475.

Joy, Maurice, and Charles Jones. 1970. Another look at the P/E ratios. *Financial Analysts Journal* 26 (September–October): 61–64.

Johnson, R. S., Lyle Fiore, and R. S. Zuber. 1989. The investment performance of common stocks in relation to their price-to-earnings ratios: An update to the Basu study. *Financial Review* 24 (August).

Malkiel, B., and J. Cragg. 1970. Expectations and the structure of share prices. *American Economic Review* 53, no. 4 (September): 365–381.

Niederhoffer, V., and P. Regan. 1972. Earnings changes, analysts forecasts, and stock prices. *Financial Analysts Journal* 28 (May–June): 65–71.

Peterson, Pamela, and David Peterson. 1996. Company performance measures of value added. Charlottesville, VA.: The Research Foundation of the Institute of Chartered Financial Analysis.

Reilly, Frank, and Keith Brown. 2003. *Investment Analysis and Portfolio Management*, 7th ed. Thomson South-Western: 486–540.

Sorenson, Eric, and David Williamson. 1985. Some evidence on the value of dividend discount models. *Financial Analysts Journal* 41 (November–December): 60–69.

Bloomberg Exercises

1. Using the BI screen (BI <Enter>) select an industry and evaluate it using the following BI Screens:
   - Comp Sheets
   - Key Indicators
   - News/Research
   - Events

- Data library
- Macro

2. Select one of the companies of interest from the industry you analyzed in Exercise 1 and evaluate it by customizing the stock's FA screen. Some customized screens to consider are:
   a. Earnings in terms of sales-per-share and profit margins.
   b. Multipliers: *P/e*, *P/S*, and *P/EBITDA*.
   c. Business Risk: margins.
   d. Financial Risk: leverage ratios.
   e. Liquidity Risk.

3. Conduct a relative analysis of the company you selected in Exercise 2 with its peers by customizing the stocks' RV screen. On the RV screen, select the index for the peers from Comp source dropdown. Some custom screens you may want to consider:
   a. Earnings in terms of sales per share and profit margins.
   b. Multipliers: *P/e*, *P/S*, and *P/EBITDA*.
   c. Business Risk: Operating and profit margins.
   d. Financial Risk: Leverage ratios.
   e. Liquidity Risk.
   f. Growth: Sustainable growth, payout ratios, and ROE.
   g. DuPont Ratios.
   h. Valuation: DDM values and market prices.

4. Select a group of stocks of interest. This could be from a portfolio you have already created, an index ((broad-based or industry/sector specific), or stocks found from a search (EQS).
   a. Conduct a relative analysis of the companies by customizing an RV screen showing the stocks' DDM values, market prices, and economic value added (EVA). Bring up the RV screen for one of the stock's in your group; on the RV screen, pull the other stocks from the Comp source dropdown (portfolio, index, or EQS search); customizes the screen, creating columns for DDM values, *EVA*s, and prices.
   b. Identify the stocks that are underpriced and have positive *EVA*s as possible buy recommendations.
   c. Compare each stock you have identified as a buy recommendation with the analysts' recommendation for that stock found on the stock's EE, ERN, and ANR screens.
   d. Conduct a SWOT analysis of one of your buy stocks. Possible screens you may want to use to obtain information to conduct your SWOT analysis:

      - BI: Bloomberg's BI screen for analysis of the industry.
      - CF: Company's 10-K reports (CF screen found on the stock's screen).
      - SPLC: Supply chain.
      - RSKC: Risk.

- DRSK: Credit risk.
- LITI: Litigation.
- CN: Company news.
- BRC: Company research.

5. Select one of the companies from the group of stocks you analyzed in Exercise 4 (or another stock of interest) and forecast its EPS forward for the next 12 months using the EPS_PE_Estimator Excel program found on the text's web site. See Bloomberg Exhibit box "Bloomberg: EPS_PE_Estimator Excel Program."

6. Screen and search for stocks using the EQS screen that meet some of the Warren Buffett Tenets, such as consistent operating history, good ROE and low debt, high profit margins, good cash position, and high *EVA*s. (see Exhibit 12.20).

    a. Screen by selecting an index and then setting the criteria for your search: market cap, ROE, profit margins, EVA (WACC EVA spread), cash-to-sale ratio exceeding a certain percentage, and the debt/equity ratio being less than a certain percentage.

    b. Analyze the stocks from your search using the RV screen for one of the stocks and importing your search from the Comp Source dropdown. Customize your screen to compare EVA, DDM values, and prices so that you can identify if the stocks are underpriced or overpriced.

7. Detailed Fundamental Analysis: Use Bloomberg to evaluate a stock of interest using fundamental analysis. Include in your analysis:

    (1) Full description of the stock: Include some of the information from the following screens:

• DES	Description
• RELS	Related securities (e.g., debt, preferred stocks)
• CF	Company Filings (10-K)
• HDS	Major holders of the stock
• OWN	Equity Ownership
• SPLC	Supply Chain
• ISSD	Issuer Description
• DDIS	Debt Distribution
• AGGD	Debt Holders
• BRC	Research on Company
• RSKC	Risk
• DRSK	Credit Risk
• LITI	Litigation
• CACS	Corporate Actions
• HRA or Beta	Characteristic Line

    (2) Brief description of the stock's sector trends (Bloomberg BI screen) and comparison of the stock relative to a sector index and the market (SPX). Use Bloomberg's Comp Sheets screen found on the BI platform.

(3) Relative analysis of the company's growth rate. Compare the company's growth rate and its components (retention rate and ROE or DuPont ratios) with a selected index. Use RV, FA, and/or GF.

(4) Relative analysis of the company's risk: liquidity risk, business risk, financial risk, and bankruptcy risk. Use RV, FA, and/or GF.

(5) Relative analysis of the company's *P/e*. Compare the company's historical *P/e* ratio with a peer index and the market (SPX). Use GF.

(6) Use your analysis of growth rates, risk, and relative *P/e* ratios to determine the stock's equilibrium *P/e*.

(7) Make a forecast of the company's *EPS*. Suggestion: $EPS(1 + g)$ or you can try the Excel multiplier program: the EPS_PE_Estimator Excel program.

(8) Compare your forecast with analysts' forecast (EE and ERN screens).

(9) Determine the stock's intrinsic value using the *P/e* multiplier approach: $V = (P/e)(E(eps))$.

(10) Make a forecast of the company's sales per share. Compare your forecast with analysts' forecast (EE and ERN screens).

(11) Determine the stock's intrinsic value using the *P/S* multiplier approach: $V = (P/S)(E(SPS))$.

(12) Determine if the stock is underpriced or overpriced.

(13) Use Bloomberg DDM model to determine the stock's value. Change assumptions from Bloomberg's default assumption if you believe they are warranted. Compare your DDM value with the market price to see if the stock is underpriced or overpriced.

(14) Make a buy, hold, or sell recommendation.

(15) Compare your recommendation with other analysts' recommendations (ANR screen).

(16) Check the news on the stock and comment on your conviction about buying or not buying the stock.

(17) Launchpad: Create a Launchpad with useful screens for analyzing and monitoring your stock and its peers.

8. Excel Exercise: Create Excel tables for analyzing a group of stocks, portfolio, or index using the Bloomberg Excel Add-In. For a guide, see the Bloomberg exhibit box: "Bloomberg Excel Add-In." Possible Excel tables are:
   a. Different Bloomberg *P/e* Ratios: Exhibit 12.2.
   b. Different Multipliers: Exhibit 12.11.
   c. DDM, Price, and Value Added: Exhibit 12.14.
   d. Duration Growth Model: Exhibit 12.15.
   e. DuPont Ratios, Growth: Exhibit 12.16.
   f. Business, Financial, Liquidity, and Bankruptcy Risks: Exhibit 12.16.

9. Excel Exercise: Create an Excel table of time series information needed to conduct a multiplier valuation on a stock of interest using the Bloomberg Excel Add-in. For a guide, see the Bloomberg exhibit box: "Bloomberg Excel Add-In." Variables to consider: *P/e*, *P/S*, *SPS*, profit margins, *EPS*, and *DPS*. See Exhibit 12.4 for a guide.

CHAPTER 13

Market and Industrial Analysis: Top-Down Approach

Introduction

In the last chapter we examined how the values of stocks can be estimated using the multiplier and discounted cash flow models. Our analysis, however, was company/stock specific, with no considerations given to the influences that the overall economy and industry have on a company's stock value. Analysis based just on company analysis is sometimes referred to as *bottom-up analysis*. Many fundamental stock analysts, however, incorporate a *top-down, three-step approach*, in which economic and industry analyses are used as inputs in evaluating a stock. This approach starts with an analysis of the aggregate economy: future gross domestic product, or *GDP* (aggregate output), prices, and the general level of interest rates. The macroeconomic analysis is followed, in turn, by an industry assessment to determine those sectors that will do well given the overall economic outlook. Finally, there is assessment of companies within industries to try to determine those stocks that investors should buy and those they should sell. Many security analysts and academics advocate this top-down approach to stock selection and portfolio management. Their justification is based, in part, on evidence that shows that general economic conditions tend to affect all companies. A recession, for example, not only adversely affects the earnings of bad companies, but also good companies. The top-down approach is also empirically supported: Studies have shown that there is a significantly high percentage of both company and industry earnings that can be attributed to aggregate economic activity.

In this chapter, we extend our examination of fundamental analysis by first looking at aggregate economic and industry factors. Consistent with the top-down approach, we start with a macroeconomic analysis in which we examine how monetary and fiscal policy, global economic conditions, labor and energy costs, and technology impact aggregate output, prices, and interest rates, as well as the impact changes in these factors have on the overall stock market. Next, we look at how industries develop over time and their relationships with each other and with the overall economy. After examining the macroeconomy and industry, we then apply the valuation approach that we examined in Chapter 12 to the valuation of the overall stock market and to an industrial sector. Finally, we conclude the chapter by presenting an example of the management of an equity portfolio that uses a top-down fundamentalist approach.

Macroeconomic Environment

The values of most stocks are affected by macroeconomic factors. Among the determining factors are (1) the overall state of the economy; (2) government policies, such as monetary and fiscal policy; (3) international factors, such as global economic growth and exchange rates; (4) labor, energy, and primary resource costs and technological advances that affect the production side of the economy; and (5) expected inflation and deflation.

Economic Conditions

Economies grow through the saving, investment, and capital formation process. In this process, aggregate output in time period 0, GDP_0, gives rise to a certain level of aggregate savings, S_0, and new capital investment expenditures, I_0; the new level of investment expenditures, in turn, changes the economy's existing capital stock, ΔK (plants, equipment, machines, etc.), and the new level of capital changes the level of aggregate production (shifting to the right, the aggregate supply curve described in macroeconomics), leading to a new level of aggregate output in the next period, GDP_1. The new level of output gives rise to a new savings and investment level, I_1, which changes the capital stock and leads to a new aggregate output level, GDP_2, new investment levels and capital, and so on:

$$GDP_0 \rightarrow S_0 \rightarrow I_0 \rightarrow \Delta K \rightarrow GDP_1 \rightarrow S_1 \rightarrow I_1 \rightarrow \Delta K \rightarrow GDP_2$$

This dynamic investment and capital formation process will lead to economic growth in aggregate output provided the return on capital (that is, the increases in aggregate output resulting from the increases in the economy's capital), creates a level of investment expenditures that is greater than the level needed to replace the economy's depreciated or obsolete capital. For the United States and other industrial countries, the twentieth century is a testimony to how economic growth occurs through the investment and capital formation process: the 1910 model-T Ford to the 2013 Mercedes, from the Wright brothers' first flight to the space shuttle; from Royal typewriters to laptop computers; from Alexander Bell's first telephone to the cell phone. Economies such as that in the United States do experience, however, periodic declines in economic growth. In terms of the investment and capital formation process, economic decline can occur when the levels of investment expenditures are not sufficient to replace depreciated capital. In such a case, there is often a decline in the capital stock and the level of aggregate production. The 1970s was a period of stagnant economic growth. Not only was there recession and inflation—stagflation—brought about by high energy prices, but also the increase in interest rates decreased the aggregate level of investment expenditures to a level in which the United States was not making the necessary investments in its manufacturing facilities (steel plants, automobile facilities, etc.) to maintain its production advantages.

When an economy is expanding, earnings tend to increase and the value of assets and their financial claims tend to rise. In addition, when economies grow, business demand for both short-term assets, such as inventories and accounts receivable, and long-term assets, such as plants and equipment, tend to increase. As a result, companies find themselves issuing new stock and selling more bonds (demanding more loans) to finance the increases in their short-term and long-term capital formation. Aggregate economic growth is also likely to increase both the purchase of cars and homes by household and the number of public projects by municipal government (e.g., roads), augmenting the supply of bonds by financial intermediaries and state and local governments. Thus, the demand for funds tends to increase in periods of economic growth, causing interest rate rates to increase. By contrast, in recessionary periods, earnings tend to decrease and stock values tend to fall. There is also less capital formation, causing rates to decrease.

It should be noted that the direct impact of economic growth on stock value can be explained not only by the growth in *GDP*, but also a wealth effect that often accompanies economic conditions or in some cases precedes economic changes; that is, a country's economic state is measured not only in terms of the aggregate production of final goods and services (i.e., the flow of *GDP*), but also on the value of its assets or aggregate wealth: the value of its equity, real estate, business debt, and government debt. Typically, when economies grow, aggregate wealth also tends to increase, raising stock market values and increasing housing and real estate values (see Exhibit 13.1). Conversely, when economies decline, aggregate wealth also tends to decrease. There are also times when changes in aggregate wealth precede changes in economic growth. For example, in 2008, the decline in real estate values and the subsequent decrease in equity value preceded the slowdown that occurred in the United States and globally.

Government Monetary and Fiscal Policy

Fiscal Policy

Fiscal policy can be defined as government actions that alter the levels of government expenditures and taxes. Expansionary fiscal policy consists of increasing government expenditures or decreasing taxes, and contractionary policy includes decreasing government spending or increasing taxes. Similar to the impact of an increase in investment expenditures, an increase in the level of government expenditures or a decrease in taxes increases aggregate demand, increasing average prices and aggregate output. The extent of the prices and output increases depends on the degree of excess capacity and

EXHIBIT 13.1   GDP and S&P 500, 1970–2013

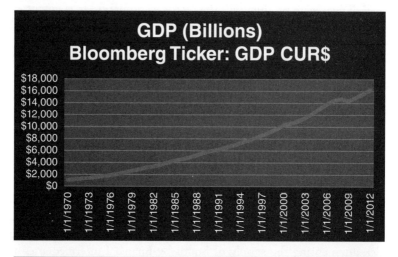

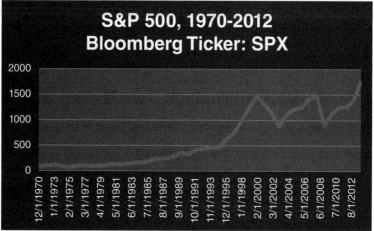

employment in the economy. For example, an economy operating at or near full production capacity with full employment would likely find the impact of an expansionary policy to be inflationary with only a small impact on increasing aggregate output; an economy with high excess capacity and unemployment, however, would likely find the impact of an expansionary fiscal policy to be one of increasing aggregate output without creating inflation.

The Obama administration's fiscal policy stimulants starting in 2008 were aimed at pulling the economy out of the recession and possibly averting a second one. The Administration's fiscal policy actions were on a scale similar to FDR's policies of the 1930s; they included government spending increases as part of the $800 billion American Recovery and Reinvestment Act, increases in direct transfers (food stamps, unemployment insurance, and subsidies to state and local government for Medicaid), and a $600 billion fiscal stimulant that included a two-year payroll tax reduction. The

Obama administration's fiscal actions, however, significantly increased the federal government deficit (government revenue minus government expenditures). The deficit went from $459 billion in 2008 to $1.8 trillion in 2009 and to $1.258 trillion in 2010 before declining to $1.089 trillion in 2012. These deficits, in turn, pushed the U.S. debt from $10.7 trillion in 2008 to $16.4 trillion in 2012 and increased the percentage of debt to *GDP* from 40.5 percent in 2008 to 72.6 percent in 2012 (see Exhibit 13.2). These high debt levels, in turn, led to a temporary credit downgrade,

EXHIBIT 13.2 U.S. Government Deficits, Debt, and Debt/GDP

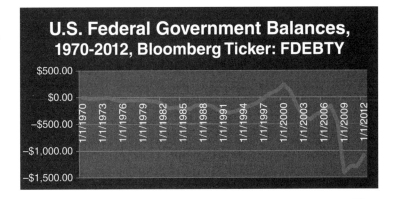

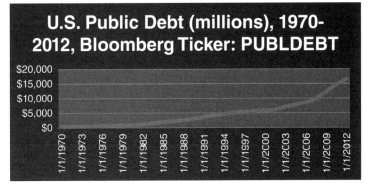

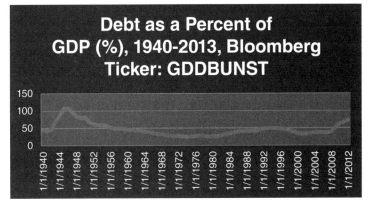

brought into question the U.S. government's ability to continue incurring debt, and raised the possibility of a potentially deeper fiscal crisis in which the United States would have to implement more robust austerity programs.

In the short run, the impact of expansionary fiscal policy depends on the nature of government spending and taxes. Some economists point out that while the size of the U.S. fiscal stimulant in 2008–2012 was large, many of the government expenditures were direct transfer payments that typically have GDP multiplier effects that are smaller and of shorter durations than the multiplier effects resulting from government capital expenditure increases. From 2009 to 2012, the growth rate in the U.S. economy was only 2.2 percent, making it one of the slowest economic recoveries on record—an economic recovery rate that was not able to bring about job growth. At the end of 2012, the unemployment rate was 7.9 percent and underemployment rate was 14 percent.

In the long run, deficit spending can lead to higher interest rates and high inflation once the economy moves back to full capacity. The long-run cost can be a lower steady-state economic growth accompanied by inflation and relatively high equilibrium levels of unemployment. In a seminal work by Reinhart and Rogoff (*This Time Is Different*), the authors found that public debt above 90 percent can reduce average growth rates by more than 1 percent.

Monetary Policy

Technically, monetary policy can be defined as central bank actions that alter the composition of asset holdings in the economy. In the U.S., one of the major monetary tools is an *open market operation* (OMO) in which the Federal Reserve (the Fed) either purchases (expansionary OMO) or sells (contractionary OMO) its holdings of Treasury securities. Such actions change not only the public's holdings of securities, but also the general level of interest rate in the economy. Monetary policy can be either expansionary (increasing the money supply) or contractionary (decreasing the money supply). It can also be consistent with fiscal policy, such as an expansionary monetary/fiscal policy mix in which the deficits resulting from increases in government expenditures and/or tax cuts are financed by the Treasury issuing new debt that is later purchased from the public by the central bank—*monetizing the debt.* Consider, for example, the case of an expansionary OMO in which the Fed buys Treasury securities held by the public. As they try to buy existing Treasury securities, their actions push the price of such securities up and their rates down. As the rate on Treasury securities decreases, investors (those investors selling their Treasuries, as well as other investors), begin to find other securities relatively more attractive. This security preference, in turn, increases the demand for other securities, causing their prices to increase and their rates to decrease. Thus, through a substitution effect, the rates on other securities also tend to fall. Finally, the sellers of Treasury securities deposit their proceeds in banks or financial institutions or use them to buy bank certificates of deposit (CDs); this can lead to an increase in the funds banks and other financial institutions make available for loans, causing lending rates to fall. Thus, the initial impact of an expansionary

OMO is to lower not only the rates on Treasury securities, but also interest rates in general.

Lower interest rates, in turn, tend to increase capital investment expenditures in the economy; that is, lower rates decrease the cost of capital, making more potential investment projects acceptable, and the lower lending rates increase household purchases of new homes and other consumer durables. The increased demand for new capital goods and consumer durables and houses increases the demand for other goods and services, increasing the demand for aggregate output and leading to a higher level of price and aggregate output levels. As with expansionary fiscal policy, the extent to which prices and output increase depends on the degree of excess capacity and the level of unemployment in the economy.

In addition to open market operations and monetizing the debt, the central bank can also affect the level of interest rates by changing the discount rate it charges banks for borrowing and by reducing the amount of reserves banks are required to maintain with them or other banks to secure their deposits. Similar to OMO, these monetary tools change interest rates and the level of capital expenditures, and by so doing change the level of aggregate output demand at any price level, thus shifting the aggregate demand curve.

For an advanced economy, monetary policy can be an effective tool provided interest rates are not too low or too high. Often contractionary policies are implemented when an economy is experiencing inflationary pressures, while expansionary policies are used when the economy is beset by unemployment, excess capacity, and recessionary pressures. Beginning in October of 1979 and extending through October 1982, for example, the Federal Reserve raised the discount rate, increased reserve requirements, and set lower monetary growth targets in an effort to combat high inflation and balance of payments problems in the United States. These actions, in turn, represented a directional change in the Fed's policies from the preceding three-year period in which they maintained lower discount rates and reserve requirements. Even though high energy prices had already contributed to inflation and high interest rates, these contractionary monetary actions served to push rates up even higher. By 1982, rates of Treasury bonds were 10 percent, mortgage rates were 15 percent, the prime rate was 21 percent, and the Dow Jones Average was at 700!

By contrast, the Fed implemented an expansionary monetary policy and undertook extraordinary monetary measures in dealing with the 2008 financial crisis. In an effort to stabilize financial markets and avert a recession in the aftermath of the subprime mortgage meltdown, the Federal Reserve cut interest rates from 4.25 percent at the start of 2008 to 2.00 percent by June 2008.[1] (Other central banks around the world took similar actions by also cutting rates.) The Federal Reserve also took action by pumping billions of dollars into the banking system via new lending programs. In aggregate, these programs provided over $500 billion in lending capacity to U.S. and foreign financial institutions. By September 2008, however, the subprime mortgage meltdown had developed into a global credit crisis, culminating in a dramatic 10-day period from September 7 to September 17: The trillion dollar mortgage giants Fannie Mae and Freddie Mac were placed into conservatorship by the Treasury;

Lehman Brothers filed for the largest bankruptcy in U.S. history ($600 billion); and American International Group received an emergency $85 billion lifeline from the Federal Reserve. During this period, the Federal Reserve took emergency steps by guaranteeing money market funds, backstopping commercial paper programs, coordinating a global interest rate cut with other central banks, making loans to institutions collateralized by mortgage-backed and asset-backed securities, and purchasing such securities as part of their open market operation. Similarly, the Treasury structured the Troubled Asset Relief Program (TARP) to shore up U.S. bank balance sheets with capital injections. The impacts of these unprecedented liquidity measures were to increase the Fed's balance sheet from $850 billion in August to $2.2 trillion in November and to lower rates from their already existing low levels. In fact, short-term Treasury rates were at one point at negative levels, while credit spreads on BBB credits over Treasuries had widened to 7 percent.

From 2009 to 2013, the Fed implemented its *quantitative easing* policy of keeping short-term rates near zero, injecting cash into the financial system, and purchasing mortgage-backed securities and debt from FNMA, FHMC, and GNMA. As part of the quantitative easing policy, the Fed began selling short-term securities and purchasing long-term securities; a policy referred to as *Operation Twist*. These monetary actions all served to stabilize the banking industry, lower intermediate rates, support a fragile housing market, and monetize the U.S. government's debt (see Exhibit 13.3). Similar monetary and fiscal policy actions were also undertaken in other developed countries in which central banks lowered rates, implemented programs to support banks and guarantee assets, and increased their government budgets with fiscal policy stimulants. The recovery, as described by the *Economist* (January 9, 2010) was one in which many governments responded to the crisis by in effect taking the debt burden off the private sector's balance sheet and putting it on their own.

EXHIBIT 13.3   U.S. Monetary Base, 1970–2012

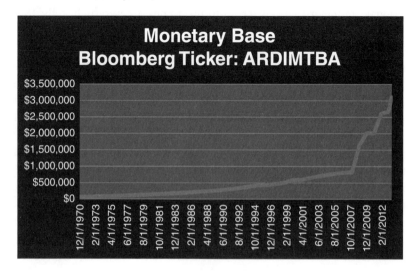

Foreign Sector

For advanced economies, the foreign sector is an important factor in determining aggregate demand, direct investments of multinationals, and corporate revenues and costs. One of the major economic factors contributing to global economic growth over the last three decades has been the economic expansions that have occurred in China, India, and other advanced emerging economies.[2]

The globalization of financial markets over the past 25 years has also led to significant increases in investment flows in and out of countries. For example, China has invested a significant amount of its international currency reserves (U.S. dollars) resulting from its balance of payment surpluses in intermediate-term U.S. Treasury securities.[3] China and other emerging countries also have sovereign-wealth funds that also invest in foreign assets. In China, for example, there is the state-owned China Development Bank that buys foreign assets as a sovereign-wealth fund.

The earnings of multinational companies and the demands for foreign goods and services are also influenced by exchange rates. For a number of subperiods between 2000 and 2013, the dollar prices of the British pound and euro were increasing (*dollar depreciation*). For dollar investors, the dollar depreciations over these periods made investments in foreign securities very attractive, whereas for British pound investors, the dollar depreciation made investments in dollar-denominated assets less attractive. For example, from January 3, 2006, to January 3, 2007, the dollar/British pound exchange rate increased 12.03 percent from \$1.7404/BP to \$1.9498/BP (see Exhibit 13.4). In January 2006, the one-year U.S. Treasury rate was yielding

EXHIBIT 13.4   Exchange Rates, \$/BP and \$/€, 1970–2012

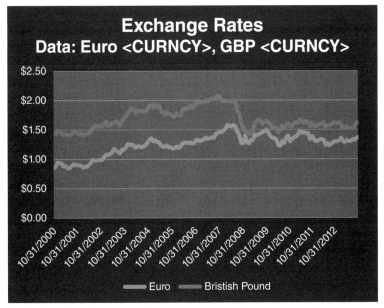

4.46 percent and the one-year British Treasury rate was at 4.30 percent. With perfect foresight, a dollar investor would have earned 17.027 percent from investing in the British Treasury security. To attain 17.027 percent, the investor would have had to convert each of her investment dollars to 1/($1.7404/BP) = 0.57458BP/$ and invested the 0.57458BP at $R_F = 4.46$ percent. One year later, the investor would have 0.6002BP [=0.57458BP (1.0446)], which she would have been able to convert at the spot exchange rate of $1.9498/BP to earn to $1.17027 [=(0.6002BP) ($1.9498/BP)]. Thus, the dollar investment in the foreign security would have yielded a dollar rate of 17.027 percent, compared to the U.S. Treasury yield of 4.30 percent.

$$\text{Rate} = \frac{(\$1.9498/\text{BP})[0.57458\text{BP}(1.0446)]}{\$1} - 1 = \frac{\$1.17027}{\$1} - 1 = 0.17027$$

Note that the same strategy would have yielded a negative rate if implemented on September 9, 2007, when the dollar/British pound exchange rate was at $2.0278/BP£, and then liquidated one year later on September 9, 2008, when the exchange rate was at $1.7543/BP (−13.49 percent).

In contrast, British pound investors would find investing in dollar-denominated assets less attractive when the dollar is depreciating (or the pound is appreciating). For example, from January 3, 2006, to January 3, 2007, a British pound investor would find the British pound/dollar exchange rate (BP/$) decreasing from 0.57458BP/ $ (=1/$1.7404/BP) to 0.512873BP/$ (=1/$1.9498/BP), a 10.74 percent decrease. Such an investor would have seen a loss of 6.90 percent if he were to have converted 1BP to $1.7404, invested the dollar at 4.30 percent for the year to earn $1.8152, and then converted back to pounds at 0.512873BP/$ to receive only 0.93098615BP:

$$\text{Rate} = \frac{[(\$1.7404)(1.043)][0.512873\text{BP}/\$]}{1\text{BP}} - 1 = \frac{0.93098615\text{BP}}{1\text{BP}} - 1 = -0.069$$

In general, when a currency like the dollar is experiencing sustained depreciation, more investment dollars can flow out as global institutional funds try to take advantage of the expected dollar depreciation and less investment dollars can flow in. Just the opposite occurs when the currency is experiencing sustained appreciation.

Exchange rates can also have a significant impact on companies that have foreign markets for their products but who produce domestically and for companies that purchase materials and inputs for manufacturing or who buy goods to be sold from foreign suppliers. For example, an increase in the dollar price of the British pound from $1.50/BP to $2.00/BP would increase the dollar cost of buying British pounds to buy British goods and services denominated in British pound. On the hand, the dollar increase from $1.50/BP to $2.00/BP would lower the British pound price of a dollar from 0.6667BP/$1 to 0.50BP/$1. British consumers and businesses, in turn would find a lower cost of buying dollars to purchase U.S. goods and services denominated in dollars.

Labor and Energy Cost

At an aggregate level, an increase in labor cost, caused by a decline in labor productivity, an increase in average wages and salaries, or an increase in benefits or an increase in the cost of natural resources such as energy, increases the overall cost of producing aggregate output. Producers often try to pass such cost increases onto spenders by increasing prices. At a macroeconomic level, an increase in labor, energy, or other resource production cost can cause aggregate output to decrease and overall prices to increase (in macroeconomics, such cost increases shift the aggregate supply curve to the left). By contrast, a decrease in labor, energy, or resource costs would lead to lower prices and greater aggregate output.

Note that monetary and fiscal policy and exogenous changes in exports affect aggregate demand. As such, they can lead to prices and aggregate output changing in the same direction. In contrast, changes in energy or labor cost affect the production side of the economy, causing opposite changes in prices and output. An increase in energy or labor cost can cause higher prices and lower aggregate output; a decrease in such cost can cause lower prices and greater output. Thus, in the case of cost increases, an economy can experience not only inflationary pressures but also recession. Nobel Laureate Paul Samuelson described such an economic state in which there is both inflation and recession as *stagflation*. The 1970s was a period in which the U.S. economy experienced severe stagflation resulting from the increases in energy prices. Specifically, the price of OPEC oil increased from $3 per barrel in 1972 to approximately $35 per barrel in 1980. These energy price increases led to increases in the overall costs of production (which was passed on in the form of higher prices), lower demand and aggregate output, and higher interest rates (as a result of the higher prices). The U.S. suffered recessions in 1973, 1975, and 1978, with each of the recessions accompanied by increases in the inflation rate. For the decade, the annual inflation rate averaged over 10 percent, the growth rate in real *GDP* for the decade was only 5 percent (by contrast from 1982 to 1995, real *GDP* doubled), and in 1979 the prime rate interest charged by banks was at 15 percent.

The higher energy prices of the 1970s also encouraged greater world oil exploration, the development of alternative energy sources, and the implementation of energy conservation policies. By the mid-1980s, a worldwide oil surplus had developed, which began to bring energy prices down. Energy prices were relatively stable for most of the 1990s. For the period from 1983 to 2004, the average price of crude oil was $22.61, with the range between $10.40 (3/31/1986) and $37.05 (6/31/2004). Since 2004, however, there has been a reversal, with energy prices increasing significantly. In 2012, crude oil prices averaged $96 per barrel for (NYMEX WTI crude oil index), with a range between $79.47 and $109.8 (see Exhibit 13.5). Many economists, in turn, have argued that the economic recovery following the financial crisis was slowed partly because of the rise in oil prices. The higher energy prices from 2004–2012 also encouraged greater energy exploration, the development of alternative energy sources, and a greater adoption of new technologies for extracting energy, such as hydraulic fracturing—fracking.[4]

EXHIBIT 13.5   Crude Oil Prices

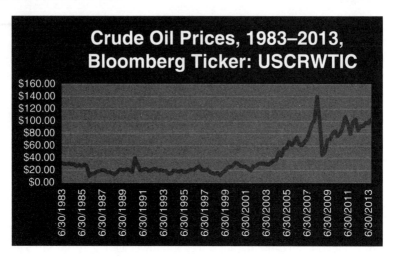

Technological Changes

From 1970 to 2013, America's gross domestic product rose from $1.076 trillion to $16.246 trillion, and the stock market, as measured by the S&P 500, increased from 92.15 in 1970 to 1,703 on 10/11/2013 (see Exhibit 13.1). While some of this extraordinary growth can be explained by expansionary monetary and fiscal policy and energy prices, much can be attributed to the advances in science and technology in such areas as computer technology, genetic engineering, and telecommunications. Over the last 40 years, the U.S. and other developed and emerging economies have evolved into economic engines. The macroeconomic impacts of these advances in technology and science have served to increase the productivity of labor and capital, analytically shifting the economy's aggregate supply. Consistent with a positive supply-side change, the U.S. and other economies has enjoyed over this time period significant growth in *GDP* and relatively stable prices.

Expected Inflation and Deflation

Expected inflation is an important factor influencing investment and consumption demand. If investors expect the prices of consumer goods and services, as well as cars, houses, and other durables, to be higher in the future, they will decrease their holdings and current purchases of fixed-income securities, and possibly equity securities, to buy more consumption goods and consumer durables. This reduction will decrease bond prices and increase yields. The expected inflation may also increase aggregate output if there is excess capital capacity and unemployment. It is also possible in an inflation climate that investors will invest more funds in equity, where they expect the returns on stock to increase with the anticipated inflation rate.

EXHIBIT 13.6 U.S. Inflation Rate

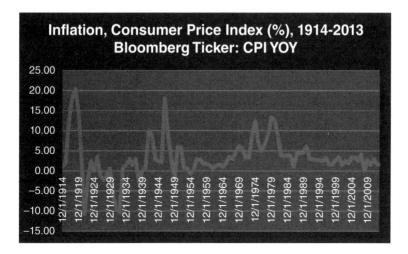

In contrast, when there is an expectation of deflation, consumers and businesses find it advantageous to defer spending in expectation of lower prices for durable and nondurable goods and capital in the future. In the financial markets, expected deflation can increase the holdings and demand for fixed-income securities and possibly the demand for equity. That is, if investors expect the prices on goods and services, cars, houses, and other durables to be lower in the future, they will increase their current purchases of bonds and other securities so that they can buy more consumption goods and consumer durables later, after prices have fallen. It is also possible, that investors will invest fewer funds in equity where they expect the returns on stock to decrease with the expected deflation. The expected deflation is also likely to decrease aggregate output as consumers and businesses cut their current purchases, creating excess capacity and unemployment (see Exhibit 13.6).

Business Fluctuations: Overshooting, Corrections, and Financial Crisis

Although the industrial economies have experienced significant economic growth over the last century, such long-run trends have also been characterized by business cycles in which economies have experienced peaks and troughs as they moved along their long-run growth trend. Economists have debated the cause of business cycles. In his classic 1939 work, the Austrian economist, Joseph Schumpeter, argued that fluctuations are the result of innovations, or the setting into use of new technological advancements. He argued that "what dominates the picture of capitalistic life and more than anything else is responsible for disequilibria is innovation, the intrusion into the system of new production functions."

On a more contemporary level, Schumpter's business cycle theory can be explained in terms of an *overshooting* phenomenon in which businesses have a tendency to overproduce when aggregate demand is high, leading to an excess supply and an equilibrium adjustment in which they have to cut output. On the other hand, businesses have a tendency to underproduce in response to declines in aggregate demand, leading to an excess demand and an eventual equilibrium adjustment in which they increase output. This overshooting phenomenon has also been explained by different financial lending and investing behaviors during different economic periods: when the economy is expanding, financial institutions tend to extend credit more liberally and investors tend to buy more securities, resulting in more loans, investments, and ultimately overproduction and overpriced asset values; when the economy is declining, financial institutions tend to tighten credit and investors tend to curb their investments, which results in underproduction and underpriced asset values. Thus, banks, financial institutions, and investors, by their lending and investing behaviors, tend to exacerbate the current economic trend, leading to an overshooting of the trend.

Many economists argue that the 2008 financial crisis and recession were a correction to a major overshooting of the U.S. and world economies. From 2000 to 2006, expansionary U.S. monetary actions, the uncontrolled expansion of derivatives and securitization, and the liberal credit policies by financial institutions led to excessive overshooting, especially in the housing industry. Prior to 2000, most potential homebuyers who did not meet strict qualification standards were denied loans. As a result, most mortgages were considered prime. In 2000, the Mortgage Bankers Association estimated that 70 percent of all loans were prime conventional, 20 percent were FHA-insured loans, 8 percent were VA-insured, and 2 percent were subprime. With the combination of the growth in securitization, the push by Congress to increase home ownership, and the introduction of innovative mortgage loans such as teasers, stretch loans, piggyback loans, and stated income loans, subprime mortgages accelerated from 2000 to 2006. In 2006, the Mortgage Bankers Association estimated that 70 percent of all mortgage loans were conventional, with 17 percent of those being subprime. As a rule, if property values increase, subprime borrowers are in a position to sell their properties and payoff their loans. Unfortunately, the real estate market, which had been accelerating since 2001, cooled in 2006 when a number of the innovative loans were reset at higher rates that many borrowers could not make. This led to defaults, bankruptcies, the decline in property values, and ultimately the collapse of the subprime market and the beginning of the financial crisis of 2008.

After the recession ended in mid-2009, U.S. *GDP* grew at an annualized rate of just 2.2 percent from 2009 to 2012. The slow recovery rate from the collapse of the real estate market in the United States is consistent with recovery rates from previous financial crises. Normally, recoveries from financial crises such as Japan's asset bubble, the 1980's emerging market crisis, or the 1930's stock market crash take longer than so-called V-shaped recoveries following cyclical recessions. From 2009 to 2012, the growth in the residential real estate market was sluggish. In 2013, however, the housing market did begin to pick up, with new home sales increasing to their highest level since 2008, housing inventories approaching an eight-year low, new construction increasing, foreclosures decreasing, housing prices starting to increase, and credit relaxing. See Exhibit 13.7 for housing trend indicators.

EXHIBIT 13.7   U.S. Housing Industry Indicators

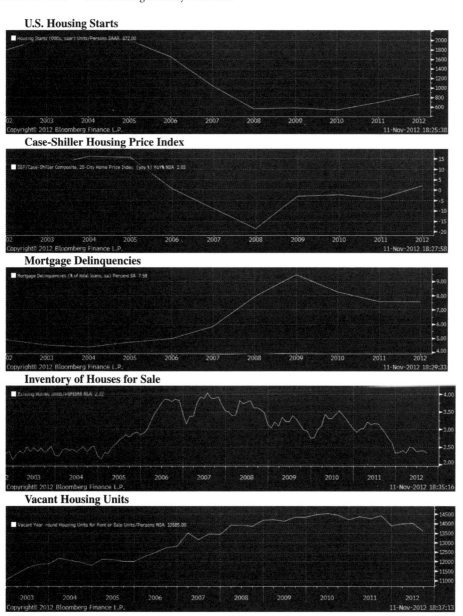

Corporate Earnings and Cash Positions

Often during periods of slow economic growth, and even recession, the earnings of many corporations are positive and their cash positions relatively large. This was the case for many companies during the slow economic recovery period from 2008 to 2012. The positive corporate earnings can be attributed to workforce reductions and to lower interest rates that had reduced corporate borrowing costs. During this period, many firms also reduced their investment expenditures. This decrease, coupled with earnings increases, resulted in significant increases in corporate cash positions. Many U.S. companies become net suppliers of funds instead of net users. As of June 2012, S&P 500 firms had approximately $900 billion of cash, 40 percent higher than their holdings in 2008 (see Exhibit 13.8). In 2012, GE reported that they expected to have $100 billion in cash holdings over the next few years, which they, in turn, estimated would be sufficient to finance their new investments, acquisitions, and share buybacks. Similar phenomena were also occurring in 2012 in other countries, such as Japan, Britain, and Canada, where corporate liquidity holdings had increased.

The large corporate cash positions also reflected an economic environment of uncertainty, leading, in turn, to lower levels of corporate investments. For investors, the large cash position of corporations creates uncertainty: On the one hand, large cash positions—liquid wealth—represents the potential for future corporate investments; on the other hand, large cash positions are also an indicator of a lack of

EXHIBIT 13.8   S&P 500 Financials: Cash per Share, Profit Margins, EPS, and Return on Equity

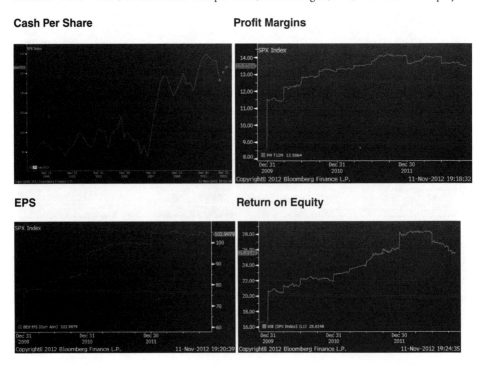

corporate investments—*dead money*—that could possibly lead to lower growth rates in earnings–per-share (*EPS*) in the future.

BLOOMBERG ECONOMIC INFORMATION AND DATA

Bloomberg Data Copied to Clipboard

The economic data in the exhibits in this section were copied into a clipboard on the Bloomberg's GP graph and imported into Excel. On the Bloomberg QP screen, right-click to "Copy/Export Options" and click "Copy Data to Clipboard."

Bloomberg Economic Information Screens

ECOF	Macroeconomic information (inflation, employment, economic indicators, housing prices) by country and region.
ECO	Calendar of economic releases.
WECO	World economic calendar and economic indicators.
FOMC	Information on policy changes of the Federal Open Market Committee.
FED	Calendar of Federal Reserve releases.
ECST	Key economic statistics by country.
EIU	Economist Intelligence Unit.
IECO	Global comparison of economic statistics.
BRIEF	Daily Economic Newsletter.
AV	Bloomberg's media links.
CENB	Central Bank menu: Use to access platforms of Central Banks.
ECB	European Central Bank portal.
BOE	Bank of England portal.
GGR	Finds global summary of government bill and bond rates for countries.
YCRV	Finds current and historical yield curves for government and corporate bonds.
IYC	Finds yield curves for different countries using IYC.
CG	Curve graph: Finds difference curves.

Bloomberg Economic Indicators

The statistic series for many economic variables can be accessed from ECOF, ECST, and other economic screens. Many of the series can be analyzed further by going to the series menu page: Ticker <Index> <Enter>; clicking Description, GP, or other screens.

Bloomberg: Excel Templates for Economic Analysis

Bloomberg has a number of Excel templates for conducting economic analysis. Use DAPI to see a listing and to download: DAPI <Enter>; Click "Excel Template Library"; Click "Economics." Templates of note:

(Continued)

- Country Risk Assessment, XCRA.XLS.
- Economic Forecast, XECF.XLS.
- Custom Economic Forecast, XCEF.XLS.
- Emerging Market Overview, XEEM, XLS.
- Granger Causality Tests, XGCS.XLS.

Economic Indicators

Economies over time do experience peaks and troughs. Given the importance of the economy to stock prices, many security analysts follow a number of economic indicators to try to predict such trends.

There are three types of indicators: *leading, coincident,* and *lagging.* The leading economic indicators are economic series that reach their peaks and troughs before aggregate economic activity reaches its peak or trough. In using leading indicators, analysts often use a *composite indicator* (e.g., an average of all the leading indicators) and diffusion indexes. A *diffusion index* measures how pervasive the economic trend is. An example of such an index is the percentage of companies reporting higher orders. This index can be combined with a leading indicator such as new orders and the composite leading indicator to determine both the direction and breadth of the movement. Coincident indicators include time series that have peaks and troughs that roughly coincide with the peaks and troughs of the business cycle. Lagging indicators, in turn, include time series that experience their peaks and troughs after the economy does. Country economic indicators can be accessed from Bloomberg's ECO, ECST, and ECOF screens. Exhibit 13.9 shows the trends in the components of leading economic indicators from 2003 to 2012.

It should be noted that no leading index can be expected to be a perfect predictor of future economic activity. Also, there are numerous political and economic events that occur that can significantly influence an economy that are not incorporated in economic time series. Given these limitations, one should always be aware that there are times when a series can give a false signal.

Leading Indicators of the Stock Market

As noted previously, the 2.2 percent growth rate in the U.S. economy from 2009 to 2012 represented one of the slowest economic recoveries on record—an economic recovery rate that had not been able to bring about job growth. In the fourth quarter of 2012, the U.S. unemployment and underemployment rates still remained high, with unemployment at 7.9 percent and underemployment at 14 percent. In contrast, however, the S&P 500 was trading at 1,426 at the end of 2012 and around 1,700 in October of 2013. The 1,700 level represented a 131 percent increase from the S&P 500's low of 735 in October 2008, with the market regaining and surpassing the value

EXHIBIT 13.9   Leading Economic Indicators—Components

Jobless Claims

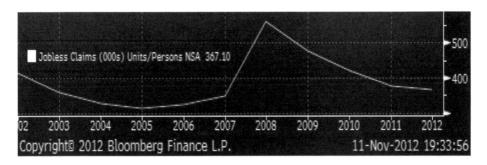

New Orders Consumer

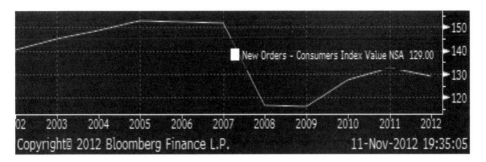

New Orders Capital

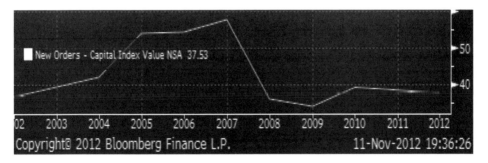

Building Permits

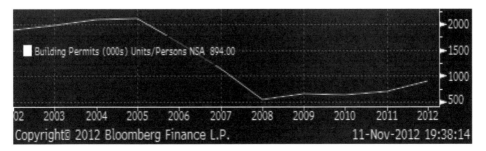

it had lost when it plunged 53 percent from its 2007 S&P high of 1,549 in late 2007 to its low of 735 in October 2008.[5] This bullish market was, in turn, leading the overall economy.

The stock market has historically been a leading indicator of the economy. Given this, a pertinent question for equity investors is: What is a leading indicator of the stock market? For years, changes in the money supply were thought to lead the stock market. In their book *Monetary History of the United States*, Friedman and Schwartz reported that declines in the rate of growth of the money supply consistently preceded business contractions, in some cases as much as 20 months, whereas increases in the rate of growth of the money supply consistently preceded economic expansions.[6] A study by Moore and others, however, found that monetary changes actually lag the stock market. These studies suggest that the market looks at leading indicators of monetary changes or looks at events or Fed announcements in an effort to portend changes in the money supply. If this is the case, then the market would respond to the anticipated changes in the money supply.[7] Some analysts believe that a possible leading stock market indicator is the ratio of the composite of coincident index to the composite lagging index. This index is thought to be a leading indicator of the leading economic indicators.[8]

BLOOMBERG ECONOMIC INDICATORS

Economic indicators can be found on Bloomberg's ECOF and ECST screens. Bloomberg's ECO screen provides information on past, current, and future releases of economic information.

See Bloomberg Web Exhibit 13.1.

Industry Analysis

Industry analysis is the next step in the top-down, three-step approach to fundamental stock analysis. In evaluating industries, it is important to note that if there is little difference in the performance among different industries, then there is no need to study industries. If the aggregate stock market, for example, is expected to generate a 10 percent rate of return, while the returns among all industries only range between 9 percent and 11 percent, then there would not be much purpose in conducting an industry analysis: One could get a 12 percent expected return by just randomly selecting industries. Studies of industrial performance, however, do show a wide dispersion in the rates of return among industries. This suggests industry analysis is important. Moreover, it is easier to find a stock from a good industry than to find a good stock from a bad or declining industry.

From an investment perspective, the identification of good industries comes from finding those sectors whose expected returns exceed their required returns. As a starting point, it is helpful to understand the nature of the industry in terms of its current stage of development and its interrelationship with other industries in the economy, as well as its relationship with the overall economy.

Stages of Industrial Development

Industrial organizational theory describes industries in terms of the five stages of development that define the typical industry's life cycle. These stages include pioneering, rapid accelerating growth, mature growth, stabilization, and deceleration and decline.

Pioneering Stage: This is the start-up stage of the industry. It is the stage in which firms in the industry are just beginning to identify their markets. The stage is characterized by high development costs, small or modest sales, and small or negative profit margins. Examples of the pioneering stage would be the car industry at the beginning of the twentieth century or the computer industry in the 1950s.

Rapid Accelerating Growth Stage: In this stage, the market for the industry starts to develop. From a low sales base, sales begin to increase at an increasing rate, often resulting in excess demand for the industry's product. During this phase, firms in the industry respond to their growing market by developing their production capacity. The rapid accelerating growth stage is characterized by high profit margins, with profit increasing significantly from a low sales base. The car industry in the 1950s, the computer industry in the 1970s, and the Internet and biotech industries of the 1990s would be examples of this second stage of industry development.

Mature Growth Stage: This is a stage in which sales continue to increase, but not at an accelerating rate. From a relatively high sales base, sales growth tends to be above the growth rate of the economy, but below the rates experienced in the previous stage. For example, if the economy were growing at 5 percent, the industry might be growing between 7 percent and 10 percent during this stage. The mature growth stage is the period when the industry's profit attracts other firms into the industry. The increased competition resulting from the entry of new firms often causes prices to decrease in the industry during this time, lowering profit margins. The greater competition also may lead to increases in advertising expenditures and other costs related to differentiating a firm's product or to constraining entry of new firms into the industry.

Stabilization Stage: This is a stage where the industry reaches an equilibrium in which the number of firms in the industry is set, demand is stable, and production capacity is at a level to meet demand. In this stage, the industry growth rate matches that of the economy and profit margins are tight but stable. For many industries, the stabilization stage is the longest period in their life cycle.

Deceleration and Declining Growth Stage: In this stage, the industry's sales growth may increase at a decreasing rate or decline. It is a period in which there is a switch in demand brought about by better substitutes (e.g., home computers and word processing software for typewriters or cars for horses).

As we discussed in Chapter 11, finding a good company in a good industry does not necessarily mean that the stock of that company is a good investment. A good company in a growing industry may be experiencing high sales and profit margins, but it could also be selling at a price that yields a return below its required return; that is, the good company's stock could be overpriced.

Interindustry and Interfirm Relations: Supply Chain

Macroeconomic analysis is concerned with what determines broad aggregates: total output, total employment, total investment, and overall prices. In the 1930s, Wassily Leontief developed a general theory of production based on economic interdependence and later gave his theory empirical content by developing the first input-output model.[9] Today, the interindustry and interfirm relations are captured by supply-chain models.

Exhibit 13.10 shows Bloomberg's supply chain chart (SPLC) for Apple Inc. Examining Apple's supply chain, we find the company has 255 suppliers, 149 customers, and three peers (based on Bloomberg's Mobile Handset Manufacturers Index (BRMOB-HVP). Suppliers are sorted in decreasing order by the percentage of their revenue generated from Apple. As shown in the exhibit, Cirrus Logic generates 77 percent of its revenue from Apple. Apple's customers are sorted in descending order by the percentage of their cost paid to Apple. As shown, 24.81 percent of Verizon's costs of goods sold are paid to Apple, and 21.11 percent of AT&T's costs of goods sold are paid to Apple. The lower screen of Exhibit 13.10 shows the supply chain table for Apple. The table shows Cirrus Logic with a market cap $1.62 billion and a projected sales growth of 17.32 percent, with 77 percent of its revenue coming from Apple. Cirrus designs and manufactures precision integrated circuits. The company, in turn, has seven suppliers and 14 customers, with one of its principal suppliers being United Microelec. It is interesting to note that over the four-year period from 10/30/2009 to 9/30/2013, the total return from Apple stock was an impressive 159.96 percent (annualized return of 27.59 percent). Even more impressive, however, was the total return from the less well-known Cirrus Logic stock of 368.18 percent (annualized return of 48.25). See Exhibit 13.11.

> **BLOOMBERG SUPPLY CHAIN ANALYSIS, SPLC**
>
> Bloomberg's SPLC platform provides a comprehensive supply chain breakdown for a selected company. You can analyze revenue and cost for a loaded company, its suppliers,

and its customers. You can also access functions that allow you to further analyze the performance of the selected company or peer companies.

- **Loaded Company** appears in the middle of the screen. The values in the central company box allow you to see how much of the company's spending and revenue has been quantified, as well as how much of the relationship data is based on proprietary Bloomberg analysis. This allows you to see what percentage of the company's supply chain is accounted for in the analysis, as well as how much of the data from the analysis is not available from other sources.
- **Suppliers** are listed vertically along the left side of the screen and represent the companies that receive revenue from the loaded company under analysis. The Rev percentages in each company box indicate the percentage of total revenue that the supplier company receives from the central company. The COGS, CAPEX, and SG&A percentages indicate the percentage of total spending that the loaded company paid to the supplier in cost of goods sold, capital expenditures, and selling, general, and administrative, respectively. You can click the up or down arrows to display more suppliers.
- **Customers** are listed vertically along the right side of the screen and represent the companies from which the loaded company under analysis receives revenue. The Rev percentages of revenue in each company box indicate the percentage of total revenue that the central company receives from the customer. The COGS, CAPEX, and SG&A percentages indicate the percentage of spending that the customer company paid to the central company in cost of goods sold, capital expenditures, and selling, general, and administrative, respectively. You can click the up or down arrows to display more customers.
- **Peers** appear across the bottom of the screen and represent the companies in the same competitive peer group as the loaded company under analysis. You can click the left or right arrow to display more competitors.
- **Control Area**: The tabs at the top of the screen allow you to adjust the data parameters, as well as display your data using different formats and sorting options. The toolbar at the top of the screen allows you to create supply chain alerts, set up supply chain monitors, and display company case studies. The menus and buttons below the toolbar allow you to select display options, the relationship between the companies that appear, and company filters.

See Exhibit 13.10.

Aggregate Stock Market Analysis and Valuation

The objective of aggregate stock market analysis is to estimate the intrinsic value and expected rate of return of a major market series such as the S&P 500 using the discounted cash flow (DCF) or multiplier approaches that we examined in Chapter 12. Using the multiplier approach, this would require estimating the expected price of the index based on forecasting its EPS and estimating its price-to-earnings ratio (*P/e*) ratio.

EXHIBIT 13.10   Bloomberg Supply Chain for Apple Inc., 10/21/2013

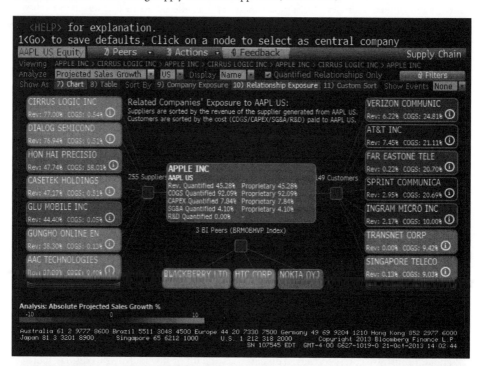

EXHIBIT 13.11   Total Return, Apple Inc. and Cirrus Logic, 10/30/2009–9/30/2013

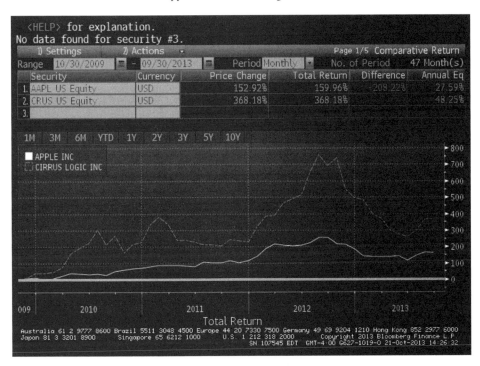

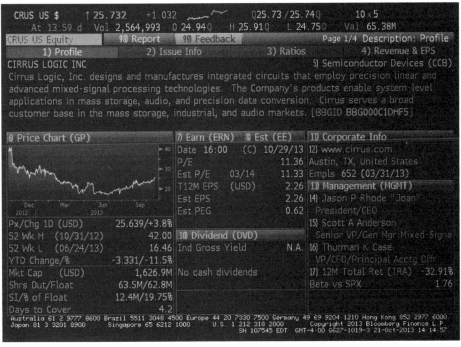

Example: Intrinsic Value and EPS Forecast of the S&P 500

Exhibit 13.12 shows annual data from 2000 to 2012 for the S&P 500 for sales per share (*SPS* or *S*), *EPS*, dividends per share (*DPS*), dividend-payout ratio (*D/E*), profit margin (*EPS/S*), *P/e* ratios, and the S&P 500 index values. Exhibit 13.13, in turn, shows macroeconomic data on *GDP*, capital capacity, industrial production in manufacturing, and personal consumptions expenditures. The sales, *DPS*, *EPS*, and *P/e* data were accessed from Bloomberg's FA and GF screens, and the economic information was pulled from Bloomberg's ECST screens.

As shown in Exhibit 13.12, *EPS* for the S&P 500 increased each year from 2001 to 2006, followed by three years of decreases in the aftermath of the 2008 financial crisis, reaching $61.94 per share in 2009. The index then increased again each year from 2009 to 2012, reaching $103.81 in 2012. From 2000 to 2012, the average annual percentage change in *EPS* was 5.92 percent, with a relatively large standard deviation of 15.73. During this period, *GDP* increased from $10.29 trillion in 2000 to $16.244 trillion in 2012 (see Exhibit 13.13). The average percentage change in *GDP* (3.9%) was smaller than the changes in *EPS* (5.92%), and the fluctuations in *GDP* (standard deviation of 2.37%) over this period were smaller than the fluctuation in *EPS* (15.73%).

The disparity in fluctuations in *EPS* and *GDP*, suggests that *EPS* cannot be explained solely in terms of the aggregate economy. As we examined in Chapter 12, many analysts forecast the individual components of *EPS* instead of forecasting *EPS* directly in terms of *GDP* or some other economic aggregate. One approach, discussed in Chapter 12, is to estimate *EPS* by forecasting sales based on an economic forecast and profit margins–based on economic productivity.

A first-pass forecast made by the author on 12/31/2012 of *EPS* for the S&P 500 series for the next year (12/31/2013), along with an estimate of the *P/e* ratio and intrinsic value of the index as of 12/31/2012, is shown in Exhibit 13.14. The forecast for *EPS* is based on projecting sales and the profit margin, and the estimate of the *P/e* ratio is based on the Gordon-Williams model.

1. **Sales:** The first row in Exhibit 13.14 shows projected *SPS* increasing by 6.74 percent from $1,098.99 per share on 12/31/2012 to $1,173.06 per share on 12/31/2013. The *SPS* projection is based on a forecasted 4.5 percent increase in *GDP* and on the following estimated relationship between the proportional change in *SPS* and the proportional change in *GDP*:

$$\Delta S/S = -0.0581 + 2.7896(\Delta GDP/GDP)$$

Proportional Δ Sales per Share	Coefficients	*t* Stat
Intercept	−0.05805	−2.3611773
Δ GDP/GDP	2.789567	5.12313908
R Square	0.724112	
Observations	12	

EXHIBIT 13.12 S&P 500: Sales, *EPS*, *DPS*, Profit Margin, Payout, and *P/e* Ratio

Date	Sales per Share	Proportional Change	EPS	Proportional Change	Profit Margin EPS/Sales	DPS	Dividend Payout DPS/EPS	P/e	S&P 500	Proportional Change
12/29/00	$622.21		$58.85		0.09458	$15.816	0.26875	22.44	1320.28	
12/31/01	$624.48	0.0036	$52.98	−0.0997	0.08484	$15.532	0.29316	21.67	1148.08	−0.1304
12/31/02	$622.90	−0.0025	$55.22	0.0423	0.08865	$15.713	0.28455	15.93	879.82	−0.2337
12/31/03	$668.22	0.0728	$61.78	0.1188	0.09245	$17.273	0.27959	18.00	1111.92	0.2638
12/31/04	$763.60	0.1427	$69.41	0.1235	0.09090	$19.959	0.28756	17.46	1211.92	0.0899
12/30/05	$886.48	0.1609	$76.07	0.0960	0.08581	$22.468	0.29536	16.41	1248.29	0.0300
12/29/06	$921.64	0.0397	$90.41	0.1885	0.09810	$25.131	0.27796	15.69	1418.30	0.1362
12/31/07	$978.72	0.0619	$89.09	−0.0146	0.09103	$28.388	0.31865	16.48	1468.36	0.0353
12/31/08	$1,032.22	0.0547	$71.79	−0.1942	0.06955	$28.462	0.39646	12.58	903.25	−0.3849
12/31/09	$888.65	−0.1391	$61.94	−0.1372	0.06970	$23.593	0.38089	18.00	1115.10	0.2345
12/31/10	$961.91	0.0824	$85.39	0.3786	0.08877	$23.595	0.27632	14.73	1257.64	0.1278
12/30/11	$1,059.70	0.1017	$99.14	0.1610	0.09355	$26.616	0.26847	12.69	1257.60	0.0000
12/31/12	$1,098.99	0.0371	$103.81	0.0471	0.09446	$31.970	0.30797	13.74	1426.19	0.1341
Average	$856.13	0.05132	$75.07	0.0592	0.08788	$22.655	0.30275	16.60	1212.83	0.0252
Standard Deviation	$175.73	0.07759	$17.03	0.1573	0.00888	$5.469	0.04088	3.01	182.69	0.1906

Bloomberg: *EPS* = Best *EPS*; Sales = Best Sales; *P/e* = Best *P/e*

Bloomberg *P/e* Ratio Calculations:

Date	PE_RATIO	BEST_PE_RATIO	EST_PE_NEXT_YR_AGGTE
12/29/2006	16.606	15.688	14.4147
12/31/2007	17.3435	16.4823	14.2991
12/31/2008	15.3955	12.5819	11.6914
12/31/2009	18.2208	18.0017	14.1652
12/31/2010	15.0866	14.7281	12.9394
12/31/2011	12.7557	12.6854	11.6019
12/31/2012	14.1222	13.7382	12.4442

- **PE_RATIO**: Price of a stock as last price by trailing 12-month EPS.
- **BEST_PE_RATIO**: Ratio calculated by dividing the price of the security by BEst (Bloomberg Estimates) earnings per share.
- **EST_PE_NEXT_YR_AGGTE**: Index estimated P/e (price/earnings) next year. Calculated as Last Price divided by estimated index earnings next year.

(*Continued*)

EXHIBIT 13.12   (*Continued*)

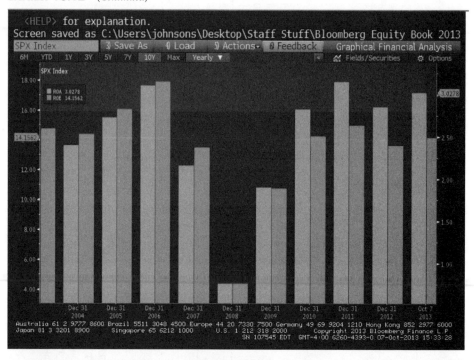

EXHIBIT 13.13 Macroeconomic Data: GDP, Capacity Utilization, Industrial Production, and Personal Consumption Expenditures

Date	GDP (billion)	Proportional Change	Capacity Utilization Index	Industrial Production Manufacturing Index	Personal Consumption Expend., PCE (billions)	PCE Per Capita	Proportional Change
12/29/00	$10,289.70				$6,989	$26,608	
12/31/01	$10,625.30	0.03262	73.80	−5.00	$7,190	$27,188	0.02180
12/31/02	$10,980.20	0.03340	75.30	2.60	$7,549	$28,363	0.04322
12/31/03	$11,512.20	0.04845	76.60	1.70	$7,970	$29,711	0.04753
12/31/04	$12,277.00	0.06643	79.00	3.90	$8,514	$31,356	0.05537
12/30/05	$13,095.40	0.06666	79.90	3.30	$9,021	$32,399	0.03326
12/29/06	$13,857.90	0.05823	80.00	2.50	$9,508	$33,994	0.04923
12/31/07	$14,480.30	0.04491	80.40	2.10	$9,941	$35,211	0.03580
12/31/08	$14,720.30	0.01657	73.20	−14.60	$9,737	$35,803	0.01681
12/31/09	$14,417.90	−0.02054	69.50	−3.30	$10,001	$35,687	−0.00324
12/31/10	$14,958.30	0.03748	75.40	6.80	$10,438	$36,781	0.03066
12/30/11	$15,533.80	0.03847	77.10	3.90	$10,887	$37,981	0.03263
12/31/12	$16,244.60	0.04576	77.50	3.20	$11,301	$39,727	0.04597
Average	$13,307.15	0.03904	76.48	0.59	$9,157	$33,139	0.03409
Standard Deviation	$1,984.59	0.02370	3.25	5.74	$1,414	$4,234	0.01637

Source: Bloomberg; Tickers: GDP CUR$; Capacity = CPTI CHNG; Ind. Prod. = IPM GYOY; PCE = PCE CUR$; PCE per Capita = PIDSDPC

515

EXHIBIT 13.14 Valuation and Forecast of S&P 500

	2012 12/31/12	2013 12/31/13	Reason
(1) Sales (S)	$1,098.99	$1,173.06	2013 Forecast: $\Delta GDP/GDP = 0.045$
			$\Delta S/S = -0.0581 + 2.7896(\Delta GDP/GDP) = 0.0674$ $S_{13} = (1 + \Delta S/S)S_{12}$ $S_{13} = (1 + 0.0674)(\$1,098.99) = \$1,173.06$
(2) Profit Margin $m = EPS/S$	9.49%	9.08%	• Operating profit margins will decrease marginally • Economy from 2012 to 2013 will continue to increase its capacity utilization rate (77.5% to 77.8%) but industrial manufacturing will stay at its 2012 level of 3.2%.
			$m = -0.01979 + 0.001393$ (Capacity Utilization) $+ 0.00077$ (Industrial Production Manufacturing Index) $m = -0.01979 + 0.001395(77.5) + 0.00077(3.2) = 0.0908$
(3) EPS	$103.81	$106.52	$EPS_{13} = m_{13} S_{13}$ $EPS_{13} = (0.090802) (\$1,173.06) = \$106.52$
(4) Payout Ratio (d/e)	0.30797	0.3027	Dividend payout will equal its 12-year average of 0.3027
(5) DPS	$31.97	$32.24	$DPS_{13} = (d/e)_{13} EPS_{13}$ $DPS_{13} = (0.3027) (\$106.52) = \$32.24$
(6) g		8.5%	• Increase in retention ratio from 69.20% to 69.73% • Increase in ROE from 11.4% to 12.19% • Projected sustainable growth: $g = (0.6973)(0.1219) = 0.085$
(7) k_e	10.486%	10.5%	Estimated market rate in 2013 will increase slightly from 10.486% to 10.5%.
(8) P/e	15.135	15.135	Estimate based on Gordon-Williams model and the estimates of d/e, g, and k_e: $\frac{P}{e} = \frac{d/e}{k_e - g} = \frac{0.3027}{0.105 - 0.085} = 15.135$
(9) Value, V	1,612	1,749	$V_t = (P/e)E(EPS_t)$ $V_{12} = (15.135)(\$106.52) = 1,612$ $E(EPS_{14}) = E(EPS_{13})(1 + g) = (106.52)(1.085) = 115.57$ $V_{13} = (15.135)(115.57) = 1,749$
(10) Market Price	1,426		Market underpriced by 11.54% ($= (1,426/1,612) - 1$)
(11) Expected Rate, E(R)		24.91%	Expected price equal to estimated intrinsic value of 1,749 $E(R) = [(1,749 + 32.24)/1,426] - 1 = 0.2491$
(12) Expected Rate, E(R)		15.30%	Expected price equal to current intrinsic value of 1,612 $E(R) = [(1,612 + 32.24)/1,426] - 1 = 0.1530$

Buy Recommendation: Market underpriced, so increase the investment fund's equity allocation.

The sales and *GDP* relation was estimated by regressing data on the proportional change in *SPS* of the S&P 500 series against proportional changes in *GDP* from 2000 to 2012 (see Exhibit 13.13). The forecast of a 4.5 percent increase in *GDP*, in turn, was based on a composite of forecasts:

$$\Delta S/S = -0.0581 + 2.7896(\Delta GDP/GDP)$$
$$\Delta S/S = -0.0581 + 2.7896(0.045) = 0.0674$$

$$S_{13} = S_{12}(1 + \Delta S_t/S)$$
$$S_{13} = \$1,098.99(1.0674) = \$1,173.06$$

2. **Profit Margin**: As shown in the second row of Exhibit 13.14, the forecast projects a small decrease in the profit margin from 9.49 percent to 9.08 percent. For this forecast, profit margins for the market were assumed to be determined by the overall economy's capacity utilization rate (i.e., the percentage of total plant and equipment capacity that is in use (Bloomberg ticker = CPTI CHNG) and by industrial manufacturing productivity, as measured by the U.S. Industrial Production Groups Manufacturing index (Bloomberg ticker = IPMGYOY). Historically, as the economy's capacity utilization rate increases, profit margins have tended to increase at a decreasing rate, with the margins leveling off around the 80 percent capacity utilization rate. The regression coefficient for profit margin was estimated by regressing the profit margin against capacity utilization and the industrial manufacturing index from 2000 to 2012:

$$m = -0.01979 + 0.001395 \text{ (Capacity Utilization)}$$
$$+ 0.00077 \text{ (Industrial Production Manufacturing Index)}$$

Profit Margin	Coefficients	*t* Stat
Intercept	−0.01979	
Capacity Utilization	0.001395	2.55735
Industrial Production Manufacturing Index	0.00077	2.49379
R Square	0.76885	
Observations	12	

The projected profit margin of 9.08 percent is based on an assessment that the economy from 2012 to 2013 would continue to increase its capacity utilization rate (77.5 percent to 77.8 percent) but industrial manufacturing would stay at its 2012 level of 3.2 percent:

$$m = -0.01979 + 0.001395 \text{ (Capacity Utilization)}$$
$$+ 0.00077 \text{ (Industrial Production Manufacturing Index)}$$
$$m = -0.01979 + 0.001395(77.5) + 0.00077(3.2) = 0.0908$$

3. **EPS:** The third row in Exhibit 13.14 shows projected *EPS* increasing by 2.61 percent from \$103.81 on 12/31/2012 to \$106.52 on 12/31/2013. The projected *EPS* of \$106.52 is based on the projected profit margin of 9.080 percent and the *SPS* of \$1,173.06:

$$EPS_{13} = m_{13}S_{13}$$
$$EPS_{13} = (0.090802)(\$1,173.06)$$
$$EPS_{13} = \$106.52$$

4. **DPS:** Given the forecasted *EPS*, *DPS* were estimated by first estimating the dividend-payout ratio for the S&P 500 for 2013 and then multiplying that estimate by the forecasted *EPS*. Exhibit 13.12 shows the annual dividend payout ratios for the period 2000–2012 for the S&P 500. The payout ratios range from 26.847 percent to 39.646 percent, with an average of 30.27 percent and standard deviation of 4.088 percent. For this forecast, the *DPS* were projected to equal their average of 30.27 percent. With an estimated payout of 30.27 percent, the *DPS* for 2013 were projected to be \$32.24:

$$DPS_{13} = EPS_{13}(D/E)_{13}$$
$$DPS_{13} = \$106.52(0.3027)$$
$$DPS_{13} = \$32.24$$

5. **Multiplier Estimate:** For the period from 2000 to 2012, the average multiplier value was 16.6, with a standard deviation of 3.013 percent. The fluctuations in the multiplier reflect, in part, investors' changing expectations about the long-run performance of the market, future earnings prospects, and future interest rates. The author estimated the multiplier in terms of the Gordon-Williams model. The author assumed that the payout ratio for the S&P 500 would equal its 12-year average of 0.3027; that the expected market rate, k_e, would be equal to Bloomberg's estimated expected market rate of 10.5 percent; and that the sustainable growth rate in *EPS* would be 8.5 percent. The 8.5 percent was approximately equal to the product of the S&P 500's *ROE* in 2012 of 11.4 percent, and the retention ratio was 69.20 percent. Based on these estimates, the author's estimated the equilibrium *P/e* value for the S&P 500 was 15.135:

$$\frac{P}{e} = \frac{d/e}{k_e - g} = \frac{0.3027}{0.105 - 0.085} = 15.135$$

The *P/e* of 15.135 was greater than the three Bloomberg *P/e* ratios on 12/31/2012 of 13.74, 14.12, and 12.44 that are shown in Exhibit 13.12.

6. **Intrinsic Value:** With a *P/e* of 15.135 and a projected *EPS* for 2013 of \$106.52, the author's estimated intrinsic value of the S&P 500 on 12/31/2012 was 1,612.

$$V_{12} = \frac{P}{e}E(EPS_{13})$$
$$V_{12} = (15.135)(\$106.52) = 1,612$$

On 12/31/2012, the S&P 500 was at 1,426. Based on this estimated intrinsic value of 1,612, an analyst confident in this analysis would consider the market underpriced on that date by 11.54% [=(1,426/1,612) − 1] and would recommend a bullish position on the market.

Using the estimated growth rate of 8.5 percent, the projection for *EPS* in 2014 would be 115.57 ([=106.52(1.085)]. Assuming no change in the equilibrium *P/e* ratio of 15.135, the projected intrinsic value for 2013 would be 1,749:

$$V_{13} = \frac{P}{e}E(EPS_{14}) = \frac{P}{e}E(EPS_{13})(1+g)$$
$$V_{13} = (15.135)(\$106.52)(1.085) = 1,749$$

Expected Market Value and Rate of Return Forecast

If the S&P 500 were priced on 12/31/2012 at its equilibrium value of 1,612, and not at its market price of 1,426, then with a projected DPS of $32.24 and an estimated 2013 intrinsic value of 1,749, the expected one-year rate of return from investing in the market would be equal to the required rate of 10.5 percent.

$$E(R) = \frac{1,749 + 32.24}{1,612} - 1 = 0.105$$

The 10.5 percent expected return would consist of an expected price yield of 8.5 percent and an expected dividend yield of 2 percent:

$$\frac{\Delta P}{P} = \frac{1,749}{1,612} - 1 = 0.085$$
$$\frac{E(d)}{P} = \frac{32.24}{1,612} = 0.02$$

Given the lower market price of 1,426 on 12/31/2012, the expected market rate would be 24.91 percent, given the projected *DPS* of $32.24 and an expected price equal to the estimated 2013 intrinsic value of 1,749:

$$E(R) = \frac{1,749 + 32.24}{1,426} - 1 = 0.2491$$

The projected 24.91 percent consists of an expected price yield of 22.65% [=(1,749/1,426) − 1] and an expected dividend yield of 2.26% [=(32.24/1,426)].

With an expected rate of 24.91 percent exceeding the required rate of 10.5 percent, a portfolio manager confident in this forecast would recommend increasing the investment fund's allocation to equity. The 24.91 percent rate, however, is based on an assessment that the market is underpriced now but would be equal to its intrinsic value one year later. It is possible that the market could continue to be underpriced one year later. If we assume, however, that the market would increase by 8.5 percent from its current level of 1,426 and that the expected dividend yield would be 2 percent, then on 12/31/2013 the projected value of the S&P 500 would be 1,547, dividends would be 28.52, and the expected return would still be equal to the required rate of 10.5 percent:

$$E(R) = \frac{1,547 + 28.52}{1,426} - 1 = 0.105$$

Thus, to obtain an expected rate greater than the required rate, a combination of expected price yield and dividend yield would have to exceed 10.5 percent. For example, if the estimated intrinsic value of 1,612 for 12/31/2012 is the projected value for 12/31/2013 and dividends were expected to be 28.52, then the expected price yield would be 13.04 percent [=(1,612/1,426) − 1], the expected dividend yield would equal 2 percent, and the expected rate of return would be 15.04 percent, exceeding the 10.5 percent required return:

$$E(R) = \frac{1,612 + 28.52}{1,426} - 1 = 0.1504$$

Ex-Post Analysis

In our example, the market was underpriced on 12/31/2013 by 11.54 percent [=(1,426/1,612) − 1]. This was based on a forecast of EPS for 2013 reaching 106.52 and an estimate of the market's equilibrium P/e ratio of 15.135. As shown in Exhibit 13.12, the S&P 500 on 10/4/2013 reached 1,690—an 18.5 percent increase from its 1,426 level on 12/30/2012. This price increase plus three quarters of dividends totaling $27.35 equates to a periodic rate of return of 20.43% (= [(1,690 + $27.35)/1,426] − 1) and an annualized rate of 27.24% [=(4/3) (20.43%)]. Thus, the realized rate exceeded the expected market rate of 10.5 percent, justifying the bullish position taken on 12/31/2012. In retrospect, this ex-post analysis suggests that the bullish forecast of the market was correct. Recall that the driver for the optimistic forecast was an expectation of an improved economic climate, with GDP expected to grow by 4.5 percent, leading to a 6.74 percent expected increase in sales for S&P 500 stocks. As of 10/4/2013, GDP was at $16.661 trillion (a 2.53 percent YTD periodic rate and 3.42 percent YTD annualized rate), and after the first three quarters of 2013, SPS were at $1,124/share (a 2.84 percent increase). The estimate P/e of 15.135 was also greater than the P/e of 13.74, suggesting the market was underpriced relative to its earnings—at least based on the author's assessment.

Valuation Using the P/S Multiplier

On 12/31/2012, the price-to-sales ratio, P/S, for the S&P 500 was 1.305. Multiplying this ratio by the projected sales for 2013 of $1,173.06, we obtain an intrinsic value of the index of 1,531. The sales forecast, in turn, calls for sales to grow at 6.74 percent based on a projected 4.5 percent growth in *GDP*. If we project the same sales growth in 2014, then expected sales for 2014 would be $1,252.12. Assuming the same *P/S* multiplier for 2013, the estimated 2013 value for the market would be 1,634. Based on a market price of 1,426, a projected end-of-the-year 2013 value of 1,634, and the forecasted *DPS* of 32.24, the expected rate of return would be 16.85 percent:

$$S_{13} = S_{12}(1 + \Delta S_t/S)$$
$$S_{13} = \$1,098.99(1.0674) = \$1,173.06$$

$$V_{12} = \frac{P}{S}E(S_t)$$
$$V_{12} = (1.305)(\$1,173.06) = 1,531$$

$$S_{14} = S_{13}(1 + \Delta S_t/S)$$
$$S_{14} = \$1,173.06(1.0674) = \$1,252.12$$
$$V_{13} = \frac{P}{S}E(S_{14})$$
$$V_{13} = (1.305)(\$1,252.12) = 1,634$$

$$E(R) = \frac{1,634 + 32.24}{1,426} - 1 = 0.1685$$

With an intrinsic value of 1,531 exceeding the market price of 1,426, and with an expected rate of 16.85 percent that exceeds the required rate of 10.5 percent, we would again consider the market underpriced and recommend a bullish position based on the *P/S* multiplier analysis. Note, however, that the *P/S* multiplier approach values the market less than the *P/e* approach (1,531 compared to 1,612). The difference in the two multiplier approaches is that the *P/e* model takes into account profitability and *P/S* does not. The forecasted profit margin of 9.08 percent used in forecasting *EPS* for 2013, in turn, is relatively high when compared to the 6.97 percent margin in 2009 (see Exhibit 13.12). The higher 1,612 value using the *P/e* multiplier captures the assumption that earnings will increase as a result of *GDP* growth and also because of a relatively high profit margin, while the 1,530 value using the *P/S* multiplier is based on just the growth in sales and not profitability. Recall that following the 2008 financial crisis economic growth was in fact slow, whereas corporate earnings were relatively strong. Many financial analysts attributed the positive earnings to companies improving their operations.

Industry Analysis and Valuation

Like the market series, the value and expected rate of return for an industry or an economic sector can be estimated by using the multiplier approach. For the multiplier approach, we need to estimate next year's *EPS* and estimate the equilibrium *P/e* ratio for the industry. An industry's expected *EPS* can be projected using the same approach used to estimate the market series' *EPS*: estimating the industry *SPS* (*S*) and profit margin ($m = EPS/S$).

In applying this model to a particular industry, industry *SPS* can be related to a more disaggregated economic series than *GDP*. For a consumption-related industry like department stores that was examined in Chapter 12, its *SPS* may be better explained in terms of personal consumption expenditures. For a heavy-metal industry like steel, a high correlation might be found between its sales and aggregate capital expenditures, and for some industries, such as those in stage 4 of industrial development, *GDP* may still be the best explanatory variable. Like the market series, profit margins for an industry can be related to capacity utilization and unit labor cost for that industry. For an industry such as department stores, commodity cost related to textiles and apparel, hourly labor cost, and costs related to health care insurance can also influence profit, as well as can international factors, such as exchange rates, since many of the goods sold by large department stores are imported.

There are two common ways of estimating the industry multiplier. First, it can be forecasted based on its relationship to the market multiplier. In this case, an analyst would regress the percentage changes in the industry's multiplier against the percentage changes in the multiplier for the market series:

$$\%\Delta(P/e)_I = a + b\%\Delta(P/e)_M$$

Using this relation, one would first forecast the multiplier for the industry and then use the regression relation to forecast the industry's multiplier. A second approach is to estimate the industry's *P/e* by forecasting the *d/e*, k_e, and *g* values for the industry. As we did with the market series, k_e can be estimated using the CAPM, estimating R_f, the market risk premium, and the industry's beta.

Example: Department Store Industry

In Chapter 12, we valued Macy's, using both the multiplier and DCF approaches, and we did a relative analysis of Macy's with some of its peers in the industry. In addition to conducting a relative analysis of the companies in the industry, industry analysis can also include estimating the value of the industry as a whole. Exhibit 13.15 shows a forecast made by the author on 12/31/2012 of the Bloomberg Department Store North American Index (BRUSDEPC). This index consists of 11 companies, including Macy's, Belk, Kohl's, and Sears. The forecast projects *EPS* of $5.18 for 2013 and estimates the intrinsic value of the index to be 167.78 on 12/31/2012. Data on *SPS*, *EPS*, *DPS*, profit margins, and *P/e* ratios that were used to make the forecast and estimate *P/e* was pulled from Bloomberg's FA and GP screens for the index (see Exhibit 13.16).

On 12/31/2012, the department store index was at $149.30. An analyst confident in the author's analysis would consider the industry underpriced by 11 percent [$=(149.30/167.78) - 1$] and would recommend a bullish position on the industry.

EXHIBIT 13.15 2013 Forecast of Department Store Index North America

	2012 12/31/12	2013 12/31/13	Reason
(1) Sales (S)	$613.78	$631.15	2013 Forecast: $\Delta PCE/PCE = 0.05$
			$\Delta S/S = 0.566(\Delta PCE/PCE) = 0.0283$ $S_{13} = (1 + \Delta S/S)S_{12}$ $S_{13} = (1 + 0.0283)(\$613.78) = \$631.15$
(2) Profit Margin $m = EPS/S$	0.821%	0.821%	• Profit margin for 2013 will equal the low profit margin for 2012. • The low margin reflects the expected increases in cost of apparel and textile cost, the increases in labor cost, and exchange rates.
(3) EPS	$5.04	$5.18	$EPS_{13} = m_{13} S_{13}$ $EPS_{13} = (0.00821)(\$631.15) = \$5.18$
(4) Payout Ratio (d/e)	0.27579	0.2267	Dividend payout will equal its 8-year average of 0.22676
(5) DPS	$1.39	$1.17	$DPS_{13} = (d/e)_{13} EPS_{13}$ $DPS_{13} = (0.22676)(\$5.18) = \$1.17$
(6) g	11.6%	11.6%	The growth rate in the industry is projected to be 11.6%, close to projected growth rates of Macy's and Kohl's.
(7) k_e	12.3%	12.3%	$k_e = R_f + [E(R^M - R_f]\beta$ $k_e = 0.0171 + [0.0875]1.210 = 0.1230$
(8) P/e	32.39	32.39	Estimated based on Gordon-Williams model and the estimates of d/e, g, and k_e: $$\frac{P}{e} = \frac{d/e}{k_e - g} = \frac{0.2267}{0.123 - 0.116} = 32.39$$
(9) Value, V	167.78	187.24 or 172.44	$V_{12} = (P/e)E(EPS_{13}) = (32.39)(\$5.18) = 167.78$ $V_{13} = (P/e)E(EPS_{13})(1 + g) = (32.39)(\$5.18)(1.116) = 187.24$ $V_{13} = \frac{P}{e}E(EPS_{13})(1 + g) = (32.39)(\$5.18)(1.0278) = 172.44$
(10) Market Price, P	149.30		Industry underpriced by 11% (= (149.30/167.78) 1)
(11) Expected Rate, E(R)		16.28% or 26.20%	$E(R) = [(172.44 + 1.17)/149.3] - 1 = 0.1628$ $E(R) = [(187.24 + 1.17)/149.3] - 1 = 0.2620$

Buy Recommendation for industry with the investment focused on industry leaders.

The forecast also estimates an expected rate for 2013 of 16.28 percent and a required return of 12.3 percent. This assessment is based on an industry expected to have only a moderate sales increase for the coming year and a low growth rate in *EPS* for two years, but a relatively high long-term growth rate (reflected in the *P/e*) that is projected to approach the growth rates of the leaders in the industry. A portfolio manager confident in this forecast would recommend increasing the investment fund's allocation to department stores, but with a caveat that the investment focus on the leaders of the

EXHIBIT 13.16 Bloomberg Department Store Index North American, BRUSDEPC Sales, *EPS*, *DPS*, Profit Margin, Payout, and *P/e*

Date	Sales per Share	Proportional Change	EPS	Proportional Change	Profit Margin EPS/Sales	Dividend Payout			Dept. Store Index	Proportional Change
						DPS	DPS/EPS	P/e		
12/30/05	$297.91		$8.92		0.02994	$0.75	0.08408	19.22	171.50	
12/29/06	$380.94	0.2787	$9.81	0.0998	0.02575	$9.39	0.95719	25.71	252.28	0.4710
12/31/07	$433.53	0.1381	$8.95	−0.0877	0.02064	$0.95	0.10615	17.39	155.57	−0.3833
12/31/08	$777.70	0.7939	−$2.26	−1.2525	−0.00291	$1.22	−0.53982	34.05	49.56	−0.6814
12/31/09	$669.24	−0.1395	$2.18	−1.9646	0.00326	$1.26	0.57798	50.71	110.49	1.2294
12/31/10	$491.36	−0.2658	$6.91	2.1697	0.01406	$1.01	0.14616	20.78	143.54	0.2991
12/30/11	$510.92	0.0398	$6.68	−0.0333	0.01307	$1.38	0.20659	18.19	121.39	−0.1543
12/31/12	$613.78	0.2013	$5.04	−0.2455	0.00821	$1.39	0.27579	29.61	149.30	0.2299
Average	$521.92	0.14950	$5.78	−0.1877	0.01400	$2.17	0.22676	26.96	144.20	0.1443
Standard Deviation	$157.88	0.34223	$4.08	1.2890	0.01116	$2.93	0.42908	11.27	57.56	0.6278

Bloomberg: *EPS* = Best *EPS*; Sales = Best Sales; *P/e* = Best *P/e*

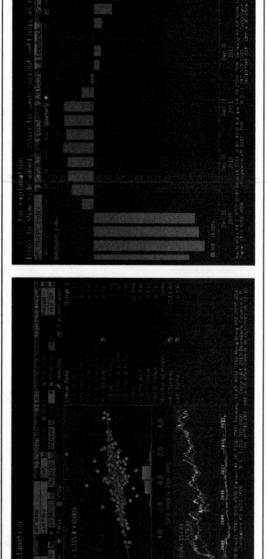

524

industry, such as Macy's, Kohl's, Dillards, or Nordstrom. The details of the forecast are described in Appendix 13A (text Web site).

An ex-post analysis of this 12/31/2012 buy recommendation shows that on 4/1/2013, the index hit 153.24 and paid a dividend of $1.62 for a quarterly return of 3.72 percent [=(153.24 + $1.62)/$149.30] − 1 and annualized return of 14.90 percent (see Exhibit 13.17). The return exceeded the required return of 12.3 percent. The index did hit a high on 5/23/2013 of 184.90, for a 23.84 percent gain. At that point, the analyst with a buy recommendation would have been very happy. On 10/4/2013, however, the index was at 159.75. This 7.00 percent price increase combined with $4.80 in dividends equated to a rate of return for the period of 10.21 percent and an annualized rate of 13.62 percent, modestly exceeding the required rate of 12.3 percent.

It should be noted that the annualized total return for the period from 1/04/2013 to 10/18/2013 (based on weekly returns) was 10.97 percent (see lower screen in Exhibit 13.17), which was significantly less than the 27.38 percent total return for the S&P 500. The drivers for the forecast, however, were for an industry moving toward consolidation, where its growth rates would reflect those of its leaders. The bullish position taken on the industry required selecting the correct stocks that make up the index, such as Macy's, which was analyzed in Chapter 12. Macy's total return for the period was, in turn, 24.53 percent, closer to the return of the S&P 500.

The last step in the top-down, three-step approach is to analyze and forecast the performances of each company in the industry. This entails conducting a relative analysis of the companies in the industry and then applying the same type of analysis and forecast for each company. In Chapter 12 we applied this type of analysis to Macy's. Recall from that analysis that Macy's was a strong buy; the stock, in turn, generated a total return of 23.3 percent for the period.

BLOOMBERG SECTOR AND INDUSTRY SCREENS AND TEMPLATES

Bloomberg Excel Add-In:
  The data in Exhibits 13.12, 13.13, and 13.16 were imported into Excel using Bloomberg's Excel Add-In and the "Import Data" tab.

- On the Bloomberg Add-In in Excel, click "Historical End of the Day" from the "Import Data" and the follow the Wizard's steps.

Bloomberg FA Screen for Indexes
- The income statements, balance sheets, valuation, and other information for indexes can be accessed from Bloomberg's FA screen. You can also create customized screens: Index Ticker <Index> <Enter>; FA.
- Note: To compare a company to the index, enter the company's ticker in the Compare box.

(Continued)

Bloomberg RV Screen for Indexes

- Relative analysis screens, RV, for companies in an index can be found by using the RV screen for one of companies and then importing the index from the Comp source dropdown. The RV screen can also be customized (Custom Tab, "Create Templates," and click "Save as" tab to save the screen). The Bloomberg RV screen can be used to do a relative analysis of companies in the industry in terms of valuation, ratios, and earnings.
- BI comparative analysis screens of the stock in an index can be accessed from the BI screen: BI <Enter>, select sector (e.g., "Consumer Discretionary"), select industry (e.g., Department Stores, North America), and select "Comp Sheets." The industry of a company can also be found by entering the company's name (or ticker) in the "Search BI" box.

Bloomberg: Excel Templates for Industry Analysis

Bloomberg has a number of Excel templates for conducting industry analysis and relative analysis of a company with its peers. Use DAPI to see a listing and to download: DAPI <Enter>; Click "Excel Template Library"; Click "Fundamentals." Templates of note are as follows:

- Bloomberg Comparable Volatility Analysis, XCVA.XLS.
- Financial Statements of Equity Indexes, XFAI.XLS.
- Multiple Securities Total Return Applications, XTOT.XLS.
- Company Snapshots with Financial Analysis, XCSF.XLS.
- Energy Company Snapshot, XNRG.XLS.
- Company Snapshot 5, XCS5.XLS.
- Portfolio Classification by S&P 500 Sectors, XPC.XLS.
- Historical Financial Template for an Industrial Company, XHFN.XLS.
- Insurance Company Snapshot, XICS.XLS.
- Fundamentals and Estimates Report, XFAE.XLS.
- Product/Geographical Segmentation, XPGE.XLS.
- Top 5 Bloomberg Peers Estimates Comparisons, XPGR.XLS.
- Index Performance and Peer Ranking, XTIR.XLS.
- Bloomberg Industries Global Aluminum Supply Model, XGSA.XLS.
- Natural Gas Basis, XNGB.XLS.
- Bloomberg Drug Prescription Data, XDRG.XLS.
- MSCI Country Weights Matrix Grouped by Sectors/Industry Groups, XMSX.XLS.
- Historical Template for an Energy Company, XHFG.XLS.
- Historical Financials for a Mining Company, XHFN.XLS.
- Historical Financial Template for a Utility Company, XHFU.XLS.
- Equity Fundaments and Peer Group Comparison, XFCT.XLS.

   See Bloomberg Web Exhibit 13.2.

EXHIBIT 13.17   Bloomberg Department Store Index North American, BRUSDEPC: Bloomberg GP and COMP Screens

(a)

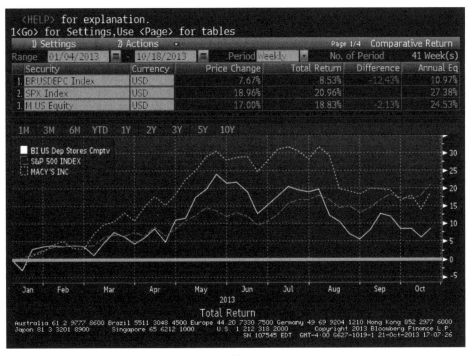

(b)

Top-Down Portfolio Management

Many fundamental stock analysts incorporate a *top-down, three-step approach* in which economic, industry, and company analyses are used as inputs in evaluating stocks. Top-down does not necessarily have to be sequential. Many portfolio managers require economic, industry, and company analysis. They then use the collective information to make their investment decisions. We conclude this chapter by summarizing the management of a student equity fund that uses economic, industry, and firm analysis to manage a $1 million equity fund.

Student Investment Equity Fund: Philosophy, Construction, and Guidelines

Philosophy
- The Student Equity Investment Fund manages a portion of the university's endowment as a tactical index fund using economic, sector, and company fundamental analysis. The fund uses the S&P 500 index as its benchmark.
- The stocks selected are based on sector analysis. Stocks in a sector that are expected to be strong have a greater allocation than that sector's allocation to the index. The overweighting or underweighting of sectors relative to the index takes into consideration current and expected economic and sector conditions. Stocks selected in different sectors are those that are considered to have good fundamentals.

Construction
- **Sector allocation** decisions are based on the following types of analysis:
  - Macroanalysis of the sectors to determine how the sectors relate to the business cycle and what factors drive the industry.
  - Strategic rotation analysis to determine how different sectors perform in different stages of a business cycle.
  - Economic analysis of structural changes to determine when the economy is experiencing major changes (e.g., globalization, downsizing, and political changes) and the implications they hold for the sector.
  - Macroeconomic analysis to determine the current and forecasted economic conditions.
- **Stock Selection**: Stocks selected in different sectors are those that are considered to have sound fundamentals. Among the quantitative and qualitative factors that are considered in determining a stock's fundamental value are the following:
  - Relative valuations.
  - Expected earnings and sales growth.
  - Sustainable growth.
  - Fundamental risk factors: liquidity risk, business risk, financial risk, exchange-rate risk, and external liquidity risk.
  - SWOT.
  - Stocks are selected based on technical or efficient market considerations when such opportunities are believed to exist.

Guidelines Approved by the University

- Stocks in the portfolio can be selected outside the index's (S&P 500) universe provided they meet the index's features of market capitalization and marketability.
- Sectors are identified by the S&P 500 Global Industry Classification Standard (GICS).
- The proportion of a sector's allocation is limited to a range equal to plus or minus 50 percent of the sector's allocation to the index.
- Sector ETFs are included in the fund.
- The cash position of the fund can be no more than 10 percent.
- No more than 8 percent of the market value of the portfolio may be invested in any single security.
- The portfolio must have a minimum of 25 holdings.
- The fund can invest in preferred stock.

Student Fund Managers' Report: Portfolio Management of the Fund, 2010, First Quarter—Economic Considerations

In January, the portfolio consisted of 55 stocks with a market value of $1,145,963, beta of 0.937, and a *P/e* of 18.96. The portfolio's top holdings were Microsoft (5.44 percent), Apple (5.15 percent), Cognizant (4.74 percent), Federal Express (3.41 percent), and Total (3.33 percent).

In early January, the release of the fourth-quarter *GDP* figure showed that the U.S. economy had grown at an annualized rate of 5.5 percent. In spite of the good economic numbers, there were still major concerns. A number of economists pointed out that the U.S. *GDP* figures were driven by government spending and the rebuilding of depleted inventories. There was also no positive indicator on job growth, household debt was still high, and U.S. bankruptcy rates were high and increasing. In China, there was growing concern over the increasing excess production capacity and excessive real estate property development, raising apprehension about a possible "China Bubble." In Europe, there was sluggish economic recovery in Spain, Ireland, Portugal, and Greece. Greece faced a fiscal crisis, potential sovereign debt default, and a credit squeeze.

The overriding concern underlying the economic climate in January and February of 2010 was that the U.S. and global economies, as well as equity values, were being maintained by an unsustainable fiscal and monetary stimulus. The relevant question was: Could the recovery be sustained? Given the uncertain economic climate in the months of January and February, the fund managers became concerned with a possible correction in the stock market. Accordingly, the managers decided to adjust the portfolio by implementing the following strategy:

1. Sell some holdings of stocks meeting their sell criteria; this would include some stock holdings that were purchased at low prices and were trading either near their 52-week high, their target value, or their 2007 peak.
2. Increase the fund's cash position.

3. Increase the fund's allocation to preferred trust stocks (these preferred stocks traded close to the subordinated debt underlying the issue and provided a more stable asset class for the fund).

4. Increase the fund's allocation to the financial sector (given the stronger balance sheets of banks).

As the result of these trades, the adjusted portfolio on February 26 consisted of an 83 percent allocation to common stocks and ETFs, 7 percent to preferred stocks, and 10 percent to cash. The adjusted portfolio was positioned to underperform the market if the market were to increase or stay flat and outperform if there was a market correction. At that time, the managers took the position that the current economic conditions would, at best, lead the market sideways around its February level, but with greater price volatility. With this investment climate, the managers' strategy moving forward was to increase the stock allocation of the portfolio based on strong fundamentals as opposed to market factors.

From February 26 to April 21, the market increased 9.3 percent, going from to 1,106 to 1,209. During this period, the fund managers increased their stock holdings by 5 percent (from the cash position) with the following stock purchases: Kohl's, Archer Daniels Midland, Abbott, Tiffany, Progress, Devon, and SalesForce. As the result of these trades, the portfolio on April 21 consisted of a 91 percent allocation to common stocks and ETFs, 6.5 percent to preferred stocks, and 2.5 percent to cash. The portfolio was overweight in the consumer staples, information technology, utilities, and telecommunication sectors, underweight in the consumer discretionary, financials, energy, industrials, and materials sectors, and approximately equal weight in the health care sector. The portfolio consisted of 57 securities with a market value of $1,259,907, beta of 0.891, and a *P/e* ratio of 17.53, compared to the *P/e* of 18.40 for the S&P 500. The portfolio's top holdings were Apple (6.20 percent), Microsoft (5.25 percent), Cognizant (5.05 percent), Federal Express (3.28 percent), and PepsiCo (3.16 percent).

For the period from November 30, 2009, to April 4, 2010, the total return of the fund was 8.67 percent compared to the index return of 9.57 percent. The fund's lower return reflects the portfolio beta of 0.829 during this period when the market was increasing. The current portfolio was positioned to slightly underperform the market if the market were to increase or stay flat, and outperform if there was a market correction.

BLOOMBERG PORT SCREEN

Bloomberg's PORT screen can be used to breakdown a portfolio in terms of sector allocations: PORT, Performance tab, and Main View Tab.

Bloomberg's PORT screen can be used to analyze a portfolio in terms of its features relative to the market: PORT, Add index, Characteristics tab, and Characteristics Summary tab.

See Bloomberg Web Exhibit 13.3.

Conclusion

This completes our investigation into fundamental analysis. Over the last three chapters, we have examined the financial anatomy of a company and the fundamental factors that determine its equity, looked at different quantitative and qualitative approaches that can be used to estimate the intrinsic value of stock, and in this chapter, examined the aggregate economic and industry factors influencing equity values and the valuation of the overall market and industries. Recall that the objective of fundamental analysis is to earn abnormal returns by purchasing stocks considered to be underpriced and selling or shorting stocks considered to be overpriced. In the next chapter, we examine technical analysis. Different from the fundamental approach, technical analysis is not directly concerned with determining a stock's value, but rather in identifying trends in stock prices that could lead to profitable trading strategies.

Web Site Information

Economic Information
1. Federal Reserve sites:
   - www.federalreserve.gov/releases/h15/data.htm
   - FRED: www.research.stlouisfed.org/fred2
2. For information on Federal Reserve policies, go to www.federalreserve.gov/policy.htm.
3. For information on European Central Banks, go to www.ecb.int.
4. For information on the U.S. Treasury's debt, go to www.publicdebt.treas.gov.
5. For information on the distribution of U.S. debt, go to the Treasury Bulletin: http://www.fms.treas.gov/bulletin/.
6. For information on U.S. government's expenditures, revenues, deficits and debt, go to: www.federalreserve.gov/releases/z1/current/data.htm.
7. For tables on U.S. government's expenditures, revenues, deficits and debt to download, go to: www.federalreserve.gov/releases/z1/current/data.htm.
8. For information on government information submitted by Congress, go to: www.gpo.gov/fdsys/search/home.action.
9. Information on the Federal Reserve System can be found by going to the Federal Reserve site: www.federalreserve.gov/pubs/Frseries/frseri.htm. The site has useful information on important monetary actions such as open market operations, changes in the discount rate, and reserve requirement changes.
10. For the Federal Reserve report on the state of the economy, go to the Federal Reserve "Beige Book": www.federalreserve.gov/monetarypolicy/beigebook. The book provides analysis of current and futures economic condition for the nation and regions.
11. For information on exchange rates and euro and yen bond yields, go to FXStreet.com: www.fxstreet.com.
12. For information on U.S. security holdings by foreigners, go to Treasury tic information: www.treas.gov/tic.

13. For information and report from the U.S. Treasury, go to www.treas.gov/.
14. For information on economic indicators and economic performance from the Council of Economic Advisors at the Federal Reserve Archival System for Economic Research (FRASER), go to http://fraser.stlouisfed.org/publications /ei/.

Notes

1. In June 2008, the subprime mortgage meltdown that began in August 2007 had developed into a global credit crisis. This crisis gained steam throughout the first half of 2008 with the fire sale of Bear Stearns to JP Morgan Chase, substantial asset value write downs by many global financial institutions, and a subsequent panic by these firms to raise billions of dollars in new capital from a variety of sources to repair their balance sheets. By September 29, 2008, asset write downs exceeded $590 billion and capital raised by financial firms totaled over $430 billion.

2. China grew at a rate of 8.9 percent in 2011 and a slightly slower rate of 8.4 percent in 2012. This contrasts with a growth rate of 11.5 percent in 2007. There were also growing concerns about China's investment expenditures and export growth occurring at the expense of consumption, its growing wealth gap, and its excessive misinvestments. In addition to China, the International Monetary Fund (IMF) reported in 2012 that the growth rates of emerging market countries had slowed and those world economic indicators showed a slowing global economy.

3. In general, when a country operates with a persistent balance of payments surplus, then there is often an accumulation of foreign currency by the country's central banks. In an effort to keep their currency values low (to maintain their export sales), such countries often invest their currency reserves in the country whose currency they are holding. Such actions describe the policies of China over the last 10 years, as well as a number of energy-producing countries in the Middle East.

4. According to the *Economist*, fracking in the 600-mile Marcellus Shale formation reserve— an area that encompasses Ohio, Pennsylvania, New York, and West Virginia—created over 100,000 jobs in energy and related industries, such as steel. The shale-gas boom also took hold in Texas, Louisiana, Arkansas, Oklahoma, and North Dakota. The increase in fracking and drilling led to significant decreases in domestic gas prices (from $13 per million BTUs in 2008 to $2 in 2012). Cheap energy prices, combined with the U.S. extensive pipeline network, also contributed to lower electric prices, increased exports, greater foreign direct investment, and increased investments in energy-intensive industries, such as liquid fuels, plastics, fertilizers, steel, and chemicals. The growth in unconventional oil and gas exploration and development in the United States accounted for $238 billion in economic activity and 1.7 million jobs. Moreover, over the next decade this growth was expected to lead to a "manufacturing renaissance" that could contribute an additional 0.5 percent to GDP growth.

5. Global equity markets had also rebounded strongly, and in the credit market, rates were relatively low, and credit spreads had narrowed.

6. Studies by Sprinkle (1971) and others conducted in the 1960s and 1970s also provide empirical evidence of the money supply as a strong leading indicator of the stock market. In

general, these empirical findings support the liquidity transmission mechanism hypothesis as an explanation of how monetary changes affect the economy. The liquidity transmission mechanism posits that changes in the money supply precede changes in interest rates and security prices that, in turn, precede changes in aggregate output.

7. In the 1980s and early 1990s, many analysts believe that Federal Reserve Chair Alan Greenspan's primary goal was to offset any inflationary pressure. This led to many looking at capacity utilization and other factors that would portend inflation.

8. Some scholars argue that the ratio of the composite of coincident index to the composite lagging index consistently leads the leading indicators, including the stock market.

9. See Wassily W. Leontief (1936 and 1951) and William Miernyk (1965).

Selected References

Chen, Nai-Fu, Richard Roll, and Stephen Ross. 1986. Economic forces and the stock market. *Journal of Business* 59 (July): 383–403.

Cooper, Richard. 1974. Efficient capital markets and the Quantity Theory of Money. *Journal of Finance* 29 (June): 887–908.

Fama, Eugene. 1981. Stock returns, real activity, inflation, and money. *American Economic Review* 71 (November): 545–565.

Friedman, Milton, and Anna J. Schwartz. 1963. Money and business cycles. *Review of Economics and Statistics* 45 (February): 32–78.

Hagstrom, Robert G. 2001. *The Essential Buffett*. Hoboken, NJ: John Wiley & Sons.

Jensen, Gerald R., Jeffrey Mercer, and Robert Johnson. 1996. Business conditions, monetary policy, and expected security returns. *Journal of Financial Economics* 40 (February): 213–237.

Keran, Michael W. 1971. Expectations, money, and the stock market. Federal Reserve Bank of St. Louis, *Review* 53 (January): 16–31.

Leontief, Wassily W. 1936. Quantitative input-output relations in the economic system of the United States. *The Review of Economics and Statistics*, 63: 105–125.

Leontief, Wassily W. 1951. *The Structure of the American Economy, 1919–1939*. New York: Oxford University Press.

Livingston, Miles. 1977. Industry movements of common stocks. *Journal of Finance* 32 (June): 861–874.

Lynch, Peter. 1989. *One Up on Wall Street*. New York: Simon & Schuster.

Lynch, Peter. 1993. *Beating the Street*. New York: Simon & Schuster.

Miernyk, William H. 1965. *The Elements of Input-Output Analysis*. New York: Random House.

Myers, Stephen L. 1973. A re-examination of market and industry factors in stock price behavior. *Journal of Finance* 28 (June): 695–705.

Niederhoffer, V., and P. Regan. 1972. Earnings changes, analysts forecasts, and stock prices. *Financial Analysts Journal* 28 (May–June): 65–71.

Patelis, Alex D. 1997. Stock returns predictability and the role of monetary policy. *Journal of Finance* 52 (December): 1951–1972.

Porter, Michael. 1980. *Competitive Strategy: Technique for Analyzing Industries and Competitors*. New York: Free Press.

Porter, Michael. 1980. Industry structure and competitive strategy: Keys to profitability. *Financial Analysts Journal* 36 (July–August): 30–41.

Shiskin, Julius. 1963. Business cycle indicators: The known and the unknown. *Review of the International Statistical Institute* 31: 361–383.

Sprinkel, Beryl W. 1971. *Money and Markets: A Monetarist View*. Homewood, Ill.: Irwin.

Bloomberg Exercises

1. General economic conditions, inflation, the size of the government debt, monetary and fiscal policies, and international capital flows all have impacts on the macro-economy. Examine some of the economic trends using the ECOF screen or by pulling up the economic indicator's screen: Ticker <Index> <Enter>. Examples:
   - U.S. Nominal GDP: GDP CUR$ <Index>.
   - U.S. Real GDP: GDP CQOQ <Index>.
   - U.S. Inflation: CPI YOY <Index>.
   - S&P/Case-Schiller: SPCS20 <Index>.
   - U.S. Unemployment Rate: USURTOT <Index>.
   - U.S. Deficit: FDEBTY <Index>.
   - Government Debt: PUBLDEBT <Index>.
   - Money Supply (M1): M1NS <Index>.
2. Provide some economic and policy analysis using information from the Federal Reserve sites (FED <Enter>; FOMC <Enter>) and some of the economic indicators from ECOF or ECST. Possible indicators are as follows:
   - U.S. Nominal GDP: GDP CUR$ <Index>.
   - U.S. Real GDP: GDP CQOQ <Index>.
   - U.S. Inflation: CPI YOY <Index>.
   - S&P/Case-Schiller: SPCS20 <Index>.
   - U.S. Unemployment Rate: USURTOT <Index>.
   - U.S. Deficit: FDEBTY <Index>.
   - Government Debt: PUBLDEBT <Index>.
   - Money Supply (M1): M1NS <Index>.
   - Balance of Payments: USCABAL <Ticker>.
   - Energy Services Price Index: CPRPENER <Ticker>.
3. Using the ECST screen, provide some analysis of recent trends in the following markets and sectors:
   - Labor market
   - Housing market
   - Industrial sector
   - Service sector
   - Demographics
4. Using the ECST screen, provide some analysis of current and future economic conditions using the following indicators:
   - Business conditions
   - Consumer confidence
   - NBER business cycle indicators
   - Leading indicators
   - Leading indicators components

5. Using the ECO screen, identify some of the current economic releases. Study some of releases by reading the analysis of some of them provided at the bottom of the ECO screen.

6. Using the BI screen, select an industry sector and evaluate the sector using the following BI screens:
   - Comp Sheets
   - Key Indicators
   - News/Research
   - Events
   - Data Library
   - Analysis

7. Analyze the industry sector you selected in Exercise 6 by examining the sector's index on the index's menu screen. The following are some possible screens to examine:
   - DES   Description
   - Mov   Equity movers
   - GP   Price graph (activate events and volume)
   - FA   Financials
   - GF   Fundamental graphs
   - TRA   Total return analysis
   - COMP   Comparative returns

8. Do a relative analysis of the companies in an industrial or peer index. The RV screen for companies in an industrial can be created by using the RV screen for one of companies and then importing the index from the Comp source dropdown on the company's RV screen.

9. Do a relative analysis of the companies in the sector or industry index you selected in Exercise 8 by customizing the RV screen. Some custom screens you may want to consider are the following:
   - Earnings in terms of sales per share and profit margins
   - Multipliers: *P/e* and *P/S*
   - Business Risk: margins
   - Financial Risk: leverage ratios
   - Liquidity Risk
   - Growth: Sustainable growth, payout ratios, and *ROE*
   - DuPont Ratios

10. Supply chain analysis:
    a. Analyze the supply chain of a large market cap company (SPLC) in terms of its suppliers, customers, and peers.
    b. Analyze the supply chain of the supplier with the greatest percentage of its revenue generated from your selected company.
    c. Analyze the supply chain of the customer with the greatest percentage of its cost paid to your selected company.
    d. Analyze one of the peers of your selected company to see if it has similar customers and suppliers.

     e. Use your selected company's COMP screen to compare its total returns with the total returns to one of its suppliers and one of its customers.

11. In the slow economic recovery following the 2008 financial crisis and recession, many companies had positive earnings and cash positions for the period from 2008 to 2012. Study this trend by examining the following ratios for the S&P 500 on Bloomberg's FA screen (SPX <Index>; FA):
   - Cash-per-share
   - *EPS*
   - Profit margins
   - *ROE*
   - *ROA*

   You may want to customize your FA screen: Cash-per-Share, Profit Margin, *EPS*, *ROE*, and *ROA*.

12. Conduct an FA analysis that is similar to the one you did Exercise 11 for a large cap company like GE.

13. Analyze an equity portfolio that you have constructed (possibly one from an exercise in a previous chapter) in terms of its sector allocations relative to the allocations of broad-based index (DJIA, Russell 3000, or S&P 500). Use Bloomberg's PORT screen and the following tabs:
   - PORT, Performance tab, and Main View Tab
   - PORT, Characteristics tab, and Main View Tab
   - PORT, Characteristics tab, and Characteristics Summary tab

14. Select a major currency (e.g., British pound, euro, yen, or Swiss franc) and study the dollar price of the currency over the last 10 years (currency ticker <CRNCY> <Enter>; GP).

   Questions:
   a. Identify periods in which a U.S. investor (dollar investor) could have made significant returns from investing in securities denominated in that currency.
   b. Identify periods in which a foreign investor (e.g., a British pound investor) could have made significant returns investing in dollar denominated securities.
   c. Identify periods in which a U.S. company with foreign sales would have had its products or services priced lower in the currency you selected. Identify periods in which its products or services would have been priced higher in that currency.
   d. Identify periods in which a U.S. company with inputs, resources, or goods purchased in the currency you selected would have had greater cost. Identify periods in which it would have had smaller cost.

CHAPTER 14

Technical Analysis

Introduction

There are two main approaches to analyzing stocks: fundamental analysis and technical analysis. Fundamental analysis looks at economic, industry, and firm factors to determine the intrinsic value of a stock or index and whether it is underpriced (buy decision) or overpriced (sell decision). Technical analysis, on the other hand, looks for patterns or trends in security prices. Different from fundamental analysis that uses economic, industry, and company data, technical analysis looks at just market data: high and low prices, closing prices, volume, moving averages, short interests, and volatility.

As an alternative approach to fundamental analysis, technical analysis is based on the premise that all fundamental information is captured in the market price and that market statistics reveal all information—the market is its own best predictor. As a complement, technical analysis when used in conjunction with fundamental analysis provides a more complete picture of the stock or market. In practice, many analysts and investment firms use fundamental analysis to determine what to buy and sell and technical analysis to determine when to buy and sell. Other market participants combine both approaches to reinforce or to check their positions.

The theory underlying technical analysis is based on fundamental supply and demand and can be summarized as follows:

- The market price is determined by supply and demand.
- Supply and demand are affected by both rational and irrational factors.
- Changes (shifts) in supply and demand change price trends.
- Price trends tend to repeat themselves—history repeats itself.

Technical analysis, in turn, tries to identify those recurring or predictable patterns and from those recurring patterns establish trading rules to obtain abnormal returns.

For technical analysis to be profitable, the market has to be inefficient. For example, suppose there is a detectable trend in the market in which a stock is consistently trading low on Monday and high on Friday. In an efficient market, technicians will see this trend and accordingly buy the stock on Monday, pushing its price up, and sell on

Friday, pushing its price down. By these trades, technicians will eliminate the trend of the stock being high on Monday and low on Friday. In contrast, in the absence of that market efficiency, the trend would continue, and the technician would profit. Many advocates of technical analysis argue that fundamental and technical information is embodied in the price of the stock, but not completely; It takes times for market prices to hit their intrinsic values as well as time for the market to identify trends. Many technical advocates also point to the behavioral finance school of thought. Behavioral finance is a psychology-based branch of finance that looks at the systematic impact that human frailties and biases, such as overconfidence or a conservative bias, have on a stock's price pattern. Again, in the absence of market efficiencies, such biases in turn would lead to discernible trends that technical investors could exploit.

In this chapter, we examine technical analysis in terms of the tools and strategies that technicians employ. We begin by defining stock price trends observed by charting stock and index prices over time. We then look at price trends combined with volume information and moving averages as a way to examine the strength or the momentum of the trend, as well as to identify the possible buy and sell signals that technicians often use. We then look at other metrics that technicians use to measure momentum; these measures include the breadth of the market (advance minus declines), confidence indicators, relative strength indicators, put/call ratios, relative strength indicators, and rate of return. We extend the application of technical indicators to foreign markets, currency, commodities, and portfolios. Finally, we conclude the chapter by moving from empirical analysis to theory, looking at behavioral finance and market inefficiencies as a possible theoretical explanation of stock price trends.

Price Trends

Charts

In trying to uncover trends in security prices, technicians study line, bar, and candle charts. A simple *line chart* connects period prices (e.g., daily closing stock prices or daily opening prices) with a continuous line. Line charts can also connect moving averages (*MA*), such as a four-day moving average based on closing prices, (P_t):

$$MA_4 = \frac{P_t + P_{t-1} + P_{t-2} + P_{t-3}}{4}$$

Bar charts show a vertical bar at each time increment. The length of the bar represents the trading range between the low and high prices for that period of time (day, week, month, or year); a line cutting through the bar represents a close or open; or in some bar charts (e.g., those on Bloomberg) there is left tick on the bar showing the opening price, and right tick showing the close. Bar charts can be generated with different periodicities, such as daily, weekly, or monthly. Compared to line charts, they provide more information. Like bar charts, *candle charts* show a candlestick at each time increment. The price information on the candle is color coded: A candle without color (or open) represents a higher closing price than the opening price; a candle with color (or solid) represents a lower close than open. The candle has two parts, a thick part or body and thin part or shadow. The body shows the open and close and will be either colored (solid) or without color (open). The shadow or thin line above the body (upper shadow) shows the high, and the shadow below (lower shadow) shows the low. Like bar charts, candle charts provide more information and can be generated for different periodicities.

Dow Theory

The Dow Theory is the most well-known theory explaining price trends. It is generally used to explain the overall market, although it can be used to explain securities and indexes. It was named after Charles Dow, the founder of the Dow Jones company, and the editor of the *Wall Street Journal*.[1] The theory explains the market in terms of three trends: primary or major, intermediate or secondary, and minor, tertiary or short-run:

- *Primary trends* are the long-run movements of prices (several months to years). They are commonly referred to as bull and bear markets and are explained by fundamental economic factors.
- *Intermediate trends* are deviations from the primary trend. They are explained as corrections, with prices reverting back to their major trend.
- *Minor trends* or short-run (day-to-day) trends are random. They are devoid of meaning. They are generally considered to be of little importance, although their movement could provide signals for changes in intermediate trends.

The three trends that make up the Dow Theory are often described in terms of an ocean analogy where the primary trend is like the ocean tide, the intermediate as a wave, and the minor as a ripple. Exhibit 14.1 shows an upward primary trend or bull market for a stock occurring from time t_0 to t_1 and a downward primary trend or bear market occurring from time t_1 to t_2. During the bull market, the price trend is characterized by each peak being higher than the previous (i.e., the tops are ascending) and with each trough being higher than the preceding trough. On trading day, t_1, there is a reversal of the primary bull trend and the start of the bear primary trend. In the bear trend each trough is lower than the previous trough (the tops are descending). Finally, note after t_2, the price fails to reach a new bottom, signaling the beginning of a new bull market. Exhibit 14.1 shows a bull trend characterized by ascending tops and a bear trend characterized by descending top. The other possible price trend would be flat tops and bottoms. This would be a *trendless* market—a market moving sideways.[2]

Resistance and Support Levels, Channels, and Breakouts

Bull, bear, and sideways trends are also described by resistance and support levels. A *resistance level* is the ceiling above which the price is not expected to rise. When a price

EXHIBIT 14.1   Dow Theory: Primary and Secondary Trends

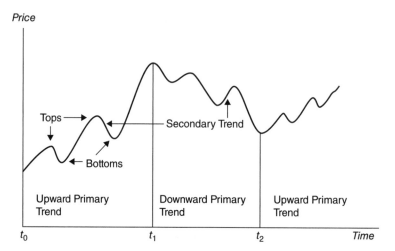

rises to its resistance level, an increase in selling and an excess supply is expected, caus-ing a price reversal. A *support level* is a floor beneath which the price is not expected to fall. When the price falls to its support level, an increase in buying and an excess demand is expected, causing the price to reverse. Price trends are characterized by prices rising until they meet their resistance level and falling back until they meet their support level. When a strong buying surge pushes the stock's price past its resistance level, it is consider a *breakout*, with the stock expected to rise to a new higher resistance level and a new support level that is often the old resistance level (see Exhibit 14.2). In contrast, when a strong selling surge pushes the stock's price below its support level,

EXHIBIT 14.2   Support and Resistance Levels and Breakouts

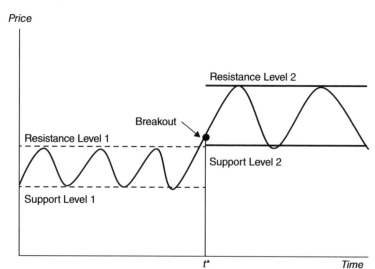

there is a breakout with the stock expected to fall until it reaches a new support level and new resistance level. Technicians, in turn, try to define trends in terms of resistance and support levels to help them identify breakouts. Often they look at volume information to confirm a breakout. That is, a stock breaking above its resistance level on heavy volume is a stronger bull sign than one breaking out on low volume.

Resistance and support levels can also be defined in terms of price ranges covering peaks and reversals and troughs and reversals. In this case, a resistance level (or ceiling level) is the price range that would lead to a reversal (from increasing to decreasing). The support line or floor line is the price range that would lead to a reversal (from decreasing to increasing). For bull markets, the support and resistance lines are positively sloped; for bear markets, they are negative; and for sideways markets they are horizontal. Moreover, stocks tend to trade in channels or bands defined by these upper and lower resistance and support lines. Technicians, in turn, try to identify the bands and look for price breakouts as signals. Given the signals, they follow rules of when to buy or sell. One accepted rule is that a breakout occurs if the price closes on the opposite side of its support or resistance line. Another rule is to first confirm the trend change by waiting for the price to reach a specified percent (e.g., 1 percent to 3 percent) beyond the line.

Example

Exhibit 14.3 shows a price graph for a stock with three channels: a *rising trend channel* or bull market, *flat trend channel* (sideways market), and *declining trend channel* or bear market. The exhibit starts with a declining trend channel that breaks out of its channel—increases above its resistance line—at t_1, signaling a possible bull run. A

EXHIBIT 14.3   Channels and Breakouts

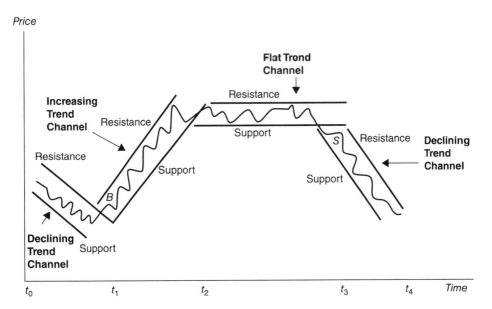

technician would have identified the t_1 breakout from the bear channel's resistance level as a reversal and might confirm a bull run at point B, where the first trough in the bull channel is higher the last trough in the bear channel. Thus, for the technician, point B is her confirmation of the reversal from a bear run to a bull run and a buy point. As shown in the exhibit, the bull trend in which the stock is in a rising trend channel lasts until t_2 where it again breaks out—decreases below its support line. The stock's price then moves sideways in a flat trend channel demarked by a resistance line equal to the bull channel's last peak and a support line equal to the bull channel's last trough. A technician would identify the t_2 breakout from the bull channel's resistance level as a reversal but would wait for a confirmation of the reversal by waiting to see whether the stock price pushes below its new support level—confirming a reversal and signaling a sell point—or if it pushes up above its new resistance level—signaling a buy or "buy more" point. At t_3, the stock does cut through its support level and begins a bear trend in a declining trend channel. The technician would identify point S as the sell point.

Trend Lines and Bands

Constructing and analyzing trend lines and channels are important to identifying if trends have been or will be broken. The resistance and support line of a channel can be thought of as points where the stock is either overbought or oversold. If a stock price breaks that level, it is a signal that something very significant is occurring and a new trend is developing. In practice, many technicians create bands around a regression trend line, moving averages, and highs and lows. A band formed using regression trends is known as an *autoregression band,* a popular band formed with moving averages is the *Bollinger band,* and a band formed using highs and lows is a referred to as a *Max/Min band.*

Autoregression Bands

An autoregression band is constructed by first identifying the price trend by regressing the stock's prices against the time periods; the band is then created by moving a certain number of standard normal deviations (e.g., +2 and −2) from the line or by setting the bands to be a certain percentage above or below the regression line. Exhibit 14.4 shows a Bloomberg bar chart of daily prices for the S&P 500 from 10/30/2006 to 10/30/2013. The graph highlights four price trend periods and two confirmation periods, each described in terms of their regression lines. Period 1 spans a 267-day period that preceded the 2008 financial crash in which the S&P 500 opened at 1,426 and closed at 1,517, with the average price changing by 0.34 points per day. Period 2 shows the bear market characterizing the crash, with the market opening at 1,181 and closing at 689, a 492-point drop over a 172-day span. In this bear trend the market dropped by 2.86 points per day. Period 3 shows a rebound period in which the market opened at 938 and then increased at a rate of 0.71 points per day for 409 days to close at 1,347. Finally, period 4 shows another bull trend, with the market opening at 1,240 and then increasing at an average of 0.85 points per day for 544 days

EXHIBIT 14.4 Auto Regression Bands for S&P 500, 10/31/2006 to 10/30/2013 Bloomberg: SPX <Enter>; Annotations; Regression

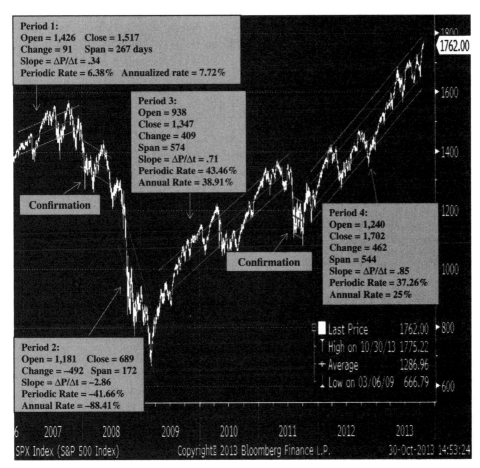

to close at 1,702. With perfect hindsight, a technician who took a long position in period 1 and then liquidated at the end of that period would have earned an annualized rate of 7.72 percent; if she later took a short position for period 2, covering the position at the end of that period, her return would have been 88.41 percent; if she then reversed and took a long position in period 3, liquidating it at the end, her return would have been 38.91 percent; and finally, if she took another long position in period 4 and liquidated it at the end, she would have earned a 25 percent annual return. This outstanding performance, however, is predicated on hindsight.

Bollinger Bands

Popularized by John Bollinger, Bollinger bands are formed by creating lines that are two standard normal deviations above and below a 20-day or 30-day moving average. The usefulness of the bands is that the price of a security, in turn, should remain within

EXHIBIT 14.5 Bollinger Bands for S&P 500, 11/1/2011 to 10/30/2013 Bloomberg: SPX <Enter>;
BOLL

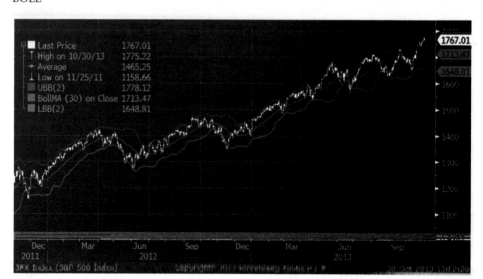

the bands 95 percent of the time provided the underlying variability does not change
significantly. A price breaking decidedly through either the upper (resistance) band or
lower (support) band would represent significant momentum that would propel the
price in the same direction of the breakout. Exhibit 14.5 shows Bloomberg price graphs
(bar chart) of daily prices (white line) for the S&P 500 from 11/1/2011 to 10/30/2013.
Also shown are the 30-day moving average, upper Bollinger band (UBB2), and lower
Bollinger band (LBB2).

Max/Min Bands

A maximum and minimum band, Max/Min band, is formed by taking the maximum
price and the minimum in the last X days (e.g., 20 days or 100 days) to set the upper
and lower bands. The Max/Min band is designed to point out the highest high and
lowest low. Like other bands it is used to identify breakouts. If a stock is trading in
a downtrend and is near a potential bottom, a break above the max line would be a
confirmation of a change in trend. In contrast, if a stock is trending up, a break down
below the minimum line is confirmation of a change in trend. Exhibit 14.6 shows
a Max/Min band formed around the S&P 500 for the period from 10/27/2006 to
10/28/2010 (a time period covering precrash, crash, and postcrash). The bands were
set using the highs and lows going 100 days back. The white line shows the price
movement of the S&P 500; other lines show the Max and Min bands. As shown in
the exhibit, the S&P 500 is closer to the minimum (approaching or hitting the Min
line) and further from the Max line for the second half of 2008 and the first quarter of
2009, indicating a number of sell breakthrough signals. By contrast, the S&P 500 is
closer to the maximum (approaching or hitting it) and further from the Min line for

EXHIBIT 14.6 Max/Min Bands for S&P 500, 10/27/2006 to 10/28/2010

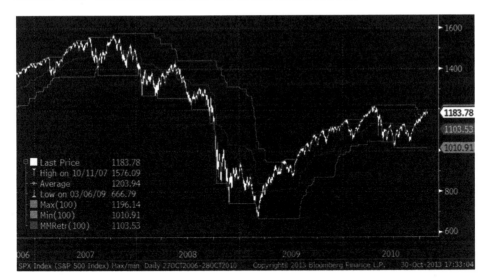

the last three quarters of 2009 and for first quarter of 2010, indicating a high number of buy breakout signals.

BLOOMBERG CHARTS, ANNOTATIONS, TECHNICAL STUDY SCREENS, CANDLE CHART, AND POINT-AND-FIGURE CHART

CHARTS HOMEPAGE: GRAPH <Enter>

The chart homepage has five box areas: custom charts, sample charts, new charting analytics, chart resource, and chart of the day newswire.

Custom Chart, G <Enter>

On the Custom Chart screen, you can create and customize charts representing different relationships, showing various technical studies. Charts created on other screens, such as GP, can also be saved to the Custom Chart screen by clicking the "Save as" tab on that screen. To create a new chart click "Create Chart" tab and then select type.

Annotations

Lines: Regression lines, bands, and other drawings can be included on a graph by clicking the "Annotate" button on the gray toolbar at the top of the price chart (GP). Clicking the button will bring up an annotations palette showing all of the tools for drawing on the chart, editing, and deleting. Trend lines, trend channels, and the regression line on the Bloomberg screen in Exhibit 14.4 were drawn from the annotation palette.

(Continued)

News: Also on the gray toolbar is the "News" button. Clicking this button will bring up an orange vertical bar. You can move the bar to a date of interest and then click to bring up a news box of stores related to your loaded security or index.

Technical Study Screens, TECH

A number of Bloomberg screens in this chapter relating to volume, moving averages, types of bands, breadth of the market, and the like are from Bloomberg's technical studies browser. The screens for these studies can be accessed from the "Technical Study Browser" found on the Graph home page (Graph <Enter>) or directly by typing TECH: TECH <Enter>. If the technical analysis study screen is not listed on the "Technical Study Browser" you can type the name of the study (e.g., Moving Averages) in the "Find a Study" box and click the name in the dropdown to bring up the screen's description page. On the description screen, press the "Launch" tab to bring up the screen. Once you're on the screen, you may want to save the screen for future use by clicking the "Save as" tab. This will save the screen to your G Screen.

Information on Bloomberg Technical Screens

For an excellent guide on technical analysis, see *Technical Analysis Handbook*, May 2010, Editor. Paul Ciana. This handbook and other information on technical analysis can be found on the Graphs homepage: Graph <Enter>, click "Charts Education."

Candle Charts

As noted earlier, *candle charts* show a candlestick at each time increment: A candle body without color (or open) represents a higher closing price than the opening price; a candle body with color (or solid) represents a lower close than open. The upper shadow or thin line above the body shows the high, and the lower shadow below the body shows the low. Candle patterns are used to depict price trends. A bull market is characterized by a series of long open candles and a bear market by long solid candles. A *hammer candle*, for example, has a small body, suggesting little difference between the close and the opening, but a long lower shadow. A series of these candles following a bull trend could signify a downturn. The opposite of a hammer is the hanging man. It has a small body and a long upper shadow.

Point-and-Figure Charts

Bar and candle charts show ending prices. *Point-and-figure* charts show only significant price changes, irrespective of the timing. The charts are set up to record a significant price change (e.g., 2 or 3 points) and to indicate reversals. For example in constructing a point-and-figure chart for a stock currently trading at $50, a technician using 2-point increments would do nothing if the stock increased to $51, but would place an X in the box if it increased to $52, and if it increased to $54, would place an X in the $52 box and $54 box. If the stock dropped from $54 to $48, a 6-point reversal, then the technician would move to the next column and place Xs in the boxes for $54, $52, $50, and $48. Point-and-figure charts that are horizontal would be considered trendless, indicating a period of consolidation; those that are vertical and above the starting price would indicate an uptrend; those that are vertical and below the starting price would indicate a downtrend. Breakouts would be when the chart moves up or down after a trendless period.

- Bloomberg's Point-and-Figure Chart, PFP: PFP <Enter> for a loaded security.
- Box Size refers to the price scale. It can be automatic or customized.
- Reversal is set as a multiple of box size. The reversal determines when you move to a new column. If the box size is 1 and the reversal is 2, then the price would have to move against the trend by 2 points to move to the next column.
- The numbers 1–9 and the letters A, B, and C represent the months January through September and October through December.

See Bloomberg Web Exhibit 14.1.

Price Trends Combined with Volume and Moving Averages

Market volume and moving averages are often used to measure the strength of a price trend. A market advance or decline is considered stronger if it also is accompanied by an increase in trading volume. Similarly, when a price breaks through its moving average from below, it is considered a bullish sign, and when it breaks through its moving average line from above, it is consider a bearish indicator.

Volume

When a strong buying surge pushes a stock's price past its resistance level on heavy volume, then one could reasonably deduct that there is bullish information that will push the price further to a new resistance level. By contrast, if a price decrease surges past the support level on heavy volume, it is a strong sell signal.

In addition to identifying buy and sell points, volume information also is used to better define the price trend. Typically, increasing volume and increasing price is a strong uptrend; increasing volume and falling price is a strong downtrend; decreasing volume and increasing price is a weak rally, and decreasing volume and decreasing price is a weak pullback. Recall, the Dow Theory defined a bull market as one characterized by ascending peaks, where each peak is higher than the previous, and a bear market as one characterized by descending peaks, where each trough is lower than the previous. These definitions can be refined by including volume. Specifically, a bull market is characterized by (1) each peak being higher than the previous, (2) the price increases being accompanied by heavier volume (strong uptrend), and (3) the price decreases being accompanied by lower volume (weak pullback). A bear market, in turn, is characterized by (1) each trough being lower than the previous, (2) the price decreases being accompanied by heavier volume (strong downturn), and (3) the price increases being accompanied by lower volume (weak rally).

In general, volume patterns help technicians to confirm the direction of the price trend and provide signals. One always needs to be cautious, however, in interpreting signals. A price decrease accompanied by heavy volume is generally interpreted as a strong downturn and a sell signal. However, a bear market with very heavy volume could also mean that the last of the bearish investors are selling and that the downward trend is reaching a *selling climax*. Thus, a heavy volume surge in a downtrend in which volume had been increasing could be a breakout signal and a possible buy point. Similarly, in the case of a strong uptrend in which price and volume are increasing, a strong surge in volume may push the price to its final peak in the bull trend. This last surge in volume in a bull run is referred to as a *speculative blow off*. It would mark the end of the run with the large volume increase signaling a sell point or a hold point.

Volume Measures

Volume at Time Measure

For a stock or market index, volume momentum is often measured in terms of actual volume to an average volume based on a specified number of periods back. Exhibit 14.7 shows Bloomberg's *Volume at Time* chart for Macy's for the period from 7/15/2013 to 10/31/2013. The top panel shows Macy's bar chart, the white histogram in the middle panel shows Macy's trading volume with the line graph showing Macy's 30-day moving average of volume, and the bottom panel shows the volume differentials between daily volume and average volume. Note that on 8/14, there was a surge in volume (the white histogram exceeding the average line), with 17.05 million shares traded compared to a 30-day average volume of 5.327. As shown in the exhibit, Macy's closed on 8/13 at $48.50 and opened on 8/14 at $46.69 before closing the day at $46.33. On 8/15, the stock opened lower at $45.85, but closed the day up at $46.30. It is interesting that the top news related to Macy's on 8/13 was a financial report that retail sales growth had fallen short of expectation. The next noticeable volume surge shown in Exhibit 14.7 occurred on 10/16. On 10/15, Macy's closed at $42.48, and on 10/16, it closed at $43.79, with 8.338 million shares traded on that day compared to an average 30-day volume of 5.69 million shares. On 10/17 the stock closed at $44.46 with the momentum in volume slowing. The top news on 10/15 was Macy's announcement that it was giving up its long tradition of being closed on Thanksgiving.

On-Balance Volume Measure

Another measure of volume momentum is the *on-balance volume* (OBV) statistic. Popularized by Joe Granville, the OBV measure is calculated by adding a previous day's volume to a cumulative volume if the stock closed higher the previous day and subtracting the previous day's volume if the stock closed lower the previous day. The measure can be used to gauge the overall strength of a trend, such as a strong bull run with prices and OBV lines increasing. Some technicians look at the

EXHIBIT 14.7 Bloomberg Volume-At-Time Screen, VAT Macy's Price, Volume, and 30-day Moving Average Volume, 7/15/2013–10/31/2013

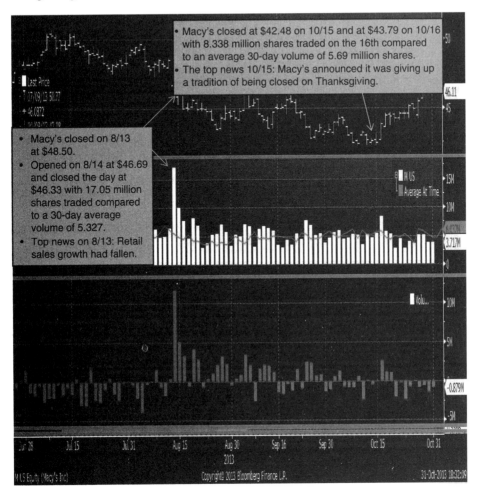

price and OBV lines for forecasting or for confirmation of a reversal.[3] Exhibit 14.8 shows the Bloomberg block charts and OBV graph for Macy's for the 7/15/2013 to 10/31/2013 period.

Market Volume Measures

A common measure of volume momentum for the overall market or a sector is the volume of stocks that have increased to the volume of stocks that have decreased. The market is considered overbought when the ratio exceed 1.5, and oversold when the ratio is less than 0.75. A similar measure is the *Trin ratio*. The ratio measures the average volume in declining issues to the average volume in advancing issues:

$$\text{Trin Ratio} = \frac{\text{Volume Declining/Number Declining}}{\text{Volume Advancing/Number Advancing}}$$

EXHIBIT 14.8 Bloomberg On-Balance Volume Screen, Macy's Price and OBV Measure, 7/15/2013–10/31/2013

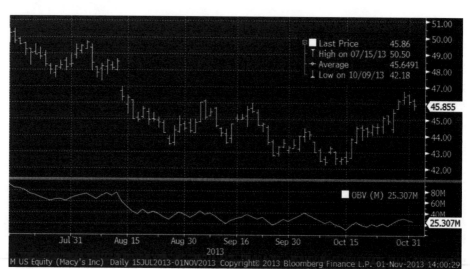

A Trin ratio above 1 is considered a bearish trend with selling pressure.

BLOOMBERG PRICE AND VOLUME SCREENS

Volume at Time, VAT

VAT screen shows prices along with trading volume, a moving average of volume, and the difference between volume and the average. You can select the number of days back to determine the moving average. To bring up the VAT screen for stock or index, type VAT. See Exhibit 14.7.

On Balance Volume, OBV

OBV measures the strength of momentum and signs for shifts in sentiment. OBV adds a previous day's volume to a cumulative volume if the stock closed higher the previous day and subtracts the previous day's volume if the stock closed lower the previous day. To bring up the OBV screen for a stock or index, type OBV.

Accessing OBV from Technical Study Screens

The OBV screen like the one shown in Exhibit 14.8 and other screens used in technical studies can be accessed from the "Technical Study Browser" found on the Graph home page (Graph <Enter>) or directly by typing TECH: TECH <Enter>. See the previous Bloomberg exhibit box for more information.

Volume Bar Distribution Screen, VBAR

VBAR shows volume at price over time. A total volume histogram is shown at the bottom of the screen; it will highlight in green if the volume is greater than the average and red if it is less than the average. You can use the chart to see the range in volume each day. To bring up the VBAR screen for a loaded stock or index, type VBAR.

Volume-Weighted Average Price, VWAP

VWAP provides historical and real-time information on price, volume, and other trades for the selected security. You can select the source(s) of the data, including an exchange or a combination of exchanges and use different price, volume, and time/date filters. The screen displays the volume-weighted average price, number of trades, and average trade size for a specified time, price, and volume range. To bring up the VWAP screen for a loaded stock or index, type VWAP.

Block Trades

- MBTR monitors block trades for stocks composing an index or portfolio.
- GIMB: Block money flow chart.

Moving Averages

There are several types of moving averages. A *simple moving average* is the average price of a stock or an index over a given interval, with the average recalculated each new time increment by adding the latest observation and deleting the oldest. With a simple moving average, equal weight is given to each observation. A *weighted moving average* weighs newer observations more than older. For example, a 30-day weighted moving average would weigh the most recent date by 30, the day before by 29, and so on. A *triangular moving average* weighs the data in the middle dates more. When used as signals for price trend changes, a weighted moving average generates the first signal, followed by the simple moving average, and then the triangular average. Other types of moving averages are exponential averages and variable moving averages that incorporate volatility. Moving averages also vary by the length of the time intervals (30-day or 100-day), with shorter intervals reflecting shorter trends, and they vary by periodicity (e.g., 52-week average and a 30-day average).

Moving average lines are used to determine the overall price trend. If the overall trend is decreasing, then the moving average line is above the price line because it averages the new lower prices with previous higher prices. When the overall price trend is increasing, the moving average line is below the price line. Technicians identify price trend reversals whenever a price line breaks its moving average line. Specifically, a signal to a technician of a reversal of a declining trend would be when prices start increasing such that the price line breaks through the moving average line from below. A technician might see this as a strong signal if it breaks the moving average line from below on heavy volume. A signal of a reversal of a rising trend would be when prices start decreasing such that the price line breaks through the moving average line from above. Again, if the breakthrough is accompanied with heavy volume, then the reverse signal may be considered a strong indicator. Exhibit 14.9 shows the bar chart, 30-day

EXHIBIT 14.9 Bloomberg GP Graph: Price, 30-Day Moving Average, and Volume: S&P 500, 11/2/2006 to 11/4/2010

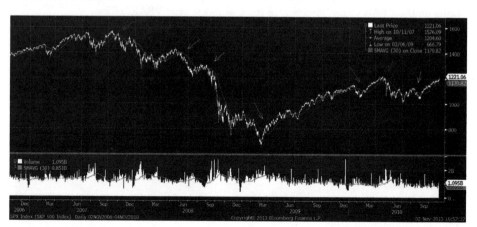

moving price average line, total volume, and 30-day moving volume average (lower pane) for the S&P 500 from 11/2/2006 to 11/4/2010 (period covering before and after the crash). As indicated in the graph, there are a number of periods from the third quarter of 2007 to the first quarter of 2009 where there are bear signals in which the price line cuts the moving average from above followed by a bear trend. From the second quarter of 2009 through 2010, there are several bull signals in which the price line cuts the moving average line from below.

Price reversal signals can vary with the length of time over which the moving average is calculated. Technicians often compare moving averages with different intervals, such as comparing a 30-day moving average with a 200-day moving average. Comparing short-run moving averages with long run may help a technician discern whether or not an issue is overbought or oversold. For example, a bullish trend market, where the 30-day moving average is above the 200-day and where the gap is widening, could be taken as an indicator of a fast run up in prices and an indication the stock is overbought. As noted previously, technicians also compare simple moving average lines with weighted and triangular lines for signals as well. It is worth keeping in mind that an early signal does not mean it is a correct signal.

Moving Average Bands

Recall, the Bollinger band is formed by adding and subtracting two standard normal deviations to a 20-day or 30-day moving average. Moving average bands, also called *moving average envelopes*, can be constructed from different moving average intervals, from weighted and triangular moving averages, and with different percentage increases and decreases from the averages. As discussed, bands help to identify resistance and support levels. They also can be used to confirm a price reversal. For example, a strong buy signal in a downtrend market would be when the price increases in that trend

EXHIBIT 14.10   Bloomberg Moving Average Envelope, GPO MAENV Macy's Price, 30-day
Moving Average, 7/22/2013–11/1/2013

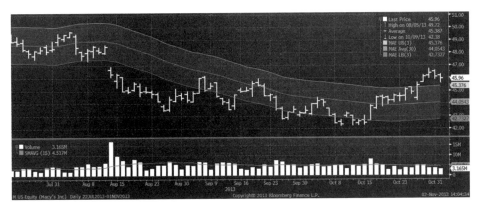

cause the stock's price line to first cut its moving average line from below and then
to cut its upper resistance level (maybe on heavy volume). If, however, the price cuts
its moving average line, but fails to push past its resistance line, then the stock would
be reverting back to either its downward trend or a new sideways trend; it could also
decrease past its support line, indicating a strengthening of the downward trend. Thus,
the resistance line helps the technician confirm if a movement past the moving average is or is not a reversal. Similarly, a strong sell signal in an uptrend market would
occur when a stock's price decreases cause its price line to first cut its moving average line from above and then cut its lower support level (maybe on heavy volume).
If, however, the price cuts its moving average line, but fails to push below its support line, then the stock would revert back to either its upward trend, a new sideways
trend, or a stronger uptrend if it pushes past its resistance line. In this case, the support
line helps the technician confirm if a movement past the moving average is or is not
a reversal.

Exhibit 14.10 shows Bloomberg's Moving Average Envelopes chart (GPO
MAENV) for Macy's for the period from 7/22/2013 to 11/1/2013. The screen shows
Macy's bar chart, 30-day moving average, and upper bound and lower bound set at
3 percent of the 30-day moving average (1.03 X MA and 0.97 X MA). We earlier discovered using Macy's volume-at-time graph (Exhibit 14.7) that on August 14, there
was a surge in volume with 17.05 million shares traded compared to a 30-day average
volume of 5.327. Also recall that the news on the August 13 was the report of lower
department store sales. Examining the moving average band, we see that Macy's also
crossed its moving average support line from above on the August 14 and continued
its downtrend to August 28. The stock hit a low for this period on October 15. It
then started an upward trend, crossing its 30-day moving average on October 17 and
its resistance level on October 28. Note that if the moving average bands had been
set at 2 percent instead of 3 percent, then it would have crossed the upper band on
October 24.

BLOOMBERG MOVING AVERAGE SCREENS

- GPO MA: Moving average screen for simple moving average. For a loaded security or index, type GPO MA.
- GPMA is a moving average price graph screen. For a loaded security or index, type GPMA.

Moving Average Envelopes: GPO MAENV

Similar to Bollinger bands, moving average envelopes are plotted by calculating percentage bands above and below a moving average. To bring up the screen for a loaded stock or index, type GPO MAENV. See Exhibit 14.10.

Accessing Moving Average and Other Technical Study Screens

Moving average screens used for studies can be accessed from the "Technical Study Browser" found on the Graph home page (Graph <Enter>) or directly by typing TECH: TECH <Enter>.

See Bloomberg Web Exhibit 14.2.

Market and Stock Metrics

Breadth of the Market

The breadth of the market refers to the degree of market participation or pervasiveness in an overall market trend. A bull (bear) market in which there are a large number of stocks increasing (decreasing) would be considered a strong bull (bear) market compared to one in which a small number are advancing (falling). In fact, an uptrend (downtrend) market in which the number of stocks participating in the increase (decrease) is decreasing is often taken as a signal of a directional change.

Advances minus declines, cumulative net advances, and moving cumulative averages are metrics used to measure the breadth of the market. The advances minus declines measure is the spread between the number of stocks that have advanced (A) and the number that have declined (D) in price: A − D. When the market is increasing and advances exceed declines by a large margin, then the uptrend is considered strong, especially if the widening positive spread is accompanied by heavy volume. When the market is in a decreasing trend and declines exceed advances by a large margin, the downtrend market is considered strong, especially if the widening negative spread is accompanied by large volume. Finally, a sign of an end to either an uptrend or downtrend is when the positive or negative spread begins to narrow.

In addition to net advance, some analysts use a moving cumulative measure of advances minus decline, adding the day's net advances to previous days going back X number of days: $\sum(A - D)$. Analysts also use a moving average of cumulative spreads. Both provide a measure of the broader trend of the market's depth. Exhibit 14.11

EXHIBIT 14.11   Bloomberg Price and Advance minus Declines Graphs for the S&P 500, 11/6/2006–11/4/2013

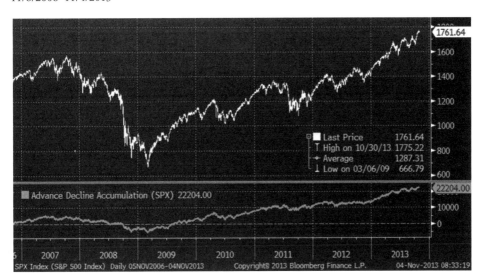

shows the price graph and cumulative advance-declines graph for the S&P 500 for the period from 11/6/2006 to 11/4/2013.

Number of Stocks Above or Below Their Moving Averages

In addition to the breadth of the market, technicians also try to determine the strength of the market and when it could be overbought or oversold. As we noted earlier, when the market or a stock hits a resistance level, it may be overbought, and when it hits its support level, it may be oversold. A measure used to determine if the overall market is near its resistance or support level is the number of stocks above their moving averages as a percentage of the total number of stocks. For example, the total number of stocks in the S&P 500 that are above their 200-day moving average as a percentage of the total number of stocks in the S&P 500. As a general rule, the market is considered overbought and subject to a reversal (negative correction) when more than 80 percent of the stocks are above their 200-day moving average; it is considered oversold and subject to a reversal (positive correction) when the percentage is less than 20 percent.

Uptick-Downtick Index

Another market gauge is a comparison of upticks to downticks. When a stock's price increases above the previous price—an *uptick*—it can be assumed the price was initiated by a buyer; when the price decreases below the previous price—a *downtick*—it can be assumed the price was initiated by a seller. An uptick-to-downtick spread, or a ratio of upticks to downticks, can be used as a measure of investors' sentiment. Many

EXHIBIT 14.12   S&P 500 Uptick-Downtick Index and S&P 500, 7/5/2012–11/2/2013 TIKX = TIKX <Index>

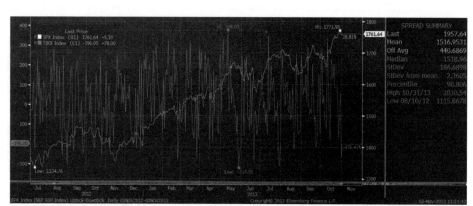

indexes and exchanges calculate an *uptick-downtick index.* The index is equal to the number of securities in the index or listed on the exchange trading on an uptick minus the number trading on a downtick. Exhibit 14.12 shows graphs of the S&P 500 and its uptick-downtick index from 7/5/2012 to 11/2/2013. The graph shows the uptick-downtick index hitting a peak of 378 on 5/10/13 before the market hits its peak (for that trend) of 1,669 on 5/21. The tick index hits a trough of −318 on 5/29, just before the market hits its low on its downtrend of 1,588 on 6/24. A perusal of Exhibit 14.12 shows other times when the index leads the market.

Since a large percentage of the volume of many markets is from institutional trades, another gauge of the market is the activities of block trades. Several exchanges track the direction of price changes that accompany a block trade. One measure of institutional sentiment is the *uptick-downtick block ratio* of the number of security blocks traded on a downtick to the number traded on an uptick. The market is considered oversold when the ratio is below 0.4 and overbought when the ratio exceeds one.

CBOE Put/Call Ratio

The put/call ratio is the ratio of the total volume of put option contracts to call option contracts. The general rule is that if the option market is bullish, then call volume will exceed put volume and the put/call ratio will be decreasing; if the market is bearish, then put volume will exceed call and the ratio will be increasing. Note that when the market is bearish the increase in put purchases can be driven not only by speculators, but also by hedgers who use long put positions to hedge their portfolios. A very low ratio is a signal of an overbought stock market, and a very high a ratio is a signal of an oversold one. The CBOE's put/call ratio is a commonly followed ratio of the option markets' sentiment that is used as an indicator of the overall stock market. Up or down deviation from the CBOE put/call ratio from 65 percent is considered a signal of market movements. Exhibit 14.13 shows the CBOE put/call ratio and prices for the S&P 500 from 11/1/2005 to 11/1/2013. For the period, the ratio hit its high of

EXHIBIT 14.13 CBOE Put/Call Ratio and S&P 500, 11/1/2005–11/1/2013 CBOE Put/Call Ratio = PCUSEQTR <Index>

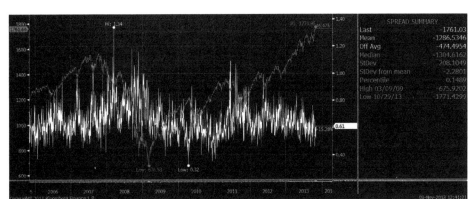

1.34 on 3/11/2008 (prior to the crash), with the market hitting its low of 676.53 on 3/4/2009; the put/call ratio hit its low of 0.32 on 4/20/2010, and the market hit its high of 1,771.95 on 10/24/2013.

In addition to using the option market's put/call ratio to evaluate the stock market, the put/call ratio of individual stocks are also used as a measure and indicator of that stock's trends. Exhibit 14.14 shows the Bloomberg's *Erlanger put/call ratio* for Macy's for the period between 7/22/2013 and 11/1/2013 that was analyzed earlier using volume-in-time graphs (Exhibit 14.7) and moving-average envelopes (Exhibit 14.10). In examining the graphs, notice how the put/call ratio increases as Macy's stock decreases and how the how the ratio decreases as its stock goes up.

Confidence Index

In addition to the option market, technicians also look to the bond market for indicators of the overall stock market. An indicator of the economy and the equity market

EXHIBIT 14.14 Bloomberg's Erlanger Put/Call Ratio Screen for Macy's 7/22/2013–11/1/2013, GPO ERPCR

is the yield on high-quality bonds to low-quality ones. When investors are confident in the economy or start to see signs of improvement (e.g., leading economic indicators rising), they often make a quality swap of their bond portfolios, swapping their higher-grade bonds for lower-grade ones to increase their portfolio's expected yield. In the bond market, these swaps, in turn, cause the prices of lower quality bonds to increase and their yields to fall, and the prices of higher quality bonds to decrease and their yield to increase. As a result, the quality spread between the low-quality yield and the high-quality yield begins to narrow. Stock market analysts study the bond market, in the same way they do the option market, for indicators of the direction of the overall stock market. In assessing the bond market, analysts look at quality spreads between high- and low-quality bond yields and also the ratio of high-quality to low-quality bond yields. Such ratios are called *confidence indexes*:

$$\text{Confidence Index} = \frac{\text{Average Yield of High-Grade Bonds}}{\text{Average Yield of Low-Grade Bonds}}$$

One of the older and still popular of these indexes is Barron's Confidence Index, which is the ratio of the average yield on 10 high-grade bonds at time t to the average yield of the Dow Jones 40 Bond bonds at time t.

At one time, the confidence index was thought to be a leading indicator of the stock market. As a leading indicator, technicians would look for divergences in which the confidence index and the market were moving in opposite directions. For example, if the confidence index was increasing (signaling that bond investors were confident) and the stock market was in a declining trend, a technician would predict a stock market reversal. Like most indicators, a confidence index provides a measure that can be used to confirm a trend. However, it may not be a leading indicator.

Short Interests

Another group of investors that technicians follow for monitoring the overall stock market, as well as stocks, are the market participants with short positions. A measure of short positions for a stock or the market is the short-interest ratio. *Short interest* is the cumulative number of outstanding shares being shorted by investors (i.e., shares borrowed that have not been covered). The *short-interest ratio* is equal to short interest divided by the average daily volume of trading. For the overall market, the ratio is equal to the number of shares shorted for stocks on an index (or on an exchange) to the average volume of trading on the index (or exchange). In general, if the short-ratio is increasing (decreasing), it would be an indication of a bearish (bullish) sentiment in the market. Exhibit 14.15 shows the short-interest ratios for the S&P 500 for all stocks in the index and by industry from 7/31/2013 to 10/15/2013, and Exhibit 14.16 shows the Bloomberg short-interest screen (SI) for Macy's. As shown in Macy's short-interest exhibit, Macy's short-interest ratio peaked on 7/31/2013, and its price hit a bottom on 8/30. The short-interest ratio, however, decreases during Macy's downtrend.

EXHIBIT 14.15   Short-Interest Ratio for S&P 500 by Industry, 7/31/2013–10/15/2013

Industry	07/31	08/15	08/30	09/13	09/30	10/15
All Securities	4.13	4.44	4.91	4.66	4.29	4.42
Energy	3.47	3.51	4.18	3.70	3.87	3.83
Materials	3.80	4.41	4.92	4.86	4.02	4.54
Industrials	4.37	4.74	5.60	5.23	4.80	4.89
Consumer Discretionary	4.73	4.55	4.91	4.92	4.60	4.53
Consumer Staples	4.79	4.74	4.63	4.60	4.14	4.61
Health Care	4.09	4.98	5.72	5.05	4.56	4.41
Financials	3.78	4.35	4.47	4.50	3.96	4.18
Information Technology	3.41	4.10	4.49	4.19	3.90	3.96
Telecommunication Services	9.06	8.48	12.78	10.55	10.02	10.21
Utilities	4.01	3.73	3.98	3.58	3.62	4.19

Source: Bloomberg, SIA Screen; SIA <Enter>

Relative Strength

Relative strength analysis measures the performance of a security to a benchmark. The most common *relative strength index* (RSI) is the ratio of stock price to the price of an index:

$$RSI = \frac{\text{Price of Stock } i}{\text{Price of an Index}}$$

When the index is rising, the stock is outperforming or leading the market, and when it is decreasing, the stock is underperforming or lagging the market. The

EXHIBIT 14.16   Bloomberg Short-Interest Screen for Macy's 7/22/2013–11/4/2013, SI

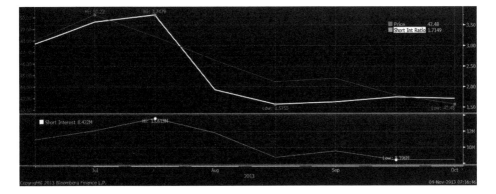

EXHIBIT 14.17   RSI Index for Apple: Price of Apple/Price of S&P 500, 11/4/2006–11/4/2013

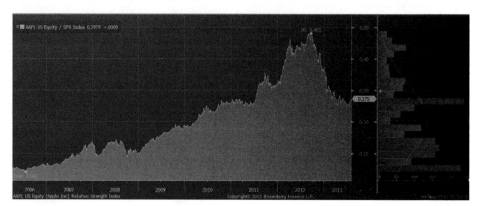

index applies to both uptrend and downtrend markets. In an uptrend market, the stock's RSI will be increasing if its price continues to increase more than the market; in a downtrend, a stock's RSI will be increasing if its price decreases less than the market.

The RSI index can be applied to an industry (price of industry index/price of market index) or to a stock relative to its industry (price of stock/price of industry index). The RSI is used to measure trends. If the prices of a stock, industry, or group of stocks are outperforming the market, it may continue to do so for some period of time. Exhibit 14.17 shows the RSI for Apple stock from 11/4/2006 to 11/4/2013. Apple's RSI increased for most of the period, hitting its maximum strength on 9/21/2012. However, from 9/21/2012 to 11/4/2103, Apple's RSI declined. In contrast, the RSI for P&G, shown in Exhibit 14.18, peaked on 12/10/2008 and then declined for the next five years.

EXHIBIT 14.18   RSI Index for Procter and Gamble: Price of P&G/Price of S&P 500, 11/4/2006–11/4/2013

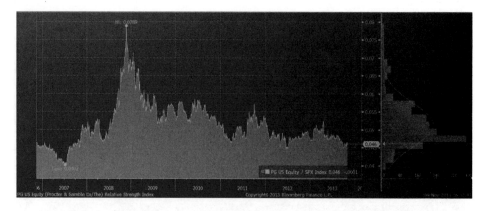

BLOOMBERG MARKET METRICS

Breadth of the Market

- **Advances Minus Declines Line, (ADL Line):** For a loaded index (e.g., S&P 500), type GPO ADL. The line can also be accessed from the "Technical Study Browser": TECH <Enter>, search for ADL or advances minus declines. See Exhibit 14.11.
- **Bloomberg NSE Advances–Declines Index:** NYADDEC <Index> <Enter>; GP.
- **McClellan Oscillator, MCCL:** McClellan Oscillator Screen shows a smooth line of the difference between advances and declines. Applicable for some indexes. For a loaded index (e.g., S&P 500) enter: MCCL <Enter>.

Uptick-Downtick Indexes:

- **TICK Index:** TICK <Index> <Enter>: Tick is equal to the number of NYSE securities trading on an uptick minus the number trading on a downtick.
- **TIKX Index:** TIKX <Index> Enter: The TIKX index is equal to the number of S&P 500 stocks trading on an uptick minus the number trading on a downtick. See Exhibit 14.12.
- **TIKI Index:** TIKI <Index> Enter: The TIKI index is equal to the number of Dow Jones stocks trading on an uptick minus the number trading on a downtick.
- **TICKUSE Index:** TICKUSE <Index> Enter: The TICKUSE index is equal to the number of all U.S. stocks trading on an uptick minus the number trading on a downtick.

Put/Call Ratio

- **CBOE Put/Call Ratio:** PCUSEQTR <Index>. See Exhibit 14.13.
- **Erlanger Put/Call Ratio:** For a loaded stock, type GPO ERPCR. See Exhibit 14.14.

Block Trade Screens

- **BTM:** Block Trade Monitor.
- **MBTR:** Block Trade Recap.

Short Interest

- **SI:** Short Interest and Short-Interest Ratios for a stock. For a loaded stock: SI <Enter>. See Exhibit 14.16.
- **SIA:** Short Interest platform for market indexes and exchanges.

Customize Graphs

- The graphs in Exhibits 14.17 and 14.18 were generated using Bloomberg's customized chart screen found on the Graphs or Charts Homepage: Charts <Enter> or Graph <Enter>; Click "Two-Security Spread or Ratio."

See Bloomberg Web Exhibit 14.3.

Technical Analysis of Other Markets and Portfolios

Our examples of trends and applications of technical tools in this chapter have so far been limited to U.S. indexes and stocks. The same analysis can be extended to foreign stock indexes and stocks, as well exchange rates, commodity prices, fixed-income prices and yields, and economic indexes.

Foreign Markets and Stocks

Exhibit 14.19 shows the bar chart for Bloomberg's European 500 index (BE500) for the period from 11/8/2010 to 11/4/2013, along with its 30-day moving average, moving average envelope (GPO MAENV), volume, 30-day moving volume average (middle pane), and cumulative advances minus declines (lower pane; GPO ADL).

EXHIBIT 14.19   Bloomberg European 500, BE500 <Index> Bloomberg Moving Average Envelope (GPO MAENV), 30-day Moving Average, Volume, and Cumulative Advances Minus Declines (GPO ADL) 11/8/2010–11/4/2013

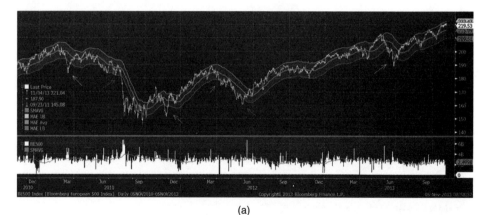

(a)

(b)

As indicated in the graph, there are a number of periods where there are bear signals in which the price line cuts the moving average from above, on heavy volume exceeding the 30-day moving average, and with cumulative advances minus declines decreasing; these signals are then followed by a bear trend. There are also several bull signals in which the price line cuts the moving average line from below, on relatively high volume, and with cumulative advances minus declines increasing.

Exchange Rates

Exhibit 14.20 shows the bar chart, moving averages, and 3 percent moving average bands for the U.S. dollar price of the euro (top panel) and Japanese yen (middle panel) from 11/8/2010 to 11/5/2013. The uptrend and downtrend for the euro is similar to the European 500 index. A currency trader using just the moving average line would find a number of signals for reversals. There are only a few confirmation points, however, where the exchange rate moves past its support and resistance levels, at least based on a 3 percent band. For the same period, the yen is characterized by a sideways trend for 2010 to the beginning of the third quarter of 2012, where it begins a significant uptrend. During both trends, the yen trades most of the time within its channel. The lower panel in Exhibit 14.20 shows a plot of both exchange rates and a correlation plot. For the period, the average correlation was –0.7731. For currency traders who use the options, futures, and forward markets, these technical trends are important in helping to identify long and short futures positions and long and short call or put positions.

Commodities

Exhibit 14.21 shows the bar chart and price charts, moving averages, and 3 percent moving average bands for spot crude oil prices (WIT cushing crude oil spot price, USCRWTIC <Index>) and corn spot prices (yellow kennel corn, dollar per bushel, CORNILNC <Index>) for the period from 11/5/2010 to 11/5/2013. For this three-year period, crude oil prices ranged between approximately $80 and $112 and had three significant peaks, each near $110, and three significant bottoms, each near $80. For the same period, corn prices ranged from $8.44 per bushel to $4.43 per bushel, with a two moderate uptrends from 11/5/2010 to 7/20/2012 and a significant downtrend for the period from 7/20/2012 to 11/4/2013.

Portfolio Management Using Technical Metrics

As noted in the introduction, technical analysis when used in conjunction with fundamental analysis provides a more complete picture of the stock or market. In practice, many analysts and investment firms use fundamental analysis to determine what to buy and sell and technical analysis to determine when to buy and sell.

EXHIBIT 14.20   Euro and Japanese Yen Bloomberg Moving Average Envelope and Correlation 11/5/2010–11/5/2013.

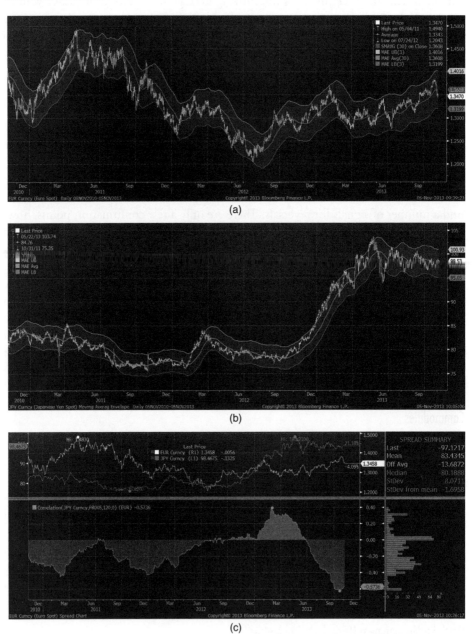

(a)

(b)

(c)

(a) Euro: EUR <Curncy>; GPO MAENV <Enter>. (b) Yen: JPY <Curncy>; GPO MAENV <Enter>. (c) The graph is generated from Bloomberg's customized chart: Charts Homepage: Charts <Enter>; Click "Two-Security Spread or Ratio."

EXHIBIT 14.21   Crude Oil and Corn Spot Prices Bloomberg Moving Average Envelope 11/5/2010–11/5/2013.

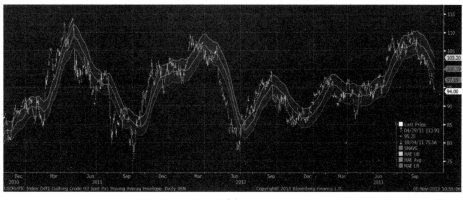

(a)

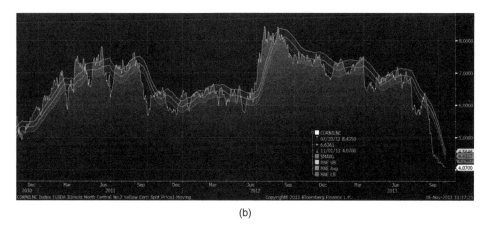

(b)

(a) Crude Oil: WIT Cushing Crude Oil Spot Price USCRWTIC <Index>; GPO MAENV <Enter>.
(b) Corn: Corn Spot Prices CORNILNC <Index>; GPO MAENV <Enter>.

Other market participants combine both approaches to reinforce or to check their positions.

In managing and monitoring an active portfolio, portfolio managers who combine financial and economic information with technical tools are better able to confirm their overall equity allocation decisions and to reinforce their buy, hold, and sell stock recommendations. In Chapter 12, we analyzed Macy's in terms of its fundamentals—sales, earnings, margins, growth rates, and investment opportunities. Such analysis is only enhanced when technical indicators such as price trends, volume, put/call ratios, short-interest ratio, and relative strength indicators are included as part of the analysis. Even when the fundamentals and technical signs conflict, they still provide a useful red flag that forces an analyst to ask questions and to look deeper.

EXHIBIT 14.22 Student Investment Fund and S&P 500 Bloomberg Moving Average Envelope 1/1/2010–6/4/2010.

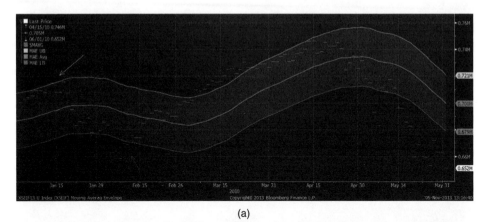

(a)

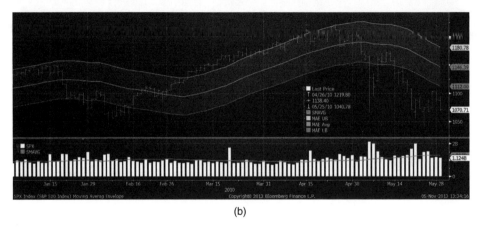

(b)

(a) Investment Fund: XSEIF13 <Index> the Bloomberg CIXB screen was used to make the fund an index. (b) S&P 500: SPX <Index>

In the last chapter, we presented the investment decisions made in the first quarter of 2010 of a student investment fund that focused on fundamentals. Recall, that in January and February, the fund managers became concerned with a possible correction in the stock market. They decided to adjust the portfolio by selling some of their stocks meeting their sell criteria based on fundamentals. Based on their technical monitors of these stocks, a number of stocks sold were also near their 52-week high and near their 2007 peak. Exhibit 14.22 shows the student fund's portfolio values and the S&P 500 from the beginning of January to June of 2010, along with the fund's 30-day moving average and moving average envelopes (GPO MAENV). As shown in the exhibit, the fund and the market were both close to their resistance levels on January 18, reinforcing the decision to sell some stocks and increase the fund's cash position. The January 1 portfolio subsequently crossed its support level at the beginning of

EXHIBIT 14.23   RSI Index: Salesforce.com Inc, Kohl's, and Progress, 1/1/2010–6/4/2010

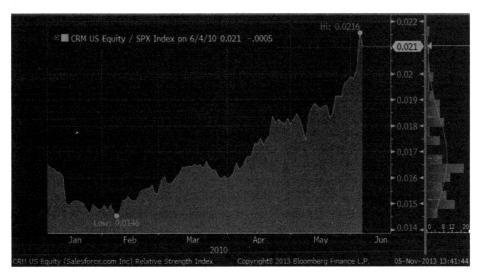

(a)

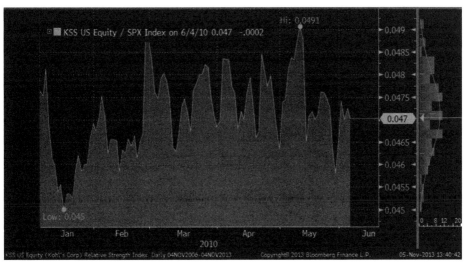

(b)

February. At that time, the fund managers increased their stock holdings by 5 percent (from the cash position) by purchasing Kohl's, Archer Daniels Midland, Abbott, Tiffany, Progress, Devon, and SalesForce.com. Each of the stocks was considered to be underpriced and a good buy based on the fundamentals. In addition, four of the stocks had very strong buy technical indicators, such as rising relative strength indexes (see Exhibit 14.23).

EXHIBIT 14.23   (*Continued*)

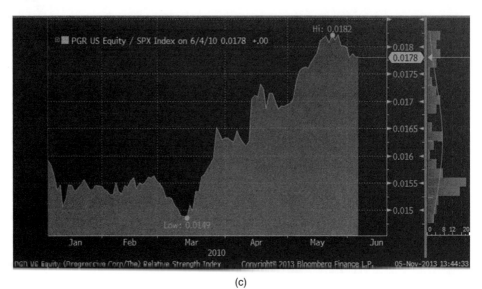

(c)

(a) Salesforce.com Inc. (b) Kohl's. (c) Progress.

BLOOMBERG: OTHER TECHNICAL INDEXES

There are numerous other indicators that technicians use. Some of note on Bloomberg include Rate of Change, Money Flow, Relative Strength Analysis, and True Range.

Rate of Change

The rate of change (ROC) is the percentage change in price from N-periods back to the current: ROC = (Current Price/Price N-Periods back) − 1. For most price trends, the price and ROC will move together. When there is a divergence, the ROC is considered the strong indicator. Thus, if the price is increasing and ROC is decreasing, it is a signal that price will reverse and decrease.

- ROC: For loaded stock or index, type ROC.

Relative Strength Analysis

Bloomberg's relative strength index (RSI) was developed by Wells Wilder. The index is based on the average of up closes to the average of down closes:

RSI = 100 − [100/(2 + (Average Up/Average Down)]

- RSI: For loaded stock or index, type RSI.

Money Flow

A money flow is equal to price multiplied by volume. For most upticks, the money flow will increase, and for most downticks the flow will decrease. The technical theory is that the money flow will lead price. If prices are decreasing (increasing) and money flow is increasing (decreasing), then price will go up (down).

- GM: For a loaded stock, type GM.

True Range

True range compares a security's high and low to the preceding day's close instead of that day's opening.

- Average True Range screen, ATR, can be accessed from the "Technical Study Browser": TECH <Enter>; search for ATR.

Bloomberg: Excel Templates for Technical Analysis

Bloomberg has a number of Excel templates for conducting technical analysis. Use DAPI to see a listing and to download: DAPI <Enter>; Click "Excel Template Library"; Click "Technicals." Templates of note:

- Historical Technical Analysis, XGDX.XLS.
- Multi Technical Analysis Screen, XMCD.XLS.
- Trader's Technical Analysis Dashboard, XTAS3.XLS.
- Above/Below Ratio, XABR.XLS.
- Intraday RSI Monitor, XRSI.XLS.
- Market Breadth Monitor, XMBM.XLS.
- Trader's Technical Analysis Dashboard for Commodities, XTAC.XLS.

See Bloomberg Web Exhibit 14.4.

Behavioral Finance

Bubbles

From the beginning of 1995 to April 2000, the S&P 500 increased 230 percent from 461 to 1,523; even more impressive, the NASDAQ 100 index (NDX (<Index>) increased 1,082 percent, from 398 to 4,704. This was the Dot-Com boom period, described by Fed Chair, Alan Greenspan, at the time as one of "irrational exuberance." After peaking in April of 2000, the market crashed. One year later, the S&P was at 1,100 and the NASDAQ 100 index had decreased to approximately 1,400; by April 2002, it had declined to approximately 1,000—the bubble had burst (see Exhibit 14.24).

In general, a speculative bubble occurs when the price of an asset, such as stock, gold, or houses, increases beyond a level that can be justified on economic grounds, and once past that level it still continues to rise. History is replete with speculative bubbles. Whether it is the South Sea Bubble, the Internet bubble, or the more recent

EXHIBIT 14.24   NASDAQ 100 Index (NDX <Index>), 1995–2009

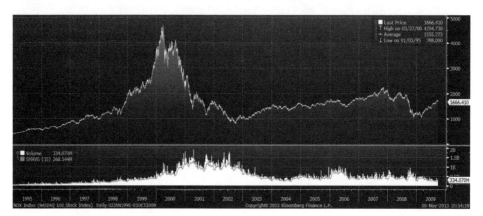

housing bubble, bubbles tend to have stages: an initial period in which an event, development, or invention changes expectations; next a period of abnormal returns for early investors, which attracts other investors; third, a boom period in which prices increase as more investors try to get rich even though fundamentals no longer make sense; fourth, the bust. In his book, *Dot.Con*, John Cassidy captures the essence of the Internet bubble with the story of Priceline.com:

> "In March 1999, Priceline.com … was preparing to do an initial public offering … The word on Wall Street was that Priceline.com would follow the path of America Online, Yahoo!, and eBay to become an "internet blue chip." The only question people in the investment community were asking was how much stock they would be able to lay their hands on .... On the morning of March 30, 10 million shares of Priceline.com opened on the Nasdaq National Market at $16 each, but the price immediately jumped to $85. At the close of trading, the stock stood at $68; it had risen 425 percent on that day. Priceline.com was valued at almost $10 billion—more than United Airlines, Continental Airlines, and Northwest Airlines combined.... Priceline.com started operating on April 6, 1998. By the end of the year it had sold slightly more than $35 million worth of airline tickets, which cost it $36.5 million .... The loss did not include any of the money Priceline.com spent developing its web site .... A few weeks after Priceline.com's IPO, its stock reached $150, at which point the tiny company was worth more than the entire U.S. airline industry. Two years later, the stock was trading at less than $2, and the entire capitalization of Priceline.com would not have covered the cost of two Boeing 747s." (Cassidy, *Dot.Con*, pp. 2–8)

Behavioral Finance Models

As noted in the introduction, behavioral finance is a psychology-based branch of finance that looks at the systematic impact human frailties and biases have on stock price patterns. In the absence of market efficiencies, behaviorists try to show how such biases lead to anomalies and discernible trends that technical investors, as well as fundamentalists, could exploit. Some of these biases include conservativeness, overconfidence, framing, and memory biases.

Conservative Bias

A *conservative bias* refers to individuals that are slow to change their positions or beliefs in the presence of new evidence. A market with a conservative bias would be slow to react to information. This bias would lead to a pattern in which it takes time for new information to be fully reflected in the price. For example, suppose an oil company just finds its oil reserves are three time greater than originally estimated and reports that the firm's earnings will be three times greater than the current level as a result of the discovery. When the company announces the reserve increase, the market would push up the company's stock price. Suppose that after the announcement is made it takes two weeks for the stock price to increase from its current level of $50 to its new equilibrium level of $75. This gradual increase in share prices may be due to the presence of a *learning lag* in which some investors respond immediately to the auspicious earnings information, but others with a conservative bias take more time to react. Since it takes some time before the impact of the information is fully reflected in the stock's price, a trend would emerge in which the stock begins to slowly trade away from its initial level to its new equilibrium one.

Overconfidence

Overconfidence occurs when individuals overestimate their knowledge, skill, or abilities. In the financial market, a dominance of overconfident investors would lead to overshooting.

For example, in the case of the new oil reserve, suppose the market is dominated by overconfident investors who overestimate the impact or exaggerate the favorable information and by their buying activities push the stock price to $80. Later, after reassessing, the market pushes the price back to its new equilibrium price of $75.

Framing Bias

Framing bias refers to how decisions or actions are influenced by how the choices are framed. A market influenced by investors with a gain-oriented frame of mind, and therefore overconfident, would tend to overshoot. On the other hand, a market influenced by investors with a loss-oriented frame of mind, and therefore conservative, would tend to lag. The frame of mind may also be different with respect to gains and losses. For example, some individuals may be more gain-oriented when it comes to gains, thus becoming more risk-seeking and aggressive as the market goes up, and then be more loss-oriented when it comes to losses, in turn becoming more risk-averse as the market declines. However, it may be the opposite, where investors become more risk-averse the more they gain, and more risk-seeking the more they lose.[4]

Another form of framing bias is mental accounting in which an investor separates decisions, for example, investors that are risk seeking when it comes to certain types of investments and risk-averse to others.

Memory Bias

Memory bias refers to individuals who place too much weight on more recent events instead of their beliefs or convictions. For example, an investor that places more weight on a forecast of good earnings than to his knowledge of the company's poor long-term prospects or his knowledge of the company's declining market share.

Behavioral Finance and Efficient Markets

As a school of thought, *Behavioral Finance* develops behavioral models that provide some support for technical analysis, provided the markets are inefficient. Behavioral biases that impact the market are irrelevant if markets are efficient. For example, in the oil well scenario where a conservative bias led to a learning lag, a technician studying such trends would be able to earn abnormal returns by buying the stock a day or two after it begins to trade away from its historical level ($50), then selling it when it stabilizes two weeks later around its new equilibrium ($75). Excess profit in this case is realized by technicians who profit from discerning learning lag trends in the market. However, if the market is efficient, then such technicians by their actions would push the price up before the laggers enter the market, thereby eliminating the trend.

Behaviorists counter the efficient market argument by pointing to *fundamental risk* that limits investors from taking advantage of mispricing. That is, a stock that is considered to be underpriced by fundamentalists would earn an abnormal return if the stock moves to its intrinsic value. The fundamental risk, however, is that the stock could continue to be underpriced. Recall, the example of Macy's in Chapter 12, in which we applied fundamental analysis to determine Macy's intrinsic value. In that example, Macy's was underpriced, but our gain from buying it depended on the market pushing its price toward its future intrinsic value. Behavioral advocates contend that because of fundamental risk, it takes time for a stock to reach its intrinsic value. They also point to how such risk explains bubbles. Consider an analyst during the dot-com bubble who argued that Priceline.com was overpriced at $68 and recommended a sell or no buy, only to later see it reach $150! Contrast her to the analyst who said Priceline.com is overpriced, but we still should buy. It is worth noting the epilogue to the Priceline.com story: From 2002 to 2008, Priceline.com traded between $50 and $65. From 2009 to 2013, the stock's price skyrocketed. On 11/6/2013, it was trading at $1,082! So maybe the technician was right. In the next chapter, we examine the efficient market theory in more detail.

Conclusion

Technical analysis looks for price trends combined with volume information, moving averages, the breadth of the market, confidence indicators, and other indicators to identify trading opportunities. As an alternative approach to fundamental analysis, technical analysis assumes that all fundamental information is captured in the market price and that market statistics reveal all information. As a complement, technical analysis when used in conjunction with fundamental analysis provides a more complete picture of the stock or market.

EXHIBIT 14.25 Bloomberg's Hurst Exponent Value for the S&P 500, 2000–2013

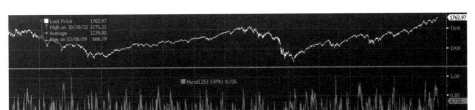

The Hurst exponent is a time-series measure named after Harold Hurst (1880–1978). The exponent was originally used in hydraulic engineering to study the volatility patterns of rain observed over a long period of time. In finance, the Hurst exponent is used to identify price patterns hidden within seemingly random stock price trends. In general, a time series can be persistent, with a tendency to continue its up or down pattern; antipersistent, in which it has a higher tendency to reverse its current pattern; or random. Bloomberg's Hurst screen (GPO KAOS) is based on the work of Christopher May who applied the Hurst exponent to nonlinear price patterns. Bloomberg's Hurst exponent screen can be used to test for randomness. If a price trend is random, the Hurst coefficient would continuously have a value close to 0.5. If not, then there is pattern to the stock price movement. For the period 2000–2013, Bloomberg's Hurst exponent value for the S&P 500 averaged 0.735 (Exhibit 14.25). Using the Hurst screen for other stocks, one will find more often than not that the stocks' price patterns have Hurst exponent values higher or lower than 0.5, suggesting patterns to their movements and providing an argument for the use of technical analysis.

BLOOMBERG ALERTS FOR TECHNICAL STUDIES

Alerts: ALRT<Enter>: The ALRT screen monitors up to 3,000 security alerts on prices, recommendations, corporate actions and filings, ratings changes, earnings, economic events, and the like. For technical analysis, you can set alerts on a number of indicators. Alerts can also be set on the G screen for a security you're analyzing.

Backtesting

Backtesting, BTST: BTST <Enter>: The BTST screen backtests a number of different technical studies and compares them to a naive buy-and-hold strategy. The tests are done on a daily basis for up to 5 years, a weekly basis for up to 25 years, and a monthly basis for up to 100 years.

(Continued)

> Each technical study can be adjusted for respective buy, sell, short, and cover signals, including multiple actions at once. On BTST, click the pencil icon to bring up a box for setting the conditions of the test. For example, click the Simple Moving Average Icon; in the condition box, set the conditions, such as long when the closing price crosses the moving average line from below and short when it crosses the line from above.
> See Bloomberg Web Exhibit 14.5.

Web Site Information

For financial information on securities, market trends, and analysis, see the following:

- http://bigcharts.marketwatch.com
- www.Finance.Yahoo.com
- http://www.hoovers.com
- http://www.bloomberg.com
- http://online.wsj.com/public/us

Notes

1. Charles Dow wrote the initial articles about price trends. After his death in 1902, William Hamilton became editor of the *Wall Street Journal* and developed the theory further. His work is explained in his book, *The Stock Market Barometer*, published in 1932. Later, Charles Rhea delineated the theory and gave it the name, "Dow Theory"—the title of his 1932 book.
2. In addition to the Dow Theory, another often-cited price trend is a *head-and-shoulders trend.* The trend has a left shoulder stage where the stock price is pushed up to a new peak before there is slowdown in volume. This is followed by a surge in buying that pushes prices to another new level before there is another slowdown in volume. This is followed by a modest rally that pushes prices up again, before retreating. The last stage is the right shoulder, in which prices fall below their support level.
3. For example, suppose the market is one in which institutional block trades initially drive the trend, followed by smaller retail investors who provide the final increments in demand. For a bull market, the OBV would be increasing with the large block and institutional purchases but would start to increase at a decreasing rate when retail investors start to buy; finally, it would decrease when institutional investors begin to sell. In most cases, OBV changes before the price change. A technician would therefore read the slowing of the OBV measure when the market is increasing as a sign of an impending peak and might sell when he sees a divergence with the price still rising and the OBV decreasing. As noted previously, it may be that the last surge in volume in a bull run is large—speculative blow; in this case, the OBV would be increasing at an increasing rate before hitting its resistance level.
4. A behavior in which investors become risk averse when their wealth increases, and become risk seeking when their wealth decreases can be explained in terms of prospect theory. The premise of prospect theory is that utility depends on changes in wealth, not on the level of wealth.

Selected References

Barber, Brad, and Terrance Odean. 2001. Boys will be boys: Gender, overconfidence, and common stock investment. *Quarterly Journal of Economics* 16: 262–292.

Barberis, Nicholas, and Richard Thaler. 2003. A survey of behavioral finance. *Handbook of the Economics of Finance*. Edited by G. M. Constantinides, H. Harris, and R. M. Stultz. Amsterdam: Elsevier.

Bollinger, John. 2002. *Bollinger on Bollinger Bands*. New York: McGraw-Hill.

Blume, Lawrence, David Easley, and Maureen O'Hara. 1994. Market statistics and technical analysis: The role of volume. *Journal of Finance* 49 (March): 153–181.

Brock, W., J. Lakonishok, and B. LeBaron. 1992. Simple technical trading rules and the stochastic properties of stock returns. *Journal of Finance* (December): 1731–1764.

Brown, David P., and Robert H. Jennings. 1989. On technical analysis. *Review of Financial Studies* 2 (October): 527–551.

Cassidy, John. 2002. *Dot.Con: The Greatest Story Ever Sold*. New York: Harper Collins.

Chopra, N., J. Lakonishok, and J. Ritter. 1992. Measuring abnormal performance: Do stocks overreact? *Journal of Financial Economics* 31: 235–268.

Ciana, Paul, ed. 2010. *Technical Analysis Handbook*. Hoboken, NJ: Bloomberg Press. (PDF document can be accessed from a Bloomberg Terminal).

DeMark, Thomas R. 1999. *The New Science of Technical Analysis*. Hoboken, NJ: John Wiley & Sons.

Edwards, R. D., and John Magee, Jr. 1966. *Technical Analysis of Stock Trends*, 5th ed. Springfield, MA: Stock Trends Services.

Fama, E. F. 1998. Market efficiency, long-term returns, and behavioral finance. *Journal of Financial Economics* 49 (September): 283–306.

Fama, E. F., and K. R. French. 1988. Permanent and temporary components of stock prices. *Journal of Political Economy* 96 (April): 246–273.

Gandar, John, Richard Zuber, Stafford Johnson, and W. Dare. 2002. "Re-Examining the betting market on major league baseball games: Is there a reverse favorite-longshot bias? *Applied Economics* 34: 1309–1317.

Gandar, John, Richard Zuber, Thomas O'Brien, and Ben Russo. 1988. Testing rationality in the point spread betting market. *The Journal of Finance* 43: 995–1008.

Glickstein, David A., and Rolf Wubbels. 1983. Dow theory is alive and well. *Journal of Portfolio Management* 9 (Spring): 28–32.

Granville, Joseph E. 1976. *Granville's New Strategy of Daily Stock Market Timing for Maximum Profit*. New York: Prentice Hall.

Grinblatt, Mark, and Bing Han. 2005. Prospect theory, mental accounting, and momentum. *Journal of Financial Economics* 78 (November): 311–339.

Hurst, H. E., R. P. Black, and Y. M. Simaika. 1965. *Long-Term Storage: An Experimental Study*. London: Constable.

Kahneman, D., and A. Tversky. 1979. Prospect theory: An analysis of decisions under risk. *Econometrica* 47: 263–291.

Karpoff, J. M. 1987. The relationship between price changes and trading volume: A survey. *Journal of Financial and Quantitative Analysis* 22 (March): 109–126.

Levy, Robert A. 1966. Conceptual foundation of technical analysis, *Financial Analysts Journal* 22 (July–August): 83.

Lo, Andrew, and Craig MacKinley. 1999. *A Non-Random-Walk Down Wall Street*. Princeton: Princeton University Press.

May, Christopher. 1999. *Nonlinear Pricing: Theory & Applications*. Hoboken, NJ: John Wiley & Sons.

Schleifer, A., and R. Vishny. 1997. The limits of arbitrage. *Journal of Finance* 52 (March): 35–55.

Sweeney, Richard J. 1988. Some new filter rule tests: Methods and results. *Journal of Financial and Quantitative Analysis* 23 (September): 285–300.

Bloomberg Exercises

1. Select a stock of interest and evaluate its price trends on Bloomberg's GP screen over a certain period of time (e.g., the most recent two years or the period before and after the financial crisis).

   a. On the GP screen, use the "Annotate" button on the gray toolbar at the top of the price chart to bring up the annotations palette. On the palette, select regression from the pointer box (top right corner of the palette), span the regression pointer over the time period of interest, and then click to create the regression band. Create several regression bands and study their beginning and ending prices and regression slope. To obtain information in a band area, move your curser to the band line to bring up an information box with price and regression information.

   b. Select the peak and trough points on your graph and study the important news at those times. To find news, click the "News" button on the gray toolbar to bring up an orange vertical bar. Move the bar to a date of interest and then click to bring up a news box.

   c. Examine some of the other drawing tools on the palette.

2. There have been two speculative-type bubbles over the last 20 years: the 1995–2000 Dot-Com bubble and the 2008 financial crisis. Using the GP graph, analyze the price trends of the Dow or S&P 500 around these periods.

   a. On the GP screen, select moving averages and identify points where the price lines cross the moving average lines.

   b. On the GP graph, select volume (dropdown box in right corner) and identify the volume at different breakout points.

   c. Create an autoregression band for the flat trends, downtrends, and uptrends. Click the "Annotate" button on the gray toolbar at the top of the price chart to bring up the annotations palette. On the palette, select regression from the pointer box (top right corner of the palette), span the regression pointer over the time period of interest and then click to create the regression band.

   d. Select primary reversal points on your graph and study the important news at those times. To find news, click the "News" button on the gray toolbar to bring up an orange vertical bar. Move the bar to a date of interest and then click to bring up a news box.

   e. Save your graph to the G screen from the "Save as" tab.

3. On the Custom Chart Screen, you can create and customize charts representing different relationships. Use the Spread Chart screen to create a relative-strength ratio for a stock of interest: G <Enter>; click "Create Charts"; select "Spread Charts" and click next; in the Chart Wizard box, input your stock and market index (e.g., S&P 500, SPX), select ratio in the dropdown box, select time period, and then click finish. To save your graph to the G screen, click "Chart Library" in the "Actions" tab.

4. Bollinger bands are formed by creating lines that are two standard normal deviations above and below a 20-day or 30-day moving average. The usefulness of the

bands is that the price of a security should remain within the bands 95 percent of the time, provided the underlying variability does not change significantly. Create Bollinger bands for a stock or index of interest and a time period of interest. To bring up a Bollinger screen for a loaded stock or index, enter: Boll <Enter>. On the Bollinger screen, change the standard normal deviation from 2 to a lower deviation (e.g., 1.5 or 1) to see if the stock breaks away from its support or resistance. Lengthen and shorten the moving average from 30 days to see if there are any breakouts.

5. Point-and-figure charts show only significant price changes, irrespective of the timing. The charts are set up to record significant price changes (e.g., 2 or 3 points) and indicate reversals. Point-and-figure charts that are horizontal would be considered trendless; those that are vertical and above the starting price would be an uptrend; those that are vertical and below the starting price would be a downtrend. Breakouts would occur when the chart moves up or down after a trendless period. On Bloomberg's Point-and-Figure Chart (PFP: PFP <Enter> for a loaded security), the "Box" size refers to the price scale (automatic or customized), and the "Reversal" is equal to a multiple of the box size and determines when you move to a new column. If the box size is 1 and the reversal is 2, then the price would have to move against the trend by 2 points to move to the next column. The numbers 1–9 and the letters A, B, and C on the PFP screen represent the months January through September and October through December.

   Use the Bloomberg point-and-figure chart screen to evaluate the price trends of a stock or index of interest. For a loaded stock, type PFP and click <Enter>. Experiment with the PFP screen by changing the size of box and reversal multiplier.

6. Volume information can be used to better define the price trend. Typically, increasing volume and increasing price is a strong uptrend; increasing volume and falling price is a strong downtrend; decreasing volume and increasing price is a weak rally, and decreasing volume and decreasing price is a weak pullback. Select a stock or index of interest and a time period of interest and examine its price and volume to determine the strength or weakness of a trend. In examining price trends and volume, use the following screens.
   a. GP screen with the volume panel.
   b. Volume-at-time (VAT) screen: This screen shows prices, along with trading volume, a moving average of volume, and the difference between volume and the average. You can select the number of days back to determine the moving average. To bring up the VAT screen for a loaded stock or index, type VAT.

7. When a strong buying surge pushes the price of a stock or index past its resistance level on heavy volume, then one could reasonably deduct that there is bullish information that will push the price further to a new resistance level. By contrast, if a price decrease surges past the support level on heavy volume, it is a strong sell signal. Select a stock or index of interest and a time period of interest and examine the volume patterns at breakout points (GPO MAENV). In retrospect, are the breakout signals correct? Study the important news around a breakout point by

clicking the "News" button on the gray toolbar to bring up an orange vertical bar. Move the bar to dates around the breakouts and then click to bring up a news box.

8. There are different types of volume measure, as well as technical studies that use volume. Volume screens used for studies can be accessed from Bloomberg's "Technical Study Browser" screen found on the Graph home page (Graph <Enter>) or directly by typing TECH: TECH <Enter> and then typing "volume" in the find box. Use the Technical Browser screen to identify the different types of volume studies. To bring up a particular screen, press the launch tab.

9. Technicians identify a possible price trend reversal whenever a price line breaks its moving average line; for instance, a reversal of a declining trend would be when prices start increasing such that the price line breaks through the moving average line from below. Moving averages can vary by length (30 days or 200 days) and periodicity (day or week). Use Bloomberg's moving average screen to create a moving average for a stock or index and a time period of interest. For a loaded stock or index, type GPO MA or use the GPMA screen (type GPMA). Once created, identify trends and reversals by comparing the price and moving average lines.

10. Moving average bands are used to identify resistance and support levels and to confirm a price reversal. Using Bloomberg's moving average envelope screen for a stock or index of interest, create a moving average band or envelope for a time period of interest and identify any breakouts from the band. To bring up the screen for a loaded stock or index, type GPO MAENV. Once created, look for trends and reversals. You may want to save your graph to the G screen; to do so, click the "Save as" tab.

11. There are different types of moving averages, such as simple, weighted, triangular, and exponential, as well as different technical studies that use moving averages. Moving average screens used for studies can be accessed from Bloomberg's "Technical Study Browser" screen found on the Graph home page (Graph <Enter>) or directly by typing TECH: TECH <Enter> and typing "moving average" in the find box. Use the Technical Browser screen to identify the different types of moving averages and moving average studies. To bring up a particular screen, click launch.

12. Breadth of the market, uptick-to-downtick index, and the CBOE put/call ratio are technical measurements used to gauge the strength or weakness of the overall market. Do an in-depth technical analysis of the overall market (use S&P 500 or Dow) for a period of interest that includes the moving average bands and volume, as well as the breadth, upticks-to-downticks ratio, and put/call volume measures. Possible Bloomberg screens to include are the following:
    a. Bands, Moving-Average Envelopes Screen: For loaded index, type GPO MAENV.
    b. Volume: Volume-at-Time Screen: For loaded index, type VAT.
    c. Advance minus Decline: For loaded index, type GPO ADL.
    d. CBOE Put/Call Ratio Screen: PCUSEQTR <Index>; GP.
    e. Uptick-to-Downtick Index Price Graph Screen: For S&P 500: TIKX <Index>; GP; for Dow: TIKI <Index>; GP.

Note: You may want to save these screens to the G screen so that you can apply them to other indexes, exchange rates, and the like.

13. Relative strength, the Erlanger put/call ratio, and the short-interest ratio are technical measures used to gauge the strength or weakness of a stock's price trend. Do an in-depth technical analysis of a stock of interest for a time period of interest that includes the stock's moving average band and volume, as well as the relative strength, put/call volume, and short-interest measures. Possible Bloomberg screens to include the following:

   a. Bands, Moving-Average Envelopes Screen: For a loaded stock, type GPO MAENV. You may want to save your moving average envelope screen to the G Screen.

   b. Volume: Volume-at-Time Screen: For a loaded stock, type VAT.

   c. Erlanger Put/Call Ratio Screen: For loaded stock, type GPO ERPCR.

   d. Short-Interest Screen: For loaded stock, type SI.

   e. Relative Strength Ratio: Create the ratio of the price of the stock to the index using the G Screen: G <Enter>; click "Create Charts"; select Spread Charts," and click next; in the Chart Wizard box, input your stock and market index (e.g., S&P 500, SPX), select ratio in the dropdown box, select time period, and then click finish. Note: If you completed Exercise 3, you may already have this chart on your G screen. If not, you may want to save the screen in the G Screen.

14. Technical analysis can be applied to study trends and breakouts for other exchanges, indexes, currencies, commodity prices, and portfolios. Select an index representing a foreign stock market or an exchange rate and construct a moving average band for a time period of interest. For a moving-average envelope for a loaded index or currency, type GPO MAENV. See if there are reversal and confirmation signals.

15. Technical analysis when used in conjunction with fundamental analysis provides a more complete picture of the stock or market. Portfolio managers and security analysts use various technical metrics to identify new stocks and to monitor their existing holdings.

   a. Select a portfolio you have created in PRTU and create an index of the portfolio using CIXB. From the index menu for your portfolio, construct a moving average band (type GPO MAENV). See how your portfolio is currently trending.

   b. Evaluate several of the stocks in your portfolio in terms of their relative strength. If you saved your relative strength screen to the G screen, use that screen to evaluate the relative strength of your stocks (see Exercise 13.e above).

   c. Evaluate several of the stocks in your portfolio in terms of their price trends within their moving average bands (type GPO MAENV). Save your MAENV screen to the G screen so that you can evaluate other stocks.

   d. Evaluate several of the stocks in your portfolio in terms of the Erlanger put/call ratio (GPO ERPCR) and the short-interest ratio (SI).

   e. Consider creating a Launchpad for your portfolio consisting of some of these technical measures as monitors. On your Launchpad, include some intraday graphs: BLP <Enter>; on the toolbar create a new view; on your other Bloomberg screens, use the Export dropdown (upper right corner) to export the screen to Launchpad.

   f. Consider setting up alerts for some of your stocks or all of your stocks using the Bloomberg ALRT screen: ALRT <Enter>.

16. Use Bloomberg's Backtest screen (BTST <Enter>) to back test a simple moving average trading strategy on a stock or index of interest. For example, set up a rule to buy when the stock cuts its moving average from below and sell or short when the stock cuts its moving average from above. On the BTST screen, click the Simple Moving Average's "Edit strategy icon" (pencil icon) to bring up a box for setting the conditions for your trade.

17. The chart homepage has five information and chart areas: Custom charts, sample G charts, Chart Resource section, and Chart of the Day. Explore some of the information on this homepage: CHART <Enter>.

18. Bloomberg's Hurst screen (GPO KAOS) is based on the work of Christopher May, who applied the Hurst exponent to nonlinear price patterns. Bloomberg's Hurst Exponent screen can be used to test for randomness. If a price trend is random, the Hurst coefficient would continuously have a value close to 0.5. If not, then there is pattern to the stock price movement. Use the Hurst screen to test whether the price patterns of some of the stocks or indexes that you have used in some of the exercises in this chapter are truly random.

CHAPTER 15

Efficient Markets

Introduction

One of the most influential theories to emerge out of the finance literature over the last 50 years is the efficient market hypothesis (EMH). Introduced by Burton Malkiel in the 1960s, the EMH precipitated a considerable amount of controversy between proponents of the EMH (primarily academicians) and practitioners who employed fundamental and technical analysis. EMH proponents argued that if the market consisted of a sufficient number of fundamentalists, then their actions would force the market price of a security to its equilibrium value. For example, if a security was underpriced, the fundamentalists would try to buy the security, pushing its market price toward its equilibrium value. In contrast, if a security was overpriced, the fundamentalists would short or sell it, pushing its market price down to its equilibrium value. Thus, according to the proponents of the EMH, with enough fundamentalists, the market price of a security is equal to its equilibrium price. Similarly, EMH proponents argued that if the market consisted of enough technicians, then their actions would eliminate the possibility of earning any abnormal return from identifying trends in security prices. As we noted in the last chapter, if a stock traded low on Monday and high on Friday, then technicians would detect this trend and would buy on Monday and sell on Friday. These actions would augment the price of the stock on Monday and lower it on Friday, thereby eliminating the trend and the possibility of earning an excess profit. If the EMH holds, in the sense that the market consists of a sufficient number of fundamentalists and technicians, then investors would be unable to earn abnormal returns from either fundamental or technical strategies. Thus, the EMH questioned the usefulness of fundamental and technical analysis. In their defense, fundamentalists and technicians argued that the efficient market theory was an oversimplification of how the market functions and that EMH proponents were naive.

One of the benefits of this controversial theory was that it spurred a considerable amount of research; in fact, there has been more research devoted to the EMH than to any other subject in investments. Moreover, the research on the EMH has helped to allay the controversy. On the one hand, studies have provided support for the use of trading strategies based on some fundamental and technical principles (though not all), justifying the contributions of fundamentalists and technicians. On the other hand, the EMH has provided fundamental and technical analysts with some new methods for selecting securities, as well as introducing statistical tools for evaluating security price trends and determining the effect of events on security prices.

In this chapter, we examine the efficient market hypothesis and studies of its validity. We begin by taking a closer look at the theory and its implications.

Efficient Market Theory

Weak, Semi-Strong, and Strong-Form Tests of the EMH

The efficient market theory addresses the question of whether or not security prices reflect information. Information contained in a security price can include both fundamental information, such as the economic, industry, and firm conditions of a company, and technical information, such as historical trends in a security's price. The information can be publicly available, such as historical data or announcements made through the media, or it can be privately available, accessible only to insiders who work, manage, or direct the company or who have special dealings or relationships with the company (e.g., lawyers, outside advisors, media, regulators, etc.). In examining the extent to which information is contained in the price of a security, the EMH subdivides the information into three categories, each considering a different type of information. Originally described by Nobel Laureate Eugene Fama as tests of informational content, the categories include the weak-form test, the semi-strong-form test, and the strong-form test.

The *weak-form tests* of the EMH test whether information contained in historical prices is fully reflected in current prices. These tests involve determining if one can earn abnormal returns (i.e., returns above the equilibrium return) from technical strategies. For example, can one earn excessive profit from detecting a trend such as a stock priced low on Monday and high on Friday, and then trading off that historical information? If there are a sufficient number of technicians in the market, they will identify such trends and by their actions eliminate the trend, or at least the ability to earn abnormal returns by employing strategies based on the trend.

Tests of the EMH are often stated in terms of a null hypothesis (H_0), which subsequent statistical tests will either reject or accept (or not reject). In the case of the weak-form test, the null hypothesis, H^{wf}_0, to be tested is:

H^{wf}_0: Investors cannot earn abnormal returns from strategies based on historical trends or return predictability patterns.

Semi-strong-form tests of the EMH test whether publicly available information is fully reflected in current prices. Two kinds of tests examine both market characteristics and the market's reaction to events or announcements. The first tests, sometimes called *cross-sectional tests*, look at whether or not abnormal returns can be realized from trading stocks with certain characteristics, such as their size or their price-to-earnings ratio. The second types of test are *event studies* or studies of announcements. Events include many factors, such as merger announcements, earnings reports, stock repurchases, new stock sales, stock splits, changes in the direction of monetary policy, or a depreciation of the dollar. Researchers usually limit their studies to events or announcements in which the information is not already reflected in the security's price; that is, the unexpected or the surprises.

When an event or announcement occurs, fundamentalists in the market reassess the equilibrium price (or value) of the security and by their subsequent trading cause the price of the security to change. For example, an unexpected good earnings announcement by a company would lead buyers and sellers of the security to value the company's stock higher, leading to a higher equilibrium price. Usually it takes some time before the market fully assesses the information and determines the new equilibrium price. For example, investors/fundamentalists may be too bullish about an unexpected good earnings announcement, causing the market price to overshoot its equilibrium value. Upon further assessment, the market may correct by slowing purchases or selling, causing the price to move down. During this reassessment period, the volatility of the stock price may increase. Semi-strong-form tests of the EMH do not rule out the possibility that during the assessment period some investors may pay less than the new equilibrium price and thus earn abnormal returns, whereas others may pay more than the equilibrium price and therefore earn returns less than the equilibrium return. Instead, the semi-strong-form tests try to determine if there are enough fundamentalists to ensure that investors, on average, do not earn abnormal returns from trading from events and announcements. As a result, the null hypothesis for the semi-strong-form tests, H^{ss}_0, is:

H^{ss}_0: Investors, on average, cannot earn abnormal returns from trading strategies based on publicly available information.

Strong-form tests of the EMH are tests of whether all information—public and private—is fully reflected in the security's price. These tests usually take two forms. One form tries to determine whether or not insiders can earn abnormal returns from their private information. That is, do the officers, managers, engineers, scientists, accountants, and others in the company, as well as those who by the nature of their business are close to the company, have private information that would allow them to earn abnormal returns? In the United States and many other countries, there are security laws that require that insiders list their trades with the SEC. The intent of the laws is to make publicly available trades that are based on privileged information. If these and other laws aimed at inside trading are effective, then a priori we would expect security prices to reflect inside information. The null hypothesis to test for this form of the EMH, $H^s_0(1)$ is:

$H^s_0(1)$: Insiders cannot earn abnormal returns from trading from private information.

The other strong-form test of the EMH tries to determine whether some non-insider groups are able to earn abnormal returns from their abilities to evaluate securities and events better than the average investor. In this strong-form test, researchers try to determine whether groups such as security analysts and portfolio managers of mutual funds and investment companies are able to earn abnormal return from being better able to value information than the average investor. The null hypothesis to test for this form of the EMH, $H^s_0(2)$, is:

> $H^s_0(2)$: Investment groups cannot earn abnormal returns from their investment strategies.

The weak-, semi-strong-, and strong-form tests of the EMH address different degrees of market efficiency. A perfectly efficient market is one in which all four hypotheses hold. In practice, a perfectly efficient market does not exist. As we will see later, evidence in support of each hypothesis is mixed.

Example

To see how information can be reflected in a security's price, consider again the case of an oil company who just finds its oil reserves are three times greater than originally estimated. Suppose that this company's accountants project that the firm's earnings will be three times greater than the current level as a result of the discovery and that the projected earnings increase is expected to be permanent. When the company announces the reserve increase, the market will push up the company's stock price. The efficient market theory, however, is less concerned with the subsequent price increase and more interested in determining whether the market is one in which investors can earn abnormal returns by using this information. The answer depends on how quickly the information is reflected in the stock's price. To see this, consider the following five scenarios.

Scenario 1

Suppose that after the announcement is made it takes two weeks for the stock price to increase from its current level of $50 to its new equilibrium level of $75. This gradual increase in share price might be due to the presence of a learning lag or the presence of a conservative bias in which some investors respond immediately to the auspicious earnings information, and others take more time to react. Since it takes some time before the impact of the information is fully reflected in the stock's price, a trend will emerge in which the stock begins to trade away from its historical level, increasing until it hits its new equilibrium, and then stabilizes. In this scenario, technicians studying such trends would be able to earn abnormal returns by buying the stock a day or two after it begins to trade away from its historical level ($50), then selling it when it stabilizes two weeks later around its new equilibrium ($75). Excess profit in this case is realized by technicians who profit from discerning learning lag trends in the market and not necessarily from the fundamental changes that are driving the price up. In this scenario, the efficient market hypothesis would not hold in the weak form (H^w_0).

Scenario 2

Suppose the market consists of fundamentalists who immediately buy the stock after the announcement and cause its price to increase sufficiently fast that technicians trading off price patterns are unable to earn excess profit. In this case, the fundamentalists' quick response to the earnings announcement eliminates the learning lag that characterized the last scenario, and the new price prevailing shortly after the announcement reflects fundamental information about the company's improved prospects. However, suppose in this case that while the stock price responds in kind to the announcement, it takes several days before the market fully assesses the impact. During this time, suppose there are overconfident investors who push the price to $80 two days after the news, then after reassessing, push the price down to $73, followed by another increase and then decrease, before settling in at the new equilibrium price of $75. Some investors buying the stock during this period will pay a price below the equilibrium of $75 and therefore realize an abnormal return; others will pay more than the equilibrium and earn less than the new equilibrium return associated with the $75 price. However, suppose that on average investors pay $75, and therefore on average realize the new equilibrium return. In this scenario, the efficient market hypothesis would hold in the weak and semi-strong forms (H^w_0 and H^{ss}_0).

Scenario 3

Suppose again that the market consists of a sufficient number of fundamentalists and technicians that the price increases quickly. This time suppose an investment group specializing in energy stocks is more adept at analyzing the news than the average investor and determines that the equilibrium price is $75. With this ability, the group is able to identify its trading strategy of buying below $75. With the stock fluctuating for several days after the announcement, suppose the investment firm buys at $72, thus earning a return above the new equilibrium level. In this scenario, the efficient market hypothesis would hold in the weak and semi strong forms (H^w_0 and H^{ss}_0), but not the strong form: $H^s_0(2)$ does not hold.

Scenario 4

Suppose this time the market is characterized by fundamentalists who are all equally adept at analyzing fundamental information. Like scenario 2, the fundamentalists again would be able to quickly push the price to its equilibrium level at $75, with a smaller accompanying variability. Unlike scenario 3, however, no investment group on average would be able to earn abnormal returns. Suppose in this case that the company's geologist, knowledgeable regarding the new reserve estimates, buys the stock several days before the announcement at $50 and then sells it sometime later at $75 when the information is fully reflected in the price. We have an insider who is able to earn abnormal return while fundamentalists and technicians are not. The efficient market hypothesis would hold in the weak and semi-strong forms (H^w_0 and H^{ss}_0), but only part of the strong form: $H^s_0(1)$, does not hold.

Scenario 5

Finally, suppose the market has the same adept fundamentalists and technicians as in the preceding cases, as well as insiders, but that the insiders, in compliance with security laws, report their stock purchases to the Securities and Exchange Commission (SEC). If insiders' trades are announced prior to the company's earnings announcement, then adept fundamentalists would push the stock price up shortly after the insider announcement and before the company's earnings announcement. If the law required that insiders report their trade intentions before they executed them (if that were possible), then with a market consisting of adept fundamentalists, the insiders would not be able to earn abnormal returns. In this case, the efficient market hypothesis would hold in the weak and semi-strong forms, H^w_0 and H^{ss}_0, as well as both strong forms, $H^s_0(2)$ and $H^s_0(1)$.

Implications

The EMH has at least three implications for investments. First, if empirical tests support the weak-form null hypothesis, then technical trading strategies based on trends would be suspect. Paradoxically, the market would have to consist of a sufficient number of technicians for a condition to exist in which there were no abnormal return opportunities from strategies based on technical trends. Similarly, if empirical tests support the semi-strong null hypothesis, then fundamental strategies based on publicly available information would also be suspect. Again, however, the market would have to consist of a sufficient number of fundamentalists for a condition to exist in which there was no opportunity to earn, on average, abnormal returns from using publicly available information. Finally, if empirical evidence supports the two forms of the strong-form hypothesis, then the use of any fundamental strategy would be suspect. Once again, however, the market would have to have a sufficient number of adept fundamentalists and insiders, as well as the appropriate security laws, for a condition to exist in which no abnormal returns could be realized from strategies based on publicly and privately available information.

Second, the EMH can be alternatively stated in terms of three conditions and their implications (see Exhibit 15.1). First, if there are enough technicians, fundamentalists, adept fundamentalists, and insiders, then the market price of the security would be equal to its equilibrium price or value (V): $P^M = V$. Second, if information is disseminated efficiently (no learning lags and no group with better information or with a comparative advantage over other investors in valuing information), then the market price will tend to equal the equilibrium price at all times, and any equilibrium price adjustments to new information will occur rapidly. Third, any new information hitting the market by definition would be random; that is, information already reflected in the price of securities includes expectation (e.g., expected earnings), thus new information

EXHIBIT 15.1 EMH: Conditions and Implications

Conditions		*Implications*
➤ The market consists of fundamentalists and technicians.	$\Longrightarrow$	➤ Stock's market price (*P*) is equal to the intrinsic value of the stock (*V*): *P* = *V*.
➤ Information is disseminated efficiently.	$\Longrightarrow$	➤ *P* = *V* at all times.
➤ News is random.	$\Longrightarrow$	➤ *P* = *V* fluctuates randomly.

would be unexpected (e.g., an unexpected good earnings announcement). Since the new information will also be reflected in the price, and since it is unexpected, it will cause the prices of securities to fluctuate randomly—a random walk.

A third implication of the EMH is that the market provides a fair game. In a fair game, the market cannot use the information available at time *t* to earn an abnormal return. If there is information that an individual (or group) has that enables him to earn abnormal returns, then the market is inefficient and the game is not fair. If the EMH holds, the security market can be deemed a fair game. Also, it should be noted that the EMH does not mean that returns are uncorrelated or independent, but rather that one cannot look at the correlations in past returns to earn excess returns. A firm, for example, could have made a series of risky investments that over several years were successful, resulting in higher realized earnings and returns. Analysts, looking at this company, would therefore see a positive correlation in return. This does not mean excess returns are increasing; rather, since risk is increasing, the company's equilibrium return is also increasing.

Studies of the Weak-Form Hypothesis

As noted earlier, since its introduction the EMH has spurred an extensive amount of empirical research. The research can be divided along the lines of the weak-form, semi-strong-form, and strong-form tests. The weak-form tests of the EMH try to examine whether information contained in historical prices is reflected in current prices. The null hypothesis to be tested is that in a weakly efficient market one cannot earn abnormal returns from trading strategies based on past price information. The empirical research on weakly efficient markets can be divided into two areas: studies of time patterns in security return (also referred to as calendar events) and studies of historical return predictability patterns.

Time Patterns

Studies of time patterns examine whether or not returns are systematically higher or lower during certain periods of time, such as a day of the week, a week of a month, or a month of a year. Surprisingly, a number of early studies discovered certain time patterns in security returns. The two most notable are the abnormally positive return pattern in the month of January, referred to as the *January effect*, and the abnormally low return pattern on Monday, referred to as the *Monday effect*.

Monday Effect

In a 1981 study, Gibbons and Hess reported that over a 17-year period from 1962 to 1978 the average annualized return on Monday was −33 percent. They also found large negative Monday returns for subperiods from 1962 to 1970 and 1970 to 1978. This Monday effect was also reported in a 1986 study by Harris. In addition to finding large negative Monday returns, Harris also found that much of the observed Monday decline occurred between the close of trading on Friday and the first hours of trading on Monday: a time trend referred to as the *weekend effect*. The Monday effect certainly questions whether markets are weakly efficient, suggesting that speculators could earn abnormal returns by shorting stocks on late Friday and covering their positions by purchasing their stocks early on Monday.

January Effect

A number of studies have found that the average returns on stocks in the month of January are significantly higher than the average returns in other months, with the stocks of smaller firms showing the largest returns. In a 1991 study, Eugene Fama found that for the period from 1941 to 1981, the average return in January for small stocks was 8.06 percent and for large stocks was 1.34 percent. In both groups, these average monthly returns were higher than the average returns in other months. Fama also found a similar January pattern from the more recent time period from 1982 to 1991, with small stocks averaging a return of 5.32 percent and large stocks a return of 3.2 percent in the month of January. Exhibit 15.2 shows monthly rates of return for the S&P 500 from 2003 to 2013, with the month in each year ranked from highest to lowest. As shown, in 8 of the last 10 years, the month of January had the highest rate of return.

The January effect is not unique to the United States. Gultekin and Gultekin in a 1983 study found average returns in January higher than in other months for the 16 countries that they studied. Brown, Keim, Kleidon, and Marsh (1983) also found a January effect extant in Australia; Berges, McConnell, and Schlarbaum (1984) documented one in Canada; and Kata and Shallheim (1985) found excess January returns for stocks traded on the Tokyo exchange, with the smaller stocks earning an average return of 8 percent.

Several theories have been advanced to explain this January anomaly. One popular explanation offered is a *tax-selling hypothesis*. According to this theory, many investors holding stocks with capital losses sell them at the end of the year to realize the tax deduction, and then buy comparable stocks at the beginning of the year. Their actions of selling at the end of the year and buying at the beginning of the year results in the

EXHIBIT 15.2 Monthly Rates of Return for S&P 500, 2003–2013

Month	Rate	Month	Rate	Month	Rate	Month	Rate	Month	Rate
4/30/2003	0.1247	1/30/2004	0.3447	1/31/2005	0.0722	1/31/2006	0.1065	1/31/2007	0.13239
10/31/2003	0.1459	11/30/2004	0.0377	7/29/2005	0.0448	10/31/2006	0.0764	4/30/2007	0.03068
5/30/2003	−0.0829	12/31/2004	0.0325	11/30/2005	0.0124	9/29/2006	−0.0305	9/28/2007	0.02994
12/31/2003	0.1539	6/30/2004	−0.0587	5/31/2005	−0.0464	8/31/2006	−0.0240	5/31/2007	0.00253
1/31/2003	−0.2304	10/29/2004	−0.0093	2/28/2005	0.0102	11/30/2006	0.0743	10/31/2007	0.01226
8/29/2003	0.1780	2/27/2004	0.0130	9/30/2005	0.0209	12/29/2006	0.0126	8/31/2007	−0.04866
7/31/2003	−0.0176	5/31/2004	−0.0212	6/30/2005	−0.0305	4/28/2006	−0.0759	3/30/2007	−0.03605
6/30/2003	−0.0160	9/30/2004	−0.0054	12/30/2005	0.0478	3/31/2006	−0.0120	12/31/2007	0.03343
3/31/2003	−0.1296	8/31/2004	−0.0093	8/31/2005	−0.0224	7/31/2006	−0.0140	6/29/2007	0.02383
11/28/2003	0.2476	3/31/2004	0.0199	10/31/2005	−0.0109	2/28/2006	0.0031	2/28/2007	−0.06421
9/30/2003	−0.0588	4/30/2004	−0.0168	3/31/2005	−0.0219	6/30/2006	−0.0082	7/31/2007	0.03444
2/28/2003	−0.1554	7/30/2004	−0.0050	4/29/2005	−0.0201	5/31/2006	−0.0001	11/30/2007	0.01778
Average	0.0133	Average	0.0268	Average	0.0047	Average	0.0090	Average	0.01403
7/31/2009	0.1018	1/29/2010	0.1681	1/31/2011	0.1806	1/31/2012	0.1600	1/31/2013	0.14331
9/30/2009	0.0705	9/30/2010	0.0627	10/31/2011	−0.0255	2/29/2012	0.0406	7/31/2013	0.12524
10/30/2009	−0.0198	7/30/2010	−0.0347	2/28/2011	0.0590	6/29/2012	−0.0026	10/31/2013	0.04201
11/30/2009	0.0574	12/31/2010	0.1416	4/29/2011	0.0274	3/30/2012	0.0340	3/29/2013	−0.10666
12/31/2009	0.0178	3/31/2010	−0.0701	12/30/2011	−0.0777	9/28/2012	0.0229	9/30/2013	0.07160
8/31/2009	−0.0847	10/29/2010	0.0118	3/31/2011	0.0543	8/31/2012	−0.0237	5/31/2013	−0.03022
1/30/2009	−0.3562	2/26/2010	−0.0666	11/30/2011	−0.0595	7/31/2012	−0.0194	4/30/2013	−0.02034
3/31/2009	−0.0339	4/30/2010	0.0744	5/31/2011	0.0788	12/31/2012	0.0340	2/28/2013	−0.05189
4/30/2009	0.0568	11/30/2010	−0.0052	6/30/2011	−0.0183	11/30/2012	−0.0070	6/28/2013	0.06047
2/27/2009	−0.1578	8/31/2010	−0.1112	7/29/2011	−0.0215	4/30/2012	−0.0129	8/30/2013	0.01662
5/29/2009	0.2504	6/30/2010	−0.0177	8/31/2011	−0.0568	10/31/2012	0.0102		
6/30/2009	0.0002	5/31/2010	0.0570	9/30/2011	−0.0718	5/31/2012	−0.0721		
Average	−0.0081	Average	0.0175	Average	0.0057	Average	0.0137	Average	0.02501

Data Source: Bloomberg

price of many stocks being lower at the beginning of the month of January and higher later in the month. Studies by Reinganum (1983) and Branch (1977) have found that stocks that reached their low in December (stocks that would have yielded capital losses for investors who purchased them during the year) on average grew faster in the month of January than any other month. Moreover, Reiganum found that a high proportion of those stocks are those of small firms. One of the problems with accepting the tax-selling hypothesis as the sole explanation of the January effect is that the effect occurs in other countries that have a different tax year (e.g., Australia) or no capital gains tax (e.g., Japan and Belgium). Another possible explanation for the January effects is a *liquidity argument* in which investors have a greater liquidity need at the end of the year and as a result are selling stock at the end of year, leading to lower stock prices at the beginning of the year.

Both the tax-selling and liquidity arguments combined may explain the January effect. If markets are weakly efficient, however, we would expect investors trading on past security price patterns to purchase stocks at the end of December and sell in January to take advantage of the abnormal returns. These actions, in turn, would serve to increase the price of the stock at the end of the year and decrease it in January, thereby eliminating the January effect. This anomaly certainly questions the weak form of the EMH.

Return Predictability Studies

In addition to time patterns, studies of weakly efficient markets also include return predictability patterns. These studies involve tests of whether or not prior returns can be used to predict future returns. The statistical tests used in many of these studies include serial correlation tests, run tests, and filter rule tests.

Serial Correlation Tests

Serial correlation (or autocorrelation) is a measure of the correlation between a series of numbers and a lagged series of numbers. In testing the weak-form hypothesis, researchers typically estimate the serial correlation between the rate of change in a security's price in one period (t) and the rate of change in the same security's price in an earlier period ($t-i$). To determine the degree of serial correlation, a security's return in one period is regressed against its return in a previous period; that is:

$$r_t = a + br_{t-i} + \varepsilon_t$$

where:

i = number of periods from t (e.g., 1, 2, ...).

In determining whether or not serial correlation exists, researchers look at the slope coefficient (b) to see if it is significantly different from zero and at the coefficient of determination (R^2) to determine the proportion of variation in returns in period t that can be explained by the variation in returns in period $t - i$.

A number of serial correlation studies have been conducted. The studies vary in terms of the securities analyzed, the lags used, and the sample periods (day, week, year, etc.). They are all unable to detect any significant pattern in security returns, finding serial correlations close to zero.

Run Tests

In a run test, a researcher looks at the number of times a security's price changes its sign; that is, goes from increasing to decreasing or decreasing to increasing. For example, from the seven closing prices shown below, there are three runs:

Day	Monday	Tuesday	Wednesday	Thursday	Friday	Monday	Tuesday
Price	52	53	51	50	49	50	49
Sign		+	−	−	−	+	−
Run			1			2	3

In an early study, Fama (1965) compared the runs from 30 Dow Jones Average stocks to the runs obtained from random number tables and found no significant difference. However, as we noted in the last chapter, the Hurst exponent is a metric used to identify price patterns hidden within seemingly random stock price trends (Bloomberg's Hurst screen: GPO KAOS). If a price trend is random, then the Hurst coefficient would continuously have a value close to 0.5. If not, then there is pattern to the stock price movement. For the period 2000–2013, Bloomberg's Hurst exponent value for the S&P 500 averaged 0.735 (Exhibit 14.25). Using the Hurst screen for other stocks shows more often than not that the price patterns of many stocks have Hurst exponent values higher or lower than 0.5, suggesting patterns to their movements and providing an argument for the use of technical analysis.

Filter Rules

Filter rules are timing strategies aimed at defining when a security should be purchased and when it should be sold. The rules are constructed based on past price behavior. For example, as discussed in Chapter 14 many technicians believe that security prices tend to randomly fluctuate within bands, until they break through their barrier, such as, an increase past their resistance line followed by an increase to a new higher level, or a decrease past their support barrier followed by a decrease to a new lower level. An X percent filter rule would be:

> If the price of the stock increases by at least X percent, buy and hold it until it reaches a peak and then drops at least X percent. When the stock drops from the peak by X percent, liquidate the position and sell short. Keep the short position until the price hits a new bottom and turns up. When the price increases by X percent from the new low, close the short position and take a new long position.

Exhibit 15.3 shows a filter rule applied to the S&P 500. The filter is set at 7.5 percent (a large filter). A long position is taken after the market increases from a bottom

EXHIBIT 15.3 A 7.5 Percent Filter Applied to S&P 500 Bloomberg: GP Graph for S&P 500

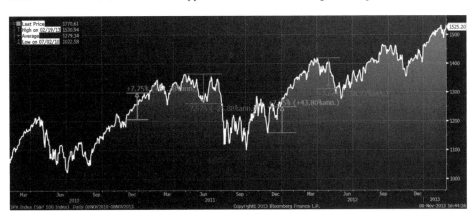

by at least 7.5 percent, and short position is taken after the stock has decreased by at least 7.5 percent from a peak.

Different filters can be applied by varying the X percent. In examining weakly efficient markets, researchers have tried to determine if filter rules based on historical patterns can earn returns significantly different from a naive buy-and-hold strategy in which one buys on the first day of the period and sells on the last day of that period. One of the first studies examining filter rules was done by Fama and Blume (1966). Using the 30 Dow Jones stocks, Fama and Blume varied their filters from $X = 0.5$ percent to $X = 4$ percent and then compared the returns obtained from each filter to the returns from a buy-and-hold strategy. They found that the only filter to outperform the buy-and-hold strategy was the one with $X = 0.5$ percent. They did find, however, that filters of 1 percent and 1.5 percent were more profitable on a before-commission cost basis than the buy-and-hold strategy when only the long positions were considered; these strategies, however, became unprofitable when transaction costs were included.

In a 1988 study, Sweeney showed that in the Fama and Blume study many of the filter rules that resulted in short positions led to trading losses, although many of the long positions were profitable. As a result, in his study of filter rules Sweeney evaluated returns using the following filter:

> If the price of a stock increases by X percent from a previous low, buy and hold until it decreases by at least X percent from a subsequent high. Then liquidate the long position and invest in a risk-free security until the stock reaches its next trough and increases by X percent.

Using this filter rule, Sweeney was able to find certain stocks that consistently yielded above average profits; unfortunately, these profits disappeared when commission costs were applied.

In a 1992 study, Brock, Lakonishok, and LeBaron tested several different breakout rules for Dow Jones stocks covering the period from 1897 through 1986. They, in turn, found the trading rules were profitable. In their 1992 study, they also reported that trading rules based on moving average were profitable. However, in a later study, Bessembinder and Chan (1998) found that over different sample periods such rules were less profitable.

A number of other studies have also been conducted to test filter rules and break-out rules. These studies vary in terms of the stocks analyzed, the filter rules tested, and the sample period examined. The conclusion reached by these studies is that, with the exception of small filters, filter rules do not outperform naive buy-and-hold strategies. Most of these studies also find that low filters (e.g., $X = 0.5$ percent) yield above average profits on a before-commission cost basis, but that the higher trading costs for implementing low filter rules negates the profits from these strategies.

Back Testing Breakout Rules, Bloomberg BTST Screen

Filter rule tests are designed to test technical rules of buying and selling when stocks break their support and resistance levels. Bloomberg's back testing screen (BTST) can

EXHIBIT 15.4   Backtests of Moving-Average Envelope, S&P 500, 11/8/2008–11/8/2013, Bloomberg, BTTS Screen

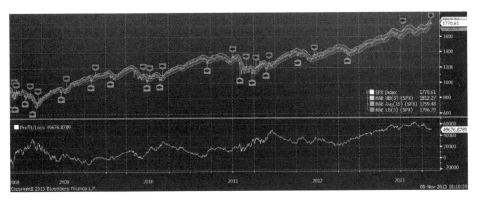

be used to back test the profitability of various technical trading rules, including when stocks hit their resistance and support line. Exhibit 15.4 shows a back test of a moving average envelope (15-day moving average with a 3 percent band) for the S&P 500, in which a long position is taken when the closing price cuts its lower band and a short positive when it cuts its upper band. The back test covered the period from 11/8/2008 to 11/8/2013. The percentage return for the moving-average envelope strategy was 49 percent. However, the percentage return from a buy-and-hold strategy for the period was 93 percent. Most of the losses, however, were from the short positions, giving some credence to the aforementioned Sweeney study. The percentage gain from a back test of the same strategy applied to the Bollinger band, which has a wider band than the moving-average envelope, however, was 122 percent for the same period (see Exhibit 15.5).

Conclusions on Weakly Efficient Markets

The tests of weakly efficient markets are mixed. On the one hand, the existence of January and Monday effects suggest abnormal returns are possible by implementing

EXHIBIT 15.5   Backtests of Bollinger Band, S&P 500, 11/8/2008–11/8/2013, Bloomberg, BTTS Screen

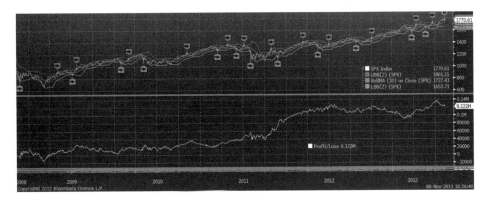

trading strategies around those periods. On the other hand, other studies suggest that the returns on securities are serially uncorrelated and that the runs observed on stocks are not significantly different from the runs obtained from a random number generator. Finally, some studies suggest that certain filter rules can yield above average profits before commission cost, but not after.

BLOOMBERG'S HURST SCREEN

Bloomberg's Hurst screen (GPO KAOS) is based on the work of Christopher May who applied the Hurst exponent to nonlinear price patterns. Bloomberg's Hurst exponent screen can be used to test for randomness. If a price trend is random, the Hurst coefficient would continuously have a value close to 0.5. If not, then there is pattern to the stock price movement. See Exhibit 14.25.

The Hurst coefficients for a number of stocks, such as those that make up an index, can be found using the RV screen for the index and then adding a column by typing in "Hurst." The coefficient for a number of stocks can also be found using the Bloomberg Excel Add In.

Back testing

Back testing, BTST: BTST <Enter>: The BTST screen back tests a number of different technical studies and compares them to a naive buy-and-hold strategy. On BTST, click the pencil icon to bring up a box for setting the conditions of the test. The back test for the moving average envelope and the Bollinger band shown in Exhibits 15.4 and 15.5, respectively, were set up using BTST.

Annotations

Lines, regression lines, bands, and other drawings can be included on a graph by clicking the "Annotate" button on the gray toolbar at the top of the price chart. Clicking the button will bring up an annotations palette showing all of the tools for drawing on the chart, editing, and deleting. The percent change lines shown in Exhibit 15.3 to identify 7.5 percent filter points were drawn from the annotation palette.

Bloomberg Excel Add-In

The data in Exhibit 15.2 was imported into Excel using Bloomberg's Excel Add-In and the "Import Data" tab.

- On the Bloomberg Add-In in Excel, click "Historical End of the Day" from the "Import Data" and then follow the Wizard's steps.
- The monthly rates shown in Exhibit 15.2 were sorted in Excel (Sort function) from "highest to lowest."

See Bloomberg Web Exhibit 15.1.

Studies of the Semi-Strong-Form Hypothesis

Semi-strong-form tests of the EMH were defined earlier as tests to determine whether or not publicly available information is reflected in current prices. According to the null hypothesis, in a semi-strong efficient market, investors, on average, cannot earn abnormal returns from trading strategies based on public information. Studies of semi-strong efficient markets can be divided into cross-sectional studies based on firm characteristics and studies of events and announcements.

Cross-Sectional Studies

Cross-sectional studies of the EMH examine whether stocks with common, observable features such as their size or price-to-earnings ratios earn abnormal returns. Three possible anomalies that have been identified by researchers examining firm characteristics are stocks with low price-to-earnings per share ratios, small-sized stocks, and stocks with high book-to-market values.

Low Price-to-EPS Ratios

A popular time-honored investment strategy among security analysts is to invest in stocks with relatively low price-to-EPS ratios (*P/e*). In a 1977 study, Basu empirically examined this investment strategy using a sample of 750 NYSE-listed stocks over a 14-year period from 1955 through 1971. Staring with the first year in his study, 1955, Basu calculated each stock's *P/e* ratio. He next ranked the 750 stocks in the order of their *P/e* ratios and formed five quintile portfolios.[1] Monthly rates of return were then calculated for the five *P/e* portfolios for the following year (1956), with each stock in the portfolio having an equal weight. Basu repeated the same calculations for the next year (1956), first arraying stocks in the order of their *P/e* ratios, next forming five *P/e* quintile portfolios, and lastly calculating the portfolio's monthly returns for the following year (1957). Basu repeated these calculations through 1971, yielding 168 monthly returns on five *P/e* portfolios. The portfolios Basu formed, in turn, could be viewed as mutual funds with a certain *P/e* size that were readjusted each year. Using the 168 monthly portfolio returns, Basu next regressed each portfolio's risk premium ($R_p - R_f$) against the market risk premium ($R_M - R_f$):

$$R_p - R_f = \alpha_p + \beta_p(R_M - R_f) + \varepsilon_p$$

He then evaluated each portfolio's performance in term of the Sharpe, Treynor, and Jensen performance measures:

$$\lambda_S = \frac{\bar{R}_p - R_f}{\sigma_p}$$

$$\lambda_T = \frac{\bar{R}_p - R_f}{\beta_p}$$

$$\lambda_J = \alpha_p$$

EXHIBIT 15.6 Basu Study, Performance Measures on *P/e* Portfolios

P/e Portfolios	1	2	3	4	5
λ_S	0.2264	0.1886	0.1475	0.0967	0.0903
λ_T	0.1237	0.1047	0.0822	0.0537	0.0508
λ_J	0.0467	0.0228	0.0017	−0.0277	−0.033

1 = lowest *P/e* portfolio, ... , 5 = highest *P/e* portfolio
Source: Basu, S. 1977. Investment performance of common stocks in relations to their price-earnings ratios: A test of the efficient market hypothesis. *Journal of Finance* 32 (June): 663–682.

The three portfolio performance measures Basu calculated for the five quintile portfolios are shown in Exhibit 15.6. In examining the table, note that there is an inverse relation between the *P/e* ratio and the portfolio ranking, with the dominant portfolio (based on all three measures) being the low *P/e* portfolio. In fact, Basu also found that based on the Sharpe index, the low *P/e* portfolio was one of only two of the quintile portfolios with a higher risk premium per level of risk than the market. The Basu study thus provided empirical support for the time-honored investment strategy of investing in stocks with low *P/e* ratios. The study also suggests a market anomaly. However, Johnson, Fiore, and Zuber (1989) found using the Basu methodology for the period from 1985 to 1989 that low *P/e* portfolios underperformed the market, as well as other *P/e* portfolios. More recent studies of low *P/e* stock performances in the period of 1990s and 2000s, however, show such stocks are again earning abnormal returns.

Exhibit 15.7 (top panel) shows the total returns based on daily percentage changes in price for the Russell U.S. Large Cap Low *P/e* index (RU1LPETR) and the S&P 500 from 11/7/2008 to 11/30/2012 when there was a bullish market trend. For that period, the low *P/e* index outperformed the S&P 500 with a total return of 70.64 percent (annualized return of 14.04 percent) compared to a 52.12 percent return (10.87 percent annualized return) for the S&P 500. However, when the market was declining from 10/1/2008 to 3/3/2009, the total return of the low *P/e* Index was −42.94 percent compared to −40.03 percent for the S&P 500 (middle panel). The lower panel of Exhibit 15.7 shows the regression line of the low *P/e* index against the S&P 500 (for the period from 10/1/2008 to 11/30/2012). The low *P/e* index has an alpha that is very close to zero and beta of 1.113. Theses regression results suggest that for at least this period, the low *P/e* index is a higher beta portfolio with no abnormal returns.

Size Effect

Another firm characteristic that has received a considerable amount of attention among researchers is firm size. In an early anomaly study, Banz (1981) formed 10 equally weighted decile portfolios based on size from the NYSE-listed stocks, and regressed each portfolio's return premium against the market premium. Using the intercept term from these regressions as an estimate of abnormal return, Banz found excess returns from the portfolio consisting of the smallest-size stocks. Banz concluded that over an

EXHIBIT 15.7   Total Return Graph Russell U.S. Large Cap Low *P/e* Index (RU1LPETR) and S&P 500 (SPX) 11/7/2008 to 11/30/2012 and 10/1/2008 to 3/3/2009

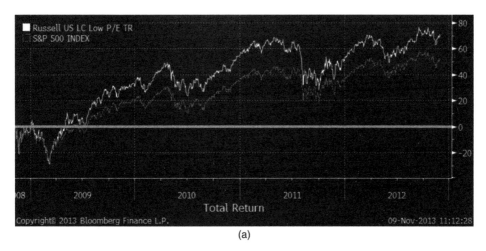

(a)

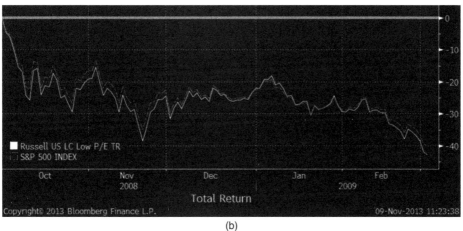

(b)

(Continued)

extended period of time, small firms earned significantly larger risk-adjusted returns than larger firms.

Similar conclusions on size and performance were also reached in another early anomaly study on the size effect for both NYSE and AMEX stocks by Reinganum (1983). For the period from 1963 to 1980, Reinganum found that a portfolio of small firms grew from $1 in 1963 to $46 in 1980 with annual rebalancing, while a portfolio of large firms grew from $1 to only $4 during that same period with annual rebalancing. Both the Banz and Reinganum studies suggest an anomaly existed over a long time period.[2] Exhibit 15.8 shows the total returns for the S&P Small Cap Core Index (DEFISCCI) and Large Cap Core Index (DEFILCCI) for the five-year period from 11/28/2008 to 10/31/2013 when there was a bullish trend. For that period, the small cap index outperformed the large cap with a total return of 183.45 percent (annualized return of 23.55 percent) compared to a 136 percent return (19.07 percent annualized

EXHIBIT 15.7 (*Continued*)

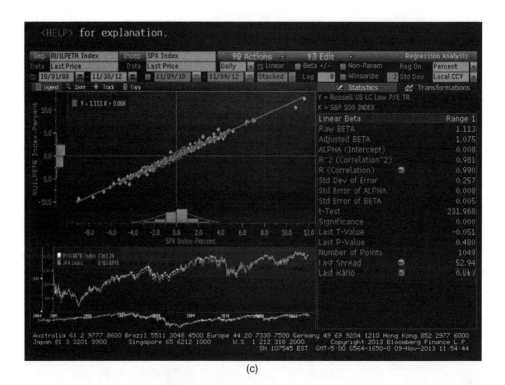

(c)

Exhibit 15.7a: 11/7/2008–11/30/2012
  Total Return:
• Low *P/e* Index = 70.64 percent (Annualized Return = 14.05 percent)
• S&P = 52.12 percent (Annualized Return = 10.87 percent)
Note: Returns are percentage price change; dividends are not included.

Exhibit 15.7b: 10/1/2008–3/3/2009
  Total Return:
• Low *P/e* index = −42.94 percent (Annualized Return = −73.78 percent)
• S&P 500 = −40.03 percent (Annualized Return = −70.47 percent)

return) for the large cap index. However, when the market was declining from
10/2/2008 to 3/3/2009, the total return of the small cap index was −48.41 percent
compared to −42.43 percent for the large cap index (lower panel of Exhibit 15.8).

A number of studies have tried to explain the size effect. James and Edmister
(1983), for example, posit that there is a lower trading volume on small-size firms that
causes them to trade with a liquidity premium over larger, more marketable stocks.
Barry and Brown (1984) argue that there is less information about small firms that
causes investors to require a higher return or an *information premium* over larger, more
well-known stocks. This information premium is also supported by a study by Arbel
and Strebel (1983) on neglected firms. Grouping stocks into three categories (highly
followed, moderately followed, and neglected), they found that not only did a small-
size effect exist, but also that there were abnormal returns for the neglected stock group.

EXHIBIT 15.8   Total Return Graph S&P Small Cap Core Index (DEFISCCI) and Large Cap Core
Index (DEFILCCI) 11/28/2008 to 10/31/2013 and 10/1/2008 to 3/3/2009

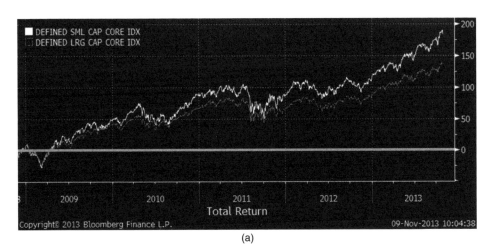

(a)

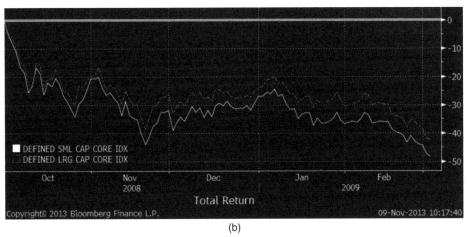

(b)

Exhibit 15.8a: 11/28/2008–10/31/2013
   Total Return:
• Small Cap index = 183.45 percent (Annualized Return = 23.55 percent)
• Large Cap index = 136 percent (Annualized Return = 19.07 percent)

Exhibit 15.8b: 10/1/2008–3/3/2009
   Total Return:
• Small Cap index = −48.41 percent (Annualized Return = −79.38 percent)
• Large Cap index = −42.43 percent (Annualized Return = −73.21 percent)

Book-to-Market Value

In a 1994 study, Lakonishok, Shleifer, and Vishny examined the performance of stock
portfolios grouped in terms of the stock's book-to-market value. To eliminate the size
effect, they first formed five quintile portfolios based on size. From each of these portfolios, they formed 10 decile portfolios based on the stock's book-to-market value.

Among the five quintile portfolios, Lakonishok, Shleifer, and Vishny found an average difference of approximately 8 percent between the high book-to-market value portfolios and the low book-to-market value ones.

Fama and French (1992) also found a significant positive relationship between the book-to-market value ratios and average returns. Running a number of cross-sectional regressions, they found that leverage and P/e ratios were significant explanatory variables of a stock's return when they were the only variables in the regression, but were insignificant when size and book-to-market values were included as explanatory variables in the regression. In contrast, they found size and book-to-market value significant when included together, as well as significant and dominant when other variables were included.

Other Anomalies

The studies by Basu, Banz, Lakonishok, Shleifer, and Vishny, and Fama and French suggest that abnormal returns may be possible from buying stocks with either low P/e ratios, relatively small sizes, or large book-to-market value ratios. Combined, these studies question whether publicly available information is reflected in security prices and therefore whether the market is semi-strongly efficient.

In addition to these studies, a number of other cross-sectional studies have also identified return irregularities. Notable anomalies were found with stocks characterized with positive skewness and stocks that had previously been poor performers. Specifically, studies by Friend and Lang (1988), Westerfield (1977), and Barone-Adesi (1985) show that there are possible gains in portfolio returns by allocating more investment funds to stocks that are characterized by positive skewness. A study by DeBondt and Thaler (1985) found abnormal returns by going long in stocks that in the previous year were the biggest losers and by going short in stocks that in the previous year were the biggest winners. In their study, they constructed portfolios each December of the 50 stocks that did the best and the 50 that did the poorest. Measuring the performance of those portfolios over the next three years, they found positive abnormal returns for the portfolio consisting of the 50 poorest stocks and negative abnormal returns for the portfolio consisting of the 50 best.

The existence of all of these anomalies certainly leads one to question the semi-strong-form of the EMH. In fact, many investors over the years have jumped on the anomaly bandwagon looking for abnormal returns. Before rejecting the semi-strong-form hypothesis, however, it is important to recognize that the anomalies reported in many of these studies are based on a CAPM framework. It could very well be that the reported irregularities are simply the result of omissions of important variables that are needed to explain equilibrium returns. This is the conclusion reached by Chan and Chen in a study of the size effect (1991). Using both CAPM and a multi-index/APT model to explain the equilibrium returns on the portfolios constructed based on size, they found that the difference in returns between the small size portfolios and the large size ones was only 1.5 percent using their multifactor model, compared to an 11 percent difference using the single-factor CAPM. Furthermore, they found that the size effect disappears when a multi-index/APT model is used and that the abnormal return observed using a CAPM framework could be explained by the risk premium term in an APT model. In addition to limitations of CAPM, another factor to consider in examining anomalies is that some may simply be proxies for others. For example, a small firm portfolio may simply be a proxy for a low *P/e* portfolio. This was the conclusion that Basu reached in a 1983 article in which he reported that the highest risk-adjusted returns were in portfolios with small firms and low *P/e* ratios. Recall, however, that Fama and French also found that *P/e* ratios were significant by themselves, but that they became insignificant when both size and book-to-market values were considered.

Event Studies

When an event such as an unexpected good earnings announcement or a merger occurs, investors reassess the value of the security and by their subsequent trading cause the price of the security to change. In addition to cross-sectional studies, empirical studies of the semi-strong-form tests of the EMH also try to determine if there are enough fundamentalists to ensure that investors, on average, do not earn abnormal returns from trading on events and announcements. Empirical studies examining this form of the semi-strong EMH are called *event studies*. These studies try to ascertain how long it takes for new information to be reflected in the price.

Methodology of Event Studies

A common methodology used in many event studies is to estimate the *cumulative abnormal returns* (*CAR*) before and after the event. A *CAR* test consists of the following steps:

1. **Step 1:** Collect a sample of companies that have experienced the event being studied.
2. **Step 2:** Determine the time of the event and the period before and after. If the period around the event is 60 days, for example, then each day prior to the event could be designated as $-30, -29, -28, \ldots, -1$, the day of the event as 0, and each of the days after the event as $+1, +2, +3, \ldots, +30$. In many studies the time periods prior to and after the event are usually equal and many use daily data.
3. **Step 3:** Determine the abnormal returns for each stock in the sample for each day, ε_i. A stock's abnormal return on a given day is equal to its actual return minus its equilibrium return, with the equilibrium return being determined by using a single or multi-index model.
4. **Step 4:** Compute the average abnormal return for each day from the abnormal returns of the stocks in the sample.
5. **Step 5:** Compute the cumulative average residual (*CAR_t*) for each period ($t = 29$, $28, \ldots, 30$) by summing the average residuals from the beginning of the sample period ($t = -30$) to that period.
6. **Step 6:** Interpret the results.

Using the *CAR* methodology, the effect of an event is examined in terms of how the *CAR* values move before and after the event. For example, if the *CAR* values prior to the event are relatively constant, then increase at or near the event, and then become stationary again after the event, it could be inferred that the market did not anticipate the event; but when it did occur, it reacted positively and efficiently. This pattern, in turn, would be consistent with a semi-strong efficient market. On the other hand, if the *CAR* values prior to the event were stationary and then increased near the time of the event, as well as after the event, then abnormal returns could be earned after the event; this trend would be inconsistent with the semi-strong efficient market. Finally, if the *CAR* values increase prior to the event and then become stationary, then it could be inferred that the market anticipated the event. In such cases, it may be that there is prior information (either public or private) that is signaling the event or it may be that the event in question is preceded by other related events or information. In either case, the presence of abnormal returns suggests market inefficiencies.

One of the early event studies using a *CAR* methodology was conducted by Fama, Fisher, Jensen, and Roll (FFJR) (1969). Their study examined the impact of stock splits and stock dividends on security returns. Taking 940 stock splits on NYSE-listed stocks over a sample period from 1927 through 1959, they first estimated each stock's characteristic line using a 60-month period around the split (30 months before and 30 months after):

$$r_i = \alpha + \beta R_M + \varepsilon_i$$

They next calculated the residual errors, $\varepsilon_{i,t}$, around the time of the split or stock dividend for each month ($-30, -29, \ldots, 0, +1, +2, \ldots +30$):

$$\varepsilon_{i,t} = r_{i,t}^{Obs} - [\alpha + \beta R_{M,t}^{Obs}]$$

where:

$r_{i,t}^{Obs}, R_{M,t}^{Obs}$ = observed returns at time t.

Note that if the residual error at the time of a stock split were positive, then the stock's return would be above the characteristic line, implying abnormal returns. To minimize the effect of factors other than the stock split or dividends on returns, FFJR next calculated the average residual error for the 940 stock splits and dividends analyzed for each of the 60 months:

$$\bar{\varepsilon}_t = \frac{1}{940} \sum_{i=1}^{940} \varepsilon_{i,t}$$

This yielded 60 average residuals: $\bar{\varepsilon}_{-30}, \bar{\varepsilon}_{-29}, \ldots, \bar{\varepsilon}_{30}$.

Finally, they computed the cumulative average residual for each period by summing the average residuals from the beginning of the sample period ($t = -30$) to that period (T):

$$CAR_T = \sum_{t=-30}^{T} \bar{\varepsilon}_t$$

EXHIBIT 15.9   Cumulative Average Residuals Error, 30 Months Before and After a Stock Split

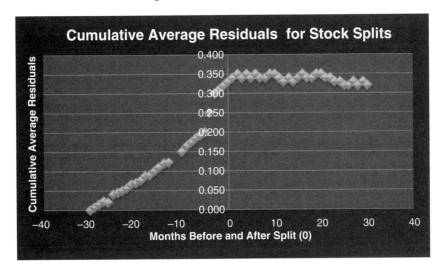

Graphical Representation of the Fama, Fisher, Jensen, and Roll Study (1969)

Exhibit 15.9 shows a representation of the *CARs* that FFJR found in each of the months before and after a stock split and stock dividend. As can be seen, the *CARs* were increasing in the months preceding the split or stock dividend and then became constant after the stock split or dividend.

In trying to interpret FFJR's results, most analysts would not conclude that the market sees a stock split or dividend as having a positive impact on the company's earnings and that it anticipates the event; stock splits and dividends are simply paper shuffling. Rather, most analysts would argue that stock splits and stock dividends are often accompanied by increases in earnings and cash dividends that, in turn, are the major factors leading to an increase in the stock's fundamental value. Thus, in the FFJR study the increase in *CAR* values prior to the splits could be interpreted as a case in which the market is already expecting higher earnings, with these expectations being reached prior to the split.

A number of event studies have been conducted using a CAR methodology similar to FFJR's. Among the events examined are unexpected earning announcements, initial public offerings, new exchange listings, corporate events, macroeconomic events, and world events. Collectively, the findings from these studies lead to mixed conclusions about the efficiency of the market.

Unexpected Earnings Announcements

A number of early studies using a CAR methodology have found that security prices tend to react quickly to anticipated earnings announcements. A more engaging question with respect to earnings, however, is how quickly the market reacts to unexpected earnings announcements.

In an early event study, Joy, Litzenberger, and McEnally (1977) used a *CAR* methodology to test the impact of unexpected earnings announcements on stock prices. They grouped the stocks in their sample into the following categories based on the differences in their actual and expected quarterly earnings: (1) plus and minus deviations of 20 percent, and (2) plus and minus deviations of 40 percent. Examining the *CAR*s for a period of 13 weeks prior to the quarterly announcement and 26 weeks following it, they found that stock prices tended to adjust quickly to the unfavorable earnings announcements, but slowly to the favorable earnings announcements, finding a 4 percent gain in the 20 percent above-expectation group and a 6 percent gain in the 40 percent above-expectation group. The Joy, Litzenberger, and McEnally study suggests that, while unfavorable earnings information is quickly reflected in a stock price, favorable information about a company's earnings takes some time before it is fully reflected, allowing investors to earn abnormal returns. Thus, their study questions the semi-strong EMH.

In a 1982 study, Rendleman, Jones, and Latane also applied a *CAR* methodology to test how the market responded to unexpected good and unexpected bad earnings announcements. To measure the unexpected earnings of a company, they calculated the company's *standardized unexpected earnings* (*SUE*) for each quarter *t*:

$$SUE_{i,t} = \frac{EPS_{i,t} - E(EPS_i)}{\sigma(\varepsilon_i)}$$

where:

$EPS_{i,t}$ = stock *i*'s announced EPS for quarter *t*

$E(EPS_i)$ = expected EPS estimated by extrapolating EPS from an estimated trend regression

$\sigma(\varepsilon_i)$ = standard deviation of the forecast error (error term from the trend regression)

A *SUE* measures the forecast error per average deviation in error. Thus, a predictable company with an average standard deviation of errors of $0.25 and a forecast error for the quarter of $1.00 (*SUE* = 4) would be considered to be a bigger earnings surprise than a less predictable company with an average standard deviation of forecast errors of $1.00 but with a forecast error of $1.00 for the quarter (*SUE* = 1).

In their study, Rendleman, Jones, and Latane obtained the quarterly earnings announcements of approximately 1,000 companies for the period from 1972 through 1980. They then calculated the *SUE* values for each company for each quarter, ranked the companies in the order of their *SUE* values, and formed 10 decile *SUE* portfolios. Rendleman, Jones, and Latane then calculated the *CAR*s for each group beginning with 20 days before the earnings announcement and 90 days after the announcement. They applied this *SUE/CAR* methodology to every quarter in the sample. The average *CAR*s for each of the 10 *SUE* groups are shown in Exhibit 15.10.

In examining the Rendleman, Jones, and Latane's findings shown in Exhibit 15.10, three trends should be noted. First, there is a direct relationship between the

EXHIBIT 15.10 Cumulative Average Residuals Error, Earnings Announcements

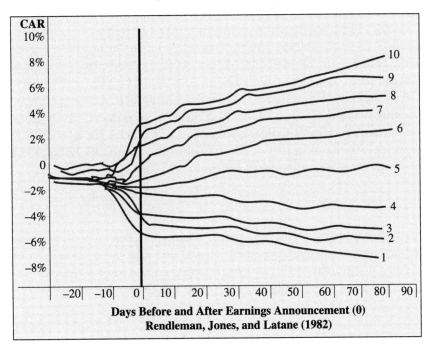

Days Before and After Earnings Announcement (0)
Rendleman, Jones, and Latane (1982)

size of the earnings announcements and the rates of returns: the greater the unexpected good earnings announcements, the greater the return; the greater the unexpected bad earnings announcements, the greater the negative returns. Second, the *CARs* tend to move a few days prior to the announcement, suggesting a market anticipation based on other information. Finally, the *CARs* continue to move up (for good earnings) and down (for poor earnings) after the announcement. Thus, like the Joy, Litzenberger, and McEnally study, the Rendleman, Jones, and Latane study also finds the market takes some time to react to good earnings announcements, and unlike the Joy, Litzenberger, and McEnally study, this study finds the market also takes some time to react to unexpected bad announcements as well. Both studies, however, suggest abnormal returns and therefore market inefficiencies.

Initial Public Offerings

When a closely held company goes public with an initial public offering (IPO) of its stock, the market determines the price of its stock. A commonly held view among many investors is that the underwriters of IPOs tend to underprice the new stock, making it possible for investors to earn abnormal returns. In an early *CAR* study, Ibbotson and Jaffe (1975) examined the return patterns of new issues over their initial 60-month period. They found average abnormal returns of approximately 12 percent in the first month after the IPO and an adjustment period of approximately three months before the stock reached its equilibrium level. Although the study suggests market inefficiencies, one should keep in mind that they estimated the abnormal returns using a single-index/ CAPM model, which may be an inappropriate model to use for a company just going public. By compiling the results of more recent studies on IPOs, one obtains a different profile of the impact of an IPO on stock prices than those determined by Ibbotson and Jaffe.[3] Specifically, studies by Ritter (1991), Lougham and Ritter (1997), and Carter, Dark, and Singh (1998) suggest that underwriters, on average, underprice IPOs by approximately 15 percent, but that the price adjustment takes place within the first few days (not three months), with most of the gains going to institutional investors. These studies thus suggest that investors who acquire IPOs after the initial adjustment would not earn abnormal returns.

Exchange Listings

Another major event for a company occurs when it decides to become listed on a national organized exchange. A common view is that such listings make a company more prestigious, make its stock more marketable, and lead to an increase in the price of the company's stock. A study by McConnell and Sanger (1989), however, finds that the marketability effect of a new exchange listing is not a significant factor in increasing the stock's value over the long run. Studies do find that around the time of a new exchange listing, the company's stock price tends to increase before the listing and decrease after the listing. Specifically, McConnell and Sanger found that abnormal returns could be realized during the period between the listing announcement and the actual listing (a period of between four to six weeks), and abnormal returns could be realized from short positions taken just after the listing.

Other Event Studies

In addition to the above studies, event studies have also been extended to global, macroeconomic, and corporate events. Studies have found that the market tends to react within hours to announcements by the Federal Reserve, the Treasury, and government agencies regarding unexpected macroeconomic information. Considerable research has also been directed toward corporate finance events, such as mergers, new security offerings, and reorganizations. For example, a study by Clifford Smith (1986) on the impact of mergers found that the price of the firm being acquired tended to increase in the market by the amount of the premium being offered by the acquiring firm, and the price of the acquiring firm tended to decrease, reflecting the market's expectation that the company paid too much. In addition, Smith also found that most of the price adjustments related to mergers occur relatively quickly.

Conclusions on Semi-Strong Efficient Markets

Studies of the semi-strong EMH are mixed. On the one hand, event studies of stock splits, IPOs, and corporate events suggest that the market tends to react quickly and efficiently to such information. On the other hand, event studies of unexpected earnings announcements and new exchange listings and cross-sectional studies on selecting stocks based on size, *P/e* ratios, book-to-market values, and neglect suggest abnormal returns are possible.

BLOOMBERG EARNINGS SCREENS

- **EEB:** The Bloomberg EEB shows projections of earnings, sales, and other income statement items from a consensus of Bloomberg contributors. You can view how the consensus has changed over time and the estimates of individual contributors.
- **ERN**: Earnings History.
- **EE**: Earnings and Estimates.
- **EM**: Earnings Trends.
- **EE SURP**: Earnings Surprises.
- **EE Z**: Zach's Earnings Estimates.

  CACS: The Bloomberg CACS screen is a good screen to use to identify a company's past and pending IPOs and new offering, stock splits, dividends, other corporate actions.

  CACT: The Bloomberg CACT screen is a good screen for investment activities for cross-sectional listings (e.g., stocks composing an index, portfolio formed in PRTU, or a search saved in EQS).

  FSCO: The FSCO screen scores and ranks funds belonging to the same peer group based on a combination of weighted indicators. Using FSCO, you can find funds that best meet your investment criteria (e.g., growth, large cap fund domiciled in the United States). You can customize your scoring templates and ratings (e.g., Sharpe, Treynor, and Jensen index). You can rank funds by setting the weights for each parameter.

  MRR: The MRR screen shows the best and worst performers for an index or portfolio.

  GP Screen and Events: On the price graphs (GPs), events such as earning announcements, stock splits, and acquisitions can be identified at the time of the announcement. The "News" box can also be brought up from the gray toolbar by clicking the News button.

See Bloomberg Web Exhibit 15.2.

Studies of the Strong-Form Hypothesis

A strongly efficient market is one in which all information—public and private—is fully reflected in security prices. As we noted earlier, tests of the strong-form EMH take two forms. The first form determines whether insiders have information that would allow them to earn abnormal returns; the second form ascertains whether certain non-insider investment groups such as security analysts or portfolio managers are able to earn abnormal returns by being able to value information better than the average investor. In testing both forms of the strong EMH, researchers have tended to focus on the performance of three identifiable investment groups: insiders, security analysts, and portfolio managers.

Insiders

Security law requires that all insiders (directors, officers, significant shareholders, and others with access to material nonpublic information) notify the Securities and Exchange Commission (SEC) within two days of all large trades they have made in their company's stock. The SEC subsequently publishes the inside trades in their publication, *Official Summary of Insider Trading*. In an early insider study, Jaffe (1974) examined the returns obtained from insider trading as reported by the SEC. He selected stocks each month from the *Official Summary* that had at least three more inside buyers than sellers (buyers' plurality) or at least three more inside sellers than buyers (sellers' plurality). Using a *CAR*-type methodology, Jaffe estimated the after-commission-cost abnormal returns for each stock meeting the plurality criterion by calculating its residual errors. He then calculated the average abnormal returns for months one, two, and eight after the trade was originated (not when it was publicly reported) and the cumulative average residual for those three months for stocks in the buyers' plurality and stocks in the sellers' plurality, as well as the average monthly and cumulative returns (in absolute value) for both plurality groups together. Jaffe found that one month after a plurality of insider trading (buying or selling), there was an average loss in value of 1 percent ($CAR = -0.0102$); after two months, a cumulative average return of approximately zero ($CAR = 0.0009$), suggesting insiders on average were breaking even; and after eight months, a cumulative average excessive return after commission cost of 3 percent ($CAR = 0.0307$). Jaffe concluded that modest abnormal returns were possible after several months as a result of trading from inside information. His study also suggested that outsiders who consistently traded with the insiders based on announced insider transactions also could have earned abnormal returns.

In a follow-up study, Seyhun (1986) examined insider trades using a larger sample than Jaffe. He also examined the profitability of trading strategies of outsiders who traded on inside information provided by investment service companies. Unlike Jaffe, he found that, on average, they were not able to profit from such trades. However, more recent studies by Chowdhury, Howe, and Lin (1993) and by Pettit and Venkatesh (1995) have looked at corporate insiders' trades to determine if insiders were long in their company's stocks before above-average uptrends and short in their stocks before above-average downtrends. They, in turn, found consistent above-average profits, especially on the purchases of their stocks. These studies suggest market inefficiencies.

Security Analysts

Several studies have investigated whether the security analysts who make buy and sell recommendations are able to earn abnormal returns for their clients. One of the early studies of buy and sell recommendations was done by Logue and Tuttle (1974). In their study, they simulated trades based on the buy and sell recommendations of six investment companies. They concluded that with the exception of Value Line, investment company recommendations would not yield returns different from a naive buy-and-hold strategy. The fact that Logue and Tuttle found Value Line to be the exception is noteworthy. Over the last twenty years, a number of studies have examined the stock recommendations of this well-respected investment advisory company.[4]

In a more recent study, Barber, Lehavy, McNichols, and Truemen (2001) found that analysts' recommendations continued to be highly skewed toward buy to strong buy. They further found that those stocks with the most-favorable recommendations tended to outperform those with the least-favorable recommendations. In a 2004 study, Jegadeesh, Kim, Krische, and Lee found positive price changes occurred when there was a change in the consensus recommendation. These more current studies suggest that analysts do provide valuable information to the market.

Portfolio Managers

Some of the earlier studies of mutual funds by Sharpe and Treynor indicated that the performance of the portfolio fund managers could not consistently outperform a naive buy-and-hold strategy on a risk-adjusted basis. These and other similar studies, however, were based on performance relative to a common benchmark and also on a CAPM or single-factor model. In a study by Grinblatt and Titmann (1992), the authors found significantly high risk-adjusted returns for growth funds. In a 1993 study, Elton, Gruber, Das, and Hlavka used a multifactor model with fund returns regressed against the excess returns of three benchmark portfolios; they, in turn, found the average alphas to be negative, implying no abnormal returns. However, in a 2005 study, Bollen and Busse ranked funds by their alpha using a multifactor model. They found a wide disparity in performance, but also found that over a short period of time, the performance differential disappears. The findings of Bollen and Busse probably also hold for some of the more well-known fund investment names such as Warren Buffett, Peter Lynch, and George Soros, who have consistently generated high returns, as well as some hedge funds.

Conclusions on the Strong-Form Efficient Markets

Conclusions regarding the strong-form of the EMH are mixed. On the one hand, there is some empirical evidence that supports the strong form of the EMH with respect to security analysts, portfolio managers, and public trading off insider trade information. On the other hand, there is evidence that indicates that some insiders are able to earn abnormal returns with private information, and some portfolio and investment managers do appear to be able to choose stocks and portfolios better than the average investor does.

BLOOMBERG INSIDER TRADING SCREENS

- INSD: Insiders Trading Monitor.
- Insider's Sentiment ETF: NFO <Equity>.
- GPTR Screen shows insider trades for a loaded stock.

Analyst Recommendations

- ANRP: Analysts Rankings.
- ANRD: Historical Consensus.
- ANR: Analyst Recommendation (for loaded stock).

See Bloomberg Web Exhibit 15.3.

Portfolios Revisited: Equity Style Portfolios

The EMH provides a methodology for not only testing for abnormal return, but also for constructing investment funds and portfolios. The weak-, semi-strong-, and strong-form tests all start with a proposed null hypothesis to test (no abnormal returns can be earned from investing in stocks with low P/e ratios or investors cannot earn abnormal returns by investing in Berkshire Hathaway, etc.). The hypothesis is then tested statistically. This methodology, in turn, provides an approach for creating new funds and investment strategies. For example, a fund manager interested in setting up low P/e portfolios could do so by following the Basu methodology by ranking the 5,000 stocks that make up the S&P in terms of their P/e and then select the lowest quintile for the low P/e fund to offer investors.

As we first discussed in Chapter 5, a number of investment funds are formed based on size and style. The origin of many of these funds, in turn, is rooted in the efficient market analysis. We conclude this chapter by revisiting portfolio analysis, examining portfolios based on style.

Value-Style and Growth-Style Portfolios

In the 1970s, *cluster analysis* was a popular approach for constructing portfolios. A cluster is a portfolio of stocks that are highly correlated with each other, but uncorrelated with other clusters or groups. Cluster portfolio included those formed with cyclical stocks, stable stocks, growth stocks, or energy stocks. Today, cluster analysis is referred to as *equity-style management*. Clusters or styles are typically broken into either value stock or growth stock categories. Sub-categories are often formed within these two groups, such as small-cap, mid-cap, and large-cap. *Value stocks* are those with low *P/e* ratios or price-to-book values (*P/B*). *Growth stocks* are those with high *P/e* or *P/B* ratios.

A common methodology used to construct value and growth funds is to rank a large sample of stocks in in terms of their *P/e* or *P/B* ratios and then select value stocks as all stocks that encompass the first half or first quarter (or some defined proportion) and growth stocks as all those encompassing the other half or last quarter (or some defined percentage).[5] For an example, see the following:

1. Select a large sample of stocks (1,000).
2. Determine the sample's total market value.
3. Compute each stock's *P/e* ratio.
4. Rank the stocks from low to high by *P/e*.
5. Define value stocks as all those stocks that encompass the first half of the market value or number (or some defined percentage).
6. Define growth stocks as all those stocks that encompass the second half of the market value (or some defined percentage).

Within a style, other groupings or substyles can be created. As noted, this could be based on market cap. Other substyles are growth and volatility. For example, within growth, funds could be set to have substyles of high growth, low growth, above-average growth.

In a 1997 study, Leinweber, Arnolt, and Luck looked at the performance of value and growth style investments. They defined value and growth by ranking stocks in terms of their *P/B* ratios. Examining monthly returns, they found that from 1975 to 1995 $1 invested in a value-grouped portfolio would have grown to $23, whereas $1 invested in a growth-grouped portfolio would have grown to $14. They also found that in 45 percent of the months in the sample, growth stocks outperformed value. Exhibit 15.11 shows Bloomberg's total return graph for the Russell 2000 Value Index (RUJ) and the Russell 2000 Growth Index (RUO). For the period from 1/31/1995 to 10/31/2013 (top panel), the value index had an annualized total return of 13.56 percent compared to an 11.63 percent return for the growth index. However, during the bear market period from 10/1/2008 to 3/3/2009, the annualized loss on the growth index was 49.49 percent, whereas the loss on the value index was 35.09 percent (middle panel). Also, for the period from 11/28/2008 to 10/31/13, when the market rebounded, the growth index outperformed the value index with an annualized return of 22.74 percent compared to 17.97 percent for the value index (lower panel).

Other Equity Styles

In addition to value and growth, portfolio style can be based simply on size, such as S&P Mid-Caps or S&P Small Caps, or just growth rates. Fund styles can be defined by a number of characteristics: for example, a fund consisting of stocks with the potential

EXHIBIT 15.11   Total Return Growth and Value Index Russell 2000 Value Index and Russell 2000
Growth Index, 1995–2013, 10/01/2008–3/3/2009, and 11/28/2008–10/31/2013

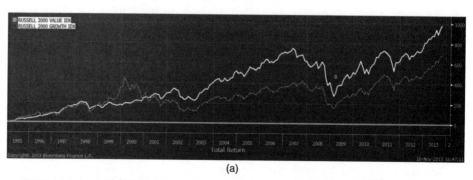

(a)

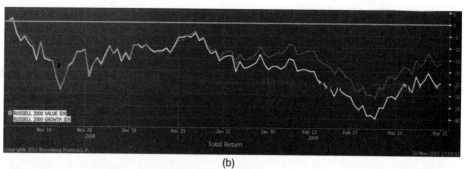

(b)

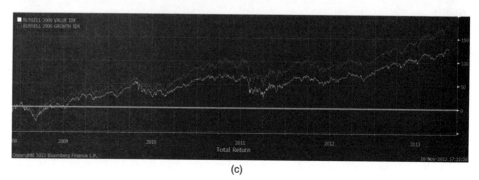

(c)

Exhibit 15.11a: Annualized Total Return
   Value Index = 13.56 percent
   Growth Index = 11.63 percent

Exhibit 15.11b: Annualized Total Return
   Value Index = −35.09 percent
   Growth Index = −49.49 percent

Exhibit 15.11c: Annualized Total Return
   Value Index = 17.97 percent
   Growth Index = 22.74 percent

EXHIBIT 15.12 Investment Styles

1. **Funds with firms with the potential for consistent earnings and dividend growth without high volatility:**
   - Market cap greater than or equal to $2.0B
   - *P/e* less than or equal to 20
   - 5-year average book value greater than 5%
   - *EPS* growth rate greater than or equal to 10%
   - Projected 5-year *EPS* growth greater than or equal to 10%
   - *ROE* greater than or equal to 20%
   - Beta less than or equal to 1.25
   - Dividend growth greater than or equal to 5%
2. **Funds with large cap companies that still have the potential for rapid earnings growth:**
   - Market cap greater than or Equal to $15.0B
   - Projected *EPS* growth greater than 20%
   - Consensus recommendation of buy or better
3. **Funds with companies with high *ROE* and good investment opportunities:**
   - Projected 1-year *EPS* growth rate greater than or equal to 15%
   - Projected 5-year *EPS* growth greater than 15%
   - *ROE* greater than 25%
4. **Funds with neglected or under-followed stocks with attractive investment opportunities:**
   - *P/e* less than 15
   - *EPS* growth rate greater than 10%
   - Projected 5-year *EPS* greater than 15%
   - Estimated analysis coverage less than 5%
5. **Funds consisting of strong companies that are trading at discounts to their growth rates. Stocks with lower PEG ratios (*P/E* divided by growth). This ratio shows how much an investor is paying for each unit of potential earnings growth:**
   - Projected 5-year *EPS* growth rate greater than 20%
   - Projected 1-year *EPS* greater than or equal to 20%
   - Daily volume greater than or 50,000
   - Zacks buy recommendation
   - PEG (*P/E* divided by growth) with lowest 20% for industry
6. **Funds consisting of companies with the potential for consistent earnings and dividend growth without high volatility:**
   - Market cap greater than $2.0B
   - *P/e* less than 20
   - 5-years average book value growth greater than 5%
   - Projected *EPS* growth rate greater than 10%
   - *ROE* greater than 20%
   - Beta less than 1.25
   - 5-year average dividend growth rate greater than 5%

for consistent earnings and dividend growth without high volatility, or funds consisting of stocks with posted positive earnings surprises in their last outings, or those with consensus broker ratings that have also recently been upgraded. Exhibit 15.12 shows several different detailed styles and the criterion for selecting them. Note how some of these are based on some of the efficient market studies we examined in this chapter.

BLOOMBERG CASE: CREATING AN EQUITY STYLE PORTFOLIO

- Search for portfolio with specific style characteristics in EQS.
- Import the EQS search to PRTU and evaluate it in PORT.

Example: Stocks with the potential for consistent earnings and dividend growth without high volatility:

- Market cap greater than or equal to $2.0B.
- *P/e* less than or equal to 20.
- Book value growth greater than or equal to 5 percent.
- 5-year *EPS* growth rate greater than or equal to 10 percent.
- *ROE* greater than or equal to 20 percent.
- Beta less than or equal to 1.25.
- Five-year average dividend growth rate greater than or equal to 5 percent.

See Bloomberg Web Exhibit 15.4

Conclusion

An efficient market is one in which all information is fully reflected in a security price. If such a market existed, then the price of the security would always be equal to its true value, and investors would not be able to earn abnormal returns from fundamental and technical strategies or from inside information. The empirical studies that have tested the weak-form, semi-strong-form, and strong-form tests of the EMH suggest that markets are not perfectly efficient. These studies have found the following:

1. Security returns are not serially correlated.
2. With the exception of small filters, strategies based on filter rules do not outperform a naive buy-and-hold strategy, and strategies using small filters do not outperform the naive strategy on an after commission cost basis.
3. A number of anomalies may exist. The most notable are the January effects, Monday effects, small-size firms, low *P/e* stocks, and high book-to-market value stocks.
4. The market appears to react quickly and efficiently to events such as IPOs, new exchange listings, and expected earnings announcements, but appears to take some time to react to unexpected earnings announcements.
5. With some exceptions, security analysts and portfolio managers do not appear to be able to outperform the market on a risk-adjusted basis.
6. Insiders appear to have information that is not fully reflected in security prices.

Notes

1. Basu actually ranked the stocks by the inverse of their *P/e* ratio. By doing this, companies with negative earnings were placed in the high *P/e* group. To address possible biases of negative earnings companies, Basu then formed a sixth portfolio that included the high *P/e* stocks without negative earnings.
2. In a 1983 study, Brown, Kleidon, and Marsh found the performance of small-size firms relative to large firms varied from period to period. They concluded that the small firm effect is unstable.
3. For a review of studies on returns from IPOs, see Ibbotson, Sindelar, and Ritter (1994).
4. In forming their recommendations, Value Line publishes weekly information on thousands of stocks in their *Value Line Investment Survey*. In their survey, the company ranks stocks from 1 to 5, where 1 represents a strong buy recommendation and 5 a strong sell recommendation. Several older studies on Value Line's recommendations have found that the stocks in group 1 consistently outperformed the market, as well as the other groups, and the stocks in group 5 significantly underperformed the market. In fact, Black and Kaplan, in a 1973 article entitled "Yes, Virginia, There is Hope: Tests of the Value Line Ranks," found that portfolios constructed with rank 1 stocks outperformed portfolios with rank 5 stocks by 20 percent on a risk-adjusted basis. Copeland and Mayers (1982) also found similar results. They also found performances that were consistent with the rankings; that is, group 1 stocks yield the highest return, followed by group 2, and so on. Finally, Stickel (1985) found that Value Line–recommended stocks that changed ranks also experienced price changes, with significant price changes occurring when a stock in group 2 moved to group 1. Unfortunately, the exceptional performance of Value Line at that time was not sustained. Over the decade of the 1990s, the Value Line Centurion Fund, which specializes in group 1 stocks, consistently underperformed the market.
5. An alternative to ranking is to use a multiple-index measure that provides a score.

   The index score is constructed so that the higher the score, the greater the growth stock. For example:

   $$S_i = c_1 \left(\frac{D}{P} \right)_i + c_2 (ROE)_i + c_3 (\text{Variation in Earnings})_i$$

Selected References

Arbel, Avner, and Paul Strebel. 1983. Pay attention to neglected firms! *Journal of Portfolio Management* 9 (Winter): 37–42.

Arnott, Robert D., and Chris G. Luck. 2003. The many elements of equity styles: Quantitative management of core, growth, and value styles. *Handbook of Equity Style Management*. Edited by T. D. Coggin, F. J. Fabozzi, and R. D. Arnott. Hoboken, NJ: John Wiley & Sons.

Banz, Rolf W. 1981. The relationship between return and market value of common stock. *Journal of Financial Economics* 9: 3–18.

Barber, B. R., M. McNichols, R. Lehavy, and B. Trueman. 2001. Can investors profit from the prophets? Security recommendations and stock returns. *Journal of Finance* 56 (April): 531–563.

Barberis, Nicholas, and Richard Thaler. 2003. A survey of behavioral finance. *Handbook of the Economics of Finance*. Edited by G. M. Constantinides, H. Harris, and R. M. Stultz. Amsterdam: Elsevier.

Barone-Adesi, G. 1985. Arbitrage equilibrium with skewed asset returns. *Journal of Financial and Quantitative Analysis*, 20: 299–313.

Barry, Christopher B., and Stephen Brown. 1984. Anomalies in security returns and the specification of the market model. *Journal of Finance* 39 (July): 807–818.

Basu, S. 1977. Investment performance of common stocks in relations to their price-earnings ratios: A test of the efficient market hypothesis. *Journal of Finance* 32 (June): 663–682.

Basu, S. 1983. The relationship between earnings' yield, market value and return for NYSE common stocks: Further evidence. *Journal of Financial Economics* 12: 129–156.

Beard, Craig, and Richard Sias. 1997. Is there a neglected-firm effect? *Financial Analysts Journal* 53 (September–October): 19–23.

Berges, Angel, John McConnell, and Gary G. Schlarbaum. 1984. The turn-of-the-year in Canada. *Journal of Finance* 39 (March): 185–192.

Bessembinder, H., and K. Chan. 1998. Market efficiency and the returns to technical analysis. *Financial Management*: 5–17.

Black, F., and R. S. Kaplan. 1973. Yes, Virginia, there is hope: Tests of the value line ranking system. *Financial Analysts Journal*: 10–92.

Black, F. 1971. Random walk and portfolio management. *Financial Analysts Journal* (March-April): 16–22.

Bollen, N. P., and J. A. Busse. 2005. Short-term persistence in mutual fund performance. *Review of Financial Studies*, 18. 569–597.

Branch, Ben. 1977. A tax loss trading rule. *Journal of Business* 50 (April): 198–207.

Brock, W., J. Lakonishok, and B. LeBaron. 1992. Simple technical trading rules and the stochastic properties of stock returns. *Journal of Finance* (December): 1731–1764.

Brown, Phillip, Donald Kiem, Allan Kleidon, W. Allan, and Terry Marsh.1983. Stock return seasonality and the tax-loss selling hypothesis: Analysis of the arguments and Australian evidence. *Journal of Financial Economics* 12: 105–127.

Chan, K. C., and Nai-Fu Chen. 1991. Structural and return characteristics of small and large firms. *Journal of Finance* 46 (September): 1467–1484.

Chopra, N., J. Lakonishok, and J. Ritter. 1992. Measuring abnormal performance: Do stocks overreact? *Journal of Financial Economics* 31: 235–268.

Chowdhury, J. S., J. S. Howe, and J. C. Lin. 1993. The relation between aggregate inside transactions and stock market returns. *Journal of Financial and Quantitative Analysis* 28 (September): 431–437.

Copeland, Thomas, and David Mayers. 1982. The Value Line Enigma (1965-1978): A case study of performance of evaluation issues. *Journal of Financial Economics* 10 (November): 289–322.

DeBondt, Werner, and Richard Thaler. 1985. Does the stock market overreact? *Journal of Finance* 40 (July): 793–805.

DeBondt, Werner, and Richard Thaler. 1987. Further evidence on investor overreaction. *Journal of Finance* 42 (July): 557–581.

Dieffenbach, R. 1972. How good is institutional research? *Financial Analysts Journal* (January-February): 54–60.

Elton, E. J., M. J. Gruber, S. Das, and M. Hlavka. 1993. Efficiency with cost information: A reinterpretation of evidence from managed funds. *Review of Financial Studies* 6: 1–22.

Fama, E. F. 1965. The behavior of stock-market prices. *The Journal of Business*, 38: 34–105.

Fama, Eugene, and Marshall Blume. 1966. Filter rules and stock market trading. *Journal of Business* 39 (January): 226–241.

Fama, E., L. Fisher, M. Jensen, and R. Roll. 1969. The adjustment of stock prices to new information. *International Economic Review* 10 (February): 1–21.

Fama, E. F., and K. R. French. 1988. Permanent and temporary components of stock prices. *Journal of Political Economy* 96 (April): 246–273.

Fama, E. F. 1991. Efficient market theory. *Journal of Finance* 46: 1575–1618.

Fama, E. F., and K. R. French. 1992. The cross-section of expected stock returns. *Journal of Finance*, 47: 427–465.

Fama, E. F., and K. R. French. 1993. Common risk factors in the returns on stocks and bonds. *Journal of Financial Economics*, 33: 3–56.

Fama, E. F. 1995. Random walks in stock market prices. *Financial Analysts Journal*: 75–80.

Friend, Irwin, and Larry Lang. 1988. The size effect on stock returns: Is it simply of risk effect not adequately reflected by the usual measures? *Journal of Business Finance* 12 (March): 13–30.

Gandar, J. M., W. H. Dare, C. R. Brown, and R. A. Zuber. 1998. Informed traders and price variations in the betting market for professional basketball games. *Journal of Finance* 53: 385–401.

Gandar, John M., Richard A. Zuber, and R. Stafford Johnson. 2004 A reexamination of the efficiency of the betting market on National Hockey League games. *Journal of Sports Economics* 5: 152–168.

Carter, R. B., F. H. Dark, and A. K. Singh. 1998. Underwriter reputation, initial returns, and the long-run performance of IPO stocks. *Journal of Finance*, 53: 285–311.

Gibbons, M. R., and P. Hess. 1981. Day of the week effects and asset returns. *Journal of Business*: 579–596.

Goetzmann, William, and Roger Ibbotson. 1994. Do winners repeat? *Journal of Portfolio Management* 20 (Winter): 9–18.

Gultekin, Mustafa, and N. Bulent Gultekin. 1983. Stock market seasonality: International evidence. *Journal of Financial Economics* 12 (December): 475–490.

Grinblatt, M., and S. Titman. 1992. The persistence of mutual fund performance. *Journal of Finance*, 47: 1977–1984.

Harris, L. 1986. A transaction data study of weekly and intradaily patterns in stock returns. *Journal of Financial Economics* 16(1): 99–117.

Ibbotson, Roger, and Jeffrey Jaffe. 1975. Hot issues markets. *Journal of Finance* 30 (September): 1027–1042.

Ibbotson, Roger, Jody Sindelar, Jay R. Ritter. 1994. The market problem with pricing of initial public offerings. *Journal of Applied Corporate Finance* 7 (Spring): 66–74.

Jaffe, Jeffery. 1974. Special information and insider trading. *Journal of Business* 47 (July): 410–428.

James, Christopher, and Robert Edmister. 1983. The relation between common stock return, trading activity, and market value. *Journal of Finance* 8 (September): 1075–1086.

Jegadeesch, N., J. Kim, S. D. Krische, and C. M. Lee. 2004. Analyzing the analysts: When do recommendations add value? *Journal of Finance* 59 (June): 1083–1124.

Johnson, R. S., Lyle Fiore, and R. A. Zuber. 1989. The investment performance of common stocks in relation to their price-to-earnings ratios: An update to the Basu study. *Financial Review* 24 (August): 499–505.

Joy, O. M., R. H. Litzenberger, and R. W. McEnally. 1977. The adjustment of stock prices to announcements of unanticipated changes in quarterly earnings. *Journal of Accounting Research*: 207–225.

Kato, K., and J. S. Schallheim. 1985. Seasonal and size anomalies in the Japanese stock market (Doctoral dissertation, Graduate School of Business, University of Utah).

Klein, Robert A., and Jess Lederman, eds. 1995. *Equity Style Management*. Chicago, Ill: Irwin Professional Publishing.

Lakonishok, J., A. Shleifer, and R. W. Vishny. 1994. Contrarian investment, extrapolation, and risk. *Journal of Finance*, 49: 1541–1578.

Leinweber, D. J., R. D. Arnott, and C. G. Luck. 1997. *The Many Sides of Equity Style. Quantitative Management of Core, Value, and Growth Portfolios*, chapter 11: 179–209.

Logue, D., and D. Tuttle. 1974. Brokerage house investment advice. *Financial Review* 8: 38–54.

Lorie, James, and Victor Neiderhoffer. 1968. Predictive and statistical properties of insider trading. *Journal of Law and Economics* 11 (April): 35–53.

Loughran, T., and J. R. Ritter. 1997. The operating performance of firms conducting seasoned equity offerings. *Journal of Finance*, 52: 1823–1850.

Malkiel, Burton G. 2003. The efficient market hypothesis and its critics. *The Journal of Economic Perspectives* 17: 59–82.

Malkiel, Burton G., and John G. Cragg. 1970. Expectations and the structure of share prices. *American Economic Review* 60 (Spring): 601–617.

Maurice Joy, O., and C. P. Jones. 1986. Should we believe the tests of market efficiency? *The Journal of Portfolio Management*, 12: 49–54.

McConnell, John J., and Gary Sanger. 1989. A trading strategy for new listings on the NYSE. *Financial Analysts Journal* 40 (January–February): 38–39.

Pettit, R. R., and P. C. Venkatesch. 1995. Insider trading and long-run performance. *Financial Management* 24 (Summer): 88–103.

Reinganum, Marc. 1983. The anomalous stock market behavior of small firms in January: Empirical tests for the tax-loss selling effect. *Journal of Financial Economics* 12 (June): 89–104.

Reinganum, Marc. 1992. A revival of the small-firm effect. *Journal of Portfolio Management* 18 (Spring): 55–62.

Rendleman, Richard, Charles P. Jones, and Henry Latane. 1982. Empirical Anomalies based on unexpected earnings and importance of risk adjustments. *Journal of Financial Economics* 10 (November): 269–287.

Rendleman, Richard, Charles P. Jones, and Henry Latane. 1985. Earnings announcements: Pre- and post-responses. *Journal of Portfolio Management* 11 (Spring): 28–32.

Ritter, Jay R. 1983. The buying and selling behavior of individual investors at the turn of the year. *Journal of Finance* (July): 701–717.

Ritter, Jay R. 1991. The long-run performance of initial public offerings. *Journal of Finance* 46 (March): 3–27.

Russo, B., J. M. Gandar, and R. A. Zuber. 1989. Market rationality tests based on cross-equation restrictions. *Journal of Monetary Economics* 24: 455–470.

Samuelson, Paul. 1989. The judgment of economic science on rational portfolio management. *Journal of Portfolio Management* 61 (December): 4–12.

Seyhun, H. Nejat. 1986. Insiders' profits, cost of trading and market efficiency. *Journal of Financial Economics* 16.

Smith, Clifford W. 1986. Investment banking and the capital acquisition process. *Journal of Financial Economics* 15 (January–February): 3–29.

Shiller, Robert J. 1981. Do stock prices move too much to be justified by subsequent changes in dividends? *American Economic Review* 71 (June): 421–436.

Shiller, Robert J. 2000. *Irrational Exuberance*. Princeton, NJ: Princeton University Press.

Shiller, Robert J. 2003. From efficient markets theory to behavioral finance. *The Journal of Economic Perspectives* 17: 83–104.

Stickel, Scott E. 1985. The effect of Value Line investment survey rank changes on common prices. *Journal of Financial Economics* 14 (March): 121–144.

Sweeney, R. J. 1988. Some new filter rule tests: Methods and results. *Journal of Financial and Quantitative Analysis*, 23(3): 285–300.

Westerfield, Randolph. 1977. The distribution of common stock price changes: An application of transaction, time, and subordinated stochastic models. *Journal of Financial and Quantitative Analysis* 10 (December): 743–756.

Womack, K. L. 1996. Do brokerage analysts' recommendations have investment value? *Journal of Finance* 51 (March): 137–167.

Zuber, R. A., J. M Gandar, and B. D. Bowers. 1985. Beating the spread: Testing the efficiency of the gambling market for National Football League games. *The Journal of Political Economy*, 93(4), 800–806.

Bloomberg Exercises

1. Filter rule tests are designed to test technical rules of buying and selling when stocks break their support and resistance levels. Bloomberg's back-testing screen (BTST) can be used to back test the profitability of various technical trading rules,

including when stocks hit their resistance and support line. Use the BTST screen to back test a moving average envelope for the S&P 500 or a stock or other index of interest. For your test, take a long position when the closing price cuts its lower band and a short positive when it cuts its upper band. Do a back test of just the long position.

- BTST <Enter>.
- On BTST screen, click the pencil icon next to "MA Envelope" to bring up a screen with several tabs.
- Click the "Strategy Definition" tab to bring up a screen for setting conditions. On the condition screen, you can edit the moving average and upper and lower bands by clicking the edit pencil icon.
- Click the "Simulation Control" tab to change the trade condition from Long & Short, Long Only, or Short Only.
- Click the "Strategy Analysis" tab to run the back test.
- On the main screen, compare the simulation result to a buy-and-hold strategy and other strategies.

2. Use the BTST screen to back test the Bollinger band for the S&P 500 or a stock or index of interest. On the BTST screen, click the pencil icon next to "Bollinger Band" to bring up a screen with several tabs for setting up your test (see Exercise 1).

3. Many of the early studies support a weakly efficient market. The Hurst exponent is a metric used to identify price patterns hidden within seemingly random stock price trends. If a price trend is random, the Hurst coefficient would continuously have a value close to 0.5. If not, then there is pattern to the stock price movement.

   a. Use Bloomberg's Hurst screen (GPO KAOS for a loaded stock or index) to see if an index or a number of stocks of interest have Hurst coefficients that are different from 0.5.

   b. Find the Hurst coefficients for stocks that make up an index (SPX or INDU) using the RV screen: INDU <Index>; RV; on the RV screen type in "Hurst" in the "Add Column" box.

4. In an early anomaly study, Banz found excess returns of portfolios consisting of the smallest size stocks. Evaluate the performance of portfolios based on size by comparing the performances over different time periods of the Russell Small Cap index (RTY <Index>) and the Russell Large Cap index (RIY <Index>) using the COMP and HS screens: RTY <Index>; COMP and HS. On the COMP and HS screens, enter the large cap index in the compare box (RIY <Index>). Use the HRA or beta screen to see the regression relationship of the indexes with the market (S&P 500): RTY or RIY <Index>; HRA. Vary the time period for your regressions. Do either of the indexes have an abnormal return (positive alpha)?

5. The Basu study provided empirical support for the time-honored investment strategy of investing in stocks with low *P/e* ratios. Many value funds and indexes are constructed with stocks with relatively low *P/e* or *P/B* ratios and many growth funds and indexes are formed with stocks with relatively high *P/e* or *P/B* ratios. Evaluate the performance of portfolios based on *P/e* or *P/B* ratios by comparing

the performances over different time period of the Russell 1000 Value index (RLV <Index>) and the Russell 1000 Growth index (RLG <Index>) using the COMP and HS screens: RLV <Index>; COMP and HS. On the COMP and HS screen enter the growth index in the compare box (RLG <Index). Use the HRA or beta screen to see the regression relation of the indexes with the market (S&P 500): RLV or RLG <Index>; HRA. Vary the time periods for your regression. Do either of the indexes have an abnormal return (positive alpha)?

6. Unexpected earnings event studies examine how the market reacts to good and bad earnings announcements. On 8/14/2013, Macy's had an unexpected bad earnings announcement of 7.46 percent below estimates and on 11/7/12 had a good earnings announcement of 22.03 percent above.

   a. Go to Macy's earnings surprise screen (EE SURP) and evaluate the impact of these announcements.

   b. Evaluate the impact of the announcements on Macy's stock price and volume around these announcement dates. On Macy's GP screen, click the "Events" tab and check "Earnings." To determine the percentage change in price, use the percentage change drawing line by clicking the "Annotations Button" on the gray toolbar and then "% Change" from the annotations palette showing all of the tools for drawing on the chart. Move the "% Change" drawer to the announcement dates and click. The line will tell you the percentage change in price.

7. The performances of funds by type can be found on the Bloomberg Fund Heat Map Screen, FMAP.

   a. Use the screen to identify several value style funds and growth style funds:
      • FMAP <Enter>, click "Objective" in "View By" dropdown and United States in "Region" dropdown, and then click "Equity" and select type (e.g., Value Broad Market and Growth Broad Market).
      • Select one of the funds and study it (the fund's ticker can be found on the description page) using the functions on the fund's menu screen (Fund Ticker <Equity> <Enter>). Functions to include are DES, historical fund analysis (HFA), and price graph (GP).

   b. Evaluate the fund using the Holdings, Performance, and Characteristics tabs on the fund's PORT screen.

   c. Examine the fund's total returns for different periods and frequencies relative to the S&P 500, Russell 3000, or Dow using the COMP screen: Fund Ticker <Equity> <Enter> and then click COMP.

   d. Using the HRA or Beta screen, determine the fund's characteristic line with the S&P 500, its systematic risk (R^2), and unsystematic risk.

   e. Using your selected fund's RV screen, compare the fund with other similar funds in terms of Sharpe, Treynor, and Jensen ranking indexes. On the RV screen, click the custom tab and then type in Sharpe, Treynor, and Jensen to find those indexes.

8. The FSCO screen scores and ranks funds belonging to the same peer group based on a combination of weighted indicators. Using FSCO, select the following types

of funds by style and categories and then score them in terms of indexes (e.g., Sharpe, Treynor, and Jensen indexes; select Risk/Return in the Model dropdown):

a. Value broad market base.

b. Growth broad market.

c. Value large cap.

d. Growth large cap.

e. Value small cap.

f. Growth small cap.

9. Use the RV screen for the S&P 500 (SPX <Index>; RV) or Russell 3000 (RAY <Index>; RV) to find the range in size (market cap), *P/e*, and *P/B* values for stocks that make up S&P 500 or the Russell 3000. On the RV screen, click the column heading of the category (e.g., market cap or *P/e*) to sort the stocks in the index in increasing or decreasing order.

10. Construct one or more of the following portfolios based on style or characteristics and evaluate it using PORT:

a. Low *P/e* Portfolio (e.g., *P/e* less than 15 or 10 or between 5 and 15 or a condition based on what you found from Exercise 9).

b. Large *P/e* (e.g., *P/e* > 25 or a condition based on what you found from Exercise 9).

c. Small Cap (e.g., market cap between $5 billion and $10 billion).

d. Large Cap (e.g., market cap greater than $100 billion).

e. Low *P/B* (e.g., price-to-book ratio less than 3).

f. High *P/B* (e.g., price-to-book ratio greater than 7).

Steps:

• Use EQS to search for stocks to form your portfolio from an index such as S&P 500 stocks or Russell 3000 stocks: EQS <Enter; select Standard and Poor's 500 or Russell 3000 from the Indexes tab; in the yellow ribbon box, type *P/e* or market cap and set your conditions; save your screen (Actions tab).

• Create a portfolio of the stocks from your search in PRTU: PRTU <Enter>; click red "Create;" from Settings Screen, click "Actions" tab and then import the stocks (on the settings screen, enable history; see Chapter 7, Bloomberg exhibit box: "Bloomberg Portfolio Screens for Evaluating Portfolios: PRTU and PORT, Steps for Creating Historical Data for Portfolios in PRTU."

• Evaluate your portfolio's past performance relative to an index (e.g., DJIA, INDU) using the PORT screen over different time periods: Performance tab, "Total Return," "Portfolio vs Index" (e.g., INDU), Time = MTD, YTD, and Custom (for Custom, the select time period must be within the period history of the portfolio created in PRTU).

• Evaluate the characteristics of your portfolio relative to an index using PORT: Characteristics tab, "Main View," "Portfolio vs Index (e.g., INDU), "by GIC Sectors" Characteristics tab, "Main View," "Portfolio vs Index" (e.g., INDU), "by GIC Sectors."

11. Several studies (Chowdhury, Howe, and Lin; Pettit and Venkatesh; and Jaffe) have found modest abnormal returns were possible for short periods from trading from

inside information. The Sabrient Insider Sentiment Index (SBRIN <Index>) consists of publicly traded companies that reflect a positive sentiment by insiders closest to the company's financials. There is also an Insider's Sentiment ETF, NFO (NFO <Equity>) that is tied to the Sabrient index. Study the relative performance of the index or ETF to the S&P 500 over different time periods using the COMP screen.

12. Studies have found that analysts' recommendations are highly skewed toward buy to strong buy compared to sell. See whether or not you find this to be the case for several stocks of interest by examining Bloomberg's analyst recommendations screens ANRP and ANRD.

CHAPTER 16

Options Markets

Introduction: Short History of the Derivative Market

In the 1840s, Chicago emerged as a transportation and distribution center for agriculture products. Midwestern farmers transported and sold their products to wholesalers and merchants in Chicago, who often would store and later transport the products by either rail or the Great Lakes to population centers in the East. Partly because of the seasonal nature of grains and other agriculture products and partly because of the lack of adequate storage facilities, farmers and merchants began to use *forward contracts* as a way of circumventing storage costs and pricing risk. These contracts were agreements in which two parties agreed to exchange commodities for cash at a future date, but with the terms and the price agreed upon in the present. For example, an Iowa farmer in July might agree to sell his expected wheat harvest to a Chicago grain dealer in September at an agreed-upon price. This forward contract enabled both the farmer and the dealer to lock in the September wheat price in July. In 1848, the Chicago Board of Trade (CBT) was formed by a group of Chicago merchants to facilitate the trading of grain. This organization subsequently introduced the first standardized forward contract, called a "to-arrive" contract. Later, it established rules for trading the contracts and developed a system in which traders ensured their performance by depositing good-faith money to a third party. These actions made it possible for speculators as well as farmers and dealers who were hedging their positions to trade their forward contracts. By definition, *futures* are marketable forward contracts. Thus, the CBT evolved from a board offering forward contracts to the first organized exchange listing futures contracts—a futures exchange.

Futures Market

Since the 1840s, as new exchanges were formed in Chicago, New York, London, Singapore, and other large cities throughout the world, the types of futures contracts grew from grains and agricultural products to commodities and metals and finally to financial futures: futures on foreign currency, debt securities, and security indexes. Because of their use as a hedging tool by financial managers and investment bankers, the introduction of financial futures in the early 1970s led to a dramatic growth in futures trading, with the users' list reading as a who's who of major investment houses, banks, and corporations. The financial futures market formally began in 1972 when the Chicago Mercantile Exchange (CME) created the International Monetary Market (IMM) division, to trade futures contracts on foreign currency. In 1976, the CME extended its listings to include a futures contract on a Treasury bill. The CBT introduced its first futures contract in October 1975 with a contract on the Government National Mortgage Association (GNMA) pass-through, and in 1977 they introduced the Treasury bond futures contract. The Kansas City Board of Trade was the first exchange to offer trading on a futures contract on a stock index, when it introduced the Value Line Composite Index (VLCI) contract in 1983. This was followed by the introduction of the Standard & Poor's (S&P) 500 futures contract by the CME and the New York Stock Exchange (NYSE) index futures contract by the New York Futures Exchange (NYFE).

Whereas the 1970s marked the advent of financial futures, the 1980s saw the globalization of futures markets with the openings of the London International Financial Futures Exchange (LIFFE) in 1982, Singapore International Monetary Market in 1986, Toronto Futures Exchange in 1984, New Zealand Futures Exchange in 1985, and Tokyo Financial Futures Exchange in 1985. Exhibit 16.1 shows the Bloomberg CTM screen that lists the major exchanges trading futures and derivatives. The increase in the number of futures exchanges internationally led to a number of trading innovations: electronic trading systems, 24-hour worldwide trading, and alliances between exchanges. Concomitant with the growth in future trading on organized exchanges has been the growth in futures contracts offered and traded on the over-the-counter (OTC) market. In this market, dealers offer and make markets in more tailor-made forward contracts in currencies, indexes, and various interest rate products. Today, the total volume of forward contracts created on the OTC market exceeds the volume of exchange-traded futures contracts. The combined growth in the futures and forward contracts has also created a need for more governmental oversight to ensure market efficiency and to guard against abuses. In 1974 the Commodity Futures Trading Commission (CFTC) was created by Congress to monitor and regulate futures trading, and in 1982 the National Futures Association (NFA), an organization of futures market participants, was established to oversee futures trading. Finally, the growth in futures markets led to the consolidation of exchanges. In 2006, the CME and the CBT approved a deal in which the CME acquired the CBT, forming the CME Group, Inc.

Formally, a forward contract is simply an agreement between two parties to trade a specific asset at a future date with the terms and price agreed upon today. A futures contract, in turn, is a "marketable" forward contract, with marketability (the ease or speed in trading a security) provided through futures exchanges that not only list hundreds of contracts that can be traded but provide the mechanisms for facilitating trades. Futures and forward contracts are known as *derivative securities*. A derivative security is one whose value depends on the values of another asset (e.g., the price of the underlying commodity or security). Another important derivative is an option. An option is a security that gives the holder the right, but not the obligation, to buy or sell a particular asset at a specified price on, or possibly before, a specific date.

EXHIBIT 16.1 Major Futures and Derivative Exchanges

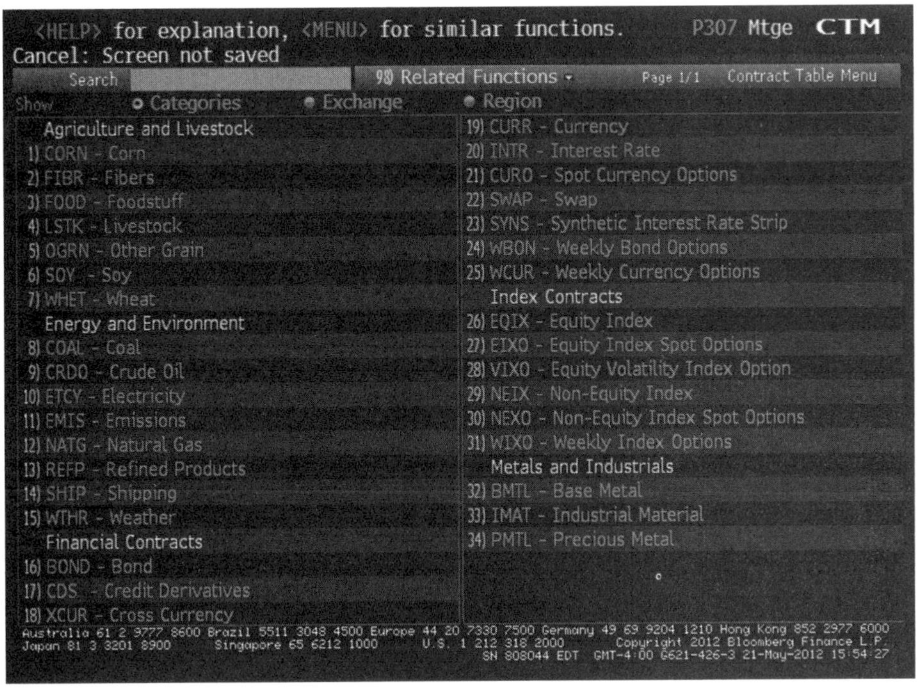

(a)

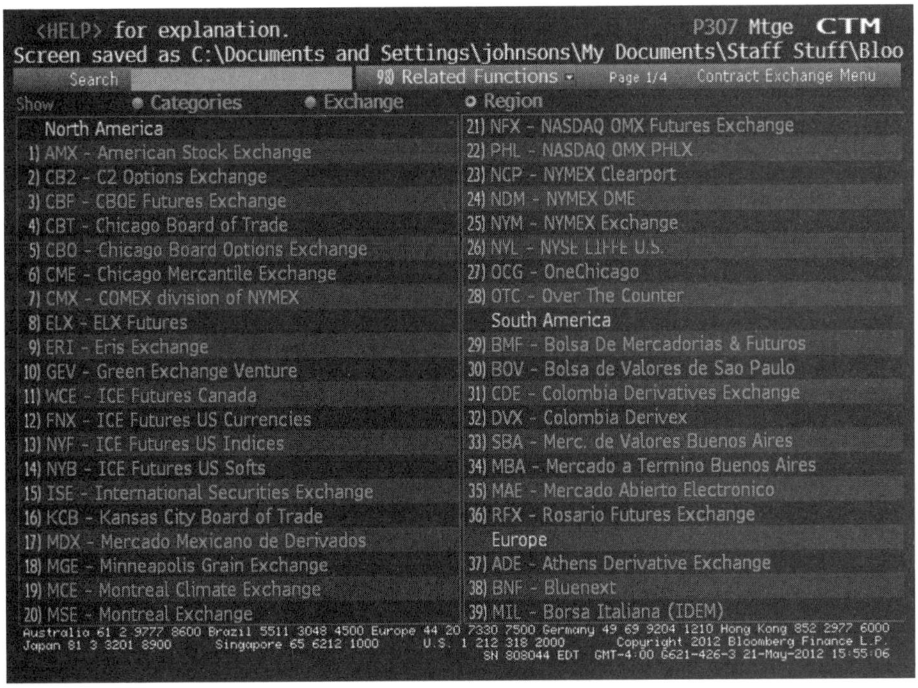

(b)

EXHIBIT 16.1   (*Continued*)

```
<HELP> for explanation.                                    P307 Mtge  CTM
Screen saved as C:\Documents and Settings\johnsons\My Documents\Staff Stuff\Bloo
      Search                           90 Related Functions ▾   Page 3/4   Contract Exchange Menu
Show           ● Categories        ● Exchange       ● Region
      Asia/Pacific                              21) OSE - Osaka Securities Exchange
 1) ACE - ACE Derivs & Cmdty Exchange           22) PMX - Pakistan Mercantile Exchange
 2) AFE - Agricultural Futures Exchange of Thailand  23) SHF - Shanghai Futures Exchange
 3) SFE - ASX Trade24                            24) SGX - Singapore Exchange (was SIMEX)
 4) ASX - Australian Stock Exchange              25) SME - Singapore Mercantile Exchange
 5) BBX - Bombay Stock Exchange                  26) FTX - Taiwan Futures Exchange
 6) CFF - China Financial Future Exchange (CFFEX) 27) TEF - Thailand Futures Exchange
 7) DCE - Dalian Commodity Exchange              28) TCM - Tokyo Commodity Exchange
 8) HKG - Hong Kong Futures Exchange             29) TFX - Tokyo Financial Exchange
 9) HKM - Hong Kong Mercantile Exchange          30) TGE - Tokyo Grain Exchange
10) INX - Indian Commodity Exchange              31) TSE - Tokyo Stock Exchange
11) ICD - Indonesia Commodity and Derivatives Exch 32) USE - United Stock Exchange
12) IDX - Indonesia Stock Exchange               33) ZCE - Zhengzhou Commodity Exchange
13) KAN - Kansai Commodity Exchange                 Africa
14) KFE - Korea Exchange                         34) YLX - JSE Interest Rate Market
15) MDE - Malaysia Derivatives Ex. (KLO)         35) GBT - Mauritius Global Board of Trade
16) MCX - MCX Stock                              36) SAF - South African Futures Exchange
17) MCI - Multi Commodity Ex. of India              Middle East
18) NDX - National Commodity & Derivatives Exchang 37) BFX - Bahrain Financial Exchange
19) NSE - National Stock Exchange                38) DGC - Dubai Gold & Commodities Exchange
20) NZX - NZX Derivatives                        39) DME - Dubai Mercantile Exchange
Australia 61 2 9777 8600 Brazil 5511 3048 4500 Europe 44 20 7330 7500 Germany 49 69 9204 1210 Hong Kong 852 2977 6000
Japan 81 3 3201 8900      Singapore 65 6212 1000      U.S. 1 212 318 2000      Copyright 2012 Bloomberg Finance L.P.
                                          SN 808044 EDT  GMT-4:00 G621-426-3 21-May-2012 15:56:04
```

(c)

```
<HELP> for explanation.                                    P307 Mtge  CTM
Screen saved as C:\Documents and Settings\johnsons\My Documents\Staff Stuff\Bloo
      Search                           90 Related Functions ▾   Page 2/4   Contract Exchange Menu
Show           ● Categories        ● Exchange       ● Region
      Europe                                    21) EOE - NYSE LIFFE - Amsterdam
 1) BTS - Bucharest Stock Exchange               22) BFO - NYSE LIFFE - Brussels
 2) BSE - Budapest Stock Exchange                23) BDP - NYSE LIFFE - Lisbon
 3) EPD - EEX Power Derivatives                  24) LIF - NYSE LIFFE - London
 4) EDX - ENDEX                                  25) EOP - NYSE LIFFE - Paris
 5) EUX - Eurex                                  26) COP - OMX Nordic Exchange Copenhagen
 6) EEE - European Energy Exchange               27) HEX - OMX Nordic Exchange Helsinki
 7) FPL - Fish Pool ASA                          28) SSE - OMX Nordic Exchange Stockholm
 8) GME - Gestore del Mercato Elettrico          29) OBX - Oslo Stock Exchange
 9) ICE - ICE Futures Europe                     30) OMP - Portugal Power Exchange
10) IGE - Istanbul Gold Exchange                 31) PXE - Power Exchange Central Europe
11) LMF - LME 3rd Wednesday Prices & Options     32) PNX - Powernext
12) LME - LME Benchmark Monitor                  33) PRG - Prague Stock Exchange
13) LMS - LME Swaps                              34) RTS - Russian Trading System
14) MFP - MEFF Power                             35) SIB - Sibiu Monetary Financial and Commodities
15) MFM - Meff Renta Variable (Madrid)           36) SPX - SPIMEX Commodity Exchange
16) MFA - MFAO Olive Oil Exchange                37) TKD - Turkish Derivatives Exchange
17) MCX - Moscow Interbank Currency Ex.          38) TQD - Turquoise Derivatives
18) N2X - N2EX UK Power Market                   39) UKR - Ukrainian Exchange
19) NPE - NASDAQ OMX Commodities                 40) WSE - Warsaw Stock Exchange
20) PMI - NASDAQ OMX Swedish Fixed Income Deriva 41) WBA - Wiener Borse
Australia 61 2 9777 8600 Brazil 5511 3048 4500 Europe 44 20 7330 7500 Germany 49 69 9204 1210 Hong Kong 852 2977 6000
Japan 81 3 3201 8900      Singapore 65 6212 1000      U.S. 1 212 318 2000      Copyright 2012 Bloomberg Finance L.P.
                                          SN 808044 EDT  GMT-4:00 G621-426-3 21-May-2012 15:55:44
```

(d)

Options Markets

Like the futures market, the option market in the United States can be traced back to the 1840s when options on corn meal, flour, and other agriculture commodities were traded in New York. These option contracts gave the holders the right, but not the obligation, to purchase or to sell a commodity at a specific price on or possibly before a specified date. Like forward contracts, options made it possible for farmers or agriculture dealers to lock in future prices. In contrast to commodity futures trading, however, the early market for commodity option trading was relatively thin. The market did grow marginally when options on stocks began trading on the over-the-counter (OTC) market in the early 1900s. This market began when a group of investment firms formed the Put and Call Brokers and Dealers Association. Through this association, an investor who wanted to buy an option could do so through a member who either would find a seller through other members or would sell (write) the option himself.

The OTC option market was functional, but suffered because it failed to provide an adequate secondary market. In 1973, the Chicago Board of Trade (CBT) formed the Chicago Board Options Exchange (CBOE). The CBOE was the first organized option exchange for the trading of options. Just as the CBT had served to increase the popularity of futures, the CBOE helped to increase the trading of options by making the contracts more marketable. Since the creation of the CBOE, organized stock exchanges in the United States, most of the organized futures exchanges, and many security exchanges outside the United States also began offering markets for the trading of options. As the number of exchanges offering options increased, so did the number of securities and instruments with options written on them. Today, option contracts exist not only on stocks but also on foreign currencies, indexes, futures contracts, and debt and interest rate-sensitive securities.

In addition to options listed on organized exchanges, there is also a large OTC market in currency, debt, and interest-sensitive securities and products in the United States and a growing OTC market outside the U.S. OTC debt derivatives are primarily used by financial institutions and nonfinancial corporations to manage their interest rate positions. The derivative contracts offered in the OTC market include spot options and forward contracts on Treasury securities, London Interbank Offered Rate–related (LIBOR-related) securities, and special types of interest rate products, such as interest rate calls and puts, caps, floors, and collars. OTC interest rate derivatives products are typically private, customized contracts between two financial institutions or between a financial institution and one of its clients.

Overview

Futures and options contracts on stock, debt, and currency, as well as such hybrid derivatives as swaps, interest rate options, caps, and floors, are an important risk-management tool. Farmers, portfolio managers, multinational businesses, and financial institutions often buy and sell derivatives to hedge positions they have in the derivative's underlying asset against adverse price changes. Derivatives also are used for speculation. Many investors find buying or selling options or taking futures positions an attractive alternative to buying or selling the derivative's underlying security. Finally, many institutional investors, portfolio managers, and corporations use derivatives for *financial engineering*, combining their debt, equity, or currency positions with different derivatives to create a structured investment or debt position with certain desired risk-return features.

In this chapter, we examine the option market, describing the markets in which equity derivatives are traded, how they are used for speculating and hedging, and how their prices are determined. In Chapter 17, we examine futures markets and how futures contracts are used for speculating, hedging, and financial engineering.

Option Strategies

Option Terminology

By definition, an option is a security that gives the holder the right to buy or sell a particular asset at a specified price on, or possibly before, a specific date. A call option would be created, for example, if on March 1, Ms. A paid $1,000 to Mr. B for a contract that gives Ms. A the right, but not the obligation, to buy "ABC Properties" from Mr. B for $100,000 on or before July 1. Similarly, a put option also would be created if Mr. B sold Ms. A a contract for the right, but not the obligation, to sell "ABC Properties" to Mr. B for $100,000 on or before July 1.

Depending on the parties and types of assets involved, options can take on many different forms. Certain features, however, are common to all options. First, with every option contract there is a right, but not the obligation, to either buy or sell. Specifically, by definition, a *call* is the right to buy a specific asset or security, whereas a *put* is the right to sell. Second, every option contract has a buyer and seller. The option buyer is referred to as the *holder* and as having a *long* position in the option. The holder buys the right to *exercise* or evoke the terms of the option claim. The seller, often referred to as the option *writer*, has a *short* position and is responsible for fulfilling the obligations of the option if the holder exercises it. Third, every option has an option price, exercise price, and exercise date. The price paid by the buyer to the writer for the option is referred to as the *option premium* (call premium and put premium). The *exercise price* or *strike price* is the price specified in the option contract at which the underlying asset can be purchased (call) or sold (put). Finally, the *exercise date* is the last day the holder can exercise. Associated with the exercise date are the definitions of European and American options. A *European option* is one that can be exercised only on the exercise date, and an *American option* can be exercised at any time on or before the exercise date. Thus, from our previous example, Mr. B is the writer, Ms. A is the holder, $1,000 is the option premium, $20,000 is the exercise or strike price, July 1 is the exercise date, and the option is American.

Exhibit 16.2 shows price quotes on a number of call and put options on Procter and Gamble stock as of 5/15/2013 from the Bloomberg OMON screen. Each option contract is characterized by its strike or exercise price, expiration, and whether it is a

EXHIBIT 16.2 Bloomberg OMON, Screen: Call Options on P&G

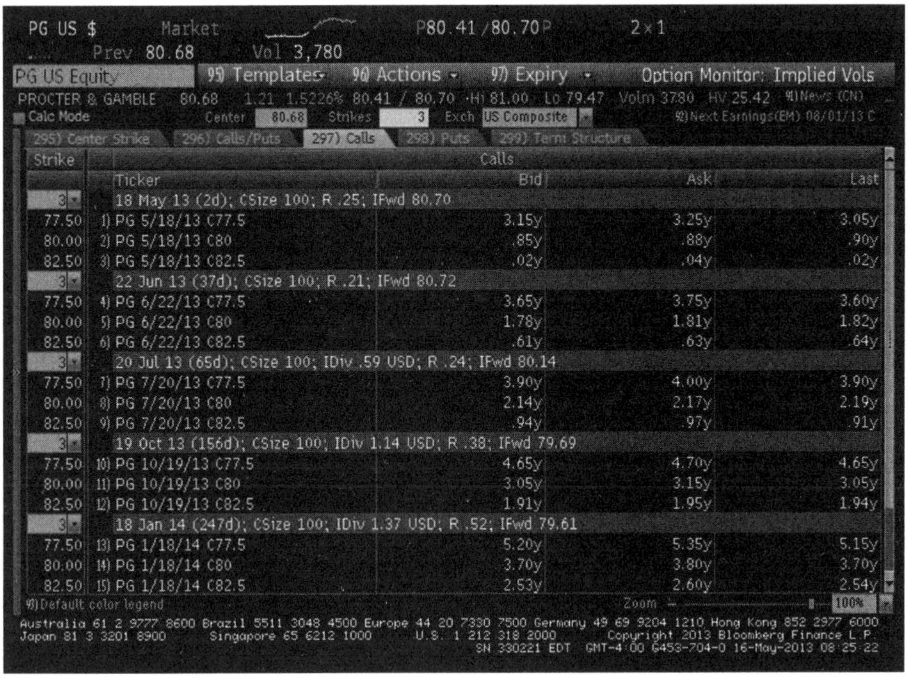

Strike	Calls: Ticker	Bid	Ask	Last
3	18 May 13 (2d); CSize 100; R .25; IFwd 80.70			
77.50	1) PG 5/18/13 C77.5	3.15y	3.25y	3.05y
80.00	2) PG 5/18/13 C80	.85y	.88y	.90y
82.50	3) PG 5/18/13 C82.5	.02y	.04y	.02y
3	22 Jun 13 (37d); CSize 100; R .21; IFwd 80.72			
77.50	4) PG 6/22/13 C77.5	3.65y	3.75y	3.60y
80.00	5) PG 6/22/13 C80	1.78y	1.81y	1.82y
82.50	6) PG 6/22/13 C82.5	.61y	.63y	.64y
3	20 Jul 13 (65d); CSize 100; IDiv .59 USD; R .24; IFwd 80.14			
77.50	7) PG 7/20/13 C77.5	3.90y	4.00y	3.90y
80.00	8) PG 7/20/13 C80	2.14y	2.17y	2.19y
82.50	9) PG 7/20/13 C82.5	.94y	.97y	.91y
3	19 Oct 13 (156d); CSize 100; IDiv 1.14 USD; R .38; IFwd 79.69			
77.50	10) PG 10/19/13 C77.5	4.65y	4.70y	4.65y
80.00	11) PG 10/19/13 C80	3.05y	3.15y	3.05y
82.50	12) PG 10/19/13 C82.5	1.91y	1.95y	1.94y
3	18 Jan 14 (247d); CSize 100; IDiv 1.37 USD; R .52; IFwd 79.61			
77.50	13) PG 1/18/14 C77.5	5.20y	5.35y	5.15y
80.00	14) PG 1/18/14 C80	3.70y	3.80y	3.70y
82.50	15) PG 1/18/14 C82.5	2.53y	2.60y	2.54y

call or put. As shown on the call screen, on 5/15/2013, P&G stock closed at 80.68, the last price on the P&G call option with an exercise price of 80 and expiration of June 13, 2013, was 1.82, and dealers were offering to sell the option (Ask) at 1.81 and to buy (Bid) the option at 1.78. Note that the contract size on the option is 100, meaning that the contract calls for buying or selling 100 options. Most stock option contracts call for 100 options. Later in this chapter, we will examine options listed on exchanges in more detail.

Fundamental Option Strategies

Many types of option strategies with names such as straddles, strips, spreads, combinations, and so forth, exist. The building blocks for these strategies are six fundamental option strategies: call and put purchases, call and put writes, and call and put writes in which the seller covers her position. The features of these strategies can be seen by examining the relationship between the price of the underlying security and the possible profits or losses that would result if the option either is exercised or expires worthless.[1]

Call Purchase

To see the major characteristics of a call purchase, suppose an investor buys a call option on P&G stock with an exercise price (X) of $80 at a call premium ($C$) of $3.

If the stock price reaches $90 and the holder exercises the option, a profit of $7 will be realized as the holder acquires the P&G stock for $80 by exercising and then sells it in the market for $90: A $10 capital gain minus the $3 premium. If the holder exercises when the stock is trading at $83, he will break even: The $3 premium will be offset exactly by the $3 gain realized by acquiring the stock from the option at $80 and selling in the market at $83. Finally, if the price of the P&G is at $80 or below, the holder will not find it profitable to exercise, and as a result, he will let the option expire, realizing a loss equal to the call premium of $3. Thus, the maximum loss from the call purchase is $3.

The investor's possible profit/loss and stock price combinations can be seen graphically in Exhibit 16.3 and in the accompanying Bloomberg table. In the graph, the profits/losses are shown on the vertical axis and the market prices of the stock at the time of the exercise and/or expiration (signified as T: S_T) are shown along the horizontal axis. This graph is known as a *profit graph* and was generated from the Bloomberg OSA screen for a P&G option with an exercise price of 80 and expiration of October 19, 2013. The line from the coordinate (80, −3) to the (90, 7) coordinate and beyond shows all the profits and losses per call associated with each stock price. That is, the (90, 7) coordinate shows the $7 call profit realized when P&G is at $90, and the (85, 2) coordinate shows a profit of $2 when the stock is at $85. The horizontal segment shows a loss of $3, equal to the premium paid when the option was purchased. Finally, the horizontal intercept shows the break-even price at $83. The break-even price can be found algebraically by solving for the stock price at the exercise date (S_T) in which the profit (π) from the position is zero. The profit from the call purchase position is:

$$\pi = (S_T - X) - C_0$$

where:

C_0 is the initial ($t = 0$) cost of the call.

Setting π equal to zero and solving for S_T yields the break-even price of S_T^*:

$$S_T^* = X + C_0 = \$80 + \$3 = \$83$$

The profit graph in Exhibit 16.3 highlights two important features of call purchases. First, the position provides an investor with unlimited profit potential; second, losses are limited to an amount equal to the call premium. These two features help explain why some speculators prefer buying a call rather than the underlying stock itself. In this example, suppose that the price of P&G could range from $60 to $100 at expiration. If a speculator purchased the stock for $80, the profit from the stock would range from −$20 to +$20, or in percentage terms, from −25 percent to +25 percent. On the other hand, the return on the call option would range from +467 percent (= [($100 − $80 − $3)/$3] − 1) to −100 percent (= [−$3/$3] − 1)! Thus, the potential reward to the speculator from buying a call instead of the stock can be substantial—in this example, 467 percent compared to 25 percent for the stock, but the potential for loss also is large, −100 percent for the call versus −25 percent for the stock.

EXHIBIT 16.3 Call Purchase

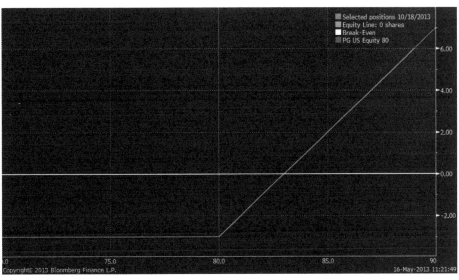

(a)

(b)

In addition to the profit graph, option positions also can be described graphically by value graphs. A value graph shows the option's value or cash flow at expiration, associated with each level of the stock price. The graph shows that if $S_T \leq X$ ($S_T \leq$ 80), then the call will have no value ($C_T = 0$), whereas if $S_T > X$ ($S_T > \$80$), then the call will have a value of $C_T = S_T - X$.

Naked Call Write

The second fundamental strategy involves the sale of a call in which the seller does not own the underlying stock. Such a position is known as a *naked call write*. To see the characteristics of this position, consider the P&G call option with the exercise price of $80 and the call premium of $3. The profits or losses associated with each stock price from selling the call are depicted in Exhibit 16.4. As shown, when the price of the stock is at $90, the seller suffers a $7 loss if the holder exercises the right to buy the stock from the writer at $80. Since the writer does not own the stock, she would have to buy it in the market at its market price of $90, and then turn it over to the holder at $80. Thus, the call writer would realize a $10 capital loss, minus the $3 premium received for selling the call, for a net loss of $7. When the stock is at $83, the writer will realize a $3 loss if the holder exercises. This loss will offset the $3 premium received. Thus, the break-even price for the writer is $83, the same as the holder's. This price also can be found algebraically by solving for the stock price in which the profit from the naked call write position is zero:

$$\pi = (X - S_T) + C_0$$
$$0 = (X - S_T) + C_0$$
$$S_T^* = X + C_0$$
$$S_T^* = \$80 + \$3 = \$83$$

EXHIBIT 16.4   Naked Call Write

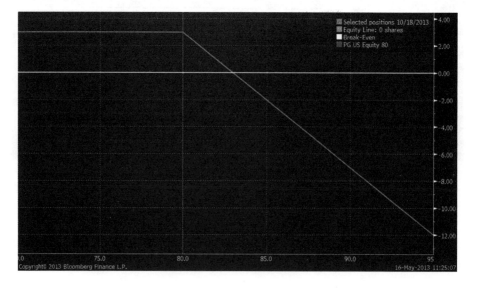

Finally, at a stock price of $80 or less the holder will not exercise, and the writer will profit by the amount of the premium, $3.

As highlighted in the graph, the payoffs to a call write are just the opposite of the call purchase; that is, gains/losses for the buyer of a call are exactly equal to the losses/gains of the seller. Thus, in contrast to the call purchase, the naked call write position provides the investor with only a limited profit opportunity equal to the value of the premium, with unlimited loss possibilities. Although this limited profit and unlimited loss feature of a naked call write may seem unattractive, the motivation for an investor to write a call is the cash or credit received and the expectation that the option will not be exercised. As we will discuss later, however, there are margin requirements on an option write position in which the writer is required to deposit cash or risk-free securities to secure the position.

Covered Call Write

One of the most popular option strategies is to write a call on a stock already owned. This strategy is known as a *covered call write*. For example, an investor who bought 100 shares of P&G stock at $80 some time ago and who did not expect its price to appreciate in the near future, might sell 100 calls on P&G (one call contract) with an exercise price of $80. As shown in Exhibit 16.5 and its accompanying Bloomberg table, if P&G is $80 or more, then the covered call writer loses the stock when the holder exercises, leaving the writer with a profit of only $3. The benefit of the covered call write occurs when the stock price declines. For example, if ABC stock declined to $70, then the writer would suffer an actual (if the stock is sold) or paper loss of $10. The $3 premium received from selling the call, however, would reduce this loss to just $7. Similarly, if the stock is at $77, a $3 loss will be offset by the $3 premium received from the call sale.

Put Purchase

Since a put gives the holder the right to sell the stock, profit is realized when the stock price declines. With a decline, the put holder can buy the stock at a low price in the stock market, and then sell it at the higher exercise price on the put contract. To see the features related to a long put position, consider the P&G put option with an exercise price $80 priced at $3 ($P_0$). If the stock price declines to $70, the put holder could purchase P&G at $70 and then use the put contract to sell the stock at the exercise price of $80. Thus, as shown by the profit graph in Exhibit 16.6, at $70 the put holder would realize a $7 profit (the $10 gain from buying the stock and exercising minus the $3 premium). The break-even price in this case would be $77:

$$\pi = (X - S_T) - P_0$$
$$0 = (X - S_T) - P_0$$
$$S_T^* = X - P_0$$
$$S_T^* = \$80 - \$3 = \$77$$

EXHIBIT 16.5   Cover Call Write

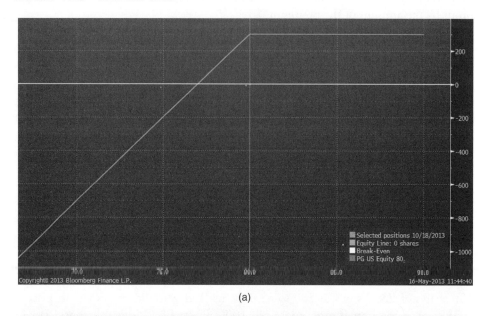

(a)

(b)

EXHIBIT 16.6   Put Purchase

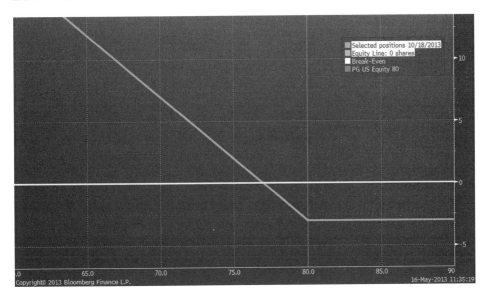

Finally, if the stock is $80 or higher at expiration, it will not be rational for the put holder to exercise. As a result, a maximum loss equal to the $3 premium will occur when the stock is trading at $80 or more. The put purchase position can also be described by its value: if $S_T < X$, then the value of the put is $P_T = X - S_T$, and if $S_T \geq X$, then the put is worthless: $P_T = 0$.

Thus, similar to a call purchase, a long put position provides the buyer with potentially large profit opportunities (not unlimited since the price of the stock cannot be less than zero), while limiting the losses to the amount of the premium. Unlike the call purchase strategy, the put purchase position requires the stock price to decline before profit is realized.

Naked Put Write

The exact opposite position to a put purchase (in terms of profit/loss and stock price relations) is the sale of a put, defined as the *naked put write*. This position's profit graph for the P&G 80 put is shown in Exhibit 16.7. Here, if P&G is at $80 or more, the holder will not exercise and the writer will profit by the amount of the premium, $3. In contrast, if P&G decreases, a loss is incurred. For example, if the holder exercises at $70, the put writer must buy the stock at $80. An actual $10 loss will occur if the writer elects to sell the stock and a paper loss if he holds on to it. This loss, minus the $3 premium, yields a loss of $7 when the market price is $70. As indicated in the

EXHIBIT 16.7 Naked Put Write

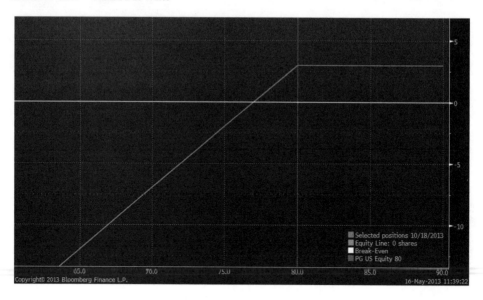

graph, the break-even price in which the profit from the position is zero is $S_T^* = \$77$, the same as the put holder's price:

$$\pi = (S_T - X) + P_0$$
$$0 = (S_T - X) + P_0$$
$$S_T^* = X - P_0$$
$$S_T^* = \$80 - \$3 = \$77$$

Covered Put Write

The last fundamental option strategy is the covered put write. This strategy requires the seller of a put to cover her position. Because a put writer is required to buy the stock at the exercise price if the holder exercises, the only way she can cover the obligation is by selling the underlying stock short. For example, suppose a writer of 100 P&G 80 puts shorts 100 shares of stock: borrows 100 shares of P&G stock and then sells it in the market at $80/share or $8,000. At expiration, if the stock price is less than the exercise price and the put holder exercises, the covered put writer will buy the 100 shares with the $8,000 proceeds obtained from the short sale and then return the shares that were borrowed to cover the short sale obligation. The put writer's obligation is thus covered, and she profits by an amount equal to the premium as shown in Exhibit 16.8. In contrast, losses from covered put write position occur when the stock price rises above $83. When the stock price is $80 or greater, the put is worthless and the holder would not exercise, but losses would occur from covering the short sale. For example, if the writer had to cover the short sale when P&G was trading at $90,

EXHIBIT 16.8 Covered Put Write

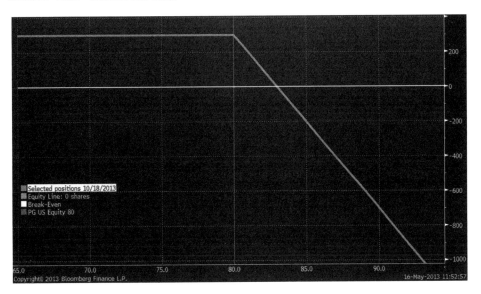

she would incur a $1,000 loss (or $1,000 paper loss if she did not have to cover). This loss, minus the $300 premium the writer received, would equate to a net loss of $700. Finally, the break-even price for the covered put write in which profit is zero occurs at $83.

Other Option Strategies

One of the important features of an option is that it can be combined with the underlying security and other options to generate a number of different investment strategies. Two well-known strategies are the *straddle* and *spread*.

Straddle

A straddle purchase is formed by buying both a call and put with the same terms— same underlying stock, exercise price, and expiration date. A straddle write, in contrast, is constructed by selling a call and a put with the same terms.

In Exhibit 16.9, the profit graphs are shown for a straddle purchase for 100 P&G calls and 100 puts with exercise prices of $80 and premiums of $3.[2] The straddle purchase shown in the figure can be geometrically generated by vertically summing the profits on the call purchase position and put purchase position at each stock price. The resulting straddle purchase position is characterized by a V-shaped profit and stock price relation. Thus, the motivation for buying a straddle comes from the expectation of a large stock price movement in either direction. For example, at the stock price of $90, a $400 profit is earned: $1,000 profit on the 100 calls minus the $600 cost of the straddle purchase. Similarly, at $70, a $400 profit is attained: $1,000 profit on the 100

EXHIBIT 16.9   Straddle Purchase

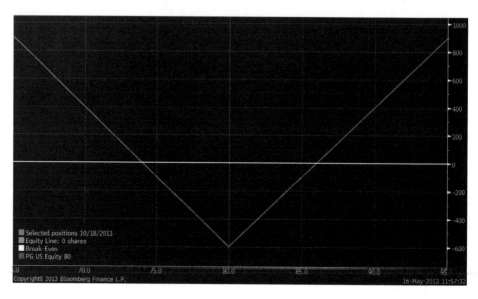

puts minus the $600 cost of the straddle. Losses on the straddle occur if the price of the underlying stock remains stable, with the maximum loss being equal to the costs of the straddle ($600) and occurring when the stock price is equal to the exercise price. Finally, the straddle is characterized by two break-even prices ($84 and $76).

In contrast to the straddle purchase, a straddle write yields an inverted V-shaped profit graph. The seller of a straddle is betting against large price movements. A maximum profit equal to the sum of the call and put premiums occurs when the stock price is equal to the exercise price; losses occur if the stock price moves significantly in either direction. A straddle write problem is included as one of the chapter problems found on the text web site.

Spread

A spread is the purchase of one option and the sale of another on the same underlying stock but with different terms: different exercise prices, different expirations, or both. Two of the most popular spread positions are the *bull spread* and the *bear spread*. A bull call spread is formed by buying a call with a certain exercise price and selling another call with a higher exercise price, but with the same expiration date. A bear call spread is the reversal of the bull spread; it consists of buying a call with a certain exercise price and selling another with a lower exercise price. (The same spreads also can be formed with puts.)

Exhibit 16.10 shows the profit graph and Bloomberg OSA table for a bull spread formed with the purchase of 100 P&G 70 calls (one contract), for $9 per call and the sale of 100 80 calls for $3 (same expirations). Geometrically, the profit and stock price relation for the spread shown in the figure can be obtained by vertically summing the

EXHIBIT 16.10   Bull Spread Purchase

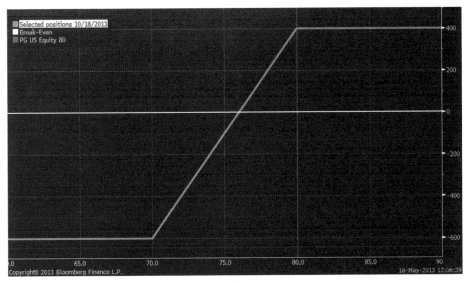

(a)

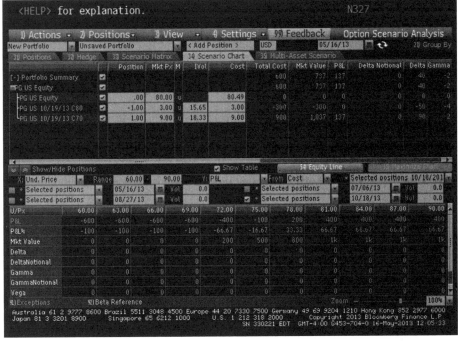

(b)

profits from the long 70 call position and the short 80 call position at each stock price. The bull spread is characterized by losses limited to $400 when the stock price is $70 or less, limited profits of $600 starting when the stock price hits $80, and a break-even price of $76.

A bear call spread results in the opposite profit and stock price relation as the bull spread: a limited profit occurs when the stock price is equal to or less than the lower exercise price and a limited loss occurs when the stock price is equal to or greater than the higher exercise price. A bear spread problem also is included as one of the chapter problems found on the text web site.

Other Positions

Between outright call and put positions, options can be combined in many different ways to obtain various types of profit relations. Speculators who expect prices on stocks to decrease in the future but don't want to assume the risk inherent in a put purchase position could form a bear call spread. In contrast, speculators who expect rates to be stable over the near term could, in turn, try to profit by forming a straddle write. Thus by combining different option positions, speculators can obtain positions that match their expectations and their desired risk-return preference. Given this, it should not be too surprising to find that options can be used to form synthetic securities such as long and short stock positions. A *simulated long position* can be formed by buying a call and selling a put with the same terms; it is equivalent to the profit and stock price relation associated with buying the underlying stock. Similarly, a *simulated short position* is constructed by selling a call and buying a put with the same terms; it is equivalent to the profit and stock price relation associated with selling the underlying stock short. Exhibit 16.11 lists some of the other option positions. Several exercises for generating profit tables and graphs for different option positions are included as part of the chapter problems found on the text web site.

EXHIBIT 16.11   Different Option Positions

---

1. **Bull Call Spread**: Long in call with low X and short in call with high X.
2. **Bull Put Spread**: Long in put with low X and short in put with high X.
3. **Bear Call Spread**: Long in call with high X and short in call with low X.
4. **Bear Put Spread**: Long in put with high X and short in put with low X.
5. **Long Butterfly Spread**: Long in call with low X, short in 2 calls with middle X, and long in call with high X (similar position can be formed with puts).
6. **Short Butterfly Spread**: Short in call with low X, long in 2 calls with middle X, and short in call with high X (similar position can be formed with puts).
7. **Straddle Purchase**: Long call and put with similar terms.
8. **Strip Purchase**: Straddle with additional puts (e.g., long call and long 2 puts).
9. **Strap Purchase**: Straddle with additional calls (e.g., long 2 calls and long put).
10. **Straddle Sale**: Short call and put with similar terms (strip and strap sales have additional calls and puts).
11. **Money Combination Purchase**: Long call and put with different exercise prices.
12. **Money Combination Sale**: Short call and put with different exercise prices.

OSA: BLOOMBERG'S OPTION SCENARIO SCREEN

Profit and value graphs for options can be generated using the Bloomberg OSA screen. To access OSA for a security, load the menu page of the security and type OSA (or click "OSA" from the menu). For example, for Procter and Gamble options do the following:

1. Go to stock or index equity menu screen: Ticker <Equity> <Return>.
2. Type "OSA."
3. On the OSA screen, click the "Positions" tab and then click "Add Listed Options" tab to bring up options listed on the stock. This brings up a screen showing the listed options from which to select, for example, 1 call contract (100 calls) and 1 put contract (100 puts).
4. After selecting the positions, type 1 <Enter> (or click) to load positions and bring up the OSA position screen.
5. On the position screen, click the "Scenario Chart" tab at the top of the screen to bring up the profit graph. The profit graph shows profits for the strategy at expiration where the option price is trading at its intrinsic value and also at time periods prior where the option price is determined by an option-pricing model. The profit graphs for different periods can be changed or deleted by clicking the select options box at the top of the screen.
6. From the position screen (click "Position" tab), you can select different positions and then click "Scenario Chart" tab to view the profit graph.
7. The scenario screen (gray "Scenario Chart" tab) shows the profit table; click "Maximize Chart" tab to see just the graph.
8. See Exhibits 16.3–16.10 for examples of tables and graphs generated from the OSA screen for P&G.

See Bloomberg Web Exhibit 16.1.

Option Price Relations

The market price of an option is a function of the time to expiration, the strike price, the price and the volatility of the underlying security, and the rate of return on a risk-free bond.

Call Price Relations

The relationship between the price of a call and its expiration time, exercise price, and stock price can be seen by defining the call's intrinsic value and time value premium. By definition, the *intrinsic value* (IV) of a call at a time prior to expiration (let t signify any time prior to expiration), or at expiration (T again signifies expiration date) is the maximum (Max) of the difference between the price of the stock (S_t) and the exercise price or zero (since the option cannot have a negative value):

$$IV = \text{Max}[S_t - X, 0]$$

Thus, if a call had an exercise price of $80 and the stock was trading at $90, then the intrinsic value of the call would be $10; if it were trading at $80 or less, the IV would be zero.

The intrinsic value can be used to define *in-the-money, on-the-money,* and *out-of-the-money* calls. Specifically, an in-the-money call is one in which the price of the underlying stock exceeds the exercise price; as a result, its *IV* is positive. When the price of the stock is equal to the exercise price, the call's *IV* is zero and the call is said to be on the money (or at the money). Finally, if the exercise price exceeds the stock price, the call would be out of the money and the *IV* would be zero:

Type	Condition	Example
In-the-Money:	$S_t > X => IV > 0$	$90 > 80 => IV = \$10$
On-the-Money:	$S_t = X => IV = 0$	$80 = \$80 => IV = 0$
Out-of-the-Money:	$S_t < X => IV = 0$	$70 < \$80 => IV = 0$

For an American call option, the *IV* defines a boundary condition in which the price of a call has to trade at value at least equal to its *IV*:

$$C_t \geq \text{Max}[S_t - X, 0]$$

If this condition does not hold ($C_t < \text{Max}[S_t - X, 0]$), then an arbitrageur could earn a riskless return by buying the call, exercising, and then selling the stock. For example, suppose an American call option on P&G stock with an exercise price of $80 was trading at $9 when the stock was trading at $90 ($IV = \text{Max}(\$90 - \$80, 0) = \$10$). In this situation we have an asset (the stock) selling at two different prices: one is $90, offered in the stock market; the other is $89 ($9 call premium plus $80 exercise price), available in the option market. In this case, an arbitrageur could realize a riskless profit of $1 (excluding commissions) per call by (1) buying the call at $9, (2) immediately exercising it (buying P&G stock at $80), and (3) selling the stock in the market for $90:

$S_t = 90, X = 80, C_t = 9$ Position	Cash Flow
Buy P&G 80 Call for 9	−9
Exercise P&G 80 Call: (Buy Stock for $X = 80$)	−80
Sell Stock in Market for 90	+90
Profit	+1

Arbitrageurs seeking to profit from this opportunity would increase the demand for the P&G call, causing its price to go up until the call premium was at least $10 and the arbitrage opportunity disappeared. Thus, in equilibrium, the American call would have to trade at a price at least equal to its *IV*.

It is important to note that the exploitation of arbitrage opportunities by arbitrageurs ensures that the price of the option will change as the underlying stock price changes. For example, if P&G stock were to increase from $90 to $95 to $100, then in the absence of arbitrage, the price of the 80 call would have to increase to a price that is at least equal to $15 when the stock is at $95 and $20 when the stock is at $100. Thus, arbitrageurs ensure that the call option derives its value from the underlying stock. Finally, note that since the above arbitrage strategy governing the price of an American option requires an immediate exercise of the call, the resulting *IV* boundary condition does not hold for European options.[3]

The other component of the value of an option is the *time value premium* (*TVP*). By definition, the *TVP* of a call is the difference between the price of the call and the *IV*:

$$TVP = C_t - IV$$

If the call premium were $12 when the price of the underlying stock on the 80 call was $90, the *TVP* would be $2. The *TVP* decreases as the time remaining to expiration decreases. Specifically, if the call is near expiration, we should expect the call to trade at close to its *IV*. If, however, six months remain to expiration, then the price of the call should be greater and the *TVP* positive; if nine months remain, then the *TVP* should be even greater. In addition to the intuitive reasoning, an arbitrage argument also can be used to establish that the price of the call is greater with a greater time to expiration (this condition is also governed by an arbitrage).

Combined, the *IV* and the *TVP* show that two factors influencing the price of a call, C_t, are the underlying stock's price and the time to expiration:

$$C_t = IV + TVP$$

Call Price Curve

The relationship between C_t and the *TVP* and *IV* is shown graphically in Exhibit 16.12. In the exhibit, graphs plotting the call prices and the *IV*s (on the vertical axis) against P&G stock prices (on the horizontal axis) are shown for an 80 P&G call option. The *IV* line shows the linear relationship between the *IV* and the stock price. The line emanates from a horizontal intercept equal to the exercise price. When the price of the stock is equal to or less than the exercise price of $80, the *IV* is equal to zero; when the stock is priced at $S_t = \$85$, the *IV* is $5; when $S_t = \$90$, the IV = $10, and so on. The *IV* line, in turn, serves as a reference for the nonlinear call price curves. As we just noted, arbitrageurs ensure that the call price curve cannot go below the *IV* line. Furthermore, the *IV* line would be the call price curve if we are at expiration since the *TVP* = 0 and thus $C_T = IV$. The call price curves in Exhibit 16.12 show the positive relationship between C_t and S_t. The vertical distance between a curve and the *IV* line,

EXHIBIT 16.12   Call and Stock Price Relation for P&G Call Option with X = $80

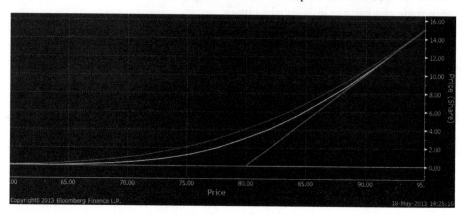

Middle Graph: Call Price Curve for Call with Six-Month Expiration
Upper Graph: Call Price Curve for Call with One-Year Expiration
45-Degree Line: Intrinsic Value (*IV*)
Bloomberg OV Screen

in turn, measures the *TVP*. Thus, the call price curve shown with one year to expiration has a call price of $1.50 when the stock is below its exercise price at $S_t = \$70$: Its $IV = 0$ and $TVP = \$1.50$. When the stock is trading at its exercise price of $80, the call is priced at $4, the $IV = 0$, and the $TVP = \$4$, and when the stock is at $85, the call is at $7, the $IV = \$5$, and the $TVP = \$2$. The call price curve for the six-month option is below the one-year call price curve, reflecting the fact that the call premium decreases as the time to expiration decreases.

In summary, the graphs in Exhibit 16.12 show (1) that a direct relationship exists between the price of the call and the stock price, as reflected by the positively sloped call price curves; (2) that the call will be priced above its *IV*, as shown by the call price curves being above the *IV* line; and (3) the price of the call will be greater the longer the time to expiration, as reflected by the distance between call price curves with different expiration periods. Finally, it should be noted that the slopes of the call price curves approach the slope of the *IV* line when the stock price is relatively high (known as a *deep-in-the-money call*), and the slope approaches zero (flat) when the price of the stock is relatively low (a *deep-out-of-the-money call*).

Variability

The call price curve illustrates the positive relation between a call price and the underlying security price and the time to expiration. An option's price also depends on the volatility of the underlying security.

Since a long call position is characterized by unlimited profits if the underlying security increases but limited losses if it decreases, a call holder would prefer more volatility rather than less. Specifically, greater variability suggests, on the one hand, a given likelihood that the security will increase substantially in price, causing the call to be more valuable. On the other hand, greater volatility also suggests a given likelihood

EXHIBIT 16.13   Price and Variability Relation

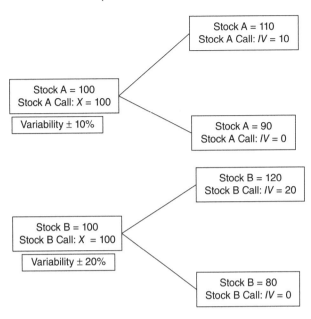

that the security price will decrease substantially. However, given that a call's losses are limited to just the premium when the security price is equal to the exercise price or less, the extent of the price decrease would be inconsequential to the call holder. Thus, the market will value a call option on a more volatile security greater than a call on one with lower variability.

The positive relationship between a call's premium and its underlying security's volatility is illustrated in Exhibit 16.13. The exhibit shows $100 call options on stocks A and B. As shown in the exhibit, Stock A is trading at $100 and has a variability characterized by an equal chance it will either increase by 10 percent or decrease by 10 percent by the end of the period (assume these are the only possibilities). Stock B, in turn, is shown trading at $100 and has a variability characterized by an equal chance it will either increase or decrease by 20 percent by the end of the period. Given the variability of the underlying stocks, the *IV* of the call option on Stock B would be either $20 or 0 at the end of the period, compared to possible values of only $10 and 0 for the call on Stock A. Since, Stock B's call cannot perform worse than Stock A's call, and can do better, it follows there would be a higher demand and therefore price for the call option on Stock B than the call on Stock A. Thus, given the limited loss characteristic of an option, the more volatile the underlying security, the more valuable the option, all other factors being equal.

Put Price Relations

Analogous to calls, the price of a put at a given point in time prior to expiration (P_t) also can be explained by reference to its *IV* and *TVP*. In the case of puts, the *IV* is defined as the maximum of the difference between the exercise price and the stock price or zero:

$$IV = \text{Max}[X - S_t, 0]$$

Similar to calls, in-the-money, on-the-money, and out-of-the-money puts are defined as follows:

Type	Condition	Example
In-the-Money:	$X > S_t \Rightarrow IV > 0$	$\$80 > \$70 \Rightarrow IV = \$10$
On-the-Money:	$X = S_t \Rightarrow IV = 0$	$\$80 = \$80 \Rightarrow IV = 0$
Out-of-the-Money:	$X < S_t \Rightarrow IV = 0$	$\$80 < \$90 \Rightarrow IV = 0$

Like call options, the IV of an American put option defines a boundary condition in which the put has to trade at a price at least equal to its IV: $P_t \geq \text{Max}[X - S_t, 0]$. If this condition does not hold, an arbitrageur could buy the put, the underlying stock, and exercise to earn a riskless profit. For example, suppose P&G stock is trading at $70 and a P&G 80 put was trading at $9, below its IV of $10. Arbitrageurs could realize risk-free profits by (1) buying the put at $9, (2) buying P&G stock for $70, and (3) immediately exercising the put, selling the stock on the put for 80. Doing this, the arbitrageur would realize a risk-free profit of $1:

$S_t = 70, X = 80, P_t = 9$	
Position	Cash Flow
Buy P&G 80 Put for 9	−9
Buy P&G Stock for 70 in the Market	−70
Exercise P&G 80 Put:	
(Sell Stock on the put for $X = 80$)	+80
Profit	+1

As in the case of calls, arbitrageurs pursuing this strategy would increase the demand for puts until the put price was equal to at least the $10 difference between the exercise and stock prices. Thus, in the absence of arbitrage, an American put would have to trade at a price at least equal to its IV.

Similar to call options, the TVP for the put is defined as:

$$TVP = P_t - IV$$

EXHIBIT 16.14 Put and Stock Price Relation for P&G Put Option with $X = 80$

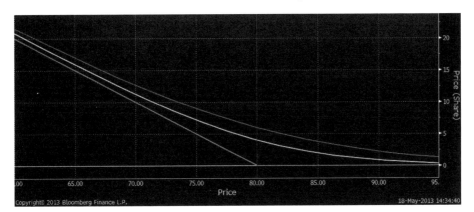

Middle Graph: Put Price Curve for Put with Six-Month Expiration
Upper Graph: Put Price Curve for Put with One-Year Expiration
Negative 45-Degree Line: Intrinsic Value (*IV*)
Bloomberg OV Screen

Thus, the price of the put can be explained by the time to expiration and the stock price in terms of the put's *TVP* and *IV*:

$$P_t = IV + TVP$$

Put Price Curve

Graphically, the put and stock price relationships are shown in Exhibit 16.14. The exhibit shows two negatively sloped put-price curves with different exercise periods, and a negatively sloped *IV* line going from the horizontal intercept (where $S_t = X$) to the vertical intercept where the *IV* is equal to the exercise price when the stock is trading at zero (i.e., $IV = X$, when $S_t = 0$). The graphs show (1) the price of the put increases as the price of the underlying stock decreases, since the put's *IV* is greater the lower the stock price; (2) the price of the put is above its *IV* with time remaining to expiration, else arbitrage opportunities would ultimately push the price up to equal the *IV*; (3) the greater the time to expiration, the higher the *TVP* and thus the greater the put price; and (4) the slope of the put price curve approaches the slope of the *IV* line for relatively low stock prices (*deep-in-the-money puts*) and approaches zero for relatively large stock prices (*deep-out-of-the-money puts*).

Variability

Like calls, the price of a put option depends not only on the underlying security price and time to expiration, but also on the volatility of the underlying security. Since put losses are limited to the premium when the price of the underlying security is greater than or equal to the exercise price, put buyers, like call buyers, will value puts on securities with greater variability more than those with lower variability.

Put-Call Parity

Consider a strategy of buying a share of stock for $50 and a put on the stock with an exercise price of $50. The cash flow from this portfolio at expiration is shown in Exhibit 16.15. As shown in Column 7, this stock and put portfolio has a minimum value of $50 (the exercise price) for $S_T \leq \$50$, and a value equal to the stock for $S_T > \$50$. Thus, an investor who purchased the stock some time ago could eliminate the downside risk of the stock by buying a put. In this case, the stock value has been "insured" not to fall below $50, the exercise price on the put. A combined stock and put position such as this is known as a *portfolio insurance* strategy or *stock insurance* strategy. Portfolio insurance represents an example of how options can be used by hedgers.

Given the values of the stock and put portfolio, consider now a portfolio consisting of a bond with a face value of $50 and a 50 call on the stock. As shown in column 4 of Exhibit 16.15, the values of this portfolio at time T are identical to the stock and put portfolio's values at each stock price. If the stock appreciates, the call becomes more valuable and the return on the bond is enhanced by the appreciation in the call price. On the other hand, if the stock falls below the exercise price, the call is worthless and the portfolio simply is equal to the face value of the bond ($50). A bond and call portfolio such as this is referred to as a *fiduciary call*, and it can be used as a substitute for buying the stock and put. The equality between the stock-put portfolio and the bond-call portfolio may be expressed algebraically as:

$$S_t + P_t = C_t + B_t$$

This expression is commonly referred to as *put-call parity*. Since the two portfolios have exactly the same cash flows at expiration, their values at any time t must be identical, else arbitrage opportunities will exist. For example, if the bond-call combination is cheaper than the stock-put portfolio, an arbitrageur can earn a profit without taking

EXHIBIT 16.15 Cash Flows on Call, Put, Stock, and Bond Positions at Expiration

			Cash Flows at Expiration			
(1)	(2)	(3)	(4)	(5)	(6)	(7)
			Bond and			Stock and Put
	Long Call		Call Portfolio	Long Put		Portfolio
S_T	(X = 50)	Bond	(3) + (4)	X = 50	Stock	(5) + (6)
$30	$ 0	$50	$50	$20	$30	$50
40	0	50	50	10	40	50
50	0	50	50	0	50	50
60	10	50	60	0	60	60
70	20	50	70	0	70	70

risk and without investing any of her own money. To expedite the strategy, the arbitrageur would have to buy the cheap portfolio (bond and call) and sell the expensive one (stock and put). The put-call parity condition is governed by the *law of one price*. This law says that in the absence of arbitrage, any investments that yield identical cash flows must be equally priced.

Option Exchanges

As with all exchanges, the primary function of derivative exchanges offering options is to provide marketability to option contracts by linking brokers and dealers, standardizing contracts, establishing trading rules and procedures, guaranteeing and intermediating contracts through a clearinghouse, and providing continuous trading through electronic matching or with market makers, specialists, and locals.

Standardization

The option exchanges standardize contracts by setting expiration dates, exercise prices, and contract sizes on options. The expiration dates on options are defined in terms of an expiration cycle. For example, the March cycle has expiration months of March, June, September, and December. In a three-month option cycle, only the options with the three nearest expiration months trade at any time. Thus, as an option expires, the exchange introduces a new option. The exchanges also offer longer maturity contracts called LEAPS. On many option contracts, the expiration day is the Saturday after the third Friday of the expiration month; the last day on which the expiring option trades, however, is Friday. In addition to setting the expiration date, the exchanges also choose the exercise prices for each option, with as many as six strike prices associated with each option when an option cycle begins. Once an option with a specific exercise price has been introduced, it will remain listed until its expiration date. The exchange can, however, introduce new options with different exercise prices at any time.

The Option Clearing Corporation

To make derivative contracts more marketable, derivative exchanges provide a clearinghouse (CH) or *option clearing corporation* (OCC), as it is referred to on the option exchange. In the case of options, the OCC intermediates each transaction that takes place on the exchange and guarantees that all option writers fulfill the terms of their options if they are assigned. In addition, the OCC also manages option exercises, receiving notices and assigning corresponding positions to clearing members.

As an intermediary, the OCC functions by breaking up each option trade. After a buyer and seller complete an option trade, the OCC steps in and becomes the effective buyer to the option seller and the effective seller to the option buyer. At that point, there is no longer any relationship between the original buyer and seller. If the buyer of the option decides to exercise, he does so by notifying the OCC (through his broker on the exchange). The OCC (who is the holder's effective option seller) will select one of the option sellers with a short position on the exercised security and assign that writer the obligation of fulfilling the terms of the exercise request.

By breaking up each option contract, the OCC makes it possible for option investors to close their positions before expiration. If a buyer (seller) of an option later becomes a seller (buyer) of the same option, the OCC's computer will note the offsetting position in the option investor's account and will therefore cancel both entries. For example, suppose in January, Investor A buys a March 50 call for 3 from Investor B. When the OCC breaks up the contract, it records Investor A's right to exercise with the OCC and Investor B's responsibility to sell ABC stock at 50 if a party long on the call contract decides to exercise and the OCC subsequently assigns B the responsibility. The transaction between A and B would lead to the following entry in the clearing firms records:

	January Clearinghouse Records for March 50 Call
1.	Investor A has the right to exercise.
2.	Investor B has responsibility.

Suppose that in early February, the price of ABC stock is trading at 60 and the price of the March ABC 50 call is trading at 12. Seeing profit potential, suppose instead of exercising, Investor A decides to close her call position by selling a March 50 call at 12 to Investor C. After the OCC breaks up this contract, its records would have a new entry showing Investor A with the responsibility of selling ABC stock at $X = \$50$ if assigned. This entry, however, would cancel out Investor A's original entry, giving her the right to buy ABC stock at $X = \$50$:

	February Clearinghouse Records for March ABC 50 Call	
1.	Investor A has the right to exercise.	
2.	Investor B has responsibility.	Closed
3.	Investor C has the right to exercise.	
4.	Investor A has responsibility.	

The OCC would accordingly close Investor A's position. Thus, Investor A bought the call for 3 and then closed her position by simply selling the call for 12. Her call sale, in turn, represents an offsetting position and is referred to as an *offset* or *closing sale*.

If a writer also wanted to close his position at this date, he could do so by simply buying a March ABC 50 call option. For example, suppose Investor B feared that ABC stock would continue to increase and therefore decided to close his short position by buying a March ABC 50 call at 12 from Investor D. After this transaction, the OCC would again step in, break up the contract, and enter Investor B's and D's positions on its records. The OCC's records would now show a new entry in which Investor B has the right to buy ABC at 50. This entry, in turn, would cancel Investor B's previous entry in which he had a responsibility to sell ABC at 50 if assigned. The offsetting positions (the right to buy and the obligation to sell) cancel each other, and the OCC computer system simply erases both entries.

February Clearinghouse Records for March ABC 50 Call

1. Investor B has <u>responsibility.</u>
2. Investor C has the <u>right</u> to exercise.   ⟩ Closed
3. Investor B has the <u>right</u> to exercise.
4. Investor D has <u>responsibility.</u>

Since Investor B's second transaction serves to close his opening position, it is referred to as a *closing purchase*. In this case, Investor B loses 9 by closing: selling the call for 3 and buying it back for 12.

Operationally, the OCC functions through its members. Referred to as clearing firms, these members are typically investment firms that are members of the exchange. Each one maintains an account with the OCC, records and keeps track of the positions for each option buyer and seller the OCC places with it, maintains all margin positions, and contributes to the special fund used to guarantee assignment. To recapitulate, by breaking up each transaction, the OCC provides marketability to options by making it easier for investors to close their positions. The OCC also enhances the marketability of option contracts by guaranteeing that the terms of a contract will be fulfilled if a holder exercises.

Margin Requirements and Trading Costs

To secure the OCCs underlying positions, exchange traded option contracts have initial and maintenance margin requirements. The margin requirements on options apply only to the option writer. On most exchanges, the initial margin is the amount of cash or cash equivalents that must be deposited by the writer. In addition to the initial margin, the writer also has a maintenance margin requirement with the brokerage firm in which he has to keep the value of his account equal to certain percentage of the initial margin value. Thus, if the value of an option position moves against the writer, he is required to deposit additional cash or cash equivalents to satisfy his maintenance requirement.

Through the option exchanges, brokers, dealers, market makers, specialists, and the OCC have created a network whereby an investor can buy and sell options in a matter of minutes. The cost of maintaining this complex system is paid for by investors through the commission costs they pay to their brokers, the bid-ask spread investors pay to market makers or specialists when they set up and then later close their positions, and the fees charged by the clearing firms of the OCC that are usually included in the brokerage commission and paid by their brokers.

Types of Option Transactions

The OCC provides marketability by making it possible for option investors to close their positions instead of exercising. In general, there are four types of trades investors of an exchange-traded option can make: opening, expiring, exercising, and closing transactions. The *opening transaction* occurs when investors initially buy or sell an option. An *expiring transaction,* in turn, is allowing the option to expire: that is, doing nothing when the expiration date arrives because the option is worthless (out of the money). If it is profitable, a holder can exercise. Finally, holders or writers of options can close their positions with *offsetting* or *closing transactions* or orders.

As a general rule, option holders should close their positions rather than exercise. If there is some time to expiration, an option holder who sells her option will receive a price that exceeds the exercise value: that is, if the holder sells the option, she will receive a price that is equal to an *IV* plus a *TVP*; if she exercises, however, her exercise value is only equal to the *IV*. As a result, by exercising instead of closing, she loses the *TVP*. Thus, an option holder in most cases should close her position instead of exercising. There are some exceptions to the general rule of closing instead of exercising. For example, if an American option on a stock that was to pay a high dividend that exceeded the *TVP* on the option, then it would be advantageous to exercise.

Since many options are closed, the amount of trading and thus the marketability of a particular option can be determined by ascertaining the number of option contracts that are outstanding at a given point in time. The number of option contracts outstanding is referred to as *open interest*. Thus, in terms of closing transactions, open interest represents the number of closing transactions on an option that could be made before it expires. The exchange, in turn, keeps track of the amount of opening and closing transactions that occur. For example, an opening order to buy 5 calls would increase open interest by 5, and a closing order to sell 5 calls would lower open interest by 5.

Stock Index Options

In March 1983, the CBOE introduced an option on the S&P 100. Because of its hedging uses by institutional investors, this option quickly became one of the most highly traded options. In late April 1983, the American Stock Exchange began offering trading on an option on the Major Market Index (MMI), an index similar to the Dow Jones Average. The introduction of the AMEX's option soon was followed by the New York Stock Exchange's listing of the NYSE stock index option and the Philadelphia exchange's Value Line index option (index of 1,700 stocks) and the National Over-the-Counter index option (index of 100 OTC stocks). Today, the most popular index options include options on the Dow Jones Average (DJX), Nasdaq (NDX), Russell 2000 (RUT), S&P 100 (OEX), and the S&P 500 (SPX).

Theoretically, an index option can be thought of as an option to buy (call) or to sell (put) a portfolio of stocks composing the index in their correct proportions. Unlike stock options, index options have a *cash settlement* feature. When such an option is exercised, the assigned writer pays the exercising holder the difference between the exercise price and the spot index at the close of trading on the exercising day. Thus, an index option can be viewed as an option giving the holder the right to purchase (call) or sell (put) cash at a specific exercise price:

> **Definition**: A call option on a stock index gives the holder the right to purchase an amount of cash equal to the closing spot index (S_t) on the exercising day at the call's exercise price. To settle, the exercising holder receives a cash settlement of $S_t - X$ from the assigned writer.

For example, a May 1,700 S&P 500 call gives the holder the right to buy cash equal to the closing spot index on the exercising day for $1,700 (as discussed below, there also is a multiplier). If the holder exercises when the spot index is $1,800, he in effect is exercising the right to buy $1,800 of cash for $X = $1,700. With cash settlement, the assigned writer simply pays the holder $100.

The put option on a stock index, on the other hand, gives the holder the right to sell cash equal to the spot index value:

> **Definition**: A put option on a stock index gives the holder the right to sell cash equal to the closing spot index on the exercising date at the put's exercise price. To settle, the exercising holder receives a cash settlement amount of $X - S_t$ from the assigned writer.

Thus, the holder of a May 1,700 S&P 500 put who exercises the put when the spot index is at 1,600 could view exercising as the equivalent to selling $1,600 cash to the assigned writer for $1,700. The writer would settle by paying the holder $X - S_t = $100.

The cash settlement feature of index options is one characteristic that differentiates them from stock options. Several other differentiating features of index options should be noted. First, the size of an index option is equal to a multiple of the index value. The S&P 100 and S&P 500 index options, for example, have contract multiples of $100. Thus, the actual exercise price on the above May 1,700 put contract on the S&P 500 is $170,000 = (1,700)($100). Second, the expiration features on many index options are similar to stock options, with most expiring on the third Friday of the expiration month. However, some index options have a shorter expiration cycle consisting of the current month, the next month, and third month from the present. Third, when an index option is exercised, the closing value of the spot index on the exercising day is used to determine the cash settlement. Since the spot index is computed continuously throughout the day, it is possible for a holder to exercise an in-the-money call early in the day, only to have it closed at the end of the day out of the money (in such a case the holder pays the writer the difference between X and S_t). Thus, an index option holder should wait until late in the day before giving his exercise notice. The assigned writer, in turn, is notified of the option assignment on the subsequent business day, at which time he is required to pay the difference in the exercise price and the closing index price. Fourth, a number of index options are European. Fifth, the tax treatment on index option positions differs from stock options in that all realized and unrealized gains on index options that occur during the year are subject to taxes, and all realized and unrealized losses occurring during the year can offset an investor's capital gains. Finally, the margin requirements for index options are similar to those for stock options, except for covered write positions, which have the same margin requirements as naked index option positions.

Managing Stock Portfolios with Index Options

One of the important uses of stock index options is in providing portfolio insurance. As previously noted, portfolio or stock insurance is combining a stock and put position. When applied to stock portfolios, it is a hedging strategy in which an equity portfolio manager protects the future value of her fund by buying index put options. The index put options, in turn, provide downside protection against a stock market decline, while allowing the fund to grow if the market increases.

To illustrate, consider the case of an equity fund manager who plans to sell a portion of a stock portfolio in September to meet an anticipated liquidity need. Suppose the portfolio that the manager plans to sell is well-diversified and highly correlated with the S&P 500, has a beta of 1.25, and currently is worth $V_0 = \$50$ million. Suppose the market, as measured by the spot S&P 500, is currently at 1,250 and that the manager expects a bullish market to prevail in the future with the S&P 500 rising. As a result, the manager expects to benefit from selling her portfolio in September at a higher value. At the same time, however, suppose the manager is also concerned that the market could be lower in September, and she does not want to risk selling the portfolio in a market with the index lower than 1,250. Suppose the CBOE has a September S&P 500 put option with an exercise price of 1,250 and multiplier of 100 that is trading at 50. As a strategy to lock in a minimum value from the portfolio sale if the market decreases, while obtaining a higher portfolio value if the market increases, suppose the manager decides to set up a portfolio insurance strategy by buying September 1,250 S&P 500 puts. To form the portfolio insurance position, the manager would need to buy 500 September S&P 500 puts at a cost of $2.5 million:

$$N_p = \beta \frac{V_0}{X}$$

$$N_p = 1.25 \frac{\$50,000,000}{(1,250)(\$100)} = 500 \text{ puts}$$

$$\text{Cost} = (500)(\$100)(50) = \$2,500,000$$

Exhibit 16.16 shows for five possible spot index values ranging from 1,000 to 1,500 the manager's revenue from selling the portfolio at the September expiration date and closing her puts by selling them at their intrinsic values. Note that for each index value shown in column 1, there is a corresponding portfolio value (shown in column 4) that reflects the proportional change in the market and the portfolio beta of 1.25. For example, if the spot index were at 1,000 at expiration, then the market as measured by the proportional change in the index would have decreased by 20 percent from its January level of 1,250 [$-20\% = (1{,}000–1{,}250)/1{,}250$]. Since the well-diversified portfolio has a beta of 1.25, it would have decreased by 25 percent [$\beta(\%\Delta$ S&P 500$) = 1.25(-0.20) = -0.25$], and the portfolio would, in turn, be worth only 75 percent of its January value of $50 million ($37.5 million). Thus, if the market were at 1,000, the corresponding portfolio value would be $37.5M ($37.5M = [$1 + \beta$ (Proportional Δ S&P 500)]$V_0 = [(1 +(-1.25)(0.20)]$ $50M). On the other hand, if the spot S&P 500 index were at 1,500 at the September expiration, then the market would have increased by 20 percent [$= (1{,}500 − 1{,}250)/1{,}250$] and the portfolio would have increased by 25 percent [$1.25(0.20)$] to equal $62.5 million [$= 1.25$ ($50M)]. Thus, when the market is at 1,500, the portfolio's corresponding value is $62.5 million. Given the corresponding portfolio values, column 5 in Exhibit 16.16 shows the intrinsic values of the S&P 500 put corresponding to the spot index values, and column 6 shows the corresponding cash flows that would be received by the portfolio manager from selling the 500 expiring September index puts at their intrinsic values. As shown in the exhibit, if the spot S&P 500 is less than 1,250 at expiration, then the manager would realize a positive cash flow from selling her index puts, with the put revenue increasing proportional to the decreases in the portfolio values, providing, in turn, the requisite protection in value. On the other hand, if the S&P 500 spot index is equal to or greater than 1,250, the manager's put options would be worthless, but her revenue from selling the portfolio would be greater, the greater the index. Thus, if the market were 1,250 or less at expiration, then the value of the hedged portfolio (stock portfolio value plus put values) would be $50 million; if the market were above 1,250, then the value of the hedged portfolio would increase as the market rises. Thus, for the $2.5 million cost of the put options, the fund manager has attained a $50 million floor for the value of the portfolio, while benefiting with greater portfolio values if the market increases.

In addition to protecting the value of a portfolio, index options also can be used to hedge the costs of future stock portfolio purchases. For example, suppose the above portfolio manager was anticipating a cash inflow of $50 million in September, which she planned to invest in a well-diversified portfolio with a beta of 1.25 that was currently worth $50 million when the current spot S&P 500 index was at 1,250. Suppose there was a September S&P 500 call option trading at 50 and that the manager was fearful of a bull market pushing stock prices up, increasing the cost of buying the well-diversified portfolio. To hedge against this, the manager could lock in a minimum cost of the portfolio of $50 million by purchasing 500 September 1,250 S&P 500 index calls at a cost of $2.5 million:

$$N_C = \beta \frac{V_0}{X}$$

$$N_C = 1.25 \frac{\$50{,}000{,}000}{(1{,}250)(\$100)} = 500 \text{ calls}$$

$$\text{Cost} = (500)(\$100)(50) = \$2{,}500{,}000$$

EXHIBIT 16.16 Stock Portfolio Hedged with S&P 500 Puts

Portfolio Hedged with S&P 500 Index Puts
Portfolio: Initial Value = $50M, β = 1.25
S&P 500 Put: X = 1,250, Multiplier = 100, Premium = 50
Hedge: 500 Puts; Cost = (500)(50)($100) = $2.5 million

1 S&P 500 Spot Index	2 Proportional Change in the Market	3 Proportional Change in the Portfolio	4 Portfolio Value	5 Put Value at T	6 Value of Put Investment	7 Hedged Portfolio Value
S_T	$g = (S_T - 1{,}250)/1{,}250$	$\beta g = 1.25g$	$V_T = (1+\beta g)\$50M$	$P_T = IV =$ Max$[1{,}250 - S_T, 0]$	CF = 500($100) P_T	Column 4 + Column 6
1,000	−0.20	−0.250	$37,500,000	250	$12,500,000	$50,000,000
1,125	−0.10	−0.125	$43,750,000	125	$6,250,000	$50,000,000
1,250	0.00	0.000	$50,000,000	0	$0	$50,000,000
1,375	0.10	0.125	$56,250,000	0	$0	$56,250,000
1,500	0.20	0.250	$62,500,000	0	$0	$62,500,000

As shown in Exhibit 16.17, if the spot index is 1,250 or higher at expiration, then the corresponding cost of the portfolio would be higher, but those higher portfolio costs would be offset by profits from the index calls. For example, if the market were at 1,500 in September, then the well-diversified portfolio with a β of 1.25 would cost $62.5million; the additional $12.5 million cost of the portfolio would be offset, however, by the $12.5 million cash flow obtained from the selling of 500 September 1,250 index calls at their intrinsic value of 250. Thus, as shown in the exhibit, for index values of 1,250 or greater, the hedged costs of the portfolio would be $50 million. On the other hand, if the index is less than 1,250, the manager would be able to buy the well-diversified portfolio at a lower cost, with the losses on the index calls limited to just the premium. Thus, for the $2.5 million costs of the index call option, the manager is able to cap the maximum cost of the portfolio at $50 million, while still benefiting with lower costs if the market declines.

OSA: PORTFOLIO INSURANCE

Importing Equity Portfolios into Bloomberg's Option Scenario Screen

On the OSA screen, you can import a portfolio and then add option positions.

To evaluate a portfolio insurance position for a portfolio you created in PRTU do the following:

- OSA <Enter>.
- From the "Portfolio" dropdown, select a portfolio.
- From red "Positions" tab, click "Add Listed Options" and then enter SPX in upper left amber area box.
- Select options and then click 1<GO>.
- On OSA screen, click portfolio summary box to include all stocks and options.
- Scroll down to options and set the number of puts needed to insure the portfolio.
- Click "Scenario Chart" tab and input setting: y box: mkt. value, range, and evaluation dates.

See Bloomberg Web Exhibit 16.2.

Black-Scholes Option Pricing Model

We described earlier how the price of an option is a function of the underlying stock's price and volatility and the option's time to expiration. An option's price also depends on other factors such as the risk-free return, whether the option is American or European, and whether the underlying stock pays a dividend during the period. Option pricing models integrate many of the relationships to determine the equilibrium price of an option.

EXHIBIT 16.17 Stock Portfolio Purchase Hedged with S&P 500 Calls

Portfolio Hedged with S&P 500 Index Calls
Portfolio: Current Cost = $50M, β = 1.25
S&P 500 Call: X = 1,250, Multiplier = 100, Premium = 50
Hedge: 500 Calls; Cost = (500)(50)($100) = $2.5 million

1	2	3	4	5	6	7
S&P 500 Spot Index	Proportional Change in the Market	Proportional Change in the Portfolio	Portfolio Cost	Call Value at T	Value of Call Investment	Hedged Portfolio Cost
S_T	$g = (S_T - 1,250)/1,250$	$\beta g = 1.25g$	$V_T = (1+\beta g)$50M	$C_T = I^F =$ Max$[S_T - 1,250, 0]$	$CF = 500($100$) C_T$	Column 4 – Column 6
1,000	−0.20	−0.250	$37,500,000	0	$0	$37,500,000
1,125	−0.10	−0.125	$43,750,000	0	$0	$43,750,000
1,250	0.00	0.000	$50,000,000	0	$0	$50,000,000
1,375	0.10	0.125	$56,250,000	125	$6,250,000	$50,000,000
1,500	0.20	0.250	$62,500,000	250	$12,500,000	$50,000,000

The two most widely used models for determining the equilibrium option price are the *Black and Scholes* (B-S) *option pricing model* (OPM) and the *binomial option pricing model* (BOPM). Black and Scholes derived their model in 1973 in a seminal paper in the *Journal of Political Economy*. The BOPM was derived by Cox, Ross, and Rubinstein (1979) and Rendleman and Bartter (1979). Each determines the equilibrium price of an option in terms of arbitrage forces. Such arbitrage models are based on the law of one price. For calls or puts, this price is found by equating the price of the call or put to the value of a replicating portfolio; that is, a portfolio constructed so that its possible cash flows are equal to the call's possible payouts. The major difference in the models emanates from the assumption each makes concerning the underlying stock price's fluctuations over time, statistically referred to as its stochastic (or random) stock process. In the BOPM, the time to expiration is partitioned into a discrete or finite number of periods, each with the same length. In each period, the stock is assumed to follow a binomial process in which it either increases or decreases. The model then determines the equilibrium price of the option in which the cash flows from an arbitrage strategy consisting of positions in the stock, call, and a bond that are zero for each discrete period. The B-S OPM, on the other hand, posits a continuous process in which the time intervals are partitioned into infinitely small periods, or equivalently, the number of periods to expiration is assumed to approach infinity. In this continuous model, the price of the option is determined by assuming that the same arbitrage strategy used in the BOPM is implemented and revised continuously. Thus, the BOPM should be viewed as a first approximation of the B-S OPM. As the lengths of the intervals in the BOPM are made smaller, the discrete process merges into the continuous one and the BOPM and the B-S OPM converge.

The mathematics used in deriving the B-S OPM (stochastic calculus and a heat exchange equation) are complex; in fact, part of the contribution of the BOPM is that it is simpler to derive, yet still yields the same solution as the B-S OPM for the case of large periods. The derivations of these models are presented in many derivative texts. The B-S model, however, is relatively easy to use.

B-S OPM Formula

The B-S formula for determining the equilibrium call and put prices is:

$$C_0^* = S_0 N(d_1) - \left[\frac{X}{e^{RT}}\right] N(d_2)$$

$$P_0^* = -S_0(1 - N(d_1)) + \left[\frac{X}{e^{RT}}\right](1 - N(d_2))$$

$$d_1 = \frac{\ln(S_0/X) + (R + 0.5\sigma^2)T}{\sigma\sqrt{T}}$$

$$d_2 = d_1 - \sigma\sqrt{T}$$

where:

T = time to expiration expressed as a proportion of the year
R = continuously compounded annual risk-free rate of return
σ = annualized standard deviation of the underlying security's logarithmic return
$N(d_1)$, $N(d_2)$ = cumulative normal probabilities

In the call and put equations, X/e^{RT} is the present value of the exercise price, $PV(X)$, continuously compounded. R is the continuously compounded annual risk-free rate. This rate can be found by taking the natural logarithm of 1 plus the simple annual rate on a risk-free security with a maturity equal to the call's expiration date. Thus, if 0.06 is the annual discrete rate, then the continuous compounded rate is $\ln(1 + 0.06) = 0.0583$; σ^2 is the annualized variance of the logarithmic return, $\ln(S_1/S_0)$. The cumulative normal probabilities, $N(d_1)$ and $N(d_2)$, are the probabilities that deviations of less than d_1 or d_2 will occur in a standard normal distribution with a zero mean and a standard deviation of 1. Tables provide such probabilities are found in many statistics and finance books. The following power function can be used instead of the table to obtain better estimations of $N(d_1)$ and $N(d_2)$:

$$N(d) = 1 - n(d), \text{ for } d < 0$$
$$N(d) = n(d), \text{ for } d > 0$$

where:

$$n(d) = 1 - 0.5[1 + 0.196854(|d|) + 0.115194(|d|)^2$$
$$+ 0.000344(|d|)^3 + 0.019527(|d|)^4]^{-4}$$
$$|d| = \text{absolute value of } d.$$

Example

Consider an ABC 50 call and an ABC 50 put that both expire in three months ($T = 0.25$). Suppose ABC stock is trading at \$45 and has an estimated annualized variance of 0.25 ($\sigma = 0.5$), and the continuously compounded annual risk-free rate is 6 percent. Using the B-S OPM, the value of the call would be \$2.88 and the value of the put would be \$7.13:

$$C_0^* = S_0 N(d_1) - \left[\frac{X}{e^{RT}}\right] N(d_2)$$

$$C_0^* = (\$45)(0.4066) - \left[\frac{\$50}{e^{(0.06)(0.25)}}\right](0.3131) = \$2.88$$

$$P_0^* = -S_0(1 - N(d_1)) + \left[\frac{X}{e^{RT}}\right](1 - N(d_2))$$

$$P_0^* = -\$45(0.5934) + \left[\frac{\$50}{e^{(0.06)(0.25)}}\right](0.6869) = \$7.13$$

where:

$$d_1 = \frac{\ln(\$45/\$50) + [0.06 + 0.05(0.5)^2](0.25)}{0.5\sqrt{0.25}} = -0.2364$$

$$d_2 = -0.2364 - 0.5\sqrt{0.25} = -0.4864$$

$$N(d_1) = N(-0.2364) = 1 - [1 - 0.5[1 + 0.196854(0.2364) + 0.115194(0.2364)^2 \\ + 0.000344(0.2364)^3 + 0.019527(0.2364)^4]^{-4}] = 0.4066$$

$$N(d_2) = N(-0.4864) = 1 - [1 - 0.5[1 + 0.196854(0.4864) + 0.115194(0.4864)^2 \\ + 0.000344(0.4864)^3 + 0.019527(0.4864)^4]^{-4}] = 0.3131$$

Comparative Analysis

The B-S call and put prices depend on the underlying stock price, exercise price, time to expiration, risk-free rate and the stock's volatility: S, X, T, R, and σ. The impacts that changes in these parameter values have on the B-S OPM price also can be seen in terms of the simulation presented in Exhibit 16.18, in which combinations of the B-S OPM call values and stock prices are shown for different parameter values. The first column in the upper table shows the call values given the parameter values used in the preceding example: $X = 50$, $T = 0.25$, $R = 0.06$, and $\sigma = 0.5$. For purposes of comparison, the other columns show the call and stock price relations generated with the same parameter values used in column 1, except for one variable: In column 2, $X = 40$; in column 3, $T = 0.5$; in column 4, $\sigma = 0.75$; and in column 5, $R = 0.08$.

In examining the exhibit, note several of the intuitive relationships that were explained earlier. First, as shown in any of the columns, when the stock is relatively low and the call is deep out of the money, the B-S OPM yields a very low call price, but as we would expect, one that is nonnegative. As the price of the stock increases by equal increments, the OPM call prices increase at an increasing rate up to a point, with the values never being below the intrinsic value. Thus, over a range of stock prices, the B-S OPM yields a call and stock price relation that is nonlinear and satisfies a lower boundary condition. The nonlinear relationship also can be seen in Exhibit 16.19, where the B-S option call values and stock prices from column 1 are plotted. As shown, the slope of this B-S option price curve increases as the stock price increases, the curve does not yield negative values, and it is above the *IV* line.

The slope of the curve is referred to as the option's *delta*. Delta is equal to $N(d_1)$ in the B-S model. For a call, the delta ranges from 0 for deep-out-of-the-money calls to approximately 1 for deep-in-the-money ones. The nonlinear call and stock price relation also can be seen by the change in the slope of the B-S option price curve as the stock price increases. In option literature, the change in slope (i.e., delta) per small change in the stock price defines the option's *gamma* (it is the second-order partial derivative of the call price with respect to changes in the stock price).

EXHIBIT 16.18 B-S OPM Call Price and Stock Price Relation Given Different Parameter Values

	1 $X = 50$ $T = 0.25$ $\sigma = 0.5$ $R = 0.06$	2 $X = 40$ $T = 0.25$ $\sigma = 0.5$ $R = 0.06$	3 $X = 50$ $T = 0.5$ $\sigma = 0.5$ $R = 0.06$	4 $X = 50$ $T = 0.25$ $\sigma = 0.75$ $R = 0.06$	5 $X = 50$ $T = 0.25$ $\sigma = 0.5$ $R = 0.08$
Stock Price	C_0^*	C_0^*	C_0^*	C_0^*	C_0^*
$ 30	$ 0.0841	$ 0.5967	$ 0.5453	$ 0.6292	$ 0.0890
35	0.4163	1.9065	1.3751	1.5028	0.4328
40	1.2408	4.2399	2.8365	2.9852	1.2826
45	2.8756	7.5682	4.9626	5.1006	2.9550
50	5.2999	11.5935	7.6637	7.7452	5.4210
55	8.5584	16.0952	10.9683	10.9782	8.7103
60	12.3857	20.8355	14.6539	14.5760	12.5702
65	16.6919	25.7002	18.7114	18.5269	16.8996
70	21.2865	30.6342	23.0555	22.7703	21.5083

Second, a comparison of columns 1 and 2 shows that for each stock price, higher call prices are associated with the call with the lower exercise price. Thus, as the exercise price decreases, the B-S OPM call price increases. Third, comparing column 3 with column 1 shows that as the B-S OPM call price increases, the greater the time to expiration. The change in an option's prices with respect to a small change in the time to expiration (with other factors held constant) is defined as the option's *theta*. Fourth, a comparison of columns 4 and 1 shows that the greater the stock's variability, the greater the call price. The change in the call price given a small change in the stock's variability is referred to as the option's *vega* (also called *kappa*). Last, comparing columns 1 and 5 shows the call price increases the greater the interest rate. The change in the call price given a small change in R is called the call's *rho*.

Exhibit 16.19 shows the combinations of the B-S put prices and stock prices for different parameters: X (column 2), T (column 3), σ (column 4), and R (column 5). In

EXHIBIT 16.19 B-S OPM Put Price and Stock Price Relation Given Different Parameter Values

	1	2	3	4	5
	$X = 50$	$X = 40$	$X = 50$	$X = 50$	$X = 50$
	$T = 0.25$	$T = 0.25$	$T = 0.5$	$T = 0.25$	$T = 0.25$
	$\sigma = 0.5$	$\sigma = 0.5$	$\sigma = 0.5$	$\sigma = 0.75$	$\sigma = 0.5$
	$R = 0.06$	$R = 0.06$	$R = 0.06$	$R = 0.06$	$R = 0.08$
Stock Price	P_0^*	P_0^*	P_0^*	P_0^*	P_0^*
$30	$19.3397	$10.0012	$19.0675	$19.8848	$19.0990
35	14.6719	6.3110	14.8973	15.7584	14.4428
40	10.4964	3.6444	11.3588	12.2408	10.2926
45	7.1312	1.9727	8.4848	9.3562	6.9650
50	4.5555	0.9979	6.1860	7.0008	4.4309
55	2.8140	0.4996	4.4905	5.2338	2.7203
60	1.6413	0.2400	3.1761	3.8324	1.5801
65	0.9475	0.1046	2.2337	2.7825	0.9095
70	0.5421	0.0387	1.5778	2.0259	0.5182

examining any of the columns in the table, observe the negative, nonlinear relationship between the B-S put price and the stock price (i.e., the put has a negative delta and nonzero gamma). Next, comparing columns 2 and 5 with column 1, observe that for each stock price, the greater the exercise price or the lower the interest rate, the greater the B-S put price. Finally, comparing columns 3 and 4 with column 1, observe that the greater the time to expiration or the greater the stock's variability, the greater the put price. Thus, the B-S put model captures the intuitive relationships described earlier. It should be noted that the B-S put model is unconstrained. That is, the B-S put model does not constrain the put value to being equal to at least its intrinsic value. Thus, for an in-the-money put, the premium can be less than its *IV*, as shown in column 1 when the stock is at $30. The possibility that $P^* < IV$ reflects the fact that the B-S model is limited to determining the price of a European put, in which negative time value premiums are possible.

Dividend Adjustments for the Black-Scholes Model

Dividends can cause the price of a call (put) to decrease (increase) on the stock's ex-dividend date and can lead to an early exercise if the option is American. The B-S OPM values European options without dividends. It therefore needs to be adjusted for dividends and for the possibility of early exercise possibility when dividends are expected. Two dividend adjustment models that use the B-S OPM are Fisher Black's pseudo-American call model, applicable to American calls when there are dividends, and Merton's continuous dividend yield approach. Both models are presented in many derivative texts.

Estimating the Black-Scholes Model

The B-S OPM is defined totally in terms of the stock price, exercise price, time to expiration, interest rate, and volatility. The first three variables are observable. The interest rate needs to be identified, and the stock's volatility needs to be estimated. In estimating the risk-free rate for the B-S OPM, the rate on a Treasury bill, commercial paper, or other money market security with a maturity equal to the option's expiration are typically used.

Two methods are often used to estimate the variance of the logarithmic return: calculating the stock's historical variance and solving for the stock's implied variance. A stock's historical variability is computed using a sample of historical stock prices (converted to logarithmic returns ($\ln(S_n/S_0)$)). The implied variance is that variance that equates the OPM's value to the market price. It is found iteratively, substituting different variance values into the B-S model until that variance is found that yields an OPM value equal to the market price. Theoretically, we should expect the implied variance for different options on the same stock to be the same. In practice, this does not occur. One way to select an implied variance is to use the arithmetic average for the different implied variances on the stock. A common approach among option traders is to select the volatility based on the option's *volatility smile* and its *volatility term structure*. A volatility smile is a plot of the implied volatilities given different exercise prices. The volatility term structure, in turn, refers to the relation between an option's implied volatility and the time to expiration. Option traders use *volatility surfaces* (graph of volatility against T and X) to help them determine the appropriate volatilities to use when pricing an option with either the B-S OPM or the binomial model.

BLOOMBERG OPTION PRICING SCREEN—OV/OVME

The Bloomberg OV screen calculates the price of an option using the Black-Scholes OPM or the Binomial (Trinomial). The user can input the variability or use the historical volatility or the implied volatility. The OV/OVME screen can be used to value existing options or an option created from an existing security. The screen shows the option's vega, theta, and rho values. The "Scenario" tab shows the price of the options given different stock price and times to expiration. The "Volatility" tab shows tables and graphs of volatility smiles, term structure, and surface. The models do incorporate dividend adjustments. Settings for dividend can be found from the "Data and Settings" tab.

See Bloomberg Web Exhibit 16.3.

Conclusion

In this chapter, we have provided an overview of options by defining option terms, examining option strategies, including portfolio insurance, looking at the functions of organized exchanges, and describing the features of the B-S OPM. Options are one of the important derivatives for speculating and hedging security and portfolio positions. In the next chapter, we examine the other important derivative—futures.

Web Site Information

- Information on the CBOE: www.cboe.com.
- Information on the Chicago Mercantile Exchange: http://www.cmegroup.com.
- U.S. Commodity Futures Trading Commission: http://www.cftc.gov.

Notes

1. As we will see later, most options are not exercised, but instead are closed by holders selling their contract and writers buying their contracts. As a starting point in developing a fundamental understanding of options, however, it is helpful to first examine what happens if the option is exercised.
2. In many of our examples, we assume calls and puts with the same terms are priced the same. We do this for simplicity. In most cases, however, calls and puts with the same terms are not priced equally.
3. The boundary condition for a European call is $\text{Max}[S_t - (X/(1 + R_f)^T, 0]$. The proof is found in many derivative texts. See Johnson, *Introduction to Derivatives* (2009).

Selected References

Arbel, Avner, and Paul Strebel. 1983. Pay attention to neglected firms! *Journal of Portfolio Management* 9 (Winter): 37–42.

Black, F. 1975. Fact and fantasy in the use of options. *Financial Analysis Journal* 31 (July–August): 61–72.

Black, F., and M. Scholes. 1973. The pricing of options and corporate liabilities. *Journal of Political Economy* 81 (May–June): 637–659.

Cox, J., and S. Ross. 1976. The valuation of options for alternative stochastic processes. *Journal of Financial Economics* 3 (January–March): 145–166.

Cox, J., S. Ross, and M. Rubinstein. 1979. Option pricing: A simplified approach. *Journal of Financial Economics* (September): 229–263.

Cox, J., and M. Rubinstein. 1983. A survey of alternative option pricing models. In *Option Pricing.* Edited by Menachem Brenner. Lexington, MA: Health.

Hull, J. C. *Options, Futures, and Other Derivatives.* 2006. Upper Saddle River, N.J.: Prentice Hall: Chapter 16.

Itô, K. 1951. On stochastic differential equations. *American Mathematical Society* 4 (December): 1–51.

Johnson, R. S. 2009. *Introduction to Derivatives: Options, Futures, and Swaps.* New York: Oxford University Press.

Johnson, R. S., J. E. Pawlukiewicz, and J. Mehta. 1997. Binomial option pricing with skewed asset returns. *Review of Quantitative Finance and Accounting* 9: 89–101.

Lantane, H., and Rendleman, R., Jr. 1976. Standard deviations of stock price ratios implied in option prices. *Journal of Finance* 31 (May): 369–382.

Merton, R. 1976. Option pricing when underlying stock returns are discontinuous. *Journal of Financial Economics* 3 (January–February): 125–144.

O'Brien, T. 1985. The mechanics of portfolio insurance. *The Journal of Portfolio Management* 14 (Spring): 40–47.

Pozen, R. 1978. The purchase of protective puts by financial institutions. *Financial Analysts Journal* 34 (July/August): 47–60.

Rendleman, R. J., and B. J. Bartter. 1979. Two-state option pricing. *Journal of Finance,* 34: 1093–1110.

Rendleman, R., Jr., and R. McEnally. 1987 Assessing the cost of portfolio insurance. *Financial Analysts Journal* 43 (May–June): 27–37.

Stapleton, R. C. and M. G. Subramanyam. 1984. The valuation of options when asset returns are generated by a binomial process. *Journal of Finance* 39: 1525–1539.

Stein, E. M. and J. C. Stein. 1991. Stock price distributions with stochastic volatility: an analytical approach, *Review of Financial Studies* 4: 727–752.

Whaley, R. 1981. On the valuation of American call options on stocks with known dividends. *Journal of Financial Economics* 9 (June): 207–212.

Whaley, R. 1982. Valuation of American call options on dividend paying stocks: empirical tests. *Journal of Financial Economics* 10 (March 1982): 29–58.

Bloomberg Exercises

1. Find descriptions, recent prices, and other information on different types of stock options: Ticker <Equity> <Enter>, click OMON. Screens to consider are DES, OTD, OMON, and OMST. To bring up an option's screen: option ticker <Equity> <Enter>.

2. Select a stock and bring up its equity screen: ticker <Equity> <Enter>). Using the Bloomberg OSA screen, select call and put options on the stock ("Positions" tab; "Add Listed Options") and evaluate the following option strategies on the stock with a profit graph:
   a. Call purchase.
   b. Call sale.
   c. Put purchase.
   d. Put sale.

    e. Covered call write.

    f. Covered put write.

    g. Straddle purchase.

    h. Straddle sale.

    i. Simulated long position.

    j. Simulated short position.

3. Identify several option strategies that you would consider if you expected stock prices to increase in the next three months. Select an option and analyze your strategies using Bloomberg's OSA screen.

4. Identify several option strategies that you would consider if you expected stock prices to decrease in the next three months. Select an option and analyze your strategies using Bloomberg's OSA screen.

5. Identify several option strategies that you would consider if you expected stock prices to be stable over the next three months. Select an option and analyze your strategies using Bloomberg's OSA screen.

6. Select exchange call and put options on an index, and evaluate the following option strategies for different holding periods with a profit table and/or graph using the Bloomberg OSA function: call purchase, put purchase, straddle purchase, straddle sale, synthetic long position, or synthetic short position.

7. Determine B-S prices of call and put options on a selected stock using the Bloomberg OV/OVME screen. Examine the model's call and put values and stock price curve generated from Bloomberg. Use either Bloomberg defaulted values for the stock's volatility, risk-free rate, and dividends, or input your own.

8. Portfolio insurance: Use Bloomberg to construct an equity portfolio or select one you have already constructed. Determine the index put positions you would need to create a portfolio insurance strategy (consider the horizon period when you select the maturity of the option). Use OSA to generate a value graph of your hedged portfolio. Include screens in you answer and bullet points on key observations. For a guide, see Bloomberg exhibit box: "OSA: Portfolio Insurance."

CHAPTER 17

Futures Markets

Introduction

A *forward contract* is an agreement between two parties to trade a specific asset at a future date with the terms and price agreed upon today. A *futures contract,* in turn, is a "marketable" forward contract, with marketability provided through futures exchanges that list hundreds of standardized contracts, establish trading rules, and provide for clearinghouses to guarantee and intermediate contracts. In contrast, forward contracts are provided by financial institutions and dealers, are less standardized and more tailor-made, are usually held to maturity, and unlike futures, they often do not require initial or maintenance margins. Both forward and futures contracts are similar to option contracts in that the underlying asset's price on the contract is determined in the present with the delivery and payment occurring at a future date. The major difference between these derivative securities is that the holder of an option has the right, but not the responsibility, to execute the contract (i.e., it is a contingent-claim security), whereas the holder of a futures or forward contract has an obligation to fulfill the terms of the contract. In this chapter, we examine the markets and fundamental uses of futures and forward contracts.

The Nature of Futures Trading and the Role of the Clearinghouse

Futures Positions

An investor or hedger can take one of two positions on a futures (or forward) contract: a long position (or futures purchase) or a short position (futures sale). In a long futures position, one agrees to buy the contract's underlying asset at a specified price, with the payment and delivery to occur on the expiration date (also referred to as the delivery date); in a short position, one agrees to sell an asset at a specific price, with delivery and payment occurring at expiration.

To illustrate how positions are taken, suppose in June, Speculator A believes that the upcoming summer will be unusually dry in the Midwest, causing an increase in the price of wheat. With hopes of profiting from this expectation, suppose Speculator A decides to take a long position in a wheat futures contract and instructs her broker to buy one September wheat futures contract listed on the CBT (one contract is for 5,000 bushels). To fulfill this order, suppose A's broker finds a broker representing Speculator B, who believes that the summer wheat harvest will be above normal and therefore hopes to profit by taking a short position in the September wheat contract. After negotiating with each other, suppose the brokers agree to a price of $3.00/bu on the September contract for their clients. In terms of futures positions, Speculator A would have a long position in which she agrees to buy 5,000 bushels of wheat at $3.00/bu from Speculator B at the delivery date in September, and Speculator B would have a short position in which he agrees to sell 5,000 bushels of wheat at $3.00/bu to A at the delivery date in September:

If both parties hold their contracts to delivery, their profits or losses would be determined by the price of wheat on the spot market (also called cash, physical, or actual market). For example, suppose the summer turns out to be dry, causing the spot price of wheat to trade at $3.50/bu at the grain elevators in the Midwest at or near the delivery date on the September wheat futures contract. Accordingly, Speculator A would be able to buy 5,000 bushels of wheat on her September futures contract at $3.00/bu from Speculator B, then sell the wheat for $3.50/bu on the spot market to earn a profit of $2,500 before commission and transportation costs are included. On the other hand, to deliver 5,000 bushels of wheat on the September contract, Speculator B would have to buy the wheat on the spot market for $3.50/bu, then sell it on the futures contract to Speculator A for $3.00/bu, resulting in a $2,500 loss (again, not including commission and transportation costs).

Clearinghouse

To provide contracts with marketability, futures exchanges use clearinghouses. Like the Option Clearing Corporation, the clearinghouses associated with futures exchanges guarantee each contract and act as intermediaries by breaking up each con-tract after the trade has taken place. Thus, in the above example, the clearinghouse (CH) would come in after Speculators A and B have reached an agreement on the price of September wheat, becoming the effective seller on A's long position and the effective buyer on B's short position:

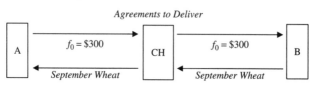

Once the clearinghouse has broken up the contracts, then A's and B's contracts would be with the clearinghouse. The clearinghouse, in turn, would record the following entries in its computers:

Clearinghouse Record:

---

1. Speculator A agrees to buy September wheat at $3.00/bu from the clearinghouse.
2. Speculator B agrees to sell September wheat at $3.00/bu to the clearinghouse.

As we earlier discussed with the Option Clearing Corporation, the intermediary role of the clearinghouse makes it easier for futures traders to close their positions before expiration. Returning to our example, suppose that the month of June is unexpectedly dry in the Midwest, leading a third speculator, Speculator C, to want to take a long position in the listed September wheat futures contract. Seeing a profit potential from the increased demand for long positions in the September contract, suppose Speculator A agrees to sell a September wheat futures contract to Speculator C for $3.25/bu. Upon doing this, Speculator A now would be short in the new September contract, with Speculator C having a long position, and there now would be two contracts on September wheat. Without the clearinghouse intermediating, the two contracts can be described as follows:

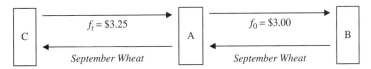

After the new contract between A and C has been established, the clearinghouse would step in and break it up. For Speculator A, the clearinghouse's record would now show the following:

Clearinghouse Record:

---

1. Speculator A agrees to buy September wheat at $3.00/bu from the clearinghouse.
2. Speculator A agrees to sell September wheat at $3.25/bu to the clearinghouse.

Thus:

The clearinghouse accordingly would close Speculator A's positions by paying her $0.25/bu ($3.25/bu − $3.00/bu), a total of $1,250 on the contract [(5,000 bu) ($0.25/bu)]. Since Speculator A's short position effectively closes her long position, it is variously referred to as a *closing, reversing out,* or *offsetting position* or simply as an *offset*. Thus, the clearinghouse, like the Option Clearing Corporation, makes it easier for futures contracts to be closed prior to expiration.

Commission costs and the costs of transporting commodities cause most futures traders to close their positions instead of taking delivery. As the delivery date approaches, the number of outstanding contracts (*open interest*) declines, with only a relatively few contracts still outstanding at delivery. Moreover, at expiration, the contract prices on futures contracts established on that date (f_T) should be equal (or approximately equal) to the prevailing spot price on the underlying asset (S_T). That is:

$$\text{At expiration: } f_T = S_T$$

If f_T does not equal S_T at expiration, an arbitrage opportunity would exist. Arbitrageurs could take a position in the futures contract and an opposite position in the spot market. For example, if the September wheat futures contract were available at $3.40 on the delivery date in September and the spot price for wheat were $3.50, then arbitrageurs could go long in the September contract, take delivery by buying the wheat at $3.40 on the futures contract, then sell the wheat on the spot at $3.50 to earn a riskless profit of $0.10/bu. Arbitrageurs' efforts to take long positions, however, would drive the contract price up to $3.50. On the other hand, if f_T exceeds $3.50, then arbitrageurs would reverse their strategy, pushing f_T to $3.50/bu. Thus, at delivery, arbitrageurs will ensure that the prices on expiring contracts are equal to the spot price. As a result, closing a futures contract with an offsetting position at expiration will yield the same profits or losses as closing futures positions on the spot by purchasing (selling) the asset on the spot and selling (buying) it on the futures contract.

Returning to our example, suppose near the delivery date on the September contract the spot price of wheat and the price on the expiring September futures contracts are $3.50/bu. To close his existing short contract, Speculator B would need to take a long position in the September contract, while to offset her existing contract, Speculator C would need to take a short position. Suppose Speculators A and B take their offsetting positions with each other on the expiring September wheat contract priced at $f_T = S_T = \$3.50/\text{bu}$. After the clearinghouse breaks up the new contract, Speculator B would owe the clearinghouse $0.50/bu and Speculator C would receive $0.25/bu from the clearinghouse:

Clearinghouse Records for Speculator B:

---

1. Speculator B agrees to *sell* September wheat to CH for $3.00/bu.
2. Speculator B agrees to *buy* September wheat from CH at $3.50/bu.

Thus:

And:

Clearinghouse Records for Speculator C:
1. Speculator C agrees to *buy* September wheat at $3.25/bu.
2. Speculator B agrees to *sell* September wheat for $3.50/bu.

Thus:

To recapitulate, in this example, the contract prices on September wheat contracts went from $3.00/bu on the A and B contract, to $3.25/bu on the A and C contract, to $3.50/bu on the B and C contract at expiration. Speculators A and C each received $0.25/bu from the clearinghouse, while Speculator B paid $0.50/bu to the clearinghouse, the clearinghouse with a perfect hedge on each contract received nothing (other than clearinghouse fees attached to the commission charges), and no wheat was purchased or delivered.

The Market and Characteristics of Futures Contracts

Microstructure

For many years, the mode of trading on futures exchanges in the United States, London (LIFFE), Paris (MATIF), Sydney (SFE), Singapore (SIMEX), and other locations was that of brokers and dealers going to a pit and using the *open outcry* method to trade. In this system, orders were relayed to the floor by runners or by hand signals to a specified trading pit. The order was then offered in open outcry to all participants (e.g., commission brokers or locals [those trading for their own accounts]) in the pit, with the trade being done with the first person to respond.

Although the open-outcry system is still used, electronic trading systems are today the primary mode used by the organized exchanges to trade derivatives. The CME and CBT developed with Reuters (the electronic information service company) the *GLOBEX* trading system. This is a computerized order-matching system with an international network linking member traders. Since 1985, all new derivative exchanges have been organized as electronic exchanges. Most of these electronic trading systems are order-driven systems in which customer orders (bid and ask prices and size) are collected and matched by a computerized matching system. In addition to linking futures traders, the futures exchanges also make contracts more marketable by standardizing contracts, providing continuous trading, establishing delivery procedures, and providing 24-hour trading through exchange alliances.

Standardization

The futures exchanges provide standardization by specifying the grade or type of each asset and the size of the underlying asset. Exchanges also specify how contract prices are quoted. For example, the contract size on most wheat contracts is 5,000 bushels.

Continuous Trading

On many futures exchanges, continuous trading is not provided by market makers or specialists, but instead through locals who are willing to take temporary positions in one or more futures. These exchange members fall into one of three categories: *scalpers,* who offer to buy and sell simultaneously, holding their positions for only a few minutes and profiting from a bid-ask spread; *day traders,* who hold positions for less than a day; *position traders,* who hold positions for as long as a week before they close. Collectively, these exchange members make it possible for the futures markets to provide continuous trading.

Price and Position Limits

Without market makers and specialists to provide an orderly market, futures exchanges can impose price limits as a tool to stop possible destabilizing price trends from occurring. When done, the exchanges specify the maximum price change that can occur from the previous day's settlement price. The price of a contract must be within its daily price limits, unless the exchange intervenes and changes the limit. When the contract price hits its maximum or minimum limit, it is referred to as being limited up or limited down. In addition to price limits, futures exchanges also can set position limits on many of their futures contracts. This is done as a safety measure both to ensure sufficient liquidity and to minimize the chances of a trader trying to corner a particular asset.

Delivery Procedures

Only a small number of contracts lead to actual delivery. Nevertheless, detailed delivery procedures are important to ensure that the contract prices on futures are determined by the spot price on the underlying asset and that the futures price converges to the spot price at expiration. The exchanges have various rules and procedures governing the deliveries of contracts and delivery dates. The date or period in which delivery can take place is determined by the exchange. When there is a delivery period, the party agreeing to sell has the right to determine when the asset will be delivered during that period.

Alliances and 24-Hour Trading

In addition to providing off-hour trading via electronic trading systems, 24-hour trading is also possible by using futures exchanges that offer trading on the same contract. A number of exchanges offer identical contracts. This makes it possible to trade the contract in the United States, Europe, and the Far East. Moreover, these exchanges have alliance agreements making it possible for traders to open a position in one market and close it in another.

Margin Requirements

Since a futures contract is an agreement, it has no initial value. Futures traders, however, are required to post some security or good faith money with their brokers. Depending on the brokerage firm, the customer's margin requirement can be satisfied either in the form of cash or cash equivalents.

Futures contracts have both initial and maintenance margin requirements. The *initial* (or *performance*) *margin* is the amount of cash or cash equivalents that must be deposited by the investor on the day the futures position is established. The futures trader does this by setting up a margin (or commodity) account with the broker and depositing the required cash or cash equivalents. The amount of the margin is determined by the margin requirement, defined as a proportion (m) of the contract value (usually 3 percent to 5 percent). For example, if the initial margin requirement is 5 percent, then Speculators A and B in our first example would be required to deposit $750 in cash or cash equivalents in their commodity accounts as good faith money on their $3.00 September wheat futures contracts:

$$m[\text{Contract Value}] = 0.05[(\$3.00/\text{bu})(5{,}000 \text{ bu})] = \$750$$

At the end of each trading day, the futures trader's account is adjusted to reflect any gains or losses based on the settlement price on new contracts. In our example, suppose the day after Speculators A and B established their respective long and short positions, the settlement price on the September wheat contract is $f_t = \$3.10/\text{bu}$. The value of A's and B's margin accounts would therefore be:

A: Account Value = $750 + (\$3.10/\text{bu} - \$3.00/\text{bu})(5{,}000 \text{ bu}) = \$1{,}250$
B: Account Value = $750 + (\$3.00/\text{bu} - \$3.10/\text{bu})(5{,}000 \text{ bu}) = \$250$

With the higher futures price, A's long position has increased in value by $500 and B's short position has decreased by $500. When there is a decrease in the account value, the futures trader's broker has to exchange money through the clearing firm equal to the loss on the position to the broker and clearinghouse with the gain. This process is known as *marking to market*. Thus in our case, B's broker and clearing firm would pass on $500 to A's broker and clearing firm.

To ensure that the balance in the trader's account does not become negative, the brokerage firm requires a *maintenance margin* (or *variation margin*) be maintained by the futures traders.[1] The maintenance margin is the amount of additional cash or cash equivalents that futures traders must deposit to keep the equity in their commodity account equal to a certain percentage (e.g., 75 percent) of the initial margin value. If the maintenance margin requirement were set at 100 percent of the initial margin, then the equity value of A's and B's accounts would each have to be at least $750. If Speculator B did not deposit the $500 required margin, then he would receive a *margin call* from the broker instructing him to post the required amount of funds. If Speculator B did not comply with the margin call, the broker would close the position.

Maintaining margin accounts can be viewed as part of the cost of trading futures. In addition to margin requirements, transaction costs are also involved in establishing futures positions. Such costs include broker commissions, clearinghouse fees, and the bid-ask spread. On futures contracts, commission fees usually are charged on a per contract basis and for a round lot, and the fees are negotiable. The clearinghouse fee is relatively small and is collected along with the commission fee by the broker. The bid-ask spreads are set by locals and represent an indirect cost of trading futures.

It should be noted that the margin requirements and clearinghouse mechanism that characterize futures exchanges also serve to differentiate them from customized forward contract positions written by banks and investment companies. Forward contracts are more tailor-made contracts, usually do not require margins, and the underlying asset is typically delivered at maturity instead of closed; they are, however, less marketable than exchange-traded futures.

BLOOMBERG COMMODITY SCREENS, CTM

Exchange-listed commodities can be found by accessing the CTM screen: CTM <Enter>. Contracts are listed by category, exchange, and region. For example, to find a stock index on the Chicago Mercantile Exchange (CME), use the CTM "Exchange" screen and click "Equity Index" from the dropdown menu in the "Category" column; to find wheat contract on the Chicago Board of Trade (CBT), use the Chicago Board of Trade "Exchange" screen and click "Wheat" from the dropdown menu in the "Category" column.

The menu screen for the contract is accessed by entering the commodity's ticker, pressing the "Comdty" key, and hitting <Enter>: Ticker <Comdty> <Enter> (e.g., for CBT wheat futures: KWA <Comdty> <Enter>. The menu includes: CT: Contract Table, GIP: Intraday Graph, EXS: Expiration Schedule, and GP: Price Graph.

See Bloomberg Web Exhibit 17.1.

Equity Index Futures

Equity Index Futures Contracts

Futures contracts on the exchanges and OTC contracts can be classified as a physical commodity, energy, stock index, foreign currency, or interest-earning asset. Of these, there are a number of futures index contracts available. Many of these contracts are on stock indexes, but there are also some on commodities (e.g., DJ-AIG Commodity Index and the GSCI index), bond indexes (e.g., Municipal Bond Index), and currencies (e.g., the U.S. dollar index). Exhibit 17.1 shows Bloomberg description and price screens on the CME's S&P 500 futures contract. The S&P 500 futures, as well as other index futures contracts, have many of the same characteristics as index options. For instance, like index options, the size of index futures contracts are equal to a multiple of the index value, and like index options, index futures are cash-settled contracts.[2]

Futures markets provide corporations, financial institutions, and others with a tool for speculating on expected spot price changes, for hedging their particular spot positions against adverse price movements, and for creating synthetic positions.

Speculative Strategies

As a speculative tool, stock index derivatives represent a highly liquid alternative to speculating on the overall stock market or on different types of stock indexes (e.g., Russell 2000, Russell 1000, Nasdaq 100 or S&P Midcap 400 index). Combined, index options and index futures give speculators a tool for generating a number of different investment strategies. As we examined in Chapter 16, option strategies such as outright call and put positions, straddles, strips, spreads, and combinations can be formed with spot index options, making it possible for investors to speculate on expected bullish, bearish, or even stable market expectations with different return-risk exposures. In the case of stock index futures, bullish (bearish) speculators can take a long (short) position in an index futures contract.

In addition to outright positions, a speculator who wants to profit from directional changes in the market, but who does not want to assume the degree of risk associated with an outright position, can instead form a spread with stock index futures. A *futures spread* is formed by taking long and short positions on different futures contracts simultaneously. Two general types of spreads exist: intracommodity and intercommodity. An *intracommodity spread* is formed with futures contracts on the same asset but with different expiration dates; an *intercommodity spread* is formed with two futures contracts with the same expiration but on different assets.

An intracommodity spread is often used to reduce the risk associated with a pure outright position. The prices on more distant futures contracts (T_2) are more price sensitive to changes in the spot price, S, than near-term futures (T_1):

$$\frac{\%\Delta f_{T_2}}{\%\Delta S} > \frac{\%\Delta f_{T_1}}{\%\Delta S}$$

A risk-averse spreader who is bullish on the stock market could form an intracommodity spread by taking a short position in a nearer-term index futures contract and a long position in a longer-term one. If the market subsequently rises, the percentage gain in the long position on the distant contract will exceed the percentage loss on the short position on the nearby contract. In this case, the spreader will profit, but not as much as she would with an outright long position. On the other hand, if the market declines, the percentage losses on the long position will exceed the percentage gains

EXHIBIT 17.1 S&P 500 Futures Contract: Bloomberg Description and Price Screens, SPA <Comdty>

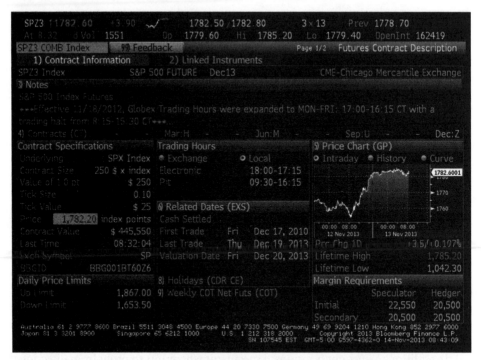

(a)

(b)

from the short position. In this situation, the spreader will lose, but not as much as she would have if she had an outright long position. Note that in forming a spread, the speculator does not have to keep the ratio of long-to-short positions one-to-one, but instead could use any ratio (2-to-1, 3-to-2, etc.) to obtain his desired return-risk combination.

Instead of an intracommodity spread, a spreader alternatively could form an intercommodity spread by taking opposite positions in different index futures. For example, suppose the relation between the Russell 2000 index and the Russell 1000 index is such that when the Russell 2000 changes by 10 percent, the Russell 1000 changes by 9 percent. A risk-averse investor who is bearish on the market could set up an intercommodity spread by going short in the Russell 2000 contract and long in the Russell 1000 contract. Thus, similar to option spreads, index futures spreads allow investors to attain lower return-risk combinations than pure speculative positions. Moreover, by changing the ratios from one long to one short or by forming intercommodity spreads with different correlations, spreaders can attain a number of different return-risk combinations.

Hedging Equity Positions

Futures markets and OTC forward contracts provide investors, businesses, and other economic entities a means for hedging their particular spot positions against adverse price movements. Two hedging positions exist: long hedge and short hedge. In a *long futures hedge* (or hedge purchase), a hedger takes a long position in a futures contract to protect against an increase in the price of the underlying asset or commodity. Long hedge positions are used, for example, by manufacturers to lock in their future costs of purchasing raw materials, by portfolio managers to fix the price they will pay for securities in the future, or by multinational corporations that want to lock in the dollar costs of buying foreign currency at some future date. In a *short hedge*, one takes a short futures position to protect against a decrease in the price of the underlying asset. In contrast to long hedging, short hedge positions are used, for example, by farmers who want to lock in the price they will sell their crops for at harvest, by portfolio managers and investment bankers who are planning to sell securities in the future and want to minimize price risk, or by multinational corporations who have to convert future foreign currency cash flows into dollars and want to immunize the future exchange against adverse changes in exchange rates.

Short Hedge Example

To illustrate how a short hedge works, consider the case of a portfolio manager, who in January knows that he will have to liquidate his stock portfolio in June and decides to hedge the value of the stock portfolio by taking a short position in the June S&P 500 futures contract. Assume in this case that the portfolio is well-diversified (no unsystematic risk), has a beta of 1.25, and in January it is worth $50,000,000 when the S&P 500 spot index (S_0) is at 1,250. Finally, suppose a June S&P 500 futures contract is

EXHIBIT 17.2 Value of the Hedged Stock Portfolio

(1) S&P 500 Spot Index at Expiration: $S_T = f_T$	(2) Proportional Change in the S&P 500: $(S_T - 1{,}250)/$ $1{,}250$	(3) Proportional Change in Portfolio Value: $\beta g = 1.25(S_T - 1{,}250)/1{,}250$	(4) Portfolio Value: $(1 + \beta g)$ $\$50M$	(5) Short Futures Cash Flow per Contract: $f_0 - S_T$ $= 1{,}250 - S_T$	(6) Futures Cash Flow: $200(\$250)$ $(1{,}250 - f_T)$	(7) Hedged Portfolio Value: $(4) + (6)$
1,000	−0.20	−0.25	$37,500,000	250	$12,500,000	$50,000,000
1,125	−0.10	−0.125	43,750,000	125	6,250,000	50,000,000
1,250	0	0	50,000,000	0	0	50,000,000
1,375	0.10	0.125	56,250,000	−125	−6,250,000	50,000,000
1,500	0.20	0.25	62,500,000	−250	−12,500,000	50,000,000

priced at 1,250 with a $250 multiple. To hedge the portfolio, the manager would need to go short in 200 S&P 500 contracts:

$$N_f = \beta \frac{V_0}{f_0} = 1.25 \frac{-\$50{,}000{,}000}{(1{,}250)(\$250)} = 200 \text{ contracts}$$

In June, the manager would liquidate his portfolio and receive or pay a cash settlement equal to the difference in the futures price (f_0) and the closing spot price on the S&P 500 (S_T) on the delivery day: $f_0 - S_T$. (The manager more likely would close the futures contract by going long in the expiring June contract trading near the spot price: $f_T = S_T$). With the short position, any loss in the market would be offset by a gain on the futures position. However, any gain in the market would be negated by a loss on the futures position. This can be seen in Exhibit 17.2. In the exhibit, the first column shows five possible S&P 500 spot index values from 1,000 to 1,500; the second column shows the proportional change in S&P 500 from the 1,250 value of the index when the hedge was set up; column 3 shows the proportion changes in the portfolio given its beta of 1.25; column 4 shows the portfolio values that correspond with the index values; column 5 shows the cash flow at expiration from one future position; column 6 shows the cash realized from the 200 short index futures contract at the June expiration; and column 7 shows the value of the futures-hedged portfolio of $50,000,000.

Note that instead of locking in a future portfolio value, the portfolio manager could have alternatively bought put options to set up a portfolio insurance position that would have provided downside protection in case the market declined, but portfolio gains if the market increased. For this, however, the manager would have had to pay an insurance premium equal to the cost of the puts (see Exhibit 16.6).

In this example, we have a perfect hedge. Part of this is because we assumed the portfolio is well-diversified and the futures price and portfolio value are such that exactly 200 contracts are needed. In most cases, we would not expect such conditions to exist. Also, if the markets are efficient, we would not expect any difference to exist between locking in the June value of the portfolio with index futures and locking in the June portfolio value by selling the portfolio in January and investing the proceeds in a risk-free security for the period. Thus, if the portfolio manager actually knew he would be liquidating the portfolio in June, then selling 200 futures contracts in January and closing the contracts and liquidating the portfolio in June should be equivalent to selling the portfolio in January and investing the funds in risk-free security for the period. If this equivalence did not hold, an arbitrage opportunity would exist.

Long Hedge Example

A portfolio manager who was planning to invest a future inflow of cash in a stock portfolio could lock in the purchase price of the portfolio by going long in a stock index futures contract. For example, suppose in January, the portfolio manager in the above example was anticipating an inflow of cash in June and was planning to invest the cash in a stock portfolio with a beta of 1.25 and currently worth \$50,000,000. If the June S&P 500 futures contract is at $f_0 = 1,250$, then the manager could hedge the purchase price by going long in 200 contracts:

$$N_f = \beta \frac{V_0}{f_0} = 1.25 \frac{\$50,000,000}{(1,250)(\$250)} = 200 \text{ contracts}$$

In June, the manager would buy the portfolio and receive or pay a cash settlement on the futures equal to the difference in the closing spot price on the S&P 500 (S_T) on the delivery day and the futures price (f_0): $S_T - f_0$. (The manager more likely would close the futures contract by going short in the expiring June contract trading near the spot price: $f_T = S_T$). With the long position, any higher portfolio cost as a result of stock market increase would be offset by a gain on the long futures position. On the other hand, any lower portfolio cost because of a market decrease would be negated by a loss on the long futures position. This is shown in Exhibit 17.3, where the long hedge position enables the manager to lock in a cost of \$50 million for purchasing the portfolio and closing the futures position in June regardless of the S&P 500 value.

Note, as we examined in Chapter 16, the manager also could lock in a maximum portfolio cost (or cap) or the minimum number of shares purchased with the possibility of lower costs or more shares if the market declines by purchasing an index call option (see Exhibit 16.7).

Hedging Risk

The above examples represent perfect hedging cases in which certain revenues or costs can be locked in at a future date. In practice, perfect hedges are the exception and not the rule. There are three types of hedging risk that preclude one from obtaining a zero risk position: *quality risk, timing risk,* and *quantity risk.*

EXHIBIT 17.3   Future Portfolio Purchase Hedged with Index Futures

(1) S&P 500 Spot Index: S_T	(2) Proportional Change in the S&P 500: $(S_T - 1,250)/$ 1,250	(3) Proportional Change in Portfolio Value: $\beta g = 1.25(S_T -$ $1,250)/1,250$	(4) Portfolio Costs: $50M $(1 + \beta g)$	(5) Long Futures Cash Flow per Contract: $S_T - f_0$ $= (S_T - 1,250)$	(6) Futures Cash Flow: 120($250) $(f_T - 1,250)$	(7) Portfolio Costs with Futures: (4) − (6)
1,000	−0.20	−0.25	$37,500,000	−250	−$12,500,000	$50,000,000
1,125	−0.10	−0.125	43,750,000	−125	−6,250,000	50,000,000
1,250	0	0	50,000,000	0	0	50,000,000
1,375	0.10	0.125	56,250,000	125	6,250,000	50,000,000
1,500	0.20	0.25	62,500,000	250	12,500,000	50,000,000

Quality risk exists when the commodity or asset being hedged is not identical to the one underlying the futures contract. In the above example, the portfolio with a beta of 1.25 was not identical to the S&P 500. The beta in the formula for N_β in turn, adjusted the number of contracts to reduce the quality risk. Timing risk occurs when the delivery date on the futures contract does not coincide with the date the hedged asset needs to be purchased or sold. For example, timing risk would exist in our long hedging example if the manager needed to invest in a portfolio at the beginning of June instead of at the futures' expiration at the end of June. If the spot asset is purchased or sold at a date that differs from the expiration date on the futures contract, then the price on the futures (f_t) and the spot price (S_t) will not necessarily be equal. The difference between the futures and spot price is called the *basis* (B_t). The basis tends to narrow as expiration nears, converging to zero at expiration $(B_T = 0)$. Prior to expiration, the basis can vary, with greater variability usually observed the longer the time is to expiration. Given this *basis risk,* the greater the time difference between buying or selling the hedged asset and the futures' expiration date, the less perfect the hedge. To minimize timing risk or basis risk, hedgers often select futures contracts that mature before the hedged asset is to be bought or sold but as close as possible to that date. For very distant horizon dates, however, hedgers sometimes follow a strategy known as *rolling the hedge forward.* This hedging strategy involves taking a futures position, then at expiration, closing the position and taking a new one. Finally, because of the standardization of futures contracts, futures hedge is subject to quantity risk. The presence of quality, timing, and quantity risk means that pricing risk cannot be eliminated totally by hedging with futures contracts. As a result, the objective in hedging is to try to minimize risk.

Portfolio Exposure — Market Timing

Instead of hedging a portfolio's value against market or systematic risk, suppose a manager wanted to change her portfolio's exposure to the market. For example, a stock portfolio manager who is very confident of a bull market may want to give her portfolio more exposure to the market by increasing the portfolio's beta. Changing a portfolio's beta to profit from an expected change in the market is referred to as *market timing*.

Without index futures (or options), the beta of a portfolio can be changed only by altering the portfolio's allocations of securities. With index futures, however, a manager can change the portfolio beta, β_0, to a new one, referred to as a target beta, β_{TR}, simply by buying or selling futures contracts. The number of futures contracts needed to move the portfolio beta from β_0 to β_{TR} can be determined using the price-sensitivity model in which:[3]

$$N_f = \frac{V_0}{f_0}(\beta_{TR} - \beta_0)$$

where:

> if $\beta_{TR} > \beta_0$, long in futures
> if $\beta_{TR} < \beta_0$, short in futures

Market-Timing Example

Consider the case of a stock portfolio manager who in September is confident the market will increase over the next three months, and as a result, wants to change her portfolio's beta from its current value of $\beta_0 = 1$ to $\beta_{TR} = 1.25$. Suppose the portfolio currently is worth $50 million, the spot S&P 500 index is at 1,000, and the price on the December S&P 500 futures contract is 1,000. To adjust the portfolio beta from 1 to 1.25, the manager would need to buy $N_f = 50$ December S&P 500 index futures:

$$N_f = \frac{V_0}{f_0}(\beta_{TR} - \beta_0) = \frac{\$50,000,000}{(1,000)(\$250)}(1.25 - 1) = 50$$

As shown in Exhibit 17.4, if the market increases, then the manager earns higher rates of return from the futures-adjusted portfolio than from the unadjusted portfolio. If the market declines, however, she incurs greater losses with the adjusted portfolio than with the unadjusted one. For example, if the market increases by 10 percent, the portfolio increases from $50M to $55M (a 10 percent increase, reflecting a $\beta = 1$) and the long futures position generates an addition cash flow of $1.25M, increasing the portfolio value to $56.25 million (a 12.5 percent increase, reflecting a $\beta = 1.25$). In contrast, if the market decreases by 10 percent, then the portfolio decreases from $50M to $45M (a 10 percent decrease, reflecting a $\beta = 1$) and the long futures position loses $1.25M, decreasing the portfolio value to $43.75M (a 12.5 percent decrease, reflecting a $\beta = 1.25$). Thus, the futures-enhanced portfolio is consistent with the characteristics of a portfolio with a β of 1.25.

EXHIBIT 17.4 Market Timing

(1) S&P 500 Spot Index: $S_T = f_T$	(2) Proportional Change: $g =$ $(S_T - 1,000)/1,000$	(3) Futures Profit: (50)($250) $[f_T - 1,000]$	(4) Portfolio Value: $50M(1+g)$	(5) Portfolio Value with Futures: (3)+(4)
800	−0.20	−$2,500,000	$40,000,000	$37,500,000
900	−0.10	−1,250,000	45,000,000	43,750,000
1,000	0	0	50,000,000	50,000,000
1,100	0.10	1,250,000	55,000,000	56,250,000
1,200	0.20	2,500,000	60,000,000	62,500,000

	Portfolio Rates of Return and $\beta = \Delta$ Portfolio Rate/Δg [+]			
S&P 500 Spot Index: S_T	Portfolio Rate: [Col (4)/$50M]−1	β	Futures-Enhanced Portfolio Rate: [Col (5)/$50M] −1	β
800	−0.20	1	0.25	1.25
900	−0.10	1	−0.125	1.25
1,000	0	1	0	1.25
1,100	0.10	1	0.125	1.25
1,200	0.20	1	0.25	1.25

[+]Portfolio Rate = $\dfrac{\text{Portfolio Value}}{\$50,000,000} - 1$

OSA: HEDGING PORTFOLIOS USING OSA

On the OSA screen, you can import a portfolio and then use the "Hedge" tab to determine the number of index futures contracts needed to hedge your portfolio. The number of contracts is based on the beta of the portfolio.

To evaluate a portfolio insurance position for a portfolio you created in PRTU:

- OSA <Enter>.
- From the "Portfolio" dropdown, select a portfolio.
- Click gray "Hedge" tab.
- On the Hedge screen, select index (e.g., SPX) and ticker (e.g., SPZ3 for December S&P 500 futures).
- The right corner box on the Hedge screen shows the portfolio value, beta, future price, contract size, and number of contracts: $N_f = \beta Vl(f_0)250$.

See Bloomberg Web Exhibit 17.2.

Pricing Futures and Forward Contracts: Carrying-Cost Model

As a derivative security, the price on a futures contract depends on the price of the underlying asset. Like options, the relation between futures and spot prices is governed by arbitrage. The arbitrage relation governing the equilibrium futures and forward prices is referred to as the *carrying-cost model*. This model determines the equilibrium futures or forward price by solving for that price that is equal to the cost of carrying the underlying asset for the time period from the present to the expiration on the contract (i.e., the net cost of buying the underlying asset and holding it for the period). If the futures or forward price does not equal the cost of carrying the underlying asset, then an arbitrage opportunity exists by taking a position in the futures or forward contract and an opposite position in the underlying asset. Thus, in the absence of arbitrage, the price on the futures or forward contract is equal to the cost of carrying the asset.

Commodity Carrying-Cost Model

The carrying-cost model for a typical commodity forward contract is:

$$F_0 = S_0(1 + R_f)^T + (K)(T) + TRC$$

where:

$K =$ storage costs per unit of the commodity per period
$TRC =$ transportation costs
$T =$ time to delivery as a proportion of a year

To illustrate, suppose in June the spot price of a bushel of wheat is $2.00, the annual storage cost is $0.30 per/bushel, the risk-free rate is 8 percent, and the cost of transporting wheat from the destination point specified on the forward contract to a local grain elevator, or vice versa, is $0.01/bu. By the cost of carry model, the equilibrium price of a forward contract on September wheat (expiration of $T = 0.25$) would be $2.124/bu:

$$F_0 = (\$2.00/\text{bu})(1.08)^{0.25} + (\$0.30/\text{bu})(0.25) + \$0.01/\text{bu} = \$2.124/\text{bu}$$

If the actual futures price is $2.16, an arbitrageur would:

1. Take a short position in the forward contract: agree to sell a September bushel of wheat for $2.16.
2. Borrow $2.00 at 8 percent interest.
3. Use the loan proceeds to buy a bushel of wheat for $2.00, and then store it for three months.
4. At expiration, the arbitrageur would transport the wheat from the grain elevator to the specified destination point on the forward contract for $0.01/bu.
5. Pay the financing costs of $2.0388/bu and the storage costs of ($0.30/bu)(0.25) = $0.075/bu.
6. Sell the bushel of wheat on the forward contract at $2.16/bu.

From this cash-and-carry strategy, the arbitrageur would earn a riskless return of $0.036/bu.[4]

Stock Index Futures Pricing: Carrying-Cost Model

The equilibrium futures price on a stock index futures contract is equal to the net costs of carrying a spot index portfolio or proxy portfolio to expiration at time T. For the case of a discrete dividend payment on the portfolio worth D_T at expiration, the equilibrium price is:

$$f_0^* = S_0(1 + R^A)^T - D_T$$

where:

S_0 = current spot index value
D_T = value of the stock index dividends at time T

If the equilibrium condition does not hold, an arbitrage opportunity will exist by taking a position in the spot portfolio, such as index ETF, and an opposite one in the futures contract. For example, if the market price on the futures contract (f_0^M) exceeds the equilibrium price, then an arbitrageur could earn a riskless profit of $f_0^M - f_0^*$ with an *index arbitrage* strategy in which she borrows S_0 dollars at the risk-free rate of R^A, buys the spot index portfolio or ETF for S_0, and locks in the selling price on the portfolio at time T by going short in the index futures at f_0^M.

Options on Futures Contracts

Option contracts on stocks, debt securities, foreign currency, and indexes are sometimes referred to as *spot options* or options on actuals. This reference is to distinguish them from *options on futures* contracts (also called *options on futures*, *futures options*, and *commodity options*). A futures option gives the holder the right to take a position in a futures contract.

A call option on a futures contract gives the holder the right to take a long position in the underlying futures contract when she exercises and requires the writer to take the corresponding short position in the futures. Upon exercise, the holder of a futures call option in effect takes a long position in the futures contract at the *current* futures price and the writer takes the short position and pays the holder via the clearinghouse the difference between the current futures price and the exercise price. In contrast, a put option on a futures option entitles the holder to take a short futures position and the writer the long position. Thus, whenever the put holder exercises, he in effect takes a short futures position at the current futures price, and the writer takes the long position and pays the holder via the clearinghouse the difference between the exercise price and the current futures price. Like all option positions, the futures option buyer pays an option premium for the right to exercise, and the writer, in turn, receives a credit when he sells the option and is subject to initial and maintenance margin requirements on the option position.

In practice, when the holder of a futures call option exercises, the futures clearinghouse will establish for the exercising option holder a long futures position at the futures price equal to the exercise price and a short futures position for the assigned writer. Once this is done, margins on both positions will be required, and the position will be marked to market at the current settlement price on the futures. When the positions are marked to market, then the exercising call holder's margin account on his long position will be equal to the difference between the futures price and the exercise price, $f_t - X$, while the assigned writer will have to deposit funds or monies worth nearly $f_t - X$ to satisfy her maintenance margin on her short futures position. Thus, when a futures call is exercised, the holder takes a long position at f_t with a margin account worth $f_t - X$; if he were to immediately close the futures, he would receive cash worth $f_t - X$ from the clearinghouse. The assigned writer, in turn, is assigned a short position at f_t and must deposit $f_t - X$ to meet her margin. If the futures option is a put, then the same procedure applies, except the holder takes a short position at f_t (when the exercised position is marked to market), with a margin account worth $X - f_t$, and the writer is assigned a long position at f_t and must deposit $X - f_t$ to meet her margin.

A spot option on a security and futures options on the same security are equivalent if the options and the futures contracts expire at the same time, the carrying-costs model holds, and the options are European. (In contrast, spot and futures options will differ to the extent that these conditions do not hold.) There are, however, several factors that serve to differentiate the spot and futures options. First, since most futures contracts are relatively more liquid than their corresponding spot security, it is usually easier to form hedging or arbitrage strategies with futures options than with spot options. Second, many futures options often are easier to exercise than their corresponding spot. For example, to exercise an option on a foreign currency futures contract, one simply assumes the futures position; exercising a spot foreign currency spot option, however, requires an actual purchase or delivery. Finally, most futures options are traded on the same exchange as their underlying futures contract, whereas most spot options are traded on exchanges different from their underlying securities. This, in turn, makes it easier for futures options traders to implement arbitrage and hedging strategies than it is for spot options traders.

Stock Index Futures Options

Some of the characteristics of futures options can be seen by examining the profit relationships for the fundamental strategies formed with these options. Exhibits 17.5 and 17.6 show the profit and futures price relationship at expiration for four fundamental option strategies using call and put options on the S&P 500 futures contract. Both the call and the put have an exercise price of 1,250 times a $250 multiple and a premium of 10 times $250, and it is assumed the futures options expire at the same time as the futures contract.

Exhibit 17.5 shows the profit and futures price relationship at expiration for the call purchase strategy. The numbers reflect a case in which the holder exercises the call at expiration, if profitable, when the spot price is equal to the price on the expiring futures contract. For example, at $S_T = f_T = 1,270$, the holder of the 1,250 futures call

EXHIBIT 17.5   Fundamental Futures Call Options Strategies

a. Long Position on S&P 500 Futures Call Option

Call on S&P 500 Futures:

- $X = 1{,}250$, Multiplier = \$250
- $C = 10(\$250) = \$2{,}500$
- Futures and option futures have same expiration.

$S_T = f_T$	π_C
1,230	−2,500
1,240	−2,500
1,250	−2,500
1,260	0
1,270	2,500
1,280	5,000
$\pi_C = \text{Max}\,(f_T - 1{,}250, 0)(\$250) - 2{,}500$	

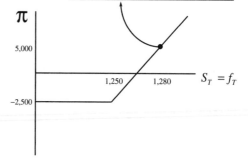

Exercise at 1,280: Holder goes long at $f_T = 1{,}280$ and then closes by going short at $f_T = 1{,}280$, and receives $f_T - X = (1{,}280 - 1{,}250)(\$250)$: $\pi = (1{,}280 - 1{,}250)(\$250) - 2{,}500 = 5{,}000$

b. Short Position on S&P 500 Futures Call Option

Call on S&P 500 Futures:

- $X = 1{,}250$, Multiplier = \$250
- $C = 10(\$250) = \$2{,}500$
- Futures and option futures have same expiration.

$S_T = f_T$	π_C
1,230	2,500
1,240	2,500
1,250	2,500
1,260	0
1,270	−2,500
1,280	−5,000
$\pi_C = -\text{Max}\,(f_T - 1{,}250, 0)\,(\$250) + 2{,}500$	

If holder exercises at 1,280: Writer takes short position at $f_T = 1{,}280$ and then closes by going long at $f_T = 1{,}280$, and pays holder $f_T - X = (1{,}280 - 1{,}250)(\$250)$: $\pi = -(1{,}280 - 1{,}250)(\$250) + 2{,}500 = -5{,}000$

would receive a cash flow of \$5,000 and a profit of \$2,500. That is, upon exercising, the holder would assume a long position in the expiring S&P 500 futures at 1,270, which she subsequently would close by taking an offsetting short futures position at 1,270, and the holder would receive \$5,000 from the assigned writer: $(f_T - X)\$250 = (1{,}270 - 1{,}250)\$250 = \$5{,}000$. The opposite profit and futures price relation is

EXHIBIT 17.6   Fundamental Futures Put Options Strategies

c. Long Position on S&P 500 Futures Put Option

Put on S&P 500 Futures:

- $X = 1{,}250$, Multiplier = $250
- $P = 10(\$250) = \$2{,}500$
- Futures and option futures have same expiration.

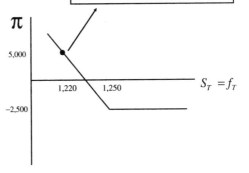

Exercise at 1,220: Holder goes short at $f_T = 1{,}220$ and then closes by going long at $f_T = 1{,}220$, and receives $X - f_T = (1{,}250 - 1{,}220)(\$250)$: $\pi = (1{,}250 - 1{,}220)(\$250) - 2{,}500 = 5{,}000$

$S_T = f_T$	π_P
1,220	5,000
1,230	2,500
1,240	0
1,250	−2,500
1,260	−2,500
1,270	−2,500

$\pi_P = \text{Max}(1{,}250 - f_T, 0)(\$250) - 2{,}500$

d. Short Position on S&P 500 Futures Put Option

Put on S&P 500 Futures:

- $X = 1{,}250$, Multiplier = $250
- $P = 10(\$250) = \$2{,}500$
- Futures and option futures have same expiration.

If holder exercises at 1,220: Writer takes long position at $f_T = 1{,}220$ and then closes by going short at $f_T = 1{,}220$, and pays $X - f_T = (1{,}250 - 1{,}220)(\$250)$: $\pi = -(1{,}250 - 1{,}220)(\$250) + 2{,}500 = -5{,}000$

$S_T = f_T$	π_P
1,220	−5,000
1,230	−2,500
1,240	0
1,250	2,500
1,260	2,500
1,270	2,500

$\pi_P = -\text{Max}(1{,}250 - f_T, 0)(\$250) + 2{,}500$

attained for a naked call write position (lower graph). In this case, if the index is at 1,250 or less, the writer of a 1,250 SP 500 futures call would earn the premium of $2,500, and if $f_T > 250$, he, upon assignment, would have to pay the difference between f_T and X and would have to assume a short position at f_T, which he would close with an offsetting long position.

Exhibit 17.6 shows the long and short put positions. In the case of a put purchase, if the holder exercises when f_T is less than X, then she will receive $X - f_T$ and a short futures position that she can offset. For example, if $S_T = f_T = 1,230$ at expiration, then the put holder upon exercising would receive $5,000 [(1,250 - 1,230)(\$250)]$ from the put writer. Her short position then would be closed by taking a long position in the S&P 500 futures contract. The put writer's position would be just the opposite.

BLOOMBERG FUTURES OPTIONS SCREENS

To Access information on futures options, do the following:

- CTM <Enter>; click "Exchange." Example: click "Chicago Mercantile Exchange," from "Category" column, select "Equity Index"; from "Type" column select futures; from "Options" column, select yes.
- Right click to bring up menu to select description (DES), contract table on futures (CT), or options on futures options (OMON).
- You can select a futures option from OMON and then bring up its menu screen: Ticker <Comdty> (e.g., SPG4C 1780 <Comdty>). The futures options screen includes options scenario analysis (OSA) and option valuation (OVL) screens.

  Alternative:

- Enter: Ticker <Comdty> to bring up futures menu; Example: SPA <Comdty> will bring up the S&P 500 futures contracts.
- On the futures menus, bring up EXS screen to find futures expirations and their tickers for futures contracts of interest (e.g., SPM4 for March 2014 S&P 500 futures).
- Bring up the futures screen: Ticker <Comdty> (e.g., SPM4 <Comdty).
- On futures menu screen, bring up the OSA screen (OSA <Enter>.
- On the futures OSA screen, select "Add Listed Options" from the red "Positions" tab; select futures options; click "Add Options" tab.
- On the OSA main screen, you can analyze positions using the "Scenario Chart" tab.

  Other option screens on the futures menu are as follows:

- OTD: Description of Futures Option.
- OSL: Option Strike List.
- OMON: Option Monitor.
- OMST: Most Active Options.
- OVL: Option valuation.

See Bloomberg Web Exhibit 17.3.

Conclusion

In this chapter, we have provided an overview of futures and forward contracts. These derivative securities are very similar to options. Like options, they can be used as speculative tools to profit from changes in asset prices and as hedging tools to minimize price risk. Also like options, futures contracts are traded on organized exchanges that have many of the same trading rules and procedures that option exchanges have. Finally, futures and forward contracts, like options, are derivative securities, and as such, their prices are determined by arbitrage forces.

The fundamental difference between the contracts is that options give holders a right, whereas futures or forward contract holders have an obligation. As a result, potential profits and losses on pure speculative futures positions are virtually unlimited compared to limited profit and loss potentials on fundamental speculative option positions. Hedging strategies with futures, while capable of eliminating downside risk, can also impact the upside potential as compared to option hedging that can provide minimum and maximum limits. Futures and options, as well as other derivative like swaps, have become a basic financial engineering tool to apply to a variety of financial problems.

We, of course, have not exhausted all derivative securities, just as we have not covered all the strategies, uses, markets, and pricing of equity securities. What we hope we have done here and in these last two chapters, however, is to develop a foundation for the understanding of derivative products and their important applications in equity management. To this extent, we also hope our odyssey into the world of stock, stock portfolios, and equity derivatives, along with our exploration into the depth and breadth of the Bloomberg system, has established a foundation and methodology for understanding the markets and uses of equity securities.

Web Site Information

- Information on the CBOE: www.cboe.com.
- Information on the Chicago Mercantile Exchange: http://www.cmegroup.com.
- U.S. Commodity Futures Trading Commission: http://www.cftc.gov.

Notes

1. Clearinghouse members are also required to maintain a margin account with the clearinghouse. This is known as a *clearing margin*.
2. Several non-U.S. exchanges offer futures trading on individual stocks, including U.S. stocks. Until 2000, U.S. security laws prohibited such trading in the United States. This law, however, was changed in 2000, resulting in proposals for such trading.
3. A portfolio's exposure to the market also can be changed by buying index call or put options. The number of options needed to change the beta is:

$$N = \frac{V_0}{X}(\beta_{TR} - \beta_0)$$

where:

    if $\beta_{TR} > \beta_0$, long in index calls
    if $\beta_{TR} < \beta_0$, long in index puts

4. For many commodities, the reverse cash-and-carry arbitrage strategy does not apply. In such cases, the equilibrium condition for the forward contract needs to be specified as an inequality: $F_0 < S_0(1 + R_f)^T + (K)(T) + TRC$.

Selected References

Figlewski, S. 1984. Hedging performance and basis risk in stock index futures. *Journal of Finance* 39 (July): 657–669.

Figlewski, S., and S. Kin. 1982. Portfolio management with stock index futures. *Financial Analysts Journal* 38 (January–February): 52–60.

Hardy, C. 1940. *Risk and Risk Bearing.* Chicago: University of Chicago Press: 67–69.

Hardy, C., and L. Lyon. 1923. The theory of hedging. *Journal of Political Economy* 31: 271–287.

Hull, J. 2005. *Options, Futures and Other Derivative Securities*, 6th ed. Englewood Cliffs, N.J.: Prentice Hall: Chapter 23.

Johnson, R. S. 2009. *Introduction to Derivatives: Options, Futures, and Swaps.* New York: Oxford University Press: Chapter 15.

Modest, D., and M. Sundaresan. 1983. The relationship between spot and futures prices in stock index futures markets: Some preliminary evidence." *Journal of Futures Markets* 3: 15–41.

Ramaswany, K., and M. Sundaresan. 1985. The valuation of options on futures contracts. *Journal of Finance* 60 (December): 1319–1340.

Shastri, K., and K. Tandon. 1986. Options on futures contracts: A comparison of European and American pricing models. *The Journal of Futures Markets* 6 (Winter): 593–618.

Whaley, R. 1986. Valuation of American futures options: Theory and tests." *The Journal of Finance* 41 (March): 127–150.

Bloomberg Exercises

1. Exchange-listed commodities can be found by accessing the CTM screen: CTM <Enter>. Contracts are listed by category, exchanges, and region. For example, to find a stock index on the Chicago Mercantile Exchange (CME), use the CTM "Exchange" screen and click "Equity Index" from the dropdown menu in the "Category" column; to find a commodity contract on the Chicago Board of Trade (CBT), use the CBT "Exchange" screen and click commodity type from the dropdown menu in the "Category" column. Using the CTM screen, find the tickers on a futures contract of interest and analyze it using screens from the contract's menu screen (Ticker <Comdty>). Screens to consider are Description (DES), Contract Table (CT), Intraday Graph (GIP), Expiration Schedule (EXS), and Price Graph (GP).

2. Select a portfolio with a market value of at least $1.5 million that you have created in PRTU. Using the OSA screen, determine the number of futures contracts needed to hedge your portfolio. For a guide, see Bloomberg box: "OSA: Hedging Portfolios Using OSA."

3. Select some put and call options on an S&P 500 futures contract using the futures contracts OSA screen:
   • Go to futures menu screen (SPA <Comdty>).
   • Look for contracts and tickers on the EXS screen.

- Bring up the futures contract menu screen (ticker <Comdty> or ticker <Index>).
- Bring up the OSA screen (OSA <Enter>).
- Use the "Position" tab on the OSA screen for the futures contract to add put and call options on the futures contract.

   Using OSA "Scenario Chart" tab, analyze a number of futures and futures options positions.
   a. Long futures position.
   b. Short futures position.
   c. Futures call purchase.
   d. Futures put purchase.
   e. Covered call write (short futures call and long futures).
   f. Covered put write (short futures put and short futures).
   g. Futures insurance (long futures contract and long futures put).
   h. Long straddle.
   i. Short straddle.

4. Select some put and call options on futures other than the S&P using the futures contracts OSA screen:
   - Go to CTM screen to find futures and futures options.
   - Go to futures menu screen (ticker <Comdty>).
   - Look for contracts and tickers on the EXS screen.
   - Bring up futures contract (ticker <Comdty> or ticker <Index>).
   - Bring up the OSA screen (OSA <Enter>).
   - Use the "Position" tab on the OSA screen for the futures contract to add put and call options on the futures contract

      Using OSA "Scenario Chart" tab, analyze a number of futures and futures options positions.
      a. Long futures position.
      b. Short futures position.
      c. Futures call purchase.
      d. Futures put purchase.
      e. Covered call write (short futures call and long futures).
      f. Covered put write (short futures put and short futures).
      g. Futures insurance (long futures contract and long futures put).
      h. Long straddle.
      i. Short straddle.

Index